Tax and the Digital Economy

Series on International Taxation

VOLUME 69

Series Editors

Prof. Ruth Mason, University of Virginia School of Law
Prof. Dr Ekkehart Reimer, University of Heidelberg

Introduction & Contents

The Series on International Taxation deals with a wide variety of topics in the global tax arena. The authors include many of the field's leading experts as well as talented newcomers. Their expert views and incisive commentary have proven highly useful to practitioners and academics alike.

Objective

The volumes published in this series are aimed at offering high-quality analytical information and practical solutions to international tax practitioners.

Readership

Practitioners, academics and policy makers in international tax law.

Frequency of Publication

2-3 new volumes published each year.

The titles published in this series are listed at the end of this volume.

Tax and the Digital Economy

Challenges and Proposals for Reform

Edited by

Werner Haslehner
Georg Kofler
Katerina Pantazatou
Alexander Rust

ATOZ Foundation
under the aegis of Fondation de Luxembourg

Wolters Kluwer

Published by:
Kluwer Law International B.V.
PO Box 316
2400 AH Alphen aan den Rijn
The Netherlands
E-mail: international-sales@wolterskluwer.com
Website: lrus.wolterskluwer.com

Sold and distributed in North, Central and South America by:
Wolters Kluwer Legal & Regulatory U.S.
7201 McKinney Circle
Frederick, MD 21704
United States of America
Email: customer.service@wolterskluwer.com

Sold and distributed in all other countries by:
Air Business Subscriptions
Rockwood House
Haywards Heath
West Sussex
RH16 3DH
United Kingdom
Email: international-customerservice@wolterskluwer.com

ISBN 978-94-035-0361-5

e-Book: ISBN 978-94-035-0335-6
web-PDF: ISBN 978-94-035-0350-9

Editors

Werner Haslehner is Professor of Law in the Faculty of Law, Economics and Finance at the University of Luxembourg, Luxembourg, where he holds the ATOZ Chair for European and International Taxation, and Director of its LLM Programme in European Union (EU) and International Tax Law. He joined the Faculty as Associate Professor in 2013, previously holding full-time academic positions in Austria at JKU Linz and in the United Kingdom at the London School of Economics and Political Sciences (LSE) and was appointed Full Professor in 2015. His research interests cover all aspects of international taxation, including the impact of EU law and tax policy.

Georg Kofler is Professor of Law and Head of the Institute for Fiscal Law, Tax Law and Tax Policy at Johannes Kepler University of Linz Law School, Austria. He previously worked with the International Department of the Austrian Federal Ministry of Finance, as acting assistant professor at New York University and as assistant professor at the University of Linz. Being an active member of several professional organizations, he serves as the chairman of the European Court of Justice Task Force of the CFE Tax Advisers Europe. His research focuses on international and European direct tax law and all aspects of Austrian tax law.

Katerina Pantazatou is an Associate Professor of Tax Law at the University of Luxembourg, Luxembourg, since September 2016. Previously, she was an FNR post-doctoral researcher at the University of Luxembourg. She received her PhD from the European University Institute (EUI), and she has been a visiting researcher at Harvard Law School and at the Institute for Austrian and International Tax law (WU) as an Ernst Mach scholar. Her research focuses on EU tax law, the digital economy and corporate governance.

Alexander Rust is Professor of Tax Law at the Institute for Austrian and International Tax Law of WU (Vienna University of Economics and Business). He previously worked as Professor of Tax Law and Director of the Master Programme in European and International Tax Law at the University of Luxembourg, as Acting Assistant Professor at New York University, and as Assistant at the University of Munich. He is a member of the editorial board of Intertax and *Internationale Steuer-Rundschau*, as well as Co-Editor of the Commentary *Klaus Vogel on Double Taxation Conventions*. His main research interests are tax treaty law, EU tax law, and tax policy.

Contributors

Andrés Báez Moreno is Associate Professor of Tax Law at the Universidad Carlos III de Madrid, Spain, and a lawyer at the Madrid Bar. He has been a visiting pre- and postdoctoral researcher at the University of Münster, Germany, the University of Cologne, Germany, the University of Padua at IBFD, Italy, and the Max Planck Institute for Tax Law and Public Finance in Munich. His areas of expertise are domestic company taxation (in particular, commercial and tax accounting) and international taxation, fields in which he has published two books and more than forty articles and contributions.

Gianluigi Bizioli is Professor of Tax Law, and International and EU Tax Law at the University of Bergamo (Department of Law), Italy. He also teaches Tax Law at the *Accademia della Guardia di Finanza* in Bergamo. He earned three degrees: (1) from the University of Bergamo in Economics and Business Administration; (2) from the University of Padua in Law; and (3) a PhD in International and Comparative Tax Law from the University of Genoa. His areas of main interests are constitutional, European and International Tax Law. He is also a member of the Board of Professors of the PhD programme in *Business and Law* of the University of Bergamo, of the Direction Committee of the *Rivista di Diritto Finanziario e Scienza delle Finanze*, of *Diritto e Processo Tributario*, and of the Editorial Board of many Italian tax law reviews, as well as the Italian Member of the Academic Committee of the European Association of Tax Law Professors (EATLP) and of the International Fiscal Association (IFA). Since June 2018, he is a Counsel of the Ministry for Regional Affairs for the implementation of the asymmetric fiscal federalism in Italy, and since 2019 a Counsel of the Italian Practice of PwC Tax and Legal Services in Milan.

Peter Bräumann is an Assistant Professor for Tax Management at Johannes Kepler University, Linz, Austria and a member of the Linz Institute of Technology's (LIT) Digital Transformation and Law Lab. His research currently focuses on fundamental legal, fiscal and social challenges for domestic and international tax law caused by the ongoing digitization of both the economy and public administration.

Yariv Brauner is the Hugh Culverhouse Eminent Scholar Chair in Taxation at the University of Florida, Levin College of Law. He joined the Florida faculty in 2006, after teaching at New York University, Northwestern, and Arizona State University. He has been a visiting professor or a guest speaker in various universities in the U.S. and abroad. He is an author of articles published in professional journals and law reviews and a co-author of *U.S. International Taxation – Cases and Materials* (with Reuven S. Avi-Yonah and Diane M. Ring), now in its 3rd. ed. He taught multiple courses in the fields of taxation, corporate taxation, international taxation, international trade law, and the law of multinational.

Tina Ehrke-Rabel is Professor of Law and since 2010 Head of the Institute for Finance and Tax Law at Karl-Franzens University, Graz. Her main areas of research interest are international, European and Austrian business tax law, including VAT and excise taxes, with a specific focus on aspects of tax enforcement and fundamental rights. She currently concentrates on the challenges of digitalization and globalization.

Joachim Englisch holds a chair for tax law and public law at Münster University, Germany. Since 2011, he is the managing director of the Institute for Tax Law at this university. At the time this book was published, he also held the Alfred-Grosser-Chair 2018/2019 at Sciences Po Paris where he carried out research on tax implications of digitalization. His main research activities are devoted to International and European tax law covering both direct and indirect taxation, and he has published and lectured extensively on a broad range of related topics. He has been invited to be a visiting professor for LLM courses on international and European tax law at several European universities.

Johannes Kofler is University Assistant at the Institute for Machine Learning at JKU since 2018. He studied Technical Physics at the Johannes Kepler University (JKU) Linz, where he graduated in 2004. He received his PhD in Theoretical Quantum Mechanics from the University of Vienna in 2009. He worked as Postdoctoral Research Scientist at the Institute for Quantum Optics and Quantum Information of the Austrian Academy of Sciences in Vienna (2009–2011) and the Max Planck Institute of Quantum Optics in Garching near Munich (2011–2017). In 2017/18, he was Researcher at AKKT, a taxation research company and cooperation partner of JKU.

Juliane Kokott holds the position of Advocate General at the Court of Justice of the European Union. Since October 2003, she has been responsible for about 1,100 cases and has delivered more than 500 opinions including about 200 on taxation. The latter covered all areas of EU Tax law, in particular the value-added tax (VAT) law and the application of the fundamental freedoms as well as the diverse EU Directives (e.g., Parent-Subsidiary Directive, Interests and Royalties Directive, and the Anti-Tax Avoidance Directive) in the field of direct taxes. Before joining the Court she was a professor at the universities of Augsburg, Heidelberg, Düsseldorf, and St. Gallen. She has also been a visiting professor at Berkeley Law, and was Deputy Chairman of the German Advisory Council on Global Change (WBGU) (1996–2003), an independent, scientific advisory body to the German government that was established 1992 in the run-up to the Rio Earth Summit. She is a graduate of the universities of Bonn, American University/Washington D.C., Heidelberg, and Harvard Law School. She has authored and co-authored a broad variety of publications on European Law, Public International Law and European Tax law, most recently 'Das Steuerrecht der Europäischen Union'. She is currently co-presiding (with Pasquale Pistone) an ILA Study Group on International Tax Law.

Marie Lamensch is Research Professor of International and European Tax Law at the Institute for European Studies and the Law Faculty of the Vrije Universiteit Brussel. She is also visiting professor at the Université Catholique de Louvain, Belgium and the Katholieke Universiteit Leuven, Belgium and a legal adviser on tax cassation cases for a Belgian law firm. Her main research topics include VAT and European Taxation. Thanks to her specific expertise in the area of VAT, she gives training for the European Commission and the European Parliament and has become a member of relevant expert groups of the OECD, the World Customs Organisation and the EU Commission. She also gives training at the IBFD's International Tax Academy and works as Technical Editor of the International VAT Monitor. She previously acted as researcher for the G20 task force on the Financial Transactions Tax, practiced as a lawyer in Brussels and Luxembourg and worked as teaching assistant in contract law at the Université Libre de Bruxelles, Belgium. Marie holds a Law degree from the Université Libre de Bruxelles and an LLM degree in international and European Law from the Vrije Universiteit Brussel, Belgium. She obtained her Doctorate at the Vrije Universiteit Brussel in July 2014, and her PhD dissertation was awarded the 2015 Maurice Lauré Prize (IFA).

Eric Robert is a tax policy advisor at the Organisation for Economic Co-operation and Development since 2014. During that period, his work has primarily focused on the direct tax challenges posed by digitalization, notably by contributing to the '2015 OECD BEPS Action 1 Report' and the 2018 OECD Interim Report on the 'Tax Challenges Arising from Digitalisation'. Before joining the OECD, he worked as a tax advisor in the corporate tax department of Taj (French law firm member of Deloitte Touche Tohmatsu Limited), where he essentially assisted French and foreign group of companies in structuring their cross-border activities, with a focus on international tax issues. He first obtained a university degree in Law in 2005 at the University Panthéon-Assas of Paris and holds since 2011 a PhD in Public Law from the same university.

Julia Sinnig is research assistant and PhD candidate under the supervision of Professor Dr Werner Haslehner at the University of Luxembourg. Her research focuses on the taxation of the digitalized economy and more specifically on destination-based corporate taxation as a potential solution to face the challenges of the digitalized economy. She published in English, French and German language on international, European and domestic Luxembourg tax-related topics.

Michael Tumpel is professor of business administration at Johannes Kepler University, Linz, Austria. His research emphasizes on Austrian, European and International tax law and tax management.

Viktoria Wöhrer, LLM, BSc, is a senior associate at Rödl & Partner in Vienna and a lecturer at the Vienna University of Economics and Business (WU) as well as the author of various publications on international, European, and domestic Austrian tax law. Her doctoral thesis on 'Data Protection and Taxpayers Rights: Challenges Created by Automatic Exchange of Information' was published by IBFD and awarded the Wolfgang Gassner Science Prize, with the prize of the Austrian Bankers' Association and with the Stephan Koren Prize.

Summary of Contents

Table of Contents

Preface and Acknowledgements

This book constitutes the latest volume in a series of publications by the University of Luxembourg's ATOZ Chair for European and International Taxation, which are based on annual conferences on current issues of international and European tax law. These conferences bring together leading tax experts from academia, various areas of tax practice, and governmental entities to facilitate high-level discussions, which are topical and foster dialogue among the different actors. This book is the result of a conference organized and funded by the ATOZ Chair for European and International Taxation at the University of Luxembourg in collaboration with the University of Linz, the Vienna University of Economics and Business, and the 'ECJ Task Force', an expert group on EU Tax Law from CFE Tax Advisers, to which the editors are grateful.

Existing tax concepts have been found increasingly outdated and incapable of meeting the tax challenges arising out of digitalization and business models and transactions that do not require physical substance. The OECD's 2018 Interim Report on Digitalization signalled the extensive permeation of digital innovation in the modern economy, which inevitably raises fundamental questions about the allocation of taxing rights on income from cross-border activities among countries. An increasing number of unilateral (and even a few coordinated) responses have been proposed and implemented by a variety of economies - rich and developing, as well as large and small - including regional economic groups such as the EU. However, no international consensus has yet been reached on how to transform the international tax system in order to address a new global norm, digitalization.

This book is the first attempt to analyse a broad set of questions that arise in this context, such as: What kind of changes are legally possible? Which changes are necessary and desirable? How feasible are certain proposed changes intended to address the challenges? And, what further challenges might arise as a consequence of the implementation of such proposed changes? Chapters 1 through 4 set out the context provided by the OECD's 2018 Interim Report on Digitalization and analyse the legal framework that proposals must abide by when trying to adapt international tax law to the digital economy. They distil legal limits on any adaption of current tax concepts for the digital economy that already exist in public international law – such as the principle of territoriality of taxation – as well as in EU-, WTO-, and national constitutional law.

Chapters 5 through 7 discuss concrete proposals for adapting the current tax systems for the digital economy. They analyse, in turn, the three main competing reform concepts brought forward: (1) the increased use of withholding taxes, (2) the creation of special taxes for digital services (with a particular focus on the proposed 2018 EU Digital Services Tax Directive), and (3) the revision of the classic concept of a permanent establishment to include a 'significant digital presence' in a state other than the taxpayer's resident state.

Chapters 8 through 10 address digital economy phenomena that demand special attention because they have revolutionized the way business relationships are construed. For instance, 'consumer-to-consumer' transactions are vital to the emergent 'sharing economy' and challenge not only traditional income tax treatment but also VAT law. Similarly, digital currencies and remote digital supply require careful consideration of existing legal doctrine and impending developments.

The final part of the book, Chapters 11 through 13, is dedicated to national tax policy concerns with a particular focus on Human Rights concerns arising from Big Data and Artificial Intelligence innovations. The advantages occasioned by these developments, both for businesses and governments, must be balanced against the risks taxpayers face with respect to their rights of defence and rights to protection of their personal data, as well as the broader threat robotization poses to present social contracts.

We would like to express our sincere gratitude to all the contributors for their commitment to the publication of this volume and for their diligent adherence to the guidelines set for the chapters by the editors. We also especially thank the ATOZ Foundation for its generous sponsorship of the research coordinated by the ATOZ Chair and the conferences organized under its aegis, which made the publication of this book possible.

We further owe thanks to our publisher Kluwer and, especially, Simon Bellamy, for their professional and kind assistance through the publication process. The timely publication of this book in its current form would not have been possible without the dedicated copy-editing work of Suzanne M. Larsen, with additional assistance from Roman Ursu and Jessica Cafferkey, as well as the staff at Newgen.

Werner Haslehner
Georg Kofler
Katerina Pantazatou
Alexander Rust

CHAPTER 1

The 2018 OECD Interim Report

Eric Robert

§1.01 INTRODUCTION

Digitalization is a transformative process driven by technology innovations that affect every aspect of our everyday lives, as well as the way our economy and society are organized and function. The breadth and speed of the change are massive, bringing in their share of disruption and uncertainty. The ensuing challenges for policymakers are complex, as they need to adapt to a changing environment while remaining principled, consistent and clear in the development and implementation of their regulations.

On the tax front, mounting evidence of the various challenges raised by said digital transformation was one of the key factors driving the launch of the Organisation for Economic Co-operation & Development (OECD)/G20 Base Erosion and Profit Shifting (BEPS) Project. In 2013, the Task Force on the Digital Economy (TFDE) was established and, through its work, that project delivered its analytical report, entitled *Addressing the Tax Challenges of the Digital Economy: Action 1 2015 Final Report* ('2015 OECD BEPS Action 1 Report'),[1] as part of the final BEPS package approved by the G20 Finance Ministers in Lima and the G20 Leaders in Antalya. The 2015 OECD BEPS Action 1 Report identified and analysed the direct and indirect tax issues raised by digitalization and developed a number of tax policy solutions to address these issues.

While that initiative was a key impetus for renovating the international tax system and tackling double non-taxation, as well as bringing major improvements to the efficiency of value added taxes (VAT)/Goods and Services Taxes (GST), it did not address (and was never intended to address) the more systemic issues that are at the heart of the traditional international income tax rules and that relate to how taxing

1. OECD, *Addressing the Tax Challenges of the Digital Economy, Action 1 – 2015 Final Report* (OECD Publishing 2015) (hereinafter '2015 OECD BEPS Action 1 Report').

rights on income generated from cross-border activities in the digital age should be allocated among countries. Since 2015, however, the global tax debate has gradually shifted from tax avoidance to policy implications that go well beyond BEPS issues: it now questions the relevance of the existing international income tax framework – notably the 'nexus' and 'profit allocation' rules – in an increasingly digitalized economy. In the absence of consensus on these systemic issues, the OECD opened a new phase of work in 2016 under G20 leadership. As part of this new phase, the recently established Inclusive Framework on BEPS published its 2018 OECD Interim Report[2] and, in 2020, it is expected to culminate in the development of a consensus-based solution that will have important ramifications for multinational enterprises (MNEs) and governments, as well as the future of our tax systems.

§1.02 THE OECD/G20 BEPS PROJECT AND THE 2015 OECD BEPS ACTION 1 REPORT

In delivering the 2015 OECD BEPS Action 1 Report, the TFDE built upon previous work on this topic, including the so-called 1998 *Ottawa Report on Electronic Commerce: Taxation Framework Conditions*[3] and considered the challenges raised by digitalization for both direct and indirect taxation.

In the area of indirect taxation, the 2015 OECD BEPS Action 1 Report recognized that new challenges arose in particular with respect to the collection of VAT/GST on the continuously growing volumes of goods and services that are purchased online by private consumers from foreign suppliers. To address these indirect tax concerns, the report recommended that countries implement its 2017 OECD International VAT/GST Guidelines,[4] particularly the destination principle for determining the place of taxation of cross-border supplies, and also consider implementing the mechanisms for effective collection of VAT/GST presented therein. The 2015 OECD BEPS Action 1 Report also identified a number of possible approaches for more effective VAT/GST collection on the ever-growing volume of imports of low-value goods from online sales.

A large number of countries around the world have already taken action to implement the 2017 OECD International VAT/GST Guidelines and other mechanisms for cross-border business-to-consumer (B2C) supplies or have announced their intention to do so.[5] While available data are relatively limited at this stage, the results in

2. OECD, *Tax Challenges Arising from Digitalisation: Interim Report 2018* 52, 167, 170 (OECD Publishing 2018) (hereinafter '2018 OECD Interim Report').
3. OECD Committee on Fiscal Affairs (CFA), *Electronic Commerce: Taxation Framework Conditions* (OECD Publishing 1998), *available at* www.oecd.org/ctp/consumption/1923256.pdf (accessed 13 November 2018).
4. OECD, *The International VAT/GST Guidelines* (OECD Publishing 2017) (hereinafter '2017 OECD International VAT/GST Guidelines') (internationally agreed standards for the application of VAT to international trade). They were approved by OECD members in 2015 and subsequently endorsed as an international standard by over a hundred countries, jurisdictions, and international organizations at the 2015 OECD Global Forum on VAT. In 2016, the 2017 OECD International VAT/GST Guidelines were adopted as a Recommendation by the OECD Council.
5. Among the latest countries to implement these solutions are G20 countries such as India & South Africa and OECD members such as Australia & New Zealand.

terms of tax revenue for countries in which customers are located are very positive, notably in the European Union (EU).[6] In addition, a number of OECD countries are currently considering the removal of their VAT exemption thresholds for the importation of low-value goods from online sales and the possible implementation of approaches to a more efficient collection of import VAT as identified in the 2015 OECD BEPS Action 1 Report.[7]

In the area of direct taxes, the 2015 OECD BEPS Action 1 Report acknowledged that, due to the pervasive nature of digitalization, it would be difficult, if not impossible, to ring-fence the digital economy from the rest of the economy. It highlighted the ways in which digitalization had exacerbated BEPS issues but suggested that the measures proposed under the other BEPS Actions were likely to address many of the double non-taxation concerns, specifically: amendments to the permanent establishment (PE) definition (Action 7); revised transfer pricing (TP) guidance (Actions 8–10 and 13); and recommendations on the design of effective controlled foreign company rules (Action 3).

In addition to BEPS issues, the 2015 OECD BEPS Action 1 Report identified a number of broader tax challenges created by digitalization, notably in relation to 'nexus, data and characterization'.[8] The report acknowledged that those challenges went beyond BEPS and recognized that they chiefly related to the question of how to allocate taxing rights on income generated from cross-border activities among countries. While identifying a number of options to address such concerns, including options that involved a new nexus of 'significant economic presence',[9] the use of a specific 'withholding tax'[10] and a 'digital equalization levy',[11] the OECD did not expressly recommend any for implementation. Instead, countries agreed to continue to monitor developments in respect of digitalization and their tax implications with the objective of producing a final report in 2020, with an interim report in 2018.

6. The EU, as the earliest adopter of these principles, has collected the most detailed information on compliance levels and revenue collected, with the total VAT revenue declared via its simplified compliance regime (Mini One Stop Shop) in its first year of operation (2015) exceeding EUR 3 billion. Approximately 70% of the total cross-border B2C supplies of services and intangibles that are in scope of this regime are captured by this simplified compliance regime. Further analysis suggests that the VAT on the remaining share of these cross-border B2C supplies of services and intangibles is remitted by foreign suppliers through the normal (non-simplified) registration and compliance regimes. The EU data also show that a relatively small number of large businesses account for the large majority of the revenues collected under the EU's simplified compliance regime. These data show that more than 99% of the VAT revenue processed through this regime is declared by about 13% of the businesses registered. The early findings of other countries that have introduced similar solutions in line with the 2015 OECD BEPS Action 1 Report are largely consistent with the EU's experiences.
7. For example, in Australia, the General Service Tax is collected from 1 July 2017 on low-value physical goods imported by consumers under a vendor collection model, by requiring non-resident businesses with an Australian turnover of AUD 75,000 or more to register and charge the tax. The twenty-eight EU Member States are also considering reform to remove of the current exemption from VAT for imports of low-value goods.
8. Chapter 7 of the 2015 OECD BEPS Action 1 Report, *see* note 1.
9. *Ibid.*
10. *Ibid.*
11. *Ibid.*

In this context, notwithstanding the important progress made after 2015 in tackling profit shifting through the widespread implementation of the OECD/G20 BEPS package, a number of countries unilaterally moved to take steps to introduce fragmented measures aimed at taxing digitalized activities and highly digitalized business models. These measures share certain common design features, as they typically seek to protect and/or expand the tax base in the country where the customers or users are located. While such measures reflect a growing discontent among some countries with the taxation outcomes produced by the current international tax system, these country-specific initiatives also increased the sense of urgency, among many other countries, to develop and adopt common policy approaches to stop the unravelling of the international income tax framework.

§1.03 RENEWED G20 INTEREST AND THE 2018 OECD INTERIM REPORT

In Baden-Baden, Germany, in March 2017, only one year after the establishment of the Inclusive Framework on BEPS,[12] ongoing concerns around the ability of the existing tax rules to meet the needs of a rapidly digitalizing economy led the G20 Finance Ministers to renew their interest in the TFDE's work. They requested an interim report thereon be delivered no later than April 2018 – a request that was reiterated by the G20 Leaders at their July 2017 summit in Hamburg, Germany. Drawing on consultations with business, academia, and civil society, and building on the 2015 OECD BEPS Action 1 Report, the Inclusive Framework on BEPS succeeded in delivering the 2018 OECD Interim Report in March 2018. That report, which included a series of important updates and findings, discussed in more detail, *infra*, was a key milestone towards developing a durable, long-term solution to the tax challenges posed by the digitalization of the economy. Not only did it show the complexity of the issues at stake (including, *inter alia*, persisting divergences among countries) but also laid down the foundations upon which a sustainable reform of the international income tax system could be developed in the coming years.

[A] Value Creation and Business Models

A robust understanding of how digitalization has changed (and continues to change) the way businesses operate and how they create value is fundamental to ensuring that the tax system responds appropriately to this ever-changing environment. In particular, looking at more highly digitalized business models, the 2018 OECD Interim Report

12. At the time of the delivery of the BEPS package, the G20 called for its timely implementation and requested that the OECD develop a more inclusive framework with the involvement of interested non-G20 countries and jurisdictions, including developing economies, on an equal footing. As a result, the Inclusive Framework on BEPS was established in June 2016 to monitor and support the implementation of the BEPS package and take forward any ongoing work arising from the BEPS Project, including on the international tax implications of digitalization. Today, more than 124 countries and jurisdictions have joined the Inclusive Framework on BEPS, whose mandate runs until end of 2020.

describes the main features of digital markets and how these shape value creation, and also identifies three characteristics that are frequently observed in certain highly digitalized business models,[13] namely:

(1) Cross-jurisdictional scale without mass. Digitalization has allowed businesses in many sectors to locate various stages of their production processes across different countries while simultaneously accessing a greater number of customers around the globe. Digitalization has also allowed some highly digitalized enterprises to be heavily involved in the economic life of a jurisdiction with or without any significant, physical presence therein, thus achieving operational local scale without local mass.
(2) Reliance on intangible assets, including intellectual property (IP). The analysis showed that digitalized enterprises are characterized by the growing importance of investment in intangibles, especially IP assets, which could either be owned by the business or leased from a third party. For many digitalized enterprises, the intense use of IP assets (such as software and algorithms) supports their platforms, websites, and many other crucial functions and, thus, is central to their business models.
(3) Data, user participation, and their synergies with IP. Data, user participation, network effects, and the provision of user-generated content are commonly observed in the business models of more highly digitalized businesses. The benefits from data analysis are also likely to increase with the amount of collected information linked to a specific user or customer. The importance of the role that user participation can play is most evident in the case of social networks, where without data, network effects, and user-generated content, the businesses would not exist as we know them today. However, the degree of user participation does not necessarily correlate with the degree of digitalization: for example, cloud computing can be considered as a more highly digitalized business that involves only limited user participation.

The reality of these business models is obviously very complex, and not all three features are necessarily present in each individual business nor are they present to the same degree. The 2018 OECD Interim Report, however, acknowledged that these characteristics are expected to become common features of an even wider number of businesses as digitalization continues to expand.

[B] Positive Impacts of BEPS Implementation

Although only two and a half years have passed since the OECD/G20 package of BEPS measures was agreed, the 2018 OECD Interim Report takes stock of progress made in their implementation. It outlined many positive developments, including, *inter alia*,

13. 2018 OECD Interim Report, 52, 167, 170.

the EU's recent adoption of its Anti-Tax Avoidance Directive,[14] as well as some aspects of the United States tax reform.[15] In response, a significant number of MNEs have already taken proactive measures to realign their tax arrangements with their real economic activity, either by reconsidering their TP positions or by relocating and onshoring valuable assets, such as intangibles. Similarly, on the critical issue of PE avoidance, some digitalized MNEs (e.g., Amazon, eBay, and Facebook) have already started changing their trade structures based on remote sales models to local reseller models.[16] With the exchange of Country-by-Country reports beginning in 2018 for the 2016 tax year, further evidence of the impact of the BEPS measures is anticipated in the coming years. These measures are, thus, effective in tackling double non-taxation but clearly do not solve the question of how rights to tax are shared among countries.

[C] Towards a Global Consensus-Based Reform of the International Income Tax System

The broader direct tax challenges of digitalization remain and raise very complex technical questions further explored in the 2018 OECD Interim Report; it generally acknowledged that the digital transformation continues to be an ongoing process and that there is a need to monitor how these changes may be impacting value creation. However, members of the Inclusive Framework on BEPS have different views on the question of whether and to what extent these features should result in changes to the international tax rules. Specifically, there is no agreement over the tax implications of scale without mass and a greater reliance on intangibles. With respect to data and user participation, there are different views on whether, and if so, to what extent, they should be considered an integral part of an enterprise's value creation process and, therefore, what impact they may have on the international tax rules.[17]

The different perspectives on these issues among the 124 members of the Inclusive Framework on BEPS can be generally described as falling into three groups.[18] The first group asserts that the reliance on data and user participation may lead to misalignments between the location in which profits are taxed and the location in which value is created. However, that first group's view is that these challenges are confined to certain business models and, thus, it does not believe that these factors undermine the principles underpinning the existing international tax framework. Consequently, countries belonging to this first group do not see a case for wide-ranging change. The second group of countries takes the view that the ongoing digital transformation of the economy and, more generally, trends associated with globalization present challenges to the continued effectiveness of the existing international tax framework for business profits. Importantly, for this second group, these challenges are not exclusive or specific to highly digitalized business models. Finally, there is the

14. *Ibid.* at 100, para. 284.
15. *Ibid.* at 100–101, para. 285.
16. *Ibid.* at 106–107.
17. *Ibid.* at 170–171.
18. *Ibid.* at 171–172.

third group of countries that believes that the BEPS package has largely addressed the concerns of double non-taxation (they do, however, highlight that it is still too early to fully assess the impact of all the BEPS measures). This third group of countries is generally satisfied with the existing tax system and does not currently see the need for any significant reform of the international tax rules.

Acknowledging these divergences, the 2018 OECD Interim Report notes that countries share a common interest in maintaining a single set of relevant and coherent international tax rules. Consequently, it embodies a commitment of all of the Inclusive Framework on BEPS member countries to undertake a coherent and concurrent review of the profit allocation and nexus rules - that is, the key concepts relating to the allocation of taxing rights between jurisdictions and the determination of the relevant share of an MNE's profits that will be subject to taxation in a given jurisdiction.[19] The objective of this review will be to work towards a consensus-based solution by 2020.

[D] Interim Measures

While making progress on a global consensus-based solution has been the TFDE's focus, a number of jurisdictions are contemplating the introduction of interim measures. In the Inclusive Framework on BEPS, there is no consensus on either the merit or need for interim measures and the 2018 OECD Interim Report does not make a recommendation for their introduction.[20]

A large number of countries believe that any interim measures will give rise to risks and adverse consequences irrespective of any limits that may be imposed on the design thereof and, therefore, oppose such measures. They believe those risks and adverse consequences would include, *inter alia*: negative impacts on investment, innovation, and growth; the possibility of overtaxation; distortive impacts on production and increasing the economic incidence of tax on consumers and businesses; and increased compliance and administration costs.

Other countries acknowledge these challenges but assert that they do not outweigh the need to ensure that tax is paid in their jurisdictions on certain digital services supplied therein and believe that at least some of the possible adverse consequences can be mitigated through the design of the measure. In other words, they believe that there is a fiscal and political imperative to act. At the same time, this same group of countries is of the view that a proliferation of different types of interim measures is undesirable and, therefore, the 2018 OECD Interim Report sets out guidance agreed by that group of countries on the design considerations that need to be taken into account when a country is considering the introduction of unilateral interim measures. These include, for instance, that any such measures should comply with existing international obligations, be temporary, targeted, and balanced, and be designed to limit compliance costs and not inhibit innovation.

19. *Ibid.* at 173.
20. *Ibid.* at 178.

[E] Beyond International Income Tax Rules

Digitalization offers new opportunities, as well as some challenges, for tax policy and administration beyond the international income tax system, which include the growth of the gig or sharing economy and how it affects tax compliance and revenues arising out of non-standard work. At the same time, technologies like blockchain give rise to both new, secure methods of record-keeping while also facilitating cryptocurrencies which pose risks to the gains made on tax transparency in the last decade.

The Inclusive Framework's work in this area is already underway; it seeks to better understand and address these developments. The 2018 Interim Report identifies new areas of work that will be undertaken by the Inclusive Framework on BEPS.[21] Given the availability of big data, international cooperation among tax administrations should be enhanced, in particular as regards the information on sharing platforms users to ensure taxes are paid by users when and where they are due. The Forum on Tax Administration,[22] working with the Inclusive Framework on BEPS, will develop practical tools and cooperation in that field and will continue its work on the tax consequences of new technologies (cryptocurrencies and blockchain technologies in particular).

§1.04 THE ROAD AHEAD

Through the Interim Report, members of the Inclusive Framework on BEPS confirmed their engagement in seeking a consensus-based solution, agreeing that the Inclusive Framework on BEPS (whose membership has now reached 117) would carry out this work with the goal to produce a final report in 2020, with another update to the G20 in 2019. The challenge for the Inclusive Framework on BEPS, and the international tax community more generally, will clearly be to bridge the divide between the various points of view and ensure that the coherence of the international income tax system remains relevant for today and the future.

In this endeavour, further work on the analysis of the valuable contribution of certain characteristics of highly digitalized business models, as well as digitalization more broadly, will be carried out. To inform the ongoing debate, technical solutions will also be explored, to test the feasibility of different options with respect to the profit allocation and nexus rules. In this process, ongoing political support will be essential to building consensus and achieving progress on these sensitive issues. In addition, gathering inputs from a broader group of stakeholders, including business, civil society, and academia, will be critical in designing solutions that are sound and ready to meet the changes prompted by digitalization while promoting investment and economic growth.

---

21. *Ibid.* at 207–208.
22. The Forum on Tax Administration (FTA) was created in 2002 and is a unique FTA for Commissioners from fifty OECD and non-OECD countries, including members of the G20. Its role is to identify, discuss and influence relevant global trends and develop new ideas to enhance tax administration around the world.

CHAPTER 2

The 'Genuine Link' Requirement for Source Taxation in Public International Law

Juliane Kokott[*]

§2.01 INTRODUCTION

My topic, the 'genuine link' requirement for source taxation in public international law, is broader than the general topic of this book, digital economy taxation. Rather, rethinking genuine link or nexus requirements is an issue concerning the modern globalized economy as such. The underlying question, i.e. in which country persons or transactions can and ought to be taxed, is not limited to the digital economy,[1] even though it seems most vital there.[2] Some, including the Confédération Fiscale Européenne (CFE),[3] therefore maintain that creating a special regime for digital companies – 'ring-fencing' them – would violate the 'principle of neutrality' espoused under the internationally agreed-upon Ottawa framework.[4] According to this Ottawa

* Many thanks to William S. Dodge, Martin Luther King, Jr. Professor of Law at the University of California, Davis, School of Law and Co-Reporter of The Restatement of the Law (Fourth), The Foreign Relations Law of the United States: Jurisdiction, for his important intellectual contribution.

1. Similarly, European Commission, *Communication from the Commission to the European Parliament and the Council: A Fair and Efficient Tax System in the European Union for the Digital Single Market*, COM(2017) 547 final, 2 (hereinafter '2017 Fair & Efficient Tax System Communication'); OECD, *Tax Challenges Arising from Digitalisation: Interim Report 2018* 52, 167, 170 (OECD Publishing 2018) (hereinafter '2018 OECD Interim Report').
2. *See, e.g.*, 2018 OECD Interim Report, *supra* note 1, at 24–25.
3. CFE Fiscal Committee, *Opinion Statement FC 10/2017: Position Paper EU Consultation on Fair Taxation of the Digital Economy* 3 (CFE 2017).
4. OECD, *Implementation of the Ottawa Taxation Framework Conditions: The 2003 Report* 12 Box 1(i) (OECD Publishing 2003).

Principle of Neutrality '[t]axation should seek to be neutral and equitable between forms of electronic commerce and between conventional and electronic forms of commerce.'[5] But, of course, the notion of genuine link can be understood differently with regard to the specific nature of the business in question.

As a starting point, let me explain the concept of genuine link in public international law (§2.02[A]), then briefly refer to the usual links in tax law (§2.02[B]), in order to reflect on links or nexus with respect to source taxation (§2.03) and, finally, on potential future developments (§2.04).

§2.02 DEFINITIONS

[A] The Genuine Link under Public International Law

In light of the principles established by the Permanent Court of International Justice (PCIJ) in its *Lotus Case*[6] and the International Court of Justice (ICJ) in its *Nottebohm Case*[7], restrictions on a state's power to tax cannot be presumed as long as there is a 'genuine link' between the taxing state and the taxpayer or the subject matter.[8]

[1] The Lotus Case *and the Principle of Territoriality*

In the *Lotus Case*, the PCIJ stressed the principle of territoriality, as did recently Advocate General Bobek in the tax case *Hornbach-Baumarkt* before the Court of Justice of the European Union (CJEU).[9] The facts underlying the *Lotus Case* were as follows: On 2 August 1926, a collision occurred on the high seas between the mail steamer *Lotus*, flying the French flag, and the collier *Boz-Kourt*, flying the Turkish flag. The *Boz-Kourt* sank and eight Turkish nationals lost their lives. Upon arrival of the *Lotus* in Istanbul, the Turkish authorities made inquiries and undertook criminal proceedings against both Lieutenant Hassan Bey, the captain of the *Boz-Kourt*, and the officer of the watch on board the *Lotus* at the time of the collision, Lieutenant Demons, a French citizen. The issue was whether Turkey had violated principles of international law by instituting proceedings against a French national acting on board a French vessel on the high seas. France maintained her exclusive jurisdiction as flag state.

According to the PCIJ:

> the first and foremost restriction imposed by international law upon a State is that – failing the existence of a permissive rule to the contrary – it may not exercise its power in any form in the territory of another State. In this sense jurisdiction is

5. *Ibid.*
6. *The Case of the SS Lotus (France* v *Turkey)* (1927) P.C.I.J. Series A, No. 9 (hereinafter '*Lotus Case*').
7. *Nottebohm (Liechtenstein* v *Guatemala)*, Judgment, I.C.J. Rep. 1955, at 4 et seq. (6 April, 1955) (hereinafter '*Nottebohm Case*'). *See also Nottebohm Case, in* 3 *Encyclopedia of Public International Law* 698 et seq. (Rudolf Bernhardt ed., North Holland 1997).
8. *See* Werner Ebke, *Double Taxation, in* 2 *Encyclopedia of Public International Law* 1099 (Rudolf Bernhardt ed., North Holland 1992).
9. *Hornbach-Baumarkt*, C-382/16, Opinion of AG Bobek, EU:C:2017:974, paras 20 et seq.

> certainly territorial; it cannot be exercised by a State outside its territory except by virtue of a permissive rule derived from international custom or from a convention[,][10]

or with the consent of the other State concerned.[11] This restriction refers to a state's jurisdiction to *enforce* rules, which cannot be exercised extraterritorially. Thus, normally, a state cannot collect taxes or undertake audits in another state's territory. Joint audits by the fiscal authorities of two different Member States of the European Union (EU) in the territory of one of those states, as they have been introduced recently, are permitted by the consent of the participating states and by the supranational law of the EU.[12]

However, the court continued, it does *not:*

> follow that international law prohibits a State from exercising jurisdiction [to prescribe or to adjudicate] *in its own* territory, in respect of any case which relates to acts which have taken place abroad, and in which it cannot rely on some permissive rule of international law.[13]

International law does *not* contain a general prohibition on states to extend the application of their laws and the jurisdiction of their courts to persons, property, and acts outside their territory. Rather, it leaves them in this respect a wide measure of discretion.[14] 'In these circumstances', the PCIJ held, 'all that can be required of a State is that it should not overstep the limits which international law places upon its jurisdiction'.[15]

The court then proceeded to hold that the territoriality of criminal law is not an absolute principle and by no means coincides with territorial sovereignty.[16] Based on those statements, one could, theoretically, read the *Lotus Case* as a basis for an unlimited extraterritorial jurisdiction to prescribe. But it is important to keep in mind that, despite those statements, the PCIJ acknowledged Turkey's jurisdiction in the *Lotus Case* on the basis of the 'effects doctrine', which is an expression of the principle of territoriality. It held that Turkey could take into consideration the fact that the offence produced its effects on the Turkish vessel and, consequently, in a place assimilated to Turkish territory. For that reason, the application of Turkish criminal law could not be challenged, even with regard to criminal offences committed in that place by foreigners.[17]

10. *Lotus Case, supra* note 6, at 18 et seq.
11. *See* Restatement (Fourth), *The Foreign Relations Law of the United States* § 402 and Reporter's Note 3 (Tentative Draft No. 3, 2017).
12. *See* Juliane Kokott, *Das Steuerrecht der Europäischen Union* s. 10 nos 95 et seq. (C.H. Beck 2018).
13. *Lotus Case, supra* note 6, at 19 (emphasis added).
14. *Ibid.*
15. *Ibid.*
16. *Ibid.* at 20.
17. *Lotus Case, supra* note 6, at 23.

[2] The Nottebohm Case *and the 'Genuine' Link*

In its 1955 *Nottebohm Case*,[18] the ICJ explicitly introduced the 'genuine link' requirement. Mr Nottebohm, a German national, settled in Guatemala in 1905 and made that country the headquarters of his increasingly prosperous business. He sometimes went to Germany on business and to Liechtenstein to visit his brother. In 1939, Mr Nottebohm became a citizen of Liechtenstein, thereby losing his German citizenship. In 1941, Guatemala joined World War II, fighting against Germany. Nottebohm was arrested as an enemy alien in 1943 and Guatemala seized and retained his property. In 1949, Guatemala expropriated by legislative decree the property of all 'private persons or corporations holding the nationality of any of the countries with which the Republic was at war, or who held such nationality on the 7th of October 1938, even though they claimed to have acquired another nationality subsequently'. On that basis, the property of Mr Nottebohm was confiscated.[19] Liechtenstein brought suit against Guatemala before the ICJ for what it argued was unjust treatment of Mr Nottebohm and illegal confiscation of his property. However, Guatemala argued that Mr Nottebohm had not gained Liechtenstein citizenship for the purposes of international law. The ICJ agreed and held inadmissible the claim submitted by Liechtenstein.[20]

The Court ruled that some link to the person or situation under the jurisdiction of a state may not be sufficient for the exercise of diplomatic protection; rather, that link had to be 'genuine'.[21] Accordingly, a state is only obliged to recognize the citizenship of a citizen of another state, for the purposes of the exercise of diplomatic protection, if there is a genuine link between the citizen and that other state.[22] That link or connection must 'be sufficiently close ... that it is possible to regard the nationality conferred upon him as *real* and *effective*, as the exact juridical expression of a social fact of a connection'.[23] For this reason, expropriations of 'enemy' property after World War II could not be put into question through diplomatic protection granted to the affected individuals. While this factual and political context relativizes the importance of the controversial *Nottebohm* judgment,[24] its underlying dogmatic approach remains interesting. The formulations in that judgment – 'real and effective', 'exact juridical expression of a social fact of a connection' – recall the CJEU's case law on abuse in tax law. The CJEU does not recognize 'wholly artificial arrangements which do not reflect

18. *Nottebohm Case*, *supra* note 7.
19. *Nottebohm Case*, *in* 3 *Encyclopedia of Public International Law* 698 et seq. (Rudolf Bernhardt ed., North Holland 1997).
20. *Nottebohm Case*, *supra* note 7, at 26.
21. *Ibid.* at 23.
22. *Ibid.*
23. *Ibid.* at 24 (emphasis added).
24. *See, e.g.*, Mads Adenas, *Jurisdiction, Procedure and the Transformation of International Law: From Nottebohm to Diallo in the ICJ*, 23 Eur. Bus. L. Rev. 128 (2012).

economic reality'.[25] Similarly, the Anti-Tax Avoidance Directive (ATAD) refers to non-genuine arrangements, which do not reflect economic reality.[26]

The question of course arises as to whether the ICJ jurisprudence can be transferred to the area of tax law. The *Nottebohm Case* deals with the issue of what kind of link entitles a state to exercise diplomatic protection based on an injury (expropriation) to its nationals: states can only protect their citizens if there is an effective link between them. But why should there be lesser requirements when it comes to imposing taxes upon individuals? If there must be an effective link entitling states to *protect* their citizens, this should be the case *a fortiori* when it comes to burdening persons who may not even be their citizens. If we transpose the ICJ jurisprudence to the area of taxation, we thus arrive at the conclusion that states must not abuse their (tax) jurisdiction by regulating situations with *no* genuine connection to their territory.[27]

[3] The Reasonable Exercise of Jurisdiction

The United States (US) Restatement (Fourth) of Foreign Relations Law also states that customary public international law governing jurisdiction to prescribe requires 'a genuine connection between the subject of the regulation and the state seeking to regulate'.[28] The US, a major tax jurisdiction, generally follows customary public international law in this respect, exercising jurisdiction to prescribe on each of the traditional bases recognized internationally.[29] Moreover, in assessing the geographic scope of federal law, US courts apply three principles of interpretation. The first one is a presumption against extraterritoriality based on 'the comity of nations'.[30] They 'interpret federal statutory provisions to apply only within the territorial jurisdiction of the United States unless there is a clear indication of congressional intent to the contrary.'[31] The second one is the principle that '[i]n interpreting the geographical scope of federal law, US courts seek to avoid unreasonable interference with the sovereign authority of other states'.[32] The third one is the principle of avoiding conflicts

25. For example, *Cadbury Schweppes*, C-196/04, Judgment, EU:C:2006:544, para. 55; *Eqiom & Enka*, C-6/16, Judgment, EU:C:2017:641, para. 30.
26. Council Directive 2016/1164 laying down rules against tax avoidance practices that directly affect the functioning of the internal market, OJ L 193/1, Art. 6(1)–(2) (2016) (hereinafter 'ATAD').
27. Restatement (Third), *The Foreign Relations Law of the United States* § 402 (1987).
28. Restatement (Fourth), *supra* note 11, § 211 (Tentative Draft No. 2, 2016).
29. Restatement (Fourth), *supra* note 11, § 201 (Tentative Draft No. 2, 2016).
30. *Am. Banana Co.* v *United Fruit Co.*, 213 U.S. 347, 356 (1909).
31. Restatement (Fourth), *supra* note 11, § 203 (Tentative Draft No. 3, 2017); *EEOC* v *Arabian Am. Oil Co.*, 499 U.S. 244, 248 (1991); *RJR Nabisco, Inc.* v *Eur. Cmty*, 136 S. Ct. 2090, 2100 (2016); *Kiobel* v *Royal Dutch Petroleum Co.*, 133 S. Ct. 1659, 1664 (2013); *Society of Composers, Authors and Music Publishers of Canada* v *Canadian Assn. of Internet Providers*, Case No. 29286 [2003], 2004 S.C.R. 45, nos 141 et seq. (S. Ct. Canada) (hereinafter 'Society of Composers').
32. Restatement (Fourth), *supra* note 11, § 204, Comment (a) (Tentative Draft No. 3, 2017); *F. Hoffmann-La Roche Ltd.* v *Empagran S.A.*, 542 U.S. 155, 165 (2004). The US Supreme Court has described this approach as a principle of 'prescriptive comity'. *See also* Restatement (Third), *supra* note 27, § 403 and comment.

with customary international law.[33] This common law presumption has its roots in an 1804 Supreme Court case according to which an act of Congress ought never to be construed to violate the law of nations if any other possible construction remains.[34] But later, customary international law rules on *prescriptive* jurisdiction became less territorial, as we have seen from the above-cited *Lotus* and *Nottebohm Cases*.[35] The more the US, as well as the EU, adopt extraterritorial rules, the more comity or friendship and respect between nations are indeed needed to resolve the resulting jurisdictional conflicts.[36]

In contrast, a state's jurisdiction to enforce rules is in principle strictly bound to its territory.[37] Consequently, tax laws may refer to persons and property outside the territory of the regulating state, but, generally, there would be no jurisdiction to enforce, i.e., to collect such taxes abroad. However, Article 11 of the Organisation for Economic Co-operation and Development (OECD) Convention on Mutual Administrative Assistance provides that 'the requested State shall ... take the necessary steps to recover tax claims' of the applicant State 'as if they were its own tax claims'. But not all states are parties to that convention and the US have entered a reservation to its Article 11. US tax treaties, generally, do not provide for the enforcement of foreign tax judgments. Nevertheless, sometimes the jurisdiction to prescribe and to adjudicate may suffice to collect tax revenues relating to persons and property outside the territory. This applies to situations where foreign debtors falling under those laws which regulate persons, property, and acts outside the territory dispose of assets inside the territory of the taxing state.

To sum up: the jurisdiction to prescribe rules and the jurisdiction to adjudicate are generally broader than the jurisdiction to enforce, which is in principle bound to the territory.[38] But the jurisdiction to prescribe also has its limits. It requires a genuine or sufficiently close connection to justify or make reasonable the exercise of prescriptive jurisdiction.[39]

33. Restatement (Fourth), *supra* note 11, § 205 (Tentative Draft No. 2, 2016).
34. *Murray* v *Schooner Charming Betsy*, 6 U.S. (2 Cranch) 64, 118 (1804).
35. For new extraterritorial duties of states, see Inter-American Court of Human Rights, *The Environment and Human Rights*, Advisory Opinion, OC-23/17 of 15 November 2016.
36. Discussing a jurisdictional rule of reason as a potential norm of international law, see Cedric Ryngaert, *Jurisdiction in International Law* 180 et seq. (Oxford Univ. Press 2d ed. 2015); *see also, e.g.*, Agreement between the European Communities and the Government of the United States of America on the Application of Positive Comity Principles in the Enforcement of their Competition Laws, June 1998, OJ L/173/28 (1998); Peter Behrens, *The Extraterritorial Reach of EU Competition Law Revisited: The 'Effects Doctrine' Before the ECJ* (Europa-Kolleg Hamburg Inst. for Eur. Integration Discussion Papers 3/16, 2016). On the different doctrines of international comity in US law, see William S. Dodge, *International Comity in American Law*, 115 Colum. L. Rev. 2071 (2015). On the tendency of Continental European countries not to frame similar doctrines in comity terms, see William S. Dodge, *International Comity in Comparative Perspective, in The Oxford Handbook of Comparative Foreign Relations Law* (Curtis A. Bradley ed., forthcoming estimated 26 June 2019).
37. Restatement (Fourth), *supra* note 11, § 401 and § 402 (Tentative Draft No. 3, 2017).
38. On the various types of jurisdiction (to enforce, to prescribe, and to adjudicate), *see* Restatement (Third), *supra* note 27, § 401; Restatement (Fourth), *supra* note 11, § 101 (Tentative Draft No. 3, 2017).
39. Restatement (Fourth), *supra* note 11, § 211, Reporters note 2, at 46 et seq. with references (Tentative Draft No. 2, 2016).

[B] Links/Nexus in Tax Law

Two types of tax jurisdiction are generally recognized: (1) the unlimited jurisdiction to tax persons on the basis of their nationality, domicile, or residence and (2) the limited jurisdiction of the source country.

[1] Residence Taxation

In most countries, it is not citizenship but rather residence that determines the tax jurisdiction over an individual (residence taxation). For the US, an individual is a taxable person if he or she is either a resident or a citizen. Usually, an individual's residence depends upon the length of his or her physical stay. Roughly, if a person spends half a year or more in a particular country, he or she is considered a resident for that year.[40] But merely maintaining a residence in a country without actually being there might suffice.

For companies, there are basically two nexus for 'residence' taxation: (1) their place of effective management or (2) their place of incorporation.[41]

---

40. Germany, for example, requires more than six months (*Abgabenordnung* (AO), per § 9); India more than 182 days (OECD, *India: Information on Residency for Tax Purposes*, s. I, oecd.org, *available at* http://www.oecd.org/tax/automatic-exchange/crs-implementation-and-assistance/tax-residency/India-Tax-residency.pdf (accessed 20 September 2018)); Luxembourg more than six months (Art. 2, *Loi du 4 décembre 1967 concernant l'impôt sur le revenu*, Mémorial A n° 79, as modified (LIR), referring to, Arts 13 & 14, *Loi d'adaptation fiscale du 16 octobre 1934* (Steueranpassungsgesetz), Mémorial A n° 901, as modified (StAnpG)); the requirements are more extensive and more complicated in the US where residents must meet the 'substantial presence test':

    > An alien individual will meet the substantial presence test if the individual is physically present in the United States for at least:
    > 1. 31 days during the current calendar year; and
    > 2. 183 days during the 3-year period that includes the current calendar year, and the 2 calendar years immediately preceding counting:
    >   a. All days of physical presence in the United States during the current calendar year, and
    >   b. 1/3 of the days the individual was present in 1st preceding year; and
    >   c. 1/6 of the days the individual was present in 2nd preceding year.

    (OECD, *US: Information on Residency for Tax Purposes* s. 1, oecd.org, *available at* http://www.oecd.org/tax/automatic-exchange/crs-implementation-and-assistance/tax-residency/United-States-Tax-Residency.pdf (accessed 20 September 2018)).
41. Germany, for example, relies on the place of effective management (*German Info*, *supra* note 40, s. II); many other states require one or the other criterion for residence taxation of companies, e.g., Luxembourg (OECD, *Luxembourg: Information on Residency for Tax Purposes* s. II, oecd.org, *available at* http://www.oecd.org/tax/automatic-exchange/crs-implementation-and-assistance/tax-residency/Luxembourg-Tax-Residency.pdf (accessed 7 September 2018)); India (*India Info*, *supra* note 40, s. II); and China (OECD, *China: Information on Residency for Tax Purposes*, s. II, oecd.org, *available at* http://www.oecd.org/tax/automatic-exchange/crs-implementation-and-assistance/tax-residency/China-Residency.pdf (accessed 20 September 2018)), while US law generally treats a corporation as a domestic corporation only if it was created or organized under the laws of the US, any of its states, or the District of Columbia, with a few voluntary or involuntary exceptions (*US Info.*, *supra* note 40, s. II).

[2] Source Taxation

The principle of source taxation, by contrast, relies on the source (country) where the income is generated.[42] There are more and more individuals and companies whose 'residence' is in one country but whose business is carried out and whose income is generated in another country. In such cases, the principle of residence-based taxation does not seem appropriate.

§2.03 THE GENUINE LINK REQUIREMENT FOR SOURCE TAXATION

Source taxation, as opposed to residence taxation, thus relies on the idea of taxation by the state within whose territory the *value is created*. Such taxation is traditionally based on business done or property located in the territory of a particular state, or transactions that occur, originate, or terminate in the territory of that state or have some other substantial connection to that state. Insofar as taxation is source-based, the nationality, domicile, residence, and presence of the parties to such transactions are irrelevant.[43]

[A] Lack of Adequate Rules

But, as EU Commissioner Moscovici has pointed out, our tax framework does not fit anymore with the development of the digital economy or with new business models,[44] unless it is understood differently. First, in the digital economy – e.g., in the advertising business – it is possible for values to be created all over the world by people from different nations, who might, in addition, move across borders. Second, as value in the digital economy can be created anywhere, companies are free to choose low-tax countries, such as Ireland, for their headquarters. That practice cannot always be said to be 'abusive', as those companies do not necessarily evade taxes in a particular country where they should be paid.[45] In principle, the lack of adequate rules cannot be attributed to – let alone be a basis for reproach of – the taxpayer in all of the cases. Therefore, it is not clear whether just applying all base erosion and profit shifting (BEPS) Action Plan[46] and EU anti-tax avoidance measures could solve the problem, as it is sometimes maintained.[47] And third, nowadays, users also contribute to the value

42. *See* 2017 Fair & Efficient Tax System Communication, *supra* note 1, at 3.
43. Restatement (Third), *supra* note 27, §§ 411 Abs. 2, 412 Abs. 1(b)–(c), Abs. 2, 3 & 4; Restatement (Fourth), *supra* note 11, regrettably, does not contain special parts on tax jurisdiction.
44. *See* Roxana Mironescu, *EU to Present 'Electroshock' Digital Tax Plan by March*, Luxembourg Times, 13 February 2018; 2017 Fair & Efficient Tax System Communication, *supra* note 1, at 6 ('has worked well for "brick and mortar" companies but ...'); European Commission, *Proposal for a Council Directive on the common system of a digital services tax on revenues resulting from the provision of certain digital services*, 21 March 2018, COM(2018) 148 final, 2018/0073 (CNS) 2 (hereinafter '2018 DST Directive Proposal').
45. *See also* Georg Kofler et al., *Digitalisierung und Betriebsstättenkonzept*, 5b RdW 369, 376–382 (2017).
46. OECD, *Action Plan on Base Erosion and Profit Shifting* (OECD Publishing 2013).
47. Relying heavily on BEPS and anti-avoidance measures, *see* CFE, *supra* note 3, at 3 et seq.

of a digital enterprise.[48] Nevertheless, even Internet giants like Amazon generally rely on a functioning state structure including courts, energy, transportation, and waste disposal, just as other tax-paying businesses do.[49] Therefore, they should also be taxed similarly to other businesses. However, many digitalized businesses can be heavily involved in the economic life of different jurisdictions without any (significant) physical presence (scale without mass).[50] Therefore, the traditional nexus rules do no longer work.

Failure to adapt international nexus rules has led to unilateral measures in many countries, including EU Member States.[51] Especially within the EU, unilateral measures tend to cause problems with regard to the functioning of the internal market, the basic freedoms, and the general prohibition of discrimination. A new perspective with regard to nexus rules is, therefore, badly needed.[52]

[B] Virtual Establishments, Place of Consumption, and the Destination Principle

This, of course, leads to the discussions about 'virtual establishments', 'significant economic presence', and 'intangible presence' and how those terms could be defined. The starting point is that tax jurisdiction relies on the idea that there should be a fair relation between state-provided services, benefits, and opportunities[53] on the one hand, and taxation on the other.

[1] Redefining Territoriality

In some types of businesses, the only reliably determinable link to the territory of a state and, thus, to the internationally recognized principle of territoriality, is consumption. But, whereas a citizen, resident or person doing business in a state can be presumed to profit from the services, benefits, and infrastructure of that state, the same does not hold true as easily when it comes to selling or providing intangible services in a country via the Internet. Sales and consumption are recognized nexus for sales taxes and value-added tax (VAT) but not, traditionally, for income taxes. Factors like sales

48. 2018 OECD Interim Report, *supra* note 1, at 171 et seq.
49. *See* Kofler, *supra* note 45, at 382.
50. *See* 2018 OECD Interim Report, *supra* note 1, at 51.
51. For example, in France, India, Israel, Italy, Taiwan, Thailand, Turkey, and the US; *see* OECD, *Digitalization Tax Interim Report: Comments Received on the Request for Input – Part II*, 1, 17–18, 25 (OECD Publishing 2017); *see also* Julia Sinnig, *Besteuerung der digitalen Wirtschaft in Großbritannien, Italien und Ungarn – ein europäischer Rechtsvergleich*, 6 Internationale Steuer-Rundschau 408 (2017).
52. 2017 Fair & Efficient Tax System Communication, *supra* note 1; EU Commission, *Proposal for a Council Directive laying down rules relating to the corporate taxation of a significant digital presence* of 21 March 2018, COM(2018) 147 final, 2018/0072 (CNS), Recital 8 (hereinafter '2018 SDP Directive Proposal').
53. *Wisconsin* v *Penney*, 311 U.S. 435, 61 (1940); *General Motors Corp.* v *Washington et al.*, 377 U.S. 436 (1964); *Goldberg* v *Sweet*, 488 U.S. 262 (1989).

and consumption can be used to apportion income among several states but, traditionally, only under the condition that the taxable person has some, even intangible, presence there. These factors alone have not been considered sufficient to establish the necessary link for income taxation.[54] However, national courts of EU Member States have occasionally recognized that the taxpayer need not have a tangible, physical presence in a state for income to be taxable there. According to that view, any corporation that regularly exploits the markets of a state should be subject to that state's jurisdiction to impose an income tax, even if not physically present there.[55]

Under Article 5 of the Commission's new proposal on taxing digital services, taxable revenues obtained by an entity are to be treated as obtained in a Member State if the users of that taxable service are located in that state.[56] Similarly, the OECD, in its 2015 OECD BEPS Action 1 Report, stated that: '[f]or consumption purposes internationally traded services and intangibles should be taxed according to the rules of the jurisdiction of consumption'.[57] Numerous tax jurisdictions are already taking their lead from the OECD's recommended approach to taxing the digital economy.[58] This indicates that these states agree on the destination principle. The destination principle has the additional advantage that it might decrease the role of tax competition, given the immobility of the consumer base as opposed to the increasing mobility of production factors. It might, thus, allow taxpayers to allocate their resources wherever they find the best business environment, instead of engaging in tax-driven allocation of production factors or in mere profit shifting between jurisdictions. At the same time, problems regarding the control of transfer pricing (e.g., on the basis of the implementation of the EU state aid prohibition) might become redundant.[59] Against this background, a few states are also introducing 'significant economic presence' tests, based on online contract conclusion, the use of digital products and services and the generation of significant revenue that is closely related to the volume of online activities performed, not by a non-resident taxable corporation, but by users located in the taxing state.[60] Collecting data in the relevant state might be another factor, even

54. *But see* 2018 SDP Directive Proposal, *supra* note 52, Art. 2 ([t]his Directive applies to entities irrespective of where they are resident for corporate tax purposes, whether in a Member State or in a third country).
55. *See also* Peter Hongler & Pasquale Pistone, *Blueprints for a New PE Nexus to Tax Business Income in the Era of the Digital Economy* 23 (IBFD, Working Paper 20 January 2015).
56. *See* 2018 DST Directive Proposal, *supra* note 44, Art. 5.
57. OECD, *Addressing the Tax Challenges of the Digital Economy, Action 1 – 2015 Final Report*, Annex D, Guideline 3.1, 222 (OECD Publishing 2015) (hereinafter '2015 OECD BEPS Action 1 Report').
58. 2018 OECD Interim Report, *supra* note 1, Annex 3.B.1. *Implementation of the Measures on VAT/GST covered by the 2015 OECD BEPS Action 1 Report*, at 118 (e.g., Argentina, Bangladesh, Brazil, Canada, Colombia, Gulf, Israel, Malaysia, Philippines, Singapore, Thailand, and Vietnam).
59. *See* Wolfgang Schön, *Destination-Based Income Taxation and WTO-Law: A Note, in Essays in Honour of Manfred Mössner* 429 (Heike Jochum et al. eds., IBFD 2016).
60. For example, Israel and India; *see* 2018 OECD Interim Report, *supra* note 1, 137 et seq., Boxes 4.1 & 4.2; *see also*, for India, s. 9(1)(i) Expl'n 2A of the Income Tax Act, 1 April 2018, according to which 'significant economic presence' can be based on any:

though its contribution to value creation is controversial.[61] For advertisement taxes, the requisite nexus might be established by the destination of the advertisement and the location of the targeted public.[62] According to the Commission's 2018 SDP Directive Proposal, a robust definition of nexus must be based on the revenues from the supply of digital services, the number of users[63] or the number of business contracts for digital services.[64]

Also, intangible property has previously been recognized as a possible way to establish nexus. Thus, a taxpayer licensing intangible Intellectual property (IP) rights[65] for use in another state and deriving income from that use has been recognized by a US court as having a 'substantial nexus' with that state.[66] According to the Commission, the destination principle appears to reflect the current legal situation in copyright law. Accordingly, 'the act of communication to the public of a copyright protected work takes place not only in the country of origin (emission-State) but also in all the States where the signals can be received (reception-States)'.[67]

[2] A Broader Understanding of Nexus

Generally, state practice is becoming more lenient with regard to the nexus requirement.[68] There is a trend to expand the tax base in the country where the customers or users are located, generally based on a broader understanding of the enterprise's engagement in that country. Also, elements linked to a market are more and more included in the tax base, notably sales, revenue, place of use, or consumption.[69] This

---

1) transaction in respect of any goods, services or property carried out by a non-resident in India including provision of download of data or software in India, if the aggregate of payments arising from such transaction or transactions during the previous year exceeds such amount as may be prescribed; or
2) Systematic and continuous soliciting of its business activities or engaging in interaction with such number of users as maybe prescribed, in India through digital means.

See also 2018 OECD Interim Report, *supra* note 1, 146, Box 4.6 (France's tax on online and physical distribution of audiovisual content focusing on the destination of the related supply, the place of performance of the sale or supply, or on whether the 'audience' of online-on-demand services is located in France (i.e., an Internet user established, domiciled, or usually resident therein)).

61. 2018 OECD Interim Report, *supra* note 1, at 25 et seq.
62. *Ibid.* at 145, Box 4.5 (Hungary's advertising tax).
63. 2018 DST Directive Proposal, *supra* note 44, at 11.
64. 2018 SDP Directive Proposal, *supra* note 52, Recital 6 & Art. 4, para. 3.
65. On intangibles as drivers of business value, 2018 OECD Interim Report, *supra* note 1, 52 et seq.
66. *See* Supreme Court of South Carolina, *Geoffrey, Inc.* v *SC Tax Comm'n*, 47 S.E.2d 13 (1993).
67. Commission Decision of 8 October 2002, Case No. COMP/C2/38.014 – IFPI 'Simulcasting', notified under doc. Number C(2002) 3639, 2003/300/EG, No. 21. *See also Society of Composers*, *supra* note 31, No. 68 (national practice confirms that either the country of transmission or the country of reception may take jurisdiction over a 'communication' linked to its territory, although whether it chooses to do so is a matter of legislative or judicial policy), and No. 76.
68. *See also* the recent US Supreme Court decision in *South Dakota* v *Wayfair, Inc.* 138 S. Ct. 2080 (2018) (concerning state sales taxes).
69. 2018 OECD Interim Report, *supra* note 1, at 159; Peter Hongler & Pasquale Pistone, *Blueprints for a New PE Nexus to Tax Business Income in the Era of the Digital Economy*; *IBFD Working Paper*

approach was first elaborated in competition law with its well-known effects doctrine[70] and can now also be found with regard to intellectual property[71] and in the law of data protection.[72] In view of the mobility of data, there seems to be no alternative to extraterritorial jurisdiction in data protection law.[73] In tax law, we are rather confronted with redefining nexus, territoriality and extraterritoriality.

However, tax enforcement may prove difficult without the physical presence of the taxpayer in the taxing country.[74]

---

20 January 2015 (IBFD 2015); *see* Schön, *supra* note 59, at 430 et seq. (apodictically '[f]rom the perspective of international customary law, this move towards a destination basis does not pose a problem: selling goods and services to a local customer base forges a "genuine link". between the taxpayer and the destination country, which is a legitimate basis for taxation.'); *see also* Kolja van Lück, *Besteuerung der 'Digital Economy' – Neue Vorstöße der EU und der OECD/G20-Staaten zur steuerlichen Erfassung digitalisierter Geschäftstätigkeiten*, 5 ISR 158 et seq., 168 et seq. (2018).

70. *See Geigy AG* v *Comm'n*, 52/69, Judgment, EU:C:1972:73, paras 41 et seq.; *Ahlström Osakeyhtiö & Others* v *Comm'n*, Joined Cases 89/85, 104/85, 114/85, 116/85, 117/85, 125/85, 126/85, 127/85, 128/85, 129/85, Judgment, EU:C:1993:120, paras 3 et seq., paras 15 et seq.; *Intel* v *Comm'n*, C-413/14, Judgment, EU:C:2017:632, paras 40, 45, 49 (the effects test).
71. *See* Alexander Peukert, *Territoriality and Extra-territoriality in Intellectual Property Law, in* 11 *Beyond Territoriality: Transnational Legal Authority in an Age of Globalization* 189, 196. (Gunther Handl et al. eds., Queen Mary Stud. in Int'l Law, Brill/Nijhoff 2012):

> In a globalized, Internet-connected world, however, in which innovations are often the result of cross-border collaboration and the use of inventions, works, signs, etc., occurs everywhere, these basic principles have become the subject of fundamental criticism. According to most observers, the territoriality principle in IP Law is based on an outdated focus on isolated national-sovereigns that are less and less able – as a matter of fact and of law – to regulate exclusively the conduct of their citizens.

72. *See Google Spain and Google*, C-131/12, Judgment, EU:C:2014:317, para. 55:

> The processing of personal data for the purpose of the service of a search engine such as Google Search, which is operated by an undertaking that has its seat in a third State but has an establishment in a Member State, is carried out 'in the context of the activities' of that establishment if the latter is intended to promote and sell, in that Member State, advertising space offered by the search engine which serves to make the service offered by that engine profitable.

Wirtschaftsakademie Schleswig-Holstein, C-210/16, Opinion of AG Bot, EU:C:2017:796, para. 92 ('"context of activities" – and not the location of the data – is a determining factor in identifying the ... applicable law'). A broad definition of territoriality can be found in Art. 3(1) of Regulation (EU) 2016/679 of the European Parliament and of the Council of 27 April 2016 on the protection of natural persons with regard to the processing of personal data and on the free movement of such data, and repealing Directive 95/46/EC (General Data Protection Regulation) (Text with EEA relevance) (2016) OJ L 119/1 (the 'Regulation applies to the processing of personal data in the context of the activities of an establishment of a controller or a processor in the Union, regardless of whether the processing takes place in the Union or not'). Björn Steinrötter, *Feuertaufe für die EU-Datenschutz-Grundverordnung – und das Kartellrecht steht Pate*, 9 EWS 61, 62 et seq. (2018).

73. *See* Philip Uecker, *Extraterritoriale Regelungshoheit im Datenschutzrecht* 250, IX (Nomos 2017).
74. EU plans on a withholding of tax or a levy on revenues generated from the provision of digital services take this into account.

§2.04 THE FUTURE: APPORTIONMENT OR MOVE TOWARDS INDIRECT TAXATION?

Two problems, thus, remain: First, as mentioned above, sales and turnover may provide an important factor for apportioning the tax load of a *taxable* person in a particular state. Yet, those factors are not generally recognized as a sufficient link for income taxation in the first place, even though state practice seems to be in the process of changing. Second, as turnover does not equal profits, a destination- or consumption-based nexus leaves us with the problem of determining the profits of the corporation.

[A] Apportionment

If those two problems can be overcome – that is, if there is some (potentially intangible) presence and if a corporate taxpayer's business income or 'apportionable income' can be determined – apportionment could mitigate the problem of 'unfair' distribution of tax revenues between the Member States of the EU.[75] Member States would have to use an apportionment formula to calculate the percentage of any income that is subject to their income tax. Apportionment, which has been practiced in the US, Canada, and Switzerland[76] for decades, was already suggested to the European Commission at the beginning of this century[77] and underlies the Commission's 2018 DST Directive Proposal.[78] However, it presupposes the adoption of the Common Consolidated Tax Base.[79]

Though the US Supreme Court upheld California's proportionate taxation of the *worldwide* income of unitary businesses,[80] California soon repealed its unitary business tax and such apportionment is rather used in interstate relations, but not when one of the taxing entities is a foreign sovereign.[81] In any case, unitary taxation with apportionment but without a common consolidated tax base creates a risk of double taxation.

But, if generally applied within the EU on the basis of a common consolidated tax base, taxing only the relevant percentage could avoid double taxation without any need to conclude double taxation agreements. EU Member States would then have to agree on an apportionment formula. In the US, there has been a development over the past

75. *Similarly*, Maarten de Wilde, *'Sharing the Pie': Taxing Multinationals in a Global Market*, 43 Intertax 438 et seq. (2015).
76. *See* Katerina Krchniva, *Comparison of European, Canadian and U.S. Formula Apportionment on Real Data*, 12 Procedia Econ. & Fin. 309 et seq. (2014).
77. Joann Martens Weiner, *Formulary Apportionment and Group Taxation in the European Union: Insights From the United States and Canada* (European Commission Taxation Papers, Working Paper No. 8/2005, 2005), *available at* https://ec.europa.eu/taxation_customs/sites/taxation/files/resources/documents/taxation/gen_info/economic_analysis/tax_papers/2004_2073_en_web_final_version.pdf. (last accessed 26 February 2019).
78. 2018 DST Directive Proposal, *supra* note 44, Art. 7.
79. European Commission, *Proposal for a Council Directive on a Common Consolidated Corporate Tax Base (CCCTB)*, COM(2016) 683 final, 2016/0336 (CNS), Recital (10) & Arts 28 & 32 et seq. (hereinafter 'CCCTB Proposal').
80. *Barclays Bank Plc.* v *Franchise Board of California*, 512 U.S. 298 (1994).
81. *Ibid.* at 332, 337–338, O'Connor J., dissenting (referring to the opposition of all EU Member States of the European Union to California's approach).

twenty years, from a formula with three equally weighted factors – (1) sales, (2) payroll, and (3) property[82] – to an enhanced or single sales factor. This mirrors the development of the modern, digitalized economy where sometimes only sales or consumption can be linked with certainty to a specific state territory.[83] The sales factor is the ratio of the taxpayer's sales within the territory of the taxing state to the taxpayer's total sales.

Even though apportionment is conceptually simple, it may prove difficult in practice to calculate with precision the amount of income that is properly taxable in a particular state. Nevertheless, the apportionment rules developed in the US do provide a 'reasonable approximation' of a corporation's in-state level of activity and therefore sufficiently calculate the 'fair share' of multistate income that a state may tax.[84] They also seem to comply with the public international law requirement of a genuine link.[85] Admittedly, American trading partners have opposed US apportionment schemes as based on worldwide income[86] and, so far, apportionment has not met with success within the OECD.[87] But apportionment might still be a reasonable solution within the EU.[88]

[B] Move Towards Indirect Taxation

As consumption typically relates to indirect taxes, an alternative would be to globally enhance VAT and to work on its effective collection worldwide.[89] Both source and residence taxation have become more and more difficult to handle for a growing category of cross-border economic activities. VAT, on the contrary, is successfully

82. For example, *Container Corp.* v *Franchise Tax Bd.*, 463 U.S. 159, 182 et seq. (1983); *see also CCCTB Proposal, supra* note 79.
83. Early cases concern interstate railway building, *see, e.g., Western Union Telegraph Co.* v *Taggart*, 163 U.S. 1 (1896); more recent cases relate to telecommunications, *see, e.g., Goldberg* v *Sweet*, 488 U.S. 252 (1989).
84. *See CCH White Paper: State Apportionment of Business Income, September 2014*, 784 (Wolters Kluwer 2014).
85. The US Supreme Court upheld the use of the worldwide unitary tax method, which uses the worldwide income of a 'unitary business' as the basis for tax assessment; it also upheld California's apportionment scheme as fair and as taking into account the undesirability of double taxation. *Container Corp.*, 463 U.S. 159, 193 (1983); *but see Japan Line* v *County of L.A.*, 441 U.S. 453 (1979) (A California *ad valorem* property tax law, even though apportioned, was found unconstitutional as applied to foreign-owned instrumentalities of foreign commerce due to the potentially immitigable risk of multiple taxation and its frustration of the federal government's ability to address foreign commerce with a unitary voice under the Commerce Clause). Due to the rather limited nature of the *Japan Line* ruling, it does not appear that, to date, the US Supreme Court has specifically ruled on the constitutionality of international apportionment. *See also* Restatement (Third), *supra* note 27, § 412 (Reporter's Note 7).
86. *See, e.g.*, Franklin Latcham, *Worldwide Combination and the Container Case: A Perspective on Unitary Taxation*, 2 Berkeley J. Int'l L. 89 et seq. (1984).
87. For example, OECD, *Review of Comparability and of Profit Methods, Revision of Chapters I-III of the Transfer Pricing Guidelines* 9 et seq. (OECD Publishing 2010).
88. *See also* 2018 DST Directive Proposal, *supra* note 44, Arts 5 & 6, particularly the rules concerning apportionment in Art. 5 No. 3.
89. Wolfgang Schön, *Der digitale Steuer-Irrweg*, FAZ (6 April 2018), *available at* http://www.faz.net/aktuell/wirtschaft/unternehmen/der-digitale-steuer-irrweg-15527941.html, at 16 (accessed 20 September 2018).

being introduced in more and more countries and is constantly becoming more important.[90] With respect to the present issue, businesses whose value creation cannot be localized reliably could be obliged to collect a potentially higher VAT on their goods and services.[91] That approach, combined with the destination principle, would also affect the allocation of tax revenues between the state of the corporation and the state of consumption; tax revenue in the countries of the shareholders might decrease whereas tax revenues in the countries of consumption might increase. Such a result would meet some of the concerns underlying the quest for an adaptation of the nexus requirement by recognizing the concept of a significant economic presence while posing a significantly lower risk of double taxation. However, the trend from direct towards indirect taxation may hit the wrong persons, namely consumers instead of big business.

§2.05 CONCLUSIONS

The foregoing leads to the following two conclusions:

(1) *Income* taxation presupposes a genuine link to the taxing state. Just providing or selling services via the Internet has not generally been considered sufficient. However, state practice is becoming more lenient. The notion of user- or consumption-based value creation is gaining ground.
(2) Insofar as some link to the taxing state can be established through at least an *intangible* presence, apportionment can contribute to a fairer distribution of tax revenues between EU Member States. However, it presupposes a common consolidated tax base and at least similar apportionment formulas.

90. *See, e.g.*, Alan Schenk, Victor Thuronyi & Wei Cui eds., *The Proliferation of VATs, in Value Added Tax: A Comparative Approach* 12 et seq. (Cambridge Univ. Press 2d ed. 2015).
91. *See also*, Marc Wolf, *La TVA pour surmonter la crise de la territorialité fiscal,* 3 Revue européenne et internationale de droit fiscal 94, 96 (2017).

CHAPTER 3

EU and WTO Law Limits on Digital Business Taxation

Werner Haslehner

§3.01 INTRODUCTION

This chapter addresses the challenges and limits posed by two sets of supranational law for any reform of international tax systems aimed at capturing profits made in specific digital business models. By way of background, it first analyses the policy challenges arising from digitalization and lists a few policy responses that have been proposed or implemented recently (§3.02). Specifically, it will focus on specific withholding taxes (WHT) tailored to 'digital transactions', new source rules ('digital nexus', 'virtual permanent establishment' (VPE), 'significant digital presence' (SDP)) and specific new taxes directly targeting 'digital business' ('equalization levies' (EL) and 'digital services tax' (DST)). As these ideas are all subject to more detailed review in other chapters in this volume, they are described here only to the extent necessary to perform a generic analysis of potential incompatibilities with supra- and international law. The chapter then reviews well-known limits imposed by European Union (EU) law for tax policy-making with specific reference to such proposed policy responses, distinguishing between limits imposed on EU Member States (§3.03[A]) and on the EU as an independent actor (§3.03[B]). It then follows a less well-trodden path, discussing limitations on reforms arising from World Trade Organization (WTO) law (§3.04), before offering a brief concluding summary of the insights gained from the chapter (§3.05).

§3.02 DIGITAL BUSINESS TAXATION REFORM: BACKGROUND

[A] Tax Policy Challenges Arising from Digitalization

The challenges posed by the digitalization of modern business to the design of a fair and efficient tax system are threefold. As the Organisation for Economic Co-operation and Development (OECD) pointed out in the 2018 OECD Interim Report[1] (the focus of Chapter 1, *supra*), digitalization allows businesses to 'create value' without a physical presence in a country on whose market and, thus, whose public goods, it implicitly or explicitly relies. Second, although they may be conceptually sound and capable of addressing transactions regardless of physical presence, current transfer pricing rules are poorly adapted to digital transactions, especially, the (dis-)location of intellectual property as a key determinant for income flows in both intra- and intercompany relations. Third, payments made for the provision of digital services are often lacking and, when they exist at all, their characterization along traditional lines (i.e., business income, royalties, capital gain) is particularly difficult since these categories were created with a very different kind of economy in mind.

Both the first and second challenges identified in the 2018 OECD Interim Report relate to a disconnection between taxation and value creation. Thus, they reflect the continuing nature of the problems the OECD described in its various 2015 Base Erosion and Profit Shifting (BEPS) reports, specifically taxpayers shifting their profits to countries where they do not 'truly' belong by means of tax structures that take advantage of the gaps in international tax rules, the lack of coherence between national rules on cross-border investment and the lack of information transparency in the field. The peculiarity with respect to digital business models is that the outcome, which is perceived to be 'incorrect',[2] is less often (or, at least, less obviously) the consequence of deliberate tax structuring by an enterprise than the result of tax systems failing to account for business models that are naturally characterized by fragmentation and its attendant dislocation of economic activity. This is particularly the case for businesses that heavily rely on (i) collecting and exploiting data and (ii) multi-sided platforms. As the 2018 OECD Interim Report noted, such 'key features [of digitalization], while not generating unique BEPS issues, can exacerbate BEPS risks'.[3]

The separate and broader third challenge identified in the 2018 OECD Interim Report relates to the ongoing viability of the existing paradigm that underlies the international tax system's allocation of taxing rights. The still relatively simple question in this context was whether new digitalized business models could fit neatly into that system's existing categories reflected in the allocation rules set out in Articles 6 through 21 of the OECD Model.[4] Arguably, it would require only relatively small

1. OECD, *Tax Challenges Arising from Digitalisation: Interim Report 2018: Inclusive Framework on BEPS* (OECD Publishing 2018) (hereinafter '2018 OECD Interim Report').
2. That is to say, the result of a shifting of profits that is not in line with the intentions of Contracting States.
3. 2018 OECD Interim Report, at 18, m.no. 17.
4. OECD, *OECD Model Tax Convention on Income and on Capital (Condensed Version)* (OECD Publishing 2017) (hereinafter 'OECD Model'). The OECD Model includes, among other things,

changes to the OECD Model Commentary on the relevant provisions to ensure a common understanding and application of tax treaties to such businesses in the future.[5] The far more difficult issue to resolve is whether the existing architecture underlying bilateral tax treaties can be made to fit the demands of fair taxation in the digital age.

[B] Tax Policy Responses

At the OECD level, no concrete conclusions or policy recommendations have yet been made as to the appropriate response(s) to the threefold challenges it identified in its latest contribution to the debate: the 2018 OECD Interim Report. That report is confined to a description of the challenges' roots and an assessment of existing national measures taken to address them. Thus, the OECD's main contribution has been to drive the debate towards a common (or at least coordinated) reform of the international tax system, through what the report calls a 'consensus-based solution' to be found by 2020.[6] That solution will not be proposed by the OECD itself, however, but by the so-called Inclusive Framework, which the report indicates comprises more than 110 members.[7] Indeed, it is clear from reading the 2018 OECD Interim Report that the OECD is hardly more than a forum for discussion between countries with rather different perspectives on both the need for and the appropriate direction of any change(s) to the international tax system.[8]

At the same time, a number of countries have already implemented legislative measures to address the perceived shortcomings of the international tax system, in what the OECD refers to as 'unilateral and uncoordinated actions'[9] that, it asserts, are 'likely to have adverse impacts on investment and growth, and risk ... increasing double taxation and complexity'.[10] Such measures (a) aim generally to protect or expand the taxable base in 'market countries' (i.e., countries in which *consumers* of (digital) goods or services or *users* of digital infrastructure are located), (b) often rely on taxation of sales or place of consumption and (c) are adopted in response to a certain level of discontent with the tax revenue resulting from existing allocation rules.[11]

More concretely, such unilateral and uncoordinated national measures fall into four categories:[12] (1) extended 'nexus' thresholds, particularly in form of alternatives

---

article-specific commentaries, and for the purposes of this Chapter, said commentaries will be collectively referred to as the 'OECD Model Commentary'.

5. For an assessment of some of the challenges in this respect, *see, e.g.*, Chapter 5, *infra*.
6. 2018 OECD Interim Report, at 212, m.no. 513.
7. *Ibid.* at 173, m.no. 398.
8. The 2018 OECD Interim Report frequently notes a lack of consensus and points to the diverging positions of countries participating in the discussions, e.g., *ibid.* at 25, m.no. 36–40 on the relationship between value creation and digitalized business models; *ibid.* at 171, m.no. 387 on the need to change international tax rules.
9. For example, *ibid.* at 134, m.no. 343.
10. *Ibid.* at 212, m.no. 511.
11. *Ibid.* at 159, m.no. 367.
12. *Ibid.* at 134, m.no. 342.

to the classic permanent establishment (PE) threshold, such as the 'significant economic presence' tests already adopted (India) or being discussed (Israel)[13] and the expansive interpretation of existing PE definitions to encompass 'virtual service PEs' embraced in Saudi Arabia and India;[14] (2) broadened application of WHT regimes, by way of, for example, expanded interpretations of 'royalties' to include payments for the use or right to use software,[15] an exception to the PE threshold for 'technical services fees',[16] and entirely new WHT regimes (e.g., on income from online advertising);[17] (3) new gross-basis 'turnover taxes' on income streams related to 'digital services' such as India's 'Equalization Levy',[18] Italy's 'Levy on Digital Transactions',[19] Hungary's advertisement tax[20] and France's tax on audiovisual content;[21] (iv) new tax regimes specifically targeting large multinational enterprises (as opposed to specific income streams or activities), such as the United Kingdom's so-called Diverted Profits Tax (DPT),[22] Australia's 'Multinational Anti-Avoidance Law'[23] and its DPT,[24] and the United States' 'Base Erosion and Anti-abuse Tax' (BEAT).[25]

Finally, the EU is expected to respond with its own tax policy. The EU Commission, for example, has made concrete efforts to coordinate legislative action, which requires agreement among all twenty-eight Member States;[26] it published a two-step legislative proposal that would, first, impose a DST (i.e., a special tax regime imposed on the revenue made by large multinational enterprises providing specified digital services)[27] and, second, harmonize the definition of a PE in the tax treaties concluded among Member States to include an SDP (SDP)[28] that would be defined by indicators linked to the location of the digital service users.[29]

These developments form the backdrop for this chapter's legal analysis. Its objective is to reveal the legal limits of such developments imposed by both EU law and international trade rules that the EU (as well as individual Member States) are obliged to adhere to when adopting such measures and the implications of such limits on any concrete design thereof. Separating the above-described proposals into three baskets,

13. *Ibid.* at 137–138.
14. *Ibid.* at 139.
15. *Ibid.* at 140 (referring to the prevailing interpretation in, e.g., Greece and the Philippines).
16. *Ibid.*
17. *Ibid.* (specifically referring to draft legislation from Thailand and India).
18. *Ibid.* at 142.
19. *Ibid.* at 143.
20. *Ibid.* at 145.
21. *Ibid.* at 146–147.
22. *Ibid.* at 149–152.
23. *Ibid.* at 153–154.
24. *Ibid.* at 155–157.
25. *Ibid.* at 158–159.
26. At the time of writing, the United Kingdom was still a Member of the EU.
27. EU Comm'n, *Proposal for a Council Directive on the Common System of a Digital Services Tax on Revenues Resulting from the Provision of Certain Digital Services*, COM(2018) 148 final 2018/0073 (CNS) (hereinafter '2018 DST Directive Proposal'), *see* Chapter 6, *infra*.
28. *See* EU Comm'n, *Proposal for a Council Directive Laying Down Rules Relating to the Corporate Taxation of a Significant Digital Presence*, COM(2018) 147 final 2018/0072 (CNS) (hereinafter '2018 SDP Directive Proposal'), Art. 4. (hereinafter, the 2018 DST Directive Proposal and the 2018 SDP Directive Proposal, are collectively referred to as the '2018 EU Digital Proposals').
29. For a more detailed analysis, *see* Chapter 7, *infra*.

this chapter will examine WHTs on payments for digital services by characterizing income as royalties/technical service fees, new 'nexus' rules, such as those in the 2018 SDP Directive Proposal, and special tax regimes, such as the 2018 DST Directive Proposal.

§3.03 EU LAW LIMITS

[A] Limits on EU Member States

[1] Member States Legislative Competence

The first potential limitation on any tax policy response at the national level arises from a lack of competence to adopt a particular legislative measure. However, because competence to adopt legislative tax measures remains squarely with Member States in the EU's constitutional framework,[30] EU law generally poses no real obstacle to any national-level action. Although the Court of Justice of the European Union (CJEU) has consistently held that Member States must exercise their retained powers 'consistently with Community [= EU] law',[31] that holding must be understood as a limitation on the law's content, primarily through Internal Market rules, and not as a limitation on the Member States' competence as such, which will be considered further below.[32]

Nevertheless, the Member States' competence can still be substantively impaired, at least to some extent, in those areas in which the EU has both competence to act and has already acted. The first such instance arises in the field of indirect taxation, where the EU's exercise of its own competence,[33] through its various VAT directives and directives on excise duties, curtails the Member States' ability to act in a field already occupied by the EU legislature. As the direct conflict here is between the Member States' competence and secondary EU law, the detailed implications thereof is considered below.[34] The second instance arises in the field of international tax law, specifically, the competence of Member States to allocate taxing rights among themselves as well as between them and third countries in double taxation conventions (DTCs).

As DTCs concern direct taxation, they fall squarely within the Member States' national competence. However, some legal scholars have raised a question as to the Member States' ability to still act freely in that realm in light of increasing EU-level direct taxation harmonization via directives adopted pursuant to Article 115 of the Treaty on the Functioning of the European Union (TFEU), that is the EU's Internal

30. This follows from the fact that the EU treaties do not name direct taxation within the competences conferred on the EU; it thus remains with Member States by default. *See* Art. 5 para. 2 TEU.
31. *See, e.g., Finanzamt Köln-Altstadt* v *Schumacker*, C-279/95, Judgment, EU:C:1995:31, para. 21; *Marks & Spencer*, C-446/03, EU:C:2005:763, para. 29.
32. *See infra* §3.03[A][2].
33. Laid down in Art. 113 TFEU.
34. *See infra* §3.03[A][3].

Market competence.[35] As part of the curious architecture of the EU external powers – that is, its competence to act on the international stage by concluding agreements with third countries or international organizations – Article 3(2) TFEU endows the EU with the exclusive competence to conclude any treaty if it 'is necessary to enable the Union to exercise its internal competence, or in so far as its conclusion may affect common rules or alter their scope'. As a consequence, regardless of the basis for common rules within the EU, their very existence and potential interference with an international treaty concerning a third country may trigger a shift of the external competence from the individual Member States to the EU. Such a shift of competence, if it were sufficiently comprehensive, would not only allow the EU to conclude DTCs but would also pre-empt Member States from continuing to do so, even before the EU has exercised that competence.[36] At this stage of EU integration in the area of direct taxation, however, the doctrine of constitutional external-sphere pre-emption cannot yet affect the Member States' ability to amend their existing DTCs in ways that alter the definition of a PE to account for a business presence that is more digital than physical.

[2] Internal Market Rules

The second potential limitation on the Member States' ability to adopt specific solutions for challenges raised by digital business arises from the EU's Internal Market rules, particularly the fundamental freedoms and the prohibition of State aid. A key element thereof is the prohibition of discrimination based on nationality, which finds its specific expression in the free movement of persons, the freedom to provide services and the free movement of capital. Although no Member State has suggested adopting taxes directly targeting select nationalities or countries, the EU-level prohibition also patently extends to various forms of indirect discrimination. Most prominently, the CJEU held that a gross WHT levy on payments made to non-resident taxpayers, when resident taxpayers did not bear such a tax (or only bore a lower tax) was unjustifiably discriminatory.[37] That decision put a clear limit on one tax policy response to perceived tax inequities, namely an increased use of gross-based WHT to reach globally active digital businesses. The concrete extent of said limit remains somewhat unclear; however, the CJEU has accepted that Member States can apply different systems of

35. *See, e.g.*, Adriana Capobianco & May Zaidan, *The External Tax Treaty Making Powers of the Member States: Defining Limits and Obligations under the Current European Legal Order*, 41 Intertax 274 (2013); Werner Haslehner, *EU-US Relations in the Field of Direct Taxes from the EU Perspective: A BEPS-Induced Transformation?*, *in The Implementation of Anti-BEPS Rules in the EU: A Comprehensive Study* 54–60 (Pasquale Pistone & Dennis Weber eds., IBFD 2018).
36. *See* Thomas Verellen, *The ERTA Doctrine in the Post-Lisbon Era: Note under Judgment in* Commission *v* Council *(C-114/12) and Opinion 1/13*, 21 Colum. J. Eur. L. 383 et seq. (2015); Amedeo Arena, *Exercise of EU Competences and Pre-emption of Member States' Powers in the Internal and the External Sphere: Towards 'Grand Unification'?*, 35 Y.B. Eur. L. 28, 64 et seq. (2016).
37. *Gerritse*, C-234/01, Judgment, EU:C:2003:340; *Denkavit*, C-145/02, Judgment, EU:C:2005:9; *Amurta*, C-379/05, Judgment, EU:C:2007:655; *Miljoen*, C-10/14, Judgment, EU:C:2015:608.

taxation to non-residents and residents, provided that the overall burden on non-residents is not higher.[38] Moreover, the CJEU has also acknowledged that a Member State can justify applying such a tax pursuant to a bilateral agreement that ensures that the foreign taxpayer receives a full and effective credit for any additional burden it may suffer as a consequence of a WHT.[39] Nevertheless, a merely theoretical possibility for such compensatory credit is insufficient; the CJEU held that the Member States must ensure that a credit will actually be given. Increased use of WHTs on royalties paid to foreign residents, however, may not offer such guaranteed compensatory credits, especially where an 'IP box' regime is available in the residence state, resulting in particularly low taxes on royalty income (and thus severely limited crediting ability). Extending WHTs for any form of royalty payment thus seems to be particularly flawed policy response, as its compatibility with EU fundamental freedoms is highly doubtful.

While WHT frequently target foreign taxpayers directly, singling out non-residents is not a prerequisite for indirect discrimination based on nationality: as the CJEU's decision in *Hervis Sport* demonstrated, a technically uniform turnover tax can nevertheless be identified as discriminatory, if size thresholds apply that ensure that the majority of entities caught by the tax are either foreign or linked to foreign companies.[40] *Hervis Sport* concerned a highly progressive Hungarian turnover tax on retail companies that used group turnover as its reference point. Ultimately, in practice, the tax only had a significant impact on companies that were part of a multinational group but left purely domestic businesses largely unaffected. Although one may dispute the case's characterization as one of 'turnover discrimination',[41] it nevertheless indicates that adopting special DSTs that ultimately result in a levy only on companies that reach a certain size in terms of turnover is likely to be problematic.

But, even if such digital business turnover taxes were not designed to reach, effectively, only foreign taxpayers, the very fact that such a progressive tax on turnover does not comport with a fundamental principle of tax law – that is, the ability-to-pay principle – is likely to create validity difficulties. If it is applied on a sector-selective basis, such difficulties are of course more likely to arise under the EU's prohibition of State aid.

Another would-be difficulty with such WHTs arises from the potential for double taxation that follows the imposition of a new WHT that is levied in an uncoordinated manner, as it is probably not creditable under existing DTCs.[42] However, the CJEU, since its judgment in *Kerckhaert and Morres*,[43] has consistently rejected the argument that double taxation violates the fundamental freedoms, when it held that:

38. *Miljoen*, C-10/14, paras 70–71; *Brisal and KBC Finance Ireland*, C-18/15, Judgment, EU:C:2016:549, para. 22.
39. *Miljoen*, C-10/14, paras 75–87.
40. *Hervis Sport*, C-385/12, Judgment, EU:C:2014:47, para. 39.
41. *See* Ruth Mason & Leopoldo Parada, *The Illegality of Digital Services Taxes under EU Law – Size Matters*, 16 Virginia Law and Economics Research Paper 10 (2018).
42. For this conclusion, see EU Council Presidency's Working Paper WK 12665/2018 INIT of 22 October 2018 on DST and Art. 2 of the OECD Model Convention; *see also* Roland Ismer & Christoph Jescheck, *Taxes on Digital Services and the Substantive Scope of Application of Tax Treaties: Pushing the Boundaries of Article 2 of the OECD Model?*, 46 Intertax 573 (2018).
43. *Kerckhaert & Morres*, C-513/04, Judgment, EU:C:2006:713.

> Community law, in its current state and in a situation such as that in the main proceedings, does not lay down any general criteria for the attribution of areas of competence between the Member States in relation to the elimination of double taxation within the Community.[44]

Although Kemmeren[45] had argued that the CJEU could reassess that position following the TFEU's entry into force in 2009 (as it abolished Article 293 of the Treaty Establishing the European Community[46] that arguably prevented the Court from forcing Member States to prevent double taxation), the CJEU has not taken up his suggestion, making it unlikely that double taxation could amount to an obstacle for the Member States, if they chose to adopt DSTs.

The EU's State aid prohibition set out in Article 107 TFEU, on the other hand, which prohibits Member State aid that only benefits certain companies or sectors, establishes a potentially more robust, second limitation on the Member States' ability to adopt taxes that target specific sectors or structures. A tax burden that is imposed on only a select category of undertakings can be characterized as illegal State aid that is being provided to all other comparable undertakings that are not subject to that same burden.[47] This is a common feature of taxes that attempt to steer behaviour, such as environmental taxes.[48]

A recent example of a sectoral tax that ostensibly aimed at capturing value created by companies that would not be reached by traditional income taxes is the Hungarian Advertisement Tax, which is imposed on the turnover made by enterprises from advertising activity. This closely resembles a turnover tax on digital businesses and, indeed, appears to have had a similar motivation. The EU Commission challenged that tax as illegal State aid. Notably, however, it did so merely on the basis that the tax's progressive rate structure and the exclusion of non-profit entities from its scope unjustifiably favoured certain undertakings falling within the personal scope of the tax, not on the basis that the exclusion of businesses not engaged in advertisement activities were entirely excluded from the substantive scope of the tax.[49] The Commission's approach appears thus still less radical than that endorsed by the CJEU in its

44. *Ibid.* at para. 22.
45. Eric Kemmeren, *After Repeal of Article 293 EC Treaty under the Lisbon Treaty: The Objective of Eliminating Double Taxation Can Be Applied More Widely*, 17 EC Tax Rev. 156 (2008).
46. *See* Treaty establishing the European Community (consolidated) OJ 2002/C 325/01 (24 December 2002).
47. The latest authoritative statement by the CJEU Grand Chamber came in the case *World Duty Free*, C-20/15 P, Judgment, EC:C:2016:981, para. 79: 'All that matters in that regard is the fact that the measure, irrespective of its form or legislative means used, should have the effect of placing the recipient undertakings in a position that is more favourable than that of other undertakings, although all those undertakings are in a comparable factual and legal situation in the light of the objective pursued by the tax system concerned.'
48. For examples of such selective environmental taxes, *see, e.g.*, *Adria-Wien Pipeline*, C-143/99, Judgment, EU:C:2001:581; *British Aggregates*, C-487/06 P, Judgment, EU:C:2008:757; and *ANGED*, C-233/16, EU:C:2018:280.
49. *See* Comm'n Decision SA.39234 (COM(2015) 1520 final), at para. 28: the Commission 'considers all undertakings which derive turnover from the publication of advertisements in Hungary to be in a comparable legal and factual situation, in light of the objective of the Hungarian advertisement tax'.

British Aggregates decision,[50] in which it analysed the substantive scope of a tax as a whole. Since the law in that decision was intended to reduce the environmental impacts of aggregate mining, yet only applied the tax to certain types of aggregate, it was inconsistent with its own objective and thus constituted a selective measure.

In light of the CJEU's case law addressing special taxes imposed on select sectors of the economy, it is clear that such taxes may well be justified, as long as they pursue a legitimate objective and are imposed in an internally consistent way. Thus far, however, both the Commission and the CJEU have emphasized the importance of the second condition in justifying such special taxes (i.e., the internally consistent implementation of the legitimate objective it pursues). It remains to be seen how much discretion the Member States ultimately possess when drawing a line around certain sectors with sector-specific taxes. Arguably, if such taxes do not aim to address particular negative externalities, but are instead merely an attempt to capture profit, the reference framework should not be defined so narrowly as to exclude, *a priori*, all undertakings outside that sector. If the tax's objective is to capture profit, on the other hand, the reference framework, naturally, ought to consist of *all* taxes intended to capture profit.[51]

[3] Secondary EU Law

Finally, prevailing secondary EU law may counter the Member States' attempts to adopt specific tax legislation intended to tackle challenges arising from digital business models. As a starting point it is worth noting that this is neither an automatic nor necessary consequence of the EU covering a certain part of tax law with secondary legislation. By contrast to field pre-emption with respect to external competences discussed above (which derives from explicit provisions in the TFEU[52]), the Member States generally remain at liberty to retain and adopt national tax rules as long as these do not *violate* contrary EU laws.[53] Thus, in principle, even if the EU were to adopt the currently proposed DST, that would not - per se - prohibit a Member State from adopting levies with similar objectives or characteristics.

Nonetheless, even though no general pre-emption principle exists in the context of taxation, secondary EU legislation, at times, explicitly prohibits Member States from adopting similar taxes to those covered thereby. The most salient examples arise in the

50. *British Aggregates*, C-487/06 P.
51. An issue arises in situations where a tax is motivated by several aims, including both profit taxation and environmental or other objectives. In this case, the relevant reference framework ought to include all these objectives, which opens the possibility to compare undertakings subject to different taxes. It need not mean that different taxation amounts to selective advantages; rather, a proportionality analysis ought to reveal whether the different treatment is justified by (all) the objectives pursued by the relevant taxes. This is the same approach as ought to be applied when specific regimes within a general income tax system are motivated by seemingly 'external' objectives, such as the promotion of R&D. *See* further Paloma Schwarz Martinez, *IP Box Regime in Europäischen Steuerrecht* 75–83 (Nomos 2017).
52. *Supra* §3.03[A][1].
53. On the different types of pre-emptive effects of secondary legislation, *see, e.g.*, Robert Schütze, *European Constitutional Law* 363–378 (CUP 2012).

field of indirect tax law. For example, Article 401 of the VAT Directive[54] bars Member States from levying a tax with the characteristics of a VAT and Article 1 of the General Excise Duty Arrangements Directive prohibits them levying turnover taxes on the supply of services.[55] Another explicit example can be found in the Capital Duty Directive,[56] whose Article 5 defines transactions that Member States cannot subject to an indirect tax in respect of operations affecting a company's capital.[57] Due to the narrow scope of both the General Excise Duty Arrangements Directive and the Capital Duty Directive, only compatibility with the VAT Directive needs to be considered here.

No special tax on turnover of digital businesses imposed by any one Member States, such as the ELs discussed in a number of countries to compensate for low exposure to corporate income taxes within Europe, could be maintained if it fell under the VAT Directive's Article 401 definition of a turnover tax.[58] While that prohibition may appear to be very broad (i.e., covering all taxes 'characterized as turnover taxes'), the CJEU has since come to interpret its scope quite narrowly. According to its consistent case law,[59] the provision merely limits a Member State's competence to impose a tax that displays the four essential characteristics of a VAT: (1) a general application to goods and services, (2) a rate that is proportionate to the price charged for such goods or services, (3) a collection mechanism that applies at each stage of the production or distribution process and (4) the existence of an input-tax deduction mechanism.

The CJEU's case law gives a great deal of leeway to the Member States to introduce indirect taxes that are technically not – in its interpretation – turnover taxes, by equating the VAT Directive's term with the notion of VAT. As a consequence, particularly because of the essential characteristic of the VAT being a general tax, more

54. Council Directive 2006/112/EC on the common system of value added tax, OJ L 347/1 (2006) (hereinafter 'VAT Directive') Art. 401:

> Without prejudice to other provisions of Community law, this Directive shall not prevent a Member State from maintaining or introducing taxes on insurance contracts, taxes on betting and gambling, excise duties, stamp duties or, more generally, any taxes, duties or charges which cannot be characterised as turnover taxes, provided that the collecting of those taxes, duties or charges does not give rise, in trade between Member States, to formalities connected with the crossing of frontiers.

55. Council Directive 2008/118/EC concerning the general arrangements for excise duty and repealing Directive 92/12/EEC, OJ L 9/12 (2009), Art. 1(3)(b).
56. *See* Council Directive 2008/7/EC concerning indirect taxes on the raising of capital, OJ L 46/11 (2008), Art. 5 (hereinafter 'Capital Duty Directive').
57. The extent of the prohibition is here limited by the general scope of the Capital Duty Directive as defined in its Art. 1 as encompassing 'indirect taxes in respect of ... (a) contributions of capital-to-capital companies; (b) restructuring operations involving capital companies; (c) the issue of certain securities and debentures'.
58. While the wording of Art. 401 VAT directive does not directly prohibit the levying of turnover taxes, but instead authorizes the levy of taxes that cannot be characterized as turnover taxes, the prohibition follows indirectly from that authorization. *See Hervis*, C-385/12, AG Opinion, EU:C:2013:513, para. 89, with case law references.
59. *See, e.g., Banca Popolare di Cremona*, C-473/03, Judgment, EU:C:2006:629; *EKW & Wein & Co*, C-437/97, Judgment, EU:C:2000:110; *KÖGÁZ & others*, C-283/06, Judgment, EU:C:2007:598; *Krawczyński*, C-426/07, Judgment, EU:C:2008:434.

specific (turnover) taxes are not prohibited by these rules,[60] which arguably means that a tax designed to tax a company's turnover from a specific type of service provided in the market (e.g., online advertising or the provision of online platform services) does not fall within Article 401's general definition of a turnover tax. Moreover, digital turnover taxes are unlikely to implement other essential VAT characteristics such as fractional tax collection or an input deduction mechanism. As the rationale behind such specific taxes lies in the difficulty of reaching digital business's profits, they are not intended to be shifted to the ultimate consumer; any mechanism designed to achieve that goal would make little sense. Although several Advocates General (AGs) have encouraged the CJEU to broaden its interpretation of the prohibition found in Article 401,[61] it has, thus far, resisted such calls.

Like indirect tax directives, direct tax directives include certain limits on the Member States' competence to tax. For example, the Interest and Royalty Directive[62] prohibits WHT levies between associated companies; that prohibition could negatively affect the Member States' ability to broaden the reach of their WHT systems for royalties as identified by the 2018 OECD Interim Report.[63] The actual impact of said limitation, however, is probably negligible since the Interest and Royalty Directive only concerns intragroup payments and defines royalties in accordance with the traditional understanding of the term found in Article 12(2) OECD Model[64] and, therefore, leaves taxes levied on payments falling outside the traditional definition unaffected.

The Parent-Subsidiary Directive,[65] for its part, could also affect the Member States' ability to impose a special tax on companies engaged in digital business, at least to the extent that such a tax would burden profits distributed within the scope of that directive. Article 4(1) thereof requires Member States to refrain from taxing[66] profits received by a resident company from a subsidiary in another Member State. A turnover tax on digital activity might contravene that prohibition under certain circumstances (e.g., if a company receiving qualifying dividends were otherwise subjected to such tax despite it being profitable only by virtue for those dividends).[67] The fact that such a turnover tax was not designed as a tax on those distributed profits cannot justify the effect thereof. The CJEU already found that the Belgian 'fairness tax' ran counter to

60. *Cf.* Ben Terra & Peter Wattel, *European Tax Law* 475 (Wolters Kluwer 6th ed. 2012).
61. *See Hervis*, C-385/12, AG Opinion, paras 93–100; *Solisnor-Estaleiros*, C-130/96 Navais, AG Opinion, EU:C:1997:152, paras 37–45.
62. Council Directive 2003/49/EC on a common system of taxation applicable to interest and royalty payments made between associated companies of different Member States, OJ L 157/49 (2003) (hereinafter 'Interest and Royalty Directive').
63. *See* 2018 OECD Interim Report, *supra* note 1, at 139.
64. *See* Art. 2(b) Interest and Royalty Directive.
65. Council Directive 2011/96/EU on the common system of taxation applicable in the case of parent companies and subsidiaries of different Member States, OJ L 345/8 (2011) (hereinafter 'Parent-Subsidiary Directive').
66. While they also have the option to, instead, apply a credit method system, once opted for exemption, Member States have to do so consistently; *see Cobelfret*, C-138/07, Judgment, EU:C:2009:82, para. 50.
67. It is easy to see how this may be the case: if revenues from digital business activity were matched by costs so that the activity itself were unprofitable, any tax payable by the company would have to be financed other profits, including those from dividends that the Parent-Subsidiary Directive seeks to exempt.

Article 4 Parent-Subsidiary Directive even though it was not intended to tax received profits, but only to tax the difference between distributed profits and taxable profits; the Court found it was sufficient that the tax actually had 'the consequence of subjecting those profits to taxation'.[68] The CJEU also explicitly stated, in *AFEP*,[69] that 'it is irrelevant whether or not the tax measure is classified as corporation tax' for it to come within the scope of the Parent-Subsidiary Directive. Nevertheless, the limitation imposed by the Parent-Subsidiary Directive on the design of a turnover tax for digital business remains relatively insignificant since the latter typically attempt to reach non-resident companies without a PE in the Member State seeking to impose the tax while Article 4(1) Parent-Subsidiary Directive only applies to the taxpayer's residence state or the state in which it maintains a PE.

[B] Limits on the EU Legislature

[1] EU Legislative Competence

As mentioned above, the 2018 EU Digital Proposals contain rules specifically intended to tackle the challenges of the digital economy, through the adoption of a DST[70] and the inclusion of an SDP test to bolster a VPE concept in the Member States' DTCs. Without analysing the 2018 EU Digital Proposals in detail, as they are the subject of Chapters 6 and 7 in this volume, the question of the potential limits on their adoption is of interest for this chapter.

Under the EU Treaties, the EU possesses an explicit competence only to harmonize indirect taxes,[71] but not direct taxes. This has not, however, stopped the EU legislature from adopting a number of direct tax harmonization measures. Such measures – for taxes *other than* turnover taxes – must be based on Article 115 TFEU,[72] which imposes relatively few restrictions on the lawmaking power of the EU.[73] It

68. *X*, C-68/15, Judgment, EU:C:2017:379, para. 82.
69. *AFEP*, C-365/16, Judgment, EU:C:2017:378, para. 33.
70. *See* further Chapter 6, *infra*.
71. Article 113 TFEU:

> The Council shall, acting unanimously in accordance with a special legislative procedure and after consulting the European Parliament and the Economic and Social Committee, adopt provisions for the harmonisation of legislation concerning turnover taxes, excise duties *and other forms of indirect taxation* to the extent that such harmonisation is necessary to ensure the establishment and the functioning of the Internal Market and to avoid distortion of competition.

(Emphasis added).

72. While there is an ongoing debate on the potential use of Art. 116 TFEU, which aims at the removal of distortions, this has not yet attracted majority support. *See, e.g.*, Terra *supra* note 60, at 23; Daniel Smit, *The Influence of EU Tax Law on the EU Member States' External Relations, in EU Tax Law and Policy in the 21st Century* 215 at 222 (Werner Haslehner et al. eds., Kluwer 2017).
73. *Cf. C*, C-122/15, AG Opinion, EU:C:2016:65, para. 52: 'There is hardly any restriction, from the point of view of substance, on the competence enjoyed by the Community or the European Union under that provision.'

merely requires that the proposed legislative measure 'directly affect the establishment or functioning of the Internal Market'.[74] More substantive limitations on the exercise of that competence, however, arise from the requirements of subsidiarity and proportionality.[75] The principle of subsidiarity demands that the EU adopt legislative measures *only if* (a) the Member States are not themselves able to achieve the objective of such legislation and (b) the EU is, in fact, better able to do so. When those two conditions are met, the principle of proportionality further restricts EU legislative action to the minimum necessary to achieve the particular legislative objective. The CJEU accords the EU institutions broad discretion when assessing an EU measure's fulfilment of both the subsidiarity and proportionality conditions, only striking down manifestly inappropriate measures.[76]

Considering these limits, the pending 2018 EU Digital Proposals would appear, prima facie, to fall squarely within the competence limits set by the TFEU. First, there can be little doubt that a harmonized VPE definition adds value to both unilateral and bilateral attempts by the Member States to extend their taxing rights over non-resident digital businesses. In particular, as the EU Commission pointed out in the 2018 SDP Directive Proposal, a common approach guaranteed by a directive ensures 'a level-playing field for all Member States and provides taxpayers with legal certainty'.[77] A coordinated, EU-wide approach to the allocation of taxing rights would certainly contribute to the functioning of the Internal Market. Arguably, the fact that the directive, if adopted as proposed, would not affect a situation in which a taxpayer is resident in a third country covered by an existing DTC with a Member State does not reduce the effectiveness of the measure in a way that would raise concerns under the principles of subsidiary or proportionality. While it is certainly true that the measures' effectiveness would be significantly reduced if a multinational enterprise could avoid paying taxes anywhere in the EU by taking residence in a third country that has concluded a DTC with at least one Member State, it is equally certain that partial harmonization would contribute to the stated objective: to 'ensure a harmonised application of the rules on a significant digital presence within the Union'[78] (i.e., to better align taxation with value creation within the EU).[79] The exclusion of third-country resident taxpayers protected by a DTC can be justified by the fact that (a) the EU ought to have rules regarding international law and (b) a unilateral deviation from agreed allocation rules would run counter to the stated goals of the OECD/G20 BEPS Project, which informs the 2018 SDP Directive Proposal.

Second, since several Member States have already adopted or announced the adoption of unilateral measures to tax digital revenue streams, the 2018 DST Directive Proposal to harmonize the field in an attempt to prevent fragmentation in the internal market as a consequence of unilateral and uncoordinated Member State action is not

74. Article 115 TFEU.
75. *See* Art. 5(1) TEU.
76. *See, e.g., British American Tobacco (Investments) Ltd*, C-491/01, Judgment, EU:C:2002:741, para. 123; *S.P.C.M. SA et al.*, C-558/07, Judgment, EU:C:2009:430, para. 42.
77. 2018 SDP Directive Proposal *supra* note 28 at 5.
78. *Ibid.* at 12 (Recital 8).
79. *Ibid.* at 11 (Recital 3).

objectionable from the perspective of the principle of subsidiarity. A question mark could be added to that statement, however, insofar as the 2018 DST Directive Proposal, if adopted as proposed, would not contain an explicit prohibition that would prevent Member States from applying additional unilateral measures.[80] Even without an explicit prohibition, however, it seems likely that the proposed DST directive would contribute to that result, which, under the CJEU's case law, would be sufficient to safeguard the EU's competence with respect thereto.[81]

More concrete questions arise from the EU Commission's purported legal basis for the 2018 DST Directive Proposal: it has stated that the proposal is based on Article 113 TFEU, which appears the natural choice, considering that the DST is designed to tax revenue from certain 'digital' services. Article 113 TFEU covers the 'harmonisation of legislation concerning turnover taxes, excise duties and other forms of indirect taxation'. Questions have been raised, however, as to the appropriateness of said legal basis. First, it is not clear that the proposed DST falls under the technical definition of a turnover tax, and second, it is equally unclear that it can be qualified as an indirect tax at all, which is a prerequisite for it to come within the scope of Article 113 TFEU.

The CJEU has not yet defined either of those terms in any case law touching on Article 113 TFEU. As outlined above,[82] it has, however, come to equate the term 'turnover tax' with that of VAT in its extensive case law on Article 401 VAT Directive. In that context, the CJEU established four essential characteristics that must be present for a measure to qualify as a turnover tax, two of which the DST, if adopted as proposed, would not fulfil: first, it would not be a general tax on goods or services, and second, it would not possess a mechanism for input-tax deduction that would ensure that the ultimate consumer bears the tax burden.

In the context of determining the EU's competence to adopt harmonizing measures under Article 113 TFEU, it makes little sense, however, to define 'turnover tax' in accordance with the Court's essential criteria of a VAT. In fact, the CJEU's narrow understanding has already been rightly criticized in the context of Article 401 VAT Directive, despite the fact that it, at least, has an unquestionable direct connection to that tax. It is difficult to find a reason why the EU legislature's choice concerning the design of a particular tax (the VAT) adopted under Article 113 TFEU should come retrospectively to define the ambit of that legal basis in such a way as to limit its scope to a tax that is exactly so designed.[83]

---

80. *See*, however, the different estimation of the EU Council Legal Service, which in para. 16 of its Opinion on the proposal for the directives states that the DST would 'introduce a harmonised system and replace the diverging measures taken (or, potentially, to be taken) unilaterally by Member States' (Interinstitutional File 2018/0073(CNS), not officially published document, on file with the author).
81. For a considerably more critical assessment with respect to both the subsidiarity and the proportionality requirement, see João Félix Pinto Nogueira, The Compatibility of the EU Digital Services Tax with EU and WTO Law: *Requiem Aeternam Donate Nascenti Tributo*, 1 *International Tax Studies* 1 (2019) (at 4.5).
82. *See supra* §3.03[A][3].
83. The EU Council Legal Service argues that, since VAT is intended to 'harmonise national legislation on turnover taxes in a global and comprehensive manner' (*see* Recital (4) of the VAT Directive), the CJEU's interpretation of Art. 401 VAT Directive can be used to ascertain the generic meaning of 'turnover taxes' for purposes of Art. 113 TFEU. But the fact that the VAT

In the alternative, could the proposed DST be adopted under Article 113 TFEU as an indirect tax? According to the EU Council Legal Service, three features evince an indirect tax: first, such a tax is imposed on transactions, such as consumption, production or transfer of ownership; second, it does not take account of the taxpayer's overall ability to pay tax; and, third, the method of taxation presupposes a difference between the formal taxpayer and the person ultimately bearing the economic burden of the tax.[84] While the first and second of these may be said to be present in the case of the proposed DST, the third – which is often considered to be the decisive element of an indirect tax[85] – is not. It should be noted that the relevant characteristic is not, as may easily be misunderstood, the mere existence of a divergence between the formal taxpayer and the person who bears, economically, the burden of the tax (i.e., the economic incidence thereof) since some divergence is inevitable for virtually any tax; rather, an indirect tax is characterized by the legislative purpose behind such divergence.[86] In the case of the proposed DST, it is clear that the EU legislature did not intend any such divergence or any shift of the burden of the tax;[87] rather, it instead aimed to directly reach profits that would otherwise remain untaxed where the 'value is created', making the proposed DST a backstop for corporate tax rules otherwise intended, economically, to burden the formal taxpayer.[88]

In light of this analysis, it seems inappropriate to suggest that the proposed DST would fall within the indirect tax competence provided by Article 113 TFEU as anything other than a turnover tax. Nevertheless, since the formal requirements of Article 115 TFEU are exactly the same, which would certainly cover the proposed DST as a 'direct tax', there can be little doubt that the EU possesses the power to adopt such legislation as a matter of right under the EU Treaties' competence rules as long as it can be shown to contribute to the 'establishment and the functioning of the internal market'.[89] This condition can be assessed very critically in light of the risks of multiple taxation, undue burdening of loss-making enterprises and various distortions of competition that may

Directive was meant to harmonize all existing turnover taxes in the EU by itself indicates already that it is not the only possible form of turnover tax that could have been adopted under Art. 113 TFEU.

84. EU Council Legal Service, *supra* note 80, at para. 25.
85. *See Banca Popolare di Cremona*, C-475/03, AG Opinion, EU:C:2005:183, para. 54.
86. For the origins of this distinction, *see* Alice Pirlot, *Environmental Border Tax Adjustments and International Trade Law* 190 (Edward Elgar 2017), who traces this back to John Stuart Mill, *Principles of Political Economy with Some of Their Applications to Social Philosophy* (Longmans, Green & Co. 1848).
87. The Commission itself answers the question whether consumers would have to bear the cost of the tax by stating: 'There is no reason why this should happen, provided that companies behave responsibly towards their customers. The Commission's goal is to ensure that all companies contribute their fair share to public revenue. This aim is to secure a level playing field between different types of companies, which is important for fair competition.' *See* European Commission – Fact Sheet, Q&A on a Fair and Efficient Tax System in the EU for the Digital Single Market (21 March 2018), http://europa.eu/rapid/press-release_MEMO-18-2141_en.htm (accessed 24 December 2018).
88. The EU Council Legal Service further points to the fact that the DST is proposed as a mere 'temporary measure', to be replaced with the SDP proposed under Art. 115 TFEU. EU Council Legal Service, *supra* note 80, at para. 29.
89. For this requirement, see both Arts 113 and 115 TFEU.

result from it.[90] A full analysis of this question is beyond the scope of this chapter; such an analysis would have to take into account not only the generous margin of discretion afforded to the EU legislature by the CJEU but also the impact of impending unilateral measures by individual Member States in the absence of EU-level action as a yardstick for improving the Internal Market.

[2] Internal Market Rules

A measure of secondary EU law would be fully subject to the EU Treaties' primary rules, particularly the limits they set in the Internal Market provisions mentioned above, which means that any EU legislative measure must, in principle, comply with the same conditions applicable to the Member States when they act within their exclusive competence.[91] In practice, however, the limits set by EU fundamental freedoms, on the one hand, and State aid rules, on the other, might apply quite differently to the EU than to the Member States.

The reason for that divergence lies, in the case of the fundamental freedoms, in at least two factors. First is the fact that any measure taken by the EU – such as the proposed DST – is likely to discriminate, if at all, only against enterprises residing in non-Member States. In this situation, only the freedom of capital movement would be applicable, which will likely not cover taxation measures that directly aim at the provision of digital services.[92] Second is the fact that the breadth of the discretion granted to the EU legislature is necessarily wider than that given to individual Member States since the risk of Internal Market fragmentation is undoubtedly lower when the EU establishes a set of common rules for the whole of the Internal Market.[93] As a consequence, prima facie discriminatory measures adopted by the EU may be found to be justified by an overriding reason in the general interest far more easily than in the case of a unilateral measure taken by a Member State.[94] Arguably, such a different level of scrutiny should only be warranted when the particular EU measure truly aims to improve the Internal Market and not in cases where Member States are permitted to

90. *See infra* Chapter 6. *See* also Pinto Nogueira, *supra* note 81, at 4.4.
91. *See* with respect to the free movement of goods, *Kieffer and Thill*, C-114/96, Judgment, EU:C:1997:316, para. 27; *Meyhui*, C-51/93, EU:C:1994:312, para. 11; *Denkavit Nederland*, 15/83, Judgment, EU:C:1984:183, para. 15. With respect to the freedom to provide services, *see Schmelz*, C-97/09, Judgment, EU:C:2010:632, para. 50.
92. Pinto Nogueira, *supra* note 81, at 4.3.1.
93. Some authors take this as a reason completely to deny the applicability of the freedoms to the EU legislature. *See* Thorsten Kingreen, *Fundamental Freedoms, in Principles of European Constitutional Law* 543 (Armin von Bogdandy & Jürgen Bast eds., Hart/Beck/Nomos 2d ed. 2009); for a recent review of the arguments, see Herbert Rosenfeldt & Aike Würdemann, Schöpfer des Binnenmarktes im Käfig der Verträge – Die grundfreiheitliche Bindung des EU-Gesetzgebers, 51 *Europarecht* 453 (2016).
94. The CJEU appears to deny the proportionality of an EU measure impacting the freedoms only in cases of manifestly inappropriate measures, emphasizing the EU legislature's discretion. *See, e.g.*, *Kieffer and Thill*, C-114/96, Judgment, EU:C:1997:316, para. 37, referring also, to that effect, to *Meyhui*, C-51/93, EU:C:1994:312, para. 21.

add individualistic exceptions into the common rules; however, the CJEU has yet to make such a distinction when examining EU-level measures.[95]

With respect to the prohibition of State aid, the application of different standards of judicial review due to the different level of risk to the Internal Market is far more explicit: Article 107 TFEU only addresses actions taken by the Member States (any aid granted *by a Member State* or through State resources[96]), thereby explicitly excluding measures taken directly by the EU from its scope. The CJEU has also confirmed that interpretation in cases in which a Member State granted tax advantages in order to implement an obligation under secondary EU law.[97] In such situations, the Court determined that the measure in question could not be imputed to the Member State and, thus, could not constitute State aid. In that context, it rightly ignored questions as to whether other characteristics of 'aid' were fulfilled because Article 107 TFEU did not bind the EU institutions at whose behest the Member State was acting.

[3] Public International Law

Finally, limits on the EU legislature's lawmaking power may result from certain of its public international law obligations. Such limits do not question the existence of EU-level competence (i.e., whether the EU *can* adopt legislative measures to address challenges of the digital economy),[98] but rather address whether it *may* adopt such laws without violating higher norms of public international law to which it may be bound. This section addresses the general relationship between EU law and public international law, as well as the potential relevance of customary international law, in the context of digital economy taxation. Specific aspects of WTO law, however, are addressed in §3.04, *infra*.

The relationship between public international law and EU law is not yet entirely settled in the CJEU's case law:[99] the Court appeared to have abandoned its initial approach (i.e., accepting customary international law as binding on the EU)[100] for a more subtle position, whereby even seemingly superior international law instruments are now necessarily subject to the Court's review in order to ensure proper protection of the EU's core principles. Thus far, however, the expression of that nuanced position

95. For a negative example, which was nevertheless accepted by the CJEU, see Case C-475/01, *Commission* v *Greece*, EU:C:2004:585 (the 'Ouzo-case'). This case concerned the reduced excise tax levied by Greece on Ouzo alone to the detriment of other (foreign) spirits, which, despite its discriminatory nature, was upheld by the CJEU on the basis that it is protected by an exception in directive 92/83, which was presumed to be lawful without further investigation as to its effects.
96. Article 107(1) TFEU.
97. *See Puffer*, C-460/07, Judgment, EU:C:2009:254, para. 70.
98. This question has been addressed *supra*, at §3.03[A][1] and §3.03[A][2].
99. *See* Juliane Kokott & Christoph Sobotta, *The Kadi Case – Constitutional Core Values and International Law – Finding the Balance?*, 23 Eur. J. Int'l L. 1015–1024 (2012).
100. *See Racke*, C-162/96, Judgment, EU:C:1998:293, para. 45; *Anklagemindigheden* v *Poulsen and Diva Navigation*, C-286/90, Judgement, EU:C:1992:453, para. 9: 'the European Community must respect international law in the exercise of its powers'.

has been limited to exceptional cases, such as *Kadi and Al Barakaat*[101]). Citing both its earlier case law and the *Kadi* decision, the CJEU more recently emphasized that 'international law is part of the European Union legal order and is binding on the institutions'.[102] The Court's assertion that the EU is bound by customary international law in exercising its powers is further reflected in Article 3(5) TEU, according to which 'the Union ... shall contribute to ... the strict observance and the development of international law, including respect for the principles of the United Nations Charter'.

Nevertheless, even taking the obligation to comply with public international law as a given, it is still not clear whether that imposes any limits on the EU's taxing jurisdiction. Indeed, finding instances of customary international law applying to tax rules is particularly difficult under the traditional understanding thereof.[103] The most commonly accepted limitation on taxation arising from customary international law is the need for a *genuine link* between a particular taxpayer and the territory of the state seeking to tax that taxpayer before the latter can assert its tax jurisdiction.[104]

In light of that customary law limitation, it is tempting to ask whether a proposal that would allow an EU Member State to tax non-resident entities without any physical presence within the EU on revenues connected to a 'user base' in that Member State could possibly comply with that internationally accepted condition. As Kokott points out in Chapter 2, *infra*, while that question has not yet been definitively addressed, it appears that international opinion has, perhaps, become more tolerant and accepting of the assertion of tax jurisdiction in such circumstances.[105] Schön, for example, expanded on the content of that principle in the context of destination-based taxation by reference to the 'economic allegiance' to a country that arises from a transfer of financial means from customers residing in that country to the taxpayer.[106] Taking Schön's formulation as the benchmark, a proposal that relies solely on the existence of a user base within the country seeking to tax may well be regarded as insufficient to establish a genuine link between the country and the foreign business taxpayer because, in the absence of a financial transfer from those users to the taxpayer that reduces the users' ability to pay tax (and, thus, the ability of their residence state to tax them), the country seeking to tax is unaffected by the existence/non-existence of that user base within its territory. Nevertheless, as the genuine link principle is certainly

101. *See Kadi*, C-402/05 P & C-415/05 P, EU:C:2008:461, paras 300–304.
102. *Evans*, C-179/13, Judgment, EU:C:2015:12, para. 35.
103. *See* Guglielmo Maisto, *On the Difficulties Regarding the Formation of Customary Law in the Field of Taxation, in EU Law and the Building of Global Supranational Tax Law* 21–35 (Dennis Weber ed. IBFD 2017).
104. *See, e.g.*, Klaus Vogel & Alexander Rust, *Introduction, in Klaus Vogel on Double Taxation Conventions* m.no. 8 (Ekkehart Reimer & Alexander Rust eds., Kluwer 4th ed. 2015); Wolfgang Schön, *International Tax Coordination for a Second-Best World (Part I)*, 1 World Tax J. 67, 90–91 (2009); *see also* Maisto, *supra* note 103, at 34 (who considers the principle of non-interference to affirm the prohibition of taxation without territorial nexus); in more detail, *see* Kokott, Chapter 2, *supra*.
105. *See* Chapter 2, *supra* (Conclusion).
106. Schön, *supra* note 104 at 92: 'it cannot be disputed that the existence of a customer base in a territory, leading to the transfer of financial means from customers to the taxpayer, forms a strong economic allegiance. This is not dependent on the total amount of sales. International law does not require a certain "threshold" to be passed'.

fluid, alternative reasoning may be applied: specifically, the mere existence of such a user base is, without doubt, valuable to the foreign business and depends on the (digital) infrastructure provided by the users' residence state. The use of such infrastructure may, in and of itself, be regarded as a sufficiently close link to tax that foreign business, with the size of the user base acting as a convenient proxy for the value derived from its use.

It should be noted here, in passing, that the Member States will be subject to both the limits on taxation imposed by public international law and any future obligation to impose a DST pursuant to an EU directive, such as that proposed in the 2018 DST Directive Proposal. In case of a conflict between those obligations, EU law would generally take precedence (except for pre-accession treaties, which have been grandfathered by Article 351 TFEU), thereby forcing the Member States to violate their international law obligations if necessary. The 2018 SDP Directive Proposal's exception for taxpayers protected by an existing DTC shows that the EU Commission is sensitive to that potential conflict.

§3.04 WTO LAW LIMITS

[A] The WTO Legal Framework: Application to Tax Law

This part of the chapter outlines the relevant limitations arising from WTO law regarding tax rule design. It is well understood that the WTO rules laid down in a number of international agreements (e.g., the General Agreement on Tariffs and Trade (GATT),[107] the General Agreement on Trade in Services (GATS)[108] and the Agreement on Subsidies and Countervailing Measures (ASCM)[109]) have an important, but limited, impact on national tax law, due to a number of partial and complete carve-outs from their scope.[110] For example, both GATT and GATS prohibit discrimination, via their respective most-favoured-nation rules[111] and national treatment rules.[112]

In reality, their respective most-favoured-nation rules are of little consequence for taxation since most countries' tax regimes do not typically distinguish between the places of origin of 'products'. What is more, even when such a difference can be more easily detected, for example, in the context of taxing services provided by taxpayers from different countries, GATS Article XIV(e) provides a specific exception to its most-favoured-nation rule, provided that said difference is the result of a DTC.

107. Available at https://www.wto.org/english/docs_e/legal_e/gatt47.pdf (accessed 28 February 2019).
108. Available at https://www.wto.org/english/docs_e/legal_e/26-gats.pdf (accessed 28 February 2019).
109. Available at https://www.wto.org/english/docs_e/legal_e/24-scm.pdf (accessed 28 February 2019).
110. *See* Wolfgang Schön, *World Trade Organization Law and Tax Law*, Bull. Int'l Tax'n 283 (2004); Wolfgang Schön, *Destination-Based Income Taxation and WTO Law: A Note, in Practical Problems in European and International Tax Law – Essays in Honour of Manfred Mössner* 430 (Heike Jochum et al. eds., IBFD 2016).
111. GATT Art. I and GATS Art. II.
112. GATT Art. III and GATS Art. XVII(1).

Similarly, for here-relevant types of taxes on revenues and profits, Article III GATT's national treatment requirement appears equally inconsequential, as such taxes do not distinguish between 'products'. Moreover, although WTO case law (particularly the *Foreign Sales Cooperation* case[113]) shows that the national treatment provision also covers differences in taxation of foreign 'producers' when compared to domestic ones,[114] its importance for the taxation scenarios considered in this chapter is limited since the specific issue related to taxation of 'digital businesses' is not related to either the production or sale of goods and, to date, no measures undertaken or under consideration in the Member States are likely to violate the requirement for equal treatment of products or producers.[115]

It is somewhat more likely that the equivalent GATS provision might be relevant, as digital businesses under scrutiny are service providers. Moreover, it has been suggested that destination-based taxation (which resembles the certain suggested resolutions discussed in the 2018 OECD Interim Report) may contravene GATT Article III (and, by analogy, one may argue, GATS Article XVII(1)), as it discriminates against foreign companies selling into the market where the taxation would take place.[116] However, as Schön pointed out,[117] it is not clear how a shift to such destination-based taxation would result in less favourable taxation in the destination state, a precondition for any purported violation of the national treatment clause. In addition, as far as it concerns taxation of services, GATS Articles XIV(d) and XXII(3) provide for exceptions to the national treatment requirement to the extent that a different taxation is covered by a DTC, which would protect measures such as a bilaterally agreed-upon change in the PE definition, even if it would otherwise be considered problematic.

The most likely WTO law challenge, therefore, would appear to come from the anti-subsidy rules found in the GATT and, most specifically, the ASCM. The general rule of ASCM Article 1(1)(a)(1)(ii) defines the non-collection of 'government revenue that is otherwise due' as a subsidy. The list of examples of subsidies falling under the general rule can be found in the ASCM's Annex I (e) to (i). According to those explanatory provisions, different benchmarks are to be applied to direct and indirect taxes. Any 'full or partial exemption, remission or deferral specifically related to exports' in the context of direct taxes is qualified as a subsidy (with an exception for exemptions intended to avoid double taxation)[118] while in the context of indirect taxes,

113. *See* the reports of the Panel and the Appellate Panel, US – FSC; Recourse to Art. 21.5 (WT/DS108/RW) of 20 August 2001; US – FSC; Recourse to Art. 21.5 (WT/DS108/AB/RW) of 14 January 2002 (hereinafter 'FSC case').
114. *See* Schön, *supra* note 104 at 435 with references to literature.
115. Indeed, if they did violate that principle, such measures are far more likely to be held incompatible with the stricter non-discrimination standard required by the CJEU's interpretation of the fundamental freedoms, including the freedom of capital movement, which also covers investment to and from non-EU Member States.
116. Charles McLure & Walter Hellerstein, *Does Sales-Only Apportionment of Corporate Income Violate the GATT?* (NBER Working Paper 9060, 2002) https://www.nber.org/papers/w9060 (accessed 18 February 2019).
117. Schön, *supra* note 104 at 438.
118. ASCM, *supra* note 109, fn 59.

only an exemption or remission in excess of those levied on domestic consumption count as such. An easy way to conceptualize the difference is the common view that 'border adjustments' are acceptable for indirect taxes but not for direct taxes.[119]

[B] Potential Application to Digital Tax Proposals

When considering the three different proposals for new tax measures discussed in this chapter, it is fairly obvious that neither (a) an extension of the PE concept to an SDP or other form of VPE nor (b) a treaty-based extension of WHT to returns on digitally provided services create serious issues with respect to WTO law. Since either extension would have to be based on DTCs and would fall under the rules concerning direct taxes, such measures would benefit from the carve-outs found in GATS Article XIV(d) for measures intended to ensure the 'equitable and effective imposition or collection of direct taxes in respect of services or service suppliers of other Members' and in GATS Article XIV(e) for measures intended to apply DTC provisions.

By contrast, a special DST could be problematic, depending on its concrete design. If it were designed as an indirect tax, the above-mentioned carve-outs could not apply, which would leave a measure that only applied to foreign service providers in violation of GATS Article XVII(1). It is notable that, in contrast to the EU Treaties, GATS defines the notion of direct taxes as 'taxes on total income, on total capital or on elements of income or of capital, including taxes on gains from the alienation of property, taxes on estates, inheritances and gifts, and taxes on the total amounts of wages or salaries paid by enterprises, as well as taxes on capital appreciation rules'.[120] One may conclude that a tax on revenue such as the EU's proposed DST would qualify as a direct tax under this provision, considering revenue an 'element of income'. The more convincing interpretation, however, would be to exclude such taxes from the definition: a tax on an 'element of income', when juxtaposed with a tax on 'total income', is better interpreted as covering only charges on certain types or categories of income (i.e., the constituent parts of *total* income under a schedular tax system), rather than the constituent parts of income (i.e., revenues, on the one hand, and expenses, on the other). Such an interpretation is also more consistent with the definition of direct and indirect taxes set forth in ACSM Footnote 58. According to that footnote, direct taxes are taxes on 'wages, profits, interests, rents, royalties, and all other forms of income, and taxes on the ownership of real property' while indirect taxes are 'sales, excise, turnover, value added, franchise, stamp, transfer, inventory and equipment taxes, border taxes and all taxes other than direct taxes and import charges'.

For an indirect tax, divergent application to resident and non-resident service providers cannot be justified. The objective of providing substantive protection against trade discrimination makes it likely that this prohibition is not to be understood too

119. For an extensive review of the existing legal framework concerning tax border adjustments, *see* Pirlot, *supra* note 86, Chapter 5.
120. GATS Art. XXVIII(o).

formally. It should, thus, cover taxes that do not explicitly target non-resident businesses, but end up only burdening them, for example, because no domestic service providers exist who surpass the size thresholds for the tax's application, making the 2018 DST Directive Proposal vulnerable to a WTO violation challenge.

Even if the EU's proposed DST were imposed in both a de jure and de facto non-discriminatory manner, it could still run counter to the ASCM's export-subsidies prohibition, due to its sector-specific nature and its tax burden shifting effect (i.e., shifting the tax burden from the residence state to the state in which the digital service is provided). Could that shift be characterized as an export exemption for resident digital service providers? As noted above, a destination-based direct tax may seem problematic. It is not obvious that an internally consistent direct tax designed to apply as backstop to a traditional corporation tax for cases where the latter insufficiently captures value created within a jurisdiction could not be designed in a way that shifts the place of taxation to a new 'source' country, such as the country where users of a digital platform are resident, without this being considered as an export subsidy, on the assumption that the relevant service provider would escape taxation on the same tax base at home. Such a situation comes closest to that Schön argued would be in line with the ASCM: he considers a sales-only apportionment formula compatible with the anti-subsidy rule and concludes that a shift to pure destination-based taxation – as a general paradigm shift for corporate taxation – would fall outside the scope of Article 3 ASCM, insofar as it is to be assessed against itself as the new benchmark. To be sure, the proponents of the potential changes to be wrought by a special DST levied in the user state do not contemplate the general paradigm shift in corporate taxation that Schön had in mind; instead, their aim is to introduce a narrow and sector-specific shift, which would bring the situation closer to that of the *FSC* case.

Yet the final analysis is not so simple. For example, the fact that the new tax would be proposed as an added tax burden on one sector rather than as tax relief for all other sectors could be important: if the benchmark corporate tax system remains that of residence taxation, and entities paying the DST remain fully subject to that tax at home, no advantage can be said to arise for them as a consequence of their 'export' when compared to resident non-digital businesses. This contrasts with the facts of the FSC case, where selected companies (the name-giving 'foreign sales corporations') were relieved from part of the normal corporate tax burden in connection with their exporting activity. In addition, the DST would not make an exemption in the business's residence state contingent on domestic production linked to exports; in contrast, it aims to tax domestic production of value through resident users. If one may rightly be critical of the view that users can be said to produce value from which the business derives its revenue, it remains certainly the case that the DST does not distinguish between domestic production (in the business's residence state) and foreign production (in any other state, including the users' residence state), an element that was important in the FSC case for the finding of an export subsidy under ASCM Article 3.[121] If a digital

121. ASCM Footnote 4 states specifically that for a subsidy to fall within the prohibition of Art. 3, it has to be tied to anticipated exportation or export earnings. The fact that a subsidy is granted to companies that export is not by itself sufficient to trigger that provision.

business derives advertising revenue from companies in its own jurisdiction, that revenue would still not be taxed if linked to users in another jurisdiction,[122] but as the service is provided to a resident company, it can hardly be considered an export.

Even if the special DST levied in the user state were creditable against the corporate tax due in the resident state, such a partial remission of tax could be covered by the exception in ASCM Footnote 59[123] and, as such, would not be problematic. Taxation at the location of the users of an online platform may not be considered to give rise to 'taxation of foreign-source income' in a traditional sense because no income may be said to arise at that location under traditional source rules (i.e., revenue streams related to services provided to a user may actually arise in another country, including the residence State of the service provider). However, as 'foreign-source income' is not otherwise defined, it is reasonable to follow the approach under domestic law. If the residence State imposes the DST on the basis of user location, this ought to be covered by the exception in ASCM Footnote 59, the purpose of which is to keep relief intended to avoid double taxation unaffected by the ASCM. In this context, it ought thus also not to matter that the tax is not technically levied on income.

The situation is clearer and less problematic if the DST were to be classified as an indirect tax (as it arguably should be, for purposes of the ASCM, if it were designed as a tax on turnover). In that case, an exemption (not to exceed the indirect tax imposed on domestic consumption) would be allowed by ASCM Annex I(g), leaving a partial tax reduction for digital service providers with an exclusively domestic user base unchallengeable.

§3.05 CONCLUSION

This chapter analysed the broader legal framework within which proposals for taxing digital business need to be embedded. It has shown that both EU Member States and the EU itself are subject to a number of existing legal constraints that must be carefully assessed in parallel with tax policy considerations. Those legal constraints primarily concern the division of competences between the EU and its Member States but also relate to discrimination rules imposed at both the EU and WTO law levels.

The picture that emerges from the analysis is diverse. On the one hand, it demonstrated that the EU has far broader discretion than its Member States when it comes to the application of EU-level non-discrimination rules in the context of digital economy taxation, but, on the other, it showed that the EU has much less room to manoeuvre under the existing competence framework established by the EU Treaties.

Ultimately, none of the currently discussed and variously proposed measures (be they additional WHTs, extended VPE thresholds or special DSTs) are either definitely

122. *See* Chapter 6, *supra*.
123. 'Paragraph (e) is not intended to limit a Member from taking measures to avoid the double taxation of foreign-source income earned by its enterprises or the enterprises of another Member.'

prohibited or entirely legal in all circumstances. Inevitably, the detailed features of each and every concrete proposal with respect to digital economy taxation must be carefully and fully considered against both the EU- and international-level prohibitions on discrimination and inappropriate subsidies.

CHAPTER 4

Fairness of the Taxation of the Digital Economy

Gianluigi Bizioli

§4.01 INTRODUCTION

In the 2015 Final Report on Action 1, the Organisation for Economic Co-operation and Development (OECD) Task Force on the Digital Economy agreed to evaluate any potential options for taxing the digital economy according to 'the basic principles of neutrality, efficiency, certainty and simplicity, effectiveness and fairness, flexibility and sustainability, and in light of the overall proportionality of the changes in relation to the tax challenges they are intended to address'.[1] Although 'no single principle can be given greater priority than any other',[2] fairness, as well as neutrality, should play a decisive role in the design of the proposals for the taxation of the digital economy since they address the issues of the distribution of the tax burden among the taxpayers and the relative proportion.

This interpretation is – at least indirectly – confirmed by the primary aim of the assignment given to the OECD by the G20 Leaders in St. Petersburg on 5–6 September 2013, where the need to ensure that 'all taxpayers pay their fair share of taxes' was underlined as a priority for the future years.

Even more evidence of this interpretative approach is found in the harmonization process in the field of direct taxation that the European Commission (Commission) started in 2017, where the ultimate emphasis lies on the fairness and efficiency of the tax system for the 'Digital Single Market'. In particular, the Commission highlights the inadequacy of the current international tax rules to address the tax challenges arising

1. OECD, *Addressing the Tax Challenges of the Digital Economy, Action 1 – 2015 Final Report* 1, 134 § 351 (OECD Publishing 2015) (hereinafter '2015 OECD BEPS Action 1 Report').
2. *Ibid.*

from the digital business models and, therefore, indicates that such rules cannot implement the principle under which businesses should pay their taxes where profits and value are generated.[3]

The theoretical justification offered by the two international organizations for a significant change in the international direct tax regime is, thus, grounded in the mismatch between the place where the profits - or, perhaps better, according to the wording of official documents, the value - are/is generated and where profits and/or value are/is taxed and, ultimately, the unfair and ineffective taxation of those profits and value that follows in the new digital business models.[4]

The aim of this chapter is to analyse such a theoretical background and, in particular, depict the meaning (or the meanings) of tax fairness in the domestic and international contexts and assess whether the solutions proposed by the OECD and the Commission effectively aim at restoring the fairness of the tax system.

Based on the findings, §4.02, *infra*, then deals with the concept of fairness. After a brief summary of the current debate about the taxation of the digital economy, §4.03 tests the coherence of the solutions and proposals presented by the international organizations with tax fairness. §4.06 draws some conclusions.

§4.02 THE (SLIPPERY) MEANINGS OF TAX FAIRNESS

[A] Tax Fairness in the Economic and Legal Literature: A Review

[1] The Roots: The Principle of Tax Equality

The necessary starting point for any analysis concerning fairness in taxation is Adam Smith's famous canon:

> The subjects of every State ought to contribute towards the support of the Government as nearly as possible in proportion to their respective abilities, *i.e.* in proportion to the revenue which they respectively enjoy under the protection of the State.[5]

---

3. Comm'n, *Communication from the Commission to the European Parliament and the Council: A Fair and Efficient Tax System in the European Union for the Digital Single Market*, COM(2017) 547 final, 2–3, 7 (hereinafter '2017 EU FETS Communication'). This theoretical framework is fostered by: (a) Comm'n, *Proposal for a Council Directive Laying Down Rules Relating to the Corporate Taxation of a Significant Digital Presence*, COM(2018) 147 final 2018/0072 (CNS) (hereinafter '2018 EU SDP Directive Proposal') and (b) Comm'n, *Proposal for a Council Directive on the Common System of a Digital Services Tax on Revenues Resulting from the Provision of Certain Digital Services*, COM(2018) 148 final 2018/0073 (CNS) (hereinafter '2018 EU DST Directive Proposal').
4. Unfairness and ineffectiveness are often measured in terms of (effective) tax rates applied to the profits earned by the multinational enterprises of the digital sector. *See, e.g.*, Centre for European Economic Research (ZEW) of the European Commission Directorate General for Taxation and Customs Unions, *The Impact of Tax Planning on Forward-Looking Effective Tax Rates*, 64 Tax'n Paper (2016).
5. Adam Smith, *An Inquiry into Nature and Causes of the Wealth of Nations* 891 (Clarendon Press 1979).

This statement reflects, first of all, the prevalent conception of the state or the government within the English-speaking world at the end of the eighteenth century and, in particular, the idea of a 'covenant' among citizens whose object was to surrender a portion of their freedoms and properties in exchange for protection. Accordingly, the consent of the governed citizens was the basic justification for government.

In this theoretical framework, Smith characterizes taxation as the compensation paid by citizens for the protection of life and ownership warranted by the state or government. At the beginning of the modern state, therefore, taxation was understood as the cost for public protection. The deprivation of property through taxes mirrors the deprivation of freedoms produced by the social compact.

Once the existence of the state or government and of taxation has been justified, the fundamental problem for the state or government lies in the criterion (or the criteria) for the distribution of public expenditure (or the costs of the public services) among the citizens. Smith's position was to link taxation with the (economic) abilities of the subjects since that criterion is the best compensation for the protection received from the state or government. To Smith's mind, therefore, the abilities of each subject are the best proxy for the economic translation of the advantages that he/she receives from the state or government.

Needless to say, on the basis of this idea, the tax burden should have been equally distributed among the subjects (i.e., subjects with the same ability should bear the same amount of taxes).[6]

In Smith's opinion, therefore, fair taxation requires that burdens be equal. Since being transposed following the French Revolution in the *Déclaration des Droits de l'Homme et du Citoyen* of 1789,[7] the principle of tax equality has been universally accepted as the cornerstone for a theory of tax justice.[8]

---

6. Both the justification and principle concerning the distribution of the tax burden can be also found in Thomas Hobbes, *Leviathan* ch. XXX (Penguin Books 1985) (*available at* https://ebooks.adelaide.edu.au/h/hobbes/thomas/h68l/chapter30.html) ('[t]o equal justice appertaineth also the equal imposition of taxes; the equality whereof dependeth not on the equality of riches, but on the equality of the debt that every man oweth to the Commonwealth for his defence', although the conclusions were in favour of a poll tax: '[s]eeing then the benefit that every one receiveth thereby is the enjoyment of life, which is equally dear to poor and rich, the debt which a poor man oweth them that defend his life is the same which a rich man oweth for the defence of his; saving that the rich, who have the service of the poor, may be debtors not only for their own persons, but for many more.')
7. Article 13 of the Déclaration: '[p]our l'entretien de la force publique, et pour les dépenses d'administration, une contribution commune est indispensable: elle doit être également répartie entre tous les citoyens, en raison de leurs facultés'.
8. In this sense, see Liam Murphy & Thomas Nagel, *The Myth of Ownership. Taxes and Justice* 12 (Oxford Univ. Press 2002):

   > [a]part from economic efficiency, the social value that has traditionally been given weight in tax design is fairness; the task of the tax designer is to come up with a scheme that is both efficient and fair. Fairness, in the traditional conception, is thought of specifically as a standard for evaluating differences in the tax treatment of different people: the principle that like-situated persons must be burdened equally and relevantly unlike persons unequally.

[2] *The Two Versions of the Benefit Principle*

If the principle of (tax) equality is considered to be a necessary prerequisite for defining what tax fairness means, it does not suffice on its own. Equality, in fact, needs a benchmark for the apportionment of public expenditure among the subjects. In this sense, '[a] tax fairness norm is a principle according to which the aggregate tax burden is to be apportioned among the population'.[9] The most commonly adopted tax fairness benchmarks (or norms) are the benefit principle and the ability-to-pay principle.[10]

According to the former, there is a strict connection between contribution and the state or government public expenditure. Prima facie, people are required to contribute 'to government on account of the benefits obtained from government on the latter's 'spending side'.[11] The benefit principle is, therefore, the plainest application of the state or government contractarian doctrine, where '[t]axes [are] looked upon as premiums of insurance which individuals paid to the collective insurance company – the state – in order to enjoy their possession in peace and security'.[12] As already mentioned in §4.02[A][1], *supra*, the benefit principle, from the outset, has been the norm legitimizing the social compact between the state or government and civil society. The former exists solely to provide services that, for a variety of reasons linked to market failure,

9. Joseph Dodge, *Theories of Tax Justice: Ruminations on Benefit, Partnership, and Ability-to-Pay Principles*, 58 Tax L. Rev. 399, 401 (2005). Similarly, Nancy Kaufman, *Fairness and the Taxation of International Income*, 29 L. & Pol'y Int'l Bus. 145, 157 (1998):

> [t]wo competing theories of interindividual equity – benefit theory and ability-to-pay theory – have historically dominated discussions of tax equity. Benefit theory and ability-to-pay are not principles of entitlement and economic justice. Rather, they have their origins in such principles

10. *See, inter alia*, Edwin Seligman, *Progressive Taxation in Theory and Practice*, 9 Am. Econ. Ass'n 150 et seq. (1908); Richard Musgrave & Peggy Musgrave, *Public Finance in Theory and Practice* 218 et seq. (McGraw-Hill Book 1989); Jeffrey Schoenblum, *Tax Fairness or Unfairness? A Consideration of the Philosophical Bases for Unequal Taxation of Individuals*, 12 Am. J. Tax Pol'y 221, 225 et seq. (1995); Murphy & Nagel, *supra* note 8, at 12 et seq., and Dodge, *supra* note 9, at 401 et seq. (author includes within the 'most commonly cited substantive tax fairness norms' not only the benefit and the ability-to-pay principles, but also the equal-sacrifice norm and the 'well-being' (or 'standard-of-living') norm). *Contra*, Stephen Utz, *Ability to Pay*, 23 Whittier L. Rev. 867 (2002) ('[t]here is broad, if not universal, agreement that fair taxation should be in accordance with "ability to pay", or the capacity of the taxpayer to bear the tax burden'). This unidirectional approach, however, ignores that, even in the modern tax systems, many forms of levies are strictly connected to the services provided by the state or government and, as such, shaped according to the benefit principle. The clear-cut position espoused by Andrés Baez & Yariv Brauner in *Withholding Taxes in the Service of BEPS Action 1: Address the Tax Challenges of the Digital Economy* 8 (IBFD Working Papers 2 February 2015) that 'what might be taxed – either in an international or a pure domestic context – is a rather artificial and arbitrary decision' should also be rejected. The authority to tax is neither artificial nor arbitrary, at least in a rule of law system; conversely, this authority is discretionary and the constitutional law framework limits the state's or government's discretion. In this sense, the constitutional law is the fundament and the limit to the authority to tax.
11. Dodge, *supra* note 9, at 402.
12. Seligman, *supra* note 10, at 150.

cannot be provided optimally by private, voluntary agreement.[13] In brief, 'taxes are what we pay for civilized society'.[14]

A second meaning of the same principle is grounded on a more specific idea of exchange between the benefits received from the state or government and the taxes paid by the subjects who belong to the polity.[15] The issue of the distribution of public expenditure among citizenry is, thus, solved through the market mechanism, without considering the utility a person derives from consuming a given quantity of government services (and how much disutility is caused by paying a certain amount of taxes). In this sense, similarly to the first version of the principle, the fair (or just) distribution of taxes among subjects is based on the exchange with the public expenditure, but, in this second version, this exchange follows the value of the overall services provided. Taxes are consideration paid for the totality of state or government services by all subjects taken together.[16]

However, because the beneficiaries of state or government activities are often indirect and diffuse,[17] the advocates of this second version of the benefit principle address the measurement issue relying on the financial well-being of the persons.[18] The financial well-being 'is said to be made possible by government institutions, laws, and

13. *See* Barbara Fried, *The Puzzling Case for Proportionate Taxation*, 2 Chapman L. Rev. 157, 160 (1999). According to Murphy & Nagel, *supra* note 8, at 16 fn 12, this understanding can be attributed to Grotius, Pufendorf, Hobbes, Locke, Rousseau, and Smith. In the twentieth century, it was still advocated by Friedrich Hayek, *The Constitution of Liberty* 315-316 (Univ. of Chi. Press 1960) (as well as by Milton Friedman, *Capitalism and Freedom* (Univ. of Chi. Press 1962) & Richard Epstein, *Takings. Private Property and the Power of Eminent Domain* (Harv. Univ. Press 1985)).
14. *Compania General de Tabacos de Filipinas* v *Collector of Internal Revenue*, 275 U.S. 87, 99–100 (1927) (J. Holmes, dissenting).
15. A depiction of the two meanings can be found in Richard A. Musgrave, *The Theory of Public Finance* ch. 4 (McGraw-Hill 1959).
16. *Ibid.*, at 62 (since the relation is one of exchange, the rules of the public household are taken to be more or less the same as those of the market); *see also*, Lorenz von Stein, *Lehrbuch der Finanzwissenschaft* Part II s. 1 (Brockhaus 1885); James Buchanan, *The Pure Theory of Government Finance: A Suggested Approach*, 57 J. Pol. Econ. 496 (1949).
17. Antonio De Viti de Marco, *Scienza delle finanze* 54 (Società Tipografica Aldo Manuzio 1923) defined the individual consumption of public services as '*un incognita*' (an unknown).
18. In this sense, *see* De Viti de Marco, *supra* note 17: ([d]acchè esiste Finanza, si è preso il reddito di ogni cittadino come indice misuratore della domanda e del consumo dei servizi pubblici, e in base a questa presunzione si è fissata l'imposta come una percentuale del reddito). The most mature systematization of this justification is due to Benvenuto Griziotti and to the so-called School of Pavia. *See, e.g.*, Benvenuto Griziotti, *Principii di politica diritto e scienza delle finanze* 50 (Cedam 1929):

> vi è un limite all'esercizio della sovranità fiscale dello Stato, affinchè l'imposta non sia uguale all'atto arbitrario e violento del bandito, che tiene in suo potere il viandante. La distribuzione delle spese pubbliche, in base al principio di capacità contributiva, deve farsi in misura dei vantaggi generali prodotti ai contribuenti, tanto dallo Stato, quanto dalla Società e dall'Economia nazionale, che lo Stato stesso rappresenta.

Benvenuto Griziotti, *Il principio della capacità contributiva e sue applicazioni*, 9 Rivista di Diritto Finanziario e Scienza delle Finanze 19 (1949); *see also* Walter Blum & Harry Kalven, *The Uneasy Case for Progressive Taxation* 35–39 (Chic. Univ. Press 1953) and for a recent

programs that create an environment or set of conditions under which private wealth accumulation is cultivated and allowed to flourish'.[19]

It is worth noting, considered the purpose of this article, that this concept of the benefit principle has been used from the outset for the justification of corporate income tax, understood as the privilege provided by the state or government for the limited liability and the other specific features granted to these subjects. This reasoning is plainly manifest in the United States Supreme Court decisions, in which Justice Day characterized the 1909 Federal Corporation Tax as:

> a tax upon the doing of business, with the advantages which inhere in the peculiarities of corporate or joint stock organization of the character described. As the latter organizations share many benefits of corporate organization, it may be described generally as a tax upon doing business in a corporate capacity.[20]

According to this syllabus, the two versions of the benefit principles differ both for the role of the state or government *and* for the criterion (or norm) concerning the distribution of the public expenditure among subjects.

Following the original idea, the role of the state or government should be restricted to the protection of subjects and, therefore, the public functions limited to (the traditional) guarantee of life, liberty and property. Differently, the second version does not address a precise limit to that role, which is strictly linked to the utility provided to subjects and due to the market failures.

As to the criteria for the distribution of the public burdens, the traditional version of the principle considers the cost of the services for each subject whereas the revised version takes into account the utilities or the advantages enjoyed by the subjects and measured according to their wealth (or income).[21]

In conclusion, the benefit principle provides a first, traditional, fair norm for taxation justifying mandatory payments because people owe their financial well-being, to a significant degree, to the state or government.[22] In other words, the state or government is justified for the 'public' use of coercion since the production of income and the maintenance of wealth are possible solely within the framework of such a political organization. Accordingly, the principle governing the distribution of public expenditure among citizens belongs to the realm of the 'social justice theory'.

---

reappraisal of the benefit principle within the Italian constitutional system, see Dario Stevanato, *La giustificazione sociale dell'imposta. Tributi e determinabilità della ricchezza tra diritto e politica* 61 et seq. (il Mulino 2014).

19. Dodge, *supra* note 9, at 406.
20. *Flint* v *Stone Tracy Co.*, 220 U.S. 107 (1910). For more on this understanding, see Charles McLure, *Source-Based Taxation and Alternatives to the Concept of the Permanent Establishment in, 2000 World Conference Report* 1, s. 6.3 (Can. Tax Found. Toronto 2000).
21. On this second version of the principle, see also Dale Pinto, *The Need to Reconceptualize the Permanent Establishment Threshold*, 60 Bull. Int'l Tax'n 266, 267 (2006).
22. In these terms, Dodge, *supra* note 9, at 407.

[3] The Ability-to-Pay Principle

The theoretical alternative[23] or, according to a different outlining, the complementary solution[24] to the benefit principle is the ability-to-pay norm.

The first feature of the latter principle lies in the constitutional status that it has attained in many European constitutions (e.g., Germany, Italy and Spain). In these jurisdictions, the interpretation of the principle is deeply influenced by the constitutional legal framework in which it is inserted as well as by the interpretations provided by the supreme (constitutional) courts.

The second feature concerns the abandonment of any link between the principle and the state or government spending side.[25] As seen in §4.02[A][2], *supra*, both versions of the benefit principles are strictly dependent on, and derive from, the justifications of and the functions exercised by the state or government. Taxation can, therefore, be characterized either as the price for the protection provided by the state or government or the compensation for the advantages and the utilities received from the state or government. Conversely, according to the ability-to-pay principle:

> [f]aculty was declared to consist not alone in the power of production or the extent of product, but also in the power to use the product in order to satisfy all one's wants. The conditions which limit faculty are to be found not only in the amount of the income, but in the demands that are upon the individual in disposing of his income. In other words, the idea of burden, or of sacrifice, was introduced. ... and faculty, or capacity to pay taxes, was henceforth declared to be measured by that proportion of his product or income, the loss of which would impose upon the individual an equal burden or sacrifice with his neighbor.[26]

Taxation according to ability (or capacity) depends solely on the number of the subject's possessions and is grounded on the justification that people with a greater number of possessions suffer a relatively limited loss compared with poorer subjects. In these terms, the systematization of which can be traced back to J.S. Mill,[27] the benchmark adopted to establish fair taxation is that of the sacrifice suffered by the

23. Utz, *supra* note 10, at 889:

> it is worthwhile to notice that ability to pay can only serve as the touchstone for spreading tax responsibility if we abandon the goal of making people pay in accordance with the governmental benefits they receive. Ability to pay theories are inconsistent with benefit taxation and with every form of quid pro quo allocation of tax liability.

24. Schoenblum, *supra* note 10, at 233–234 ([a]bility to pay is not an entirely distinct alternative to benefit theory. Any number of benefit theorists have justified differentials in taxation founded on benefit theory by reference to ability to pay). Similarly, Stevanato, *supra* note 18, at 61 et seq., highlights the *intreccio* (interlacement) of the two principles, which are not mutually incompatible, as they partially overlap.
25. Concurrently, Dodge, *supra* note 9, at 450.
26. Seligman, *supra* note 10, at 209.
27. 5 John Stuart Mill, *Principles of Political Economy: With Some of Their Applications to Social Philosophy* ch. 2 (William Ashley ed., Longmans, Green & Co. 1920).

subjects from the coercive takings of their possessions.[28] For Mill, each subject is required to bear his/her 'fair share' since anything less would require others to bear more than their fair shares.[29] Accordingly:

> [a] government ought to make no distinction of persons or classes in the strength of their claims on it', leading to the statement that whatever sacrifice is required of subjects 'should be made to bear as nearly as possible with the same pressure upon all, which, it must be observed, is the mode by which the least sacrifice is occasioned on the whole.[30]

In a nutshell, tax burdens should be designed to impose an equal sacrifice on all subjects in the same conditions, and this sacrifice should be measured in terms of means.[31]

In conclusion, the ability-to-pay principle measures the distribution of the costs of public expenditure according to the bearable economic sacrifice of the subject (i.e., according to his/her overall possessions). In this sense, the most evident difference with the benefit principle is that the ability-to-pay norm does not rely on the economic subjective utility of the taxpayer. In other words, the justification for taxation lies solely in the possessions, although subjects' possessions can be considered as the indirect measure (or value) of the government services or, putting it differently, a proxy of the enjoyment (or utility) of public expenditure.

This conclusion requires two further clarifications. The first concerns the evolution of the meaning of the ability-to-pay principle due to the interpretation made in the literature and by judges in Germany, Italy and Spain. Despite the fact that the starting point is grounded on the idea of economic sacrifice, the Italian and Spanish literature and case law primarily characterize the ability-to-pay principle in terms of 'participation' of the subject to a territorial polity.[32] In this sense, the subject's possessions form the benchmark for the distribution of the costs of the public services whereas his/her participation to the community represents the justification for taxation. The basic idea of the subject's contribution is, therefore, based on the 'solidarity' among subjects.[33]

The second clarification regards the development of a broader concept of ability to pay which, in addition to monetary possessions, also considers what economists refer to as 'human capital' (e.g., knowledge, ability, personality and connections) that enable people to act productively. According to this stand, the correct notion of ability

---

28. In similar terms, Utz, *supra* note 10, at 886–887 (the ability-to-pay approach adopted by Mill was 'backed by an analysis of taxpayer welfare in terms of utility' and that '[t]ax burdens should be designed to impose an equal sacrifice on all individuals, and this sacrifice should be measured in terms of means').
29. Mill, *supra* note 27, at 804.
30. *Ibid.* at 804.
31. Utz, *supra* note 10, at 887.
32. For the Italian system, see Francesco Moschetti, *Il principio della capacità contributiva* (Cedam 1973); An introduction of the Spanish is contained in Martín Queralt et al., *Curso de Derecho Financiero y Tributario* 1, 122 et seq. (Editorial Tecnos 2016).
33. Concurring, Wolfgang Schön, *International Tax Coordination for a Second-Best World (Part I)*, 1 World Tax J. 67, 71 (2009) ([t]he ability-to-pay principle is deeply rooted in the Western tradition of taxation being a citizen's contribution to the common good by reason of solidarity among the members of a society).

to pay is 'endowment' in the complete sense, which includes a person's potential income.[34]

[B] The International Scenario

This dialectical theoretical perspective of tax fairness can also be extended to international (or extraterritorial) taxation.[35] Worldwide taxation may be justified on the ground of the ability-to-pay principle, and, in particular, of the special intensity of the subject's participation in the residence jurisdiction;[36] similarly, source taxation may either be justified according to the benefit principle, and, in particular, for the utility non-residents derive from the public expenditure in the jurisdiction where the economic activity is carried on (or the consumption occurs),[37] or to the ability-to-pay principle (i.e., for the possessions situated in that jurisdiction that reveal the (limited) participation of the subject to the economic life of the jurisdiction).[38]

The ability-to-pay principle was clearly endorsed by the Report on Double Taxation submitted to the Financial Committee of the League of Nations by the Experts in 1923 (the '1923 DT Report'). In Part II, section 1 of the 1923 DT Report, the experts pointed to the application of the 'entire exchange theory' in modern times in favour of the 'faculty theory or theory of ability to pay': In fact, '[t]his theory is more

34. The definition is provided by Murphy & Nagel, *supra* note 8, at 21, who cite Francis Walker, *The Base of Taxation* 3 Pol. Sci. Q. 1, 14–16 (1888) & David Bradford, *Untangling the Income Tax* ch. 8 (Harv. Univ. Press 1986). Murphy & Nagel conclude that the idea of ability to pay 'has only an indirect relation to the value of fairness' using the following example:

> [i]f two people, Bert and Kurt, earn the same amount, in fact, but Bert is earning at his full capacity and Kurt below his capacity, why might it be thought unfair to tax them the same absolute amount? We cannot say that Kurt has more money available, since he does not. Perhaps he has more leisure and is for that reason better off than Bert. But this is not necessarily so: Perhaps Kurt and Bert work the same hours, but Kurt is earning less than he might because he has chosen to be a teacher rather than a lawyer.

35. Concurring, Michael Graetz, *Taxing International Income: Inadequate Principles, Outdated Concepts and Unsatisfactory Policies*, 54 Tax L. Rev. 216, 294 & 307 (2001) & Clifton Fleming et al., *Fairness in International Taxation: The Ability-to-Pay Case for Taxing Worldwide Income*, 5 Florida Tax Rev. 299, 308 (2001).
36. Concurring, Schön, *supra* note 33, at 72 (and the cited contributions) ([w]ordlwide taxation is meant to include the global income of a person in a literal sense, enabling the taxpayer to set off profits and losses from different sources and enabling the tax authorities to apply personal deductions and a progressive tax rate to the aggregate).
37. Critically, Johanna Hey, *'Taxation Where Value Is Created' and the OECD/G20 Base Erosion and Profit Shifting Initiative*, 72 Bull. Int'l Tax'n 203, 205 (2018) (the use of public goods is neither a good justification for taxing income nor does it provide any guidance for measuring and attributing the income of a MNE to different jurisdictions).
38. In this sense, see Klaus Vogel, *World-wide vs. Source Taxation of Income: A Review and Reevaluation of Arguments (Part III)*, 16 Intertax 393 (1988) and, recently, Baez & Brauner, *supra* note 10, at 4.

comprehensive than the preceding theory, because it includes what there is of value in the benefit theory'.[39]

The abandoning, or the overcoming, of the benefit principle was not based on heuristic arguments, but to its final incorporation into the ability-to-pay principle, since the latter, in the understanding of the 1923 DT Report, comprehends the utility provided by the state or government services. In other words, addressing a syncretic concept of ability to pay, the 1923 DT Report fostered a theory of fair taxation based on the sacrifice of the subject, who surrenders a portion of his/her possessions, and on the economic utility received from the state or government. The role of the state or government could, therefore, be appreciated by the increase in the subjects' economic means.

It is worthwhile noting that, at the international level, fair taxation has also been analysed as a matter of economic justice among states (i.e., as the distribution of the authority to tax and, ultimately, tax revenue among states).[40]

The conceptual distinction between the interindividual and internation equity was first introduced by P. Musgrave over forty years ago. This perspective is based on the commonly accepted distinction between source and residence taxation. In particular, foreign and domestic income should be considered as income of the residence jurisdiction whereas the taxation of the source jurisdiction should require some kind of justification.[41]

A different solution to the issue of the distribution of the authority to tax among different jurisdictions was advanced by the 1923 DT Report, which considered economic allegiance to be the foundation of the state's competence in taxation:

> [a] part of the total sum paid according to the ability of a person ought to reach the competing authorities according to his economic interest under each authority. The ideal solution is that the individual's whole faculty should be taxed, but that it should be taxed only once, and that liability should be divided among tax districts according to his relative interests in each (Part II, Section I).[42]

---

39. League of Nations Economic and Financial Commission, *Report on Double Taxation Submitted to the Financial Committee* Doc. E.F.S. 73.F.19, 1, 20 (1923) (hereinafter the '1923 DT Report'). It stated that:

    > [s]o far as the benefits connected with the acquisition of wealth increase individual faculty, they constitute an element not to be neglected. The same is true of the benefits connected with the consumption side of faculty, where there is room even for a consideration of the cost to the government in providing a proper environment which renders the consumption of wealth possible or agreeable. The faculty theory is the more comprehensive theory.

40. The two dimensions of fairness in the international scenario are acknowledged also by Filip Debelva, *Fairness and International Taxation: Star-Crossed Lovers?* 10 World Tax J. 1, para. 3 (2018).
41. Peggy Musgrave, *Taxation of Foreign Investment Income. An Economic Analysis* 1, 16, 22, & 104 (John Hopkins Press 1963); Richard Musgrave & Peggy Musgrave, *Inter-Nation Equity, in Modern Fiscal Issues: Essays in Honour of Carl S. Shoup* 63, 68–78 (Richard Bird & John Head eds., Univ. of Toronto Press 1972).
42. 1923 DT Report, *supra* note 39, at 20.

The 1923 DT Report took the position that the authority to tax should be exercised according to the place of origin and the place of residence of the owner of the wealth. The origin of income corresponds to the place (or places) where it is created.[43] In this sense, the Experts suggested that income should be taxed only once where it was created, i.e., according to the economic allegiance.

In conclusion, leaving aside any issue concerning the internation equity, the benefit and ability-to-pay principles can be addressed as the guidelines in assessing the fairness of the international tax system or, in other words, the exercise of extraterritorial state authority to tax. These principles, as seen in §4.02[A][2] and [A][3], *supra*, justify the exercise of the authority to tax according to a social justice theory.

§4.03 TAX FAIRNESS AND THE PROPOSALS FOR THE TAXATION OF THE DIGITAL ECONOMY

[A] The Meaning of Tax Fairness Raised by the OECD and EU Documents on Digital Economy Taxation

Comparing the different official documents published by the OECD and the European Union (EU), the more elaborated attempt to define tax fairness and its implications in the digital economy context is contained in the 2017 EU FETS Communication.[44] After putting forward the modern tax mantra that profits should be taxed where the value is created, the Commission explicitly introduces the two main policy challenges raised by the changing paradigms of the international economy:

> - **Where to tax? (nexus)** – how to establish and protect taxing rights in a country where businesses can provide services digitally with little or no physical presence despite having a commercial presence; and
> - **What to tax? (value creation)** – how to attribute profit in new digitalised business models driven by intangible assets, data and knowledge.
>
> These challenges need to be looked at together to find a meaningful solution for determining where economic activities are carried out and value is created for tax purposes.[45]

A fair tax system, according to this approach, would, therefore, require the determination of the economic contribution given by the digitalized business models, and, in particular, by data and knowledge, and, *if any*, the alignment between the profits (or the value) generated and the jurisdiction where they arise (and should be taxed). As clearly summarized by the dichotomy 'nexus' and 'value creation', the concept of fairness does not impose only a change, either in the sense of a revision or complete overhaul, of the current international rules on the allocation of the taxing rights, but, *first and foremost*, an economic analysis of the digitalized models to figure

43. *Ibid.* at 19–20, 24.
44. 2017 EU FETS Communication, *supra* note 3.
45. *Ibid.* at 7.

out the new items of taxable income (or, according to the international mantra, to the new taxable value).[46]

A similar meaning can be drawn from the 2015 OECD BEPS Action 1 Report, where the fact that the 'growing reliance in certain new business models on data may raise challenges both in terms of characterisation of and attribution of value from data, and in terms of the changing ways in which users and customers interact with businesses' has been stressed.[47] And again, the issues are summarized according to the categories of 'nexus', 'data' and 'characterization'.

On these latter issues, the 2018 OECD Interim Report[48] offers some further descriptive elements for the analysis of the income (or value) dimension of the issue:

> Finally, data and user participation, and, more generally, the ongoing and interactive relationships between digitalized businesses and their customers, may represent additional tax challenges, in and to the extent that they can be considered a source of a firm's value creation. This could be the case, for instance, if a large base of active online users producing substantial amounts of content and data is considered a material contribution to the value creation of a business, distinct from the algorithms and other intangible assets used for analyzing and processing this content and data.[49]

According to this brief selection of the hundred pages published by the OECD and the Commission, it can be concluded that the concept of tax fairness addressed is no more than the simple enforcement of the principle of tax equality. The purpose of the aforementioned documents is, therefore, to foster an equal tax treatment of the new business (digital) models and the traditional (or 'brick and mortar') ones, by means of:

(a) the updating of traditional concepts that are no longer in line with the economic reality;
(b) the measurement of new forms of wealth, arising from the new economic reality.[50]

---

46. This dichotomy is further developed by the 2018 EU DST Directive Proposal, *supra* note 3, in which the Commission states that fairness is heavily undermined by the fact that:

> the input obtained by a business from users, which actually constitutes the creation of value for the company, could be located in a tax jurisdiction where the company carrying out a digital activity is not physically established (and thus not established for tax purposes according to the current rules) and where therefore the profits generated from such activities cannot be taxed. Secondly, even where a company has a permanent establishment in the jurisdiction where the users are located, the value created by user participation is not taken into account when deciding how much tax should be paid in each country.

47. 2015 OECD BEPS Action 1 Report, *supra* note 1, at 98–99 § 247.
48. OECD, *Tax Challenges Arising from Digitalization – Interim Report 2018* 170, § 386 (OECD Publishing 2018) (hereinafter '2018 OECD Interim Report').
49. *Ibid.*
50. This distinction is also highlighted by Hey, *supra* note 37, at 204 (the concept of value creation is not limited to the attribution of profits for the application of the existing corporate income tax, but is also a fundamental reason for the invention of new taxable items).

The reference to tax fairness contained in the official documents of the international organizations is, therefore, an exercise of rhetoric (or, in other words, rather pleonastic) since it purports the need to re-establish the tax equality in a changed (and changing) economic world. However, the same documents do not contain any attempt or show any effort to assess the fundamental criteria according to which the tax burden should be (equally) distributed among the taxpayers. Any reference to the 'value' created through the digital businesses is, in fact, a reference to an empty concept that is not defined either by the international documents or by the OECD Member States tax jurisdictions.

A pragmatic attempt to assign some content to that concept is provided by the proposals to tax the digital economy, which are considered in the following paragraphs.

§4.04 DO THE PROPOSED SOLUTIONS COMPLY WITH TRADITIONAL CONCEPTS OF TAX FAIRNESS?

[A] Introduction: A Brief Summary of the Proposed Solutions

In the 2015 OECD BEPS Action 1 Report, the OECD suggested three different hypotheses for coordinating the direct taxation of the digital economy.

The first concerns the updating of the criteria for the definition of the non-resident taxable presence in the source jurisdiction, able to 'evidence a purposeful and sustained interaction with the economy of that country via technology and other automated tools.'[51] In detail, the economic taxable presence considers both a number of digital factors and a series of quantitative thresholds, in order to capture only the most significant cases. Of the latter, only revenues generated with in-country customers through an enterprise's digital platform, a minimum amount of revenues generated from remote transactions concluded with customers in the country concerned and the introduction of a mandatory registration system for enterprises meeting the previous criteria are suggested.[52]

As far as the digital presence is concerned, a series of 'digital factors' and 'user-based factors' are considered, including the existence of a local domain name, a local digital platform, local payment options, monthly active users, online contract conclusion and data collected.[53]

The alternative approaches suggested by the 2015 OECD BEPS Action 1 Report include:

(a) a withholding tax on payments by residents (and local PEs) of a country for goods and services purchased online from non-resident providers;[54]

51. 2015 OECD BEPS Action 1 Report, *supra* note 1, at 107 § 277.
52. *Ibid.* at 107–108 § 278.
53. *Ibid.* at 109 §§ 279 et seq.
54. *Ibid.* at 113 §§ 292 et seq.

(b) an equalisation levy.[55]

The proposed withholding tax is, in the 2015 OECD BEPS Action 1 Report, rather generic and undefined. It would cover 'certain payments made to non-resident providers of goods and services ordered online … or to all sales operations concluded remotely with non-residents' and would be levied on the gross-basis payments made.

Finally, the 'equalization levy' is addressed to tax remote sales transactions concluded with in-country customers when the business maintains a significant economic presence (as mentioned above) in the market jurisdiction.

It is well known that the 2018 OECD Interim Report does not implement any specific proposal, due to the lack of necessary consensus among the OECD Members.

The most detailed proposals for the taxation of the digital economy arose from the Commission.

Following the strategy drawn up in the 2017 EU FETS Communication, on 21 March 2018, the Commission published a short-term proposal and a long-term (or systemic) proposal.

With the 2018 EU DST Directive Proposal,[56] the Commission intends to tax revenues stemming from the supply of certain digital services provided by non-resident suppliers. According to Article 3 of the Proposal, only those services for which the participation of a user constitutes an essential input for the business carrying out that activity are subject to taxation.[57] The taxable revenues are those resulting from the monetization of the user input (i.e., the revenues obtained by a taxable person by means of the inputs gathered or collected in the user's residence jurisdiction).

The long-term proposal, the 2018 EU SDP Directive Proposal,[58] conversely, aims at introducing into the EU tax system the concept of 'significant digital presence (SDP)', which is grounded on three different elements: (1) revenues from supplying digital services, (2) the number of users of digital services and (3) the number of contracts for a digital service.[59] If these requirements are fulfilled, a permanent establishment (PE) is deemed to exist.[60] Finally, the 2018 SDP Directive Proposal deals with the rules for allocating profits to a SDP confirming the extension of the current guidelines developed in the authorized OECD approach (AOA).[61]

---

55. *Ibid.* at 115 §§ 302 et seq.
56. 2018 EU DST Directive Proposal, *supra* note 3.
57. The explanatory notes to the 2018 EU DST Directive Proposal, *supra* note 3, at 7, state that:

> the business models captured by this Directive are those which would not be able to exist in their current form without user involvement. The role played by users of these digital services is unique and more complex than that traditionally adopted by a customer. These services can be provided remotely, without the provider of the services necessarily being physically established in the jurisdiction where the users are and value is created.

58. 2018 EU SDP Directive Proposal, *supra* note 3.
59. *Ibid.* Art. 4(3).
60. *Ibid.* Art. 4(1).
61. *Ibid.* Art. 5.

§4.05 ARE THE SOLUTIONS AND THE PROPOSALS FOR DIGITAL ECONOMY TAXATION FAIR? A PRELIMINARY CONCLUSION

Once the meanings of tax fairness or, at least, the fundamental meanings of tax fairness have been defined, the next step is the assessment of the compliance of the international Proposals on the taxation of the digital economy with these meanings.

In general terms, two different profiles should be considered. The traditional problem relates to the justification of the taxation of resident and non-resident, or domestic or foreign wealth (income). Restricting the analysis to the digital economy, the core question regarding tax fairness is the justification for the activities carried on by non-residents in the source jurisdiction without any physical presence.

On the other side, a complementary issue concerns the measurement of the income (or, in the modern understanding, of the value) generated in the source jurisdiction through digital business models.

These profiles must be treated separately.

As far as the 'SDP' is concerned, the taxation of the income generated in the source jurisdiction without any physical presence can be sufficiently justified according to the utility non-residents derive from the market where the economic activity is carried out. In other words, taxation of the non-residents can be understood as the utility stemming from the (legal and economic) protection granted by that jurisdiction. In these terms, the 'SDP' represents a sharp revaluation of the benefit principle, understood not as the price for the services received but as the utility derived from the legal and economic system where the business is carried on. The legal and economic system should, therefore, be understood as the essential requirement for the exercise of the digital business models.[62]

Considering the 2018 EU SDP Directive Proposal, the mentioned economic and legal utility can be primarily inferred from the business contracts concluded in the tax period requirement (Article 4(3)(c)).

Instead, it is hard to justify the taxation of non-residents according to the ability-to-pay principle since the absence of any physical link with the source jurisdiction excludes any tangible participation of the subject to the polity and, therefore, it impedes to assign any specific duty of solidarity to the non-resident economic operator.[63] It is difficult, in other words, to identify a qualified participation to the polity

62. According to these conclusions, Baez & Brauner's position cannot be shared ('[t]he profit as taxable base bears no relation to the use of public goods by non-resident taxpayers; in a nutshell, the benefit theory and profit taxation, under whatever PE design, embody a *contradictio in terminis*', *supra* note 10, at 9). The relation considered by the benefit principle, in the version accepted above, is between the economic and legal system and the economic activity carried on, not directly between 'the use of public goods' and profits. Taxation should be justified for the advantages and the privileges businesses receive from public expenditure; in these sense, public utility is deemed to be the proxy for the allocation of the tax burden among taxpayers. In the mentioned authors' view of the benefit principle, conversely, taxation should be characterized as the price for the services received.

63. Concurrently, Baez & Brauner, *supra* note 10, at 5: 'source taxation is not warranted in most cases of the digital economy since its principal participation in the source economy is supplying goods and services to local customers, and such participation is not sufficient to constitute

in the mere presence of the domain or the digital platform or, again, in the gathering of the users' data.

In conclusion, the 'SDP' can be considered as a sufficient proxy to justify the taxation in the user's jurisdiction and to apportion the income generated through the digital business models. If the pragmatic consequences of such a solution would be to lower the PE threshold,[64] from the fairness perspective the introduction of the 'SDP' would lead to a change of the theoretical paradigm of the justification for taxation, shifting from the ability-to-pay to the benefit principle.

As already stated,[65] the use of different PE thresholds may give rise to issues of compliance with the tax equality principle. This deemed discrimination, however, should be rejected due to the non-comparability of the 'brick-and-mortar' and the 'digital' economy business models.

The challenging issue of this concept lies in the determination of the income attributable to the SDP. Any attempt to deviate from the AOA,[66] in fact, may create a clash with the tax treatment of the traditional PE and, therefore, the violation of the tax equality principle.[67] Again, however, the issue can be overcome considering these situations not comparable.

The justification for the withholding tax (or, in the wording of the EU, of the 'Digital Services Tax') presents more difficulties. The only way this levy could be coherent with the benefit principle is the demonstration that the source jurisdiction concurs with the production of the income (or concurs with the generation of the *taxable* value). This demonstration would also prevent the withholding tax on digital services from violating the tax equality principle and, in particular, the discrimination between traditional and digital models.

Both the OECD and the Commission focus on the user's role in the creation of the value for the non-resident.[68] However, the information or the data gathered by non-residents are not sufficient to generate *profits* since they derive from the processing performed by the non-resident, normally by means of algorithms. In this sense,

---

source taxation jurisdiction'. However, *see* the 2015 OECD BEPS Action 1 Report, *supra* note 1, at 107 § 276, which states that the:

> elements of the three potential options could be combined into a new concept of nexus for net-basis taxation (a 'significant economic presence'), with the intent to reflect situations where an enterprise leverages digital technology to participate in the economic life of a country in a regular and sustained manner without having a physical presence in that country.

64. See, in this sense, the sophisticated analysis provided by Peter Hongler & Pasquale Pistone, *Blueprints for a New PE Nexus to Tax Business Income in the Era of the Digital Economy* 23 et seq. (IBFD, Working paper, 20 January 2015), *available at* https://www.ibfd.org/sites/ibfd.org/files/content/pdf/Redefining_the_PE_concept-whitepaper.pdf.
65. Baez & Brauner, *supra* note 10, at 6.
66. As proposed by the 2015 OECD BEPS Action 1 Report, *supra* note 1, at 111 §§ 284 et seq.
67. Concurring, Georg Kofler et al., *Taxation of the Digital Economy: 'Quick Fixes' or Long-Term Solution?*, 58 Eur. Tax'n 523, 529 (2017).
68. *See* Baez & Brauner, *supra* note 10, at 15: '[t]he more serious challenge, however, is not technical, but conceptual, as it provides a dominant destination basis for the tax, determined by the user not the provider'.

information and data are a necessary part of the chain for the creation of the value, but not sufficient for the process of profit generation and, thus, they cannot be qualified as taxable income in the source jurisdiction. If this reasoning is right, the withholding tax on digital services, or the EU DST, cannot be justified either according to the ability-to-pay principle, due to the lack of participation of the non-resident to the polity, or to the benefit principles since the source jurisdiction does not provide a sufficient utility for the creation of the income attributable to the non-resident.

A related issue concerns the determination of the final taxation of the digital services provided. Any final withholding tax, which cannot be credited in the residence tax jurisdiction, violates the net-basis income principle that can be inferred from the tax equality principle.[69]

Finally, the equalization levy, in one form proposed as 'excise tax', is intended to impose a burden on non-resident enterprise's significant economic presence in a jurisdiction. The purposes of such a levy is to place domestic and foreign providers on the same level.[70]

Since the significant economic presence is a necessary requirement for the application of the equalization levy, the justification for such a taxation can be found in the benefit principle, in the terms stated *supra* in this paragraph. For the same reasons, it is hard to provide any good argument for justifying such a tax lacking the economic presence.

§4.06 CONCLUSIONS

The analysis developed in the previous paragraphs allows three main conclusions:

(1) the widespread use of the expression 'tax fairness' in the OECD and EU documents is not much useful in the justification of the rationale for the taxation of the digital economy. Such an expression is not defined and, where it is, is done in a rather rhetoric or pleonastic manner;
(2) the benefit principle – as norm of a tax fairness theory – permits to justify the taxation of the significant economic presence in the source tax jurisdiction, understood as the compensation for the economic and legal utility provided by such jurisdiction;
(3) a final withholding tax cannot find the justification either in the benefit principle, nor in the ability-to-pay principle, unless levied on the basis of a significant economic presence in the source jurisdiction.

69. In such terms, *see also* Kofler, *supra* note 67, at 529, who added that '[u]nder a withholding tax, ... the assessment of a uniform, final gross withholding tax, all business models in the digital economy would ultimately be "lumped together". This would disregard the fact that value creation and margins under various business models are very different'.
70. *Ibid.* at 530.

CHAPTER 5

Tax Policy for the Digitalized Economy under Benjamin Franklin's Rule for Decision-Making

Andrés Báez Moreno & Yariv Brauner

§5.01 INTRODUCTION AND SCOPE

In 1772, Joseph Priestly went to Benjamin Franklin seeking advice on an affair of great importance to him. The brilliant polymath, however, taught him how to fish instead of just giving him the fish; he did so in a letter that deserves, at the very least, a literal quotation:

> I cannot for want of sufficient Premises, advise you what to determine, but if you please I will tell you how.
>
> When these difficult Cases occur, they are difficult chiefly because while we have them under Consideration all the Reasons pro and con are not present to the Mind at the same time; but sometimes one Set present themselves, and at other times another, the first being out of Sight. Hence the various Purposes or Inclinations that alternately prevail, and the Uncertainty that perplexes us.
>
> To get over this, my Way is, to divide half a Sheet of Paper by a Line into two Columns, writing over the one Pro, and over the other Con. Then during three or four Days Consideration I put down under the different Heads short Hints of the different Motives that at different Times occur to me for or against the Measure. When I have thus got them all together in one View, I endeavour to estimate their respective Weights; and where I find two, one on each side, that seem equal, I strike them both out: If I find a Reason pro equal to some two Reasons con, I strike out the three. If I judge some two Reasons con equal to some three Reasons pro, I strike out the five; and thus proceeding I find at length where the Ballance lies; and if after a Day or two of farther Consideration nothing new that is of Importance occurs on either side, I come to a Determination accordingly.

> And tho' the Weight of Reasons cannot be taken with the Precision of Algebraic Quantities, yet when each is thus considered separately and comparatively, and the whole lies before me, I think I can judge better, and am less likely to take a rash Step; and in fact I have found great Advantage from this kind of Equation, in what may be called Moral or Prudential Algebra.[1]

This decision-making model, which has also been subject to recent academic scrutiny,[2] remains largely valid today, particularly for the potential discrete options whose pros and cons are readily identifiable. In the authors' view, this is the case for the identified alternative solutions for the tax challenges related to the digitalized economy. Such alternatives were first presented by the Organisation for Economic Co-operation and Development (OECD) as part of the OECD/G20 Base Erosion and Profit Shifting (BEPS) Project, in its report entitled *Addressing the Tax Challenges of the Digital Economy: Action 1: 2014 Deliverable* ('2014 OECD BEPS Action 1 Deliverable')[3] and, with certain nuances,[4] they remain in play in the Post-BEPS era.

For many observers, the BEPS Project's final report, entitled *Addressing the Tax Challenges of the Digital Economy, Action 1: 2015 Final Report* (the '2015 OECD BEPS Action 1 Report')[5] was a disappointment. Indeed, it, unlike all of the other final reports from the BEPS Project, contained no specific recommendations for adoption,[6] but invited countries to a certain extent to unilaterally introduce, in their domestic law solutions and from among the tax policy options it described, additional safeguards against BEPS.[7] However, that final result is hardly surprising, if we take into account

1. Benjamin Franklin, *Mr. Franklin: A Selection from His Personal Letters* (Yale Univ. Press 1956).
2. Jean Czerlinski et al., *How Good Are Simple Heuristics?, in Simple Heuristics That Make Us Smart* 97–118 (Gerd Gigerenzer et al. eds., Oxford Univ. Press 1999).
3. OECD, *Addressing the Tax Challenges of the Digital Economy, Action 1: 2014 Deliverable* 143–147, 153–154 (OECD Publishing 2014) (hereinafter '2014 OECD BEPS Action 1 Deliverable').
4. A withholding tax (WHT) solution, however, seems to have lost OECD and EU support. *See* OECD, *Tax Challenges Arising from Digitalisation: Interim Report 2018: Inclusive Framework on BEPS* (OECD Publishing 2018) (hereinafter '2018 OECD Interim Report') and the 2018 EU Proposals, *infra* notes 13–15, released in March 2018.
5. OECD, *Addressing the Tax Challenges of the Digital Economy, Action 1: 2015 Final Report* 285 (OECD Publishing 2015) (hereinafter '2015 OECD BEPS Action 1 Report').
6. It is in fact remarkable that BEPS Action 1 has been ironically re-baptized as BEPS (In)Action 1: Gianni, Monica, *OECD BEPS (In)Action 1: Factor Presence as a Solution to Tax Issues of the Digital Economy (July 8, 2018)*, Tax Lawyer 72 (2018). Available at SSRN: https://ssrn.com/abstract=3211971. Equally critical in this respect: Eva Escribano López, *A Preliminary Assessment of the EU Proposal on Significant Digital Presence: A Brave Attempt That Requires and Deserves Further Analysis in Combating Tax Avoidance in the EU. Harmonization and Cooperation in Direct Taxation* 561 (José Manuel Almudí et al. eds., Wolters Kluwers 2018).
7. Somehow contradicting the very fundamental insight of the whole BEPS Project that international coordination of tax policies is a condition for the success of any substantial reform and that, by definition, unilateral action, regardless of its substance, cannot succeed; Yariv Brauner, *BEPS: An Interim Evaluation*, 6 World Tax J. 1 (2014); Yariv Brauner, *What the BEPS?*, 16 Fla. Tax Rev. 55, 58–59 (2014). This contradiction becomes apparent in the OECD's recent *Request for Input on Work Regarding the Tax Challenges of the Digitalised Economy*, http://www.oecd.org/tax/tax-policy/tax-challenges-digital-economy-request-for-input.pdf (accessed 14 November 2018) (hereinafter '2017 OECD Input Request') in which, after acknowledging the invitation to adopt domestic solutions from the tax policy options considered in the 2015 OECD BEPS Action 1 Report, the OECD appears to be upset that an increasing number of countries have begun taking steps towards the implementation of unilateral and uncoordinated measures aimed at taxing

that the BEPS Project aspired, in the first place, to restore a predetermined level of residence and source taxation, without changing the existing international standards on the allocation of taxing rights on cross-border income.[8]

However, once it became apparent that the implementation of the BEPS package (particularly Actions 3, 6, 7, 8, 9 and 10) did not address the BEPS issues created by digitalization or, at least, a number of broader direct tax challenges related thereto,[9] it became equally clear that the pursuit of a solution worthy of recommendation must continue. In response, the G20 leaders, in March of 2017, showed their ongoing support for the OECD's work on the digital economy, asking the OECD's Task Force on the Digital Economy to deliver an interim report by April 2018 on digitalization's implications for taxation. To that end, the OECD issued, in September 2017, a request for input on key issues related to the tax challenges raised by digitalization and the potential options to address them (2017 OECD Input Request),[10] which was completed by a significant number of commentators.[11] The 2018 OECD Interim Report was finally published in 2018 accompanied by the promise of an update of progress in 2019 and a final report in 2020.

In the same vein, the European Commission, on 21 September 2017, issued a communication, entitled *A Fair and Efficient Tax System in the European Union for the Digital Single Market* (2017 EU Comm'n Comm. on Fair/Efficient Tax).[12] Six months later, on 21 March 2018, the European Commission proposed new solutions for taxing the digital economy, including: (i) a Proposal for a Council Directive laying down rules relating to the corporate taxation of a significant digital presence (2018 SDP Directive

---

digitalized activities and highly digitalized business models. Some echoes of this 'regret' are also visible in the 2018 OECD Interim Report 177–191 when it describes the considerations for the design of interim measures.

8. As clearly demonstrated by the following statement contained in the OECD's original Action Plan:

> In the changing international tax environment, a number of countries have expressed a concern about how international standards on which bilateral tax treaties are based allocate taxing rights between source and residence States. This Action Plan is focused on addressing BEPS. While actions to address BEPS will restore both source and residence taxation in a number of cases where cross-border income would otherwise go untaxed or would be taxed at very low rates, these actions are not directly aimed at changing the existing international standards on the allocation of taxing rights on cross-border income.

(OECD, *Action Plan on Base Erosion and Profit Shifting* 11 (OECD Publishing 2013) (emphasis added)).

9. Something the OECD predicted in the 2015 OECD BEPS Action 1 Report, *supra* note 5, at 12–13.
10. 2017 OECD Input Request, *supra* note 7.
11. All such comments are published in OECD, *Public Comments Received on the Tax Challenges of Digitalization*, http://www.oecd.org/tax/beps/public-comments-received-on-the-tax-challenges-of-digitalization.htm (accessed 22 August 2018).
12. EU Comm'n, *Communication from the Commission to the European Parliament and the Council: A Fair and Efficient Tax System in the European Union for the Digital Single Market*, COM(2017) 547 final, 11 (hereinafter '2017 EU Comm'n Comm. on Fair/Efficient Tax').

Proposal),[13] (ii) a Proposal for a Council Directive on the common system of a digital services tax on revenues resulting from the provision of certain digital services (2018 DST Directive Proposal)[14] and (iii) a recommendation relating to the corporate taxation of a significant digital presence (collectively, with the directive proposals, the '2018 EU Proposals').[15]

The objective of this chapter is to offer to the OECD (for the design of its 2020 final report), the EU Institutions (for structuring future EU legislative action) and any States considering or reconsidering unilateral measures in the field, a decision-making table, in the style of Franklin, of the pros and cons that might help them better calibrate the three available policy options. Our task, of course, must be carried out under certain assumptions, as follows:[16]

(1) Doing nothing is not an option. At both the institutional and the academic levels, there is global consensus that the current system requires changes. We are well aware of recent academic work that still questions the need for a change in the international tax regime as regards the digitalized economy.[17] Nevertheless, this problem goes beyond the remit of this chapter.
(2) The basic architecture of the international tax regime (i.e., reliance on the source-residence paradigm and total rejection of alternatives to the current transfer pricing rules) will remain intact. Even if radical alternatives – some of them particularly focused on the digitalized economy[18] – are becoming more widespread, they will not be considered herein.
(3) The tax policy options considered herein are those contained in the 2015 OECD BEPS Action 1 Report[19] and the 2017 EU Comm'n Comm. on Fair/Efficient Tax,[20] which are (a) the use of a new tax nexus concept based on 'significant economic presence' (SEP) or 'significant digital presence' ('SDP', collectively with SEP, 'SEP/SDP'), (b) the use of a withholding tax (WHT) on certain types of transactions (which may, or may not, be 'digital' or even 'remote' transactions) and (c) the use of a 'digital equalization levy' (DEQL). Other specific measures, such as specific regimes targeting large

13. Eur. Comm'n, *Proposal for a Council Directive Laying Down Rules Relating to the Corporate Taxation of a Significant Digital Presence*, COM(2018) 147 final 2018/0072 (CNS) (hereinafter '2018 SDP Directive Proposal').
14. Eur. Comm'n, *Proposal for a Council Directive on the Common System of a Digital Services Tax on Revenues Resulting from the Provision of Certain Digital Services*, COM(2018) 148 final 2018/0073 (CNS) (hereinafter '2018 DST Directive Proposal').
15. Eur. Comm'n, *Recommendation Relating to the Corporate Taxation of a Significant Digital Presence*, COM(2018) 1650 final.
16. The authors of this contribution do not necessarily share all of these assumptions in their entirety; rather, they are only used as a starting point for achieving the objectives of this chapter.
17. Wolfgang Schön, *Ten Questions About Why and How to Tax the Digitalized Economy* 2017-11 Max Planck Institute for Law & Public Finance 1–6 (2017).
18. Michael Devereux & John Vella, *Implications of Digitalization for International Corporate Tax Reform*, 46 Intertax 550 (2018).
19. 2015 OECD BEPS Action 1 Report, *supra* note 5, at 107–117.
20. 2017 EU Comm'n Comm. on Fair/Efficient Tax, *supra* note 12, at 9–10.

multinational enterprises (MNEs),[21] will not be considered in this chapter, at least not in any particular detail.[22]

The structure of this chapter is as follows: §5.02 provides a description of the tax policy options to be compared according to their basic characteristics as contained in the 2015 OECD BEPS Action 1 Report, the 2017 EU Comm'n Comm. on Fair/Efficient Tax, the 2018 EU Proposals and several national initiatives that have been adopted in line (allegedly) with them; §5.03 provides a description of the particular WHT we propose, describing its advantages compared to alternative digital transaction WHT designs; §5.04 compares all of those policy options, describing their pros and cons in relation to implementation issues (e.g., definition and control of thresholds, scope of attribution of profits, method of taxation and compliance), and other legal concerns (i.e., double tax convention (DTC) law, European Union (EU) law and World Trade Organization (WTO) law; and, finally, in §5.05, we map our conclusions in our decision-making table.

§5.02 DESCRIBING THE PROPOSED TAX POLICY OPTIONS

We must first acknowledge that the BEPS Project's approach to Action 1 has evolved over time, which has allowed the OECD to gradually propose more specific tax policy options intended to deal with the so-called broader direct tax challenges raised by the digital economy. Indeed, the fact that certain original options have disappeared,[23] other, already-existing alternatives have developed in remarkable ways[24] and completely new solutions have been suggested in the 2015 OECD BEPS Action 1 Report[25] collectively offer a general idea of the different tax policy options we compare in this chapter. However, the proposals contained in the 2015 OECD BEPS Action 1 Report are still too crude to support the comparative analysis provided in this chapter.[26] Thus, the basic alternatives mentioned herein will be complemented, as necessary, with a brief description of some unilateral domestic measures that have already been implemented

21. We refer to a specific category of unilateral measures, recently mentioned by the OECD, including: the 'Diverted Profit Tax' in the UK and Australia; the enhanced procedure for cooperation and collaboration for PEs in Italy; and the Base Erosion and Anti-Abuse Tax (BEAT) in the United States (2018 OECD Interim Report, *supra* note 4, at 147).
22. For further discussion of these alternatives, *see* Andrés Báez Moreno, *A Note on Some Radical Alternatives to the Existing International Corporate Tax and Their Implications for the Digital(ised) Economy*, 46 Intertax 560 (2018).
23. Such as the new nexus based on SDP, a bandwidth tax, or a 'Bit Tax', contained in the 2014 OECD BEPS Action 1 Deliverable, *supra* note 3, at 143–145, 146–147.
24. The 2015 OECD BEPS Action 1 Report, *supra* note 5, in contrast to the 2018 OECD Interim Report, *supra* note 4, contains substantial developments as regards the *new nexus based on the concept of significant economic presence* (at 107–113) and, to a lesser extent, in relation to a *WHT on digital transactions* (at 113–115).
25. The concept of an 'equalization levy' (DEQL) is a creation of the 2015 OECD BEPS Action 1 Report, *supra* note 5, at 115–117.
26. The 2018 OECD Interim Report, *supra* note 4, has not significantly altered said landscape, with the exception of DEQLs (as an interim measure) that are considered in detail in Chapter 6 thereof (at 177–191).

by some jurisdictions and some models developed by academics. In line with this approach, we examine the main features of these different alternatives discussed below.

[A] A New Tax 'Nexus' Concept: SEP

Despite its terminology, this SEP policy option is really about modifying the concept of a permanent establishment (PE) for the digital age, suggesting that there can be a virtual PE (VPE), meaning a PE that is fully dissociated from the current physical and/or personal presence requirements that have traditionally characterized PEs. The existence of a SEP depends on: (i) a revenue factor identified with a (preferably) high[27] threshold of gross revenues generated from 'remote' transactions,[28] calculated on a related-group basis;[29] combined with either (ii) digital factors either in the form of local domain names, local digital platforms or local payment options;[30] or (iii) user-based factors, such as monthly active users, online contract conclusion or data collected.[31]

This new SEP definition of a VPE is actually not much different from that proposed in recent academic work[32] in the '2018 SDP Directive Proposal'[33] and, to a lesser extent, from the only national regulation in place to date referring to SEP.[34]

---

27. Intended to minimize administrative burdens for tax administrations, as well as compliance burdens for the taxpayer. 2015 OECD BEPS Action 1 Report, *supra* note 5, at 108.
28. A reference to 'digital' transactions is avoided in order not to treat other 'remote' transactions (mail-order or telephone transactions) differently (2015 OECD BEPS Action 1 Report, *supra* note 5, at 108).
29. A separate-entity basis should be avoided in order to prevent artificial fragmentation of distance selling activities (2015 OECD BEPS Action 1 Report, *supra* note 5, at 108).
30. *Ibid.* at 109.
31. *Ibid.* at 110–111.
32. Hongler and Pistone refer to the provision of digital services used by more than one thousand monthly users if the total amount of revenue due to the aforementioned services in the other Contracting State exceed a yet-to-be-determined minimum turnover (Peter Hongler & Pasquale Pistone, *Blueprints for a New PE Nexus to Tax Business Income in the Era of Digital Economy*, *White Paper Series* 25 (IBFD 2015)). In fact, their proposal combines a revenue factor with a user-based factor; *see also* Yariv Brauner & Pasquale Pistone, *Adapting Current International Taxation to New Business Models: Two Proposals for the European Union*, 71 Bull. Int'l Tax'n 681, 683 §3 (2017).
33. Article 4(3) of the 2018 SDP Directive Proposal provides that 'significant digital presence' shall be considered to exist in a Member State if digital services are provided through a digital interface and one or more of the following conditions is met: (a) the proportion of total revenues obtained in that tax period and resulting from the supply of those digital services to users located in that Member State in that tax period exceeds EUR 7,000,000; (b) the number of users of one or more of those digital services who are located in that Member State in that tax period exceeds 100,000; (c) the number of business contracts for the supply of any such digital service that is concluded in that tax period by users located in that Member State exceeds 3,000.
34. On 1 February 2018, the Indian Finance Minister presented the country's then-latest budget containing a new sourcing rule that referred to SEP based upon two alternative factors: (1) the aggregate of payments arising from a transaction carried out by a non-resident during the financial year exceeding a yet-to-be-prescribed amount or (2) systematic and continuous soliciting of business activities or engaging in interactions with a yet-to-be-prescribed number of Indian users through digital means. For its part, the Indian budget proposal defined SEP by, alternatively: (a) a mere revenue factor (on a transaction by transactions basis) or (b) a combination of a user-based factor and a totally undefined concept of 'continuous soliciting of

As with any PE, determining the threshold for its existence is just a first step in the VPE analysis, inasmuch as the attribution of profits to the VPE arises immediately after it is found to exist. In this regard, the 2015 OECD BEPS Action 1 Report acknowledged that the traditional attribution rules, which are based on functions performed, assets used and risk assumed, would not permit a significant profit attribution to a VPE.[35] Moreover, after rejecting substantial departures from the existing PE standards - such as treating customers and users as performing certain functions or replacing a functional analysis with an analysis based on game theory - the report proposed a modified *deemed-profit method* articulated through a ratio of presumed expenses nuanced by industry-specific profit percentages, together with rebuttable presumptions given to taxpayers in a loss-making position at the end of the fiscal year.[36] Whether or not that methodology amounts to a predetermined formula[37] or to a predetermined margins system goes well beyond the scope of this chapter.

Academic work in relation to this new VPE threshold has also advocated for a departure from the current PE attribution system by proposing a 'modified profit split' based on an upfront allocation of one-third of the profit of an enterprise acting in the digital economy to the market jurisdiction (i.e., the country in which the VPE is 'located'),[38] a 'deemed attribution of risks, assets and functions' combined with a profit split method[39] or, finally, a full attribution of the income generated by fully dematerialized activities in the Source state in combination with an aliquot expense deduction.[40]

For its part, the 2018 SDP Directive Proposal departs significantly from the current orthodox OECD attribution practice,[41] by expanding the functions allegedly performed by a VPE - to cover the 'economically significant activities' performed by the taxpayer through the digital interface - and imposing the preferential use of the profit split method by means of special splitting factors.[42] India's new SEP regulation, on the other hand, has simply ignored the problem.[43]

---

business'. The Indian SEP threshold has been rightly criticized for its vagueness and ambiguity (Shilpa Goel, *Indian 2018 Budget: New Nexus to Tax Based on Virtual Presence* (Kluwer International Tax Blog 2018)), *available at* http://kluwertaxblog.com/2018/02/05/indian-2018-budget-new-nexus-tax-based-virtual-presence/ (accessed 22 August 2018).

35. 2015 OECD BEPS Action 1 Report, *supra* note 5, at 111–112.
36. *Ibid.* at 112–113.
37. *Ibid.* at 112 (rejecting the concept).
38. Hongler & Pistone, *supra* note 32, at 34–36. A subsequent proposal suggested using the profit split method adapted by replacing the risk-taking function and the geographical presence of assets with other criteria, which could include the revenue from the contracts concluded in the country of the VPE and others that more closely correspond to the dynamics of the new business models. Brauner & Pistone, *supra* note 32, at 3.
39. Daniel. W. Blum, *Permanent Establishments and Action 1 on the Digital Economy of the OECD Base Erosion and Profit Shifting Initiative – The Nexus Criterion Redefined?*, 69 Bull. Int'l. Tax'n 314, 322–323 (2015).
40. *Ibid.*
41. Contrary to what one might think in view of para. 2 of Art. 5 of the 2018 SDP Directive Proposal.
42. For a good description of the proposed system, *see* Escribano López, *supra* note 6, at 594–598.
43. As denounced by Goel, *supra* note 34. In this connection however certain authors explain how the attribution of profits in the Indian context has been based on intuition rather than on the

[B] A WHT on Certain Types of (Digital) Transactions

The 2015 OECD BEPS Action 1 Report was rather inconclusive when defining the WHT tax policy option, leaving its final setting open. First, it acknowledged that a WHT could be imposed as a stand-alone, gross-basis final WHT *or* as a primary-collection mechanism to support the new VPE nexus approach mentioned earlier.[44] However, for legal reasons analysed in greater detail, *infra*, the 2015 OECD BEPS Action 1 Report finally saw the use of a WHT as more of a back-up mechanism for net-basis taxation enforcement.[45] Second, when it described the scope of transactions to be covered by such a WHT, the 2015 OECD BEPS Action 1 Report eschewed the adoption of a detailed list of transactions covered by the WHT, instead favouring a more general definition, such as one related to transactions for goods or services ordered online or simply all sales operations concluded remotely with non-residents.[46] Third, although the 2015 OECD BEPS Action 1 Report toyed with the possibility of requiring intermediaries processing payments made to digital economy actors to withhold taxes on payments made in business-to-consumer (B2C) contexts, it still appeared to veer towards a WHT limited to business-to-business (B2B) transactions.[47] Finally, the 2015 OECD BEPS Action 1 Report acknowledged that a WHT on gross revenues might not be a good proxy for tax on net income, such that the only solution it put forward in this regard was to fix the tax rate at a relatively low level, to address the many concerns about such WHTs; however, as already stated, due to (apparently insurmountable) WTO and EU law concerns, the 2015 OECD BEPS Action 1 Report only supported a WHT as a back-up enforcement mechanism for the net-basis taxation it considered a more viable approach.

In 2018, Italy introduced its so-called Web Tax, effective as of 1 January 2019 (*Imposta sulle Transazione Digitale*), which will apply a tax rate of 3% to some yet-to-be-specified[48] Internet services provided by both Italian resident businesses and non-resident businesses to local business recipients. A condition for such transactions to be subject to the tax is that the provider must put in place at least three thousand transactions per year (likely on behalf of Italian resident taxpayers[49]).

---

application of the 'authorized OECD approach' or an orthodox attribution practice: Anandapadmanabhan Unnikrishnan & Meyyappan Nagappan, *Virtual Permanent Establishment: Indian Law and Practice*, 46 Intertax 530 (2018).

44. 2015 OECD BEPS Action 1 Report, *supra* note 5, at 113.
45. *Ibid.* at 113.
46. *Ibid.* at 113–114.
47. *Ibid.* at 114.
48. The digital transactions hit by the tax will be identified by a decree of the Italian Tax Agency to be issued before 30 April. To the best of our knowledge this decree has not been approved yet. Current law refers to 'supply of services via electronic means, namely the Internet or other networks' and defines the latter services as those whose supply is, by nature, automated, requiring the use of information technology but minimal human intervention. Some commentators have prognosticated that the tax will just cover Internet advertisement and similar services. Patrizio Braccioni, *Italian Finance Law 2018: Focus on the New Tax on Digital Transactions ('Web Tax') and on the New Features of the Italian Permanent Establishment*, https://www.paulhastings.com/publications-items/details/?id=ccd5ed69-2334-6428-811c-ff00004cbded (accessed 23 August 2018).
49. However, this does not seem to be entirely clear according to the letter of the law. *Ibid.*

[C] A Digital Equalization Levy

It is quite obvious that the DEQL policy alternative is the least developed among those referred to in the 2015 OECD BEPS Action 1 Report, most likely due to it being the only one that was not in discussed in the 2014 OECD BEPS Deliverable; it could not, therefore, benefit from the discussion process that followed its publication.[50] Consequently, the description of the DEQL policy alternative could be little more than a presentation of the many uncertainties still surrounding it, which include the following: First, some commentators are perplexed by what the DEQL would equalize.[51] Nevertheless, it seems that the DEQL is likely intended, at least theoretically, to ensure equal treatment of foreign and domestic suppliers, but that has not yet been made clear.[52] Second, except for references in the 2015 OECD BEPS Action 1 Report to 'equalization levies *in the form of excise taxes*',[53] it is difficult to ascertain exactly what the nature of a DEQL is. However, there appears to be a broad consensus that such a DEQL should be neither an income tax nor a general turnover tax; it would, therefore, be an additional tax on top of existing direct and indirect taxes.[54] This second aspect of a DEQL is fairly consistent with the idea that the DEQL should be paid, in principle, by in-country customers and users.[55] Third, with regard to the eventual scope of the DEQL, uncertainties become dramatic. When it comes to the DEQL's objective scope, the 2015 OECD BEPS Action 1 Report stated that it would be applied only in cases where it is determined that a non-resident enterprise has a SEP, but it also considered the possibility of applying the DEQL to all transactions concluded remotely with in-country customers.[56] With respect to the means of conducting transactions, the 2015 OECD BEPS Action 1 Report did not decisively come down on either side of the issue related to which transactions would be taxable: be it all transactions concluded remotely or just those effectuated through a digital platform.[57] Finally, and despite the fact that the DEQL appears to have been designed to cover cross-border transactions alone, the 2015 OECD BEPS Action 1 Report also appears to suggest that the DEQL could be imposed on both domestic and foreign entities.[58] The DEQL would be imposed on the gross value of the goods and services provided.[59] Finally, it suggested that the

50. In fact, the disappearance of the '*bandwidth*' *or* '*Bit Tax*' initially mentioned in the 2014 OECD BEPS Action 1 Deliverable and the subsequent emergence of the DEQL option in the 2015 OECD BEPS Action 1 Report has never been explained.
51. Michael Devereux, *A Marxist Approach to International Taxation* (Oxford Univ. Centre for Business Tax'n 2017) (http://business-taxation.sbsblogs.co.uk/2017/11/17/a-marxist-approach-to-international-taxation/ (accessed 14 November 2018)).
52. 2015 OECD BEPS Action 1 Report, *supra* note 5, at 115; Georg Kofler et al., *Taxation of the Digital Economy: 'Quick Fixes' or Long-Term Solution?*, 57 Eur. Tax'n 523, 528 s. 4.4.1 (2017).
53. 2015 OECD BEPS Action 1 Report, *supra* note 5, at 115 (emphasis added) (DEQL parallels are drawn to equalization levies in the insurance area).
54. Schön, *supra* note 17, at 14; Brauner & Pistone, *supra* note 32, at 2.
55. 2015 OECD BEPS Action 1 Report, *supra* note 5, at 116.
56. *Ibid.* at 116.
57. *Ibid.*
58. *Ibid.* at 117.
59. *Ibid.* at 116.

DEQL would be collected by the foreign (or domestic) enterprise via a simplified registration regime or by a local intermediary.[60]

India's DEQL, introduced on 29 February 2016,[61] is regarded as the best example of the 2015 OECD BEPS Action 1 Report's DEQL policy option. In fact, India's new DEQL shares many of the features just mentioned in relation to the OECD's general discussion of the DEQL policy option, such as being, at least theoretically, outside the scope of income and general consumption taxes, only being imposed on transactions effectuated through a digital platform,[62] being applicable only if a non-resident enterprise has a SEP in India,[63] and only covering cross-border transactions.[64] However, India's DEQL differs from the original OECD policy option in some significant respects: it is to be collected by the service *recipient* (not by the foreign enterprise or a local intermediary), it is only chargeable on certain services[65] and, perhaps due to the foregoing, it is only collected on B2B transactions.[66] The DEQL contained in the '2018 DST Directive Proposal' also shares some of the features just mentioned, namely being, again, allegedly outside the scope of income and general consumption taxes, only being imposed on transactions effectuated through a digital platform and requiring the fulfilment of threshold(s) referred to the quantitative amount of services provided in the EU or the total amount of worldwide revenues[67]or being collected by the service provider.[68]

§5.03 OUR PROPOSAL TO ESTABLISH A STAND-ALONE GROSS-BASIS FINAL WHT ON (CROSS-BORDER) SERVICES IN B2B CONTEXTS

Our goal in this chapter is not only to compare the three policy options contained in the 2015 OECD BEPS Action 1 Report but also to elicit the pros and cons of our proposed

60. *Ibid.*
61. On this new tax: Sagar Wagh, *The Taxation of Digital Transactions in India: The New Equalization Levy*, 70 Bull. Int'l. Tax'n 538 (2016); Mansi Agrawal, *India at the Forefront in Implementing BEPS-Related Measures: Equalization Levy in Line with Action 1*, 23 Int'l Transfer Pricing J. (2016); Amar Mehta, *'Equalization Levy' Proposal in Indian Finance Bill 2016: Is It Legitimate Tax Policy or an Attempt of Treaty Dodging?*, 22 Asia-Pac. Tax Bull. 2 (2016); Ashok Lahiri et al., *Equalization Levy*, Brookings India Working Papers 1, 39 (2017).
62. India's DEQL is only imposed on certain *online* services, meaning that a facility, service, right, benefit or access is obtained through the Internet or any other form of digital telecommunication network.
63. Measured in this case by a revenue factor inasmuch as the aggregate amount of consideration received in a financial year must not exceed INR 100,000.
64. India's DEQL is only charged on certain services received from non-residents in India.
65. India's DEQL is exclusively charged on *specified services*, meaning online advertisement, any provision of digital advertising space or any other facility or service for the purpose of online advertisement, and includes any other service that has been notified by the government of India in this regard. Even though the original proposal presented by the Indian Committee on the Taxation of E-Commerce covered a long list of digital services and goods (*see* Wagh, *supra* note 61, at 547–548) and despite a possible future expansion by simple notification by the Indian Government, in its current state, India's DEQL is just imposed on digital advertising services.
66. The 2015 OECD BEPS Action 1 Report made no reference to an eventual exclusion for B2C transactions when describing the DEQL, unlike in its WHT policy option discussion.
67. *See* Art. 4 of the 2018 DST Directive Proposal.
68. *See* Arts 4 and 9 of the 2018 EU DST Directive Proposal.

WHT solution vis-à-vis VPEs and DEQLs. Thus, in this section, we present our argument in favour of a low tax rate, stand-alone, gross-basis final WHT on services in the B2B context. We will then compare our model to the other tax policy options in §5.04, *infra*. Here, however, we merely examine the advantages of our proposed model against other potential or existing WHT regimes.[69]

[A] A Stand-Alone Final WHT

All research done to date in relation to WHT solutions to the challenges posed by the digital economy has concluded that the nexus-based solution (i.e., the VPE) is superior to a WHT and has, consequently, only showed support for WHT as a collection mechanism, albeit a primary mechanism, to enforce the new nexus approach.[70] However, we believe that that instrumental design does not overcome many of the disadvantages[71] linked to the eventual creation of a new nexus in the form of a VPE,[72] while squandering many of the benefits of a WHT.

[B] A WHT on (Cross-Border) B2B Services

Limiting the application of a WHT intended to address digital economy challenges only to (cross-border) B2B services has a significant number of implications that, at the same time, entails some of its main advantages in comparison to other legal designs.

[1] The Exclusion of Goods

All of the various WHT variants contained in the 2015 OECD BEPS Action 1 Report defined the scope of the ultimate WHT on digital transactions to include both goods *and* services (i.e., digital sales transactions or sales operations concluded remotely with non-residents).[73] Our proposal does not because there are a number of good reasons to exclude the sale of goods from our proposed WHT. First, the problem of online retailers has already been adequately addressed under OECD BEPS Action 7[74] and Article 13 of the Multilateral Instrument (MLI).[75] Indeed, the significant reduction

69. This is an evolved proposal, built upon a previous proposition by the authors: Andrés Báez Moreno & Yariv Brauner, *WHT in the Service of BEPS Action 1: Address the Tax Challenges of the Digital Economy*, *in White Paper Series* 33 (IBFD 2015).
70. 2015 OECD BEPS Action 1 Report, at 115. Kofler et al., *supra* note 52, at 530; Hongler & Pistone, *supra* note 32, at 10; Brauner & Pistone, *supra* note 32, at 1. The authors have defended this idea in a previous publication: Báez Moreno & Brauner, *supra* note 69, at 2.
71. To which we will be make a detailed reference in §5.04, *infra*.
72. Some authors have suggested that a WHT is merely a back-up mechanism that would address all the challenges – including under DTC law – that emerge out of a redefined SEP concept (*see* Kofler, *supra* note 52, at 529–530).
73. 2015 OECD BEPS Action 1 Report, *supra* note 5, at 113–114.
74. OECD, *Preventing the Artificial Avoidance of Permanent Establishment Status, Action 7 – 2015 Final* 285 (OECD Publishing 2015).
75. OECD, *Multilateral Convention to Implement Tax Treaty Related Measures to Prevent Base Erosion and Profit Shifting* (OECD Publishing 2017) (hereinafter 'MLI').

of PE exceptions in Article 5(4) OECD Model[76] will allow the Source state – that is, the state in which the 'logistic PE' is located – to tax many 'digital sales of goods' that had been untaxed before its implementation.[77] To the extent any new WHT also covers digital sales of goods, its interaction with the extended 'logistic PE' should be resolved. One possible solution might be a rule similar to the PE proviso in Articles 10(4), 11(4) and 12(3) of the OECD Model that would place income derived from digital sales of goods back in the category of PE taxation. However, to achieve that same result, it would be simpler to exclude all goods from the new WHT. Without such a special rule addressing such potential conflict, the coexistence of 'logistic PEs' and a WHT covering sales of goods will inevitably raise characterization issues.

Second, it has become almost commonplace to declare that the digital economy's new business models blur the line between goods and services[78] and that, according to the 2015 OECD BEPS Action 1 Report,[79] results in new characterization issues for both domestic and tax treaty purposes. However, that broad, general declaration is partially inaccurate. In reality, these new business models (a) enlarge the very space of services (*servitization*) and (b) in certain cases, expand their quantitative importance. The advent of 'cloud computing', which has actually turned software into service, is a classic example of servitization.[80] Despite the doubts expressed by the 2015 OECD BEPS Action 1 Report on characterization,[81] it is quite clear that cloud computing arrangements qualify as service contracts. As for expanding the quantitative importance of certain new business models, online advertising is just one case in point; the advantages of Internet advertising in comparison to traditional channels – by means of 'user-generated content' provided for 'free' by customers in two-sided platforms and subsequent tailored advertising – has provoked a dramatic increase in these services, with an expected growth rate of 12.1% per year over the period from 2014 to 2019.[82] Similarly, digitalization has increased the importance of intermediation services, both

76. OECD, *OECD Model Tax Convention on Income and on Capital (Condensed Version)* (OECD Publishing 2017) (hereinafter 'OECD Model').
77. Of course, the problem remains for suppliers without logistic centres in the market jurisdictions. *See* Kofler, *supra* note 52 at 527; Georg Kofler et al., *Taxation of the Digital Economy: A Pragmatic Approach to Short-Term Measures*, 58 Eur. Tax'n 123, 124 s. 2.2 (2018). Some authors do not consider this problem to be an urgent one (e.g., Hongler & Pistone, *supra* note 32, at 24); however, it deserves further attention.
78. 2015 OECD BEPS Action 1 Report, *supra* note 5, at 53; 2017 EU Comm'n Comm. on Fair/Efficient Tax, *supra* note 12, at 4; *see* Kofler, *supra* note 52, at 523.
79. Particularly with regard to cloud computing and 3D printing (2015 OECD BEPS Action 1 Report, *supra* note 5, at 104–106).
80. Schön, *supra* note 17, at 9.
81. 2015 OECD BEPS Action 1 Report, *supra* note 5, at 104–106. Some authors have correctly pointed out that both the 2014 OECD BEPS Action 1 Deliverable and the 2015 OECD BEPS Action 1 Report overstate the alleged lack of guidance regarding cloud computing, probably reflecting an invigorated revenue interest of the Source state (Matthias Valta, *Article 12 Income from Royalties*, *in* 1 *Klaus Vogel on Double Taxation Conventions* 1000 (m.note 107) (Ekkehart Reimer & Alexander Rust eds., Walters Kluwer Law & Business 4th ed. 2015).
82. 2015 OECD BEPS Action 1 Report, *supra* note 5, at 113–114. Additionally, figures show that online advertising may only be in its infancy! *See* Assaf Prussak, *The Income of the 21st Century: Online Advertising as a Case Study for the Implications of Technology for Source-Based Taxation*, 16 Tul. J. Tech. & Intell. Prop. 39, 53 (2013).

between businesses and consumers[83] and among consumers themselves.[84] In this context, it seems safe to say that the digitalized economy is, by and large, an economy of services.[85]

[2] A Mere Reference to Services

The 2015 OECD BEPS Action 1 Report assumed that any new WHT would cover either (a) transactions ordered 'online' or (b) all sales operations concluded remotely with non-residents.[86] In contrast, our proposal merely refers to 'services', without adding any qualifiers (such as, 'digital' or 'remote' services). A number of reasons explain our simple design.

First, it avoids the significant degree of complexity and eventual characterization problems often linked to scopes listing specific types of transactions.[87] The existing unilateral measures in the form of a WHT or a DEQL clearly show these difficulties.[88] Second, a reference to all services – regardless of their remote, digital or 'traditional' nature – avoids potential accusations of favouring traditional means of doing business and, thereby, removes any hint of ring-fencing the digital economy.[89] Third, it avoids characterization issues and potentially abusive arrangements, particularly with regards to complex contractual relationships that include both remote and physical services.

[3] Cross-Border (or Also Domestic) Services

All of the alternative designs for an eventual digital transaction WHT presented in the 2015 OECD BEPS Action 1 Report appear to have been designed to apply exclusively to cross-border transactions.[90] Nevertheless, and perhaps fuelled by legal criticism of

83. A good example would be digital travel agencies, such as Booking.com.
84. This is the model of platforms within the collaborative economy such as Airbnb & Uber.
85. In the same vein: Jinyan Li, *Protecting the Tax Base in a Digital Economy, in United Nations Handbook on Selected Issues in Protecting the Tax Base of Developing Countries* 407, 424 (Alexander Trepelkov et al. eds., UN 2015); BEPS Monitoring Group, Comment, in OECD, *Tax Challenges of Digitalisation: Comments Received on the Request for Input Part I* 20, 27 (OECD Publishing 2017); David Orzechowski, *The Taxation of Fees for Technical, Managerial and Consultancy Services in the Digital Economy with Respect to Art 12A of the 2017 UN Model, in* Committee of Experts on International Cooperation in Tax Matters Fifteenth Session, E/C.18/2017/CRP.23 1, 29 (UN 2017).
86. 2015 OECD BEPS Action 1 Report, *supra* note 5, at 113–114.
87. *Ibid.* at 113 (setting out the advantages of general definitions).
88. For India's DEQL, *see* section 5.02[c]; for Italy's Web Tax, *see* Braccioni, *supra* note 48.
89. This criticism has been made, either explicitly or implicitly, with respect to DEQLs and WHTs designed to cover only just 'digital' transactions: Pistone & Brauner, *supra* note 32, at 2; Schön, *supra* note 17, at 14–15.
90. In fact, the 2015 OECD BEPS Action 1 Report refers to a WHT on payments by residents (and local PEs) of a country for goods and services *purchased online from non-resident providers* (at 113) (emphasis added). It is, therefore, surprising that the 2015 OECD BEPS Action 1 Report poses the problem of unequal treatment of domestic and foreign entities when dealing with DEQLs – even proposing to impose the tax on both domestic and foreign entities (at 117). And, what is even more astonishing is that the 2015 OECD BEPS Action 1 Report explicitly indicates that this problem also arises with the imposition of a gross-basis final WHT (at 116). It is hard

purely cross-border solutions,[91] a significant number of unilateral reactions to the tax challenges posed by the digital economy contemplate expanding such measures to purely domestic transactions.[92] Some commentators have claimed that extending the scope of 'digital taxes' to also cover purely domestic transactions would have a dramatic, anti-technology impact[93] placing European businesses at a disadvantage.[94] This might hold true for DEQLs, not creditable either in the Residence State or in the Source state. Indeed, it is extremely improbable that the Residence state will accept to credit a liability labelled as *indirect tax* by the Source state. In the context of a DEQL also covering domestic transactions, it is also unlikely that the DEQL will be credited against Corporate Tax. Therefore, the deduction of the DEQL as a cost from their corporate tax base is the best the companies can reasonably hope for in this context.[95] Things are different as regards WHTs. In a treaty context -of course if the treaty provides for source taxation of cross-border services[96] – the tax withheld at source would be credited in the Residence State. Although this will depend on the domestic regulation, in a non-treaty context, the tax withheld at source would be creditable, in principle, in the Residence State according to the corresponding unilateral foreign tax credit method. The situation is not any different in a purely domestic scenario. If the WHT is extended to also cover domestic situations the tax withheld will be creditable against domestic mainstream Corporate Income Tax. Therefore, there seems to be no trace of the deep anti-technology effect allegedly originated by the extension of a WHT on services to pure domestic transactions.

In any case the material outcome of this extension would be rather irrelevant if one takes into account that Companies performing domestic transactions would normally have to make advance payments which, in financial terms, may be equivalent to an eventual new WHT on domestic services. Indeed, expanding the scope of WHTs or DEQLs to embrace domestic transactions is typically justified by fear of violating EU or WTO law by means of cash flow disadvantages for non-residents generated by gross WHTs or DEQLs as opposed to net-oriented advance payment for domestic Corporate Tax purposes.[97] However, particularly with respect to a WHT on cross-border services, this potential for violation is not self-evident, as will be shown below.[98]

---

to understand why – being a problem common to both DEQLs and WHTs – the report just refers to it when dealing with the former policy alternative.

91. Brauner & Pistone, *supra* note 32, at 2; Schön, *supra* note 17, at 15–16; Kofler et al., *supra* note 52, at 531.
92. A case in point would be Italy's Web Tax (*see* Braccioni, *supra* note 48, at 2); *see also*, the 2018 DST Directive Proposal, *supra* note 14 (covers cross-border *and* purely domestic constellations).
93. Schön, *supra* note 17, at 16.
94. *Ibid.*
95. In fact this is also formulated as a mere hope in Recital 27 of the 2018 DST Directive Proposal when stating: *In order to alleviate possible cases of double taxation where the same revenues are subject to the corporate income tax and DST, it is expected that Member States will allow businesses to deduct the DST paid as a cost from the corporate income tax base in their territory, irrespective of whether both taxes are paid in the same Member State or in different ones. See* §5.04[B][2] and §5.04[B][3], *infra.*
96. *See* §5.04[B][1], *infra.*
97. This is particularly evident in the 2018 DST Directive Proposal, *supra* note 14.
98. *See* §5.04[B][2] and §5.04[B][3], *infra.*

In a nutshell, an eventual extension of our WHT to also embrace pure domestic services would be fairly harmless in terms of final collection while perhaps reporting certain advantages in terms of DTC, EU and WTO law consistency.

[4] Exclusion of B2C Services

The 2015 OECD BEPS Action 1 Report made significant efforts to address tax collection issues raised by a future WHT on digital transactions, particularly in connection with B2C transactions. Despite having explored the only available solution to this problem in a WHT context – that is, requiring intermediaries who process consumer payments to withhold the tax from said payments in the B2C context – the 2015 OECD BEPS Action 1 Report did not seem to recommend this option due to several technical concerns.[99] Their reflections seem sufficient to exclude B2C transactions from the scope of any new WHT on digital transactions.

However, this practical exclusion has generated widespread criticism, as it seems at odds with any of the theoretical foundations upon which such a WHT is supposed to be based (i.e., to achieve fair competition between domestic and cross-border suppliers or to shift taxing rights between countries).[100] In our view, this criticism loses sight of the following facts: First, the achievement of fair competition or the shift of taxing rights between countries are not the only grounds upon which a WHT on (digital) services might be grounded. Indeed, the so-called base-erosion approach has often been presented as the starting point for several proposals to expand market countries' taxing rights, both generally[101] and specifically, in the field of the digitalized

99. Indeed intermediaries would generally not have access to transaction-identifying information needed to correctly perform their WHT obligations and, even in the presence of a mandatory registration system whereby all remote sellers must designate a dedicated bank account for payments received from local customers, important challenges may arise when these intermediaries are situated in third countries with no connection to the jurisdiction of the customer (2015 OECD BEPS Action 1 Report, *supra* note 5, at 114). Similar concerns were expressed in several submissions made in response to the 2018 OECD Input Request, e.g., by the Italian Banking Association (ABI), Comment, in OECD, *Tax Challenges of Digitalization: Comments Received on the Request for Input Part I, supra* note 11, at 4; and AFME/UK Finance, Comment, in *ibid.* at 9.

100. Schön, *supra* note 17, at 12. In the same vein, but referring to the neutrality principle: Dale Pinto, *Options to Address the Direct Tax Challenges Raised by the Digital Economy: A Critical Analysis*, 65 Can. Tax J. 291, 325 (2017).

101. Such as the UN Services Taxation Project, to which we make reference in several subsequent sections. Since the very beginning of the UN Services Taxation Project, this background has appeared repeatedly: Committee of Experts on International Cooperation in Tax Matters (hereinafter 'CEICTM') Sixth session, Note on the Taxation of Services Under the United Nations Model Tax Convention E/C.18.2010/CRP.7 1, 26 (UN 2010); Brian J. Arnold, Note by the Secretariat: Additional Note on the Tax Treatment of Services E/C.18.2010/CRP.7/Add.1 1, 4 (CEICTM, UN 2013); CEICTM, Report on the Eighth Session (15–19 October 2012) E/2012/45 1, 11 (UN 2013); Brian J. Arnold, Note on a New Article of the UN Model Convention Dealing with the Taxation of Fees for Technical and Other Services E/C.18/2013/CRP.5 1, 4 (in, CEICTM, UN 2013); Brian J. Arnold, Note from the Coordinator of the Subcommittee on Tax Treatment of Services: Draft Article and Commentary on Technical Services, E/C.18/2014/CRP.8. 1, 6–7 (UN 2014). This idea, with varying degrees of concerns and practical consequences, has also been present in the work of Professor Arnold, who might well be considered the intellectual father of the UN Service Project. *See* Brian J.

economy.[102] We, however, do not mean to undermine a previously fair level of source taxation, in the sense typically used by the BEPS Project, but rather highlight the fact that income derived by non-residents might be deductible against the tax base in the source country (i.e., base-erosion principle). In B2C transactions, it seems fairly obvious that, in the absence of a deduction by the payer against his local tax base, no withholding should be made.[103]

Second, according to the available information, the dominance of B2B transactions in the global digitalized economy remains hegemonic. The 2015 OECD BEPS Action 1 Report noted that the vast majority of e-commerce consists of transactions in which a business sells products or services to other businesses.[104] More precise analyses indicate that B2B transactions account for somewhere between 75%,[105] 80%[106] or 90%[107] of the total value of e-commerce activity. The discrepancy in figures, the proliferation of business models beyond traditional e-retail and the progressive mass access of individuals to information technology resources worldwide may indicate that B2C transactions are not as insignificant as previously thought. Be it as it may, the predominance of B2B transactions in the digitalized economy remains clear and, thus, any tax policy option should rely upon the rule rather than the exception, particularly when taking the exception into account involves serious collection problems.[108]

§5.04 A WHT SOLUTION VIS-À-VIS OTHER POLICY ALTERNATIVES

Having set out the fundamental aspects of our proposal for a WHT on (cross-border) B2B services, we must undertake the essential task of this article which, as we already

Arnold, *Threshold Requirements for Taxing Business Profits under Tax Treaties*, 10 Bull. Int'l Tax'n 476, 489–490 (2003); Brian J. Arnold, *The Taxation of Income from Services Under Tax Treaties: Cleaning Up the Mess (Expanded Version)*, 65 Bull. Int'l Tax'n 66 (2011); Brian J. Arnold, *The Taxation of Income from Services, in United Nations Handbook on Selected Issues in Protecting the Tax Base of Developing Countries* 47, 48–49 (Alexander Trepelkov et al. eds., UN 2015).

102. Richard Doernberg, *Electronic Commerce and International Tax Sharing*, 16 Tax Notes Int'l 1013, 1016 (1998); Jinyan Li, *International Taxation in the Age of Electronic Commerce: A Comparative Study* 592–593 (Canadian Tax Foundation 2003); Báez Moreno & Brauner, *supra* note 69, at 9–10.
103. Andrés Báez Moreno, *The Taxation of Technical Services under the United Nations Model Double Taxation Convention: A Rushed – Yet Appropriate – Proposal for (Developing) Countries?*, 7 World Tax J. 1, 30 s. 3.2.1.2.4 (2015).
104. 2015 OECD BEPS Action 1 Report, *supra* note 5, at 55. In support of this proposition, it simply refers to previous OECD guidance (i.e., OECD, *OECD Guide to Measuring the Information Society 2011* 204 (OECD Publishing 2011)).
105. *See* EMarketer, *B2C Report on US Consumer Shopping, Buying & Demographics*, http://www.bus.umich.edu/KresgePublic/Journals/EmarketerReports/2001/eCommerce%20B2C%20Report%20September%202001.pdf (accessed 14 November 2018) and the EMarketer, *B2C Report*, http://www.bus.umich.edu/KresgePublic/Journals/EmarketerReports/2001/eCommerce%20B2B%20Report%20July%202001.pdf (accessed 14 November 2018) (quoted by Robert Doernberg et al., *Electronic Commerce and Multijurisdictional Taxation* 6 (Kluwer Law International 2001).
106. OECD, *Economic and Social Impact of Electronic Commerce: Preliminary Findings and Research Agenda* 36 (OECD 1999).
107. *See* Li, *supra* note 85, at 418 (quoting the 2014 OECD BEPS Action 1 Deliverable, *supra* note 3).
108. These compliance issues will be considered in detail in the next paragraph of this contribution.

anticipated, is not other than comparing its pros and cons vis-à-vis the other policy alternatives contained in the 2015 OECD BEPS Action 1 Report. In order to proceed systematically, we will divide the features to be compared between design and implementation issues (§5.04[A]) and legal consistency issues (§5.04[B]).

[A] Design and Implementation Issues

Our proposal for a WHT on cross-border B2B services will be compared with the other two policy alternatives suggested in the 2015 OECD BEPS Action 1 Report (i.e., the new SEP nexus and DEQLs) with respect to five key aspects of design and implementation: (1) definition and control of thresholds, (2) attribution of profits, (3) scope, (4) method of taxation and (5) compliance.

[1] Definition and Control of Thresholds

According to OECD's last proposal,[109] and in view of some of the existing domestic measures adopted so far,[110] designing a new VPE concept or, more generally, a new SEP nexus concept would, in any event, require a legal determination of a (revenue) threshold, which would likely have to be combined with additional qualitative and/or quantitative benchmarks.[111] For a number of reasons,[112] setting-up a threshold – however defined – might well be considered connatural to any rational design of a new nexus rule. Conversely, thresholds are not actually needed when designing other policy options such as WHTs or DEQLs.[113]

109. 2015 OECD BEPS Action 1 Report, *supra* note 5, at 107–111. The 2018 OECD Interim Report, *supra* note 4, has not further insisted on this idea or its detailed development as far as the exploration of potential changes to the current nexus and profit allocation rules has been referred to future work.

110. *See, e.g.*, India's new nexus-based SEP concept, discussed in §5.02[A], *supra*; *see also* the 2018 OECD Interim Report, *supra* note 4, at 138. Israel's tax circular introducing an SEP test (*ibid.* at 137) is a notable exception in this regard, listing a number of alternative factors of digital presence (online contract conclusion, use of digital products and services, localized website and multi-sided business models), but not incorporating a revenue-threshold requirement based on domestic sales.

111. *See* §5.02[A], *supra*.

112. In our view, in the absence of the traditional qualitative features of a Permanent Establishment (i.e., a fixed place of business or a dependent agent) the only way to define a 'virtual' nexus is by means of quantitative thresholds normally defined according to revenue- or user-based factors or a combination thereof. A definition based exclusively upon qualitative (digital) factors would be easily avoidable and not very indicative of an SEP.

113. The description of the WHT option in the 2015 OECD BEPS Action 1 Report, *supra* note 5, does not make a single reference to an eventual threshold. However, as regards equalization levies, the Report indicates that in order to provide clarity, certainty and equity to all stakeholders, and to avoid undue burden on small- and medium-sized businesses, the equalization levy would be applied only in cases where it is determined that a non-resident enterprise has a SEP (2015 OECD BEPS Action 1 Report, *supra* note 5, at 116). In fact, several 'turnover' taxes (as these have been redubbed in the 2018 OECD Interim Report, *supra* note 4) include a quantitative threshold (e.g., India's DEQL, Italy's Web Tax and France's tax on online and physical distribution of audiovisual content). Additionally, the 2018 OECD Interim Report clearly indicates that any interim tax measure would need to have a threshold (at 188). Finally, a

There has been a spirited defence of threshold requirements for taxing business profits.[114] However, when comparing the different policy options regarding tax challenges of the digitalized economy, the following reflections should be taken into account: First, the elimination of thresholds for source taxation under a WHT or a DEQL would eliminate the current 'all-or-nothing rule' typical of any type of existing concept of the PE. The breach of the continuity requirement (i.e., the non-existence of a PE leads from full to zero taxation), that is present in traditional physical and personal PEs, would become even more dramatic in new nexus VPEs, where the lack of one threshold unit (day, dollar, user or consumer) could lead from full taxation of income attributable to the VPE to no source taxation at all.[115] Second, shaping any such threshold(s) might prove to be a difficult task;[116] as a result, the final rules would be complex and difficult to interpret. In fact, rules defining thresholds in relation to existing proposals on VPEs and DEQLs have been criticized for being, on the one hand, vague and ambiguous,[117] or a nightmare of complexity and a mess of legal uncertainty, on the other.[118] Third, thresholds, particularly revenue- or user-based factors, may be easy for a potential taxpayer to avoid, which will, inevitably, lead to such thresholds being designed on a related-group basis rather than on a separate-entity basis[119] and, for any domestic sales thresholds, to the application of anti-avoidance rules to address artificial (or resale) arrangements with non-group members.[120] Although theoretically effective for ensuring the integrity of the system, such rules would add complexity to already-cumbersome threshold rules.

Traditionally, thresholds for taxing cross-border business profits have been justified by pointing to the legal certainty they provide for non-resident taxpayers and tax authorities alike, particularly when compared to sourcing rules for business profits based on limited case law and administrative practices.[121] However, as previously noted, that traditional view no longer seems valid, at least when it comes to thresholds in relation to several existing proposals. Those who support thresholds for taxing

---

double threshold (annual worldwide total revenue above EUR 750 million and annual revenue form the provision of digital services above EUR 50 million) was introduced in the 2018 DST Directive Proposal, *supra* note 14.

114. Arnold, *Threshold Requirements*, *supra* note 101, at 482–483.
115. For more on the continuity approach and the avoidance of the all-or-nothing rule, even if unrelated to a VPE, see Wolfgang Schön, *International Tax Coordination for a Second-Best World (Part I)*, 1 World Tax J. 67, 99–101 (2009). For the same reasoning regarding 'service PEs or VPEs', *see* Báez Moreno & Brauner, *supra* note 69, at 18; Báez, *supra* note 103, at 3.2.1.1.1.
116. For a good description of these difficulties, *see* Blum, *supra* note 39, at 318–321.
117. In relation to the new Indian nexus to be taxed on virtual presence, *see* Goel, *supra* note 34.
118. In relation to the 2018 DST Directive Proposal, *supra* note 14; Johannes Becker & Joachim Englisch, *EU Digital Services Tax: A Populist and Flawed Proposal* (Kluwer International Tax Blog 2018).
119. As recognized in the 2015 OECD BEPS Action 1 Report, *supra* note 5, at 108, and the 2018 OECD Interim Report, *supra* note 4, at 188, for revenue-based factors. Both the 2018 SDP Directive Proposal, *supra* note 13, at 4(3,) and the 2018 DST Directive Proposal, *supra* note 14, at 4(6), follow this recommendation.
120. Recognized by the 2018 OECD Interim Report, *supra* note 4, at 188–189, for domestic sales thresholds.
121. Arnold, *Threshold Requirements*, *supra* note 101, at 482. This also seems to be the reason for the thresholds contained in the Explanatory Memorandum to the 2018 DST Directive Proposal, *supra* note 14.

business profits indicate that a WHT, as an alternative used to reduce compliance costs and ease the administration of profit taxation, comes with its own set of problems, in particular, gross taxation and frequently arbitrary and unfair outcomes (such WHT solution disadvantages will be considered separately, *infra*). At this point, suffice it to say that the absence of those thresholds in the WHT policy option provides greater simplicity, certainty and even policy advantages - particularly the elimination of the current 'all-or-nothing approach' typical of the threshold approach, particularly for VPEs.

[2] Profit Attribution

Under current PE profit attribution rules - typically based on the (*significant people*) functions the PE performs, the assets it uses and the risks it assumes - it would be extremely difficult to attribute any profit to a VPE. Indeed, the problem of attribution is almost uniformly acknowledged to be the Achilles' heel of all of the current proposals that favour the new SEP nexus concept.[122] Perhaps the best evidence of the magnitude of the challenges posed by the use of said concept is the general lack of conviction with which the OECD presented it and its two alternative implementation methods (i.e., the fractional apportionment method[123] or the modified deemed-profit method[124]) to traditional attribution rules. Other methods suggested in more recent literature (e.g., the Modified Profit Split Method with an Upfront Income Allocation of a Partial Profit to the Market Jurisdiction,[125] the Sales-Based Transactional Profit Split,[126] or the New Transfer Pricing Guidance for the Digital Economy[127]) are still far from being universally accepted, as they come with their own technical problems.[128] To date, legislative initiatives at both the national and European levels have either completely ignored the issue[129] or have only come up with rather objectionable regulatory

122. *See* Li, *supra* note 85, at 445; Blum, *supra* note 39, at 322–323; Kofler, *supra* note 52, at 529; Pinto, *supra* note 100, at 322; Schön, *supra* note 17; Matteo Cataldi. *The Attribution of Income to a Digital Permanent Establishment, in Taxation in a Global Digital Economy* 143, 149 (Ina Kerschner & Maryte Somare eds., Linde 2017); Adolfo Martín Jiménez, *BEPS, the Digital(ized) Economy and the Taxation of Services and Royalties*, 46 Intertax 620, 624 (2018). 2015 OECD BEPS Action 1 Report, *supra* note 5, at 111–112.
123. Quickly discarded for being a departure from current international standards (2015 OECD BEPS Action 1 Report, *supra* note 5, at 112).
124. Theoretically presented as a superior alternative but riddled with numerous technical and practical problems according to 2015 OECD BEPS Action 1 Report, *supra* note 5, at 113.
125. Hongler & Pistone, *supra* note 32, at 34–36.
126. Ulrich Schreiber & Lisa Fell, *International Profit Allocation, Intangibles and Sales-Based Transactional Profit Split*, 9 World Tax J. 99, 99–115 (2017).
127. Marcel Olbert & Cristoph Spengel, *International Taxation in the Digital Economy: Challenge Accepted?*, 9 World Tax J. 6, 8 2.2.2 (2017) (more hesitant at 35. 5.2.2).
128. A synthesis of these new methods, accompanied by some critical remarks in Cataldi, *supra* note 122, 154–159.
129. For instance, India's new nexus based on a concept of 'SEP'. Israel's Circular introducing a 'significant economic presence' test for the purpose of attributing profits merely refers to the domestic rules based on the arm's length principle and leaves unresolved the issue of whether meaningful profits could be attributed to the defined taxable presence (2018 OECD Interim Report, *supra* note 4, at 137).

solutions.[130] The rules to attribute profits in respect of the SDP contained in Article 5 of the '2018 EU SDP Directive Proposal' are a case in point. The idea, according to Article 5(4) and 5(5) of the Proposal, that economically significant activities[131] are performed by the SDP is a mere fiction aimed at the removal of the requirement of significant *people* functions under common attributions standards and the systematic capture of automated functions by the VPE.[132] Indeed just fictitiously may be stated that a (revenue-users-contracts) threshold *performs* functions whatever these functions may be. This fiction becomes particularly evident when attributing storage, processing, analysis, deployment and sale of user-level data[133] or storage, processing and display of user-generated content[134] to the SDP; the same is true with regard to the attribution to the VPE of 'any digital service'.[135] The second main departure of the VPE attribution system from the regular attribution standards – i.e., the preferential use of the profit split method by means of special splitting factors – also poses serious questions. Article 5(6) of the 2018 EU SDP Directive Proposal imposes the preferential use of the profit split method *unless the taxpayer proves that an alternative method based on internationally accepted principles is more appropriate*; this proof would not be really difficult in practice.[136] Moreover, it is not clear whether more appropriate splitting factors different from those explicitly mentioned in Article 5(6) of the 2018 EU SDP Directive Proposal would be admissible under this provision.[137] Be that as it may, and apart from purely technical details, the proponents of the alternative methods for profit attribution to VPEs have not been able to convince academics or policymakers, for that matter, that such methods do not generate the kind of digital economy ring-fencing against which all stakeholders warn and claim to want to prevent.[138]

The truth is that the alternative methods' acknowledged vagueness, as well as the general lack of consensus regarding them, should come as no surprise if data collected from users in the VPE State are to become key value drivers for profit attribution under any new VPE approach.[139] Indeed, one of the stickiest issues raised in response to the

130. This is the case as regards the rules to attribute profits in respect of the significant digital presence contained in the 2018 SDP Directive Proposal, *supra* note 13, at 5.
131. Including, according to Art. 5(5): the collection, storage, processing, analysis, deployment and sale of user-level data; the collection, storage, processing and display of user-generated content; the sale of online advertising space; the making available of third-party created content on a digital marketplace; and, finally, the supply of any digital service different from the aforementioned.
132. Escribano López, *supra* note 6 at 596.
133. 2018 SDP Directive Proposal, Art. 5.5(a).
134. *Ibid.* Art. 5.5(b).
135. *Ibid.* Art. 5.5(e).
136. Martín Jiménez, *supra* note 122, at 635.
137. Rafaele Petruzzi & Vasiliki Koukoulioti, *The European Commission's Proposal on Corporate Taxation and Significant Digital Presence: A Preliminary Assessment*, 58 Eur. Tax'n 391, 398 (2018).
138. Schön, *supra* note 17, just referring to the profit split method proposed by Hongler and Pistone (*see* Hongler & Pistone, *supra* note 32); Kofler, *supra* note 52, at 529 warning that an alternative method for profit attribution should be embedded in an overall concept in order not to lead to unequal treatment in comparison to the 'classical' economy.
139. See, for example, the great importance attached to user-level data and user-generated content for the attribution of profits under a new Digital PE according to 2018 SDP Directive Proposal, Art. 5(5).

2017 OECD Input Request was how, exactly, value would be attributed to raw digital data, data collection and data analysis, in the context of the definition of the new VPE and, particularly, how would profit be attributed to that VPE.[140] If there has not been even minimal consensus on the relative value to be attributed to the different stages in which data can be made available and used, the prospect of designing new consensual rules for attribution based, essentially, upon the value of data might prove a difficult, if not impossible, task.

It is obvious that under a WHT or a DEQL[141] approach, there is no need to attribute profits, as those policy options completely sidestep the question.

[3] Digital and Non-digital Transactions, B2B and B2C Transactions and Domestic and Cross-Border Transactions

With respect to their scope, all of the potential policy options compared herein appear focused on the provision of services, apparently under the assumption that the use of other 'trade structures' based on remote sales of physical goods has already been adequately addressed under other, earlier BEPS Actions.[142] As far as other aspects of their respective scopes are concerned, however, the available policy options vary widely, which requires yet another, more detailed comparison, which, for the sake of clarity, follows.

[a] Digital and Non-digital Transactions

The digital and non-digital transactions policy option question, which has two parts, first asks if the particular policy option is limited to digital services or if it embraces non-digital services and then, second, asks whether it ought to. To be fair in any such comparison, that question must be examined in those two steps. First, we must decide if the policy option has a 'natural' scope, which means asking, as a matter of principle, whether it is likely to cover all provided services or only those labelled 'digital' (however that term may be defined). So far, the vast majority of legislative measures and proposals relating to VPEs or DEQLs auto-define their particular scope to some sort of digital channel.[143] On the other, our WHT proposal, even though it could be

140. Barry Larking, *A Review of Comments on the Tax Challenges of the Digital Economy*, 72 Bull. Int'l Tax'n. 1 (2018); Sylvia de Jong et al., *Dealing with Data in a Digital Economy*, 25 Int'l Transfer Pricing J. (2018).
141. In fact the 2015 OECD BEPS Action 1 Report (*supra* note 5, at 115) decided to introduce an DEQL to avoid some of the difficulties arising from creating new profit attribution rules for purposes of the new SEP nexus.
142. As the OECD concluded 2018 OECD Interim Report, *supra* note 4 at 105–107.
143. As regards VPE proposals, this is true for both legislative proposals (e.g., the Israel's Circular introducing a 'significant economic presence test'), India's SDP regulation and the EU SDP Directive Proposal, *supra* note 13) and academic suggestions (Hongler & Pistone, *supra* note 32, at 24–25). As regards DEQL, this holds true for India DEQL and the EU DST Directive Proposal, *supra* note 14.

conceived to only cover digital services,[144] covers all services, without adding any limiting qualifiers, such as 'digital' or 'remote'.[145]

Second, we must ask whether a broad scope, one that also covers non-digital services, is preferable to a more limited reach. All of the arguments set forth above[146] that favour a broad WHT on services can be used here to shed light on the issue (e.g., arguments in favour of simplicity and neutrality, in the sense that the policy option does not generate undesirable ring-fencing effects or prevent robust measures against tax avoidance). Further still, as discussed above, some of the ring-fencing effects of the various policy options might be exacerbated by the scope of certain designs, particularly DEQLs. Indeed, the already-inherent ring-fence effect of restricting the policy option's scope to digital services could be substantially aggravated if that scope is further restricted to just some of such digital services. India's current DEQL (only covering advertising services) and the 2018 DST Directive Proposal's limited scope (only covering advertising and intermediation services[147]) are cases in point, as they result in 'double or triple ring-fence[s]'.[148] Whether or not such double (or triple) ring-fencing may have a solid theoretical foundation is a different question. As recently stated by Professor Schön, some tax regimes that are frequently blamed for generating negative ring-fence effects really only implement general principles in a specific, real-world situation.[149] That might be the case for the 2018 DST Directive Proposal, which targets digital services according to its Explanatory Memorandum, as the user's participation in a digital activity constitutes an essential input for the business carrying that activity.[150] Be that as it may, such explanations cannot justify the loss of simplicity and negative impact on robustness against artificial avoidance strategies generated by policy options just covering (certain) digital services.

[b] B2B and B2C Transactions

Under the SEP (or VPE) nexus approach, both B2B and B2C transactions could be attributed to the VPE and, thus, be taxed accordingly. By contrast, a decision to include B2C services under a DEQL will depend, to a large extent, on how the taxable event is

144. In fact the 2015 OECD BEPS Action 1 Report, *supra* note 5, referred to transactions for goods or services *ordered online* or to all sales operations concluded remotely with non-residents. The Italian *Web Tax*, for its part, refers to a supply of services *via electronic means* even if the services falling within its scope are still to be specified.
145. *See* §5.03[B][2], *supra*.
146. *Ibid.*
147. In December 2018 France and Germany proposed to even further restrict the scope of a future DST to just cover digital advertising sales.
148. A 'triple ring-fence' would arise if an otherwise targeted solution also only applied to so-called digital 'giants' and not to SMEs selling digital products. Schön, *supra* note 17, at 7.
149. *Ibid.*
150. In the same vein, *see* Kofler, *supra* note 52, at 526. However, the clearest proof that this alleged justification of ring-fencing effects is not without controversy is that these authors merely focus on advertising and similar activities (as the Indian Equalization Levy) assuming that 'intermediation services' entail 'hybrid categories of the digital economy' in which the collection of personal data does not constitute something unique.

designed[151] and who is ultimately liable for payment and fulfilment thereof,[152] whereas a WHT on (digital) services would ideally have to be limited to B2B transactions due to obvious pragmatic implementation issues (e.g., asking individual consumers to first withhold and then pay the tax is simply not practical!).

If, however, all of the arguments mentioned above that favour excluding B2C services from any WHT proposal (e.g., consistency with alternative foundations for a WHT on cross-border services and the scant (relative) importance of B2C services in the digitalized economy) are found to be insufficient support for the adoption of such a WHT over one of the other options the alternative collection methods recently proposed for B2C transactions in a destination-based model or in a value-added tax (VAT) context (i.e., based upon customer-collection rules[153]) would work equally well for a WHT on services.[154]

[c] *Domestic and Cross-Border Transactions*

Another problem with defining the scope in the different policy options compared herein relates to the transaction each would cover. Does a policy option only cover cross-border transactions or should its scope be extended to embrace domestic services? This question must only be answered in connection with the WHT and DEQL policy options, inasmuch as a VPE approach is inherently focused on cross-border transactions.

Our discussion on potentially covering purely domestic transactions is almost, per se, immaterial. In fact, if extending the scope of a WHT or a DEQL to cover domestic transactions is more thoroughly explored, the purported reasons therefor seem to be related more to potential infringement of EU and/or WTO law constraints than to any intrinsic advantage (or disadvantage) from such extended coverage.[155] Therefore, we have opted to discuss the advantages or disadvantages of such an extended coverage design separately when we deal with legal consistency issues, *infra*. Nevertheless, there is still one domestic versus cross-border issue that we must address now.

---

151. Due to its exclusive focus on advertising services the Indian Equalization Levy is just referred to B2B services (Wagh, *supra* note 61, at 549). On his part, the Proposed EU Tax on Digital Services, covering services consisting in the making available of multi-sided digital interfaces to users (intermediation services), might also include B2C services under its objective scope; this does not hold true for advertising services also covered by the Proposed EU Tax on Digital Services.
152. Under the Indian Equalization Levy the obligation to deduct the tax and transfer it to the tax authorities falls on the payer and this makes an eventual coverage of B2C transactions difficult. On his part, the Proposed EU Tax on Digital Services shall be payable and the corresponding obligations fulfilled by the taxable person providing the taxable services facilitating the inclusion of business to consumers transactions especially with regard to intermediation services.
153. Marie Lamensch, *Destination Based Taxation of Corporate Profits: Preliminary Findings Regarding Tax Collection in Cross-Border Situations*, Oxford Univ. Centre for Business Taxation, Working Paper No. 17/16, 15–18 (2017).
154. In the same vein Martín Jiménez, *supra* note 122, at 634.
155. 2015 OECD BEPS Action 1 Report, *supra* note 5, at 115 & 117; Kofler, *supra* note 52, at 531 (only as regards DEQLs); Schön, *supra* note 17, at 15–16, 27; Brauner, *supra* note 32, at 71; 2018 OECD Interim Report, *supra* note 4, at 183 (regarding so-called interim measures).

Some initiatives recently implemented, unilaterally, by EU Member States (e.g., Italy's Web Tax) or proposed at the EU level (e.g., the 2018 DST Directive Proposal) have effectively expanded the scope of the particular WHT or DEQL to include purely domestic transactions. Such expansion, done in an attempt to avoid EU law constraints, has generated serious consistency questions. If a WHT on digital services or, even more problematic, a DEQL is intended to act as a compensatory tax ensuring a level playing field for digital MNEs and their local competitors,[156] any expansion of such 'compensatory tax' to purely domestic transactions would, by definition, ruin the intended equalization.[157] Of course, an obvious question to be answered would be whether the alleged non-taxation of digital MNEs (particularly United States MNEs) still persists after the implementation of all of BEPS Actions.[158] Be that as it may, trying to equalize the different treatment of two groups of taxpayers by imposing the same burden on both groups is utter nonsense.

[d] *Method of Taxation (Net Versus Gross Taxation)*

Even if this is not a clear issue in the literature,[159] the truth is that net taxation is assumed in relation to business profits covered by Article 7 of both the OECD Model[160] and the United Nations (UN) Model[161] and, therefore, a net tax basis might well be labelled a necessary feature (and an advantage) of the VPE approach to taxation of (digital) services. Detractors of WHTs[162] and DEQLs[163] commonly assume that the gross basis upon which such proposals are based is one of their main defects, which, in turn, makes the VPE approach their preferred option. Indeed, the existence of very different profit margins under various business models, particularly in the digital

156. This is particularly prevalent in the rhetoric of the 2018 DST Directive Proposal, *supra* note 14 (e.g., the definition of its general objectives set out in its Explanatory Memorandum).
157. *See* Becker & Englisch, *supra* note 118.
158. Indeed the 2018 OECD Interim Report (*supra* note 4, at 106) affirms quite categorically:

> The implementation of the measures described in this Part (BEPS package) has made a number of cross-border tax planning schemes unfeasible or no longer financially attractive, including for highly digitalized business. ... There are also expectations that this should help establishing a more level playing field where domestic SMEs and MNEs are taxed similarly.

159. Jacques Sasseville & Richard J. Vann, *Article 7: Business Profits, in Global Tax Treaty Commentaries* s. 5.1.3 (Richard J. Vann ed., IBFD 2014).
160. And, in relation to PE taxation according to domestic law.
161. United Nations Model Double Taxation Convention between Developed and Developing Countries (2017).
162. 2015 OECD BEPS Action 1 Report, *supra* note 5, at 114–115; Pinto, *supra* note 100, at 327; Kofler, *supra* note 52, at 529, Schön, *supra* note 17, at 26; also according to input received in response to the 2017 OECD Input Request, *supra* note 7, as reported by Larking, *supra* note 140, at 10.
163. 2018 OECD Interim Report, *supra* note 4, at 187; Kofler, *supra* note 52, at 531; Kofler, *supra* note 77, at 126, s. 3, also according to input received by the OECD in response to the 2017 OECD Input Request, *supra* note 7, as reported by Larking, *supra* note 140, at 11.

sector,[164] implies that taxation on a gross basis would lead to unequal results. The most extreme case, of course, would be that of loss-making companies, among which one should not only think about the typical example (i.e., start-ups and small and medium-sized enterprises) but also 'digital giants' that have generated losses year after year since their inception. Certainly, relying on the entity's gross income, rather than net income, is the Achilles' heel of WHTs and DEQLs.

Both proponents and detractors of WHTs and DEQLs frequently call for low tax rates – which allegedly reflect typical profit margins – as one potential way to reduce the negative effects of gross taxation.[165] This solution, however, deserves several criticism: First, the notion of 'high' or 'low' tax rates seems rather imprecise and arbitrary, as evidenced by the fact that several rates have been proposed as 'reasonable' by the supporters and drafters of WHTs and DEQLs.[166] Second, a very low nominal rate applied on gross basis may disguise a much higher rate of net taxation.[167] Third, an arbitrary tax measure or tax outcome does not cease to be arbitrary by imposing it at a very low rate; it remains arbitrary though less burdensome. And, finally, it makes no sense to refer to 'typical profit margins' since, as we have pointed out, there is no 'typical' profit; an arithmetic average would tell us nothing and, thus, would not solve the problems raised by gross taxation.

Other options to reduce the negative effects of gross taxation operating on the taxpayer's taxable base, in our view, are hardly more convincing. Indeed, taxing only a certain percentage of the gross amount of payment would perform, in reality, in almost the same way as imposing a low tax rate but would be, perhaps, more transparent.[168] Thus, both alternatives suffer from the same problems. Moreover, although well-meant, a recent proposal to establish different presumptive profit rates for classes of trade and industries based on historical relationships between gross income and profits in specific fields of activity in relation to cross-border taxation of services in general[169] would also generate significant regulatory difficulties, complicate the control tasks of the tax authorities and may also invite serious qualification issues.[170]

Taxation on a gross basis appears to be an inevitable evil under WHT or DEQL approaches. While that is true, the degree of importance frequently attached to this

164. Not to mention the case of companies who offer similar services but declaring immense disparities with regard to their profits, with *Google* and *Yahoo* being cases in point (Schön, *supra* note 17, at 26).
165. 2015 OECD BEPS Action 1 Report, *supra* note 5, at 115.
166. Indeed, actual and proposed rates vary dramatically. For example, France's so-called You Tube Tax imposes 2% for ordinary audiovisual content, but 10% for pornographic or violence-inciting content; the 2018 DST Directive Proposal (*supra* note 14) and Italy's Web Tax (*see* Braccioni, *supra* note 48, at 2) chose to impose 3%; Hungary's so-called Advertisement Tax imposes 5%-7.5%, and India's DEQL uses 6%. As for domestic and treaty tax rates related to cross-border services, the variations are quite significant. *See* Arianne Pickering, *General Report: Subject 1 Enterprise Services*, 97A IFA Cahiers 17, 50 (2012).
167. For a useful example, *see* Kofler, *supra* note 77, at 126 s. 3.
168. Arnold, *Cleaning Up the Mess*, *supra* note 101, at 61.
169. Fernando Souza de Man, *Taxation of Services in Treaties Between Developed and Developing Countries: A Proposal for New Guidelines* 7.2 (IBFD 2017).
170. Báez Moreno, *supra* note 103, at s. 3.2.1.2.1.

disadvantage should be nuanced, particularly if we take the following into account: for example, even though developing the technology required to provide services online can require substantial initial investment, once it has been created, providing subsequent services frequently requires limited marginal costs.[171] Nevertheless, in many services business models, providing such subsequent (digital) services could require significant ongoing expenditures, for which a WHT on gross revenues could be inadequate.[172] If source (or residence!) countries are seriously concerned about the impact of gross-basis taxation, they could further counteract the perceived negative impact in other ways, such as: (a) creating special rules for start-up companies, companies in transition, loss-making companies and low-margin companies,[173] and/or (b) allowing carry-forward for foreign tax credits or special exemptions, or even adopt tax refund schemes.[174]

[e] Compliance and Enforcement

It is commonly assumed that VPEs pose major challenges with regard to compliance and enforcement.[175] Indeed, according to current proposals defining SDP, the state in which the PE is located should become aware and be able to control that a non-resident taxpayer effectively exceeds the threshold(s) upon which the very concept of PE is based and, once this has been done, to also control the income generated and attributable to that SDP.[176] In the context of a company with no physical presence in the Source state this might prove extraordinarily problematic.[177] Academic proposals to alleviate these concerns, such as the creation of (Mini) One-Stop Shop obligations,[178] would certainly temper excessive compliance but it is still questionable whether it would be useful to align substantive and enforcement jurisdiction.[179] In this context, it has to be borne in mind that the level of compliance of the Mini One-Stop Shop for VAT purposes in the EU has been extremely low due, precisely, to the lack of practical means to require the collection of the taxes from businesses located beyond the jurisdictional reach of the tax authorities.[180]

Compliance and enforcement issues are not connatural to equalization levies as their existence largely depends on the very design of the levy. In principle, an equalization levy, such as the Indian one, will not pose special enforcement issues; being a tax on advertisement services, and covering by nature just B2B transactions,

171. 2015 OECD BEPS Action 1 Report, *supra* note 5, at 114. Wei Cui, *The Digital Services Tax: A Conceptual Defense* 21–22 (https://papers.ssrn.com/sol3/papers.cfm?abstract_id=3273641).
172. 2015 OECD BEPS Action 1 Report, *supra* note 5, at 114.
173. Báez Moreno & Brauner, *supra* note 69, at 22.
174. *Ibid.*
175. Kofler, *supra* note 52, at 529.
176. Blum, *supra* note 39, at 323.
177. Walter Hellerstein, *Jurisdiction to Tax in the Digital Economy: Permanent and Other Establishments*, 68 Bull. Int'l Tax'n. 346, 348 (2014).
178. *Ibid.* at 350 (referred though to effective collection of VAT in the digital economy). Hongler, *supra* note 32, at 36–37.
179. Following the popularized by Hellerstein, *supra* note 177, at 346–351.
180. Lamensch, *supra* note 153, at 11.

the service recipient would deduct the equalization levy when paying the service provider for the rendered services. If the deduction of payments for domestic income tax purposes of the services recipient is made conditional on the effective deduction and remittance of the equalization levy,[181] the system would work in a reasonable manner. However, the existence of a threshold in this levy might significantly alter this simple functioning scheme. The proposed EU Digital Services Tax, by making the service provider liable for payment and fulfilment of obligations, presents all the difficulties previously described in relation to Virtual PEs and, maybe for this reason, it also incorporates a 'simplification' mechanism in the form of a One-Stop Shop. Everything we said before in relation to compliance and enforcement of the Virtual PE solution remains applicable to equalization levies designed as the proposed EU Digital Services Tax.

A stand-alone gross-basis final WHT on services in B2B contexts is self-enforcing. If the deduction of payments to non-residents for services is made conditional on the effective withholding, it seems evident that the system will work on its own.[182] Of course, in a treaty context, this mechanism can pose compatibility problems with, in particular, Article 24(4) of both OECD- and UN Model-patterned DTCs. However an extension of the WHT to also embrace domestic services – and the corresponding limitation of deduction in case of no or improper withholding – would easily solve the problem.

[B] Legal Consistency Issues

Our proposal for a WHT on (cross-border) B2B services will be compared with the other two policy alternatives found in the 2015 OECD BEPS Action 1 Report (i.e., the new SEP concept of nexus and DEQLs) with regard to three key aspects of consistency with higher-ranking legal rules: (1) DTC law, (2) WTO law and (3) EU law.

[1] Double Taxation Conventions (DTCs)

Among DTC law specialists, there is almost universal consensus that the introduction of a new VPE nexus would require existing bilateral DTCs to be renegotiated.[183] A

181. And this seems to be the case, *see* Wagh, *supra* note 61, at 549.
182. This advantage has been reported both under the auspices of the UN Project on services and other more general proposals of WHT founded on the base erosion approach; this advantage is even reported by opponents of the new provision. In this respect, *see* Doernberg, *supra* note 102, at 1017; *see* Li, *supra* note 85, at 594; Dale Pinto, *E-Commerce and Source-Based Income Taxation* 6.4.4 (IBFD 2003); Pickering, *supra* note 166, at 35.
183. The recent proposal by Pistone and Brauner suggesting an intervention at the level of interpretation to extend the fixed place of business requirement under Art. 5(1) of the OECD/UN Model Tax Conventions to also embrace virtual presence (Pistone & Brauner, *supra* note 32, at 3) which is certainly beyond the limits of interpretation (Schön, *supra* note 17, at 10). In any case, an eventual adoption of the 2018 SDP Directive Proposal would automatically override PE provisions in bilateral tax treaties between Member States (*see* Kofler, *supra* note 52, at 528) & 2018 SDP Directive Proposal, Explanatory Memorandum.

similar concern has been expressed in relation to any WHT on (digital) services.[184] Conversely, the specialists appear to agree that DEQLs fall outside the scope of DTCs based on the OECD and UN Models.[185] Against this background, it may be (rashly) concluded that a DEQL would represent a better alternative than either the VPE or the WHT solutions.[186] However, this conclusion should, at the very least, be tempered by the following reflections: first, there has been a growing tendency in DTCs concluded between developing countries and, to a lesser extent, between developing and developed countries, to include separate provisions allowing source taxation of 'fees for technical services'.[187] In 2017, the UN Model was revised to include new provision attributing taxing rights to the Source state for fees for technical services, which will almost certainly lead to an increase in the bilateral DTCs that incorporate these kind of attribution rules.

Some commentators, particularly those commenting on India's DTCs, have signalled that, according to India's settled case law, standard or general services provided *en masse* to a company's clients are excluded from the objective scope of DTC provisions referring to *fees for technical services* because of the requirement that technical services involve specialized knowledge, skill or expertise on behalf of a particular client.[188] That interpretation would mean that the taxation imposed on a significant volume of digital services would not be covered by any particular DTC provisions, even on *fees for technical services,* which would speak in favour of alternative solutions such as DEQLs.[189]

However, others,[190] including the authors, cannot find, either in the precise wording of the DTC provisions referring to technical services or in its alleged ordinary meaning (i.e., applying specialized knowledge, skill or expertise on behalf of a client as reflected in the UN Model Commentary on its new provision on *fees for technical services*)[191] any clear and reasonable basis for excluding automated, standard, general,

184. Schön, *supra* note 17, at 27; *see* Kofler *supra* note 52, at 529.
185. *See* Kofler, *supra* note 52, at 531; Schön, *supra* note 17, at 14 (though hesitantly); Pistone & Brauner, *supra* note 32, at 2.
186. In fact, the *Indian Committee on Taxation of E-Commerce* did not recommend either a Virtual PE or a WHT because these would require changes in tax treaties. Instead, an equalization levy, so the Committee, provided a simpler option under domestic laws without needing amendment of a large number of tax treaties (Lahiri, *supra* note 61, at 15–16).
187. This growth is clearly visible by comparing the treaties containing these kind of provisions in the survey carried out by Wijnen, de Goede and Alessi in 2011 (Wim Wijnen et al., *The Treatment of Services in Tax Treaties*, 66 Bull. Int'l Tax'n. 27, 27–33 (2012) and the later work by Angharad Miller, *Taxing Cross-Border Services: Current Worldwide Practices and the Need for Change* 1, 147. 6.6 (IBFD 2016).
188. This is particularly the view taken by Falcão and Michel when stating that many of the services provided through an online interface are 'generic' in nature and not of the required technical and specialized nature to be caught by Art. 12[a] in the first place (Tatiana Falcão & Bob Michel, *Scope and Interpretation of Article 12 A: Assessing the Impact of the New Fees for Technical Services Article*, 4 Brit. Tax Rev., 422, 438 (2018)).
189. Lahiri, *supra* note 61, at 3–4.
190. The OECD seems to also share this view when stating that: *While this definition* (that of *fees for technical services*) *is not specifically targeted at digital products and services, it generally includes a broad range of cloud computing services* (2018 OECD Interim Report, *supra* note 4, at 140).
191. UN Model Commentary, para. 62, Art. 12 A.

routine or 'canned' services, whose performance requires the application of specialized knowledge, skill or expertise on behalf of a client, sometimes in an even more intense fashion than in tailored services, from new inclusion in the term. Things would be different if a reference were made to an immediate application of specialized knowledge, skill or expertise on behalf of a client; in that case, there would be a legal basis for a distinction between standard and tailored services. But again, this nuance is not found in the proposed Commentaries nor, more importantly, in the UN Model's text.[192]

Second, in view of the fact that the concept of 'taxes on income' under both the OECD and UN Models remains problematic, it might prove more daring to simply assert that, regardless of the specifics of any particular DEQL, as DEQLs are not a tax on income, the DEQL is outside the scope of DTCs. In fact, if the concept of income, as generally agreed, is centred on both the receipt and the recipient of payments,[193] some DEQLs, such as the one proposed in the 2018 DST Directive Proposal, still run the risk of being qualified as income taxes and, therefore, incompatible with DTC obligations.[194] Indeed, if the service provider is the person liable for the DEQL's payment and fulfilment obligations,[195] and, at least for these purposes, the fact that the tax is levied on gross revenue is not relevant, it seems difficult *not* to consider DEQLs as a tax on income.[196] Moreover, in relation to DEQLs that are less focused on the recipient of income, such as India's DEQL,[197] considering them income taxes is not inconceivable either,[198] as it could even be argued that a domestic DEQL law, without ever involving a DTC override, could still be labelled 'treaty dodging'.[199]

Therefore, on balance, although it is clear that any new VPE would require a systematic revision of all bilateral DTCs in force, the compatibility of WHTs and DEQLs

192. For more details on this issue, *see* Báez, *supra* note 103, at s. 3.2.1.2.2.
193. Roland Ismer & Alexander Blanck, *Article 2 Taxes Covered, in Klaus Vogel on Double Taxation Conventions*, *supra* note 81, at 143, 159 m.note 36; Marjaana Helminnen, *General Report, in The Notion of Tax and the Elimination of International Double Taxation or Double Non-Taxation*, 101 B IFA Cahiers 19, 36 (2016).
194. Of course, this would not be a problem among the Member States if the 2018 DST Directive Proposal is finally approved as written, inasmuch as bilateral DTCs among the Member States would automatically be overridden by the Directive. However, this might be a problem when the service provider is a resident in a third State, which will often be the case, particularly in relation to digital MNEs targeted by the new tax. It is likely that the EU Commission either ignored this problem or simply considered the 2018 DST Directive Proposal as outside the scope of DTCs if we recall that, unlike it did for the 2018 SDP Directive Proposal, it did not make a recommendation that Member States adapt their third-state DTCs to the DST.
195. 2018 DST Directive Proposal, *supra* note 14, at 9.
196. In the same vein: Martín Jiménez, *supra* note 122, at 636. Adolfo Martín Jiménez, *The Concept of Tax in Treaties in the Post-BEPS World, in Tax Treaties After the BEPS Project. A Tribute to Jacques Sasseville* 165, 189–190 (Brian J. Arnold ed., Canadian Tax Foundation 2018).
197. Under India's DEQL, the service recipient must withhold the levy when paying the non-resident service provider, but a failure to withhold does not allow India's tax authorities to send notices or otherwise penalize the non-resident service provider (Wagh, *supra* note 61, at 549). Therefore, the service provider (and recipient of the payments) seems relatively unaffected thereby.
198. Wagh, *supra* note 61, at 550; *see* Mehta, *supra* note 61, at 5.
199. Mehta, *supra* note 61, at 5.

with DTC obligations will depend largely upon the specific design of the measure in domestic law and the specific wording of the applicable DTC.

[2] WTO Law

Unlike the VPE solution, both the WHT[200] and DEQL solutions[201] have been accused of violating international commerce laws (i.e., the General Agreement on Tariffs (GATT)[202] and the General Agreement on Trade in Services (GATS)),[203] which, once again, gives the VPE solution the preferential air described, *supra*, with respect to DTC consistency issues. But, once again, that rushed conclusion must confront two significant realities. First, both GATT and GATS require their signatories to tax foreign suppliers of goods and services no less favourably than its own domestic suppliers. However, GATS provides broad exceptions when the signatory applies direct tax measures.[204] More specifically, GATS Article XIV(d) provides that nothing in the Agreement is to be construed to prevent the adoption or enforcement by any Member of measures inconsistent with Article XVII (i.e., the national treatment rule) provided that the difference in treatment is aimed at ensuring the equitable or effective imposition or collection of direct taxes in respect of services or service suppliers of other Members; Article XIV(d)'s footnote 6 expands on that concept, to cover measures that include, in particular, the application of WHTs to non-residents.[205] Therefore, a gross WHT, like the one we propose in this chapter, would not violate GATS.[206] (ii) As regards DEQLs on services (e.g., the 2018 DST Directive Proposal and India's DEQL), the application of GATS Article XIV(d)'s carve-out would very much depend on the DEQL's qualification as an income tax.[207] Be that as it may, the DEQL could always be imposed on both resident and non-resident service providers to avoid any such concerns.[208] However, as previously reported,[209] this expansion might cause serious inconsistencies, particularly in the field of 'compensatory' DEQLs.

200. 2015 OECD BEPS Action 1 Report, *supra* note 5, at 115 (making though an accurate distinction between GATT and GATS); *see* Kofler *supra* note 52, at 529; Schön, *supra* note 17, at 27.
201. 2015 OECD BEPS Action 1 Report, *supra* note 5, at 116–117; *see* Kofler *supra* note 52, at 531; Schön, *supra* note 17, at 15.
202. General Agreement on Tariffs and Trade 1994, 15 April 1994, Marrakesh Agreement Establishing the World Trade Organization, Annex 1A, 1867 U.N.T.S. 187, 33 I.L.M. 1153 (1994).
203. General Agreement on Trade in Services, 15 April 1994, Marrakesh Agreement Establishing the World Trade Organization, Annex 1B, 1869 U.N.T.S. 183, 33 I.L.M. 1167 (1994).
204. 2015 OECD BEPS Action 1 Report, *supra* note 5, at 115.
205. Jennifer E. Farrell, *The Interface of International Trade Law and Taxation: Defining the Role of the WTO* 1, 192 8.4.2.1 (IBFD 2013).
206. In the same vein, with certain nuances on services rendered outside the Source state, *see* Brian J. Arnold, *The Taxation of Income from Services*, in *United Nations Handbook on Selected Issues in Protecting the Tax Base of Developing Countries*, *supra* note 101 at 47 & 99–101.
207. *See supra* Chapter 3. However Professor Schön, very much in favour of considering these levies as coming on top of existing direct and indirect taxes, categorically concludes that the carve-out in Art. XIV paras d & e of the GATS would not protect such legislation (Schön, *supra* note 17, at 15–16).
208. This is the case for example of the *Proposal for a Common System of a Digital Services Tax*.
209. *See* §5.04[A][3][c].

[3] EU Law

That a VPE approach does not raise EU law concerns is, for the most part, taken for granted,[210] while both WHT[211] and DEQL[212] solutions are routinely accused of infringing EU law, particularly with respect to EU fundamental freedoms protected by the Treaties. Once again, certain realities counter that accusation. First, at the time of this writing, VPE proposals have yet to satisfactorily resolve the problem of how to attribute profits to a VPE. Hence, unless new attribution rules like those contained in Article 5, 2018 SDP Directive Proposal are further developed, there would be ample reason to claim unacceptable (i.e., unjustifiable) discrimination under EU fundamental freedoms, if only on the basis of the uncertainty surrounding the new 'rules'.[213]

Second, when analysing the compatibility of WHTs and DEQLs with EU law, particularly with regard to the available policy alternatives for taxing the digital economy, many scholars frequently refer to their potential for different treatment of domestic and cross-border (digital) services and, based solely upon that different treatment, deduce therefrom that the solutions will result in EU law violations. In light of recent decisions coming out of the Court of Justice of the European Union (CJEU) on WHT, particularly its *Brisal* decision,[214] certain WHT critics[215] have become more specific and more strident in their criticisms. Indeed, *Brisal* and other contemporary decisions[216] have made it clear that the CJEU's *Truck Center*[217] judgment could not be understood as an excuse to apply different tax collection systems to residents and non-residents.[218] In fact, with respect to the main issue at stake in the application of a WHT on services (i.e., creating different rules for the taxable bases for domestic and cross-border transactions[219]), it is clear from the CJEU's *Brisal* decision (as well as

210. *See* Kofler, *supra* note 52, at 529, these referring to (Joachim Englisch. *BEPS Action 1-EU Law Implications* 3 Brit. Tax Rev. 280, 285–286 (2015)). However this last author referred to 'crude' version of BEPS Action 1 merely analysing potential extensions of the PE concept under BEPS Action 7.
211. 2015 OECD BEPS Action 1 Report, *supra* note 5, at 115; *see* Kofler *supra* note 52, at 529; Schön, *supra* note 17, at 27.
212. 2015 OECD BEPS Action 1 Report, *supra* note 5, at 116; 2018 OECD Interim Report, *supra* note 4, at 183 (if not equally applied to residents and non-residents); *see* Kofler, *supra* note 52, at 531; Pistone & Brauner, *supra* note 32; Schön, *supra* note 17, at 15.
213. In this context, a reference to the decision of the CJEU *SIAT*, C-318/10, Judgment, EU:C:2012:415.
214. Case C-18/15.
215. Italian Banking Association (ABI), in *Tax Challenges of Digitalization: Comments Received on the Request for Input Part I*, *supra* note 11, at 5.
216. Such as *Hirvonen*, C-632/13, Judgment, EU:C:2015:765; *Miljoen*, Joined Cases C-10/14, C-14/14 & C-17/14, Judgment, EU:C:2015:608.
217. *Truck Center*, C-282/07, Judgment EU:C:2008:762.
218. CFE ECJ Task Force, *Opinion Statement ECJ-TF 2/2016 on the Decision of the Court of Justice of the European Union of 13 July 2016, in* Brisal & KBC Finance Ireland *(Case C-18/15), on the Admissibility of Gross WHT of Interest*, 57 Eur. Tax'n 30, 32–33 (2017).
219. As regards the existence of different techniques for charging tax on residents and non-residents, AG Kokott states correctly that the Court held on a number of occasions that the specific technique of deducting tax at source for non-resident service providers in principle does not infringe freedom to provide services (*Brisal & KBC Finance Ireland*, C-18/15, AG Opinion, EU:C:2016:182, para. 22).

many others)[220] that, in principle, it is an infringement of the freedom to provide services if non-resident taxpayers, in contrast to resident taxpayers, cannot deduct expenses directly connected to the activity that is being taxed, which difference could well be found to be an insurmountable obstacle to the application of a WHT on services, like the one we propose herein.[221] However, that hasty conclusion would not reflect reality, as a significant number of Member States already allow deductions for expense directly related to the respective income obtained by (certain) service providers resident anywhere within EU/EEA countries.[222] In fact, some of these EU/EEA service provider regimes are the result of the various Member States' attempt to implement the CJEU's criteria for an EU-law-compatible WHT. In any case, an extension of our WHT proposal to also cover domestic services in the manner described above would eliminate different treatment between domestic and cross-border transactions and, therefore, any possible violation of EU law.

Finally, though, it seems a foregone conclusion that the implementation of a DEQL would violate EU law. It is difficult to envisage a DEQL that is not designed as (excise) tax on the gross, rather than the net, amount of the supply, demonstrating that the detrimental effects of the DEQL method of taxation are connatural to that particular policy option. Additionally even if a DEQL is extended to also embrace domestic transactions – like in the EU proposal for a DST – some authors have been claiming possible discriminatory effects resulting from the existence of size thresholds in the proposal.[223]

§5.05 CONCLUSIONS

We firmly believe that an academic work's conclusion, such as this one, should be more than a condensed repetition of the research, arguments and outcomes set forth in the main body thereof. Rather, we believe that the conclusion should offer the reader a schematic overview of the points of arrival of the research and allow him or her – together with the concluding summary – to decide whether or not the work merits

220. See an exhaustive list of this case law in Opinion of Advocate General Kokott delivered on 17 March 2016 in *Brisal & KBC Finance Ireland*, C-18/15, AG Opinion, EU:C:2016:182, para. 27.
221. Particularly if these conclusions can be expanded to other sources of income such as royalties or service fees. In the affirmative as regards royalties: Eric Kemmeren, *Gross WHT: Is the Court of Justice of the European Union Back on Track with Regard to Deductible Expenses*, EC Tax Rev. 2, 7 (2017).
222. In particular Andreas Hable & Christian Wimpissinger, *Austria*, *in* 97A *Enterprise Services* 116 (IFA Cahiers 2012); Claudine Devillet & Xavier Van Vlem, *Belgium*, *in* 97A *Enterprise Services* 144 (IFA Cahiers 2012) (referred to entertainers for which a limited lump-sum cost deduction is allowed); Lenka Fialkova, *Czech Republic*, *in* 97A *Enterprise Services* 260 (IFA Cahiers 2012); Anders Norgaard & Philip Noes, *Denmark*, *in* 97A *Enterprise Services* 277 (IFA Cahiers 2012) (for entertainers); Borbála Kolozs & Annamária Köszegi, *Hungary*, *in* 97A *Enterprise Services* 344 (IFA Cahiers 2012) (for individual service providers); René Monfrooig & Linda Ten Broeke, *The Netherlands*, *in* 97A *Enterprise Services* 501–502 (IFA 2012); Rita Calcada Pires, *Portugal*, *in* 97A *Enterprise Services* 571–572 (IFA Cahiers 2012); José Manuel Calderón Carrero, *Spain*, *in* 97A *Enterprise Services* 629 (IFA 2012) (only for services carried out physically in Spain).
223. Ruth Mason & Leopoldo Parada, *The Illegality of Digital Services Taxes Under EU Law: Size Matters*, Virginia Law and Economics Research Paper No. 2018-16, https://papers.ssrn.com/sol3/papers.cfm?abstract_id=3279639.

further attention, as well as guide him or her on where he or she can find the reasoning that leads to a particular outcome. In short, a researcher should write his or her conclusions at the end of the work, whereas the reader, in many cases, may use the conclusion as his or her starting point. With that in mind, our readers will find herein just a bare table of outcomes from our research and analysis, accompanied by footnote references to the point in this contribution he or she can trace the detailed arguments upon which we base those conclusions. Such outcomes are synthesized into a decision-making table (Table 5.1), in which the clearly objectionable options are marked with an **X**, the options for which our evaluation of the policy option depends on its design are marked with **Y** and the best options are marked with a **Z**.

Table 5.1 Decision-Making Table

Issue to Be Compared	*VPE*	*WHT*	*DEQL*
Thresholds[1]	X	Z	Y
Attribution[2]	X	Z	Z
Scope			
Digital/Non-Digital[3]	Y	Z	Y
B2B/B2C[4]	Z	X	Y
Cross-border/domestic[5]	Z	Z	Y
Method of Taxation			
Gross/net[6]	Z	X	X
Compliance[7]	X	Z	Y
Double Taxation			
Conventions[8]	X	Y	Y
WTO Law[9]	Z	Z	Y
EU Law[10]	Z	Y	X

1. Ruth Mason & Leopoldo Parada, *The Illegality of Digital Services Taxes Under EU Law: Size Matters*, Virginia Law and Economics Research Paper No. 2018-16, https://papers.ssrn.com/sol3/papers.cfm?abstract_id=3279639. §5.04[A][1].
2. *Ibid.* §5.04[A][2].
3. *Ibid.* §5.03[B][2] & §5.04[A][3][a]
4. *Ibid.* §5.03[B][4] & §5.04[A][3][b]
5. *Ibid.* §5.04[A][3] & §5.04[A][3][c] & §5.04[B][2] & §5.04[B][3].
6. *Ibid.* §5.04[A][3][d] & §5.04[B][3][d].
7. *Ibid.* §5.04[A][3][e].
8. *Ibid.* §5.04[B][1].
9. *Ibid.* §5.04[B][2].
10. *Ibid.* §5.04[B][3].

Making our conclusions based solely on the number of negative (**X**), mediocre (**Y**) and positive (**Z**) ticks on the table would be a rather superficial approach to choosing the appropriate policy alternative, particularly if we take into account that, perhaps, not all of the parameters we considered should be given equal importance. Nevertheless, Table 5.1 suggests some quick conclusions:

(1) DEQLs are generally an inferior option.
(2) There are major (normally reflex) advantages and disadvantages with both the VPE and WHT solutions:
    (a) the structural weaknesses of the VPE solution appear manifold, with some being insurmountable; and
    (b) Our proposal for a stand-alone gross-basis final WHT on (cross-border) B2B services also has a few serious drawbacks that, while less numerous, may only be surmountable if the WHT is designed properly.
(3) In any case, any solution must be counterbalanced by simpler, more certain and more easily enforceable measures.

CHAPTER 6

Equalization Taxes and the EU's 'Digital Services Tax'

Georg Kofler & Julia Sinnig[*]

§6.01 INTRODUCTION AND BACKGROUND

[A] Tax Challenges of the Digital Economy

In the 'Rome Declaration' of March 2017, twenty-seven of the Member States of the European Union (EU), the Council of the European Union (EU Council), the European Parliament (EU Parliament), and the European Commission (EU Commission) pledged to work toward 'embracing technological transformation', such a transformation being an essential element for ensuring a prosperous and sustainable future.[1] Indeed, technological transformation and digitalization profoundly affect a great many of society's elements - jobs, industries, education, and social welfare systems.[2] However, they also create challenges for existing tax systems.

The new business models of the so-called digital economy are based on modern information and communication technologies and the exploitation of large amounts of data, which frequently blur the lines between goods and services and vary widely in their approach, form, impact, and monetization (e.g., online retailers, social media

* This chapter was finalized in November 2018 and, with minor differences, was previously published in 47 Intertax 176–200 (2019).

1. EU Council Press Release, *Declaration of the Leaders of 27 Member States and of the European Council, the European Parliament and the European Commission*, 25 March 2017, consilium.europa.eu, http://www.consilium.europa.eu/en/press/press-releases/2017/03/25/rome-declaration/ (accessed 12 November 2018).
2. For an instructive analysis, *see, e.g.*, OECD, *Measuring the Digital Economy – A New Perspective* (OECD Publishing 2014).

platforms, subscriptions to digital services, and collaborative platforms[3]). Nevertheless, they have a common view that value creation is largely decentralized and decoupled from a 'physical presence'. Especially in times of intensifying international tax competition, those new business models reveal possible weaknesses in the current international direct tax framework, which was originally designed for 'brick and mortar' businesses and still largely relies on physical presence as a threshold for the international allocation of taxing rights. Thus, it comes as no surprise that such weaknesses have entered the limelight of international policy discussions.[4]

Recently, the United States (US) Supreme Court, in *South Dakota* v *Wayfair, Inc.*,[5] added fuel to that discussion by abandoning its long-standing physical presence test under its Commerce Clause case law. Overruling its prior line of reasoning regarding an out-of-state seller's obligation to collect and remit sales tax, which culminated in its 1992 *Quill Corp.* v *North Dakota* opinion,[6] the Court found that a US State could oblige out-of-state sellers with no physical presence in that State to collect and remit sales taxes on goods the seller ships to consumers in that State. Although addressing a sales tax question, the Court's finding that a 'substantial nexus' to a particular State does not depend on its physical presence therein could be extended to political and policy considerations related to the broader, direct tax challenges posed by the digital economy.[7]

Policymakers, including EU policymakers, struggle to 'find solutions which would ensure fair and effective taxation as the digital transformation of the economy

3. For the EU's fundamentally positive approach to the sharing economy, *see, e.g.*, Giorgio Beretta, *The European Agenda for the Collaborative Economy and Taxation*, 56 Eur. Tax'n 400 et seq. (2016).
4. For a general analysis of policy options, *see, e.g.*, Michael Devereux & John Vella, *Implications of Digitalization for International Corporate Tax Reform*, 46 Intertax 550 (2018). *See also* the authors' earlier contributions to that discussion: Georg Kofler, Gunter Mayr & Christoph Schlager, *Digitalisierung und Betriebsstättenkonzept*, 36 RdW 369 (2017); Georg Kofler, Gunter Mayr & Christoph Schlager, *Taxation of the Digital Economy: 'Quick Fixes' or Long-Term Solution?*, 57 Eur. Tax'n 523 (2017); Georg Kofler, Gunter Mayr & Christoph Schlager, *Taxation of the Digital Economy: A Pragmatic Approach to Short-Term Measures*, 58 Eur. Tax'n 123 (2018); Daniela Hohenwarter, Georg Kofler, Gunter Mayr & Julia Sinnig, *Qualification of the Digital Services Tax Under Tax Treaties*, 47 Intertax 140 (2019); Julia Sinnig, *The Reflection of Data-Driven Value Creation in the 2018 OECD and EU Proposals*, 27 EC Tax Rev. 325 (2018); Jens Schmittmann & Julia Sinnig, *Aktuelle Entwicklungen im Steuerrecht in der Informationstechnologie 2017/2018 – Teil 1*, 22 Kommunikation & Recht 88 (2019); Julia Sinnig, *Die steuerrechtlichen Herausforderungen der digitalen Wirtschaft – Was passiert in Europa?, in Tagungsband Herbstakademie 2017: Recht 4.0 – Innovationen aus den rechtswissenschaftlichen Laboren* 903, 915 (Jürgen Taeger ed., OlWIR 2017); Julia Sinnig, *Besteuerung der digitalen Wirtschaft in Großbritannien, Italien und Ungarn – ein europäischer Rechtsvergleich*, 6 ISR 408 (2017); Julia Sinnig, *Tax and the Digital Economy – Bericht zur Konferenz vom 20.4.2018, Universität Luxemburg*, 7 ISR 225 (2018). Parts of this contribution are based on these earlier works.
5. *S.D.* v *Wayfair, Inc.*, No. 17-494, 585 U.S. ___ (2018).
6. *Quill Corp.* v *N.D.*, 504 U.S. 298 (1992).
7. Compare Reuven S. Avi-Yonah, *Designing a 21st Century Taxing Threshold: Some International Implications of* South Dakota vs. Wayfair (Univ. of Mich. Public L. Res. Paper No. 611, 2018), *available at* https://ssrn.com/abstract=3201418 (accessed 12 November 2018) (arguing broader implications) with Ruth Mason, *Implications of Wayfair*, 46 Intertax 810 (2018) (arguing for a more cautious reading of *Wayfair* with regard to direct taxation).

accelerates'.[8] They argue that nothing less than global '[economic] efficiency is at stake, as well as tax fairness and sovereignty'.[9] Thus, debates regarding the 'fitness' or 'outdatedness' of the current international tax system in the digital age substantially overlap discussions regarding the tax avoidance and aggressive tax planning practices of well-known technology corporations.[10] Such discussions, as well as the perceived global 'undertaxation' of digital business models,[11] however, should not inform the policy decisions lying ahead, as the economy as a whole has been, and will continue to be, digitalized: reports from the Organisation for Economic Co-operation and Development (OECD) and the EU have impressively outlined the various new business models, their growth, their size, and their impact on the global economy, as well as the differences in tax burden between companies that offer classic cross-border physical services and companies that offer digital ones.[12] Given the increasingly pervasive nature of digitalization, however, it might be difficult, if not impossible, to 'ring-fence' the digital economy from the rest of the economy for tax purposes.[13] Indeed, attempts to single out the digital economy always raise a question as to whether they comply with the established so-called Ottawa Taxation Framework, according to which, *inter alia*, '[t]axation should seek to be neutral and equitable between forms of electronic commerce and between conventional and electronic forms of commerce'.[14] While

8. EU Comm'n, *Communication from the Commission to the European Parliament and the Council. A Fair and Efficient Tax System in the European Union for the Digital Single Market*, COM(2017) 547 final, 2 (hereinafter '2017 EU Comm'n Comm. on Fair/Efficient Tax').
9. *Political Statement–Joint Initiative on the Taxation of Companies Operating in the Digital Economy* (9 September 2017), *available at* http://www.mef.gov.it/inevidenza/banner/170907_joint_initiative_digital_taxation.pdf, which has originally been signed by France, Germany, Italy and Spain and to which six more Member States – Austria Bulgaria, Greece, Portugal, Romania and Slovenia – have acceded (hereinafter 'Political Statement–Joint Initiative').
10. *See, e.g.*, the State aid procedure against Ireland with regard to purported tax benefits for Apple Inc. in Eur. Comm'n Press Release, *State Aid: Ireland Gave Illegal Tax Benefits to Apple Worth up to €13 Billion, available at* http://europa.eu/rapid/press-release_IP-16-2923_en.htm (accessed 12 November 2018) and the pending cases *Ireland* v *Comm'n*, T-778/16, Action for annulment and *Apple Sales Int'l* v *Comm'n*, T-892/16, Action for annulment.
11. For an in-depth discussion of the worldwide level of taxation of digital businesses and the argument that the picture drawn in public debate is misleading, as there is no systemic difference in income taxes paid by digital corporations compared to their traditional peers, *see* Matthias Bauer, *Digital Companies and Their Fair Share of Taxes: Myths and Misconceptions* (ECIPE Working Paper No. 3, 2018), *available at* http://ecipe.org//app/uploads/2018/02/ECI_18_OccasionalPaper_Taxing_3_2018_LY08.pdf.
12. *See, e.g.*, Eur. Comm'n, *Report of the Commission Expert Group on Taxation of the Digital Economy* (Eur. Union 28 May 2014); OECD, *Addressing the Tax Challenges of the Digital Economy, Action 1 – 2015 Final Report* (OECD Publishing 2015) (hereinafter '2015 OECD BEPS Action 1 Report'), and OECD, *Tax Challenges Arising from Digitalisation – Interim Report 2018: Inclusive Framework on BEPS* (OECD Publishing 2018) (hereinafter '2018 OECD Interim Report'); 2017 EU Comm'n Comm. on Fair/Efficient Tax, *supra* note 8. Impressively, in 2017, for example, nine out of the top twenty companies by market capitalization were technology companies, with Apple, Alphabet, Microsoft, and Amazon taking the first four spots (compared with only one technology company, Microsoft, was in the top twenty in 2006), and between 2008 and 2016 revenue of the top five e-commerce retailers grew 32% per year on average (compared with a 1% annual growth of the entire EU retail sector). *See, e.g.*, 2017 EU Comm'n Comm. on Fair/Efficient Tax, *supra* note 8 at 4.
13. 2015 OECD BEPS Action 1 Report, *supra* note 12, paras 115 & 364.
14. OECD Committee on Fiscal Affairs, *A Borderless World: Realising the Potential of Electronic Commerce* (OECD 1998) (hereinafter '1998 OECD Electronic Commerce Potential Report'); *see*

some argue that specific taxation based on digital presence would not give rise, per se, to an infringement of the neutrality principle,[15] others take the opposing view.[16] Apart from those direct and indirect tax challenges, the new business models also raise a number of additional tax issues connected with mobility and dematerialization, among them the potential to decrease the States' ability to collect revenues from payroll taxes, environmental taxes, real property taxes, and wealth taxes.

The current international tax framework – even after the modifications by the OECD Base Erosion and Profit Shifting (BEPS) project[17] – still puts emphasis on physical presence in the form of a permanent establishment (PE) in the source country as a nexus-defining criterion (*see, e.g.*, Article 5 OECD Model[18]). While that concept has generally proven successful for reasons of (relative) clarity, certainty, and enforcement, the prevalence of the digital economy has certainly triggered the question if an expansion or reconsideration of this traditional concept or, perhaps, even some other form of source taxation is warranted. Indeed, many States take the position that traditional approaches largely fail in levying a (presumed) adequate level of tax on the digital economy and, further, that neither the OECD BEPS project nor the EU Anti-Tax Avoidance Directive (ATAD)[19] addresses that issue comprehensively. While some of

also 2015 OECD BEPS Action 1 Report, *supra* note 12; para. 7, with an overview of the subsequent developments in appendix A.

15. *See, e.g.*, Peter Hongler & Pasquale Pistone, *Blueprints for a New PE Nexus to Tax Business Income in the Era of the Digital Economy* 41 et seq. (IBFD White Paper, Working Paper, 2015), *available at* https://www.ibfd.org/sites/ibfd.org/files/content/pdf/Redefining_the_PE_concept-whitepaper.pdf.
16. *For example*, AmCham EU, *in* OECD, *Comments Received on Public Discussion Draft: BEPS Action 1: Address the Tax Challenges of the Digital Economy* 3 (OECD Publishing 2014).
17. Action 7 of the OECD BEPS project (OECD, *Preventing the Artificial Avoidance of Permanent Establishment Status, Action 7 – 2015 Final Report* (OECD Publishing 2015)) regarding the artificial avoidance of PEs relates to the definition of 'PE' (particularly with respect to commissionaire structures and warehouses), barely touches on the basic structural problems: To be sure, it lowers the threshold – under treaty law – from which the source country can start taxing business profits (*see also* Arts 12–15 of the Multilateral Instrument) (*see* OECD, Multilateral Convention to Implement Tax Treaty Related Measures to Prevent BEPS, oecd.org, http://www.oecd.org/tax/treaties/multilateral-convention-to-implement-tax-treaty-related-measures-to-prevent-BEPS.pdf (accessed 12 November 2018)). However, this does not address the basic question of business models under which the company needs no physical presence in the country in which sales are made, contractual relationships arise without the involvement of personnel, value is created (e.g., through advertising) based on uncompensated user contributions (particularly in 'multi-sided' business models) or by collecting and exploiting data (especially user data). *See also* Lisa Spinosa & Vikram Chand, *A Long-Term Solution for Taxing Digitalized Business Models: Should the Permanent Establishment Definition Be Modified to Resolve the Issue or Should the Focus Be on a Shared Taxing Right Mechanism?*, 46 Intertax 476 (2018).
18. OECD, *OECD Model Tax Convention on Income and on Capital (Condensed Version)* (OECD Publishing 2017) (hereinafter 'OECD Model'). The OECD Model includes, among other things, article-specific commentaries, and for the purposes of this chapter, said commentaries will be referred to as the 'OECD Model Commentary' (if not referring to specific articles) or the 'OECD Model Comm. on Art. [*X*] [the relevant article]' together with the relevant paragraphs thereof, as appropriate.
19. Council Directive 2016/1164 laying down rules against tax avoidance practices that directly affect the functioning of the internal market, OJ L 193/1 (2016), as amended by Council Directive 2017/952 as regards hybrid mismatches with third countries OJ L 144/1 (2017) (hereinafter 'ATAD').

those challenges may be addressed, at least in part, by adjustments to or refinements of the transfer pricing framework and approaches to profit allocation in general,[20] a broader policy debate remains.

There is a visible and increasing trend in political and technical discussions to operationalize the so-called utility theory or to view income taxation as being connected more to the demand component of the market jurisdiction and less with the supply component of the residence jurisdiction,[21] as is, for example, evidenced by the existing broad discussion of a destination-based corporate tax (focusing on the customer's residence)[22] and the introduction of a new distributive rule for fees for technical services in the 2017 update of the United Nation's Model.[23] Indeed, the lines between the objects of income taxation and those of consumption taxation might become increasingly blurred. As one of the largest potential challenges facing national and international taxation, ideas and viewpoints on those issues are abundant[24] and its political momentum has become enormous over the last few years.

---

20. Marcel Olbert & Christoph Spengel, *International Taxation in the Digital Economy: Challenge Accepted?*, 9 World Tax J. 3 (2017).
21. Hongler & Pistone, *supra* note 15, at 15 et seq.
22. *For example*, Alan Auerbach et al., *Destination-Based Cash Flow Taxation* (Oxford Univ. Centre for Bus. Tax'n, Working Paper No. 17/01, 2017); *see also Commission Expert Group on Taxation of the Digital Economy*, *supra* note 12 at 50.
23. United Nations, *United Nations Model Double Taxation Convention Between Developed and Developing Countries: 2017 Update* 1, 322 et seq. Art. 12A (New York, 2018). For further discussion on the topic, *see, e.g.*, Franziska Sixdorf & Sebastian Leitsch, *Taxation of Technical Services Under New Article 12A of the UN Model – Improved Taxation or a Step in the Wrong Direction?*, 57 Eur. Tax'n 234 (2017).
24. For more recent discussions in literature, *see* the contributions in this volume and, e.g., Walter Hellerstein, *Jurisdiction to Tax in the Digital Economy: Permanent and Other Establishments*, 67 Bull. Int'l Tax'n 346 (2013); Hongler & Pistone, *supra* note 15; Yariv Brauner & Andres Baez, *Withholding Taxes in the Service of BEPS Action 1: Address the Tax Challenges of the Digital Economy* (IBFD 2015); Daniel Blum, *Permanent Establishments and Action 1 on the Digital Economy of the OECD Base Erosion and Profit Shifting Initiative – The Nexus Criterion Redefined?*, 69 Bull. Int'l Tax'n 314 (2015); Eva Escribano Lopez, *An Opportunistic, and yet Appropriate, Revision of the Source Threshold for the Twenty-First Century Tax Treaties*, 43 Intertax 6 (2015); Olbert & Spengel, *supra* note 20; Kofler, Mayr & Schlager, *Digitalisierung und Betriebsstättenkonzept*, *supra* note 4; Claus Staringer, *Virtual? Reality!*, 27 SWI 341 (2017); Kofler, Mayr & Schlager, *Taxation of the Digital Economy: A Pragmatic Approach to Short-Term Measures*, *supra* note 4; Sinnig, *The Reflection of Data-Driven Value Creation in the 2018 OECD and EU Proposals*, *supra* note 4; Wolfgang Schön, *Ten Questions About Why and How to Tax the Digitalized Economy*, 72 BIT 278 (2018); Johanna Hey, *'Taxation Where Value Is Created' and the OECD/G20 Base Erosion and Profit Shifting Initiative*, 72 BIT 203 (2018); Stephan Eilers & Florian Oppel, *Die Besteuerung der digitalen Wirtschaft: Trends und Diskussionen*, 27 IStR 361 (2018); Lee Sheppard, *Digital Permanent Establishment and Digital Equalization Taxes*, 72 Bull Int'l Tax'n (2018); Barry Larking, *A Review of Comments on the Tax Challenges of the Digital Economy*, 72 Bull Int'l Tax'n (2018); Spinosa, *supra* note 17; Alessandro Turina, *Which 'Source Taxation' for the Digital Economy?*, 46 Intertax 495 (2018); Devereux & Vella, *supra* note 4; Ana Paula Dourado, *Digital Taxation Opens the Pandora Box: The OECD Interim Report and European Commission Proposals*, 46 Intertax 565 (2018).

[B] Potential Approaches: OECD and EU

As exemplified by the various business models in the digitalized economy (e.g., online retailing and Internet advertising) and the different modes of value creation (i.e., chain, network, and shop),[25] any attempt to redefine nexus (from the perspective of domestic law as well as from tax treaty law) will, of course, face the question of what intensity of domestic value creation or market participation must exist to conclude that taxation in the non-residence State is justified, with the latter being, for example, the State of consumption, the State of users' residence or, perhaps more generally, the destination or 'market' State.[26] Hence, if profits should be taxed 'where value is created',[27] one needs to identify what that value is and how to measure it, before deciding where it was created. This is already a troublesome endeavour.[28] The OECD addressed a number of these points most recently in its 2015 OECD BEPS Action 1 Report[29] – particularly with regard to the concept of a 'significant digital presence (SDP)'. That report discusses three possibilities to cover 'digital added value' based on the characteristic challenges of the digital economy:

(1) conceptualizing a 'significant economic presence' as a threshold for source taxation;[30]
(2) creating a withholding tax for digital transactions (i.e., on payments by residents and local PEs of a country for goods and services purchased online from non-resident providers);[31] or
(3) introducing 'equalization taxes or levies' in order to ensure equal treatment of foreign and domestic suppliers.[32]

However, the OECD did not issue a recommendation for any such measure[33] but rather left it to the States to take unilateral measures if treaty law obligations are met

25. For comprehensive analysis, *see* 2018 OECD Interim Report, *supra* note 12, paras 30 et seq.
26. It must be pointed out that the traditional notion of 'source country' does not necessarily coincide with the concept of 'market country' as discussed in the context of the digitalized economy. First, the notion of source country is generally used when a taxpayer has established a presence which goes beyond the supply of goods and services, whereas the market country might be the mere country of destination, consumption or users' residence (*see, e.g.*, Schön, *supra* note 24 at 288–289). Second, even when a traditional source country is present (e.g., because of a PE in that State), it does not necessarily mean that this is also the 'market' State (e.g., because the PE deals with customers in yet other countries).
27. Which alone seems to be a new concept in international tax law. *See, e.g.*, Hey, *supra* note 24, at 203; Schön, *supra* note 24, at 280.
28. *See, e.g.*, Hey, *supra* note 24.
29. *See also* the OECD's extensive analysis in the Technical Advisory Group on Monitoring the Application of Existing Treaty Norms for Taxing Business Profits, *Are the Current Treaty Rules for Taxing Business Profits Appropriate for E-Commerce? – Final Report* (June 2004).
30. 2015 OECD BEPS Action 1 Report, *supra* note 12, paras 277 et seq.
31. *Ibid.* paras 292 et seq.
32. *Ibid.* paras 302 et seq.
33. This non-recommendation was based on a number of reasons: First, that certain BEPS measures will mitigate some aspects of the broader tax challenges, and that consumption taxes will be levied effectively in the market country, and, second, that all discussed options would require substantial changes to key international tax standards and would require further work. *See* 2015

(usually, they would not be met in cases involving 'virtual' PEs and withholding taxes for digital transactions). Nevertheless, the potential options identified in the 2015 OECD BEPS Action 1 Report dominate the current discussion,[34] and some jurisdictions have already taken unilateral action.[35] However, also the 2018 OECD Interim Report on 'Tax Challenges Arising from Digitalisation' clearly showed that there is no international consensus on either the merit or need of such measures.[36] While the existence of three frequently observed characteristics of digitalized businesses – (1) cross-jurisdictional scale without mass, (2) reliance on intangible assets (including intellectual property), and (3) the relevance of data, user participation, and their synergies with intellectual property – is generally acknowledged, 'there is no consensus on their relevance and importance to the location of value creation and the identity of the value creator'.[37] Indeed, the need for a new or restructured international tax regime is also a heavily discussed topic in legal and economic scholarship.[38]

That difference in perspective is clearly demonstrated in the 2018 OECD Interim Report, according to which the more than 110 countries in the Inclusive Framework can be largely divided into three groups:[39]

- The first group of countries share the view that, taken together, some characteristics frequently observed in certain highly digitalized business models – in particular, reliance on data and user participation – may lead to misalignments between the location in which profits are taxed and the location in which value is created; being generally supportive of the broad principles underpinning the existing international tax framework, these challenges are, according to that group, confined to certain business models and may be addressed through targeted changes to the existing tax rules, including a reconsideration of the rules relating to profit allocation and nexus.

OECD BEPS Action 1 Report, *supra* note 12, at 13 & paras 243 et seq. & para. 357, also noting that '[c]ountries could, however, introduce any of these three options in their domestic laws as additional safeguards against BEPS, provided they respect existing treaty obligations, or in their bilateral tax treaties'.

34. *See, e.g.*, Turina, *supra* note 24.
35. *See* §6.01[C] *infra*.
36. 2018 OECD Interim Report, *supra* note 12; for brief analyses, *see, e.g.*, Eilers & Oppel, *supra* note 24; Dourado, *supra* note 24.
37. 2018 OECD Interim Report, *supra* note 12, para. 36.
38. For a generally critical position, *see, e.g.*, Schön, *supra* note 24. For critical assessments of equalization levies, compare, e.g., Johannes Becker & Joachim Englisch, *EU Digital Services Tax: A Populist and Flawed Proposal*, kluwertaxblog.com, http://kluwertaxblog.com/2018/03/16/eu-digital-services-tax-populist-flawed-proposal/ (accessed 12 November 2018); Fred van Horzen & Andy van Esdonk, *Proposed 3% Digital Services Tax*, 25 Int'l Transfer Pricing J. 267 et seq. (2018). For a rather positive view, *see*, however, Dourado, *supra* note 24, at 565, 568 et seq. For a defence of the DST as a tax on location-specific rent earned by digital platforms, see W. Cui, *The Digital Services Tax: A Conceptual Defense* (26 October 2018), *available at* SSRN: https://ssrn.com/abstract=3273641 (accessed 12 November 2018).
39. 2018 OECD Interim Report, *supra* note 12, paras 388 et seq.

- The second group of countries take the view that the ongoing digital transformation of the economy and, more generally, trends associated with globalization present challenges to the continued effectiveness of the existing international tax framework for business profits, with these challenges not being exclusive or specific to highly digitalized business models; those challenges relate to the allocation of profits as well as the nexus issue.
- The third group of countries consider that the BEPS package has largely addressed the concerns of double non-taxation, although these countries also highlight that it is still too early to fully assess the impact of all the BEPS measures; these countries are generally satisfied with the existing tax system and do not currently see the need for any significant reform of the international tax rules.

Against this background, the EU has started along a progressive path on the issues. The 2014 report of the Commission Expert Group on Taxation of the Digital Economy advocated for improvement in the tax environment for young, innovative (especially digital) companies while simultaneously speaking out against a new concept of 'digital taxable presence',[40] and the call for new taxation approaches to the digital economy has gained enormous political momentum in the last years: the Estonian Presidency put digital economy tax issues at the forefront of its tax agenda and Austria while initially pushing for the introduction of a digital PE concept[41] followed the conclusion of the EEconomic and Financial Affairs Council (ECOFIN) ministers to pursue the Digital Services Tax (DST) in a first phase during its Presidency in the second half of 2018.[42]

The European Parliament also exercises significant political pressure of taxing digitalized business models.[43] In the Fall of 2017, France, Germany, Italy, and Spain called for the introduction of an equalization levy based on the turnover generated in Europe by digital companies as a 'quick fix' (without ruling out other long-term solutions),[44] and six more Member States joined that call at the informal ECOFIN meeting held in Tallinn on 16 September 2017.[45] At that meeting, some Member States

40. *See Commission Expert Group on Taxation of the Digital Economy, supra* note 12, at 47, noting that it had 'extensively considered this question and has come to the conclusion that there is currently no valid justification for such a fundamental change specifically for digital activities', and rather recommending to counter revenue concerns through the VAT system.
41. *See* Austrian Presidency of the Council of the European Union, *Programme of the Austrian Presidency*, 8; Bundesministerium für Finanzen, *Schelling-Plan zur Schließung der internationalen Steuerflucht-Routen: Europäische und internationale Maßnahmen zur Vermeidung von Gewinnverschiebungen und des internationalen Steuerbetruges* (BMF 2017) & for critical analysis, *see* Staringer, *supra* note, 24, 341 et seq.
42. *See* para. 5 in the Note from the Presidency to the Permanent Representatives Committee/Council, Doc. 13525/18 FISC 427 ECOFIN 968 DIGIT 205 (29 October 2018).
43. *See, e.g.*, Paul Tang & Henri Bussink, *EU Tax Revenue Loss from Google and Facebook* (September 2017), https://static.financieel-management.nl/documents/16690/EU-Tax-Revenue-Loss-from-Google-and-Facebook.pdf (accessed 12 November 2018).
44. *See* Political Statement–Joint Initiative, *supra* note 9.
45. These are Austria, Bulgaria, Greece, Portugal, Romania & Slovenia.

expressed strong opposition to, and concerns about, changing the tax framework for the digital economy while other Member States argued for a comprehensive and robust approach to taxation of the digital economy, one based on the time-tested rules of the current international corporate tax framework.[46] That would require a (general) recalibration of the nexus required for the source State to tax and would also entail a modification of the PE concept (and the rules of attributing profits reflecting the value created) as an amendment to the established international tax framework.[47] Such a 'digital business establishment' could (also) be included in the Common (Consolidated) Corporate Tax Base (C(C)CTB);[48] in early 2018, the EU Parliament had already put concrete proposals forward for its inclusion in the CCCTB[49] as well as for a needed revision of Article 5 OECD Model,[50] including an approach that weighs the collection and exploitation of data (data factor) in the CCCTB's apportionment formula.[51]

In September 2017, the Commission issued a Communication on 'A Fair and Efficient Tax System in the European Union for the Digital Single Market',[52] discussing background issues, objectives, and - on a rather abstract level - various options for both the long and short term. The Commission ultimately called 'for a strong and ambitious EU position on taxing the digital economy',[53] which would either feed into ongoing international work or occur within the EU Single Market. The Commission, however, raised two important questions:

- First, the question of nexus - that is, 'how to establish and protect taxing rights in a country where businesses can provide services digitally with little or no physical presence despite having a commercial presence' (i.e., 'where to tax?').[54]

46. Presidency Issues Note for the informal ECOFIN Tallinn, 16 September 2017 - Discussion on corporate taxation challenges of the digital economy, paras 10 et seq., eu2017.ee, https://www.eu2017.ee/political-meetings/ecofin (accessed 12 November 2018).
47. *See* the Estonian Presidency, *EU Finance Ministers Agreed to Develop New Digital Taxation rules* (16 September 2017), noting that 'Estonia is of the opinion that when bringing the tax rules up to date, it is important to abandon the requirement that companies have to be physically present in a country or own assets there, and replace this with the concept of a virtual permanent establishment'.
48. Eur. Comm'n, Proposal for a Council Directive on a Common Corporate Tax Base, COM(2016) 685; Eur. Comm'n, Proposal for a Council Directive on a Common Consolidated Corporate Tax Base (CCCTB), COM(2016) 683.
49. Eur. Parliament Committee on Economic and Monetary Affairs, Draft Report on the proposal for a Council directive on a Common Corporate Tax Base (COM(2016)0685 - C8-0472/2016 - 2016/0337(CNS)), Amendments 9, 19, 36, 37 & 38 (13 July 2017); Committee on Legal Affairs, Opinion for the Committee on Economic and Monetary Affairs on the proposal for a Council directive on a Common Corporate Tax Base (PE 602.948v03-00) Amendments 6, 12, 15, 16, 19, 26 (19 September 2017); and the amendments in the European Parliament legislative resolution of 15 March 2018 on the proposal for a Council directive on a Common Consolidated Corporate Tax Base (CCCTB), P8_TA(2018)0087 (hereinafter '2018 EU Parliament CCCTB Resolution').
50. *See* Tang, *supra* note 43, at 11.
51. 2018 EU Parliament CCCTB Resolution, *supra* note 49.
52. 2017 EU Comm'n Comm. on Fair/Efficient Tax, *supra* note 8.
53. *Ibid.* at 10.
54. *Ibid.* at 7.

- Second, the question of value creation – that is, 'how to attribute profit in new digitalized business models driven by intangible assets, data and knowledge' (i.e., 'what to tax?').[55]

To address these issues, the Commission favoured a long-term approach that would 'entail reform of international tax rules on permanent establishment, transfer pricing and profit attribution applicable to digital technologies', including the identification of '[a]lternative indicators for significant economic presence [that] are therefore required in order to establish and protect taxing rights in relation to the new digitalised business models'.[56] Accordingly, its CCCTB 'proposal offers a basis to address these key challenges'.[57] Alongside the work on this longer-term strategy, the Commission explicitly mentioned three 'more immediate, supplementary and short-term measures that should be considered to protect the direct and indirect tax bases of Member States' (i.e., an equalization tax on turnover of digitalized companies, a withholding tax on digital transactions, or a levy on revenues generated from the provision of digital services or advertising activity).[58] Indeed, one of those alternative options for shorter-term solutions mentioned by the EU Commission was an '[e]qualisation tax on turnover of digitalised companies', which the EU Commission described as a:

> tax on all untaxed or insufficiently taxed income generated from all internet-based business activities, including business-to-business and business-to-consumer, creditable against the corporate income tax or as a separate tax.[59]

A potential subset of such equalization taxes, the EU Commission argued, could be more 'targeted' levies on, for example, revenues generated from the provision of digital services or advertising activity. Moreover, such separate levies 'could be applied to all transactions concluded remotely with in-country customers where a non-resident entity has a significant economic presence'.[60] The EU Commission, however, was well aware of some of the disadvantages and shortcomings of all short-term measures.[61]

[C] EU Directive Proposals: SDP and DST

The ideas presented in the September 2017 Commission Communication were eventually incorporated in a two-prong legislative proposal in March 2018. Prefaced by the EU Commission Communication entitled 'Time to Establish a Modern, Fair and

55. *Ibid.*
56. *Ibid.* at 9.
57. *Ibid.*
58. *Ibid.* at 10.
59. *Ibid.*
60. *Ibid.*
61. Indeed, the 2017 EU Comm'n Comm. on Fair/Efficient Tax notes that '[q]uestions about the compatibility of such approaches with the double-taxation treaties, State aid rules, fundamental freedoms, and international commitments under the free trade agreements and WTO rules would need to be examined'; *ibid.*

Efficient Taxation Standard for the Digital Economy',[62] the EU Commission proposed two digital economy directives:[63]

- the first proposed directive[64] offers a long-term solution based on the creation of a SDP as a supplement to existing PE rules and was accompanied by a recommendation for Member States to renegotiate their tax treaties with third countries accordingly;[65] and
- the second proposed directive,[66] the focus of this article, offers a short-term (intermediate) solution in the form of a 3% turnover tax on certain digital services (the so-called DST), which represents, effectively, an equalization tax tailored to address value creation through user participation and not, for example, through consumption or data.

While the DST Directive Proposal is discussed in much greater detail below,[67] it should be mentioned here that the EU Commission argued that such measures are needed to alleviate potential fragmentation within the Internal Market. Such national measures, it argued, 'can be of a very diverse nature', and 'are already in place or are being planned by Member States',[68] which would make EU action necessary 'in order to mitigate the fragmentation of the Internal Market and the creation of distortions of competition within the Union due to the adoption of such divergent unilateral actions at national level'.[69] Moreover, it suggested that 'an EU solution rather than different

62. Eur. Comm'n, *Communication from the Commission to the European Parliament & the Council, Time to Establish a Modern, Fair and Efficient Taxation Standard for the Digital Economy*, COM(2018) 146 final & Annex.
63. *See also* EU Comm'n Staff, *Impact Assessment Accompanying the Proposal for a Council Directive laying down rules relating to the corporate taxation of a significant digital presence & Proposal for a Council Directive on the common system of a digital services tax on revenues resulting from the provision of certain digital services* SWD(2018) 81 final/2 (hereinafter '2018 EU Staff Impact Assessment'). For a brief analysis of the proposals, *see, e.g.*, Larisa Gerzova et al., *Taxation of the Digital Economy: The EU's Outlook* (IBFD White Paper, Working Paper, 2018), *available at* https://www.ibfd.org/IBFD-Tax-Portal/News/New-White-Paper-Taxation-Digital-Economy-EU-s-outlook.
64. EU Comm'n, *Proposal for a Council Directive laying down rules relating to the corporate taxation of a significant digital presence, COM(2018)147 & Annexes* (hereinafter '2018 SDP Directive Proposal').
65. For a more detailed analysis, *see* Peter Bräumann, Chapter 7 in this volume.
66. EU Comm'n, *Proposal for a Council Directive on the common system of a digital services tax on revenues resulting from the provision of certain digital services*, COM(2018) 148 (hereinafter '2018 DST Directive Proposal'); for a critical assessment also from a political perspective, *see, e.g.*, CFE Tax Advisors Europe, *Opinion Statement FC 1/2018 on the European Commission proposal of 21 March 2018 for a Council Directive on the common system of a digital services tax on revenues resulting from the provision of certain digital services* (CFE Tax Advisers Europe, 2018), also *available at* http://taxadviserseurope.org/wp-content/uploads/2018/06/CFE-Opinion-Statement-EU-Digital-Services-Tax.pdf (accessed 12 November 2018).
67. *See* §6.03, *infra*.
68. 2018 DST Directive Proposal, *supra* note 66, at 5.
69. *Ibid.*

national policies entails a reduction in the compliance burden for businesses subject to the new rules'.[70]

Such reasoning certainly has a number of shortcomings[71] and raises numerous issues as to the Union's competence in that area,[72] yet it is also true that, while the OECD and the EU strive for a multilateral solution,[73] a number of States have already taken unilateral action.[74] EU examples of such equalization levies are: Italy's levy on digital transactions, Hungary's advertisement tax, and France's tax on online and physical distribution of audiovisual content;[75] Spain, the United Kingdom (UK) having recently announced their own 'DSTs'.[76] Non-EU examples include, of course, India's 6% levy on payments to foreign companies for online advertising services, the most prominent international illustration of an equalization levy.[77] All such levies aim at collecting tax from foreign-based entities that are not physically present in the taxing jurisdiction such that, in general, they cannot be reached by that jurisdiction's

70. *Ibid.*
71. For one, it is not clear how the DST could avoid the potential fragmentation of the Internal Market if – unlike Art. 401 of the VAT Directive – it would not exclude that additional similar or overlapping unilateral taxes are created on the level of the Member States, and if would therefore be 'harmonization'. Moreover, it might even be doubted that the proposed DST is an 'indirect tax' within the meaning of Art. 113 TFEU in the first place; *see* van Horzen & van Esdonk, *supra* note 38.
72. It might, for example, be asked if the danger of potential distortions is enough to trigger the competence to harmonize under Art. 113 (or Art. 115) TFEU, and if, in any event, unilateral non-discriminatory destination-based taxes could lead to relevant distortions of the Internal Market at all.
73. *Compare* Angel Gurria, OECD Secretary-General, Opening Remarks at 16 September 2017 ECOFIN Meeting on International Taxation, *available at* http://www.oecd.org/about/secretary-general/ecofin-international-taxation-opening-remarks.htm with 2017 EU Comm'n Comm. on Fair/Efficient Tax, *supra* note 8, at 8 et seq.
74. For an instructive overview of the current trends, *see* Sagar Wagh, *The Taxation of Digital Transactions in India: The New Equalization Levy*, 70 Bull. Int'l Tax'n 538, 539 et seq. (2016), and the brief overview of the unilateral actions taken by Australia, China, France, India, Israel, Italy, and the United Kingdom by the UN Committee of Experts on Int'l Cooperation in Tax Matters, *The Digitalized Economy: Selected Issues of Potential Relevance to Developing Countries*, E/C.18/2017/6, un.org http://www.un.org/ga/search/view_doc.asp?symbol=E/C.18/2017/6 (accessed 12 November 2017).
75. For a brief description of these regimes, *see* 2018 OECD Interim Report, *supra* note 12, boxes 4.4.–4.6.
76. Spain and the United Kingdom are in the process of introducing levies on digital services that resemble the EU DST proposal. For details on the Spanish Draft Budget Plan for 2018, which was published on 23 October 2018 and is currently open for public consultation, *see* Gobierno de Espana, Ministerio de Hacienda, *Punto de acceso para facilitar la participación pública en el procedimiento de elaboración de normas*, *available at* http://www.hacienda.gob.es/es-ES/Normativa%20y%20doctrina/NormasEnTramitacion/Paginas/normasentramitacion.aspx (accessed 12 November 2018). For a description of HM Treasury's digital services tax, see HM Treasury, *Budget 2018 Digital Services Tax*, *available at* https://assets.publishing.service.gov.uk/government/uploads/system/uploads/attachment_data/file/752172/DST_web.pdf (accessed 12 November 2018). In total, twelve Member States have already adopted or are currently planning to adopt interim direct or indirect tax measures to target digitalized activities, *see* 2018 EU Staff Impact Assessment, *supra* note 63, 54–55.
77. *See* Wagh, *supra* note 74, at 543 et seq.

corporate tax system. Such an approach is not, however, entirely novel, as unilateral taxes for certain transactions or branches of the digital economy are already common features in existing tax systems; indeed, many countries already levy taxes on online gambling and betting or employ special tax rules for the so-called sharing economy (e.g., to collect tourist taxes).[78] Nonetheless, such unilateral action (whether broad or narrow) might not be a sensible alternative for every State, depending on its legal structure (e.g., its tax treaty obligations) or its economic situation.[79] From an EU perspective, moreover, '[d]ivergent national approaches within the EU can fragment the Single Market, increase tax uncertainty, destabilise the level playing field and open new loopholes for tax abuse'.[80]

At this juncture, it should also be noted that the EU Commission is as well outspoken about one meta-policy goal inherent in its DST proposal: it 'gives a strong sign to the international community as to the commitment of the EU to act when it comes to ensuring the fair taxation of the digital economy,'[81] which might explain why the Commission has been pushing a tax that (optimistically) might only bring in revenues of EUR 5 billion for all Member States combined.[82] Smaller Member States, in particular, with a minimal revenue stream from a DST might question the sensibility of such a measure, particularly in light of its unclear administrative and compliance costs.[83] That path to a potential EU directive (and even more so to a global approach) is not only fraught with numerous policy and technical questions but also beset with the political realities and diverging interests of the relevant (Member) States.[84]

78. For an overview on this subject, see EU Comm'n Staff, *European Agenda for the Collaborative Economy – Supporting Analysis* 41 et seq. (Working Paper, SWD 184 final 2016); *see also* Beretta, *supra* note 3, at 400 et seq.
79. *See* Kofler, Mayr & Schlager, *Digitalisierung und Betriebsstättenkonzept*, 376 et seq. (Austria), *supra* note 4; *see* Staringer, *supra* note 24, at 341, 343.
80. *See* EU Comm'n, *Fact Sheet, Questions and Answers on the Communication on a Fair and Efficient Tax System in the EU for the Digital Single Market*, http://europa.eu/rapid/press-release_MEMO-17-3341_en.htm (accessed 12 November 2018).
81. 2018 DST Directive Proposal, *supra* note 66, at 5.
82. *See* EU Comm'n Press Release, *Digital Taxation: Commission Proposes New Measures to Ensure That All Companies Pay Fair Tax in the EU*, IP/18/2041, http://europa.eu/rapid/press-release_IP-18-2041_en.htm (accessed 12 November 2018) ('An estimated EUR 5 billion in revenues a year could be generated for Member States if the tax is applied at a rate of 3 %'). According to the 2018 EU Staff Impact Assessment, *supra* note 63, at 70, the expected revenues are between EUR 4.7 to EUR 6 billion.
83. *See* the Regulatory Scrutiny Board Opinion SEC(2018) 164, 2–3, available in Doc. 7419/17 ADD 4 FSIC 150 ECOFIN 276 (23 March 2018).
84. This may also raise the subsequent issue whether enhanced cooperation might provide a suitable tool to move forward in only some and not all Member States. On the other hand, a directive would have a double harmonizing effect: It would oblige Member States to amend their domestic laws and would arguably 'override' (pre-existing and new) provisions in tax treaties between Member States. *See* Yariv Brauner & Georg Kofler, *The Interaction of Tax Treaties with International Economic Laws, in Global Tax Treaty Commentaries* ch. 2.3.3 (Richard Vann et al. eds., IBFD 2014).

§6.02 THE IDEA OF EQUALIZATION TAXES: ASSESSMENT AND CRITICISM

[A] Equalization Taxes in OECD BEPS Action 1

Since the 1998 Ottawa Ministerial Conference on Electronic Commerce,[85] it has become commonplace to argue that the digital economy cannot be separated from the traditional economy. While this might be true when it comes to classic value chains (e.g., production and/or distribution of tangible and intangible products), new business models that are prevalent in the digital economy place greater emphasis on value creation through mediating technology in multi-sided markets (e.g., social networks, online marketplaces, and sharing economy platforms) and highly specialized services in single-sided markets (e.g., cloud computing and diagnostics).[86] If one takes the position that some or all of these business models create a significant economic presence in a jurisdiction but are (or are at least perceived to be) 'undertaxed' in that State for lack of physical presence,[87] a potential option to address such 'undertaxation' is an equalization levy. Indeed, the 2015 OECD BEPS Action 1 Report mentioned the introduction of equalization levies as a potential approach to remedy that situation.[88] While there is no international consensus on either the merit of, or need for, equalization taxes,[89] the 2018 OECD Interim Report discussed, at length, a number of necessary design features for any such tax.[90]

Essentially, equalization taxes are special excise taxes – intended to compensate for 'lost' profit taxes – that target foreign economic actors with a significant economic presence in the taxing jurisdiction; their purpose is to place domestic and foreign providers on a par. Presently, several countries collect excise taxes, for example, on premiums paid to non-resident insurance providers that would otherwise remain untaxed. Another example might be the equalization levy on online advertising introduced by India in 2016, under which business-to-business (B2B) payments to non-resident taxpayers for online advertising are subject to taxation at a rate of 6%.[91] The OECD has noted that, in the digital economy, such an equalization levy serves as

85. 1998 OECD Electronic Commerce Potential Report, *supra* note 14, noting, *inter alia*, that 'taxation should seek to be neutral and equitable between forms of electronic commerce and between conventional and electronic forms of commerce'.
86. *See, e.g.*, the discussion in HM Treasury, *Corporate Tax and the Digital Economy: Position Paper*, gov.uk https://www.gov.uk/government/consultations/corporate-tax-and-the-digital-economy-position-paper (accessed 12 November 2018) (hereinafter 'HM Treasury Position Paper'). Indeed, as a starting point, the 2015 OECD BEPS Action 1 Report provides an overview of the various business models of the digital economy and analyses four typical structures: (1) online retailing, (2) Internet advertising, (3) cloud computing and (4) Internet app stores. 2015 OECD BEPS Action 1 Report, *supra* note 12, at 51 et seq. with a summary in box 4.1 at 64.
87. It should be noted that the market State (i.e., where consumption takes place) and the source State within the meaning of the international tax framework are not necessarily the same. Take for example a PE: The profits attributable to it may be taxed in the State of its location (Arts 5 and 7 OECD MC), whether or not its customers are also resident in that State.
88. 2015 OECD BEPS Action 1 Report, *supra* note 12, paras 302 et seq.
89. 2018 OECD Interim Report, *supra* note 12, para. 404.
90. *Ibid.* paras 403 et seq. & §6.02[B][2] *infra*.
91. For an overview, *see* Wagh, *supra* note 74, at 543 et seq.

a way to tax a non-resident enterprise's significant economic presence in a country while simultaneously avoiding profit attribution problems arising from a nexus based on a 'virtual' PE concept.[92] Nevertheless, a significant economic presence would be required for applying such an equalization tax because it provides clarity, certainty, and equity to all stakeholders, and avoids undue burden on small- and medium-sized businesses.[93] Hence, the baseline definitional problem (i.e., when does such 'significant economic presence' exist?) also arises in the context of equalization taxes.

As for the potential scope of such a tax, the OECD discusses a number of variations depending on the respective policy priorities:[94] if, for example, the policy priority lies in taxing remote sales transactions with customers in a market jurisdiction, one possibility is to apply the levy to all transactions concluded remotely with in-country customers; if, however, the policy priority is to tax the value considered to be directly contributed by customers and users, then the levy would be imposed on data and other contributions gathered from in-country customers and users. However, as with the scope of an equalization levy, there is currently broad consensus that, at least within the international taxation framework,[95] neither the mere consumption of goods or services in a country[96] nor the deductibility of payments for goods or services received from non-residents in that country[97] should, by itself, entitle that country to tax the profits of the business providing the goods or services.

Nevertheless, the recent focus is not on mere consumption, but is, rather, on the utilization of passively provided user-related data (e.g., search and surfing history for

92. The 2015 OECD BEPS Action 1 Report, *supra* note 12, para. 302 describes that idea as follows: To avoid some of the difficulties arising from creating new profit attribution rules for purposes of a nexus based on significant economic presence, an 'equalization levy' could be considered as an alternative way to address the broader direct tax challenges of the digital economy. This approach has been used by some countries in order to ensure equal treatment of foreign and domestic suppliers. For example, in the area of insurance, some countries have adopted equalization levies in the form of excise taxes based on the amount of gross premiums paid to offshore suppliers. Such taxes are intended to address a disparity in tax treatment between domestic corporations engaged in insurance activities and wholly taxable on the related profits, and foreign corporations that are able to sell insurance without being subject to income tax on those profits, neither in the State from where the premiums are collected nor in State of residence. As discussed below, an equalization levy could be structured in a variety of ways depending on its ultimate policy objective. In general, an equalization levy would be intended to serve as a way to tax a non-resident enterprise's significant economic presence in a country. In order to provide clarity, certainty and equity to all stakeholders, and to avoid undue burden on small- and medium-sized businesses, therefore, the equalization levy would be applied only in cases where it is determined that a non-resident enterprise has a significant economic presence.
93. *Ibid.*
94. *Ibid.* paras 303 et seq.
95. For broad policy discussions, e.g., with regard to a destination-based corporate tax (focusing on the customer's residence), *see, e.g.*, Auerbach, *supra* note 22; Devereux, *supra* note 4, at 550 et seq.
96. *See generally* for the lack of source taxation rights with regard to services rendered by non-residents Art. 5 para. 139 OECD Model Convention Commentary 2017 (hereinafter 'OECD MC Comm.').
97. There are, however, some notable exceptions, such as the introduction of a new distributive rule for fees for technical services in the 2017 update to the UN Model. For discussion, *see, e.g.*, Sixdorf & Leitsch, *supra* note 23, at 234 et seq.

targeted advertising) and of more active contributions to value creation by users (e.g., through active user participation in social media platforms, online marketplaces that match suppliers to purchasers, or user-generated content on streaming platforms),[98] regardless of whether or not those users are identical to the business's customers. It is frequently argued that the value generated by user data, participation, and creation of content 'is not captured under the existing international tax framework, which focuses exclusively on the physical activities of a business itself in determining where profits should be allocated for corporate tax purposes', meaning that significant value can be generated from a market without the profits derived therefrom being subject to tax there.[99] That said, however, it is heavily disputed whether and, if so, to what extent, data and user participation represent a contribution to value creation by the enterprise:

- Indeed, some countries hold the view that user participation is a unique and important driver of value creation in digitalized businesses, being something genuinely new and going beyond the mere consumption of a service (i.e., the provision of access to the business model).[100] This position is also endorsed by the EU Commission, which believes that:

  > [i]n the digital economy, value is often created from a combination of algorithms, user data, sales functions and knowledge. For example, a user contributes to value creation by sharing his/her preferences (e.g. liking a page) on a social media forum. This data will later be used and monetised for targeted advertising. The profits are not necessarily taxed in the country of the user (and viewer of the advert), but rather in the country where the advertising algorithms has been developed, for example. This means that the user contribution to the profits is not taken into account when the company is taxed.[101]

- Other countries strongly reject the suggestion that data and user participation should be considered value creation by the business in the user's jurisdiction and take the position that data collection from users, user participation, and the provision of user-generated content as transactions should be viewed as barter transactions: businesses provide financial or non-financial compensation (e.g., data hosting, email services, or digital entertainment) to the users in exchange for such data/content.[102] From their perspective, there should be no

98. *See, e.g.*, HM Treasury Position Paper, *supra* note 86, at paras 3.14 et seq.
99. *See, e.g.*, *ibid.* para 3.21 & HM Treasury, *Corporate Tax and the Digital Economy: Position Paper Update*, paras 2.1 et seq., gov.uk https://www.gov.uk/government/consultations/corporate-tax-and-the-digital-economy-position-paper (accessed 12 November 2018) (hereinafter 'HM Treasury Position Paper Update') (also distinguishing between user participation and the mere collection of data from users or customers).
100. 2018 OECD Interim Report, *supra* note 12, para. 38. *See also* the conclusions in HM Treasury Position Paper Update, *supra* note 99, and in Australian Government, The Treasury, *The Digital Economy and Australia's Corporate Tax System*, Treasury Discussion Paper (October 2018).
101. *See* Eur. Comm'n Fact Sheet, *Questions and Answers on a Fair and Efficient Tax System in the EU for the Digital Single Market*, http://europa.eu/rapid/press-release_MEMO-18-2141_en.htm (accessed 12 November 2018).
102. 2018 OECD Interim Report, *supra* note 12, paras 39 & 393.

profit allocated to the sourcing of data from users, as the user's supply of data is no different from other business inputs sourced from an independent third party in the business' supply chain (e.g., data storage, broadband access, or electricity).[103] Moreover, although the argument has not yet been made, applying that same perspective to equalization taxes can be intellectually justified, not as a proxy for the taxation of corporate profits, but rather as a proxy for taxing the nearly impossible-to-tax imputed income the users (arguably) accrue from all such small barter transactions (i.e., the in-kind value they receive from using, e.g., 'free' services).

These differences in perspective on a business' value creation through data and user participation, as well as the more general disagreements about whether and what changes might be needed in light of digitalization, will certainly inform the international and EU discussion on all of the issues concerning the broader tax challenges posed by the digital economy.

Additionally, there are, of course, fundamental objections to 'quick fixes' as they are likely to be temporary solutions.[104] Such a piecemeal approach only succeeds in 'patching-up' particular issues, without providing a reliable, long-term policy solution. They might not even be a reliable source of tax revenue if monetization models change. Moreover, it is not entirely clear that equalization taxes will be beneficial for the EU and its Member States (especially if third countries react by enacting similar taxes), nor is it clear how such taxes could affect growth and investment. Finally, issues of tax incidence are uncertain: ultimately, the likelihood that such equalization tax would be shifted by the intended taxpayers (i.e., digital companies) to European consumers seems high, particularly given that some digital economy players operate as quasi-monopolies. The OECD explored some of those challenges in the 2018 OECD Interim Report, but the EU Commission's DST Proposal hardly addressed them.

[B] Policy and Technical Challenges of Equalization Levies

[1] Broader Economic Risks and Challenges

While the 2018 OECD Interim Report clearly showed that there is no international consensus on either the merit of, or need for, equalization taxes,[105] the OECD nevertheless devoted a whole chapter therein to 'Interim Measures to Address the Tax Challenges Arising from Digitalization'.[106] It noted that a number of countries opposed such measures on the basis that they give rise to risks and adverse consequences irrespective of their design. While other countries acknowledge such challenges, they

103. Countries that support this view agree that the interaction between users and the digitalized business is a transaction that could be subject to income taxation, although they also observe that income tax systems today rarely capture these types of barter transactions where there is no financial compensation (i.e., cash payment) on either side of the transaction. *Ibid.* para. 39.
104. *See also* Presidency Issues Note for the informal ECOFIN Tallinn, *supra* note 46, para. 8.
105. 2018 OECD Interim Report, *supra* note 12, para. 404.
106. *Ibid.* paras 403 et seq.

did not believe they outweighed the need to implement interim measures and instead believed that at least some of the potential adverse consequences could be mitigated through the measures' design.[107]

Against this background, the OECD noted the potential risks and adverse consequences that could arise with respect to equalization taxes but also identified a number of ameliorating design considerations for them. The broader risks and challenges largely relate to the adverse economic impacts of equalization taxes.[108] The OECD, in this regard, mentioned the following considerations:[109]

- Impact on investment, innovation, and growth – any tax on the supply of particular services is likely to increase the cost of capital, reducing the incentive to invest with a resulting negative effect on growth. Moreover, a gross-basis tax only applicable to digitalized sectors would risk slowing down investment in innovation for those businesses that are subject to the tax or indirectly affected by it, and thus, could effectively penalize start-ups and other growing firms with losses or limited profitability.
- Impact on welfare – a gross-basis tax is equivalent to a tax on inputs, which implies that it is likely to distort firms' choices of inputs, thus distorting production itself, which is likely to have a negative impact on the overall welfare of an economy and on its output.
- Potential economic incidence of taxation on consumers and businesses – depending on the price sensitivities of the seller and customers, and the structure of the market, the incidence of taxation could be fully or partially passed on to local consumers in the form of higher prices for goods or services.
- Potential for overtaxation – in order to comply with its international obligations, a country could be required to apply the tax to both residents and non-residents and to limit any credit mechanism against other taxes, which could create issues of overtaxation (e.g., if payments are subject to both corporate taxation and an equalization tax) and economic double taxation via cascading effects (e.g., if a taxable service is incorporated in a taxable onward supply).
- Potential difficulties in implementing such a tax as an interim measure – taxes, once introduced, are often difficult to repeal and given the time that may be needed to develop and implement an interim measure, that raises a question as to whether it is worth introducing a completely new set of rules (with all of the related administrative procedures that necessitates) that might apply only for a limited period of time.

---

107. *Ibid.* paras 408–411.
108. *See also, e.g.*, Schön, *supra* note 24; Matthias Bauer, *Five Questions about the Digital Services Tax to Pierre Moscovici* (ECIPE Working Paper No. 04/2018, 2018), *available at* http://ecipe.org/app/uploads/2018/06/Five-Questions-about-the-Digital-Services-Tax-to-Pierre-Moscovici.pdf.
109. 2018 OECD Interim Report, *supra* note 12, para. 407.

- Compliance and administration costs – an interim measure could also give rise to significant compliance and administration costs that could be disproportionate to the amount of tax raised under the measure, particularly given that the measure is only intended to be temporary. The taxing jurisdiction might also encounter difficulties in auditing and verifying the accuracy of the returns filed and payments made by non-residents.

[2] Necessary Design Features of Equalization Taxes

[a] Compliance with International Obligations (Tax Treaties, EU Law, and WTO Law)

Compliance with international obligations (i.e., tax treaties, EU law, and World Trade Organization (WTO) law) is a primary objective of tax measures addressing the digitalized economy.[110] Indeed, if equalization taxes are structured to raise the revenues expected, they would likely create cases of (domestic[111] and international) double or even multiple taxation. Indeed, existing equalization taxes, such as the Indian tax on online advertising, are viewed as being indirect taxes falling squarely outside the scope of existing tax treaties.[112] Their imposition is neither barred in the imposing State nor subject to any relief from double taxation in the taxpayer's residence State.[113]

Nevertheless, it is sometimes undeniable that a 'connection' to corporate tax exists, either because the direct tax system serves as a backstop[114] or because double taxation with regular corporate tax and the equalization levy is mitigated (e.g., through a credit).[115] The OECD, therefore, gave considerable thought to the scope of Article 2 (Taxes Covered) OECD Model, which provides that the Convention applies to 'taxes on income' or on 'elements of income', 'irrespective of the manner in which they are levied', and that it will also apply to all new taxes that are identical or 'substantially

110. *Ibid.* paras 413–431.
111. The 2017 EU Comm'n Comm. on Fair/Efficient Tax, *supra* note 8, explicitly notes that an equalization tax might either be structured as 'creditable against the corporate income tax or as a separate tax'. If structured in the former way, however, that seems to imply that the equalization tax could be credited against the domestic corporate tax, if any. That, of course, would raise a number of technical issues, e.g., with regard to the cross-crediting of taxes over various entities in the group or over various activities within one entity.
112. *See* for India's position, e.g., Wagh, *supra* note 74, at 543 et seq. *Contra*, Roland Ismer & Christoph Jescheck, *Taxes on Digital Services and the Substantive Scope of Application of Tax Treaties: Pushing the Boundaries of Article 2 of the OECD Model?*, 46 Intertax 573, 575 (2018). Whether falling outside of the scope of tax treaties or overriding these, the result–double or multiple taxation–remains the same.
113. 2015 OECD BEPS Action 1 Report, *supra* note 12, para. 307.
114. In India, the non-resident advertiser is the taxpayer, but the Indian client has an obligation to withhold the tax; if it violates that obligation, no direct tax deduction is allowed for the advertising expense. *See* Wagh, *supra* note 74, at 543 et seq.
115. 2015 OECD BEPS Action 1 Report, *supra* note 12, para. 308.

similar' to the taxes listed.[116] However, 'a tax that is covered by tax treaties is generally one that is focusing on the supplier, rather than on the supply',[117] and arguments for a tax being outside the scope of Article 2 OECD Model may:

> be stronger where [such a tax] is: (i) levied on the supply of a certain defined category or categories of e-services and imposed on the parties to the supply without reference to the particular economic or tax position of the supplier; (ii) charged at a fixed rate, calculated by reference to the consideration paid for those services (without reference to the net income of the supplier or the income from the supply); and (iii) not creditable or eligible for any other type of relief against income tax imposed on the same payment.[118]

The borderline, however, is not clear-cut. One could, for example, argue that a typical equalization tax levied on a gross amount is close to one falling under Article 2 OECD Model if the equalization tax rate implicitly takes into account lump-sum expenses to accommodate 'different profit margins'.[119] Also, any equalization tax structured as 'creditable against the corporate income tax'[120] would likely create a 'risk' that it will fall under Article 2 OECD Model, suggesting that any such equalization tax should not be creditable, but only be tax deductible for corporate tax purposes,[121] as envisaged by the 2018 DST Directive Proposal.[122] And, even if the application of Article 2 OECD Model (and the treaty limitations to taxation) could indeed be avoided, from a policy point of view, an equalization tax would likely be at odds with the initial balance inherent in any particular tax treaty. From another perspective, however, the 2018 OECD Interim Report concluded that applying an equalization tax to non-residents would not, generally, give rise to discrimination under Article 24 OECD Model (which provision applies also to taxes not covered by Article 2 OECD Model) because such tax would not relate to one of the precise circumstances addressed by Article 24 OECD Model.[123]

Moreover, it remains to be seen if an equalization tax should only apply to cross-border transactions (i.e., only to non-resident enterprises) or to domestic transactions, too; the former approach may raise all kinds of WTO and EU law objections,[124]

116. For a detailed discussion of Art. 2 OECD MC in light of the features of equalization taxes, *see* Ismer & Jescheck, *supra* note 112, at 573 et seq.
117. 2018 OECD Interim Report, *supra* note 12, para. 421.
118. *Ibid.*
119. *See* 2018 DST Directive Proposal, para. 35 and for a critical perspective in light of Art. 2 OECD MC, *see* van Horzen & van Esdonk, *supra* note 38.
120. *See, e.g.*, 2017 EU Comm'n Comm. on Fair/Efficient Tax, *supra* note 8, at 10.
121. *See* Kofler, Mayr & Schlager, *Taxation of the Digital Economy: 'Quick Fixes' or Long-Term Solution?*, *supra* note 4, at 531 & 532.
122. The 2018 DST Directive Proposal does not contain a rule that deduction must be granted, but rather expresses the expectation 'that Member States will allow businesses to deduct the DST paid as a cost from the CIT base in their territory, irrespective of whether both taxes are paid in the same Member State or in different ones' (Preamble to 2018 DST Directive Proposal, para. 27).
123. 2018 OECD Interim Report, *supra* note 12, paras 425 & 426.
124. *Ibid.* paras 427–431.

while the latter might create the necessity to mitigate double imposition of regular corporate tax and the equalization levy.[125] Furthermore, the OECD pointed out that:

> [i]n order to ensure that the measure is not impermissible State aid when applied by individual jurisdictions, the measure would need to be designed not to provide a selective advantage to any group of taxpayers. In other words, an interim measure would need to avoid different treatment of undertakings that are in a legally and factually comparable position.[126]

Indeed, to comply with EU and constitutional non-discrimination requirements, as well as EU State aid rules, the potential threshold for the application of an equalization tax (e.g., a revenue threshold) must likely be set for both comparable cross-border and domestic situations,[127] an approach taken by the 2018 DST Directive Proposal.[128] However, the mere introduction of such thresholds (e.g., EUR 750 million of worldwide revenues) may already raise questions with regard to EU non-discrimination rules and EU State aid law,[129] although it is not entirely clear whether and in what circumstances measures based on an EU directive could violate these rules.[130]

Finally, the OECD noted that, for EU Member States, 'the interim measure should also be designed such that it is not a value added tax that would be inconsistent with the EU Directive on the Common System of Value Added Tax'.[131] It is, however, not entirely clear why such a potential inconsistency argument would be relevant from a legal perspective if the relevant equalization tax were based on an EU directive. First, it can be argued that a revenue-based equalization tax is not covered by Article 401 value added tax (VAT) Directive's[132] prohibition of 'turnover taxes' because it would not be an all-phase input deduction tax that generally applies to transactions relating to

125. 2015 OECD BEPS Action 1 Report, *supra* note 12, para. 306.
126. 2018 OECD Interim Report, *supra* note 12, para. 429.
127. *See, e.g.*, Turina, *supra* note 24, at 509.
128. *See* §6.03[C][1] *infra*.
129. *See, e.g.*, the negative Commission Decision 2017/329 on the measure SA.39235 (2015/C) (ex 2015/NN) implemented by Hungary on the taxation of advertisement turnover, OJ L 49/36 (2016), where the Commission found aid in the fact that Hungarian law 'lays down progressive rates of taxation that apply to the annual turnover derived from the publication of advertisements in Hungary depending on the brackets into which an undertaking's turnover falls. The progressive character of those rates has the effect that the percentage of tax levied on an undertaking's turnover increases progressively depending on the number of brackets within which that turnover falls. This has the result that undertakings with low turnover (smaller undertakings) are taxed at a substantially lower average rate than undertakings with high turnover (larger undertakings). Being taxed at this substantially lower average tax rate mitigates the charges that undertakings with low turnover have to bear as compared to undertakings with high turnover and therefore constitutes an advantage to the benefit of smaller undertakings over larger undertakings for the purposes of Article 107(1) of the Treaty.'
130. For a brief discussion of that issue, *see* Turina, *supra* note 24, at 510, and for a detailed analysis based on the idea of covert nationality discrimination based on company size, see Ruth Mason & Leopoldo Parada, *The Illegality of Digital Services Taxes under EU Law: Size Matters* (6 November 2018), *available at* https://ssrn.com/abstract=3279639 (accessed 12 November 2018). *See also* §6.03[D][1][b] *infra*.
131. 2018 OECD Interim Report, *supra* note 12, para. 430.
132. Council Directive 2006/112/EC of 28 November 2006 on the common system of value added tax, OJ L 347/1 (2006), as amended.

goods or services.[133] Second, that prohibition, which is addressed to the Member States, would not conflict with a tax that is on the same legislative 'level' (i.e., secondary EU law).[134]

[b] Temporary Nature of an Equalization Tax as an Interim Measure

As the OECD noted, '[a]ny interim measure should be introduced recognising the policy intent of it being temporary; ceasing to apply once a global response to the tax challenges raised by digitalisation has been agreed and is implemented',[135] as otherwise, the international preference for comprehensive global solution would be undermined.

[c] Targeted Scope of an Equalization Tax

> Given the potential adverse consequences of introducing an interim measure, it is important that the measure is as targeted as possible at those businesses that are perceived to constitute the highest risk, which for a number of countries are those businesses that combine high levels of scale without mass, and have business models that rely heavily on user participation and network effects.[136]

Thus, the OECD 2018 Interim Report argues that an interim measure should not apply to supplies of physical goods when the supplier is simply the owner of the goods transferring title in those goods to the seller under a contract that is concluded online[137] and, further, should 'be restricted to certain specified e-services and not apply to all services simply on the basis that they are provided over the Internet'.[138] Indeed, a focus of a targeted interim measure could be on Internet advertising and digital intermediation services because those activities are perceived by some countries as categories of e-services businesses that 'typically operate remotely and rely heavily on intangible property, data, user participation and network effects and believe that therefore value is being created in their jurisdiction'.[139] The 2018 DST Directive Proposal largely adopts the same approach.[140]

Scholarly discussion, however, generally argues that the substantive scope of any equalization tax should be further restricted, specifically in light of attempts to

133. *See Banca popolare di Cremona*, C-475/03, Judgment, EU:C:2006:629 (with regard to the Italian IRAP) & for brief analysis Turina, *supra* note 24, at 510 et seq.
134. *See, e.g.*, Kofler, Mayr & Schlager, *Taxation of the Digital Economy: 'Quick Fixes' or Long-Term Solution? supra* note 4 at 531. However, a turnover tax that is not all-phase might lead to cascading effects and, hence, double taxation.
135. 2018 OECD Interim Report, *supra* note 12, para. 432.
136. *Ibid.* para. 434.
137. *Ibid.* para. 436.
138. *Ibid.* para. 437.
139. *See generally, ibid.* para. 439 & in more detail paras 440–442 for Internet advertising and paras 443–445 for intermediation services.
140. *See* §6.03[A] *infra*.

'ring-fence' certain business models that are unique to the digital economy.[141] In that regard, scholars have argued that the mere use of the Internet to facilitate the sale of goods or services (e.g., retailing), as well as multi-sided intermediaries and marketplaces (e.g., app stores and platforms in the collaborative economy) seem to be mere extensions of the 'traditional economy' which may well achieve 'scale without mass' that could give rise to a myriad of delimitation issues. In contrast, the intensity of the collection, use, and exploitation of personal data as core part of a business model and value creation might serve as a narrow, but more targeted, indicator.[142] Monetizing user data is the backbone of Internet advertising, but such data plays quite a different role and is prevalent on a different level for multi-sided platforms operating as intermediaries (e.g., in the sharing economy) and, more generally, for businesses that are based on traditional value creation.

[d] Minimizing Overtaxation

The OECD's key objective for an interim measure is 'to balance the underlying policy objective of trying to address the rapidly emerging challenges raised by the digitalization of the economy while avoiding the risk of over-taxation on taxpayers caught by the measure'.[143] This relates to several aspects: First, the broader the scope of the measure, the more likely it will result in overtaxation of certain taxpayers. Second, the rate 'should be set at a low rate that is proportionate to the profit margins of the businesses that it is to apply to',[144] which is indeed a hard task. In a single-rate structure, the different business models would all be taxed at the same turnover-based level, but the profit-based effect on typical B2B and B2C (business-to-consumer) business models –

141. *See, e.g.*, Kofler, Mayr & Schlager, *Taxation of the Digital Economy: 'Quick Fixes' or Long-Term Solution?*, *supra* note 4, at 126 et seq.
142. However, while the mere collection of personal data does neither constitute something new or unique, nor seems 'worth' taxing in itself, the value created through exploitation of personal data for third-party advertisers might well be viewed as giving sufficient claim to tax to the State from whose residents the user data is collected. Indeed, if the political decision for a short-term measure was taken, there are several advantages to a rather narrow approach, i.e., to only apply a short-term measure to situations where user data is exploited to generate revenues from third parties. First, it largely avoids delimitation problems. Many companies collect personal data these days (e.g., food chains, fitness centres, etc.). However, the main business purpose of these companies is not the collection of personal data. Rather, this personal data merely supports the company's main business purpose and is analysed for this reason (e.g., food chains use the data to tailor their offerings to their customers' wishes, which – if successful – results in higher sales). Moreover, the mere collection and analysis of personal data for a company's so-defined own business purposes could scarcely be delimited. Therefore, finding no tax nexus until the personal data is exploited to generate fees from third parties avoids difficult delimitation questions. Second, it would link taxation to the exploitation of data that generates revenues from third parties (i.e., the advertisers) and hence to the value created by such exploitation (i.e., advertising income under the specific business models in question). Thinking in terms of an equalization levy, therefore, a pragmatic approach could focus on advertising and similar activities provided through the Internet that are based on the exploitation of personal data. *See* for that discussion Kofler, Mayr & Schlager, *Taxation of the Digital Economy: 'Quick Fixes' or Long-Term Solution?*, *supra* note 4, at 126 et seq.
143. 2018 OECD Interim Report, *supra* note 12, para. 446.
144. *Ibid.*

which have been extensively discussed in scholarly literature[145] – would be quite different given the different margins. Even a notionally low tax rate on a turnover basis can have huge distortive effects depending on the specific situation of the taxpayer and its profit margins[146] and could, oftentimes, translate in exorbitant tax burdens on profit.[147] Third, a gross-basis tax has the potential to result in economic double taxation, if a mere deduction from the income tax base, rather than a tax credit, is granted.[148] Fourth, cascading effects could arise 'where a supply of e-services is made to a person that incorporates those services into an onward supply that is subject to the excise tax under domestic or foreign law'.[149] That eventuality could only be avoided through special measures (e.g., an exemption) if it is proven that the e-service will be used in an onward-taxable supply.[150]

[e] Minimizing Impact on Start-Ups, Business Creation, and Small Businesses

The design of an interim measure,[151] according to the OECD, 'will also need to be calibrated to limit any undue impact on business creation arising from digitalisation, noting the positive impacts that digitalisation has had on economic growth and productivity'.[152] In light of the potential impact of a gross-basis tax on start-ups and, more generally, small businesses and the burdens caused by compliance obligations, the OECD took the view that 'an interim tax measure would need to have a threshold' to be set by reference to the results of the previous accounting period in order to promote certainty in the application of the threshold.[153] Possible approaches could be (1) to combine a gross-revenue threshold for the group as a whole with a local-country sales threshold or (2) to only apply a local-country sales threshold.[154] A gross-revenue threshold (e.g., based on the CbC-Reporting threshold of EUR 750 million) would provide a bright-line test for businesses that do not have a significant global presence, so 'that smaller businesses entering the domestic market would not need to track their

145. *See, e.g.*, Kofler, Mayr & Schlager, *Taxation of the Digital Economy: 'Quick Fixes' or Long-Term Solution?*, *supra* note 4, at 123 et seq.
146. *Ibid.* at 531.
147. *See* Bauer, *supra* note 108.
148. *See also* 2018 OECD Interim Report, *supra* note 12, para. 447.
149. *Ibid.* para. 448.
150. *Ibid.* para. 449.
151. Similar discussions are, of course, also necessary with regard to when a digital or economic presence should be deemed to be 'significant' (to give rise to source State taxing rights); here, several factors or indicators have been discussed, for example, country-specific turnover from digital transactions, 'digital' factors, such as a local domain name, a local digital platform, local payment options, or user-based factors, such as active, domestic monthly users of a platform. *See, e.g.*, 2015 OECD BEPS Action 1 Report, *supra* note 12, paras 277 et seq., and the more concrete proposal made by Hongler & Pistone, *supra* note 15, at 15 et seq. Although a short-term measure may not focus on 'significant' economic presence, the practical reasons for defining an 'entry criterion' are similar (i.e., lowering tax compliance costs), especially for innovative SMEs.
152. 2018 OECD Interim Report, *supra* note 12, para. 450.
153. *Ibid.* para. 452.
154. *Ibid.* para. 453.

level of sales in each taxing jurisdiction in order to determine whether they were subject to the interim measure'.[155] The additional local sales threshold 'would exclude those e-service suppliers with a low level of supplies of e-services in a particular jurisdiction or geographic market, where the costs of administration and compliance are likely to be too great to justify the imposition and collection of a tax'.[156]

While the 2018 DST Directive Proposal also chose such a double-threshold, alternative approaches could exempt small- and medium-sized enterprises (SMEs) (as defined by the EU Commission[157]) or provide a *de minimis* exception of revenues generated in a specific country (e.g., Hungary's revised advertisement tax provides, for example, a *de minimis* threshold of HUF 100 million, which is approximately EUR 325,000, for sales from marketing activities[158]).[159] In any event, to comply with EU and constitutional non-discrimination requirements, as well as EU State aid rules, any threshold would likely have to be set for both cross-border and domestic situations and across various forms of advertising. This is a specific consideration for countries (such as Austria) that currently levy an advertisement tax on 'offline' commercials, but are considering expanding it to online advertising.[160]

[f] Minimizing Cost and Complexity

Especially for interim gross-basis tax measures, 'administrative cost and complexity should be kept to a minimum',[161] which would, in particular, require a common place-of-supply rule that determines whether the supply of e-services has been made within the taxing jurisdiction.[162] More generally, a short-term measure must be delimited geographically, likely through a proxy for the jurisdiction, to establish which residents participate and/or provide user data. In that respect, the OECD suggested focusing on the various types of digital services. Advertising services should be treated as being supplied in the jurisdiction where the advertising communication is targeted (based, for example, on the internet protocol (IP) address),[163] intermediation services as being supplied in the jurisdiction where the customer of the intermediation service is located (as a proxy for the place of the underlying transaction), with the relevant costumer being the person that contracted for the supply of the intermediation

155. *Ibid.* para. 454.
156. *Ibid.* para. 455.
157. EU Comm'n, *Commission Recommendation concerning the definition of micro, small and medium-sized enterprises*, OJ L 124/36 (2003).
158. For a brief description of Hungary's advertisement tax, *see* Box 4.5 of the 2018 OECD Interim Report, *supra* note 12.
159. Kofler, Mayr & Schlager, *Taxation of the Digital Economy: 'Quick Fixes' or Long-Term Solution?*, *supra* note 4, at 127.
160. It should be noted, however, that the Austrian Constitutional Court recently held that taxation of 'offline' advertisement while not taxing online advertising under the Austrian advertisement tax (*Werbeabgabe*) does not violate the principle of equal treatment. *See* VfGH, 12 October 2017, E 2025/2016, AT:VFGH:2017:E2025.2016.
161. 2018 OECD Interim Report, *supra* note 12, para. 457.
162. *Ibid.* para. 458.
163. *Ibid.* paras 459–462.

services.[164] In the latter respect, the 2018 DST Directive Proposal arguably takes a slightly different approach; it focuses on the revenue stream and the parties' location, irrespective of which party to the underlying transaction is charged a fee by the intermediation service.[165]

§6.03 THE EU'S DST

The 2018 DST Directive Proposal is a concrete example of an equalization levy that would apply within the EU, if adopted. Unlike the OECD, the EU Commission and a number of Member States see a need to implement such an interim measure.[166]

[A] Policy Objectives

To achieve one of its main political priorities – that is, the Digital Single Market[167] – the EU Commission believes it is vital to implement a fair and appropriate tax framework.[168] Hence, it has stated that 'user generated contents and data collection have become core activities for the value creation of digital businesses',[169] which are not reflected in current tax rules. Because of the risk of corporate tax base erosion, as well as the public perception of unfair treatment of digital and non-digital businesses, the EU Commission has urged the Member States to act;[170] it argues that an EU-wide DST, as set out in the 2018 DST Directive Proposal, will avoid fragmentation of the Single Market that would be caused by their implementation of uncoordinated, unilateral measures and ensure that competition is not distorted thereby.[171] Moreover, the 2018

---

164. *Ibid.* para. 463. The OECD further explained:

> Thus in the case of hotel booking websites, where the commission for the intermediation service is generally paid by the hotel, the supply would then be treated as made to the hotel. Similarly, in respect of the sale of goods where the seller pays a commission to the eservice provider in respect of every sale, the intermediation service would then be treated as supplied to the seller of the goods (and, in this case, the country of residence of the goods supplier would impose the tax, and not the country of residence of the goods buyer). In those cases where the service provider charges separate fees to different parties with respect to different sides of the same transaction (e.g. in the case of an intermediation service, both the seller and the purchaser of the intermediate goods or services) then the supply would be treated as made in proportion to the consideration provided.

165. *See* §6.03[C][2] *infra*.
166. 2018 DST Directive Proposal, *supra* note 66, at 3; 2018 OECD Interim Report, *supra* note 12, para. 514; *see also* §6.01[C] *supra*.
167. 2018 DST Directive Proposal, *supra* note 66, at 1 referring to a Communication from the Commission to the European Parliament, the Council, the European Economic and Social Committee and the Committee of the Regions: A Digital Single Market Strategy for Europe, 6 May 2015, COM(2015) 192.
168. 2018 DST Directive Proposal, *supra* note 66, at 1.
169. *Ibid.*
170. *Ibid.* at 3.
171. *Ibid.*; *see also* §6.01[C] *supra*. The Commission notes that ten Member States have already adopted or plan to adopt the concrete implementation of unilateral measures.

DST Directive Proposal generally aims to achieve sustainable public finances, to ensure 'social fairness' via equal treatment of businesses active in the EU, and to combat aggressive tax planning.[172]

The 2018 DST Directive Proposal's specific objective is to tax – in a manner that is simple to administer – revenues generated by the supply of certain digital services.[173] It is intended to level the playing field until the Member States can agree on a long-term measure (ideally based on a SDP).[174] In that regard, the proposed DST only taxes activities that have a high level of user participation, which, in turn constitutes an important business input factor.[175]

[B] Legal Basis

The 2018 DST Directive Proposal is based on Article 113 TFEU,[176] which provides a special legislative procedure pursuant to which the EU Council may adopt harmonizing provisions on, *inter alia*, turnover taxes after having consulted the EU Parliament and the European Economic and Social Committee (EESC).[177] The proposed instrument is a directive, rather than a regulation, as that is the only instrument permitted under Article 113 TFEU's procedure.[178]

172. 2018 DST Directive Proposal, *supra* note 66, at 3–4.
173. *Ibid.* at 3.
174. *Ibid.*
175. *Ibid.* at 7.
176. It might be noted in passing that there is an intense discussion as to the correct legal basis of the DST proposal, i.e., whether it should be based on Art. 113 TFEU or on Art. 115 TFEU (*see* para. 8 in the Note from the Presidency to the Permanent Representatives Committee/Council, Doc. 13525/18 FISC 427 ECOFIN 968 DIGIT 205 (29 October 2018)), which largely depends how to understand the terms 'turnover taxes' and 'other forms of indirect taxation' in the former provision. Since the DST Proposal aims at the issuance of a Directive (the only instrument available under Art. 115 TFEU) and both provisions would trigger the same legislative procedure, the choice of legal basis might not have any immediate legal ramification, although it remains to be seen how the European Court of Justice (ECJ) will address that issue. The Court has the authority to review Union acts for the lack of competence or the choice of the wrong legal basis, ruling on the 'legality' or 'validity' of legislative acts (Arts 264 and 267 TFEU). The issue of 'legality' includes, under Art. 263 TFEU, 'jurisdiction in actions brought by a Member State, the European Parliament, the Council or the Commission on grounds of lack of competence' and to declare such acts 'void' (Art. 264 TFEU), but a temporal limit is put on such proceeding, as those 'shall be instituted within two months of the publication of the measure' (after which elapse the lawfulness of the Union act is presumed; *see, e.g.*, ECJ, 5 October 2004, C-475/01, *Commission/Greece* ('Ouzo'), EU:C:2004:585, paras 22–23). No such temporal limit is imposed on preliminary ruling procedures initiated by domestic courts under Art. 267 TFEU, where the ECJ reviews the 'validity' 'of acts of the institutions, bodies, offices or agencies of the Union', which may include lack of competence; such a finding by the ECJ, though only addressed to the referring national court, has quite similar effects as an annulment in a procedure under Art. 263 TFEU (*see, e.g.*, ECJ, 13 May 1981, 66/80, *SpA International Chemical Corporation*, EU:C:1981:102).
177. 2018 DST Directive Proposal, *supra* note 66, at 5.
178. *Ibid.*

According to the current wording of the 2018 DST Directive Proposal, if approved, the Member States would be obliged to transpose the new directive by 31 December 2019, with substantive application as of 1 January 2020.[179]

[C] The DST's Characteristics

[1] Tax Rate, Taxable Persons, and the Tax Base

The proposed DST is a destination-based turnover tax levied on gross revenues net of VAT (and other similar taxes[180]) arising out of certain digital services. Costs cannot be deducted from the tax base and losses cannot be carried forward. The rate, in turn, is set at 3%,[181] to achieve 'an appropriate balance between revenues generated by the tax' and to account 'for the differential DST impact for businesses with different profit margins'.[182]

DST-taxable persons will be any corporate or transparent entity[183] fulfilling two conditions. The first condition, whose objective is to exclude SMEs and start-ups and, thus, to only target companies of a certain scale able to establish strong market positions,[184] requires the entity to have a total amount of taxable revenues in the relevant financial year that exceeds EUR 750 million.[185] The second condition, whose objective is to capture only subject those entities with a 'significant digital footprint' in the EU to the DST,[186] requires the entity to have a total amount of taxable revenues obtained within the EU that exceeds EUR 50 million.[187]

To avoid potential double taxation caused by corporate tax and DST, the 2018 DST Directive Proposal expects Member States to allow 'businesses to deduct the DST paid as a cost from the corporate income tax (CIT) base in their territory, irrespective of whether both taxes are paid in the same Member State or different ones'.[188] That approach would almost certainly be systematically correct, *de lege lata,* in many of the Member States that employ a worldwide tax system, but might also lead to shifts in tax

179. *Ibid.* Art. 25(1). Note however that the dates are between square brackets, which means that they are in particular subject to change.
180. *Ibid.* Art. 3(2).
181. *Ibid.* Art. 8.
182. *Ibid.* recital (35).
183. *Ibid.* Arts 4(1) & 2(1).
184. *Ibid.* at 10. The arguments for taxing only 'big players' are of mere political nature and cannot explained by any legal rationale.
185. *Ibid.* Art. 4(1)(a).
186. *Ibid.* at 10.
187. *Ibid.* Art. 4(1)(b). These amounts are calculated at the date of when they fall due, not when they are effectively paid/received, *see* Art. 4(5) 2018 DST Directive Proposal. The text of the proposal is however not entirely clear on whether the first bracket of EUR 50 million of taxable revenues is already taxed or whether just the part of turnover above EUR 50 million is taxed (i.e., if the taxable person has a turnover of EUR 80 million, only EUR 30 million would constitute the tax base). From the wording of the proposal, it seems more likely that the first bracket of EUR 50 million is already taxed.
188. Recital (27) of the Preamble to 2018 DST Directive Proposal. The wording 'it is expected that Member States will allow business to deduct the DST' indicates that this cost deductibility is a strongly recommended option.

revenues when DST revenue accrues to one Member State when the business expense deduction is borne by another Member State. As the EU Commission, obviously, did not intend to mandate specific corporate tax rules, this expressed 'expectation' of a cost deduction is merely mentioned in the preamble and is not prescribed in the substantive body of the proposed directive.[189]

[2] Taxable Transactions and Place of Taxation

The 2018 DST Directive Proposal adopts a step-by-step approach to determining services, nexus, and revenue apportionment. First, it defines which revenue streams (i.e., revenues from which precise services) are taxable (Article 3); second, it determines the place of taxation (i.e., the nexus), by references to users' location (Article 5(2)); and third, it apportions the revenue between the relevant Member States based on user-related criteria (Article 5(3)).

The list of covered services in Article 3, which is exhaustive, includes placing user-targeted advertising on a digital interface and providing intermediation services that allow users to access a multi-sided digital interface to find and interact with each other, as well as transmitting collected user data, including data inferred from the users' activities on digital interfaces.[190] Certain services are explicitly excluded from the scope of the DST Directive Proposal, 'the making available of a digital interface where the sole or main purpose of making the interface available is for the entity making it available to supply digital content to users or to supply communication services to users or to supply payment services to users'.[191] The excluded intermediation services are different from covered intermediation services in that covered services allow users to interact without knowing each other beforehand due to software allowing for that interaction,[192] whereas covered services are based on the active involvement of users (e.g., by offering goods or services to other users); thereby creating network effects of which intermediaries benefit.[193] Further excluded services are those provided by a trading venue or a systematic internalizer of services referred to in points (1)–(9) of section A of Annex I to Directive 2014/65/EU[194] and regulated

189. This might be explained by the fact that if the cost deduction was provided for in the substantial part of the proposal, the DST is more likely to appear as a prepayment of CIT, which could lead to incompatibility issues with WTO law and double tax treaties; *see also* §6.03[D][1][a] and §6.03[D][1][c] *infra*.
190. Article 3(1) 2018 DST Directive Proposal.
191. *Ibid.* Art. 3(4)(a). The Explanatory Memorandum to the 2018 DST Directive Proposal clarifies that these services shall not be regarded as intermediation services subject to DST as user participation plays a less important role in the value creation process of companies offering these services; *see* 2018 DST Directive Proposal, *supra* note 66, at 8. This would however not apply if users make available digital content to other users on that digital interface, which would in turn again fall within the definition of services subject to DST.
192. 2018 DST Directive Proposal, *supra* note 66, at 8.
193. *Ibid.*
194. EU Parliament & EU Council, *Directive 2014/65/EU of the European Parliament and of the Council of 15 May 2014 on markets in financial instruments and amending Directive 2002/92/EC and Directive 2011/61/EU*, OJ L 173/349 (2014).

crowdfunding services as well as those facilitating the provision of a loan provided by these trading venues or internalizers of services.[195]

Hence, in contrast to the 2018 SDP Directive Proposal, which adopted a broad definition of digital services in its Article 3(5),[196] the 2018 DST Directive Proposal only covered certain digital services. Thus, the 2018 DST Directive Proposal rejected the opinion issued by the EU Commission Expert Group in 2014, which advised, at that time, against any 'ring-fencing' measures.[197]

The 2018 DST Directive Proposal makes no reference to a cross-border requirement in defining the term services so that it applies equally to domestic and international situations. That policy choice diminishes possible discrimination claims, even though in practice, the twofold revenue thresholds would almost certainly result, in a majority of cases, in taxation of cross-border business operations.[198]

The place for such taxation, pursuant to proposed Article 5(2), is to be the location of the users in any particular Member State at the moment they receive the taxable service, irrespective of whether said users have paid for the service or contributed thereto by any other means, such as providing data, whether consciously or unconsciously.[199] The taxable persons' and users' establishments, as well as their places of supply and payment (if different),[200] thus, are irrelevant, which stands in line with the notion that only user involvement as a contribution to value creation is taken into account for DST taxation, irrespective of how or when such users generally pay for a service or if only some users pay therefore.[201] The users' location is determined either by means of the IP address of the device enabling the user to access the taxable service or by any other geolocation method that achieves a more accurate determination of such location.[202]

The 2018 DST Directive Proposal goes on to provide that both the user's location (i.e., the place of taxation) and any revenue allocation among the Member States depend on the different types of services covered:

- *User-targeted advertising on a digital interface* – for advertising services, the Member State in which users viewing the advertising are located at the moment of its display must tax.[203] Taxable revenues generated from such advertising services in more than one Member State are allocated among such Member States in a proportional manner, with the number of times an advertisement has appeared on the users' devices during the given tax period located in that Member State taken into account.[204]

195. Article 3(4)(b) & (c) 2018 DST Directive Proposal.
196. *See also* the contribution of Peter Bräumann, Chapter 7 in this volume.
197. *Commission Expert Group on Taxation of the Digital Economy*, *supra* note 12, at 41.
198. *See* §6.03[D][1][ii] *infra* for the analysis of possible issues related to State aid rules in that regard.
199. Article 5(1) 2018 DST Directive Proposal.
200. *Ibid.* Art. 5(4).
201. *Ibid.* at 11.
202. *Ibid.* Art. 5(5).
203. *Ibid.* Art. 5(2)(a).
204. *Ibid.* Art. 5(3)(a).

- *Intermediation services matching users to other users for the supply of goods and services* – with multi-sided interfaces that match users and their peers for the underlying supply of goods and services, the Member State in which the user is located when using a device to access the interface and conclude an underlying transaction on that interface must tax.[205] The number of users having concluded underlying transactions on the digital interface in the relevant tax period determines each Member State's proportionate share of the tax base.[206] The EU Commission's DST proposal presumes that whether a particular user operates as the buyer or the seller in any particular transaction should not impact either the place of taxation or revenue allocation, as both actors equally contribute to value creation by the digital business.[207]
- *Other intermediation services* – in the case of any other intermediating digital interfaces, the Member State in which the user opens his or her account[208] to access the interface must tax, irrespective of how long the user account exists.[209] The EU Commission observed that, in such cases, users usually pay periodic fees to the digital business after having registered or opened an account.[210] The 2018 DST Directive Proposal obliges Member States to tax the proportion of revenues relating to the number of users holding an account allowing them to access the tax period during all or part of the tax period.[211]
- *Transmission of collected user data* – for taxable services relating to the transmission of user data, the Member State in which the users were located when using a device to access an interface resulting in the generation of data in the hands of the business must tax.[212] In that regard, the number of users from whom data have been transmitted as a result of them accessing the interface dictates the proportion of taxable revenues of any particular Member State.[213]

The rules for determining the location of users and allocating the revenue derived from the digital service may be summarized as follows:

205. *Ibid.* Art. 5(2)(b)(i).
206. *Ibid.* Art. 5(3)(b)(i).
207. 2018 DST Directive Proposal, *supra* note 66 at 12.
208. To distinguish from the registration process – it is sufficient to log in in order to be counted as a user of these intermediation services.
209. Article 5(2)(b)(ii) 2018 DST Directive Proposal.
210. 2018 DST Directive Proposal, *supra* note 66, at 12. Examples for this are certain dating websites, such as 'match.com', which make the accessibility of the full service subject to the payment of subscription fees.
211. Article 5(3)(b)(ii) 2018 DST Directive Proposal. Note that this is wider than the requirement of Art. 5(2)(b)(ii) relating to the location of users, where it is prescribed that users have opened the account to access the interface via that account during the tax period to be locatable in that Member State.
212. Article 5(2)(c) 2018 DST Directive Proposal.
213. *Ibid.* Art. 5(3)(c). The reference in this provision to the taxable period as well as previous periods should be understood as neutralizing the moment of data collection and uniquely focusing on the moment of data transmission irrespectively of when they have been collected.

Service	*Location in a Member State (IP or Geolocation)*	*Revenue Proportion*
Placing of advertisements on a digital interface (Article 3(1)(a) DST)	Advertising appears on user's device (Article 5(2)(a) DST)	Number of times an advertisement has appeared on users' devices (Article 5(3)(a) DST)
Making available multi-sided digital interfaces ('intermediation services') (Article 3(1)(b) DST)	User's device for concluding underlying supply of goods or services (Article 5(2)(b)(i) DST)	Number of users having concluded underlying transactions (Article 5(3)(b)(i) DST) –*Place of underlying transaction irrelevant* (Article 5(4)(a) DST)
	User's device for opening account in other cases (Article 5(2)(b)(ii) DST)	Number of users holding an account (Article 5(3)(b)(ii) DST)
Transmission of user data (Article 3(1)(c) DST)	Data generated from the user having used a device (Article 5(2)(c) DST)	Number of users from whom data transmitted has been generated (Article 5(4)(c) DST) –*Tax period irrelevant*

[3] Tax Collection and Enforcement

As a general rule, a taxable person must register in only one Member State in which DST is due, i.e., either in the Member State in which the taxable person is liable to DST for the first chargeable tax period or, if that would be true for more than one Member State, such one of those Member States as the taxable person chooses.[214] Hence, to facilitate tax collection, the 2018 DST Directive Proposal offers a One-Stop-Shop (OSS) mechanism that allows a taxpayer obliged to pay DST in more than one Member State to choose one Member State (the 'OSS MS') for all of its DST interactions (e.g., identifying itself, submitting annual DST returns, and making DST payments).[215] The taxable person's choice of OSS MS is binding for three tax periods, including the tax period in which it made its choice.[216] Despite having chosen an OSS MS, the taxable person remains liable for any DST due in each Member State in which it is imposed.[217]

214. Article 10(1) 2018 DST Directive Proposal. An individual identification number is provided to the taxable person by the Member State of identification; Art. 11(1) 2018 DST Directive Proposal.
215. *Ibid.* Art. 10(3); 2018 DST Directive Proposal, *supra* note 66, at 12. An information exchange is set up between Member States in that regard; *see infra* and Arts 20–23 2018 DST Directive Proposal. It seems, however, that at the Council level 'Delegations agree that, in principle, DST collection should function without the one-stop-shop'; *see* para. 7 in the Note from the Presidency to the Permanent Representatives Committee/Council, Doc. 13525/18 FISC 427 ECOFIN 968 DIGIT 205 (29 October 2018).
216. Article 13(1) 2018 DST Directive Proposal.
217. Article 18(4) 2018 DST Directive Proposal. This liability may lead to cash flow disadvantages in cases where the Member State of identification does not transmit timely the amount due in another Member State and the latter requests the taxable person to pay the DST due to it again. *See* §6.03[D][1][c] *infra*.

To further facilitate DST collection, the proposed directive allows consolidated groups to appoint a single entity to act on the group's behalf for all such DST interactions.[218]

A tax return and any DST payment due must be submitted every tax period (i.e., calendar year)[219] within thirty working days following the end thereof (e.g., 31 December).[220] The total DST payable by a taxable person must be paid to the Member State of identification or the chosen OSS MS, if applicable.[221]

The 2018 DST Directive Proposal requires Member States to establish an exchange of information system, through which all relevant information regarding the taxable person's identity, notices, annual DST returns (and amendments thereto, if appropriate), and DST payments must be transferred within ten working days.[222] The 2018 DST Directive Proposal leaves the exact configuration and implementation of the exchange-of-DST-information system up to the EU Commission, which is authorized to adopt relevant implementing acts therefore.[223]

[D] DST Challenges and Practical Issues

There is no consensus on the either merit or the need of 'equalization taxes' or, more generally, interim measures in the OECD 2018 Interim Report of March,[224] and such taxes are met with strong opposition from the US as they would violate 'the long-held principle that taxes on multinationals should be profit-based, not revenue based'.[225] Some States have, however, already moved forward with their own 'equalization taxes'[226] and, e.g., the UK as well as Australia have set out detailed policy ideas on turnover-based taxation of certain digital services.[227] Practitioners, industry and academics are, however, largely sceptical with regard to turnover-based interim solutions,[228] although it is argued that the DST could not only be defended from a political standpoint – i.e., by giving 'a strong sign to the international community as to

218. Article 9(2) 2018 DST Directive Proposal.
219. *Ibid.* Art. 2(7).
220. *Ibid.* Arts 14 & 16(2).
221. *Ibid.* Art. 16(1).
222. *Ibid.* Arts 20–22.
223. *Ibid.* Art. 23(2).
224. OECD 2018 Interim Report, paras 403 et seq.
225. *See* the letter of 18 October 2018 by Orrin Hatch and Ron Wyden from the United States Senate to Donald Tusk and Jean-Claude Juncker regarding the DST Proposal, *available at* https://www.finance.senate.gov/imo/media/doc/2018-10-18%20OGH%20RW%20to%20Juncker%20Tusk.pdf (accessed 12 November 2018).
226. *See* §6.01[C] *supra*.
227. *See* HM Treasury position paper on 'Corporate tax and the digital economy: position paper update' (March 2018), and Australian Government, The Treasury, *The Digital Economy and Australia's Corporate Tax System*, Treasury Discussion Paper (October 2018).
228. For critical assessments of equalization levies, *see, e.g.*, Pasquale Pistone & Yariv Brauner, *Adapting Current International Taxation to New Business Models: Two Proposals for the European Union*, 71 Bull. Int'l Tax 681, 682–683 (2017); Becker & Englisch, *supra* note 38; van Horzen & van Esdonk, *supra* note 38, at 267 et seq. For a rather positive view, *see*, however, Dourado, *supra* note 24, at 565, 568 et seq. For an analysis of the potential impact from a business perspective, see Helge Sigurd Næss-Schmidt, Gerdis Marquart & Palle Sørensen, *The Impact of an EU Digital Service Tax on German Businesses*, Copenhagen Economics Report (19 October 2018).

the commitment of the EU to act when it comes to ensuring the fair taxation of the digital economy'[229] – but also as a way of taxing location-specific rents earned by digital platforms.[230] At the time of writing, it is unclear if agreement on the DST will be reached at the EU level,[231] and, if so, which features will address the concerns raised over the last couple of months. There is indeed a variety of practical implementation challenges arising from the adoption of the 2018 DST Directive Proposal, and three broad groups of challenges – (1) compatibility with the international legal framework, (2) selected policy objections and (3) some broader practical issues – require deeper analysis.

[1] Incompatibility and Lack of Coordination with Existing Legal Frameworks

[a] Relationship with Double Tax Conventions: Double Taxation

'Interim measures' for the taxation of the digitalized economy, such as the DST, also have a tax treaty dimension. They raise, *inter alia*, the question whether they have to be viewed as taxes on 'income' or 'elements of income', which are core notions for the delimitation of the substantive scope of tax treaties. Relating to possible interim measures to address the tax challenges arising from digitalization, already the OECD in its 2018 Interim Report has accentuated the need for compliance of such measures with international law. 'Any new tax that a country introduces must be in compliance with its existing international obligations', including tax treaties,[232] and this compliance with tax treaties is also an essential aim of the DST proposal[233] and subject to discussions in Council.[234] If, conversely, the DST would have to be viewed as a tax on 'income' or 'elements of income' within the meaning of Article 2 OECD MC and hence generally fall within the scope of tax treaties, a possible conflict between the levy of DST and the existing rules of tax treaties, especially with regard to provisions along the lines of Articles 5, 7 and 23 OECD MC, would arise.

229. 2018 DST Directive Proposal, *supra* note 66, 5. For a critical perspective on the argument that 'while consensus is being built interim solutions may be positive to make sure that the debate continues towards a consensus type solution', see Yariv Brauner, *Taxing the Digital Economy Post-BEPS, Seriously*, 46 Intertax 462, 464 (2018).
230. Cui, *supra* note 38.
231. *See, e.g.*, para. 15 in the Note from the Presidency to the Permanent Representatives Committee/Council, Doc. 13525/18 FISC 427 ECOFIN 968 DIGIT 205 (29 October 2018).
232. 2018 OECD Interim Report, *supra* note 12, paras 413–431.
233. Indeed, the DST proposal is the Commission's reaction to the invitation to adopt proposals responding to the challenges of taxing profits in the digital economy by the ECOFIN conclusions of 5 December 2017. At this time, many Member States had expressed an interest in devising temporary measures aimed at collecting more revenues resulting from digital activities in the Union, while ensuring these measures would remain outside the scope of tax treaties. *See* Council of the European Union, *Responding to the challenges of taxation of profits of the digital economy – Council conclusions*, 15445/17, FISC 346 ECOFIN 1092 (5 December 2017), para. 24.
234. *See* para. 8 in the Note from the Presidency to the Permanent Representatives Committee/Council, Doc. 13525/18 FISC 427 ECOFIN 968 DIGIT 205 (29 October 2018).

However, based on the criteria set out by the OECD,[235] a balancing of the various factors leads to the conclusion that the DST is not a tax covered by tax treaties,[236] a position – explicitly or implicitly – shared by nearly all commentators.[237] Admittedly, the borderline drawn by Article 2 OECD MC for 'hybrid' taxes such as the DST is blurred, and legal certainty on that issue will only be achieved in the future; if it were eventually to be determined that the DST is covered by tax treaties, EU law would generally override tax treaties, but difficult questions might arise under Article 351 TFEU.[238]

Concluding that the DST would not fall under Article 2 OECD MC also means that unrelieved double burdens occur where revenues are taxed under DST and profits under a – domestic or foreign – CIT: A cross-border taxable person could be subject to double (and, hence, over-) taxation for which no relief is contemplated by Article 23 OECD Model.[239] Further, neither the double tax convention's (DTC's) mutual agreement procedure under Article 25 OECD Model nor the EU dispute resolution directive's dispute resolution mechanisms would apply.[240] Creating a new tax that falls outside the scope of existing DTCs modelled on the OECD Model is a step backwards rather than forwards toward avoiding double taxation.[241]

---

235. *See* §6.02[B][2][a] *supra*.
236. *See* for the main arguments and further references Hohenwarter et al., *supra* note 4.
237. *See, e.g.*, Ismer & Jescheck, *supra* note 112, at 577 (2018); Turina, *supra* note 24, at 518 (2018); CFE Tax Advisors Europe, *supra* note 66; Tom O'Shea, *Comments on the EU's Proposed Indirect Digital Service Tax*, 90 Tax Notes Int'l 1373, 1377 (2018); Opinion of the European Economic and Social Committee ECO/459 on the Taxation of profits of multinationals in the digital economy (EESC 2018/01556 adopted on 12 July 2018, OJ C 367/73 (10 October 2018), m.nos 1.5 and 2.4 (referring to the DST as turnover tax or indirect tax); Cui, *supra* note 38; Fadi Shaheen, *Income Tax Treaty Aspects of Nonincome Taxes: The Importance of Residence*, 71 Tax L. Rev. (2018) 583, 620 et seq. (with regard to recent examples of turnover and equalization taxes); *contra* Matthias Valta, *Verfassungs- und Abkommensrechtsfragen des Richtlinienentwurfs für eine Steuer auf digitale Dienstleistungen*, 27 IStR 765, 771–772 (2018).
238. More generally, regulating the treatment of non-EU nationals in internal legislation may create conflicts with existing bilateral tax treaties and call for an examination of the scope of Art. 351 TFEU. A potential 'treaty override' can, e.g., already be found in Art. 7 ATAD, which requires the inclusion of foreign, tax treaty exempt PEs in the scope of CFC rules, thereby arguably forcing Member States to override the exemption method in their tax treaties with third countries. On the other, the Union is usually careful not to upset the existing tax treaty network between Member States and third countries. This is clearly visible, e.g., with regard to the Commission's proposal for a significant digital presence (COM(2018) 147), where Art. 2 specifies that the Directive would, 'in the case of entities that are resident for corporate tax purposes in a third country with which the particular Member State in question has a convention for the avoidance of double taxation', only apply 'if that convention includes provisions similar to Articles 4 and 5 of this Directive in relation to the third country and those provisions are in force'. Complementing this delimitation of the Directive's scope, the Commission has simultaneously issued a recommendation to Member States to (bilaterally) amend their tax treaties with third countries and to include provisions on significant digital presences (*see* the Commission's Recommendation of 21 March 2018 relating to the corporate taxation of a significant digital presence, COM(2018) 1650).
239. CFE Tax Advisors Europe, *supra* note 66, at 7.
240. *Ibid.* 7 & 9; Council Directive 2017/1852 on tax dispute resolution mechanisms in the European Union, OJ L 265/1 (2017), at Art. 1.
241. The CFE Tax Advisors recommend the implementation of new taxes within the scope of the existing tax treaty network, *see* CFE Tax Advisors Europe, *supra* note 66, at 10. The difficulty

[b] *Interference with EU Law*

Five EU law domains could pose potential problems for implementing the DST as proposed by the 2018 DST Directive Proposal:

(1) Principles of Union Law: Member States continue to debate the subsidiarity and proportionality of the 2018 DST Directive Proposal; some argue that it does not properly respect those principles.[242]
(2) Fundamental EU Freedoms: Although these are unlikely to cause problems, as the proposed DST applies equally to domestic and cross-border situations,[243] it remains to be seen whether it might be viewed as de facto discrimination of foreign or foreign-owned companies and what consequences would derive therefrom in case of a harmonized regime.[244]
(3) VAT: The proposed DST is unlikely to interfere with Article 401 of the VAT Directive,[245] which generally prohibits other turnover taxes presenting characteristics similar to VAT;[246] the proposed DST is not an 'all-phase, input-deduction tax that generally applies to transactions relating to goods or services'.[247] Moreover, as the proposed DST would be enacted on the same legislative level as VAT (e.g., secondary EU law), it would be difficult to demonstrate that the two taxes were incompatible.[248]
(4) CCCTB: Assuming that both the CCCTB proposals[249] and the 2018 DST Directive Proposals are adopted, one might think there would be a potential conflict in their implementation and application. However, the EU Commission did not provide a detailed explanation as to how the DST fits within the proposed CCCTB framework,[250] likely because of the DST's stopgap, temporary nature, but instead explained how its CCCTB proposal should be adapted to the 2018 SDP Directive Proposal, the EU Commission's the long-term

to achieve an aptly designed equalization levy is also demonstrated by Ismer & Jescheck, *supra* note 112, at 575, comparing the Indian equalization levy and the Italian web tax.

242. *See* the negative parliamentary opinions in PE622.193 (Danish Parliament); Doc. 9139/18 FISC 221 ECOFIN 444 (Irish Parliament), PE622.196 (Maltese Parliament); PE622.197 (Netherlands House of Representatives).
243. Turina, *supra* note 24, at 509.
244. *See* Mason & Parada, *supra* note 130, arguing that DST-like taxes might cause covert nationality discrimination based on taxpayers' size. *See also* Turina, *supra* note 24, at 509, referring to ECJ, *Safir*, C-118/96, Judgment, EU:C:1998:170, where the Court found a violation of the freedom to provide services by a Swedish insurance equalization levy.
245. Council Directive 2006/112/EC of 28 November 2006 on the common system of value added tax, [2006] OJ L 347/1.
246. As clarified by the case law of the Court of Justice: *Dansk Denkavit*, C-200/90, Judgment, EU:C:1992:152, paras 11–14; *see* for further explanations Turina, *supra* note 24, at 510.
247. Kofler, Mayr & Schlager, *Taxation of the Digital Economy: 'Quick Fixes' or Long-Term Solution?*, *supra* note 4, at 531.
248. *Ibid.* 531.
249. *See also* §6.01[B] *supra*.
250. 2018 DST Directive Proposal, *supra* note 66, at 4.

solution for digital economy taxation.[251] Consequently, no interference between DST and CCCTB is expected.

(5) State Aid: The argument has been raised that State aid prohibitions and obligations under Article 107 TFEU might, potentially, interfere with the implementation of the DST as proposed in the 2018 DST Directive Proposal, as its application to only certain digital services and its revenue thresholds could amount to selectivity.[252] However, a strong argument against the DST's qualification as State aid - despite the necessity of and discretion in implementation by the individual Member States - is its approval by the Union legislator, which, first, implies that the measure cannot be imputed to the Member States (but rather stems from an act of the Union legislature) and, second, amounts to a declaration that it is not a measure 'affect[ing] trade between Member States'.[253]

[c] *Interference with WTO Law*

It has been argued that the DST, if implemented in its proposed form, might raise issues under the General Agreement on Trade in Services, as it would only cover certain digital services[254] and would, in effect, only target the 'biggest' digital services providers, which happen to be, by and large, third-country players.[255] However, it remains to be seen whether the legal application of the DST to domestic and foreign service providers effectively removes such objections.[256]

[2] *Selected Policy Objections*

As previously suggested, if the DST were to be adopted in its currently proposed form, its implementation could lead to significant legal uncertainty for a variety of reasons,

251. 2018 SDP Directive Proposal, *supra* note 64, at 3-4.
252. Turina, *supra* note 24, at 510 & 519; Mason & Parada, *supra* note 130.
253. *See* ECJ, 5 April 2006, T-351/02, *Deutsche Bahn AG* v *Commission of the European Communities*, EU:T:2006:104, paras 101-106. This case dealt with the transposition of Directive 92/81 into German law, providing in its Art. 8(1)(b) for an exemption of certain mineral oils from excise duty. The German national railway company, Deutsche Bahn, claimed that this exemption implemented into German law constituted State aid and requested the EU Commission to take measures against it, which has been rejected due to the fact that the exemption finds its origin in EU law. The Court agreed with the Commission, *see* especially para. 102: In transposing the exemption into national law, Member States are only implementing Community provisions in accordance with their obligations stemming from the Treaty. Therefore, the provision at issue is not imputable to the German State, but in actual fact stems from an act of the Community legislature.
254. Article 3(1) 2018 DST Directive Proposal, *see also* CFE Tax Advisors Europe, *supra* note 66, at 6. For a critical analysis from a US perspective, see Gary Clyde Hufbauer & Zhiyao Lu, *The European Union's Proposed Services Tax: A De Facto Tariff*, Peterson Institute for International Economics (June 2018), https://piie.com/publications/policy-briefs/european-unions-proposed-digital-services-tax-de-facto-tariff (accessed 12 November 2018).
255. Frans Vanistendael, *The Level Playing Field in Digital Taxation*, 90 Tax Notes Int'l 867, 868 (2018).
256. *See* for a brief discussion, e.g., Schön, *supra* note 24, at 286.

resulting in a *dis*incentive for cross-border trade and investment in the Member States in which the DST is imposed.[257] Why? Because the proposed DST sits outside of the Member States' 'normal' CIT system, and thus sidesteps the CIT's 'core problem', which is at the very heart of the whole digital tax debate.[258] The DST, rather, would create an additional layer of complexity on top of the already-complex CIT issues, without offering any coordinated solution to any of them.[259] The time and energy spent on developing a well-functioning, well-thought-through DST would probably be better invested in hammering out a coordinated long-term solution that addresses the broader CIT issues, like a SDP, destination-based residual market profit allocation or inbound and outbound minimum taxes,[260] as well as the CIT's subordinate issues.

The DST's likely negative impact on cross-border trade and investment may also lead one to question whether it is effectively capable of contributing to the creation and subsequent reinforcement of the EU-envisaged EU Digital Single Market;[261] its adoption would likely have adverse effects on that market. Moreover, the fragmentation risks likely to arise out of unilateral Member State measures intended to blunt the potential negative impacts of the DST as drafted would have to be carefully assessed and balanced to ensure that it does not make matters even worse.

The rationale behind the 2018 DST Directive Proposal, and the DST proposed therein, is the EU's quest for a 'fairer distribution of tax revenues between national tax administrations' and the correction of the 'existing misalignment of taxation and value creation'.[262] However, neither the concept of 'fair distribution' nor the scope of such purported misalignment have been clearly established or defined, nor has there been an adequate, transparent assessment of the overall impact of the proposed DST on growth, welfare, revenue distribution, and compliance, much less an assessment of its costs.[263] Indeed, with respect to the balance among Member States, the Opinion of the EESC expressed its concern that the proposed shift in taxation to a revenue-based system 'will benefit larger economies with many consumers at the expense of smaller exporting economies' and underlined 'that any solution, whether short or long term, to the taxation of digital business models must result in fair and equal economic outcome for all economies in the EU'.[264] Despite such concerns, the legislative process seems to

257. Brauner, *supra* note 229 at 465.
258. *Ibid.* at 464.
259. *Ibid.*
260. For a recent analysis of these proposals, *see, e.g.*, Itai Grinberg, *International Taxation in an Era of Digital Disruption: Analyzing the Current Debate* (29 October 2018), *available at* SSRN: https://ssrn.com/abstract=3275737 or http://dx.doi.org/10.2139/ssrn.3275737 (accessed 12 November 2018).
261. 2018 DST Directive Proposal, *supra* note 66, at 3.
262. *See* 2018 EU Staff Impact Assessment, *supra* note 63, at 3.
263. *See also* the critical statements in the Regulatory Scrutiny Board Opinion, Proposal for a Council Directive laying down rules relating to the corporate taxation of a significant digital presence & Proposal for a Council Directive on the common system of a digital services tax on revenues resulting from the provision of certain digital services, https://eur-lex.europa.eu/legal-content/EN/TXT/PDF/?uri=PI_COM:SEC(2018)162&from=EN (accessed 12 October 2018).
264. Opinion of the European Economic and Social Committee of 12 July 2018 on 'Proposal for a Council Directive laying down rules relating to the corporate taxation of a significant digital presence', EESC 2018/01556, [2018] OJ C 367/73.

have been driven, mainly, by the political will to set a political milestone with respect to taxation of digital business models; much of that political will being based on a vague 'perceived unfairness'.[265]

Moreover, as proposed, the 'fairness' of the DST clearly has its limits, particularly with respect to turnover taxation for the different business models with their different profit margins. From the perspective of 'profits', the 2018 DST Directive Proposal's turnover basis, of course, fails to incorporate a profitability threshold, which disregards the ability-to-pay principle[266] and creates adverse effects for companies with small profit margins, such as start-ups.[267] The worldwide turnover threshold (EUR 750 million) furthers favour start-ups with low turnover in their first years of business activity compared to already established companies, active in other fields of business, that decide to widen their offer towards digital services covered by the DST proposal. The latter companies tend to easily fulfil the turnover threshold of EUR 750 million and hence to fall within the scope of application of the DST,[268] whereas the first companies may generate higher turnover and profits with their digital activities without being liable to DST. Such outcome seems to contradict the core idea of a 'digital services' tax. To remedy that likely and correct criticism, the DST should be redesigned with respect for fundamental taxation principles firmly in mind. For example, it could be redesigned to constitute a minimum or 'default' tax, similar to the UK's 'diverted profits tax' or India's equalization levy.[269] Such a design would influence taxpayer behaviour and incentivize them to declare and pay CIT rather than to be subjected to a more expensive DST alternative (although one must acknowledge that a closer interrelation between a turnover tax and CIT could lead to stricter scrutiny in light of Article 2 OECD Model).

---

265. In the 2018 DST Directive Proposal (*supra* note 66, at 3), it is not clearly stated on whose perception the Commission relies. Related documents reveal that it deals with (voting) citizens' perception, *see, e.g.*, 2018 EU Staff Impact Assessment, *supra* note 63, at 3: The solution would improve the perception of fairness for citizens by ensuring that large companies with significant digital activities do not escape their taxes in the EU.
266. Even if the aim of the DST is certainly to tax digital companies that are 'on paper' loss making but where in reality shareholders and other stakeholders still have significant financial benefits, e.g., by the increasing share value. This is however contradictory to fundamental principles of taxation. For further explanation on such principles that also the DST should respect, *see, e.g.*, 2015 OECD BEPS Action 1 Report, *supra* note 12, paras 10 et seq. & 32 et seq.; Thomas Rödder, *Globalisierung und Unternehmenssteuerrecht: Wie ist das ertragsteuerliche Besteuerungssubstrat multinationaler Unternehmen sachgerecht auf die betroffenen Fisci aufzuteilen?, in Festschrift für Joachim Lang zum 70. Geburtstag: Gestaltung der Steuerrechtsordnung* 1147 et seq. (Klaus Tipke et al. eds., Otto Schmidt 2011); Heinz-Jürgen Pezzer, *Rechtfertigung der Körperschaftsteuer und ihre Entwicklung zu einer allgemeinen Unternehmensteuer, in Die Steuerrechtsordnung in der Diskussion – Festschrift für Klaus Tipke zum 70. Geburtstag* 419, 424 (Joachim Lang ed., Otto Schmidt 1995); Joachim Englisch, *VAT/GST and Direct Taxes: Different Purposes, in Value Added Tax and Direct Taxation – Similarities and Differences* 1, 3–9 (Michael Lang et al. eds., IBFD 2009).
267. CFE Tax Advisors Europe, *supra* note 66, at 8.
268. Provided that the additional threshold of taxable turnover within the EU (EUR 50 million) is also fulfilled.
269. Both levies do not apply in case the non-resident taxpayers maintain a PE to which the profits may be attributed and which is liable to corporate income tax. Wagh, *supra* note 74, at 549; Sinnig, *Besteuerung der digitalen Wirtschaft in Großbritannien, Italien und Ungarn*, *supra* note 4, at 410.

One particular aspect of legal uncertainty in the DST's practical application (again, assuming it is adopted as originally proposed) would arise out of its distinction between 'covered' and 'not covered' services. That distinction leaves open significant questions with respect to digital economy business models that combine different intermediation services. For any kind of intermediation services, the economic importance of the business grows alongside the number of users, as that reinforces its network effects.[270] The proposed DST, on the other hand, draws a dividing line between different types of intermediation services, attempting to tax only those that rely on value creation caused by user involvement.[271] For example, in the case of some collaborative (or sharing) economy models and online gaming business models, it is difficult to determine if payment or communication services, or the supply of digital content for that matter, are the 'sole or main purpose'[272] of the activity. If they were, such business models would be excluded from DST liability. But, such businesses may also imply an intermediation activity that facilitates the supply of goods and services between users or advertising activities and, hence, may heavily rely on user involvement and value creation on that basis, while simultaneously supplying digital content and other excluded services as an important part of their business model.[273] The definition of 'sole or main purpose', therefore, seems too vague to draw a clear and unambiguous dividing line between services covered by the DST and those excluded from its scope of application.

[3] Broader Practical Issues

Whereas, at least in the short and midterms, potential issues relate more to administrative difficulties, the proposed DST's long-term challenges put the ultimate effect of the DST, on both the market and tax incidence, into question. Of course, the definition of the covered digital services and also the sharing mechanism of revenue collected from DST raise a number of technical questions, and it seems that work on these issues in the Council has made progress to the extent that '[t]here is agreement on most of the definitions used for the purposes of the Directive, including multi-sided digital interfaces and targeted advertising',[274] while there is disagreement on whether the transmission of data collected about users and generated from users activities on digital interfaces (sale of user data) should be covered by the Directive.[275] In any event, the wording of the DST proposal makes one wonder if it overstretches the ability to comply: Revenues from advertising services under Article 3(1)(a) DST proposal, e.g.,

270. 2018 OECD Interim Report, *supra* note 12, para. 42.
271. 2018 DST Directive Proposal, *supra* note 66, at 8.
272. Article 3(4)(a) 2018 DST Directive Proposal.
273. Carrie Brandon Elliot, *Creating Value: Taxing Video Game Companies*, 90 Tax Notes Int'l 831, 833 (2018).
274. *See* para. 7 in the Note from the Presidency to the Permanent Representatives Committee/Council, Doc. 13525/18 FISC 427 ECOFIN 968 DIGIT 205 (29 October 2018).
275. *See* paras 10–11 in the Note from the Presidency to the Permanent Representatives Committee/Council, Doc. 13525/18 FISC 427 ECOFIN 968 DIGIT 205 (29 October 2018). For a narrow approach, *see* Kofler, Mayr & Schlager, *Taxation of the Digital Economy: A Pragmatic Approach to Short-Term Measures*, *supra* note 4, 123 et seq.

are effectively allocated to the EU depending on where the advertisement is displayed (i.e., 'appears on the user's device'; Article 5(2)(a) DST proposal), and between the Member States 'in proportion to the number of times an advertisement has appeared on users' devices in that tax period' (Article 5(3)a) DST proposal). Compliance with those provisions might require to divide revenue between the EU (and particular Member States) and the rest of the world and would pose the additional challenge that taxpayers – at least under current business and contractual arrangements – might not even know where the users are located (e.g., with regard to banner advertisements that are sold in bulk and placed on third-party webpages). While it might be understandable that the DST proposal does not focus on the location or 'source' of revenue derived from customers purchasing advertisement placement (information on which might be derived from VAT data) but rather 'user value creation',[276] it should also accommodate situations where compliance is either impossible or would create concerns with regard to data protection.

In the short term, moreover, high administrative costs on both sides (i.e., tax administrations and taxpayers)[277] and the acknowledged tax collection difficulties associated with tax imposed by way of self-assessments handed in by non-residents compared to withholding by resident agents will constitute the proposed DST's main implementation issues. That high cost is not likely to be proportionate to the limited expected revenues.[278] The DST's administration, including each Member State's enforcement rights when it is owed DST,[279] even when the taxable person has chosen an OSS MS pursuant to Articles 10(3)(b) and 13 2018 DST Directive Proposal, is likely to have significant negative effects on taxpayers. If, for example, a taxpayer pays the whole amount of DST due to all Member States to the OSS MS,[280] the taxpayer can still be obliged to pay a Member State's proportionate share thereof to the other Member State when the OSS MS fails to transfer the paid DST sums to other Member States. Taxpayers are thus obliged to answer for the poor practices (or even malpractice) of the OSS MS's tax administration.

For the longer term, one obvious lacuna in the 2018 DST Directive Proposal is its surprising lack of any sunset clause, even though it has been explicitly declared an 'interim' solution.[281] Some fear that, if adopted, the DST would lose its temporary nature once Member States realize that it is an effective way to generate revenue:[282] once a tax is in place, it can be very difficult to repeal it.[283] Indeed, the issue of 'timing' requires some comments:

276. *See* Recital (7) of the Preamble to 2018 DST Directive Proposal.
277. *See* §6.02[B][1] and §6.02[B][2][vi] *supra*.
278. 2018 EU Staff Impact Assessment, *supra* note 63, 2. *See also* §6.01[C] *supra*.
279. Article 18(4) 2018 DST Directive Proposal.
280. In compliance with Art. 16(1) 2018 DST Directive Proposal, which does not seem to be an optional choice for the taxable person.
281. 2018 DST Directive Proposal, *supra* note 66, at 2.
282. Lee Sheppard, *Five Takeaways from the Digital Tax Debate*, 89 Tax Notes Int'l 1251, 1252 (2018).
283. *See* §6.02[B][1] *supra*.

- The DST proposal does not contain any so-called sunset clause, although 'all delegations [in the Council] agree that the Directive should expire once the comprehensive solution at global level is in place'.[284] It is, however, debated if a sunset clause should have a fixed expiry date upon which the DST Directive would expire automatically or whether the expiry of the DST Directive should be linked to developments at the OECD/G20 level.[285] The first option would include a formal end date of the DST Directive. The second solution, i.e., the link to global developments (which are expected until summer 2020), is not unheard of in EU tax legislation[286] and there are certainly a number of technical ways to implement such condition (e.g., by linking the expiration of the DST to a new proposal by the EU Commission, which is contingent on a solution at the OECD/G20 level). However, the question remains if the mere 'sunset' of the DST Directive at the EU level would likewise (legally, not only politically) ban Member States from 'keeping' their domestic implementing legislation or to again introduce similar national taxes. It would certainly seem prudent, from an internal market perspective, that such national taxes would be explicitly 'outlawed', and the approach chosen for the EU-wide abolition of capital duties might serve as an example.[287]
- Conversely, one could also think about a vacatio legis of the DST Directive, linking the entry into force of the Directive to developments at the OECD/G20 level. Such 'inverted sunset clause' – or, more to the point, a 'sunrise clause' – would condition the DST to a non-solution at a global level. However, and apart from a number of technical issues, while such a 'sunrise' provision would potentially increase political pressure towards an international solution, it could politically create an outcome that nobody seems to wish for: That an imperfect measure that was conceptualized to be a short-term, interim solution would become permanent.

Further, as proposed, the DST is a turnover tax without any allowance for cost deduction that might distort the market due to cascading effects[288] and may shift the tax incidence to European consumers rather than to the targeted multinationals, such that the legislative intent to make the latter, and not the former, carry the financial burden

284. *See* para. 12 in the Note from the Presidency to the Permanent Representatives Committee/Council, Doc. 13525/18 FISC 427 ECOFIN 968 DIGIT 205 (29 October 2018).
285. *See* para. 14 in the Note from the Presidency to the Permanent Representatives Committee/Council, Doc. 13525/18 FISC 427 ECOFIN 968 DIGIT 205 (29 October 2018).
286. *See* Art. 11(6) ATAD, where the obligation to implement the interest barrier under Art. 4 is deferred for Member States which have national targeted rules for preventing BEPS risks at 8 August 2016, which are equally effective to the interest limitation rule set out in this Directive, as those Member States 'may apply these targeted rules until the end of the first full fiscal year following the date of publication of the agreement between the OECD members on the official website on a minimum standard with regard to BEPS Action 4, but at the latest until 1 January 2024'.
287. *See* Council Directive 2008/7/EC of 12 February 2008 concerning indirect taxes on the raising of capital, [2008] OJ L 46/11.
288. *Ibid.* §6.02[B][1].

of the DST will not be achieved.[289] Cascading effects may occur where taxable services are incorporated in a taxable onwards supply. The DST's cascading effects could also lead to double taxation.[290]

Also, as the scope of the proposed DST's application is very limited, one may wonder about its real impact, considering that monetization or service models can quickly adapt to new rules and, hence, escape the newly adopted DST.[291]

Finally, it is not entirely clear whether national 'equalization levies' with a similar scope as the EU DST, such as Hungary's advertising tax or the announced Spanish DST, would be legally pre-empted by the DST Directive, even though it seems (politically) clear that the DST should harmonize the field and prevent the fragmentation of the Internal Market by a myriad of unilateral taxes. It would therefore seem recommendable that a DST Directive explicitly spells out a prohibition of parallel national taxes, e.g., along the lines of Article 401 of the VAT Directive's prohibition of 'turnover taxes'.

§6.04 SUMMARY AND CONCLUSIONS

The digital economy challenges the very concept of tax territoriality based on physical presence in a fundamental and unprecedented way, and market jurisdictions seem to play an increasingly important role in tax revenue allocation. Proposed measures to modify the existing tax system include a modified PE concept (so as to include significant economic or digital presence), a withholding tax for digital transactions, and equalization levies. To date, no international consensus regarding any one of these measures has been found.

Nevertheless, in March 2018, the EU Commission dared to take the first step toward solving digital taxation issues via its 2018 SDP Directive Proposal for the long term and its 2018 DST Directive Proposal as an interim solution to permit taxation while work on the long-term solutions continues. That interim solution – which might be viewed as an 'equalization levy' from a political perspective – is intended to be a temporary patch over perceived 'undertaxation' of digital businesses in market jurisdictions in which those businesses lack a physical presence. Many perceive such an interim measure as a 'simpler' solution when compared to attempts to define significant economic or digital presence, which in itself is a rather delusive finding, as the question of when a sufficient nexus to tax exists remains the same. Yet, that question is decisive and subject to much debate: States still do not agree on whether or to which extent data and user participation represent a contribution to a business' value creation.

Besides broader implementation issues (such as the impact on investment, innovation, and growth, as well as on social welfare, a shift of the economic incidence of the proposed DST to consumers, the risk of overtaxation, and administrative burdens of implementing and enforcing a new tax), equalization levies raise a number

289. *Ibid.* §6.02[A]; *see also* CFE Tax Advisors Europe, *supra* note 66, at 8.
290. *Ibid.* §6.02[B][1]; CFE Tax Advisors Europe, *supra* note 66, at 8.
291. *Ibid.* §6.02[A]. For the limited expected financial impact so far, *see* 2018 EU Staff Impact Assessment, *supra* note 63, at 70.

of other issues. Concretely, as they are intentionally created to sit in between CIT systems and consumption taxes, they must still comply with existing international obligations, such as DTCs and EU and WTO law. Interim equalization levies should not undermine the development of a coordinated preferable solution on an international level, which prescribes the temporary nature of such levies. The OECD has recommended that equalization levies only apply to a limited circle of business models – that is, those constituting the highest risk for the national CIT – due to the potentially significant adverse consequences these levies have, such as overtaxation. Further, the tax rate applicable to gross revenues as well as the creation of revenue thresholds intended to exclude SMEs to promote innovation and growth need to be determined carefully, taking into account the significant economic impact such levies may have. EU law prescribes equal treatment of domestic and cross-border situations. Further, administrative cost and complexity of application should be kept to a minimum in order to ensure effective tax collection.

The 2018 DST Directive Proposal, if adopted, would create a 3% turnover tax imposed on gross revenues arising from certain digital services. It aims at levelling the playing field for businesses active in Europe but raises a number of concerns regarding its compatibility with international and EU, a number of policy questions and a myriad of technical issues, some of which were addressed in this chapter. Moreover, unilateral or EU 'equalization taxes' might prompt reactions by major trading partners, as they deviate from the historic consensus that taxation of multinationals should be based on profits rather than on turnover.

Since the time of writing this chapter, the initially strong will of certain Member States to adopt a DST at the European level seems to decrease. During the ECOFIN meeting of 4 December 2018, Member States' finance ministers could not agree on the compromise text proposed by the Austrian presidency,[292] and currently a more limited tax addressing only advertising services is under discussion.[293] The tendency of certain Member States seems to prefer waiting for agreement on a global approach at the level of the OECD/G20.[294] Despite its inherent risks, however, some Member States such as

292. Council of the European Union, Proposal for a Council Directive on the common system of a digital services tax on revenues resulting from the provision of certain digital services – General approach, Doc. No. 14886/18 FISC 511 ECOFIN 1149 DIGIT 239 (29 November 2018).

293. Council of the European Union, Economic and Financial Affairs Council, 04/12/2018, *available at* https://www.consilium.europa.eu/en/meetings/ecofin/2018/12/04/ (accessed 22 February 2019). The proposed compromise (*see supra* note 292) notably suggested a more nuanced definition of the terminology employed in the directive; modified the services covered, so as to exclude, e.g., the sale of certain data from its scope; to limit the location of users to the use of their devices' IP addresses, excluding thereby 'any other method of geolocation'; and certain modifications to the procedural rules, such as an extended deadline for the DST return submission. Further, the compromise proposed to delay the application of the DST to 1 January 2022. Moreover, in the meantime, the European Parliament has been consulted and proposed a number of amendments to the Commission proposal, see European Parliament, European Parliament legislative solution of 13 December 2018 on the proposal for a Council directive on the common system of a digital services tax on revenues resulting from the provision of certain digital services (COM(2018)0148 – C8-0137/2018 – 2018/0073 (CNS)) (13 December 2018).

294. Council of the European Union, Proposal for a Council Directive on the common system of a digital services tax on revenues resulting from the provision of certain digital services – General approach, Doc. 14885/18 FISC 510 ECOFIN 1148 DIGIT 238 (29 November 2018), para. 8.

the Austria, France, Italy, Spain, and the UK are in the process of moving forward with the enactment of unilateral equalization levies due to the failure to adopt a (modified) DST proposal at Union level by the end of 2018.[295]

295. *See, e.g.*, for Austria: *EU: Digitalsteuer für Internetriesen soll spätestens 2020 kommen*, Die Presse, *available at* https://diepresse.com/home/wirtschaft/economist/5431409/EU_Digital steuer-fuer-Internetriesen-soll-spaetestens-2020-kommen (accessed 22 February 2019); for France: David Keohane, *France Accelerates Plans for Its Own Digital Tax*, Financial Times, 17 December 2018, *available at* https://www.ft.com/content/a4881362-0216-11e9-9d01-cd4d49 afbbe3 (accessed 22 February 2019); for Italy: EY, *Italy Introduces New Digital Services Tax*, *available at* https://taxinsights.ey.com/archive/archive-news/italy-introduces-new-digital-services-tax.aspx (accessed 22 February 2019); for Spain: EY, *Spain Sends Bill on Digital Services Tax to Parliament for Approval*, 29 January 2019, *available at* https://www.ey.com/gl/en/services/tax/international-tax/alert--spain-sends-bill-on-digital-services-tax-to-parliam ent-for-approval (accessed 22 February 2019).

CHAPTER 7

Digital Permanent Establishments on Its Way to Becoming a Reality? The EU Commission's Proposal on Taxing 'Significant Digital Presence'

Peter Bräumann

§7.01 INTRODUCTION

When the European Commission unveiled its proposals for 'a modern, fair and efficient taxation standard for the digital economy' on 21 March 2018, it promised nothing less than a 'comprehensive solution to the challenge of taxing the digital economy'.[1] To deliver on this ambitious objective, the proposals include the Commission's concrete visions for a long-term and lasting redesign of the international corporate tax system to tackle the challenges of digitization. The concept of a Significant Digital Presence (hereinafter 'SDP') forms the core of these plans. The term essentially refers to a new rule for the establishment of a taxable nexus tailored to the commercial provision of digital services. The SDP is intended to serve as an addition to the existing and commonly accepted rules on Permanent Establishments (hereinafter 'PE') akin to Article 5 of the Organisation for Economic Co-operation and Development (OECD) Model Tax Convention on Income and on Capital (hereinafter 'OECD MC'), albeit without requiring any physical presence of the service provider in the jurisdiction concerned.[2]

1. EU Comm'n, Communication from the Commission to the European Parliament and the Council: Time to establish a modern, fair and efficient taxation standard for the digital economy, 6 COM(2018) 146 final (hereinafter 'EU Comm'n Tax'n Standard for the Digital Economy').
2. EU Comm'n, Proposal for a Council Directive laying down rules relating to the corporate taxation of a significant digital presence, 2 & 7 COM(2018) 147 final (hereinafter '2018 SDP Directive Proposal'); EU Comm'n Tax'n Standard for the Digital Economy, *supra* note 1, at 6.

The Commission envisions an implementation via three-way strategy:[3]

(1) as a compulsory rule within the existing European Union (EU) Member States' corporate tax systems for mandatory application in situations between Member States (and vis-à-vis third countries which have not entered into a convention for the avoidance of double taxation with a Member State in question) as soon as 2020;[4]
(2) by gradually incorporating the SDP concept into EU Member States' existing double taxation conventions with all non-EU jurisdictions;[5]
(3) and finally as integral part of the planned EU-wide Common Consolidated Corporate Tax Base (CCCTB).[6]

Eventually, the Commission hopes for the SDP to provide a model, which will be followed by many other (non-EU) nations. As such, it should feed the current discussion on adaptions of international tax law as regards the 'digital economy' currently taking place on the level of the OECD's Inclusive Framework on Base Erosion and Profit Shifting (BEPS) with the aim of providing a solution by 2020.[7] The Commission deliberately wants the EU to take a pioneering role and push the international debate forward.[8] The first of the aforementioned implementation measures – the adaption of the Member States' corporate tax regimes to the SDP in relationship to other Member States and third states they have not entered into tax treaties with – should be enforced by a Council Directive proposed as one of two central elements of the Commission's plans.[9] The corresponding changes to tax treaties with third states are outlined in a Commission Recommendation.[10]

In addition to the SDP, the second key element of the proposals is a suggested Council Directive on a Digital Services Tax[11] (hereinafter 'DST'). This DST is designated as an interim measure only until the long-term comprehensive solution in form

3. *Ibid.* at 6 et seq.
4. *See* EU Comm'n Corporate Tax'n of a Significant Digital Presence, *supra* note 2.
5. *See* EU Comm'n, Commission Recommendation relating to the Corporate Taxation of a Significant Digital Presence COM(2018) 1650 final (hereinafter 'Comm'n Recommendation on Significant Digital Presence Taxation').
6. *See* 2018 SDP Directive Proposal, *supra* note 2, at 3 et seq., wherein the Commission refers to comparable works and proposals by the European Parliament for Amendments to the Proposed Common Corporate Tax Base and CCCTB Directives.
7. OECD, *Base Erosion and Profit Shifting Project: Tax Challenges Arising from Digitalization – Interim Report 2018* para. 399 (OECD Publishing 2018) (hereinafter '2018 OECD Interim Report').
8. *See* EU Comm'n Corporate Tax'n of a Significant Digital Presence, *supra* note 2, at 7; 2018 SDP Directive Proposal, *supra* note 2, at 3 & 6.
9. *See* EU Comm'n Corporate Tax'n of a Significant Digital Presence, *supra* note 2, at 4.
10. Comm'n Recommendation on Significant Digital Presence Taxation, *supra* note 5.
11. EU Comm'n, Proposal for a Council Directive on the common system of a digital services tax on revenues resulting from the provision of certain digital services COM(2018) 148 final (hereinafter '2018 DST Directive Proposal').

of the SDP comes into effect internationally.[12] An expiration of the DST after the implementation of the SDP, however, is merely a political commitment. The proposed Council Directives do not provide any form of legally binding sunset clause or SDP implementation threshold effecting an automatic end of the DST. It is left open which level of international diffusion the SDP has to exceed before the DST will be deemed unnecessary. For now, both measures should enter into force at the same time (the proposals mention the year 2020).[13] Nonetheless, the intended relationship between the (lasting) SDP and the (interim) DST concepts as described in the Commission's proposals emphasizes, that it wishes for the SDP - a new nexus within corporate taxation for digital service providers– rather than novel kinds of taxes like the DST to shape the future of international tax law.

The SDP does not appear as a surprise or groundbreaking novelty to the ongoing debates about an appropriate taxation of contemporary (partly or fully) digitized business models. On the level of international tax policymaking, the Final Report on Action 1 of the OECD/G20's BEPS Project[14] already prominently and extensively highlighted the idea of 'a new nexus based on the concept of significant economic presence'[15] as one option to tackle the 'direct tax challenges raised by the digital economy'. The works within the BEPS project naturally drew considerable academic interest to the topic.[16] Yet, scholarly proposals on the idea of a 'digital' or 'virtual PE' or similar concepts as a taxable nexus particularly for e-commerce operations date at least as far back as the late 1990s and early 2000s.[17] In these earlier stages of

12. *Ibid.* at 3 & 16 (recitals 6 & 7 of the proposed Directive); *see also* EU Comm'n Corporate Tax'n of a Significant Digital Presence, *supra* note 2, at 9; 2018 SDP Directive Proposal, *supra* note 2, at 4.
13. 2018 SDP Directive Proposal, *supra* note 2, at 19 (proposed Art. 9 para. 1); 2018 DST Directive Proposal, *supra* note 11, at 36 (proposed Art. 25 para. 1).
14. OECD, *Base Erosion and Profit Shifting Project Action 1 Final Report: Addressing the Tax Challenges of the Digital Economy* (OECD Publishing 2015) (hereinafter '2015 OECD BEPS Action 1 Report').
15. *Ibid.* paras 277 et seq.
16. *For example*, Walter Hellerstein, *Jurisdiction to Tax in the Digital Economy: Permanent and Other Establishments*, 68 Bull. Int'l Tax'n 348 (2014); Peter Hongler & Pasquale Pistone, *Blueprints for a New PE Nexus to Tax Business Income in the Era of the Digital Economy* (IBFD White Papers 2015); Eva Escribano López, *An Opportunistic, and yet Appropriate, Revision of the Source Threshold for the Twenty-First Century Tax Treaties*, 43 Intertax 6 (2015); Daniel Blum, *Permanent Establishments and Action 1 on the Digital Economy of the OECD Base Erosion and Profit Shifting Initiative: The Nexus Criterion Redefined?*, 69 Bull. Int'l Tax'n 314 (2015); Marcel Olbert & Christoph Spengel, *International Taxation in the Digital Economy: Challenge Accepted?*, 9 World Tax J. 3 (2017); Yariv Brauner & Pasquale Pistone, *Adapting Current International Taxation to New Business Models: Two Proposals for the European Union*, 71 Bull. Int'l Tax'n 12 (2017); Georg Kofler et al., *Taxation of the Digital Economy: 'Quick Fixes' or Long-Term Solution?*, 57 ET 523 (2017); Saturnina Moreno González et al., *Adapting the Concept of Permanent Establishment to the Contest of Digital Commerce: From Fixity to Significant Digital Economic Presence*, 45 Intertax 732 (2017); Claus Staringer, *Virtual? Reality!*, 27 SWI 341 (2017); Tsutomo Endo, *Modification of a Taxable Nexus to Address the Tax Challenges of the Digital Economy*, *in Taxation in a Global Digital Economy*, 105 (Ina Kerschner & Maryte Somare eds., Linde 2017); Wolfgang Schön, *Ten Questions about Why and How to Tax the Digitalized Economy* (Max Planck Institute for Tax Law and Public Finance Working Paper 2017-11), *available at* https://papers.ssrn.com/sol3/papers.cfm?abstract_id=3091496.
17. For example, Reuven Avi-Yonah, *International Taxation of Electronic Commerce*, 52 Tax L. Rev. 507 (1997); Luc Hinnekens, *Looking for an Appropriate Jurisdictional Framework for Source-State Taxation of International Electronic Commerce in the Twenty-First Century*, 26 Intertax 192

digitization, the OECD Committee on Fiscal Affairs already conferred on the implications of the growing e-commerce sector to the definition of PEs in Article 5 of the OECD MC.[18] The Committee back then essentially concluded, however, that the PE definition did not require any fundamental modifications in light of technological advances.[19] Instead, only the Commentary on the OECD MC was amended to include guidance on the application of the unchanged PE definition to 'Electronic Commerce'.[20] A specific Technical Advisory Group even explicitly evaluated the notion of a 'virtual PE' for the OECD back then, but spoke against any material changes to the traditional PE framework with its key criterion of physical presence.[21]

Even in spite of the recent considerations within the BEPS project, the OECD seems to maintain some reluctance towards any form of 'digital PE'. While the Final Report on Action 1 extensively discussed the rationale behind and cornerstones of nexus concepts not relying on physical presence,[22] the Task Force on the Digital Economy's eventual conclusions did explicitly not recommend any implantation of measures of this kind for the time being.[23] The recent 2018 OECD Interim Report still does not take a clear position on the matter. It instead emphasizes the divergence in states' opinions and promises further analysis with the intention of arriving at a consensus-based solution by 2020[24] (which might be why the Commission wants to advance on setting standards by then).

Policymakers within the EU (who admittedly are confronted with a smaller numbers of says on the matter), however, do not seem to share the OECD's concerns about rushing this issue. In 2017, an unambiguous Commission Communication foreshadowing a major reform to the PE concept and referring to political backing from the Economic and Fiscal Affairs Council (ECOFIN) on this matter preceded the recent proposals on the SDP.[25] With this announcement, the Commission implicitly refused the recommendations by its own Expert Group on Taxation of the Digital Economy, who pleaded for particular adjustments of the PE concept rather than the creation of

(1998); Dale Pinto, *E-Commerce and Source-Based Income Taxation* (IBFD 2003); Arthur Cockfield, *Reforming the Permanent Establishment Principle Through a Quantitative Economic Presence Test*, 38 Can. Bus. L.J. 400 (2003).

18. *See* Noah Gaoua, *Taxation of the Digital Economy: French Reflections*, 54 Eur. Tax'n 10, 10 et seq. (2014).
19. OECD Committee on Fiscal Affairs, *Clarification on the Application of the Permanent Establishment Definition in E-Commerce: Changes to the Commentary on the Model Tax Convention on Article 5*, http://www.oecd.org/ctp/treaties/1923380.pdf (accessed 22 October 2018).
20. *Ibid. See also* the still existing explanations in OECD, *Commentaries on the Articles of the Model Tax Convention* Art. 5 paras 122 et seq. (OECD Publishing 2017).
21. OECD Centre for Tax Policy and Administration, *Are the Current Treaty Rules for Taxing Business Profits Appropriate for E-Commerce?: Final Report*, paras 322 et seq. and 349 et seq. http://www.oecd.org/tax/treaties/35869032.pdf (22 October 2018).
22. 2015 OECD BEPS Action 1 Report, *supra* note 14, paras 246 et seq., paras 253 et seq., paras 277 et seq.
23. *Ibid.* para. 357.
24. 2018 OECD Interim Report, *supra* note 7, paras 395 et seq.
25. Eur. Comm'n, *Communication from the Commission to the European Parliament and the Council: A Fair and Efficient Tax System in the European Union for the Digital Single Market*, 2 et seq. and 8 et seq. COM(2017) 547 final.

new forms of nexus.[26] Not long after the Commission's Communication, the Council of the EU expressed its support for fundamental reforms.[27]

Political considerations for realignments of the PE concept in individual Member States can be traced back even further.[28] These may additionally explain the present sense of urgency on the EU level, as the Commission fears a proliferation of ineffective unilateral measures bearing the danger of disruptions to the internal market.[29] This fear might not be unfounded, as the aforementioned 2018 OECD Interim Report identified at least two EU jurisdictions where such modifications to the national PE concepts have been enforced (the Slovak Republic) or resolutely announced (Austria).[30] The Report also presents similar legislative action in Israel and India. However, it expects these measures to be without large impact, as unilateral motions will most likely be constrained by factors like tax treaty obligations.[31]

This is where the EU's legal nature as a supranational organization drastically changes the picture. The European Commission's proposals are particularly noteworthy not only because they contain a more or less fully fleshed out concept for a 'digital PE' but also because they are the first motion towards such concept with a realistic chance of coordinated and thus effective implementation between multiple jurisdictions. EU Member States might also more easily be able to solve issues of enforcement.[32] While a swift passage of the SDP Directive might be doubtful from a political perspective,[33] it puts the concrete idea of a 'European digital PE' in the spotlight. Considering the European Commission's pronounced commitment and the recurring calls for a 'fair taxation of the digital economy' in the public debate, the proposal will most likely not simply disappear without effect. As the most recent development carrying such political weight, the SDP concept will certainly fuel and shape the general discussion on 'digital PEs'.

The remainder of this contribution will use these developments as a background and in a first step provide an overview and critical analysis of the key rationale behind

26. Commission Expert Group on Taxation of the Digital Economy, *Report*, 47 et seq. (European Union 2014).
27. Council of the European Union, *Council conclusions on 'Responding to the Challenges of Taxation of Profits of the Digital Economy'*, paras 10 et seq., FISC 346 ECOFIN 1092 (2017).
28. The French government, e.g., commissioned an extensive report which (among other things) recommended the need for renegotiations of the PE concept on an international level already back in 2013: Pierre Collin & Nicolas Colin, *Task Force on Taxation of the Digital Economy: Report to the Minister for the Economy and Finance, the Minister for Industrial Recovery, the Minister Delegate for the Budget and the Minister Delegate for Small and Medium-Sized Enterprises, Innovation and the Digital Economy*, https://www.hldataprotection.com/files/2013/06/Taxation_Digital_Economy.pdf (accessed 30 June 2018).
29. 2018 SDP Directive Proposal, *supra* note 2, at 5.
30. *See* 2018 OECD Interim Report, *supra* note 7, para. 351 and the explanations in footnote 5. For the Austrian plans, *see also* Staringer, *supra* note 16, at 341 et seq.
31. *See* 2018 OECD Interim Report, *supra* note 7, paras 351 et seq.
32. On such issues, *see, e.g.*, Hongler & Pistone, *supra* note 16, at 36 et seq.
33. For example, the German chancellor Angela Merkel has just recently openly questioned all notions of 'digital PEs' in the German parliament, as she fears a domino effect resulting in generally broadened PE definitions and thus potentially harming German export-oriented manufacturers; *see* German Bundestag, Minutes of plenary proceedings 19/32, Stenographic record, 2979.

the more recent 'digital PE' notions. The focus will be on conceptual questions rather than certain business models or a precise definition the 'digital economy' as such. In a second step, the SDP as proposed by the European Commission as the currently most momentous political impetus to the 'digital PE' debates will be examined in detail. As it serves as example for the specific execution of such notions, this will also highlight some general features relevant for all 'digital PE' models.

§7.02 THE QUESTIONABLE RATIONALE BEHIND 'DIGITAL PES'

[A] The Changed Stance Towards 'Physical Presence': Still Physical after All

The need for a 'digital PE' as a new form of taxable nexus for business profits is predominantly justified on the grounds that the established PE definition with its key criterion of physical presence is unfit for an increasingly digitized economy.[34] This definition is attributed to a time of 'brick and mortar' businesses in which having premises on site was considered a prerequisite for extensive commercial operations in a certain geographical market. Within these confinements of the 'traditional economy', the permanent connection of a foreign business to a certain jurisdiction as manifested by the existence of a PE had been seen as just reason for providing that jurisdiction with the right to tax a share of the profits arising from the business. This follows from the idea that parts of the business were operated within such jurisdiction, thus justifying an exemption from exclusive taxation in the country of residence (deemed the prime 'place of business') under Article 7 paragraph 1 OECD MC. Distance, however, no longer plays a role for the electronic provision of 'digital services', which could easily be operated remotely. Thus, the link between physical proximity and income generation was severed for such services, calling for a new approach in defining the reasonable 'closeness' between a non-resident business and a certain jurisdiction that raises the latter's right to taxation.[35]

Taking this argument at face value might indicate that the concept of a 'digital PE' counters the assumed weaknesses in the current PE definition with a departure from physical criteria. On closer examination, such a shift from 'physical' to 'non-physical' criteria is, however, not what the discussions and proposals truly revolve around. The envisioned concepts rather suggest the establishment of 'digital PEs' on the basis of user or customer location and criteria derived from that point, e.g., revenue attributable to the local user base, payments received from or contracts closed with local

34. *See generally* Schön, *supra* note 16, at 1 et seq.
35. *See, e.g.*, 2015 OECD BEPS Action 1 Report, *supra* note 14, para. 256; 2018 SDP Directive Proposal, *supra* note 2, at 7 et seq.; EU Comm'n, Staff Working Document: Impact Assessment Accompanying the document Proposal for a Council Directive laying down rules relating to the corporate taxation of a significant digital presence and Proposal for a Council Directive on the common system of a digital services tax on revenues resulting from the provision of certain digital services, 9 and 16, SWD(2018) 81 final/2; Hongler & Pistone, *supra* note 16, at 14; Kofler, *supra* note 16, at 523.

customers or providing localized language and payment options.[36] Despite being sometimes referred to by different names (the OECD, e.g., counts the existence of local domain names, local digital platforms and local payment options towards 'digital factors' rather than 'user-based factors', which include *inter alia* the number of active local users[37]), all these criteria boil down to nothing more than locating the demanders of a service.

Therefore, the currently considered 'digital PE' concepts still eventually revert to physical criteria. The proposed SDP Directive may serve as prime example. Whether a digitally provided service creates an SDP within a certain Member State should in essence be judged on the basis of (1) electronic devices used to access the service from within its territory and (2) the number of contracts concluded with business clients who reside in that Member State for tax purposes.[38] Hence, the proposal does not introduce any factors that are 'non-physical' (or not already contained within current taxation rules on business residence). It simply uses a different set of physical factors for establishing the location where a service is deemed rendered and thus its provider is considered 'present' for this purpose.

This continuing reliance on physical factors, however, is not merely a 'lack of vision' from the European Commission. It might actually be impossible to completely drop the decisiveness of physical factors as long as the delineation between multiple tax jurisdictions depends on concepts of territoriality. Economic activities must in one way or another be linked to specific geographical points to adequately narrow down the number of jurisdictions potentially levying taxes on these particular activities (a thought also embedded in the traditional PE concept[39]).

Digital processes themselves are mere electronic signals in the form of software and data and thus immaterial in nature, making it virtually impossible to pinpoint them to any location. However, such processes are not operated in a vacuum or purely 'virtual world'. Even electronic services require at least some physical equipment and are at one point initiated by people for catering to other people's needs. Hence, no digital process is completely without physical 'traces', either in the form of equipment or people contributing to the process or receiving its result, which may serve as 'proxies' for linking digital processes to distinct locations. Considerations like these can already be found among the reasons behind the OECD Commentary's elaborations on e-commerce, essentially concluding that a physical server hosting a website can – other than the website itself – establish a PE in the traditional sense.[40]

---

36. *See, e.g.*, 2015 OECD BEPS Action 1 Report, *supra* note 14, paras 277 et seq.; OECD, *Base Erosion and Profit Shifting Project: Accessing the Tax Challenges of the Digital Economy – Action 1: 2014 Deliverable*, 145 et seq. (OECD Publishing 2014); 2018 SDP Directive Proposal, *supra* note 2, at 7 et seq. and 16 et seq. (proposed Art. 4 paras 3 et seq.); Hongler & Pistone, *supra* note 16, at 24 et seq.
37. 2015 OECD BEPS Action 1 Report, *supra* note 14, paras 279 et seq.
38. 2018 SDP Directive Proposal, *supra* note 2, at 16 et seq. (proposed Art. 4 paras 3 et seq.).
39. *See* OECD, *Commentaries on the Articles of the Model Tax Convention*, Art. 5 para. 21 (OECD Publishing 2017) (hereinafter 'OECD Tax Convention Commentaries'); 1 Ekkehart Reimer, *Klaus Vogel on Double Taxation Conventions* Art. 5 m.n 45 et seq. (Ekkehart Reimer & Alexander Rust eds., Kluwer Law 4th ed. 2015).
40. *See* OECD Tax Convention Commentaries, *supra* note 39, Art. 5 para. 123.

As mentioned, the 'digital PE' concepts do still eventually rely on tangible, geographically attributable factors and thus are not fundamentally different from the already established PE principles on the dimension of physicality. They do, however, drastically change the physical 'proxy' used for connecting digital services to a certain jurisdiction. The defining elements of a 'digital PE' focus on the users of a service, relying on demand-side and market-based considerations while the traditional PE concept is centred on the supplier's or service provider's perspective.

[B] Shifting Income Taxation to the Demand Side of Business Operations?

The realignment 'digital PEs' could bring to the international distribution of taxation rights is not caused by a shift from 'physical' to 'digital' factors, but rather by a shift from supply-side- to demand-oriented income taxation in cross-border cases. Whereas the commercial 'presence' establishing a nexus for taxation in cases of long-distance sales and services is judged primarily based on 'physical manifestations' of the providing business under the traditional PE concept, 'physical manifestations' of the recipients serve this function under a 'digital PE' rule. Thus, the market jurisdictions as the 'destinations' of digital services may claim the conducting of commercial operations within their territory for purposes of taxation. Unsurprisingly, the concept of a destination-based corporate tax[41] is sometimes seen as closely related to the 'digital PE' in the literature[42] and was even considered an alternative to the SDP by the European Commission.[43]

With this in mind, one could go even further and argue, that the term 'digital PE' is misleading, as the true intention of a more market-based corporate taxation is not crucially dependent on digitization or distinct features of the 'digital economy' at all. Indeed, while the proponents of broadened PE definitions usually express their suggestions in the context of digitized business models, the theoretical taxation principles they invoke for justifying extended 'source taxation' by the market jurisdictions could easily be applied to 'traditional' businesses as well.[44] These arguments generally follow two lines of thought. First, market jurisdictions would provide certain

41. For comprehensive elaborations, see Michael Devereux & Rita de la Feria, *Designing and Implementing a Destination-Based Corporate Tax* (Oxford University Centre for Business Taxation Working Paper 14/07, 2014), *available at* http://eureka.sbs.ox.ac.uk/5081/1/WP1407.pdf. Alan Auerbach et al., *Destination-Based Cash Flow Taxation* (Oxford University Centre for Business Taxation Working Paper 17/01, 2017), *available at* https://eml.berkeley.edu/~auerbach/CBTWP1701.pdf.
42. *See, e.g.*, Kofler, *supra* note 16, at 524.
43. EU Comm'n, Commission Staff Working Document: Impact Assessment Accompanying the document Proposal for a Council Directive laying down rules relating to the corporate taxation of a significant digital presence and Proposal for a Council Directive on the common system of a digital services tax on revenues resulting from the provision of certain digital services, 29 et seq. & 34 et seq. SWD(2018) 81 final/2 (hereinafter 'Commission Staff Impact Assessment on Significant Digital Presence & Provision of Digital Services').
44. *See* Schön, *supra* note 16, at 17 et seq.

'benefits' to foreign businesses, i.e., public goods facilitating their commercial operations even when the latter's own premises and personnel are located abroad, e.g., social stability, a functional legal system or infrastructure allowing the delivery of goods or services.[45] Second, economic welfare could never be generated by a supplier alone. Only the existence of a demanding counterpart allowed for the creation of 'added value' profits can draw upon. In this sense, customers are viewed as inevitably participating in the production of a supplier's taxable income.[46]

This second argument draws an analogy to a point already mentioned before on the example of locating digital processes. Profit is generated as a result of commercial transactions requiring at least two parties. Such transactions, however, are abstract concepts. Thus, rules for attributing them to a single, distinct location usually rely on 'physical manifestations' in the form of (capital) goods and people involved, but always contain at least some degree of simplifying fiction. The established principles of international taxation rely on the consensus that the whole process of 'commercial income generation' primarily takes place on the premises of a business, even though profit can never be created there alone without contact to the world beyond (just as accurately pointed out by the aforementioned proponents of increased 'source taxation' rights for market jurisdictions).[47]

The resulting conceptual attribution of profit taxation to the supply side of a transaction can, however, be seen as more than just an arbitrary political decision. Provided that modern tax systems generally feature a dualism of income and consumption taxes, it appears consistent to draft the principles of income taxation (including the PE concept) with regards to the supply side, and of consumption taxation (in the form of a value added or sales tax) to the demand side of market transactions.[48] As 'digital PE' concepts deliberately create a nexus for income taxation based on demand-side factors, some authors rightly detect an advancing blur between the conceptual spheres of income and consumption taxation.[49]

Policymakers, however, appear to go great lengths to deny such consumption-oriented influences and rationalize the 'digital PE' with ideas of an unaltered focus on the operations of the suppliers of digital services. The explanations in the proposed SDP Directive, e.g., explicitly state that no taxable nexus should be created based on the place of consumption only.[50] Shifting the decisive criteria for the establishment of such a nexus to demand-side factors while maintaining the image of solely judging the

45. *See also* Commission Staff Impact Assessment on Significant Digital Presence & Provision of Digital Services, *supra* note 43, at 19.
46. Arguments like these are, e.g., elaborated by Hongler & Pistone, *supra* note 16, at 17 et seq. For a critical evaluation, *see* Schön, *supra* note 16, at 16 et seq.
47. *Ibid.*
48. Diving deep into fundamental questions, one might ask whether there truly is a fundamental border between direct income and indirect consumption taxation. No matter the legal design, the party economically facing the tax burden is decided by market forces, as the side with more market power is able to pass on the taxes it carries from a legal perspective; *see* Joachim Englisch, *Steuerrecht*, §17 m.n. 14 (Klaus Tipke & Joachim Lang eds., Verlag Dr. Otto Schmidt 21st ed. 2013).
49. *See* Kofler, *supra* note 16, at 524; Schön, *supra* note 16, at 17.
50. 2018 SDP Directive Proposal, *supra* note 2, at 7.

operations of a business itself as origin of taxable profits requires some justification. For reconciling these two rather contradictory approaches, the OECD refers to the idea of 'value creation' in the 'digital economy'. In essence, this idea elevates the users of digital services from mere demanders to active participants in the provider's operations, either by supplying their data or by generating network effects (which arise, when growing numbers of users add to the appeal of the service itself, e.g., in case of an online marketplace). The users are deemed direct contributors to the operator's intangible assets and net worth.[51] Hereby, a jurisdiction where users reside can claim the conduct of business operations within its territory without any production factors or agents of the provider being present, but yet without backing that claim on the sole basis of being the place of consumption.

[C] 'Value Creation' as Substantial Counterargument to Demand Orientation?

Building the 'digital PE' concept on this 'value creation' approach of users featuring in the service provided might be intended to curb demands for a general shift towards market-based income taxation for the time being. Additionally, this line of reasoning has another advantage from a perspective of policy justification. It aids in explaining why the taxation of the 'digital economy' requires such a user-based approach for the establishment of a taxable nexus while customer location can remain absent from the traditional PE definition. Furthermore, it resonates with the BEPS Project's results on transfer pricing, which declared 'value creation' the new guiding principle for the allocation of profits within multination groups of companies.[52]

From a historical perspective, a reorientation on these grounds can also be seen as falling in line with existing amendments to the PE concept launched by the OECD. These already show tendencies of facilitating the assumption of a PE in market jurisdictions, thus lowering the threshold for the existence of a taxable nexus in their favour. The probably most established extension to the 'traditional' PE definition is the dependent agent provision in Article 5 paragraph 5 OECD MC (which received considerable attention and was thoroughly modified under the BEPS Project[53]). Under this rule, a person acting on behalf of an enterprise by habitually concluding or principally preparing certain contracts in a foreign jurisdiction is sufficient for creating a taxable PE there.

Without going into detail, the concept bears some striking resemblances to core motives behind the 'digital PE' notion. A PE under Article 5 paragraph 5 OECD MC does

---

51. *See* 2015 OECD BEPS Action 1 Report, *supra* note 14, paras 164 et seq., 247 et seq., 257 et seq. and 280 et seq.; 2018 OECD Interim Report, *supra* note 7, paras 34 et seq., 139 et seq. and 386. *See also* EU Comm'n, *supra* note 4, at 1, 7 et seq.; Commission Staff Impact Assessment on Significant Digital Presence & Provision of Digital Services, *supra* note 43, at 12 et seq.
52. OECD, *Base Erosion and Profit Shifting Project Actions 8–10 Final Reports: Aligning Transfer Pricing Outcomes with Value Creation*, 3, 9 et seq. (OECD Publishing 2015). *See also* Olbert & Spengel, *supra* note 16, at 9 et seq.
53. *See* OECD, *Base Erosion and Profit Shifting Project Action 7 Final Report: Preventing the Artificial Avoidance of Permanent Establishment Status*, paras 5 et seq. (OECD Publishing 2015).

neither require any premises or fixed place of business on site[54] nor the person in question being an employee[55] so that the enterprise as taxpayer itself shows no physical presence. The resulting PE, however, is not treated any different from a regular PE under Article 5 paragraphs 1 and 2 OECD MC.[56] As the PE exemptions for preparatory and auxiliary functions in paragraph 4 explicitly also apply to dependent agents under paragraph 5, purchasing agents are generally not covered,[57] so the rule primarily benefits market jurisdictions. Overall, the provision already contains obvious elements of a 'sales location PE'. Yet again, the rationale given by the OECD stays in line with a supply-side perspective and describes dependent agents as partly involving the principal's business in their own activities,[58] thus quasi-carrying these operations to or manifesting them in the foreign jurisdiction. The consequently required close tie between the agent and the actually contracting taxpayer is further emphasized by the exemption for independent agents in Article 5 paragraph 6 OECD MC.

There are other provisions with clear intentions of establishing taxable PEs at customers' jurisdictions. The construction PE under Article 5 paragraph 3 of the OECD MC can be seen as an example, as it applies to activities not already covered by the standard PE definition.[59] The United Nations Model Double Taxation Convention[60] knows an own provision in its Article 5 paragraph 3 further extending the PE definition to the mere 'furnishing of services' if certain time requirements are met. The OECD Commentary contains a model for a similar provision, although generally advising against the inclusion of such 'service PEs'.[61] The OECD itself might, however, have made subtle moves towards easing the assumption of a PE at locations where services are provided by foreign businesses. It did so by including the (controversially received) example of a painter who spends three days a week over a two-year period working on a client's large office building as constituting a PE of the painter.[62] Yet, while all these provisions aim at creating a PE as taxable nexus in the market jurisdiction, they can still be easily justified with supply-side considerations, as they build on equipment or people present for the provision of services and attributable to the provider's operations. With the argument of 'value creation' by the users of digital services, the OECD obviously wants to retain this approach under the 'digital PE' notion as well.

Nonetheless, the 'value creation' argument as cornerstone for the taxation of the 'digital economy' is not fully convincing. The OECD itself admits that neither the use of client data nor network effects are completely unknown in 'traditional' business models and could thus be considered truly distinct features of the 'digital economy'. The importance of such factors for businesses models in the 'digital economy',

---

54. *See* Reimer, *supra* note 39, Art. 5 m.no. 310.
55. OECD Tax Convention Commentaries, *supra* note 39, Art. 5 paras 82 et seq.
56. *Ibid.* Art. 5 m.n. 310 et seq.; *see also* OECD Tax Convention Commentaries, *supra* note 39, Art. 5 paras 99 et seq.
57. *Ibid.* Art. 5 para. 85.
58. *Ibid.* para. 83.
59. *Ibid.* para. 50; *see also* Reimer, *supra* note 39, Art. 5 m.n. 176 et seq. & 399.
60. United Nations, *Model Double Taxation Convention Between Developed and Developing Countries* (United Nations 2011).
61. OECD Tax Convention Commentaries, *supra* note 39, Art. 5 paras 132 et seq.
62. *Ibid.* Art. 5 para. 17. *See critically* Reimer, *supra* note 39, Art. 5 m.n. 133 et seq. & 403.

however, is seen as being unprecedented.[63] Still, whether and to which extent users should be deemed participants in a firm's business operations is mentioned as one of the central dividing lines between the Members of the Inclusive Framework on BEPS[64] requiring further analysis.[65]

This divergence exposes a problem far more crucial than potential analogies to traditional (non-digitized) business models: 'Value creation' alone cannot satisfyingly justify any changes to generally accepted principles on the international distribution of taxation rights, as the term itself is not a fully fledged concept with a generally agreed-upon meaning.[66] One might even go further and argue that 'value creation' itself requires a definition first and thus yields no additional arguments for the issue of whether a taxable nexus should be assumed in a jurisdiction at all. The term rather just paraphrases the question of where to internationally locate the origin of business income for the purpose of taxation, so far simply referred to as 'source'. It seems highly doubtful whether 'value creation' is any distinct from the concept of 'source' as regards the rationale for the establishment of a taxable nexus.[67]

Whether labelled as 'source' or 'value creation', the terminology should not distract attention from the fundamental problem remaining unsolved. Business income generally results from combining multiple input factors, transforming them to an output and supplying this output to third parties for consideration, often multiple times in a row as long as the third party itself is not a final consumer. These 'value chain' processes are abstract economic concepts and thus per se immaterial. As was mentioned on the analogous example of the place of services before, locating the resulting income at distinct geographical points for taxation will thus always require some degree of simplifying fiction. It seems natural to derive such fictions from the locations of people and objects most closely related to each part of the process. Yet, which of these 'physical manifestations' is connected to specific portions of the income of an individual taxpayer and, in this regard, where the income sphere of one taxpayer ends and that of another one begins are mere conventions, having become principles through mutual recognition.

The currently recognized principles of income taxation in cross-border cases (as embodied in the PE definition in Article 5 OECD MC) are based on the general fiction that business profits arise where physical space at the disposal of a business is used for its operations with a certain degree of permanence.[68] Simply put, a business is assumed to generate all its income at the places, where its equipment or its personnel 'work' for the business, if such places somehow effectively 'belong' to the business and are not only used temporarily or coincidentally (i.e., are at the constant disposal of the

63. *See, e.g.*, 2015 OECD BEPS Action 1 Report, *supra* note 14, paras 166, 169, 259 & 262.
64. 2018 OECD Interim Report, *supra* note 7, para. 372.
65. *Ibid.* para. 397.
66. *See* Olbert & Spengel, *supra* note 16, at 12; Schön, *supra* note 16, at 5 & 21 et seq.
67. *See also* Johanna Hey, *'Taxation Where Value is Created' and the OECD/G20 Base Erosion and Profit Shifting Initiative*, 72 Bull. Int'l Tax'n 203, 204 (2018); Jonathan Schwarz, *Value Creation: Old Wine in New Bottles or New Wine in Old Bottles?*, http://kluwertaxblog.com/2018/05/21/value-creation-old-wine-new-bottles-new-wine-old-bottles (accessed 30 June 2018).
68. *See* OECD Tax Convention Commentaries, *supra* note 39, Art. 5 para. 6.

business[69]). This, however, does not necessarily require closeness to the market jurisdiction.[70] Deeming the criteria of 'physical presence' an assumption of such closeness seems like an over-interpretation (with demand-side orientation in mind).

The aforementioned dependent agent rule is an exemption to this principle, as the activity of a person alone (without 'space') is sufficient for the establishment of a PE. Yet, that person must be dependent on the business and thus quasi-'belong' to it as well. Ultimately, the whole process of 'value creation' is attributed to premises and contracting agents 'under the control' of a business by these principles (and even those are not always fully covered, as the still upheld exemptions for preparatory and auxiliary business functions with deemed minor importance in Article 5 paragraph 4 OECD MC prove). By design, they ignore any 'work' done or potentially 'valuable inputs' obtained outside that scope, even if they can clearly contribute to commercial success (e.g., distance selling, Television (TV) advertisement in a foreign country, occasional consultation at a client's location, inspiration coming to R&D personnel at a conference abroad).

Especially, all possibly beneficial inputs by persons or conditions not under control of the business are disregarded. A supplier's plant is not attributed to another business, even if all its production is bought by that business as the sole customer.[71] The place of origin of certain raw materials or intermediate products in general is not per se deemed part of a business, even if distinct qualities of these inputs clearly shape its own output and are crucial for its commercial success. Comparable examples can be mentioned for the other end of the 'value chain', as customers often play a vital part in enabling or facilitating a supplier's operations without being attributed to these. The delivery dock at a customer's warehouse may be used by a transportation company daily for multiple years without becoming assigned to the latter's business.[72] A consumer driving to a shop for getting a good implicitly aids the respective seller by saving her the need for delivery while still making the sale possible. Buyers of cars create the opportunity for follow-up sales of spare parts and workshop services. Viewers of commercial TV, cinemagoers or readers of newspapers enable media companies to sell valuable advertisement by providing their time and attention. Lottery participants raise the prize jackpot and thus the lottery's appeal to additional participants.

All these examples have in common that third parties somehow aid in the 'value creation' process in its entirety, however without being attributed to a business generating profit as only one step of that process under the prevalent taxation principles. Hence, value contributing factors beyond the control of the business itself are not seen as part of its own income-generating (and thus taxable) operations, even if they create the indispensable environment or prerequisites for these. Economically interpreted, profit embodies the portion of 'value created' a business can claim because it was added by factors committed to the process under its own risk and command (the

69. *Ibid.* Art. 5 paras 10 et seq.
70. *See* Schön, *supra* note 16, at 22.
71. OECD Tax Convention Commentaries, *supra* note 39, Art. 5 para. 12.
72. *Ibid.* Art. 5 para. 16.

extent of this claim of course being subject to market conditions). Against this background, these elements became natural proxies for locating the taxable income of that very business. Third parties and circumstances not at its disposal are, conversely, not attributed to its income-generating operations and thus do conceptually not attract any income of the business for the purpose of taxation.

Despite contrary assertions, 'brick and mortar' businesses are not fundamentally different from any providers of 'digital services' in this regard. The latter can also not operate in empty space, but need a minimum of physical input factors at their disposal (at least some computer equipment or working space for employees setting-up and maintaining the algorithms and systems). Even when the users of digital services are deemed to act like 'involuntary suppliers of value' to the business, they act in a generally non-coordinated manner and the 'net worth' of their contributions per se will often be almost negligible. Only when the business combines and uses these inputs to create a marketable product or service, which at one point has required 'traditional' work, will there be a remarkable appreciation in value from a traditional supply-side perspective.

Would, however, users truly be seen as 'suppliers' of an input that already has some worth, one has to raise the question why they would provide this value to the business without consideration. Generally, suppliers of raw materials are not attributed to the 'value creation' of a business not only because they do not act under its discretion but also because there is a market transaction, which delimits the supplier's business (and taxable income) from the sphere of the customers. If users are to be conceptually treated like suppliers, their motive for 'supporting' a digital service provider will not be sheer generosity. Their 'contribution' to the service is either mandatory for their own purposes (e.g., showing a photo to friends online requires its upload) or they even accept inconveniences as fair consideration (e.g., a website showing advertisements before providing access to videos free of monetary charges). No matter the exact reason, the users act in their own interest, generating 'value' primarily for themselves and not offering it 'for free'.

If user contribution is deemed to be a valuable 'raw material' to businesses in the 'digital economy', one has to justify why the users are attributed directly to the business and not taxed for their own 'profits' themselves. Taxation on such scale is obviously not viable. However, this thought leads back to the central issue. Justifying a 'digital PE' on grounds of existing profit taxation principles and traditional supply-side reasoning results in manifold inconsistencies. These are not deficiencies of the 'digital PE' notion itself, they result from treating it as something else than it actually is.

[D] The True Background: Tax Policy and the Sentiment of Revenue Lost by 'Importers' of Digital Services

Ultimately and notwithstanding all contrary assertions, the 'digital PE' concept is a fundamental move to demand-oriented income taxation. The arguments raised for its justification under feigned retention of existing principles in 'modern' form, especially the notion of 'value creation', can only pertain when demand-side factors are considered more decisive than before in international tax law. On close consideration, this also is an implicit key point separating Action 1 from large parts of the rest of the BEPS Project.[73] Businesses in the 'digital economy' may have some features beneficial for their tax planning (e.g., the possibility of easy relocation, as they do not require extensive physical premises). These, however, are the result of the nature of their operations, not primarily a result of tax considerations. Such businesses often do not 'avoid' the establishments of PEs with elaborate schemes (which are tackled by other parts of the BEPS Project); they simply have no reason to be physically present in many jurisdictions. The BEPS Action Plan already recognized this and admitted that even low taxation per se is not an indicator for deficiencies in tax law against this background.[74]

The true essence of tax challenges arising from the 'digital economy' is thus less a problem of tax law but rather a question of tax policy. Considering the arguments for special treatment of the 'digital economy' in the BEPS reports (e.g., the 'scale without mass' aspect, the monopoly tendencies or the elusive role of intellectual property rights[75]) with this in mind shows a rather obvious political reality. The 'digital economy' effects large parts of the world, but its most thriving 'big players' are few and they are unevenly spread from a global perspective. The nature of their operations allows for maintaining huge commercial influence from relatively small, local hubs. Some states find themselves in the unfamiliar role of one-sided importers as regards the digital economy. This raised awareness of the perhaps unfavourable position such jurisdictions face in international income taxation. Less need for physical input factors and the resulting growing mobility and long reach of the 'digital economy' also naturally fuel tax competition. Local providers in high-tax jurisdictions might not only face the sheer market power of a foreign 'big player', their perception of tax burden grew as competition has entered a more global scale and local proximity alone does not necessarily compensate for disadvantages of higher taxation any longer.

For an 'importing' nation seeking to establish a level playing field in income taxation from the perspective of local competition, it seems natural to push for more demand-oriented taxation. This is understandable and it is definitely a justifiable policy goal,[76] but a question of policy nonetheless.[77] However, dangerous discrepancies and legal uncertainties arise when this objective is covered under pretensions of maintaining the traditional supply-focused position of international income taxation. Circumventing the true rationale behind motions for 'digital PEs' adds a sense of dishonesty to the debate.[78] It might not be far-fetched to suppose that an open call for demand-oriented income taxation is avoided, as the jurisdictions 'importing' digital services often are exporters in the 'traditional economy' and would thus most likely face

73. *See, e.g.*, Blum, *supra* note 16, at 316; Staringer, *supra* note 16, at 348.
74. OECD, *Action Plan on Base Erosion and Profit Shifting*, 10 (OECD Publishing 2013).
75. *See, e.g.*, 2018 OECD Interim Report, *supra* note 7, paras 130 et seq.; 2015 OECD BEPS Action 1 Report, *supra* note 14, paras 151 et seq.
76. *See* Schön, *supra* note 16, at 17.
77. *Cf.* OECD Tax Convention Commentaries, *supra* note 39, Art. 5 para. 136. *See also* Staringer, *supra* note 16, at 344.
78. *See also* Schwarz, *supra* note 67.

disadvantages from a general realignment of international profit distribution rules. The large consumer markets of the future will be found in populous nations. Pushing for a demand-oriented PE, even when currently focused on the 'digital economy' only, might turn out as short-sighted strategy for established industrialized nations.

§7.03 SDP: THE 'DIGITAL PE' AS CONCRETELY PROPOSED BY THE EUROPEAN COMMISSION

[A] Legal Framework

As mentioned in the introduction, the European Commission just recently revealed its vision of the SDP, a 'digital PE' for mandatory implementation between EU Member States, as recommendation for their relationships towards third states and even as model for a global solution beyond the EU. The term SDP is not an original creation but was already used in the BEPS Action Plan[79] and the following Action 1 Deliverable 2014.[80] Interestingly, the following works did not continue that terminology.[81]

In a first step, a Council Directive should force Member States to include the SDP as an addition to their PE definitions for corporate tax purposes. By explicitly demanding an insertion into the existing PE concepts, the SDP as a solution for the taxation of the 'digital economy' should fit in smoothly with existing tax systems[82] instead of creating a new tax (like the equally proposed interim DST). Moreover, this strategy can be seen as an example for policymaker's aforementioned efforts to deny fundamental realignments of international tax distribution and belittle the paradigm shift caused by the introduction of a 'digital PE' model. The Commission's Impact Assessment does not consider the SDP a 'fundamental reform' of corporate taxation, as opposed to a destination-based cash flow tax, unitary taxation or a residence tax base with destination tax rates.[83]

The Commission bases its proposal on Article 115 of the Treaty on the Functioning of the European Union (TFEU),[84] which allows for the enactment of directives for the approximation of laws affecting the establishment or functioning of the internal market. The justification in the proposal seems rather peculiar, as the Commission depicts Article 115 TFEU ambiguously as quasi-catch-all clause for EU tax legislation not already covered by Article 113 TFEU on turnover taxes.[85] While it is true that Article

79. 2018 OECD Interim Report, *supra* note 7, at 29 & 35.
80. OECD, *Base Erosion and Profit Shifting Project: Accessing the Tax Challenges of the Digital Economy – Action 1: 2014 Deliverable*, 143 et seq. (OECD Publishing 2014) (hereinafter '2014 OECD BEPS Action 1 Deliverable').
81. 2015 OECD BEPS Action 1 Report, *supra* note 14, para. 277 refers to 'significant economic presence'; 2018 OECD Interim Report, *supra* note 7, para. 397 even more generally to 'nexus rules that would consider the impacts of Digitalization on the economy' instead.
82. 2018 SDP Directive Proposal, *supra* note 2, at 2.
83. *Ibid.* at 6; Commission Staff Impact Assessment on Significant Digital Presence & Provision of Digital Services, *supra* note 43, at 29 et seq. and 34 et seq.
84. Consolidated version of the Treaty on the Functioning of the European Union, Art. 115 OJ C 326, 26 Oct. 2012, 47.
85. 2018 SDP Directive Proposal, *supra* note 2, at 4 et seq.

115 TFEU normally is the only basis for EU legislation in the field of direct taxation,[86] it is not a general provision, but requires an effect on the internal market. The measure in question has to prevent obstructions of the EU's fundamental freedoms arising from differences in national legislation while an ancillary effect of harmonizing market conditions alone is insufficient.[87] Nonetheless, the explanations on the necessity of the SDP for the functioning of the internal market, although fundamentally required for the legitimacy of EU action, remain fairly vague and abstract. They refer to a cross-border nature of digital activities, equal treatment of taxpayers in all Member States, legal certainty and, in case the EU should not act, a multitude of ineffective unilateral measures with potentially disrupting effects for the internal market.[88]

The specific distortions of the internal market feared by the Commission, however, do not become clear, especially as even the existing PE concepts are not yet fully harmonized. While a coordinated multilateral approach in questions of international taxation undoubtedly entails benefits, it is hard to see why measures in the tax systems of individual Member States should automatically be a hindrance for the internal market, as long as fair competition between and equal treatment of all EU businesses within a certain jurisdiction is guaranteed. The European Court of Justice (ECJ), particularly in its decisions on double taxation, has repeatedly held that disadvantages arising from the individual Member States' different and uncoordinated rules on taxation are not per se restricting the fundamental freedoms that constitute the internal market, as long as they are non-discriminatory in nature. Neither is the parallel exercise of tax competences by multiple Member States alone a violation of EU law nor are Member States in any way obliged to adapt their own tax system to the systems of other states, if not required by harmonizing acts of secondary law.[89] Within these limits, Member States are *inter alia* free to determine the connecting factors for the allocation of fiscal jurisdiction in their bilateral agreements on taxation.[90] In determining the chargeable events of a tax, the taxable amount and the tax rates applicable to profits coming within their jurisdiction they are only restricted by the obligation to treat non-resident companies not discriminatory in comparison with national establishments.[91]

This ECJ case law is hardly compatible with the Commission's current standpoint on corporate taxation, which basically comes down to differences in the national tax

86. *See Commission* v *Council*, C-338/01, Judgment, EU:C:2004:253.
87. *See Germany* v *Parliament and Council*, C-380/03, Judgment, EU:C:2006:772, paras 36 et seq.; *Arnold André*, C-434/02, Judgment, EU:C:2004:800, paras 29 et seq.; *Germany* v *Parliament and Council*, C-376/98, Judgment, EU:C:2006:772, paras 81 et seq.; *Parliament* v *Council*, C-187/93, Judgment, EU:C:1994:265, para. 25.
88. 2018 SDP Directive Proposal, *supra* note 2, at 5.
89. *See, e.g.*, *NN(L)*, C-48/15, Judgment, EU:C:2016:356, para. 47; *X*, C-302/12, Judgment, EU:C:2013:756, paras 28 et seq.; *Banco Bilbao Vizcaya Argentaria*, C-366/10, Judgment, EU:C:2011:864, para. 31; *Block*, C-67/08, Judgment, EU:C:2009:92, paras 28 et seq.
90. *See, e.g.*, *Beker*, C-168/11, Judgment, EU:C:2013:117, para. 32; *Renneberg*, C-527/06, Judgment, EU:C:2008:566, para. 48.
91. *See, e.g.*, *X*, C-68/15, Judgment, EU:C:2017:379, para. 41; *Test Claimants in the FII Group Litigation*, C-446/04, Judgment, EU:C:2006:774, paras 123 et seq.; *Kerckhaert & Morres*, C-513/04, Judgment, EU:C:2006:713, paras 19 et seq.

systems themselves already being considered distortions to the internal market.[92] A likewise premise seems to be required for understanding why the SDP should have to be implemented uniformly in all Member States in order for the internal market to function. If different rules on taxation in different Member States and even double taxation are not per se seen as distortions to the internal market (in line with the ECJ's view), there seems to be no reason for prohibiting even partly different national strategies (or bilateral agreements) on the taxation of the 'digital economy'. It, e.g., would not distort the internal market if some Member States simply decided to generally not implement the SDP concept and retain their current PE definitions. Profits elsewise allocated to such countries by the SDP rules would simply remain taxable in the taxpayer's residence country. This would not even fuel tax competition between Member States beyond the existence of different tax rates, which explicitly remain permitted either way.[93]

The true reason for the necessity of EU legislation on the SDP might again be found in policy rather than sophisticated legal assessments. The SDP could hardly become the global model the Commission envisions it to be, if it was not even generally established throughout the EU. Moreover, an EU directive seems highly attractive from the perspective of those Member States pushing for the introduction of 'digital PEs' in their national tax laws. While unilateral moves are not prohibited by EU law, these states most likely face the problem of having entered into double taxation conventions preventing them from raising taxes for a purely 'digital PE'. The SDP directive saves these states the difficulties of having to renegotiate (or breach) their intra-EU tax treaties by acting as a general, yet lawful 'treaty override' for all cases between Member States.[94]

Joint and public action on the EU level might also raise pressure on Member States where companies affected by 'digital PE' provisions reside.[95] As these countries will potentially see parts of their tax base eroded, their willingness to change their tax treaties in bilateral negotiations might not be grand. However, Article 115 TFEU requires unanimity in the Council, so the pressure to accept the SDP proposal is again more political than legal in nature. At the same time, this prerequisite of unanimity practically relativizes the question whether Article 115 TFEU provides sufficient basis for EU legislation.

---

92. *See, e.g.*, European Commission, *Proposal for a Council Directive on a Common Corporate Tax Base*, 4 et seq. (25 October 2016), COM(2016) 685 final.
93. 2018 SDP Directive Proposal, *supra* note 2, at 5.
94. *Ibid.* at 3. This power of a directive results from the primacy of EU over national legislation in case of conflict as originally developed by the ECJ in *Costa* v *E.N.E.L.*, 6/64, Judgment, EU:C:1964:66. The resulting derogation of national provisions also applies to transnational treaties between EU Member States. For a comprehensive review, *see, e.g.*, Georg Kofler, *Doppelbesteuerungsabkommen und Europäisches Gemeinschaftsrecht*, 265 et seq. (Linde 2007).
95. The respective intra-EU disparities are, e.g., mentioned by Commission Staff Impact Assessment on Significant Digital Presence & Provision of Digital Services, *supra* note 43, at 41 et seq.

[B] Territorial Scope

In accordance with the legal framework just described, the SDP will primarily be applicable in relations between EU Member States. Article 2 of the proposed directive generally covers all entities, whether resident within the EU or in a third state for purposes of corporate taxation. This wide scope, however, is followed by an exemption for all entities resident in third countries that have entered into double taxation conventions vis-a-vis the Member State concerned, if these treaties do not (yet) contain provisions similar to the SDP.[96] This restriction was deemed necessary, as such double taxation conventions might overrule the national SDP provisions[97] and Member States should not be forced to breach their treaties.[98] The residence of a taxpayer for application of the SDP rules will thus have to be determined not under a Member State's national law, but after considering respective treaty provision (e.g., a 'tie-breaker provision' for dual-residents akin to Article 4 paragraph 3 OECD MC), even though these usually apply on the treaty level only.[99]

Actually, the restraint might less be driven by the *pacta sunt servanda* principle than the EU's severely limited authority over tax treaties between Member States and third states[100] (especially as the functioning of the internal market can hardly be invoked in these constellations). This is the likely reason why the Commission's plan is restricted to a mere non-binding recommendation[101] for SDP amendments to the bilateral tax treaties of EU members with third states.

As EU Member States usually maintain extensive networks of such conventions even with non-EU jurisdictions, the SDP will primarily result in shifts of taxable profits between Member States and not substantially enlarge the total 'EU tax base' by attracting large profits from businesses in third states. While there might also be intra-EU discrepancies between the locations of 'digital service' users and the tax residences of companies providing these services,[102] public attention usually revolves primarily around taxation of non-EU enterprises with presumed high profitability and low tax burden like Alphabet (the holding company of Google), Apple, Facebook or Amazon. The SDP Directive, however, will overwhelmingly not affect the majority of such cases. Only intra-EU tax competition or deemed unfair profit allocation might be fought. In the worst case, the SDP Directive could lead to companies relocating their residence to non-EU jurisdictions to avoid distribution of their taxable profits to multiple tax jurisdictions within the EU under the SDP provisions.

---

96. *See* 2018 SDP Directive Proposal, *supra* note 2, at 14 (proposed Art. 2).
97. *Ibid.* at 4.
98. *Ibid.* at 7.
99. *See* OECD Tax Convention Commentaries, *supra* note 39, Art. 4 para. 7.
100. *See* for a comprehensive analysis Kofler, *supra* note 94, at 288 et seq.
101. EU Comm'n, *supra* note 5.
102. *See* EU Comm'n, *supra* note 43, 41 et seq.

[C] Material Scope: 'Digital Services Through Digital Interfaces'

While most 'digital PE' concepts share similar objectives and general principles, the question which services and businesses are to be covered by such provisions in detail is essential and far from trivial. It implicitly requires policymakers to leave the realm of keywords behind and take a concrete stand on what they consider the 'digital economy', for which existing PE rules are deemed insufficient, and how to distinguish it from 'traditional' business models.

The OECD/G20's BEPS Action 1 Reports already elaborately demonstrate that it is relatively straightforward to describe the 'digital economy' by looking at specific and well-known examples and identifying similarities between them. These elaborations also show that the 'digital economy' can be thought of as having two facets, the digitization of existing 'offline' business models (e.g., online retailing or online payment services) and the emergence of radically new commercial concepts 'born' from digitization and impossible without widespread computer networks (e.g., social networks or cloud computing).[103] The line between these two sectors is, however, a blurred one.

There will hardly be any businesses with cross-border operations not making commercial use of the Internet in any way (at least as means of communication) even in the most 'traditional' industries. On the other end, some 'traditional' business models have so profoundly changed due to the possibilities offered by modern technology that they are barely still comparable to their 'offline equivalents' (e.g., online advertising personalized to individual consumer preferences using elaborate automatized analysis of user data). Thus, it might be more suitable to imagine the modern economy as a continuum of commercial activities ranging from less to more focus and dependency on digital technology. As the OECD/G20 accurately hold: 'The digital economy is increasingly becoming the economy itself.'[104]

The blurred borders of the 'digital economy' pose a fundamental problem to policymakers with the objective of designing a 'digital PE' only for specific business models they want to cover. They need to find a general definition embracing these businesses while keeping the existing PE concepts in place for the rest of the economy as to not risk complete realignments of taxation rights. The OECD/G20 expressed their concerns that such attempts of 'ring-fencing the digital economy' would be impossible or require arbitrary lines to be drawn.[105] Nonetheless, the fundamental issue from a legal perspective is not the creation of special provisions for taxpayers in a specific situation per se, as certain circumstances justifiably call for modifications of more

103. *See* 2014 OECD BEPS Action 1 Deliverable, *supra* note 80, at 69 et seq.; 2015 OECD BEPS Action 1 Report, *supra* note 14, paras 116 et seq.; 2018 OECD Interim Report, *supra* note 7, paras 100 et seq.
104. 2014 OECD BEPS Action 1 Deliverable, *supra* note 80, at 73; 2015 OECD BEPS Action 1 Report, *supra* note 14, para. 115.
105. 2014 OECD BEPS Action 1 Deliverable, *supra* note 80, at 73; 2015 OECD BEPS Action 1 Report, *supra* note 14, para. 115. *See also* 2018 OECD Interim Report, *supra* note 7, para. 375.

general rules. The challenge, however, is that these special provisions should still fall in line with the general principles and structures of international tax law.[106]

After all, even the OECD/G20's statements on the undesirability of 'ring-fencing' prove quite hollow. The BEPS Action 1 Reports themselves go great lengths to identify features distinguishing the 'digital economy' or 'more digitalized business models' from the rest of the economy,[107] which would hardly be necessary without any desire for legal separation. Furthermore, the reported concepts for a new and extended taxable nexus under the PE label contain elements perceptibly limiting the scope of such provisions to certain 'digital activities';[108] a necessity, when a general shift of the PE concept to demand-oriented factors is not intended.[109] The Members of the Inclusive Framework on BEPS, however, hold divergent views on whether such a set of specific rules tailored to the 'digital economy' is required.[110]

The European Commission's full plan for the 'taxation of the digital economy' interestingly follows two different alternatives for determining the scope of operations covered. The interim DST should apply to three exhaustively enumerated types of digital services only, namely personalized online advertising, multi-sided digital intermediary platforms (e.g., electronic market places), and sales of user data.[111] The SDP proposal follows the opposite approach and relies on a broad general definition of activities covered, followed by specific (non-exhaustive) examples and exemptions. A business can maintain a SDP, when it supplies 'digital services through a digital interface'.[112] A 'digital interface' is simply defined as any piece of software (including websites and mobile applications) directly accessible to end users, whether these are individuals or businesses.[113] 'Digital services' generally encompass all services which are delivered over computer networks, would be impossible to provide without information technology, and are designed to be rendered essentially automatically with minimal human intervention on the side of the supplier.[114]

This definition of 'digital services' is not a novel one. Its origins trace back to EU legislation on the common value added tax (VAT) system,[115] where it defines the term 'electronically supplied services'. This term and the 'digital services' under the SDP

106. *See* Schön, *supra* note 16, at 6 et seq.
107. *See, e.g.*, the conclusions in 2014 OECD BEPS Action 1 Deliverable, *supra* note 80, at 84 et seq.; 2015 OECD BEPS Action 1 Report, *supra* note 14, paras 151 et seq.; 2018 OECD Interim Report, *supra* note 7, paras 130 et seq.
108. 2014 OECD BEPS Action 1 Deliverable, *supra* note 80, at 143 et seq. proposes an *a priori* limitation to 'fully dematerialized digital activities'. 2015 OECD BEPS Action 1 Report, *supra* note 14, paras 281 et seq. recommends a combination of revenue factors with digital or user-based factors as a threshold for new PE concepts, thus making a seemingly neutral PE provision effectively applicable to certain forms of digital operations only.
109. *See* already §7.02[C] *supra*.
110. *See* 2018 OECD Interim Report, *supra* note 7, paras 388 et seq.
111. *See* with further details 2018 DST Directive Proposal, *supra* note 11, at 7 et seq. & 24 et seq. (proposed Art. 3).
112. 2018 SDP Directive Proposal, *supra* note 2, at 16 (proposed Art. 3).
113. *Ibid.* at 14 (proposed Art. 3 paras 2 and 4).
114. *Ibid.* at 7 & 14 et seq. (proposed Art. 3 para. 5).
115. Council Implementing Regulation (EU) No 282/2011 laying down implementing measures for Directive 2006/112/EC on the common system of value added tax, Art. 7 [2011] OJ L 77.

Directive are intended to include the same kind of services.[116] Even the exemplary list of services particularly covered by the definition and the list of exemptions[117] (partly moved to annexes[118]) are copied word by word from that VAT provision. It has to be noted, though, that the VAT provision is used in its original form ignoring subsequent amendments.[119] The SDP definition of 'digital services' thus differs in detail from the VAT definition as currently in force.

One aspect the SDP proposal adds to the original VAT definition is an explicit exemption for sales of (regular) goods or services, which are merely 'facilitated' by using digital networks. Thus, the SDP Directive should cover the provision of access to a digital market place, but not the sales concluded there. The Commission considers this essential, as the SDP should not establish a taxable nexus based on the place of consumption only.[120] This clearly stated objective, however, makes the borrowing of the 'digital services' definition from VAT, a consumption tax, without any fundamental adaptions seem somewhat contradictory.

Indeed, the treatment of software and digital versions of media content (e.g., e-books, electronic versions of newspapers, music or movies) seems inconsistent, considering the Commission explicitly wants the SDP concept not to cover 'mere' sales of goods and services, even when conducted online. The supply of digitized products generally, however, is, deemed a 'digital service'.[121] Providing access to or downloads of software, the digitized content of books, photographs, music, films or games are *inter alia* listed as particular examples.[122] However, supplying the same content on physical media (e.g., a data disc) is exempt (even in cases of distance selling).[123] Therefore, not the material content provided by a seller but the way of delivery or transmission determines whether this sale is covered by the SDP rules. This becomes particularly notable in cases of online retailers offering the same product (e.g., a certain music album, book or video game) on one webpage in different formats as downloadable or 'physical' version (e.g., an audiobook as download or on compact disc).

One could argue that downloads of 'digital goods' can often be processed fully automatized and over far distances once the basic system is set up while the delivery of physical media with the same content usually still requires 'brick and mortar' business operations like storage and transport. Human contribution and physical proximity to a client's location may still be beneficial for such operations, thus making them more likely to establish a 'traditional PE' close to the market jurisdiction. Such justification of the SDP, however, revealed quite obviously a reorientation of tax policy

116. 2018 SDP Directive Proposal, *supra* note 2, at 7.
117. *Ibid.* at 14 et seq. (proposed Art. 3 para. 5).
118. EU Comm'n, Annexes to the Proposal for a Council Directive laying down rules relating to the corporate taxation of a significant digital presence, 2 et seq. COM(2018) 147 final (hereinafter '2018 SDP Directive Proposal Annexes').
119. Council Implementing Regulation (EU) No 1042/2013 amending Implementing Regulation (EU) No 282/2011 as regards the place of supply of services, Art. 1 [2013] OJ L 284.
120. 2018 SDP Directive Proposal, *supra* note 2, at 7.
121. *Ibid.* at 14 (proposed Art. 3 para. 5(a)).
122. 2018 SDP Directive Proposal Annexes Taxation, *supra* note 118, at 2 (Annex II, points (f), (l), (m), (t), (v), (w)).
123. *Ibid.* at 3 (Annex III, points (d)–(h)).

towards a more market-, demand- or destination-based income taxation. The current key argument for the introduction of 'digital PEs', namely user's contribution to 'value creation'[124] or the role of intellectual property,[125] can hardly be raised in defence of a different treatment of downloads vis-à-vis physical copies of the same content. For the users, downloading is just a way of transmission but does not fundamentally change their involvement in the service. The intellectual property embodied in the content provided and monetarized by the business is also the same in both cases (only the digital platform providing and processing the downloads might constitute an additional intellectual property element).

Except the (policy-driven) desire for the establishment of a PE at or close to the place of consumption, there barely seems to be any justification for specific provisions on downloads in income taxation. The profit arising from the (distance) sale of digital content does not change its nature and origin, whether that content is transferred by download or delivery of a storage medium. The proposed directive aims to avoid application of the SDP concept to mere sales of goods or services just because the transaction is 'facilitated by using the Internet'.[126] Using the Internet as a quasi-means of transportation in essence also facilitates the underlying transaction without fundamentally changing the 'product'. The content itself usually is at the parties' central interest and embodies the actual 'value' transferred. Singling out profits from downloads just because they can more easily be provided remotely would barely be different from distinguishing between profits from sales 'ex-works' and profits from distance selling.

Under the EU's common VAT system, which differs between the 'supply of goods' and the 'supply of services',[127] different treatment of downloads and delivery of the same content on physical media may, however, be reasonable. Nevertheless, even in the area of VAT, one of the Commission's proposals presently under debate pushes for the possibility of equal treatment of downloads and physical media: E-publications (e.g., e-books) as 'electronically provided services' currently fall under the standard VAT rates while Member States may apply a reduced rate to printed books, newspapers and periodicals. As both, cross-border sales of goods and electronic services have gradually been redesigned to be taxable at the same place (consumer's location) and tax competition for the lowest VAT rate is thus no longer a prime concern, the mandatory unequal treatment of e-publications and printed content is considered outdated. The Commission explicitly mentions that both formats offer the same content for users.[128] Yet again, given the statutory place of consumption is unaffected by the 'style of delivery', the Commission itself does not recognize any material difference in the content provided that would justify different tax treatment. As the designated aim of the SDP is not to focus on the place of consumption only, one might

124. *See* §7.02[C] *supra*.
125. *See, e.g.*, 2018 OECD Interim Report, *supra* note 7, paras 135 et seq.
126. 2018 SDP Directive Proposal, *supra* note 2, at 15 (proposed Art. 3 para. 5 final sentence).
127. Council Directive 2006/112/EC on the common system of value added tax, Art. 2 para. 1(a) and (c) and Arts 14 et seq. and 24 et seq. [2006] OJ L 347, 11.
128. *See* EU Comm'n, Proposal for a Council Directive amending Directive 2006/112/EC, as regards rates of value added tax applied to books, newspapers and periodicals, 2 COM(2016) 758 final.

ask why such a differentiation deemed outdated in consumption taxation should be upheld for purposes of income taxation.

Nonetheless, this differentiation is not the only inconsistency resulting from adopting the VAT definition to the SDP concept. From the perspective of consumption taxation, it might be appropriate to treat a multitude of services which are accessed online as 'electronically supplied services' since these services are 'consumed' regardless of the degree of user involvement. When using the 'value created' by users as the central justification for attributing parts of the provider's profit to these users' locations, however, the usefulness of user input to the business has to be judged by higher standards. Besides the already mentioned software and media downloads, the list of services explicitly covered by the SDP proposal currently contains entries like search engines, subscriptions to online newspapers or journals, online news, traffic information and weather reports, information automatically generated based on user input (e.g., financial or legal information), access to automated online games or online teaching without human intervention.[129] In none of these examples is a user necessarily more than a passive consumer, who accesses certain information or entertainment.

One might rightly argue that these accesses create possibilities for interest-related advertising. However, so do newspapers, magazines, cinema attendances, TV and radio channels, waiting areas etc. without being seen as benefitting from consumer input.[130] Online services naturally create additional possibilities for the provider. User's interests can be traced or are revealed by their inputs and the service may be enhanced or advertisement targeted. This, however, does not apply to all the examples listed above. An online weather service will hardly be able to tailor its content to special interests or improve its forecasts based on user data. Moreover, simple user 'clicks' barely go beyond mere sales figures (e.g., for analysing the frequented sections of an online news service) as available to many businesses. Simply observing customers in their passive consumption or using their attention does not make them 'value creators'. This assessment might change, when user data is analysed with elaborated algorithms so that individualized offers or advertising can be presented in large scale (or sold for that purpose). However, if that were the true grounds for taxation, it would be more reasonable to limit the SDP's scope to such data collection and use (as under the DST proposal) rather than all sorts of online content that might theoretically allow for user tracing.

The examples also raise the question of which level of human involvement is required in order for a service to not be rendered essentially automated (and thus falling outside the scope of the proposed SDP Directive). Again, the answer is relatively straightforward for a consumption tax as one can ask whether the specific addressee receives some kind of notable human output (e.g., an individual answer compared to a generic piece of news). The SDP proposal, however, refers to human intervention on

129. 2018 SDP Directive Proposal Annexes, *supra* note 118, at 2 (Annex II, points (n), (p), (q), (s), (x), (y), (z)).

130. Some of these are even explicitly exempt from the definitions in the SDP proposal; *see* 2018 SDP Directive Proposal Annexes, *supra* note 118, at 3 (Annex III, points (a), (e), (m)).

the side of the supplier in its explanatory remarks.[131] Online newspapers with articles written by individuals, e.g., encompass extensive and regular human input with only the following 'online distribution' to the readers happening mostly automatized. The core operations on part of the supplier are barely 'machine work', yet the SDP proposal mentions online newspapers as particular examples for 'digital activities'.[132]

All this leads back to the conclusions already reached in the section on the rationale for 'digital PEs' and confirms these to a certain degree. The SDP Proposal attempts to hide a 'consumption shift' of income taxation but copies the scope of 'digital activities' covered from consumption taxation and thus (*inter alia*) contains clear elements of taxation at the place of consumption. The issues demonstrated can hardly be justified on the grounds of income taxation. Particularly, the services that might establish a SDP are in large parts not based on any form of 'value creation' from their users, although that very concept serves as the central argument for the SDP proposal and the creation of a new taxable nexus as a whole.[133]

[D] Thresholds for Establishing a SDP

The 'traditional' PE is often viewed as functioning as a threshold provision, marking the point at which the economic activities of a foreign business within a jurisdiction have reached a level of solidification that justifies taxation. This generally requires certain degrees of geographical and temporal permanency as well as discretionary power of the taxpayer.[134] Setting such minimum threshold for source taxation rights entails multiple benefits, which should not be completely forgone under a 'digital PE' rule, e.g., avoiding costs and legal uncertainty for both taxpayers and administrations or an excessive fragmentation of the taxable base in case of only insignificant or hardly assessable contact to an economy.[135]

As such notions generally try to leave physical criteria behind while maintaining the idea of applying to 'significant' activities within a market jurisdiction only, they usually propose different kinds of thresholds. Examples (that may be combined) include, e.g., numbers of users (or share of the population) of a digital service within a foreign country, the volume of data collected on these users, the number of contracts concluded with or payments received from customers in such country, the amounts of revenue generated within or attributable to a jurisdiction. Potential criteria could also focus on whether the service is tailored to customers in a certain jurisdiction (e.g., by offering local language, support or payment options).[136]

The European Commission's SDP proposal knows three alternative thresholds to be applied to the 'digital services' of a business as a whole. Exceeding one or more of

131. 2018 SDP Directive Proposal, *supra* note 2, at 7.
132. EU Comm'n, *supra* note 118, at 2 (Annex II, point (n)).
133. 2018 SDP Directive Proposal, *supra* note 2, at 2 & 9.
134. *See, e.g.*, OECD Tax Convention Commentaries, *supra* note 39, Art. 5 para. 6; Reimer, *supra* note 39, Art. 5 m.no. 2; Gaoua, *supra* note 18, at 11; Blum, *supra* note 16, at 315 et seq.
135. *See, e.g.*, Hongler & Pistone, *supra* note 16, at 23.
136. *Ibid.* at 24 et seq.; *see also* 2014 OECD BEPS Action 1 Deliverable, *supra* note 80, at 144 et seq.; 2015 OECD BEPS Action 1 Report, *supra* note 14, paras 277 et seq.

these limits within a Member State in one tax period establishes a SDP there. These thresholds are:[137]

(1) The local share of revenue exceeding EUR 7 million. Total revenue includes all forms of regular and one-time benefits arising from the provision of 'digital services' (net of VAT and duties).[138] Subsequently, this number is divided by the total number of times devices accessed the services worldwide and multiplied by the number of users within a Member State.
(2) The number of users in a Member State exceeding 100,000.
(3) The number of contracts with business users in a Member State exceeding 3,000.

For all these thresholds, user location is decisive. Unfortunately, only the statutory location of business users for purposes of the third threshold is clearly defined. Business users are resident in a Member State, if they are residents for purposes of corporate taxation either there or in a third state, but maintain a PE in the Member State.[139] However, the treatment of individuals running a business and being liable to income tax is left open. As business contracts cover all contracts concluded in the course of carrying on business,[140] it would be nonsensical to exclude income tax payers. The general 'user' definition, however, seems to distinguish between individuals and businesses.[141] Moreover, the taxes covered by the term 'corporate taxes' are exhaustively listed in an Annex.[142]

An even more problematic ambiguity lies within the definition of general user location, as applying to individuals and businesses for the first two of the aforementioned thresholds. A user should be deemed to be located in a Member State, if she 'uses a device' for accessing the service there.[143] The device location should be judged based on the IP address or any other more accurate method of geolocation. Leaving the (disputed) possibilities of IP-based geolocation aside for the time being,[144] the proposal does not define the 'use of a device' that serves as proxy for user location. It especially does not contain a clear rule on how to treat multiple uses of one device or *vice versa* one user accessing a single service with multiple devices. The general provision in the proposed Article 4 paragraph 4 seems to focus primarily on the individual 'user'. Therefore, one identifiable user may count as 'one' user in every Member State she uses at least one device to access the service. This seems to correspond closest with the envisioned threshold of 100,000 users. However, short-term stays of such people in other countries would raise the 'user count' there. This method of counting is also

137. 2018 SDP Directive Proposal, *supra* note 2, at 16 (proposed Art. 4 para. 3).
138. *Ibid.* at 15 (proposed Art. 3 para. 6).
139. *Ibid.* at 16 et seq. (proposed Art. 4 para. 5(b)).
140. *Ibid.* at 16 (proposed Art. 4 para. 5(a)).
141. *Ibid.* at 14 (proposed Art. 3 para. 4).
142. 2018 SDP Directive Proposal, *supra* note 2, at 14 (proposed Art. 3 para. 1); 2018 SDP Directive Proposal Annexes, *supra* note 118, at 1 (Annex I).
143. 2018 SDP Directive Proposal, *supra* note 2, at 16 (proposed Art. 4 para. 4).
144. *See, e.g.*, James Muir & Paul van Oorschot, *Internet Geolocation: Evasion and Counterevasion*, 42 CSUR Art. 4 (2009).

unreliable when a service requires no user identification or allows for multiple accounts per person or one account for multiple persons. Multiple users could be counted as 'one' because they use the same device or account; single users could be counted repeatedly because they run multiple accounts and/or devices.

Nonetheless, the proposed provision on revenue attribution for the first thresholds mentions the worldwide 'number of times that devices are used ... by users' as baseline value for comparison with the 'users' in a Member State.[145] This wording indicates a rather different approach, where each individual device or maybe even every individual use of a device is the key element. The questions resulting from this are manifold. If a single computer is used to access a digital service three times daily, the resulting 'user count' could range anywhere from one (as it is the same device) to 1,095 (the number of individual accesses in one year). If each device were counted once, users of multiple devices or devices used by multiple people would again distort the relevant figures. If devices are counted repeatedly 'per use', a time span has to be defined after which a 'new use' begins, should 'page refreshes' or frequent logons and logoffs not count as individual uses. Therefore, both approaches, whether primary based on 'users' or of 'number of times that devices are used' seem to be in dire need of further clarification. As both enter the same calculation for the revenue threshold, it is at least necessary to define a common standard of measurement.

Notably, the Commission decided to propose fixed thresholds and not leave room for adaptions to the size of the individual Member States. A 'digital service' would thus require relatively less market share in larger jurisdictions for establishing a SDP there. Such jurisdictions potentially benefitted the most from the SDP notion. Almost 25% of Malta's population would have to be counted as 'users' for establishing an SDP based on the user threshold while a little more than a thousandth of the German population would already suffice. The Commission justifies the fixed limits and their height with considerations on the compliance costs of establishing a SDP. The thresholds should not follow any ratio but signify levels of commercial activity that allow for handling tax liability under an additional jurisdiction.[146]

'Associated enterprises' are treated as a single entity for applying the thresholds.[147] This generally concerns cases, in which one enterprise has a significant impact over or holds a share of more than 20% (directly or indirectly) in another.[148] As all 'digital services' of a business are evaluated jointly under the proposed SDP Directive, minor online activities of members within a group might already establish SDPs in multiple jurisdictions, if another member already exceeds one threshold with a certain service. While a division of service provision between related businesses should of course not render the thresholds ineffective, this seems to contradict the Commission's generally proclaimed aim to ensure reasonable levels of compliance costs for taxpayers with the proposed thresholds.

145. 2018 SDP Directive Proposal, *supra* note 2, at 17 (proposed Art. 4 para. 7).
146. 2018 SDP Directive Proposal, *supra* note 2, at 8.
147. *Ibid.* at 16 (proposed Art. 4 para. 3).
148. *Ibid.* at 15 et seq. (proposed Art. 3 para. 9).

[E] Profit Attribution to an Established SDP

When a Member State finds that a foreign business falling within the territorial scope of the proposed SDP directive has exceeded at least one of the statutory thresholds with covered 'digital services' within its jurisdiction, it can assume a SDP to exist. The SDP is to be treated like any 'traditional PE'.[149] This means *inter alia* that the SDP sets the grounds for taxation rights but does not yet create a taxable base that ultimately decides the tax burden faced by the business in (and revenue generated by) that state. Thus, the question of profit attribution to a SDP (as under Article 7 OECD MC) arises in a second, no less essential step. This touches on the field of transfer pricing for the 'digital economy', which itself is still far from providing well-developed answers to the issues raised by such business models (even under the existing principles of international taxation).[150]

Scholarly works have repeatedly pointed out that the establishment of 'digital PE' provisions would have to be accompanied by fundamental revisions in the field of profit attribution to PEs. Without going into every detail, the currently accepted principles largely focus on the assumption that a PE is treated like a stand-alone enterprise dealing at arm's length with the other parts of the business. This initially requires an analysis and allocation of the functions, assets and risks of the business as 'forces of attraction' for apportioning the taxable profit between its parts in the residence state and one or more PEs. The starting point of these considerations, however, generally are 'significant people functions', i.e., actual activities performed by individuals working for the business. As a 'digital PE' is more or less defined by not having any physical input factors or personnel in the jurisdiction concerned, applying these standards would result in little to no taxable profit attributed to it and essentially render the whole concept meaningless.[151] The OECD/G20's works also recognized this problem.[152]

While the explanatory statement on the SDP proposal proclaims to set out the principles for profit attribution to a SDP,[153] the actual provisions are barely more than general guidelines. Largely, they just repeat the aforementioned standards, especially the dealing-at-arm's-length principle.[154] The analysis of the functions of the SDP, however, should focus on the 'economically significant activities performed' rather than on 'significant people functions'.[155] For judging these 'economically significant

149. *Ibid.* at 16 (proposed Art. 4 para. 1).
150. *See, e.g.*, Olbert & Spengel, *supra* note 16, at 31 et seq.
151. *See, e.g.*, Hongler & Pistone, *supra* note 16, at 32 et seq.; Schön, *supra* note 16, at 24 et seq.; Blum, *supra* note 16, at 322 et seq.; Staringer, *supra* note 16, at 349; Kofler, *supra* note 16, at 529.
152. *See*, 2015 OECD BEPS Action 1 Report, *supra* note 14, paras 284 et seq.; 2018 OECD Interim Report, *supra* note 7, paras 378 & 397.
153. 2018 SDP Directive Proposal, *supra* note 2, at 3.
154. *Ibid.* at 17 (proposed Art. 5 para. 2).
155. *Ibid.* at 8 et seq. and 17 (proposed Art. 5 para. 3).

activities', the development, enhancement, maintenance, protection and exploitation of intangible assets should be considered.[156] The proposed directive also provides examples. These show more similarity to the DST than the SDP proposal, as user data and user-generated content, online advertising space, and digital marketplaces are mentioned. Nonetheless, the list ends with a quasi-catch-all phrase referring to 'any digital service not listed' before.[157] Ultimately, the actual profit distribution should be based on the profit split method, if the taxpayer cannot offer a more appropriate internationally accepted method. The splitting factors may include expenses for R&D and marketing as well as the number of users and amount of data collected per state.[158] The Commission admits that these rules are only general principles and specific guidelines would have to be developed.[159]

The proposed rules for profit attribution barely go beyond the very basics that can be derived from the SDP concept itself, including the factors relevant for its establishments and thresholds. Even the eventually dictated profit split method essentially results from a process of elimination, as none of the other established transfer pricing methods yields results suitable for a 'digital PE' in the absence of physical input factors and considering the importance of intangible factors.[160] However, it should not be understated that this comes down to an 'upfront income allocation of a partial profit to the market jurisdiction'.[161] Whether such a bold move can realistically succeed from a policy perspective seems highly doubtful.[162] As the profit split method is also not a standard choice for profit attribution to 'traditional PEs', the further issue of equal treatment of such PEs and SDPs arises.[163] This is exacerbated by the SDP proposal's strategy of adding the SDP notion to existing PE concepts and applying both parallel,[164] potentially even to the same taxpayer.

Overall, the question of profit attribution to a SDP seems far from a comprehensive solution. However, as it is ultimately decisive for the tax base that market jurisdictions might attract with the SDP notion, its relevance is obvious. Many of the conceptual issues that seem unclear in the provisions on the establishments of SDPs will re-emerge here. Especially the question of 'value created' by user contribution has to be answered, now even requiring facts and numbers rather than general considerations. It will come down to a debate on whether the 'providers' or the 'exploiters' of user data are the key value creators. Even if the SDP notion in general is pushed through, market jurisdictions could find themselves not getting the tax revenues from the 'digital economy' they hoped for, when the generally accepted profit attribution rules are not changed accordingly.

156. *Ibid.* at 17 (proposed Art. 5 para. 4).
157. *Ibid.* at 17 (proposed Art. 5 para. 5).
158. *Ibid.* at 18 (proposed Art. 5 para. 6).
159. *Ibid.* at 9.
160. Hongler & Pistone, *supra* note 16, at 32 et seq.; Olbert & Spengel, *supra* note 16, at 40 et seq.
161. *Ibid.* at 33.
162. Staringer, *supra* note 16, at 349.
163. *See, e.g.*, Schön, *supra* note 16, at 25 et seq.; Kofler, *supra* note 16, at 529.
164. 2018 SDP Directive Proposal, *supra* note 2, at 16 (proposed Art. 4 para. 2).

§7.04 RÉSUMÉ

While 'digital PE' notions for establishing a taxable nexus without physical presence of a business in income taxation are far from new concepts, they have recently received considerable attention *inter alia* as parts of the BEPS project. While the OECD still debates on whether to implement such nexus, the European Commission launched a concrete proposal in the form of a proposed SDP Directive. An introduction of a 'digital PE' would realign international profit taxation to demand-oriented or destination-based factors. Policymakers, however, try justifying 'digital PEs' with existing principles focusing on operations of the supplying businesses for the distribution of taxation rights (e.g., by raising the argument of 'value created' for businesses by the users of digital services). The combination of fundamental demand orientation with seemingly supply-side reasoning leads to manifold inconsistencies and open questions in the 'digital PE' concepts. This also applies to the SDP proposal, which, e.g., copies definitions from VAT resulting in a hardly justifiable scope of services covered and does not solve the questions of profit attribution to the 'digital PE' established under its provisions. The legal debate would certainly benefit from treating the motive of enhancing taxation rights for market jurisdictions more openly. Such openness, however, is unlikely, as general shifts to demand-oriented income taxation would be unfavourable for nations that are 'exporters' outside the sectors of the 'digital economy'.

CHAPTER 8

Tax Treatment of Digital Currencies

Michael Tumpel & Johannes Kofler

§8.01 WHAT ARE DIGITAL CURRENCIES?

The term 'currency' refers to 'something (such as coins, treasury notes and banknotes) that is in circulation as a medium of exchange'[1] or, more simply, to money. Whereas currencies can be traced back to Sumer – the earliest known civilization in the historical region of southern Mesopotamia – and Ancient Egypt,[2] digital currencies are a rather new phenomenon. The idea of digital money (sometimes called 'cryptocurrency') goes back to a research paper from 1983,[3] but it took another twenty-five years for it to break through.

In 2008, a person or group of persons, under the pseudonym Satoshi Nakamoto, put forward a solution[4] to a century-old problem of bookkeeping: if one uses a single ledger for all transactions, one must trust the central authority that controls the ledger. Alternatively, if one uses many individual ledgers with none of them having any priority, there is no way to achieve consensus when they show deviations. The proposed solution – blockchain – is a procedure that provides access to a trustworthy network of ledgers without any central authority – and its security is guaranteed by a novel cryptographic protocol.

1. Merriam-Webster Dictionary, https://www.merriam-webster.com/dictionary/currency (accessed 29 October 2018).
2. https://en.wikipedia.org/wiki/History_of_money.
3. David Chaum, *Blind Signatures for Untraceable Payments, in Advances in Cryptology* (David Chaum et al. eds., Springer 1983).
4. Satoshi Nakamoto, *Bitcoin: A Peer-to-Peer Electronic Cash System*, https://bitcoin.org (31 October 2008), https://bitcoin.org/bitcoin.pdf (accessed 29 October 2018).

The dilemma posed by decentralized ledgers – i.e., they can be duplicated or falsified – is particularly relevant to digital currencies and is known as the 'double-spending problem'.[5] If digital tokens can easily be duplicated and spent multiple times, the currency is quickly devaluated and becomes worthless. It is, thus, no surprise that Nakamoto also put forward a digital currency, called 'bitcoin', running on a blockchain architecture. It was the first solution to the double-spending problem that did not require a clearing agent. We will explain the technical details behind bitcoin and the blockchain technology in §8.02, *infra*.

Bitcoin has dramatically increased in value over the last decade and is certainly the most widely known cryptocurrency although opinions about its intrinsic value and general importance considerably diverge.[6] In 2010, one bitcoin was worth less than USD 0.01, but then developed rather steadily, spiking at the end of 2017 at almost USD 20,000. It dropped significantly at the beginning of 2018 and, as of this writing, is priced around USD 4,100. Over the past several years, many other cryptocurrencies have come into being, such as Ethereum, Ripple and Litecoin. At the end of November 2018, there were approximately 2,100 cryptocurrencies and their total market value was about USD 140 billion,[7] down from a peak of more than USD 700 billion, and Bitcoin captured around 50% of the total crypto market. In 2017, 370 initial coin offerings (ICOs) have raised USD 6.2 billion and, in 2018 alone (from January to November), 970 ICOs have raised USD 22.1 billion.[8]

Notwithstanding the hype and risks related to cryptocurrencies, the advantageous characteristics of the blockchain architecture are compelling: distributed (public) ledgers do not require any trust; control through a network community; participants are pseudonymous (while the transactions are public, individuals are only identified via digital addresses); global consensus about what is being added to the blockchain; and fraud (e.g., changes, deletions, double-spending) is impossible, due to computational complexity. Some view blockchain as one of the most disruptive innovations since the Internet, opening up possibilities such as 'programmable money' and an 'autonomous economy of things'.

The technology is maturing and taking hold in a broad landscape of use cases. IBM, Microsoft, Apple, Berkshire Hathaway, Daimler, Allianz, Walmart and countless

5. David Chaum, Amos Fiat & Moni Naor, *Untraceable Electronic Cash*, Proceedings on Advances in Cryptology – CRYPTO '88, Lecture Notes in Computer Science, 403, Springer-Verlag, pp. 319–327.
6. While Japan accepted bitcoin as a legal means of payment (https://www.cnbc.com/2017/09/29/bitcoin-exchanges-officially-recognized-by-japan.html) and Peter Thiel called it 'a threat to fiat money' (https://www.youtube.com/watch?v=FMDlhy-ZTNo&t=670, timestamp 11:25), Warren Buffett recommended to 'stay away from it' as 'the idea that it has some huge intrinsic value is just a joke in my view' (https://www.cnbc.com/2018/05/01/warren-buffett-bitcoin-isnt-an-investment.html) and Jamie Dimon called it a 'fraud' and 'worse than tulip bulbs' (https://www.independent.co.uk/news/business/news/bitcoin-fraud-tulip-bulbs-jpmorgan-ceo-jamie-dimon-bank-investor-crypto-currency-a7943986.html), comparing the valuation to the Dutch tulip bubble in the seventeenth century.
7. CoinMarketCap, https://coinmarketcap.com (accessed 29 November 2018).
8. CoinSchedule, *Cryptocurrency ICO Stats 2018*, https://www.coinschedule.com/stats.php (accessed 29 October 2018).

other companies are investing in blockchain.[9] Blockchain technology can be employed for optimizing delivery chains, interlinking machines, facilitating real-time cross-country financial transactions, asset transfers and notary services, managing registries for insurances, simplifying settlement systems for, *inter alia*, electricity and mobility services and many other uses. Venture capital funding in the years 2015, 2016, 2017 and 2018 (until November) was USD 0.6, 0.6, 0.9 and 3.1 billion, respectively.[10] In January 2017, McKinsey published a report[11] predicting that blockchain will reach its potential within five years and impact financial institutions (banks and insurance companies) with USD 80 to USD 110 billion in potential value creation. For instance, blockchain-based automated insurance policies implemented as smart contracts would lead to automatic payout against an insurable event without manual administration. An EY report[12] predicts that governments may mandate or eventually even enforce blockchain technology for financial transactions, as the public ledger of all transactions would allow them immediate impose and collect taxes in real time. Tax fraud could be severely limited; for example, the U.K. Government Chief Scientific Advisor proposed a blockchain-based European value added tax (VAT) system, which he argued would 'make the black-market economy more difficult to conceal'.[13] At the same time, blockchain could reduce the risk of tax controversies, rendering tax audits almost unnecessary.

In September 2017, China announced a ban on ICOs as it 'seriously disrupted the economic and financial order'.[14] As cryptocurrencies can be subject to regulation, their future role in our economies will depend on legislation and the policies of central banks and fiscal authorities. Whereas, at the beginning of this decade, bitcoin was only considered as a means of payment from a tax perspective, now tax authorities are also interested in taxing bitcoin profits. In order to understand the tax implications of cryptocurrencies, some background knowledge of its technical details and the blockchain technology behind them is necessary.

§8.02 THE BLOCKCHAIN TECHNOLOGY BEHIND CRYPTOCURRENCIES

When using a credit card, one is not obliged to understand the technical details and implementations that make its use possible. The same is true for the blockchain technology, where user-friendly applications already exist. Nevertheless, we provide a

9. https://www.forbes.com/sites/michaeldelcastillo/2018/07/03/big-blockchain-the-50-largest-public-companies-exploring-blockchain/ (3 July 2018, accessed 29 November 2018).
10. https://www.coindesk.com/bitcoin-venture-capital (accessed 29 November 2018).
11. Johannes-Tobias Lorenz et al., *Blockchain in Insurance – Opportunity or Threat?* (McKinsey & Company 2016), *available at* https://www.treasury.gov/initiatives/fio/Documents/McKinsey_FACI_Blockchain_in_Insurance.pdf.
12. Channing Flynn, *Preparing for Digital Taxation in a Blockchain World*, bna.com (October 2016), https://www.bna.com/preparing-digital-taxation-n73014447764/ (accessed 29 October 2018).
13. https://www.bna.com/preparing-digital-taxation-n73014447764/ (28 November 2016, accessed 29 November 2018).
14. Jon Russell, *China Has Banned ICOs*, techcrunch.com (4 September 2017), https://techcrunch.com/2017/09/04/chinas-central-bank-has-banned-icos/ (accessed 29 October 2018).

brief overview of the main technical ideas behind blockchain, with our main focus on the specific example of bitcoin.

Let us start with introducing a public (online) ledger that keeps track of transactions. The ledger has sequentially numbered entries such as:

Line 101: *A* pays 10 to *B*
Line 102: *B* pays 20 to *C*
Line 103: *D* pays 20 to *C*
Line 104: *A* pays 10 to *B*.

As anyone can add lines to the ledger, how can anyone trust it? That issue is resolved by a well-known procedure, the so-called a digital signature. *Party A*, for example, has to sign Line 101 in the above ledger with her signature, which she produces from the message – the text of Line 101, itself – and her private key. Her private key is a bit sequence that only she knows. As all lines have labels, which belong to the lines themselves, Line 104 will require a different signature than Line 101. With *Party A*'s public key, which is openly known and mathematically linked to her private key, everyone else can check that the signature was indeed made by *Party A*.

Party B could have made up Line 104 without *Party A's* knowledge and then try to forge *Party A's* signature by trying to guess all of *Party A's* possible private keys, such that, when combined with *Party A's* public key, the false Line 104 transaction would be verified. However, with the key lengths in use as of this writing, the expected time needed to search through all of the possibilities would be astronomically large.

In a decentralized network, there is not just one ledger; each party has their own copy of it and they simply broadcast new transactions into the world. The only remaining problem with such a decentralized network was how all of these broadcasts would be received and stored in the correct (i.e., the same) order and, thus, ensure synchronized ledgers. Nakamoto solved that issue in 2008. Most importantly, as there is no physical representation such as coins or bills, the synchronized ledger *is* the currency.

For cryptocurrencies to function, of all existing ledgers trust is given to that ledger whose verification has required the most computational work, a concept called 'proof of work'. The core concept relies on so-called hash functions, which have been at the heart of many cryptographic protocols for a long time. A hash function takes an input (a text, a picture, or, in our case, a ledger) in its digital form and produces an output sequence of a predetermined length, called 'the hash'.[15] A hash of a large amount of data resembles the fingerprint of a person. It is a quasi-unique means of identification, but contains much less information, so there is now a way to reconstruct the original from its hash. A typical hash function in cryptography is the open-source Secure Hash Algorithm (SHA) 256, which puts out 256 bits in an apparently random and non-revertible way for a particular input.[16] To give specific examples, the SHA256 outputs

15. An extremely simple hash function would simply add up all bits of an input and report the digit sum (modulo 2) as a one-bit output.
16. A strict mathematical proof that the inverse direction is, indeed, not feasible does not exist; however, it is an assumption widely adopted in the scientific community. Finding a bug in a

of the strings for 'taxation' and 'Taxation' (for brevity, in hexadecimal form) read as follows:

> SHA256('taxation') = d8806ee41898c3007efd6d1a15caa3d08964b7a0ae500c7715fc750f511843a9
> SHA256('Taxation') = ba0724188508839a09d501c17557f8063b7ec4ef7f41fb4c1a49606bcedac548

Although the only difference in the inputs was the capitalization of one letter (the first 't' in the word), the SHA256 outputs appear completely random and are completely different.

Similarly, the hash function of the 'Magna Carta' on the one hand, and the hash function of the 'Magna Carta with only one single letter changed' on the other, are completely different and have no connection to each other whatsoever. This is called the 'avalanche effect'. It is straightforward to compute the hash, but it is virtually impossible to revert it to guess the original input for it. And, there is no known way to guess the hash of an input any faster than actually computing it.[17]

In the bitcoin protocol, a block needs to be verified once it reaches the length of one megabyte (8,000,000 bits). Verifying a certain block of ledger transactions takes place as follows.

First, participants in the network try to find a valid verification number which they then add to the end of the block. A verification number is valid if the hash of the ledger block, including the (guessed) verification number at its end, starts with a certain number of zeros, which is the equivalent to requiring the resulting hash to be below a certain target value. That target value can be dynamically adapted in time, such that the verification time of a block is kept roughly constant even though the number of network participants and their total computing power can change drastically. In the bitcoin protocol, the average block verification time is kept close to ten minutes. The average work required to find a verification number is exponential in the number of required zeros. However, once found, the number can be verified very quickly by executing a single hash and checking it.

Once the lucky contender finds a valid verification number – which usually requires lots of trials and, therefore, large amounts of computational effort, hardware and electricity[18] – the ledger is successfully signed, thus completing this block. The verification number is then broadcast out into the world, and the hash of the verified block becomes the header in the next block of transactions. Once that block is signed, its hash becomes the entry of the next and so on, hence the name blockchain.

---

specific hash function used in a blockchain protocol renders the whole protocol completely insecure, which is why blockchains that use open-source hash functions, and whose algorithms can be publicly analysed and discussed, are considered the most reliable.

17. *Ibid.*
18. As of this writing, the electricity consumption of the worldwide bitcoin network is about 50 TWh, close to the country-wide consumption of Bangladesh with a population of 144 million people. This is about 0.23% of the world's total electricity consumption. https://digiconomist.net/bitcoin-energy-consumption (accessed 29 November 2018).

In the bitcoin protocol, the verifier gets rewarded with a certain number of bitcoins. The reward is written into the first line of the verified block. The reward was initially set to 50 bitcoins per block, but it gets cut in half every 210,000 blocks. It is currently 12.5 bitcoins per block and will decrease to 6.25 bitcoins per block in the year 2020. This geometric decrease limits the total possible number of bitcoins to 210,000 (50 + 25 + 12.5 + 6.25 + ...) = 21 million. As reward bitcoins are newly created and added to the already existing number of bitcoins, this process is called 'mining'. As Nakamoto wrote: 'The steady addition of a constant of amount of new coins is analogous to gold miners expending resources to add gold to circulation. In our case, it is CPU time and electricity that is expended.'[19] As of this writing, there were approximately 17.4 billion bitcoins.

If two different blockchains are broadcast, the longer one (i.e., the one that encompasses the larger number of blocks) is the one being trusted. With bitcoin, an individual transaction is considered confirmed if it is part of a confirmed block and a block is considered confirmed if (a) it is in the longest branch and (b) at least five blocks follow it in the longest branch. Unconfirmed blocks are part of the so-called orphan branches (*see* Figure 8.1). Trust, therefore, is not based on a central authority (such as a central bank), rather, it stems from the amount of computational effort that has been invested.

Figure 8.1 Example of Confirmed Bitcoin Structure with Orphan Branches

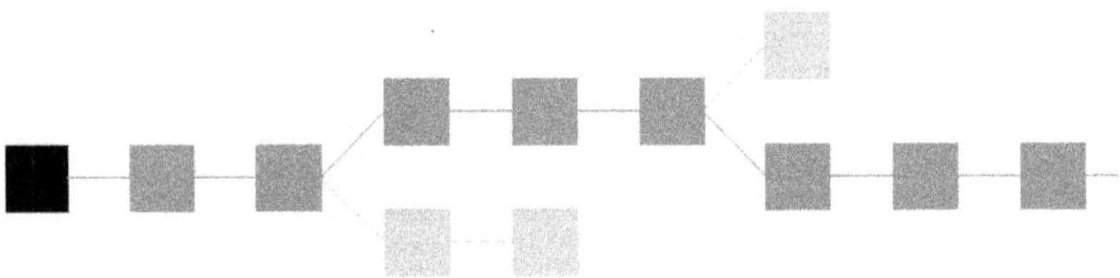

Confirmed blocks (dark gray) form a continuous chain from a single original starting block (black). The hash of each verified block becomes the header of the next block. Blocks which have been successfully verified but end up in a dying branch are unconfirmed (and thus invalid) and called orphan blocks (light gray).

Apart from mining bitcoin, there is a second way for participants to accumulate bitcoin, namely transaction fees. If *Party X*, for example, wants to transfer some amount of bitcoin to *Party Y*, *Party X* may designate a higher input value (what *X* pays) than the output value (what *Y* receives). If the input value exceeds the output value, the difference is called a transaction fee. The larger the transaction fee is, the more attractive it is, and the faster it will be verified by the network. Typical transactions use one half of one kilobyte and typical transaction fees range between 1,000 and 10,000

19. Nakamoto, *supra* note 4.

satoshi per kilobyte. A 'satoshi' is the smallest possible bitcoin unit, namely one-hundredth of one-millionth of a bitcoin.

In short, a bitcoin miner inputs his or her computing power at the disposal of the network, hoping to verify a block. If successful, the miner is rewarded with mined (i.e., newly created) bitcoins and, potentially, transaction fees (paid by the transaction parties). If unsuccessful, the miner receives nothing whatsoever.

§8.03 QUESTIONS RELATED TO THE TAX TREATMENT OF DIGITAL CURRENCIES

As far as we can tell, a significant number of people have embraced the idea of bitcoin and other digital currencies: they use it not only as a means of payment but also for other purposes, such as investment. Entire business models have evolved around digital currencies. Consequently, questions related to their tax treatment must be addressed. Several such questions must be analysed from both the direct (income tax) and indirect (VAT)tax perspectives, but for the purposes of our chapter, we will only discuss the following:

- Transferring digital currencies.
- Exchanging digital currencies.
- Exchange platforms and so-called wallet apps for digital currencies.
- Holding assets in digital currencies.
- Verifying digital currency transactions.
- Mining digital currencies.

Since digital currencies differ widely with regards to their legal structure and business model, we will continue to focus our attention on bitcoin, as it was the first digital currency and has, by far, the greatest market capitalization of all cryptocurrencies. Nevertheless, only some of the results of our bitcoin analysis can be applied to other digital currencies; not all that we deduce about bitcoin, from a legal perspective, as well as existing jurisprudence, fits other digital currencies.

Moreover, many other blockchain applications trigger tax consequences, such as:

- ICOs.
- So-called Smart contracts.
- Supply chain management.

Especially with regard to the last three issues, tax authorities and tax experts have wildly different opinions. We will analyse the facts, legal structure and business models of digital currencies, concentrating on bitcoin, to find answers to the above-mentioned questions, relying on legal texts as well as jurisprudence, as well as scholarly literature.

§8.04 DIGITAL CURRENCIES AS A MEANS OF PAYMENT

The Court of Justice of the European Union (CJEU) already encountered some VAT questions regarding digital currencies. In its first-ever ruling on digital currency, in *Hedqvist*,[20] it basically followed Advocate General (AG) Juliane Kokott's opinion.[21] AG Kokott explained that 'according to the findings of the referring court, bitcoins also constitute a pure means of payment. The only purpose of possessing them is to reuse them as a means of payment at some point.'[22] The CJEU adopted that conclusion, explicitly referring to the AG Opinion,[23]such that both the CJEU and the AG relied on the referring court's finding, that bitcoin is purely a means of payment. However, while bitcoin clearly serves as means of payment, it does not necessarily follow that its sole purpose and use is that limited. Neither the AG nor the relevant courts contemplate that bitcoin miners and holders could (or would) use bitcoin for widespread speculative and/or investment purposes.

Because bitcoins were only viewed as means of payment, the AG concluded that, in accordance with the principle of fiscal neutrality in the form of the principle of equal treatment, the transfer of bitcoin, as such, could not constitute a chargeable event,[24] relying on the CJEU's 1998 decision in *First National Bank of Chicago*.[25] In that case, the CJEU found that the transfer of legal tender constituted neither a supply of goods nor a supply of services. According to the CJEU at the time, currencies used as legal tender had no other practical use than as a means of payment; they were simply used to facilitate an economy's trade in goods and services and, thus, could not be consumed or used as goods, unlike gold or cigarettes for example, which had been and still were used, both directly and indirectly, as means of payment.[26] In conformity with the CJEU's *First National Bank of Chicago* decision, bitcoin was found to fulfil the same function as money, which is to act as the consideration for the supply of goods and/or services. Therefore, the AG opined that its transfer was not a taxable transaction falling within the scope of VAT.

However, for the reasoning the CJEU used in *First National Bank of Chicago* to work, a company would have had to provide services that included both the exchange of traditional currency for bitcoin virtual currency and vice versa. In *Hedqvist*, with reference to *First National Bank of Chicago*, the CJEU decided that buying and selling bitcoins at a price that included a markup constituted a supply of services for consideration.[27] Nevertheless, in accordance with the AG Kokott's Opinion, the CJEU ruled that the exemption set out in Article 135(1)(e) of the VAT Directive[28] covers not

20. *Hedqvist*, C-264/14, Judgment, EU:C:2015:718.
21. *Hedqvist*, C-264/14, AG Opinion, EU:C:2015:498.
22. *Ibid.* para. 17.
23. *Hedqvist*, C-264/14, para. 24.
24. *Ibid.*
25. *First National Bank of Chicago*, C172/96, Judgment, EU:C:1998:354, paras 25–35.
26. *Hedqvist*, C-264/14, AG Opinion, para. 14.
27. *Hedqvist*, C-264/14, para. 31; with reference to *First National Bank of Chicago*, C-172/96, para. 25.
28. Council Directive 2006/112/EC of 28 November 2006 on the common system of value added tax, OJ L 347, 11.12.2006, pp. 1–118.

only the supply of services regarding legal tender but also the exchange of traditional currencies for units of bitcoin and other virtual currencies (and vice versa), when the exchange is performed in return for payment of a sum equal to the difference between, on the one hand, the price paid by the operator to purchase the currency and, on the other, the price at which he sells that currency to his clients.[29] Since the CJEU did not make distinction between legal tender and bitcoin as a means of payment, it seems clear that the conclusion must be extended to the exchange of bitcoin in other digital currencies that also function as means of payment. Other services rendered by exchange platforms and wallet apps for digital currencies that also involve the exchange of traditional currencies for digital currencies should, therefore, also be exempt from VAT pursuant to Article 135(1)(e) of the VAT Directive.

§8.05 PRIVATE INVESTMENTS IN DIGITAL CURRENCIES

If a taxpayer acquires bitcoin for speculative purposes, VAT treatment may be different from that stated in §8.04, *supra*. As we know from the CJEU's decision in *EDM*,[30] the mere acquisition and sale of shares and other negotiable securities are not an economic activity. Specifically, for an undertaking, neither the scale of its sales nor its employment in connection with such sales can constitute criteria for distinguishing between its activities and that of a private investor, which fall outside the scope of the VAT Directive.[31] In contrast, drawing revenue on a continuing basis from activities that go beyond the simple acquisition and sale of securities (e.g., transactions carried out in the course of a business trading in securities) *is* covered by the VAT Directive.[32] It seems reasonable to draw the same line relating to transactions in bitcoins and other digital currencies, to determine whether particular transactions fall within or outside the scope of the VAT Directive.

Thus, buying and selling digital currencies as a private investor are not regarded as an economic activity and, therefore, should fall outside the VAT Directive's scope.[33] However, continuing, ongoing exchanges of digital currencies or incidental transactions by taxpayers may still fall under the scope of the VAT Directive but are likely to be exempt from VAT, pursuant to its Article 135(1)(e).

§8.06 VERIFICATION OF TRANSACTIONS OF DIGITAL CURRENCIES

This question deals with the tax treatment of the so-called bitcoin miners. As mentioned above, bitcoin mining is the process of adding transaction records to bitcoin's public ledger of concluded transactions (i.e., its blockchain). Mining involves a network participant (i.e., one who has provided the network access to his or her

29. *Ibid.* para. 53.
30. *EDM*, C-77/01, Judgment, EU:C:2004:243, para. 58.
31. *Ibid.* para. 61.
32. *Ibid.* para. 59.
33. Article 1 Council Directive 2006/112/EC of 28 November 2006 on the common system of value added tax, OJ L 347, 11.12.2006, pp. 1–118.

computing power) identifying a block that, when hashed twice with SHA256, yields a number smaller than the given difficulty target (recall that the hash of a block header must start with a certain number of zeros). Identifying such a hash is a random process with low probability, so that, typically, a lot of trial and error is required before a valid proof of work is generated, but the probability of long-term success can be calculated and, thus, so can the average profit derived from mining (Bitcoin Mining Profit calculators, which calculate the average profit given the hashing power, power consumption and cost per kWh of the mining activity, are readily available on the Internet[34]). Perhaps surprisingly, professional bitcoin miners – despite the fact that the process of identifying a hash is random – are not, then, in the position of the gambler at a casino; rather, they are in the position of the casino and are, therefore, performing an economic activity.

The primary purpose of bitcoin mining is to allow bitcoin nodes to reach a secure, tamper-resistant consensus. Miners render verification services for compensation: individual transaction fees and mined bitcoins. Those paying the transaction fees to bitcoin miners do so to encourage them to include their transaction in a block, as miners can decide whether to include a particular transaction in a block or exclude it. Successful bitcoin miners can claim both mined bitcoin *and* transaction fees while other miners receive nothing for their activity until their next success, if any. This compensation/reward system raises a question as to whether verifying digital currency transactions via mining should be considered the supply of a service for consideration within the meaning of Article 2(1)(a) VAT Directive and, thus, a VAT taxable transaction, the answer to which may not be as clear as one might think.

For purposes of the VAT Directive, supplying a service for consideration requires a legal relationship between the supplier of such service and the recipient thereof, pursuant to which there is reciprocal performance, that is the remuneration received by the supplier constitutes the value actually given in return for the service supplied to the recipient. A supply is done 'for consideration' within the meaning of Article 2(1)(a) VAT Directive if a direct link exists between the service supplied and the consideration received.[35] In a bitcoin transaction, the transferor essentially asks every miner participating in the network to include his or her transaction in a block and to verify the block by finding a suitable hash. By verifying the transaction (i.e., adding the transaction to his or her block and finding the correct hash), the miner and the transferor enter into a legal relationship, one in which a direct link exists between the miner's supply of service and the consideration the miner receives in form of the transaction fee for that service. Hence, the miner's verification of digital currency transactions, such as bitcoin, appears to result in a VAT taxable transaction.

Moreover, the VAT exemption set out in Article 135(1)(e) of the VAT Directive does not appear to cover such transactions because there is no exchange of virtual currency between the parties other than the transaction fee, itself. The service provided by the miner to a transferor does not involve the cryptocurrency itself, but instead,

34. CryptoCompare Currency, https://www.cryptocompare.com/mining/calculator/ (accessed 29 October 2018).
35. *Hedqvist*, C-264/14, para. 27.

involves the miner's verification of the transferor's bitcoin transaction. In that scenario, the transaction might fall within the scope of the VAT exemption set out in Article 135(1)(d) of the VAT Directive, which exempts transactions involving, *inter alia*, payments and transfers, if the transfer fulfils the specific, essential functions of the services described in said provision.[36] In its 2011 *Nordea* decision,[37] the CJEU decided that, to fulfil the requirements for an Article 135(1)(d) exemption, the services provided must have the effect of transferring funds and must entail changes of a legal and financial character; in other words, it must be distinguished from the mere physical or technical supply of services, such as making a data handling system available to the service recipient. In light of the CJEU's past decisions, it is not at all sure that the CJEU would consider the services provided by bitcoin miners exempt on the basis of either of the Article 135(1)(d) or (e) VAT Directive exemptions.

§8.07 MINING OF DIGITAL CURRENCIES

As of this writing, in addition to the transaction fees they receive for placing transactions in their block(s), miners are awarded 12.5 newly system-generated bitcoins. Some scholars are of the opinion that these awards represent remuneration for an ancillary service to the service of verifying a transaction in by including it in their block.[38] However, the bitcoins awarded to successful miners are provided to encourage those miners to keep the decentralized ledger of all transactions within the network of the digital currency and, thus, the bitcoin system alive. Since the service's recipient is the bitcoin network's community of current and future participants, the service lacks the necessary legal relationship between the provider of the service (the miner) and the recipient (the community), pursuant to which there must be reciprocal performance, with the remuneration received by the service provider constituting the actual consideration given in return for the service supplied to the recipient.[39] Failing that, the miner's award is not remuneration for a supply of service within the scope of Article 2(1)(a) VAT Directive and, thus, is a not VAT taxable transaction.[40]

§8.08 INCOME TAX QUESTIONS

Whether capital gains or losses from buying and selling digital currencies must be included in a taxpayer's income tax base depends on the specifics of the income tax law

36. *Ibid.* para. 39.
37. *Nordea*, C- 350/10, Judgment, EU:C:2011:532, para. 24.
38. David Dietsch, *Umsatzsteuerliche Behandlung von Bitcoin-Mining*, 6 MwStR 250, 252 (2018).
39. Redmar Wolf, *Bitcoin and EU VAT*, 25 Int'l VAT Monitor 254, 257 (2014).
40. *See* Letter from the German Ministry of Finance to the Supreme Financial Authorities of the Länder, *Umsatzsteuerliche Behandlung von Bitcoin und anderen sog. virtuellen Währungen; EuGH-Urteil vom 22. Oktober 2015, C-264/14, Hedqvist* (27 February 2018), *available at* https://www.bundesfinanzministerium.de/Content/DE/Downloads/BMF_Schreiben/Steuerarten/Umsatzsteuer/Umsatzsteuer-Anwendungserlass/2018-02-27-umsatzsteuerliche-behandlung-von-bitcoin-und-anderen-sog-virtuellen-waehrungen.pdf?__blob=publicationFile&v=1.

of the taxpayer's home state. From a tax treaty perspective, digital currency capital gains and losses can be considered either business income or income from capital gains, depending on whether the investment in bitcoin is a business or private asset.

Scholars generally agree that profits from services of exchange of digital currencies constitute business income.[41] However, there are still divergent views with regard to the income obtained through mining activities. As mentioned above, professional digital currency mining yields profits that can be calculated, at least to a certain extent, in advance, despite the fact that the success of verifying a block is random and, therefore, often confused with gambling.[42] Professional investors in digital currency mining ventures can generally calculate the expected revenues in advance. In contrast, those who participate in a network of digital currency as a hobby will only earn revenue by sheer chance; on average, their activity, like gambling, will result in losses – similar to a gambler – but those and such losses are not typically incorporated as part of the taxpayer's income tax base.

§8.09 CONCLUSION

Digital currencies based on blockchain technology have quickly developed over the last several years. That boom, and the purportedly huge profits that came with it, made tax authorities aware of cryptocurrency's potential. To better understand the myriad tax implications of digital currencies, one must look behind the veil of technical implementation and its different business models. With regard to the most common cryptocurrency, bitcoin, we have good, solid knowledge about its function and tax consequences. The CJEU's VAT guidance in *Hedqvist* has helped to demystify the tax treatment of digital currencies and has also encouraged tax authorities to express their opinion on how to handle this evermore common phenomenon. Nevertheless, one must always remember that the term digital currency or cryptocurrency covers many different schemes that are sold to the public. To determine the exact tax consequences of any of those schemes, one must have a good understanding of the cryptocurrency's specific legal structure as well as the business model that lies behind it. In this chapter, we provided some guidance in that regard, by looking more closely at bitcoins' operation and structure, as well as its VAT and income tax consequences, as bitcoin remains, at the time of this writing, the most recognizable example of digital currencies, which, surprisingly, abound, despite their decentralized and amorphous character.

41. Matthias Petutschnig, *Sind Bitcoins ertragsteuerpflichtig?* ÖStZ 353 (2014); Tanja Geisler, *Bitcoins und andere Kryptowährungen*, SWK 930 (2017).
42. *See* Tina Ehrke-Rabel et al., *Bitcoin-Miner Als Prosumer: Eine Frage Staatlicher Regulierung? Dargestellt Am Beispiel Des Glücksspielrechts (Legal and Regulatory Aspects of Bitcoin Mining as a Form of Prosuming)*, 4 Austrian L. J. 188 (2017); Daniel Varro, *Bitcoin-Mining: nicht steuerbares Glücksspiel?*, 2017 Taxlex 399 (2017).

CHAPTER 9

Taxing Remote Digital Supplies

Marie Lamensch

§9.01 'DIGITAL SUPPLIES': A CONCEPTUAL CHALLENGE FOR THE VAT SYSTEM

The twenty-first-century economy has largely become global and digital. A fast-growing portion of overall taxable consumption is now effected via 'digital supplies', i.e., supplies of services and intangible fully effected online.[1] The spread of the 'Internet of Things' and of cloud computing services as well as new business models based on 'big data' applications will further accelerate this development.[2] It is therefore crucial that value added tax (VAT) be effectively imposed on this key sector of the 'Digital Economy' (neutrality principle).

At the same time, businesses that offer digital supplies (digital suppliers) should not be faced with disproportionate risk and compliance burdens when assessing and collecting the VAT due on their supplies (efficiency, simplicity and proportionality principles). Compliance costs reduce productivity and hence have the potential to hamper growth. As compliance costs are thought to be larger (as a percentage of turnover) for smaller firms, this could prevent start-ups, micro-, small- and medium-size enterprises from entering into the highly promising international digital markets and thus hamper their growth and distort market competition (again: neutrality

1. *See* OECD, *OECD Digital Economy Outlook 2015* (OECD Publishing 2015), explaining how the digital economy now permeates countless aspects of the world economy, impacting sectors as varied as banking, retail, energy, transportation, education, publishing, media or health and how Information and Communication Technologies are transforming the ways social interactions and personal relationships are conducted, with fixed, mobile and broadcast networks converging, and devices and objects increasingly connected to form the 'Internet of things'.
2. *See* Communication from the Comm'n to the European Parliament, the Council, the European Economic and Social Committee and the Committee of the Regions, *A Digital Single Market Strategy for Europe*, COM(2015) 192 final.

principle). Finally, the potential for fraud and international double taxation or unintentional non-taxation should also be minimized (effectiveness principle).

Regarding the international taxation framework within which these objectives are to be achieved there is widespread agreement among tax scholars, first, that VAT should ideally be levied in the jurisdiction of presumed consumption: 'at destination'. This is also reflected in the International VAT/GST (Goods and Services Tax) guidelines issued by the Organisation for Economic Co-operation and Development (OECD) and in international practice.[3] The reason is that such an allocation of taxing rights avoids distortions of competition among suppliers from different jurisdictions, as the same VAT burden will apply in the domestic marketplace irrespective of the location of the supplier. This is particularly crucial for digital supplies that are fully remotely delivered and for which the location of the supplier is therefore not important.

Second, a major paradigm in the VAT system is that suppliers are required to assess and collect the taxes on their supplies. This 'vendor collection model' was designed in the course of the twentieth century,[4] in an era in which the great majority of transactions were domestic. In a domestic context, collecting taxes and remitting revenue to the tax administration (irrespective of whether the tax is due at origin[5] or at destination) results in acceptable compliance burden costs for businesses (efficiency simplicity, legal certainty and proportionality). In this context also States simultaneously have the right to tax (substantive jurisdiction) and the means to enforce collection (enforcement jurisdiction) – both being strictly territorially related (effectiveness).[6] In a domestic context, therefore, the vendor collection model satisfies the traditional tax systems benchmarks.

On the contrary, in a cross-border scenario, a disconnect between substantive and enforcement jurisdiction may arise when the destination principle applies, particularly with regard to cross-border digital supplies that do not cross physical borders, which excludes the possibility to enforce tax collection at the moment of import.[7] In practice, this means that States frequently have to rely on suppliers over which they have no enforcement jurisdiction to collect their taxes. This is most problematic in view of the limited capacity of States to enforce their laws beyond their territorial limits through other means such as international cooperation and assistance in tax issues. In the real world, however, these mechanisms have very limited effectiveness because

3. OECD, *International VAT/GST Guidelines* (OECD Publishing 2017).
4. Wilhelm von Siemens first proposed the concept of a value added tax in 1919. Carl Friedrich von Siemens, *Veredelte Umsatzsteuer* (n. pub 1921). In 1921, Adams developed the 'credit invoice method' to prevent tax cumulation in view of a potential implementation in the US, which, however, never materialized; Thomas S. Adams: *Fundamental Problems of Federal Income Taxation*, 35 Q. J. Econ. 527 (1921). France was eventually the first country to introduce a value added tax in 1954: Introduced by the Loi no. 54-404 of 10 April 1954, J.O. of 11 April 1954.
5. That is, in the jurisdiction of the supplier.
6. The concepts of 'enforcement jurisdiction' versus 'substantive jurisdiction' have been developed by Walter Hellerstein. *See, e.g.*, Walter Hellerstein, *Jurisdiction to Impose and Enforce Income and Consumption Taxes: Towards a Unified Conception of Tax Nexus, in Value-Added-Taxes and Direct Taxation* 545 (Michael Lang et al. eds., IBFD 2009).
7. Marie Lamensch, *Is There Any Future for the Vendor Collection Model in the 21st Century Economy?*, 27 Int'l VAT Monitor 182 (2016).

they are not in place (or are not well publicized) between major players in the global economy (United States of America, European Union (EU), China, India etc.).

Cross-border scenarios were the exception when the VAT system was designed, and the few businesses engaging into cross-border supplies in the mid-twentieth century did traditionally only trade in goods (with possible VAT enforcement at the border) and did only target a handful of foreign markets. With the development of the Internet, however, cross-border trade of digital supplies (services and intangibles) has now become mainstream. Accordingly, the development of the Digital Economy has raised serious concerns over the capacity of national tax administrations to effectively monitor and enforce the collection of VAT in line with the internationally accepted destination principle under the traditional collection model (lack of effectiveness). A particular issue is that liability risks primarily concern resident suppliers, as it is difficult to monitor and enforce compliance of the national VAT regime in the case of inbound digital supplies (not crossing physical borders) from offshore suppliers who are not subject to host state tax audits. Enforcement limitations therefore also potentially result in competition distortions between digital suppliers depending on their origin (lack of neutrality).

Another important difficulty associated with the vendor collection model in a digital era is that it creates particular VAT compliance challenges for digital suppliers. A business willing to reach customers worldwide will have to register in each jurisdiction where it has customers and file periodical tax returns (lack of efficiency, simplicity and proportionality). This inevitably comes at a cost and can be a real burden if the procedures and requirements vary. An additional difficulty concerns the identification of the customers, in particular when the customer is a non-taxable person. VAT systems were designed in times when goods constituted the bulk of international trade, and for that reason they presume a 'tangible' nature and 'physical' movement of the taxable object across borders from a known point of origin to a readily identifiable destination.[8] Services and intangibles, however, may flow from one location to another instantaneously. The contracting parties may meet only 'virtually' on the 'e-marketplace', without any form of traditional or 'physical' contact so that customers often remain anonymous or 'pseudonymous'. In addition, the Internet is a borderless medium that ignores geography and time constraints, and therefore allows for low transaction costs and an immediate high-speed supply at any time and from any origin to any destination. In practice this means that digital suppliers face serious challenges in identifying the status (business or final consumer) and the location of their customers for the purpose of correctly assessing and collecting the VAT on their supplies in the time frame that is available to them, i.e., before payment (lack of legal certainty, simplicity, proportionality and efficiency).[9] VAT is indeed a transaction-based tax, and therefore all relevant factors must be assessed by the time that the supply is carried out, and thus almost instantaneously in the case of most digital supplies. A major difference as compared to the sector of 'conventional supplies' is

8. 36 Marie Lamensch, *European Value-Added Tax in the Digital Era: A Critical Analysis and Proposals for Reform, in IBFD Doctoral Series* (Pasquale Pistone ed., IBFD 2015).
9. *Ibid.*

therefore that VAT assessment must be completed in an automated fashion and through clearly formatted procedures. Moreover, tax administrations will also face difficulties in identifying Internet users (anonymity as an obstacle to implementation by suppliers, particularly for digital supplies, and also to enforcement by tax administrations, even within jurisdictional reach).[10]

Against this background this contribution outlines, in a first part, the place of supply and related collection rules that apply to so-called electronically supplied services under the VAT Directive[11] (and the Implementing Regulation 282/2011[12] as amended by Council Regulation 1042/201314[13]). It also analyses the amendments recently adopted under the 'e-commerce VAT package' that will be effective as of 2019 and 2021 (section §9.02).[14] In a second part, the special rules regarding the (non-)applicability of reduced rates to electronically supplied services and relevant Court of Justice of the European Union (CJEU) case law will be discussed. General thoughts will also be shared regarding the possible impact of the Proposal recently tabled by the European Commission (EC), aimed at offering further flexibility to the Member States regarding VAT rates (section §9.03). Final comments are offered in section §9.05.

As a preliminary note of caution, the author would like to highlight that the concept of 'electronically supplied services' is defined in a relatively narrow way under Article 7(1) of the Implementing Regulation 282/2011, as follows:

> 'Electronically supplied services' as referred to in Directive 2006/112/EC shall include services which are delivered over the Internet or an electronic network and the nature of which renders their supply essentially automated and involving minimal human intervention, and impossible to ensure in the absence of information technology.

10. *See, e.g.*, Arthur Cockfield, *Designing Tax Policy for the Digital Biosphere*, 34 Conn. L. Rev. 333, 335–336 (2001); Arthur Cockfield, *Transforming the Internet into a Taxable Forum: A Case Study in E-Commerce Taxation*, 85 Minn. L. Rev. 1172 (2001); Walter Hellerstein & Charles McLure, *Sales Taxation of Electronic Commerce: What John Due Knew All Along*, 93 Nat'l Tax Ass'n 216 (2001).
11. Council Directive 2006/112 on the common system of value added tax, OJ L 347, 1 [2006] (hereinafter 'VAT Directive').
12. Council Regulation 282/2011 laying down implementing measures for Directive 2006/112/EC on the common system of value added tax, OJ L 77/1 [2001] (hereinafter 'Implementing Regulation 2011').
13. Council Regulation 1042/2013 amending Implementing Regulation (EU) No 282/2011 as regards the place of supply of services, OJ L284/1 [2013] (hereinafter 'Implementation Regulation 2013').
14. The e-commerce VAT package consists of one directive (Council Directive 2017/2455 amending Directive 2006/112/EC and Directive 2009/132/EC as regards certain value added tax obligations for supplies of services and distance sales of goods, OJ L 348 [2017]) and two regulations Implementing Regulation (EU) 2017/2459 amending Implementing Regulation (EU) No. 282/2011 laying down implementing measures for Directive 2006/112/EC on the common system of value added tax and Council Regulation (EU) 2017/2454 amending Regulation (EU) No. 904/2010 on administrative cooperation and combating fraud in the field of value added tax). It covers all B2C 'e-commerce transactions', including supplies of intra-EU and inbound B2C electronically supplied services, intra-EU B2C distance sales of goods and B2C imports, but only electronically supplied services will be addressed in this contribution.

Annex II of the VAT Directive contains an indicative list of qualifying services. It includes, *inter alia*, the supply of images, text and information and making available of databases; the supply of music, films and games, including games of chance and gambling games, and of political, cultural, artistic, sporting, scientific and entertainment broadcasts and events; website supply, web hosting and distance maintenance of programmes and equipment. This list was eventually inserted in the Implementing Regulation 282/2011. A negative list of examples (i.e., of supplies that do not qualify as electronically supplied services) was also added that includes: CD-ROMs, floppy disks and similar tangible media; video cassettes and DVD), games on a CD-ROM; services of professionals such as lawyers and financial consultants, who advise clients by email; teaching services, where the course content is delivered by a teacher over the Internet or an electronic network (namely via a remote link); offline physical repair services of computer equipment. All supplies fully effected online but that do not qualify as electronically supplied service (e.g., because they require more than minimal intervention) are governed by the general rules for services (e.g., webinars, dating websites that offer personalized treatment of customers). This results in legal uncertainty and practical difficulties that will not be addressed in this contribution.[15]

§9.02 ELECTRONICALLY SUPPLIED SERVICES: EU VAT DIRECTIVE PLACE OF SUPPLY AND RELATED COLLECTION RULES

[A] B2B Electronically Supplied Services

[1] Destination-Based Taxation and Reverse Charge

In accordance with the general place of supply rule for business-to-business (B2B) services (Article 45 of the VAT Directive), B2B supplies of electronically supplied services are taxed at destination. In accordance with Article 196 of the VAT Directive, the customer is liable to self-assess and pay the VAT in cross-border situations (reverse charge).

As mentioned already a difficulty of the vendor collection model under a destination-based system is that taxable persons should be able to identify and locate their customers on a transaction basis. Identification, i.e., confirmation of the taxable or non-taxable status, is required because the reverse charge mechanism applies in B2B situations. Location is also required because reverse charging only applies in cross-border situations. Fact is that identifying and locating customers may be difficult in the case of electronically supplied services, which are made remotely, in a fully automated way and 24/7.

15. For more on this question, see Madeleine Merckx, *VAT and E-Services: When Human Intervention Is Minimal*, 29 Int'l VAT Monitor 17 (2018); *see also* Giorgio Beretta, *VAT on Financial and Insurance Services at the Dawn of the Fourth Industrial Revolution*, 29 Int'l VAT Monitor 142 (2018).

[2] Customer Identification

In cases of intra-EU and inbound[16] B2B supplies in which the business customer does not communicate a VAT number, Article 18(2) of the Implementing Regulation 282/2011 allows, as a general rule, suppliers to deny him status as a taxable person 'unless (the supplier) has information to the contrary'.

Since 1 January 2015, pursuant to the entry into effect of Council Regulation 1042/2013 amending the Implementing Regulation 282/2011, suppliers 'may' deny taxable status to an EU customer who has not communicated a VAT number, without having to consider 'information to the contrary'.[17] This amendment was no doubt meant to provide relief to suppliers. In practice, however, the risk of losing the customers to which a supplier would deny taxable status should not be underestimated because a taxable person who is refused the benefit of the reverse charge system would not be able to eventually deduct any VAT charged to him.

The EC has issued 'explanatory notes' with respect to Council Regulation 1042/2013.[18] These notes (hereinafter 'EC explanatory notes') confirm that a customer initially treated as a non-taxable person should not be able to eventually recover his input VAT. The EC explanatory notes, however, add that he should be given the possibility – within a reasonable time –[19]to rectify the situation with the supplier, who would need to make the necessary adjustments, which may imply refunding any VAT previously charged.[20] This clarification is not entirely satisfactory in the first place because the possibility of a late adjustment may not be entirely convincing for a customer who still might be tempted to look for another supplier who would immediately treat him as a taxable person. Second, numerous adjustment demands would substantially increase the compliance burden and costs for digital suppliers.

Surprisingly, the EC explanatory notes further provide that even when a customer communicates a VAT number that has been successfully verified and there is no information suggesting that the customer is not a taxable person, the supplier may still,

16. From a supplier not established and not having a fixed establishment in the EU to a customer established or having a fixed establishment in the EU.
17. With effect as of 1 January 2015, Implementation Regulation 2013, adds the following second subparagraph to Art. 18(2) of the Implementing Regulation: 'However, irrespective of information to the contrary, the supplier of ... electronic services may regard a customer established within the Community as a non-taxable person as long as that customer has not communicated his individual VAT identification number to the supplier'.
18. EU Comm'n, Explanatory notes on the EU VAT changes to the place of supply of telecommunications, broadcasting and electronic services that enter into force in 2015 (2014), *available at*: https://ec.europa.eu/taxation_customs/sites/taxation/files/resources/documents/taxation/vat/how_vat_works/telecom/explanatory_notes_2015_en.pdf (accessed 9 October 2018) (hereinafter 'EC explanatory notes'). The EC Explanatory Notes, 48, confirm that Art. 18(2) is optional for suppliers, as long as the customer has not communicated his VAT number.
19. *Ibid.* at 50.
20. *Ibid.* The notes highlight that only the circumstances existing at the time of the taxable event are relevant. It is thus only when the customer qualified as a taxable person at the moment of the taxable event but was not able to provide a VAT number at that time that a rectification is possible, and not when the customer was not yet a taxable person at the time of the taxable event but becomes one shortly after.

in case of doubt, decide that the communication of the VAT number is not sufficient.[21] If, on the basis of these notes, Member States would consider that in some cases even a verified VAT number is not enough, it would obviously increase the legal uncertainty surrounding customer identification.

In the cases where a business customer does communicate a VAT number, this information may unfortunately not always be verifiable because of the limits of the VAT information exchange system (VIES), through which taxable persons are expected to verify the validity of their customers' VAT numbers. For example, the current VIES only allows for the uploading of VAT numbers attributed to suppliers who are themselves engaged in intra-EU supplies, so that a supplier who only supplies domestically (but who buys his input cross-border) will not be able to prove that he has a valid VAT number through the VIES system.

Another delicate situation occurs when the VIES confirms the validity of a VAT number but does not display the corresponding name and address. In that case, the question arises whether and how suppliers are expected to verify that the VAT number corresponds to the name and address given by the customer, as required by Article 18(1) of the Implementing Regulation 282/2011.[22] It may also be possible that the customer is using a VAT number and matching name and address that do not belong to him at all. Finally, in a sector in which transactions are concluded 365 days per year, and 24 hours a day, any temporary unavailability of the VIES would be most problematic.[23] Summing up, whenever the VIES cannot be relied on for whatever reason, digital suppliers will have difficulties to verify EU VAT numbers on a real-time basis. More fundamentally, transaction-based verification requirements seem unrealistic for digital suppliers, and surprising in view of the fact that these supplies are defined under the Implementing Regulation 282/2011 as 'automated' in their delivery and content and made with 'minimal human intervention'.

In the case of outbound B2B supplies to third countries, suppliers are expected to obtain a certificate issued by the customer's competent tax authorities as confirmation

---

21. *Ibid.*

22. EU Comm'n, FAQ on the VIES, http://ec.europa.eu/taxation_customs/vies/faq.html (accessed 9 October 2018), Question no. 17: 'Is it possible to have the name and/or the address linked to a VAT number?' Answer:

> Certain Member States permit the display of the name and address of the taxable person where the VAT number is currently valid. If no name/address is displayed, this means that the relevant Member State does not permit the display of this data.
>
> Customers have the right to get confirmation from their own tax administration if a VAT identification number is associated with a name and/or address.

23. *Ibid.* Question no. 14: 'What do I have to do if the web site doesn't run?' Answer:

> The Commission's web site is a real-time system which checks the validity of VAT identification numbers against the databases maintained by Member States. In other words, when you check a number, it is the database of that Member State that is being checked. Some parts of the system may be unavailable at certain times due to the necessity to back-up the Member States' databases.
>
> This is a known problem, and the Commission is working with Member States to ensure that the length of time that their databases are down for updating is kept to a minimum.

that the customer is engaged in economic activities (as these customers' VAT number will not be stored in the VIES).[24] In the absence of such a certificate, they should obtain a VAT number or a similar number that is attributed to the customer by the country of establishment and that is used to identify businesses or they should rely on: 'any other proof which demonstrates that the customer is a taxable person and if the supplier carries out a reasonable level of verification of the accuracy of the information provided by the customer, by normal commercial security measures such as those relating to identity or payment checks'.[25] There is no specific provision to address the situation of digital suppliers, even though these general verification requirements are very difficult, if not impossible, to implement in a digital context.[26] This having been said, the scope of application of Article 18(3) is actually quite limited because outbound supplies to third countries are generally not subject to EU VAT. Accordingly, once the supplier has determined that a client is established or resides outside of the EU, he can proceed to a VAT-free supply, without further need for status verifications (*see* below, however, the question of customer location is not always so easy to settle).

[3] Customer Location

In the case of intra-EU B2B supplies to customers located in a single jurisdiction, suppliers must identify the place of establishment or usual residence of their customers.[27] For that purpose, they must rely on information received from those customers (self-identification), but should then verify that information by: 'normal commercial security measures such as those relating to identity or payment checks.'[28]

24. Implementation Regulation 2011, Art. 18(3)a), provides that:

    3. Unless he has information to the contrary, the supplier may regard a customer established outside the Community as a taxable person:
       (a) if he obtains from the customer a certificate issued by the customer's competent tax authorities as confirmation that the customer is engaged in economic activities in order to enable him to obtain a refund of VAT under Council Directive 86/560/EEC of 17 November 1986 on the harmonization of the laws of the Member States relating to turnover taxes – Arrangements for the refund of value added tax to taxable persons not established in Community territory.

25. Implementation Regulation 2011, Art. 18(3)b).
26. As may be illustrated by some basic questions. First, on what basis does the EU legislator assume that third countries are at all prepared to issue such certificates (in particular in the absence of international mutual assistance agreements), and if so, what information should be contained in these certificates and in what language should they be drawn up? Second, the notion of a VAT number or a similar number may not even exist in certain third countries and even if it does and the number can be obtained, how can it possibly be verified by the supplier that the number actually corresponds to a specific taxpayer. Third, the requirement that 'any other proof' be considered casts doubt on the extent of suppliers' verification obligations (does it refer to any other proof that the supplier 'has' or that he should 'look for'?), and also seems unrealistic in view of the context in which supplies of electronically supplied services are taking place. In that respect, such extensive verification obligations are actually quite surprising in view of the fact that 'electronically supplied services' are defined under the VAT Directive as 'automated' in their delivery and content and made with 'minimal human intervention'.
27. That is, the place of taxation in VAT Directive, Art. 44.
28. Implementation Regulation 2011, Art. 20 provides that:

Possible limitations to the availability and reliability of VAT numbers for identification purposes were already discussed above, and the same conclusions can be drawn regarding the location information that a customer's VAT number can provide. Other identity information could possibly be drawn from the billing address provided by the customer, but this type of data can, in the author's view, not be considered as a reliable indicator in the context of electronically supplied services because the customer does not need the supplier to know where he resides, and giving a wrong billing address with the objective to obtain a lower VAT rate will have no consequences for him. Finally, suppliers do not always have access to payment details (e.g., when the transaction passes through intermediaries such as PayPal) and in any case only have access thereto after the payment has been completed (which is too late for the supplier who needs to take a decision whether or not to charge VAT to the customer).

In more complicated situations of intra-EU B2B supplies to customers located in several countries, verification obligations are even more challenging. When the supply is made to a fixed establishment of the customer located in another jurisdiction that is receiving the service and using it for its own needs, the supply is indeed deemed to take place there.[29] Beyond the question of the costs associated with these verifications, legal certainty is not ensured because the concept of fixed establishment itself which is defined as:

> Any establishment other than the place where the taxable person has established his business characterized by a certain degree of permanence and suitable structure in terms of human and technical resources to enable it to receive and use the services supplied to it for its own needs or to provide the services which it supplies, respectively.[30]

> Where a supply of services carried out for a taxable person, or a non-taxable legal person deemed to be a taxable person, falls within the scope of Article 44 of Directive 2006/112/EC, and where that taxable person is established in a single country, or, in the absence of a place of establishment of a business or a fixed establishment, has his permanent address and usually resides in a single country, that supply of services shall be taxable in that country. The supplier shall establish that place based on information from the customer, and verify that information by normal commercial security measures such as those relating to identity or payment checks. The information may include the VAT identification number attributed by the Member State where the customer is established.

29. Implementation Regulation 2011, Art. 21 provides that:

> Where a supply of services to a taxable person, or a non-taxable legal person deemed to be a taxable person, falls within the scope of Article 44 of Directive 2006/112/EC, and the taxable person is established in more than one country, that supply shall be taxable in the country where that taxable person has established his business. However, where the service is provided to a fixed establishment of the taxable person located in a place other than that where the customer has established his business, that supply shall be taxable at the place of the fixed establishment receiving that service and using it for its own needs. Where the taxable person does not have a place of establishment of a business or a fixed establishment, the supply shall be taxable at his permanent address or usual residence.

30. Implementation Regulation 2011, Art. 11.

may be interpreted differently by each Member State (it being understood that this issue is not specific to electronically supplied services).[31]

More fundamentally the question also remains open how suppliers of electronically supplied services are at all able to determine whether a fixed establishment has: 'a sufficient degree of permanence and a suitable structure in terms of human and technical resources to receive and use the service', or whether it acquires a given supply for its own need or is acquiring (or paying) the supply for mere organizational reasons within the company, and therefore whether it should effectively benefit from a zero-rated supply under reverse charging. For example, a provider of electronically supplied services providing market reports or statistics should be able to determine whether the fixed establishment acquiring one of his products is able to, and is effectively going to, use it for its own needs, and is not simply acting as paymaster among the several entities of the company. The Implementing Regulation 282/2011 clarifies that in order to determine that a customer's fixed establishment is going to use a supply, suppliers are expected to consider the 'nature and use' of the supply provided.[32] Where the nature and use of the supply provided do not allow identifying the fixed establishment to which the service is provided, suppliers are expected to:

> Pay particular attention to whether the contract, the order form and the VAT identification number attributed by the Member State of the customer and communicated to him by the customer identify the fixed establishment as the customer of the service and whether the fixed establishment is the entity paying for the service.[33]

Finally, in cases in which the customer's fixed establishment to which the supply is made cannot be determined in accordance with these elements, or in cases in which supplies are made under: 'a contract covering one or more services used in an unidentifiable and non-quantifiable manner', suppliers may legitimately consider that the supply has been provided at the place where the customer has established his business.[34] It is clear that these implementing provisions regarding multiple location customers were adopted with 'traditional services' (i.e., not digital) in mind. It is regrettable that no specific rules were adopted to address the specific situation of digital suppliers.

[4] Changes to Come with the Adoption of the E-Commerce Package?

The e-commerce package has been adopted on 5 December 2017. It will bring substantial changes to the rules that apply to Business to consumer (B2C) supplies of electronically supplied services, as will be discussed in the next section (§9.02[B]). It does, however, not concern B2B supplies at all. Accordingly, the specific situation of

31. Ine Lejeune et al., *Implementing Measures Relating to EU Place-of-Supply Rules: Are Business Issues Solved and Certainty Provided?*, 22 Int'l VAT Monitor 144, 147 (2011).
32. Implementation Regulation 2011, Art. 22 para. 1.
33. *Ibid.* para. 2.
34. *Ibid.* para. 3.

B2B digital suppliers is not likely to be better taken into consideration in the coming years and the current difficulties discussed above are here to stay.

[B] B2C Electronically Supplied Services

[1] Destination-Based Taxation and the MOSS System

In accordance with the general place of supply rules of Article 45 of the VAT Directive, B2C services are taxed at origin. While most B2C services used to be domestic (and origin- and destination-based rules would, in practice, have a similar outcome), an increasing number of them are now supplied on a cross-border basis. For what concerns B2C supplies of electronically supplied services, an origin-based system would not be tenable as it would bear major risks of distortions of consumption decision (i.e., consumers choosing to buy from suppliers located in low VAT jurisdictions) and consequently also distortions of establishment decisions (i.e., suppliers deciding to establish themselves in low VAT jurisdictions).

In 2003 the EU VAT legislator then introduced an exception to Article 45 of the VAT Directive for what concerns inbound[35] supplies of electronically supplied services to non-taxable EU customer (in line with the 1998 OECD Ottawa Framework for e-commerce transactions).[36] It is noteworthy that until 2015, Article 45 of the VAT Directive continued to apply to intra-EU supplies until 2015 (for political reasons, hence distortions of competition were arising and being located in a low VAT jurisdiction allowed to offer lower prices). Since 2015, all B2C supplies of electronically supplied services (intra-EU and inbound) are taxable at destination (and the distortions have thus been removed).

In order to streamline collection at destination, a Mini One Stop Shop (MOSS) is available that allows both EU and non-EU taxable persons to register once in the EU (in the so-called Member State of identification) and to declare and pay the VAT related to all their supplies of electronically supplied services made to EU non-taxable person through the Member State of identification.[37] The Member State of identification is then required to redistribute the revenue among the different Member States of consumption. The MOSS system, which is optional, was initially conceived to streamline tax collection by non-EU taxable persons (and has been in application for them since 2003). The same system is now available for both EU and non-EU taxable persons, even if two separate schemes coexist (a 'Union Scheme' and a 'Non-Union Scheme').[38] MOSS returns must be submitted quarterly, at the latest on the twentieth day after the end of the taxable period. There is no threshold (i.e., VAT is due from the first cent,

35. That is, supplies made by a non-EU supplier to an EU customer.
36. OECD, *Electronic Commerce: Taxation Framework Conditions* (Draft Ministerial Report) (1998) https://www.oecd.org/ctp/consumption/1923256.pdf (accessed 20 August 2018).
37. VAT Directive, Arts 359 et seq.
38. Council regulation (EU) 967/2012 of 9 October 2012 amending Implementing Regulation (EU) No 282/2011 as regards the special schemes for non-established taxable persons supplying telecommunications services, broadcasting services or electronic services to non-taxable persons, OJ L 290/1 (2012).

irrespective of the supplier's turnover). Quarterly returns must be submitted even if no supply has taken place in a given taxable period.

A centralized point of registration certainly simplifies the remittance process. It is noteworthy, however, that this has not been sufficient to incentivize compliance. The number of registrations is indeed not very high, in particular for what concerns non-EU taxable persons.

In 2016, 12,900 EU taxable persons had registered to the MOSS (one year after it became available to them).[39] Although the question may be raised whether 12,900 registrations correctly reflect the number of non-EU taxable persons supplying electronic services to EU no-taxable persons, this is at least a much higher figure than the number of registration by non-EU suppliers. As a matter of fact, only 539 businesses were registered under the MOSS in January 2014 (thus eleven years after the scheme had been put into place).[40] Massive information campaigns were then run in 2014 in order to better inform non-EU taxable persons of their obligations and of the facilitation offered to them via the MOSS (in view of the implementation of a similar system for EU suppliers).[41] Unfortunately, the number of registrations by non-EU taxable persons has remained relatively low (a bit more than 1,000). This difference in the number of registration by EU and non-EU taxable persons can be explained by the greater possibility for Member States to enforce the registration requirement over EU taxable persons, in view of the existence of instruments of cooperation between the Member States. Moreover, for EU taxable persons, the MOSS registration is to be made in their Member State of establishment, which is always simpler than to register in a foreign country. EU businesses are therefore more likely to be compliant. In contrast, EU Member States have no enforcement jurisdiction beyond their borders. In practice this creates an unlevelled playing field between EU and non-EU businesses. This is one of the reasons why the EC made the 'e-commerce package' proposal (adopted in December 2017, *see* section (§9.02[B][4].):

39. EU Comm'n, Impact Assessment accompanying the EC proposal for Council Directive amending Directive 2006/112/EC as regards harmonizing and simplifying certain rules in the value added tax system and introducing the definitive system for the taxation of trade between Member States, SWD(2017) 325 final, 74 (hereinafter 'Impact Assessment').
40. Most of them in the United Kingdom (266), followed by the Netherlands (111), Germany (43), Ireland (41), and Luxembourg (28). Only fifteen had registered in France, fourteen in Italy, eight in Sweden, four in Malta, three in Denmark, two in Spain, one in Belgium, Bulgaria, Cyprus and Greece, and none in Austria, the Czech Republic, Croatia, Estonia, Finland, Hungary, Latvia, Lithuania, Poland, Portugal, Romania, and Slovakia (figures communicated by the UK Treasury in January 2014).
41. Impact Assessment, 70. The Commission, in collaboration with Member States and business organization, participated in a number of seminars to explain to business how the new rules would work, and what it can offer them in terms of simplicity. The Commission made a keynote presentation at the OECD Global VAT Forum in Japan in April 2014. Further events took place in Luxembourg, the UK, Poland, Germany and the US. In addition, the Commission has a dedicated web portal with all the relevant information on the 2015 changes and MOSS, https://ec.europa.eu/taxation_customs/business/vat/telecommunications-broadcasting-electronic-services/content/mini-one-stop-shop_en (accessed 19 October 2018).

> There are in essence three reasons to act: ... the current system is not neutral as EU businesses are at a clear disadvantage to non-EU businesses which can legitimately and through high levels of non-compliance make VAT-free supplies into the EU. Given that VAT rates can be as high as 27%, there is a substantial distortion in favour of non-EU business if VAT is not applied.[42]

High setting-up costs probably also have an impact on compliance (in particular for non-EU taxable persons, which are outside jurisdictional reach of the EU Member States). The final version of the impact assessment accompanying the e-commerce package proposal (hereinafter 'Impact Assessment')[43] does not provide an estimate of the setting-up costs for the MOSS (in particular for adapting information technology systems). It only mentions running costs (EUR 2,200 per year per business, only for the technicalities of using the MOSS, which is already quite a lot).[44] However, a provisional figure of EUR 2.5 million setting-up cost per business and an average annual administrative burden estimated at EUR 2,172 for EU suppliers and EUR 41,623 for non-EU suppliers had been communicated in February 2016 (but has apparently been removed from the final version of the Impact Assessment).

[2] Customer Location

In the case of B2C supplies, self-identification verified by suppliers is again the rule.[45] In the absence of 'official' information available for non-taxable persons (such as a VAT number), verifications must be made on the basis of: 'normal commercial security measures such as those relating to identity or payment checks'.[46] Fact is, however, that suppliers again do not always have access to payment details (e.g., when the transaction passes through intermediaries such as PayPal or if the customer uses e-cash), and it remains unclear what the EU legislator means by 'identity checks' that could be performed by the supplier of electronically supplied services to non-taxable persons, be it from a legal, commercial or timing perspective (once again taking into account that the category 'electronically supplied services' only covers supplies that are 'automated, made with minimal human intervention').[47] In fact, even when the customer uses a simple credit card, the payment information will only be known to the

42. EU Comm'n, Proposal for Council Directive amending Directive 2006/112/EC as regards harmonizing and simplifying certain rules in the value added tax system and introducing the definitive system for the taxation of trade between Member States: Explanatory Memorandum, 4 October 2017, COM(2017) 569 final, 2.
43. Impact Assessment.
44. A provisional figure of EUR 2.5 million setting-up cost per business and an average annual administrative burden estimated at EUR 2,172 for EU suppliers and EUR 41,623 for non-EU suppliers had been communicated in February 2016 in a draft version of the report but has apparently been removed from the final version of the report.
45. In accordance with Implementation Regulation 2011, Art. 23(1).
46. Implementation Regulation 2011, Art. 23(2).
47. Would 'identity check' relate to the customer's Internet Protocol (IP) address? IP addresses are not reliable as proxies as they can be manipulated. Also to be noted that in *Scarlet Extended*, C-70/10, Judgment, EU:C:2011:771, para. 51, the CJEU decided that IP addresses are personal data because they allow those users to be precisely identified. The European Commission also took the view that IP addresses are personal data in its recent proposals to reform the EU data

supplier once the payment has been completed (while the location information is needed at the time when the correct amount of VAT must be calculated, i.e., before payment).

Additional verifications are furthermore needed when the consumer is established in more than one country or has his permanent address in one country and his usual residence in another (multiple location customer). In that case, the supplier must determine the: 'place that best ensures taxation at the place of actual consumption'.[48] Council Regulation 1042/2013 clarified this concept by introducing a hierarchy. For non-taxable legal persons central administration comes first, unless there is evidence that the service is used at a fixed establishment. For non-taxable natural persons, the place of residence comes first, unless there is evidence that the service is used at the permanent address. Quite unfortunately, Council Regulation 1042/2013 did not give any guidance either on how to determine where these places are effectively located or on how to determine that consumption occurs at a fixed establishment or at a permanent address (i.e., the lowest ranked proxy).[49] In B2C supplies in particular, a related element that should not be underestimated is the average sales price and profit margin of electronically supplied services and the high number of daily transactions (low value high volume). Many electronically supplied services are indeed cheap (e.g., a few cents or a couple of euros for a song), and the number of daily cross-border transactions is much higher than in conventional commerce. This means that imposing transaction-based verifications may risk to cause costs equal to or even exceeding the benefit of most transactions.

Council Regulation 1042/2013 however provides for a series of presumptions that should apply when it proves: 'extremely difficult, if not practically impossible, for the supplier to know where the customer is actually established, has his permanent address or usually resides'.[50] It remains unclear whether to 'know' in this case actually means 'to verify' customer location on the basis of the rules described above. However, we assume that it is indeed only when these verifications have remained unfruitful that suppliers should rely on the presumptions. The questions may nevertheless be raised whether suppliers are aware of the fact that they cannot directly rely on the presumptions but should first try to apply the normal rules, and whether they will have to demonstrate to the tax administration that their efforts have remained unfruitful to

protection framework. EU Comm'n (2012a), Data protection reform: Frequently asked questions, in MEMO/12/403, Electronic identification, signatures and trust services: Questions & Answers (2012), http://europa.eu/rapid/press-release_MEMO-12-403_en.htm?locale=en (accessed 9 October 2018).

48. Implementation Regulation 2011 before its amendment by Implementation Regulation 2013, Art. 24(2).

49. For example, a provider of electronically supplied services may not in all reasonableness be expected to be able to determine whether a consumer will listen to the music or watch the movies he has downloaded from his principal or secondary residence. Nor may he be expected to be able to determine whether a private customer is a multiple or single location customer, hence whether the tax should be assessed in accordance with the rules applicable in the country of residence or establishment of the customer or whether further investigation should be performed to determine the place that: 'best ensures taxation at the place of actual consumption' (as required under Art. 24(2) of the Implementing Regulation 2011.

50. EC explanatory notes, 55.

justify the use of the presumptions at the stage of the audit. More importantly the question may also be raised whether the presumptions are an improvement, i.e., whether they effectively facilitate suppliers' task and increase legal certainty.

A number of presumptions could in principle apply, but in practice the presumption that is most likely to apply requires from the taxable person that he collects two pieces of non-contradictory evidence to determine location (including for example an Internet Protocol (IP) address, a billing address, a credit card number or any other element that would allow determining the residence of the customer).[51] This presumption still does not offer the legal certainty to which taxable persons are entitled because it assumes that the taxable persons are able to proceed to real-time verifications and arbitrages (e.g., such as taking a decision if the IP address and the billing address are different).[52] It is therefore not surprising that the EC itself acknowledged that: 'The concerns raised during the consultation process by businesses and business associations, including small and medium enterprises, mainly relate to the 2015 place of supply rules and application of the MOSS for the services concerned.'[53]

Another issue is that the Member States of consumption remain competent to audit the suppliers (and not the Member States of identification). Therefore, taxable persons may be confronted to different expectations in terms of compliance. The Commission tried but failed to convince the Member States to adopt a standard audit file.[54] This potentially further increases compliance costs and legal uncertainty for businesses.

[3] A Deeming Provision for Platforms

Last but not least, Council Regulation 1042/2013 has rendered platforms liable for the collection of VAT in supplies made through them in specific circumstances. More precisely, building on the legal fiction laid down in Article 28 of the VAT Directive, Article 9a in Council Regulation 282/2011 (as amended by Council Regulation 1042/2013) foresees that any taxable person who 'takes part' in the supply of electronically supplied services is deemed to be acting in his own name albeit on behalf of the initial provider of these services.[55]

---

51. Implementing Regulation 2011 as amended by Implementation Regulation 2013, Art. 24(a) d).
52. *See* Marie Lamensch, *Tax Assessment in a Digital Context: A Critical Analysis of the 2015 EU Rules*, *in* 46 *Value Added Tax and the Digital Economy: The 2015 EU Rules and Broader Issues, EUCOTAX Series on European Taxation* 39 (Marie Lamensch, Edoardo Traversa & Servaas van Thiel eds., Kluwer 2015).
53. EU Comm'n, Proposal for Council Directive amending Directive 2006/112/EC as regards harmonizing and simplifying certain rules in the value added tax system and introducing the definitive system for the taxation of trade between Member States, Explanatory Memorandum, *supra* note 42, at 5.
54. EU Comm'n, Withdrawal of Commission Proposals (2016/C 155/04), List of Withdrawn Proposals, OJ C 155/3 (2016).
55. Implementation Regulation 2011 as amended by Implementation Regulation 2013, Art. 9(a) provides that:

    1. For the application of Article 28 of Directive 2006/112/EC, where electronically supplied services are supplied through a telecommunications network, an interface or

The presumption does not apply (i.e., can be rebutted) when the initial service provider is explicitly indicated as the supplier by the taxable person taking part in the supply,[56] and this is reflected in the contractual arrangements with the customer, either because the initial supplier is identified on the invoice issued by each person taking part in the B2B supply or in the customer's bill or receipt in the case of a B2C supply.[57] When these (cumulative) conditions are met, the initial provider of the electronically supplied service will remain the one liable for assessing and collecting the tax.[58]

A taxable person taking part in the supply by authorising payment or delivery[59] or setting the terms and conditions of the supply will, however, have no possibility to escape from the application of the presumption, even if he/she fulfils these conditions (one of the three events is enough to exclude the rebuttal of the presumption).[60] In contrast, a taxable person only processing the payment will not be covered by the presumption.

---

a portal such as a marketplace for applications, a taxable person taking part in that supply shall be presumed to be acting in his own name but on behalf of the provider of those services unless that provider is explicitly indicated as the supplier by that taxable person and that is reflected in the contractual arrangements between the parties. In order to regard the provider of electronically supplied services as being explicitly indicated as the supplier of those services by the taxable person, the following conditions shall be met:

(a) the invoice issued or made available by each taxable person taking part in the supply of the electronically supplied services must identify such services and the supplier thereof;

(b) the bill or receipt issued or made available to the customer must identify the electronically supplied services and the supplier thereof. For the purposes of this paragraph, a taxable person who, with regard to a supply of electronically supplied services, authorizes the charge to the customer or the delivery of the services, or sets the general terms and conditions of the supply, shall not be permitted to explicitly indicate another person as the supplier of those services. (b) ...

3. This Article shall not apply to a taxable person who only provides for processing of payments in respect of electronically supplied services or of telephone services provided through the internet, including voice over internet Protocol (VoIP), and who does not take part in the supply of those electronically supplied services or telephone services.

56. EC explanatory notes, 33, clarify that the identification of the supplier must be clear and unambiguous (i.e., can be made by a code provided it is clear enough for all the parties, does not need to include full coordinates). European Commission.
57. EC explanatory notes, 24.
58. *Ibid.* at 32–33.
59. *Ibid.* at 34. According to the EC explanatory notes, authorizing the payment means deciding that the customer's account, credit or debit card can be debited as payment for the electronically supplied service while authorizing the delivery refers to deciding whether, at what time or under which preconditions the delivery is made. In practice, a taxable person authorizes a delivery when he either sends approval to start the delivery of the service, delivers the service himself or instructs a third party to do so (in practice the person authorizing the delivery is likely to be the one who controls the technical platform over which the services are provided).
60. *Ibid.* at 34–35. According to the EC explanatory notes, this for example includes the terms and conditions set by marketplaces and similar platforms requiring users to agree to general terms and conditions for doing business with that website or platform (such as maintaining an account) as well as the general terms and conditions (including licence agreements) which the final consumer has to agree with before receiving access to the app or content. Illustrative charts of the scenario in which all the intermediaries rebutted the presumption and in which some intermediaries are caught and not others are offered on the following pages.

According to the EC explanatory notes, if at any stage an intermediary is covered by the presumption (either because one or two above conditions are not met or if he/she authorizes the payment or delivery or sets the terms conditions), it will not be possible for intermediaries further down the chain to indicate the original supplier as the supplier of the service. In that case, it will only be possible to go back up to the first intermediary covered by the presumption.

The EC explanatory notes also give several examples (with illustrative charts) of situations in which a taxable person is, in the EC's opinion, 'taking part' in the supply for the purpose of Article 9a of the Implementing Regulation. This includes the case in which the taxable person owns or manages the technical platform over which supplies are provided, controls or exerts influence on the pricing, issues a VAT invoice, receipts, or bills to the customer, provides customer support in relation to the service supplied, owns the customer data, or exerts influence over the presentation and format of the virtual market place 'so that the brand and identity of the taxable person are significantly more prominent than those of the other persons involved in the supply' (and here the explanatory notes explicitly refer to app stores).[61]

The EC explanatory notes also stress that the assessment of the chain supply should start at the level of the final consumer and move upstream in the chain.[62] In other words, in case several intermediaries could be covered by the presumption, it is the intermediary covered by the presumption under 9a of the Implementing Regulation that is the closest to the customer that will be the taxable person. The explanatory notes further hold that a taxable person should normally be deemed to be taking part in the supply if contractual or legal arrangements stipulate clearly that this person is acting in his own name but on behalf of the initial provider and this reflects reality, but that if the contractual or legal arrangements may be not sufficiently clear on that question, all the factual features of the transaction need be taken into account. The notes also clarify that it is not sufficient to insert a clause in the contract that would exclude a taxable person from the chain of transaction if this does not reflect economic reality.[63] Because a taxable person only processing the payment will not be covered by the presumption, the EC explanatory notes analyse more concrete situations where the Internet provider or mobile operator facilitates the flow of cash and/or content.[64] In short, the question in these cases is whether the participation of these intermediaries is sufficiently predominant.

Shifting the tax liability to the successive intermediaries taking part in such chain supplies seems a logical and desirable improvement that increases legal certainty. As a matter of fact, when a digital supplier relies on several intermediaries to market his products (including for example a marketplace for applications), he will in many cases not have any contact whatsoever with final customers. In these circumstances, he cannot reasonably be expected to correctly assess and collect VAT on final supplies. In contrast, intermediaries will in many cases have easier access to relevant and reliable

61. *Ibid.* at 28–29.
62. *Ibid.* at 35.
63. *Ibid.* at 27.
64. *Ibid.* at 29.

information regarding customers, obtained in the context of more established relationships (e.g., if the intermediary covered by the presumption is a marketplace for applications to which all the devices of the customer are connected, e.g., Apple store).

This having been said, because of the complexity of some transaction chains, and the high number of intermediaries possibly involved in an online supply, implementing Article 9a of the Implementing Regulation 282/2011 may not always be so easy and the EC explanatory notes are in this case extremely useful, provided the interpretations given therein are fully endorsed by the Member States and would be confirmed by the CJEU. In the author's view, however, the EC explanatory notes offer a rather disputable interpretation of this provision. As a matter of fact, even though Article 9a of the Implementing Regulation provides that an intermediary, who authorizes the charge to the customer or the delivery of the services or sets the general terms and conditions of the supply, cannot indicate another person as the supplier of those services (and therefore is automatically to be considered as the taxable person in the supply), it does not say anything that, in the author's view, can be interpreted as including intermediaries who, for example, provide customer support in relation to the service supplied, exert influence over the presentation and format of a marketplace or own customers data.

Some cases will also remain more difficult to handle, for example when, at the end of the chain, two intermediaries 'taking part' in the supply can be considered as equally close to the final customer, or when the different intermediaries are not aware of the others' 'interventions', and therefore cannot assess how close they are to the final consumer. However, it can be assumed that in the great majority of the cases, intermediaries 'taking part' to a supply will know who else is involved in the supply and how 'close' they are to the customers. Moreover, even if Article 9a of the Implementing Regulation 282/2011 may be complex to implement, the complexity in fact mostly comes from the transactional scenario chosen by the taxable persons involved.

[4] Changes to Come with the Adoption of the E-Commerce Package?

[a] An 'E-Commerce Package for All B2C E-Commerce Transactions'

On 5 December 2017 the VAT 'e-commerce package' was adopted. The package is composed of one directive (Council Directive 2017/2455 amending Directive 2006/112/EC and Directive 2009/132/EC as regards certain VAT obligations for supplies of services and distance sales of goods) and two regulations (Implementing Regulation (EU) 2017/2459 amending Implementing Regulation (EU) No. 282/2011 laying down implementing measures for Directive 2006/112/EC on the common system of VAT and Council Regulation (EU) 2017/2454 amending Regulation (EU) No. 904/2010 on administrative cooperation and combating fraud in the field of VAT). The e-commerce package covers all B2C 'e-commerce transactions', including supplies of intra-EU and inbound B2C electronically supplied services, intra-EU B2C distance sales of goods and B2C imports. The next subsections summarize the amendments that are made to the provisions that concern electronically supplied services only.

[b] Availability of the Non-union Scheme for Non-EU Suppliers with an EU VAT Number

At the moment, non-EU taxable persons who do have a VAT number in the EU (for occasional supplies) are allowed to use neither the non-EU scheme nor the EU scheme. As a consequence, they have to register in each jurisdiction of consumption. As of 2019, a taxable person not established in the EU but having an EU VAT number will be able to use the MOSS (non-Union scheme). A loophole of the current MOSS system will thus be fixed.

[c] A First Threshold of EUR 10,000 (as of 2019)

As of 2019, a threshold of EUR 10,000 will be applied below which the place of supply of B2C supplies of electronically supplied services will be in the Member State of the supplier (only B2C supplies are taken into account for the application of the threshold).[65] We will thus have a comeback of the origin principle in the case of intra-EU B2C supplies when the supplier has a small cross-border turnover. This move goes at odds with the OECD VAT/GST guidelines that services and intangibles should be taxed at destination in order to ensure neutrality in cross-border trade.[66] As a result thereof, distortions of competition may again arise in favour of taxable persons located in low VAT Member States. In addition, this step backward reintroduces a discrimination towards non-EU businesses that will still be required to collect the tax at destination (with the related compliance burden) irrespective of the volume of sales to the EU.

From a government perspective the risk also exists that taxable persons with a low cross-border turnover under-declare VAT in order to remain under the threshold (which they might not be tempted to do if the consequences of exceeding the threshold were not as substantial as having to register to the MOSS and make periodical returns even in the absence of sales in a given period).

On the positive side, the threshold is likely to be a relief for EU taxable persons making a few sales cross-border. Origin taxation should moreover remain optional. In other words, small and medium-sized enterprises (SMEs) should be 'allowed to use the MOSS anyhow, e.g., if during a calendar year their turnover is exceptionally below the threshold'.

Another positive aspect is that it mitigates to a certain extent the non-applicability of the SME exemption scheme at a cross-border level (at least for what concerns digital suppliers). As confirmed by the CJEU in the *Schmelz* case,[67] Member States are indeed not obliged to grant the benefit of their domestic SME scheme to taxable person located

65. Paragraphs 2 to 5 to be added to VAT Directive, Art. 58. This means that a company with a large domestic turnover but a small cross-border turnover will also be able to benefit from the option.
66. OECD, *International VAT/GST Guidelines*, *supra* note 3.
67. *Schmelz*, C-97/09, Judgment, EU:C:2010:632.

in another Member State (according to the CJEU, this is an obstacle to the free movement of services that is justified by the effectiveness of tax controls).[68] While a simplified registration via the MOSS would already be easier than a traditional registration for small digital suppliers that are exempt at home, an origin-based taxation (exemption) is even easier.[69]

[d] Home Country Rules for Invoicing and Record-Keeping

Also as of 2019, the invoicing rules of the Member State of identification will apply.[70] In other words, while the Member States of consumption have the taxing rights, they should accept to audit taxable persons on the basis of invoices drawn up in accordance with other Member States rules. This is likely to be a major relief for businesses. On the downside, however, they will have to keep records of all transactions for a period of ten years, which largely exceeds the record-keeping requirements of most Member States.

From a government perspective, it remains to be seen how tax administrations will audit taxable persons on the basis of invoices of a very different format (and in different languages).

[e] Relaxed Customer Identification Requirement below a Second Threshold of EUR 100,000

The requirements regarding customer location in the case of electronically supplied services will also be relaxed as of 2019. From that date, a single piece of evidence will be sufficient (instead of two as mentioned above) where the total annual value of intra-EU B2C supplies, exclusive of VAT, does not exceed EUR 100,000.[71] This threshold does thus again only apply to intra-EU supplies (in the same way as the first threshold of EUR 10,000 discussed above). Accordingly, it again provides for a less favourable treatment of non-EU businesses. The question then arises how are small non-EU taxable persons supposed to comply with the two pieces of evidence requirement when it is clearly acknowledged that small EU taxable persons cannot?

In general, also, it seems that only requiring one piece of evidence means that it will be very easy for fraudulent customers to obtain VAT-free supplies (e.g., by changing their IP address or by providing a false billing address). For the sake of clarity, and as already written elsewhere, the author believes that the two pieces of evidence requirement were difficult to abide by SMEs.[72] However, the solution does, in the

68. For an analysis of this decision, see Marie Lamensch (2013) *Lenient Constitutional Control of the VAT Exemption for Small- and-Medium Sized Enterprises? – Commentary on the European Court Decision in the Schmelz case, in Tax Law in the Light of Judgments: Interaction Between European law and Domestic Courts – 2012; Tax Planning: What Is (Un)acceptable – 2013, in* 5 *Forum Reports on European Taxation* (Servaas van Thiel ed., CFE 2013).
69. As of 2021, the same threshold will apply for intra-EU distance supplies of goods.
70. VAT Directive, Art. 219(a).
71. Implementing Regulation 2011, Art. 24(b), paras 2 & 3.
72. Marie Lamensch, *The 2015 Rules for Electronically Supplied Services – Compliance Issues*, 26 Int'l VAT Monitor 11 (2015).

author's view, not lie in the relaxing of this requirement but rather in the design of an alternative method of assessing and collection VAT on electronically supplied services.[73]

[f] *Longer Deadlines to Submit MOSS Returns and Easier Procedure to Correct VAT Returns*

As of 2021, the deadline to submit MOSS returns will be extended, from twentieth to the last day of the month following the end of the tax period.[74]

Another positive change for business is that, from 2021 on, it will also be possible to correct previous VAT returns in a subsequent return (instead of in the returns of the tax periods to which the corrections relate).[75]

[g] *Final Comments on the E-commerce Package*

We already noted that the newly adopted e-commerce package does not address the flaws of the current rules applicable in the case of B2B supplies.

With respect to B2C supplies, although it does contain several amendments, it is regrettable that nothing is foreseen to address the key issue of the low level of compliance by non-EU taxable persons (as reflected in the very low number of MOSS registrations by non-EU suppliers). In this context, it is also regrettable that difficult and costly verification requirements are being maintained on non-EU taxable persons regarding customer location (while they are being softened for the smaller EU suppliers because the EC itself acknowledges that the current requirements are difficult to comply with). This will certainly not help increasing the level of compliance from non-EU taxable persons. Consequently, the EU Member States will continue to lose substantial VAT revenue.

§9.03 ELECTRONICALLY SUPPLIED SERVICES: EU VAT DIRECTIVE PROVISIONS ON REDUCED RATES AND RECENT EC PROPOSAL

[A] Current Rules

In accordance with Article 98(2) of the VAT Directive, electronically supplied services cannot be subject to reduced rates. In 2015, the CJEU had to confirm that both French and Luxembourg legislation providing for the application of reduced rates to e-books were infringing the VAT Directive and thereby causing distortions of competition with the twenty-six other Member States.[76] The Court further decided that Article 98(2) of

73. Lamensch, *supra* note 8.
74. VAT Directive Art. 369(f) for the EU scheme; *and* VAT Directive Art. 364 for the non-EU scheme.
75. VAT Directive Art. 365 for the non-EU scheme; *and* VAT Directive Art. 369(g)(4) for the EU scheme.
76. *Commission* v *France*, C-479/13, Judgment, EU:C:2015:141; *and Commission* v *Luxembourg*, C-502/13, Judgment, EU:C:2015:143. To be noted that the distortions of competition in question

the VAT Directive could not be challenged on the basis of the principle of fiscal neutrality because this principle 'cannot extend the scope of reduced rates of VAT to the supply of electronic books' and because 'Point 6 of Annex III to the VAT Directive is not a provision which, unequivocally, extends the scope of reduced rates of VAT to the supply of electronic books'.[77] The Court here referred to its decision in C-174/11 Zimmermann,[78] that:

> The principle of fiscal neutrality – a particular expression of the principle of equal treatment at the level of secondary EU law and in the specific area of taxation ...[79] is not a rule of primary law against which it is possible to test the validity of an exemption provided for under Article 13 of the Sixth Directive. Nor does that principle make it possible for the scope of such an exemption to be extended in the absence of an unequivocal provision to that effect.

The Court thus decided that France and Luxembourg were not justified in applying reduced rates to e-books under the arguments, first, that the text of the VAT Directive as currently drafted does not allow for the application of reduced rates to e-books and, second, that the principle of fiscal neutrality cannot overrule the text of the VAT Directive. As written elsewhere, the author is of the opinion that the principle of neutrality is not breached in this case because books and e-books are not similar and therefore a different treatment cannot be found discriminatory.[80] In her opinion, the decision to apply different rate may be disputable from a tax policy perspective (why not also encouraging reading e-books?) but not on the ground of equal treatment.

The CJEU eventually adopted a different view in the C-390/15 *RPO* case. The referring Court was asking the CJEU whether Article 98(2) of the VAT Directive read in conjunction with point 6 of Annex III would not be invalid on the ground that, by ruling out any possibility for the Member States of applying a reduced rate of VAT to the

---

have naturally disappeared on 1 January 2015, when all intra-EU supplies of electronically supplied services to non-taxable persons became taxable at destination in accordance with VAT Directive, Art. 58(c), as amended by Council Directive 2008/8 amending Directive 2006/112/EC as regards the place of supply of services, Art. 5, [2008] OJ L 44/11.

77. *Commission* v *Luxembourg*, C-502/13, para. 51.
78. *Zimmermann*, C-174/11, Judgment, EU:C:2012:716; Same decision in *Deutsche Bank*, C-44/11, Judgment, EU:C:2012:484, in which the Court endorsed Advocate General Sharpston's (ad absurdum) reasoning (*Deutsche Bank*, C-44/11, AG Opinion, EU:C:2012:276, pt. 60) that:

> If all activities partly in competition with each other had to receive the same VAT treatment, the final result would be – since practically every activity overlaps to some extent with another – to eliminate all differences in VAT treatment entirely. That would (presumably) lead to the elimination of all exemptions, since the VAT system exists only to tax transactions.

79. Reference is made to *NCC Construction Danmark*, C-174/08, Judgment, EU:C:2009:669, para. 44.
80. Marie Lamensch, *Different VAT Rates for Digital and Paperback Publications in the EU, a Breach of 'Fiscal Neutrality'? A Tentative Answer and Broader Reflection on the Coherence of the EU Rules Prohibiting Indirect Tax Discrimination*, 4 World J. VAT/GST L. 1 (2015). *See also*, *K Oy*, C-219/13, Judgment, EU:C:2014:2207, that did not concern electronically supplied services but books supplied in a physical format other than a paper format (i.e., an electronic file on a physical support).

supply of e-books, that article would infringe the principle of equal treatment as set out in Article 20 of the EU Charter of Fundamental Rights. In a first step the CJEU found that, in the light of the objective pursued by Article 98(2) of the VAT Directive, read in conjunction with point 6 of Annex III, the supply of digital books on all physical means of support and the supply of digital books electronically amount to comparable situations.[81] The CJEU, however, still did not conclude to a breach of neutrality because it considered that the discrimination resulting from the non-applicability of reduced rates to the latter situation is justified.[82]

According to the CJEU, when the EU legislature adopts a tax measure:

> it is called upon to make political, economic and social choices, and to rank divergent interests or to undertake complex assessments. Consequently, it should, in that context, be accorded a broad discretion, so that judicial review of compliance with the conditions set out in the previous paragraph of this judgment must be limited to review as to manifest error.[83]

Based on the preparatory documents for Directive 2002/38 (which introduced the first provisions as regards electronically supplied services in the VAT Directive), the CJEU highlighted that the amendments then proposed were 'a first step in implementing a new policy on VAT, intended to simplify and strengthen the VAT system in order to encourage legitimate commercial transactions within the internal market'[84] and that 'it was considered necessary to make electronically supplied services subject to clear, simple and uniform rules in order that the VAT rate applicable to those services may be established with certainty and, thus, that the administration of VAT by taxable persons and national tax authorities is facilitated'.[85] It is therefore on the basis of the principle of legal certainty (in the sense that EU rules should enable those concerned to know unequivocally the extent of their rights and obligations so that they are in a position to order their affairs with the benefit of full information)[86] and simplicity (considering that it is a legitimate objective to lay down general rules which can be easily applied by economic operators and are easily verified by the competent national authorities)[87] that the non-applicability of reduced rates to electronically supplied services, which 'spares taxable persons and national tax authorities from an obligation to examine, for each type of electronic service that is supplied, whether it falls within one of the categories of services that qualify for such a rate under Annex III to the VAT' and the resulting discrimination would be justified. The CJEU further confirms that the measures are appropriate and proportionate to reach that objective.[88]

---

81. *RPO*, C-390/15, Judgment, EU:C:2017:174, para. 49.
82. *Ibid.* para. 52; with reference to *Arcelor Atlantique and Lorraine & Others*, C-127/07, Judgment, EU:C:2008:728, para. 46.
83. *RPO*, C-390/15, para. 54; with reference to (*see*, to that effect, judgments *British American Tobacco (Investments) and Imperial Tobacco*, C-491/01, Judgment, EU:C:2002:741, para. 123; *and Billerud Karlsborg and Billerud Skärblacka*, C-203/12, Judgment, EU:C:2013:664, para. 35).
84. *RPO*, C-390/15, para. 56.
85. *Ibid.* para. 57.
86. *Ibid.* para. 59.
87. *Ibid.* para. 60.
88. *Ibid.* paras 63–64.

While the general prohibition laid down under Article 98(2) of the VAT Directive still remains valid, on 6 November 2018, the Member States have adopted a Directive that allows them to apply reduced, super-reduced, or zero VAT rates to 'electronic publications', thereby allowing future alignment of VAT rules for electronic and 'physical' publications.[89] Although this Directive only concerns 'electronic publications', this might be actually be the first step towards a generalization of reduced rates on electronically supplied services as the EC subsequently issued a proposal which would allow Member States more flexibility as regards rates in general, in the context of the 'definitive' VAT system (the 6 November Directive will only apply until such a broader liberalization is achieved). The key features of this EC proposal will be sketched and briefly commented in the next section.

[B] EC Proposal: Possibility to Apply Reduced Rates in the Future?

On 18 January 2018, the EC tabled an ambitious Proposal regarding VAT rates.[90] The EC indeed proposes that more flexibility be offered to the Member States regarding the applicable rate structure in general – not only with respect to electronic publications. The reasons is that the historical ambition to set up a 'definitive VAT system' based on the principle of origin (which required a certain level of harmonization of rates in order to avoid distortions of competition) was abandoned, and the Commission is now proposing a 'definitive VAT system' based on the destination principle (under which different rates would not distort competition).

The main points of this proposal can be summarized as follows.

A first important point is that no amendment of Articles 96 and 97 of the VAT Directive is foreseen, which means that even in the new VAT rate system a standard rate of at least 15% will have to be applied to both supplies of goods and services.

A second point is that a new Article 98 of the VAT Directive, which combines the current Articles 98 and 99 of the VAT Directive, would allow Member States to not only maintain the two existent reduced rates (of a minimum of 5%) but to also add an additional reduced rate with no minimum requirement and a zero rate. However, these reduced rates should always benefit the final consumer and should be in the general interest. In practice, it means that reduced rates should not apply to supplies that are only used as intermediate input and will not eventually be sold to final consumers. Moreover, the new Article 99a would require from Member States that take into account that the weighted average VAT rate, which should in any case exceed 12%.

A third and most important point is that the method of listing supplies for which a reduced rate can be applied (current Annex III) would no longer apply. A reverse

89. Council Directive amending Directive 2006/112/EC, as regards rates of value added tax applied to books, newspapers, and periodicals, OJ L 286, 14.11.2018, pp. 20–21. The proposal for this Directive was adopted on the same day as the proposal for the e-commerce VAT package.

90. *Ibid.* (SWD(2018) 7 final) – (SWD(2018) 8 final COM(2018) 20 final).

method is proposed instead: a new Annex (Annex IIIa) would indeed list the supplies to which reduced rates could not apply (e.g., supply of excise goods, precious metals, jewellery, alcoholic beverages and tobacco products, to the supply of weapons, oil, computers, watches, furniture, musical instruments, works of art and surprisingly even financial and insurance services).[91]

An in-depth analysis of this proposal would go beyond the scope of this manuscript. A general comment may, however, be made that is relevant for electronically supplied services: although the initial idea that the EU VAT system would eventually become 'origin based' was abandoned, the author shares the opinion of other scholars[92] that it remains necessary to maintain a certain level of approximation with respect to rates for the sake of the achievement of the Internal Market, i.e., an area without internal borders where goods and services move freely. As a matter of fact, the possibility that VAT rates schemes would greatly vary among the Member States is a clear obstacle to cross-border trade within the EU. For what concerns electronically supplied services in particular, the arguments of legal certainty and simplicity raised by the CJEU in the RPO case are extremely relevant. In the case of a digital supplier serving customers in potentially all Member State, not being able to apply the standard rate would indeed be extremely complex. All the more so if different rates were adopted depending on the type of electronically supplied services (e.g., Music, videos, e-books, audiobooks).

§9.04 CONCLUSIONS AND FINAL COMMENTS

After setting the scene by summarizing the challenges to which the VAT system in general is confronted with the development of the Digital Economy and the apparition of 'digital supplies', this contribution sought to provide a detailed analysis of the place of supply and related collection rules that apply to 'electronically supplied services' under the EU VAT Directive and the Implementing Regulations. While pointing at the flaws of the current legislation, it also discussed the positive and less positive amendments that will enter into effect in 2019 and 2021. A main conclusion that can be drawn from this analysis is that enforcement, in particular on non-EU taxable persons making supplies to EU non-taxable consumers, remains a major weakness. In the author's view, only a complete change of approach - and the reliance on new technologies - would enable the Member States to effectively collect their VAT on such digital supplies.

91. EU Comm'n, Annex to the Proposal for a Council Directive amending Directive 2006/112/EC, *supra* note 91, COM(2018) 20. The European Commission justifies this list by stating that a standard rate in these domains prevents distortions of competition and serves as a counterbalance against the increased flexibility that is given to the Member States.

92. *See* Rita de la Feria & Max Schofield, *Towards an [Unlawful] Modernized EU VAT Rate Policy*, 26 EC Tax Rev. 89 (2017). The authors conclude that: 'Article 113 TFEU could not be used as a legal basis for a Directive aimed at disharmonizing VAT rates, and that any such Directive, would lack legal basis and, consequently, be unlawful under the EU constitutional principle of conferral of powers.'

This contribution also presented an overview of the situation regarding the application of reduced rates, recalling that under the current state of the law, the Member States are not allowed to apply reduced rates to electronically supplied services, but noting that this may change in the future, with a potentially substantial impact for digital suppliers.

CHAPTER 10

The Taxation of the Sharing Economy

Katerina Pantazatou

§10.01 INTRODUCTION

The Organisation for Economic Co-operation and Development (OECD) focused its attention on how to tax the digital economy more than three years ago. In light of the increasing digitalization of what used to be the traditional economy and despite the many tax and regulatory challenges posed thereby, the OECD concluded in its Base Erosion and Profit Shifting (BEPS) Action 1 Final Report that it would not be feasible to ring-fence the digital economy from the rest of the economy for tax purposes.[1] If national and supranational actors follow suit, then their existing tax rules ought to be adjusted to address digital economy challenges. Nevertheless, in order to ensure that the European Union (EU) gets its fair share of the revenue pie, the EU Commission (Commission) recently issued two legislative proposals addressing the digital economy, both of which attempt to ring-fence digital economy taxation from traditional economy taxation: the 2018 SDP Directive Proposal and the 2018 DST Directive Proposal (collectively, the '2018 EU Proposals').[2]

The 'sharing economy' constitutes a sub-area of the digital economy.[3] It has been classified as a 'hybrid' model, based on multi-sided platforms that rely heavily on user

1. OECD, *Addressing the Tax Challenges of the Digital Economy, Action 1 – 2015 Final Report* (OECD Publishing 2015) (hereinafter '2015 OECD BEPS Action 1 Report').
2. European Union Commission (EU Comm'n), *Proposal for a Council Directive laying down rules relating to the corporate taxation of a significant digital presence*, 21 March 2018, COM(2018) 147 final (hereinafter '2018 SDP Directive Proposal') & EU Comm'n, *Proposal for a Council Directive on the common system of a digital services tax on revenues resulting from the provision of certain digital services*, 21 March 2018, COM(2018) 148 final (hereinafter '2018 DST Directive Proposal' and collectively, with the 2018 SDP Directive Proposal, the '2018 EU Proposals').
3. Georg Kofler et al., *Taxation of the Digital Economy: A Pragmatic Approach to Short-Term Measures*, 58 Eur. Tax'n 123 (2018).

data and combining traditional and new elements.[4] Variously called the sharing, collaborative, gig or 'peer-to-peer' (P2P) economy, and sometimes described as collaborative consumption or crowd-based capitalism,[5] all intend to describe an economic model in which individuals are able to borrow or rent assets owned by someone else.[6] It is, usually, a collaborative platform model, whereby digital platforms act as 'matchmakers'. They connect spare capacity with demand for such capacity, enabling individuals to share 'access' to assets rather than own them outright.[7] Such platforms charge either a fixed or a variable fee on each transaction. Therefore, the so-called sharing economy is really nothing of the sort; it is, rather, an access economy,[8] whereby online, multi-sided platforms facilitate transactions between individual 'sellers' or renters of goods and services to individual consumers, that is P2P transactions, which occur outside of traditional business structures (e.g., the case of marketplaces).

This chapter presents the challenges arising out of the sharing economy from a conceptual perspective and then addresses the main questions regarding the taxation of, first, the platforms themselves and, second, the service providers. While the former relates to taxation of the *digital* economy as a whole, the latter presents a distinctly sharing economy problem, as a large part of sharing economy activities avoid taxation due to the non-visibility of service provider action.

§10.02 WHAT IS THE SHARING ECONOMY?

It is hard to define the sharing economy. The Commission defines it as 'encompassing business models where activities are facilitated by collaborative platforms that create an open marketplace for the temporary usage of products and services often provided by private individuals'.[9] Different platforms may employ completely different features and still fall within the 'sharing economy' umbrella term. Platform revenue models vary significantly, even within the same commercial sector, but most adopt a fixed or

---

4. *Ibid.*
5. This term was coined by Arun Sundararajan, *The Sharing Economy: The End of Employment and the Rise of Crowd-Based Capitalism* 1, 27 (Mass. Inst. Tech Press 2016).
6. Henrique Schneider, *Creative Destruction and the Sharing Economy: Uber as Disruptive Innovation* 1, 6 (Edward Elgar 2018).
7. EU Comm'n, Communication from the Commission to the European Parliament and the Council, A Fair and Efficient Tax System in the European Union for the Digital Single Market, COM(2017) 547 final, 21 September 2017, *available at* https://eur-lex.europa.eu/legal-content/EN/TXT/PDF/?uri=CELEX:52017DC0547&from=en (accessed 9 October 2018).
8. Giana Eckhardt & Fleura Bardhi, *The Sharing Economy Is Not About Sharing at All*, Harv. Bus. Rev., hbr.org, https://hbr.org/2015/01/the-sharing-economy-isnt-about-sharing-at-all (accessed 3 September 2018).
9. EU Comm'n, Communication from the Commission to the European Parliament, the Council, the European Social and Economic Committee and the Committee of the Regions, A European Agenda for Collaborative Economy COM(2016) 356 final, 2 June 2016 (hereinafter 'EU Collaborative Economy Agenda'), *available at* https://ec.europa.eu/transparency/regdoc/rep/1/2016/EN/1-2016-356-EN-F1-1.PDF(accessed 3 September 2018).

variable commission approach, with commissions ranging from 1% to 2% of transaction value for crowdlending, to as high as 20% for ride-sharing.[10] On average, over 85% of the transaction value is received by the service provider rather than the platform.[11]

In an attempt to put some limits on this broad concept, Sundararajan describes some of its key characteristics:

- it is largely market-based;
- it creates new opportunities (high-impact capital);
- the networks created therein are crowd-based instead of corporations or centralized institutions;
- the lines between the 'personal' and the 'professional' remain blurred; and
- the lines between 'casual labour' and 'full employment' also remain blurred.[12]

Despite the inherent difficulty in defining the term, the sharing economy's key characteristics remain important in any attempt to systematize the business models that fall under its broad umbrella. In other words, it remains unclear whether platforms that span from accommodation to funding to the provision of other services, which are more or less well known, such as Booking.com, Uber, Airbnb, Lyft, BlaBlaCar, CouchSurfing, JustPark[13] and AngelList,[14] fall equally within the sharing economy, and the question is neither definitional nor merely rhetorical. If there could be one common definition of the sharing economy, there would be no need for such a diverse and disjointed (tax) treatment of the different platforms and service providers.[15] Instead, a common understanding of what, exactly, is the sharing economy would permit taxation of platforms and service providers, based on common principles and, thus, should suffice to cover the whole spectrum of the sharing economy activities. Similarly, such a common understanding would facilitate appropriate legislation and regulation addressing other issues arising out of such activities, such as the legal relationship between the platform and service providers.

One category of online platform that one must eliminate from the concept of the sharing economy is the 'retail exchange market', exemplified by platforms such as Amazon and eBay. Rather than focusing on selling items to the ultimate consumer, the sharing economy generates revenue by providing services. Some similar platforms, such as Craigslist, may provide both: Craigslist, for example, offers a platform for buying and selling products as well as services. In that sense, Craigslist is 'a slightly closer cousin ... to the sharing economy', yet a highly salient element of the sharing

10. Carrie Brandon Elliot, *Taxation of the Sharing Economy: Recurring Issues*, 72 Bull. Int'l Tax'n 1 (2018).
11. *Ibid.*
12. Sundararajan, *supra* note 5, at 27.
13. JustPark is a P2P marketplace that matches people who have empty parking spaces with those looking for a space to park.
14. AngelList is a crowdfunding platform that puts start-ups in contact with investors who make investments in early-stage companies.
15. As will be discussed later in the chapter, states currently have different tax rules that apply, for instance, only to one platform within a given sector, e.g., Airbnb. Other platforms operating within the accommodation sector, for instance, might not be caught by these rules.

economy – trust – is missing.[16] Craigslist, unlike the Uber and Airbnb platforms, does not offer background screening or service provider ratings, making it less popular for those seeking services.

The difficulty in separating sharing economy activities from other economic activities can also be attributed to the myriad differentiating elements within sharing economy platforms that operate in the same 'area'. Such differences include, for example:

- how the service provider is compensated (Lyft, for instance, in its early years, did not require a payment for the service rendered, rather the service receiver was expected to give a 'donation' or 'gift' to the service provider);
- how the price is determined (i.e., by the individual service provider or the platform);[17]
- whether the platform provides day-to-day operational input to service providers;
- the amount of control the platform exercises over the service provider; and
- the availability of a P2P feedback system.

Obviously, these variable features are particularly relevant to taxation: they affect whether, and if so, to what extent, different kinds of taxes apply to the platform and the service providers. The sheer variability (and creativity) in platform features demonstrates how difficult (and potentially futile) it is to attempt to devise an 'all-encompassing' tax system that catches all platforms and different business models within the sharing economy. Such futility may well justify why no particular legal framework is currently envisaged for addressing the *sharing economy's* specific tax challenges; instead, to date, the approach to addressing them has been to address them, if at all, in the context of taxing the broader *digital economy*.

§10.03 TAXING THE PLATFORM AND THE SERVICE PROVIDERS: RECURRING ISSUES

Due to the aforementioned variation in platforms included in the sharing economy, it would be impossible (and, perhaps, even futile) to attempt to describe all of the tax-related issues associated with each business model. Thus, this contribution will only look at the issues raised by two of the most well-known representative models: (1) Uber and (2) Airbnb.

The relationship in the sharing economy context is a triangular one. The platform, the 'matchmaker', connects the service provider to the potential consumer. In principle, legal and natural persons engaging in sharing economy activities should be subject, under certain conditions, to either personal or corporate income tax and value added tax (VAT). In some cases, depending on the area within which they operate and the country at issue, the platforms are required to pay one or more special

16. Sundararajan, *supra* note 5, at 50.
17. For example, Airbnb has a pricing tool built into its platform.

taxes (such as a tourist tax, a municipality tax, social security contributions, and license fees).

I will use an example from a typical sharing economy representative, Airbnb, to illustrate the potential taxes triggered in the sharing economy's typical triangular relationship. Airbnb matches service providers who are willing to rent out their dwellings to consumers. For the use of the platform, both the service provider and the consumer pay a fee to Airbnb for its connecting services. The tremendous expansion of Airbnb in the past ten years has led to protests by hotel owners who allege a huge drop in reservations because of the digital platform, similar to the complaints taxi drivers made against Uber.[18] This expansion is partly due to the shadow economy that arises from the inability of states and/or platforms to monitor service provider activities in the sharing economy and to tax them accordingly. This is why, in most cases, the principal tax problem in this triangular relationship lies with the service provider rather than the platform itself. I turn, now, to explore the major issues that arise with regard to the taxation of the platforms (§10.03[A]) and the taxation of the service providers (§10.03[B]).

[A] The Platform

Platform taxation is the most common problem in the digital economy context, and two recent EU Directive proposals aim to address it.[19] The reason is that most worldwide digital platforms enjoy low effective tax rates on their commission income due to their tax-efficient structures, which generally report most of their income as royalties in low- or zero-tax jurisdictions. The same thing happens with the biggest sharing economy platforms.

Uber and Airbnb, two of the most representative sharing economy platforms, use similar structures to benefit from low effective taxation. Uber's case demonstrates the problems usually faced in the context of the digital economy and platform taxation.[20] Uber's parent company, in Delaware, owns a Dutch limited partnership (Commanditaire Vennootschap, 'CV'), a reverse hybrid treated as a controlled foreign corporation in the United States (US) and as a pass-through entity in the Netherlands. In 2013, the CV paid its US parent a one time fee of about USD 1 million and agreed to pay a royalty of 1.45% of its net revenue to the US parent, where is it also taxed for the right to use Uber's intellectual property outside the US. A Dutch limited liability company (Besloten Vennootschap met beperkte aansprakelijkheid, 'BV'), a pass-through entity for both US and Dutch tax purposes, processes the worldwide payments for all rides and keeps 20% after paying 80% to the drivers (the service providers). From that, the BV

18. *See, e.g.*, Deborah Kyvrikosaios & Alkis Konstantinidis, *Taxi Drivers Protest Against Uber 'Invasion' in Greece*, Reuters (6 March 2018), https://www.reuters.com/article/us-greece-protests-taxis-uber/taxi-drivers-protest-against-uber-invasion-in-greece-idUSKCN1GI1ST; Gwyn Topham, *London's Black-Cab Drivers Consider Suing Uber for £1bn*, The Guardian (24 July 2018), https://www.theguardian.com/technology/2018/jul/24/londons-black-cab-drivers-consider-suing-uber-for-1bn.
19. *See infra* §10.04.
20. Elliot, *supra* note 10 (description of structure).

pays the local operating subsidiaries their costs plus a markup, and pays a royalty to the CV, leaving the BV with just 1% of its revenue. The markup paid to the local subsidiaries may be reduced by interest payments on intercompany start-up loans. The CV's headquarters is in Bermuda, where there is no corporate income tax. The Dutch view the CV as a company controlled by US owners and having Bermuda headquarters and no business operations or taxable income in the Netherlands, thereby completely escaping taxation in Europe.

That complete escape from taxation (replicated by other platforms) where all the 'value is created' has led the Commission to propose two solutions, in the form of directives, one long term and one short term, to allow Member States to tax such platforms' profits and/or revenue. Those developments will be briefly analysed in the context of the sharing economy, in §10.04, *infra*.

[1] VAT

The Commission has acknowledged the many complications that have arisen and continue to arise in the application of VAT[21] in the *digital economy*.[22] While it has also identified the many challenges that arise in the context of applying the existing VAT rules in the *sharing economy*, it has only published two relevant Working Papers on the topic.[23] The two, non-binding, Working Papers provide guidelines on the application of existing EU VAT rules to the *sharing economy*. The package of legislation on modernizing VAT for cross-border e-commerce proposed by the Commission in December 2016 does not include any sharing economy-specific rules.[24]

21. Council Directive 2006/112/EC on the common system of value added tax, OJ L 347/1 (2006) as amended (hereinafter 'VAT Directive'). The VAT Directive recast the Sixth Council Directive 77/388/EEC on the harmonization of the laws of the Member States relating to turnover taxes – Common system of value added tax: uniform basis of assessment, OJ L 145/1 (1977).
22. In December 2017, in an attempt to modernize VAT for cross-border e-Commerce, the Commission proposed a *VAT Digital Single Market Package* (EU Comm'n, Digital Single Market – Modernising VAT for cross-border e-Commerce, ec.europa.eu, https://ec.europa.eu/taxation_customs/business/vat/digital-single-market-modernising-vat-cross-border-ecommerce_en. (accessed 24 September 2018)) (hereinafter 'VAT Digital Single Market Package'). In the same context, it had previously issued several other relevant, non-binding documents: e.g., EU Comm'n, Communication from the Commission to the European Parliament, the Council and the European Economic and Social Committee on an Action Plan on VAT, Towards a Single EU VAT Area: Time to Decide, COM(2016) 148 final. Eur. Comm'n, Proposal for a Council Directive amending Directive 2006/112/EC and Directive 2009/132/EC as regards Certain Value Added Tax Obligations for Supplies of Services and Distance Sales of Goods, COM(2016) 757 final.
23. Eur. Comm'n Value Added Tax Committee, *VAT treatment of sharing economy* (Eur. Comm'n, Working Paper No. 878, 2015), *available at* https://circabc.europa.eu/sd/a/878e0591-80c9-4c58-baf3-b9fda1094338/878%20-%20VAT%20treatment%20of%20sharing%20economy.pdf. While not directly connected to the sharing economy, the Commission's Working Paper on the treatment of crowdfunding addresses similar issues to the ones arising in the context of the sharing economy Eur. Comm'n Value Added Tax Committee, *VAT treatment of crowdfunding* (Eur. Comm'n, Working Paper No. 836, 2015), *available at* https://circabc.europa.eu/sd/a/c9b4bb6f-3313-4c5d-8b4c-c8bbaf0c175a/836%20-%20VAT%20treatment%20of%20Crowd%20funding.pdf.
24. For an overview of the package, see *VAT Digital Single Market Package*.

What seems to be commonly acknowledged is that the supply of goods and services provided by 'collaborative' (i.e., sharing economy) platforms and through such platforms by/to their users are, in principle, VAT-taxable transactions.[25] Hence, as VAT applies to the provision of services and goods, one has to distinguish between, on the one hand, the services provided by the sharing economy platforms/intermediaries themselves (e.g., Uber) to the service providers using the platform to provide their services (e.g., the Uber drivers) and, on the other, the provision of those services by the latter to the ultimate consumer or end user thereof (e.g., the Uber users/passengers) facilitated by the platform. The two types of transactions should be considered *separately* for VAT purposes. In this undertaking, different configurations of both types should be taken into account, notably, whether access to the platform is provided with or without consideration and/or whether the services provided through the platform are subject to a price.[26]

Collecting VAT from the platform is the easiest task for national tax authorities. The Airbnb website, for example, states that Airbnb collects VAT in all Member States by reference to the services provided through the platform.[27] This, however, excludes any VAT the service providers (i.e., the hosts) are obliged to pay concerning the services they provided to the end users (i.e., their guests). A platform's tax structure (such as Uber's described in §10.03[B][1], *supra*) can also affect its VAT liability. Uber's failure to pay VAT in London, for example, became an issue when Uber was seeking to renew its licence to operate.[28] As Uber booked (and still books) all of its United Kingdom (UK) rides through its Dutch subsidiary, it avoided (and still avoids) paying the 20% VAT charged on goods and services provided in the UK, despite its 'services being London-based for the purposes of the Taxi and Private Hire Act 1998, but non-UK based for the purposes of taxation, in particular VAT'.[29]

Other loopholes can also be found for avoiding paying VAT. The Uber example is demonstrative; Uber avoided paying VAT in the UK by asserting that it had no obligation to collect VAT on rides because it only acted as an agent for self-employed drivers, rather than a service provider.[30] Consequently, the legal status of the platform and the legal relationship between the platform and the service provider become fundamental in defining the platform's tax liability, as the OECD stressed in its 2018 Interim Report on tax challenges arising from digitalization.[31]

---

25. EU Collaborative Economy Agenda, *supra* note 9.
26. *See* Eur. Comm'n, *VAT Treatment of Sharing Economy, supra* note 23.
27. For instance, in Greece, Airbnb collects a tax rate of 5% VAT per night.
28. The ban on Uber in London did not relate to tax reasons.
29. Conor Sullivan & Leslie Hook, *Transport for London Board Member Raised Questions on Uber and Tax*, Financial Times (27 September 2017), https://www.ft.com/content/1c4e11ea-a35d-11e7-b797-b61809486fe2.
30. In this case, Uber would have to collect VAT equal to 20% of every fare and give it to HM Revenue & Customs.
31. OECD, *Tax Challenges Arising from Digitalisation – Interim Report 2018* 1, 196 (OECD Publishing 2018) (hereinafter '2018 OECD Interim Report').

[2] *Enforcement/Collection*

In terms of enforcement and collection of taxes, a successful strategy requires the cooperation of all the three parties: (1) the platform, (2) the service provider and (3) the consumer. As the Commission suggests, 'raising awareness on tax obligations, making tax administrators aware of collaborative business models, issuing guidance, and increasing transparency through online information can all be tools for unlocking the potential of the collaborative economy'.[32]

At the platform level, there are three different ways to contribute to better enforcement and collection of taxes. The three ways can be separated into: (1) direct collection and payment of different taxes due by the platform itself, (2) cooperation between the platform and the national tax authorities with regard to the service provider's data and (3) promotion (by the platform) of tax compliance through new technologies and by reducing compliance burdens for the service provider taxpayers through automated compliance processes. This latter point will be discussed, *infra*, in §10.03[B][4].

Direct collection and payment by the platform of certain taxes due has already been implemented in some cities in the context of Airbnb. For instance, in Amsterdam, the authorities have concluded an agreement with Airbnb to collect its tourist tax. Similarly, Airbnb has, in many cities around the world (including Lisbon and Paris in Europe), agreed to collect and remit occupancy taxes. The same applies to VAT, as Airbnb collects VAT in all Member States by reference to the services provided through the platform.[33] Loopholes, however, with regard to the legal status of the platform and/or the legal relationship between the platform and the service provider may allow the platform to avoid paying VAT.[34]

At this stage, facilitation through Airbnb or through the tax authorities could provide an incentive for the *service providers* (i.e., the *hosts*) to pay VAT. Another way for Member States, in cooperation with the platforms, to force such service providers (e.g., the Airbnb hosts) to pay VAT and other applicable taxes is to oblige those who want to provide their services through the platform to register on a special register.[35] This strategy is becoming increasingly common in countries and cities around the world, but it is not free of problems.[36] The drawback with this solution is that it cannot monitor the frequency nor the duration of the services provided, and, hence, it can be easily rendered ineffective. In other words, while an Airbnb host might be registered in the relevant register, he might not report all of his transactions in order to fall within the *de minimis* rules.[37] To avoid this problem, the register must be directly connected to, and informed and updated by, the platform. This, however, would cost the platform in

32. EU Collaborative Economy Agenda, *supra* note 9, at 13.
33. For instance, in Greece Airbnb collects VAT at a tax rate of 5% per night.
34. *See supra* §10.03[A][1], the Uber example in the UK.
35. Greece, for instance, is one of the countries that adopts this system.
36. *See infra* §10.03[B] the examples of New York and Japan.
37. Most Member States have established minimum annual turnover for VAT imposition (VAT registration threshold).

two ways: first, in terms of administrative costs, and second, in terms of a potential loss of service providers and consumers.

The collection of direct taxes poses challenges that are more significant. Currently, it is up to the Member States to ensure that effective mechanisms are in place to monitor the service providers' business activities in the sharing economy and to tax them accordingly. Under the EU legal framework for information exchange, there is no obligation forcing the platforms to share information with the tax authorities.[38]

While, practically, cooperation between the platform and the national tax authorities could again be of help, it might clash with the EU's data protection legal framework.[39] According to that legislation, it could be contrary to EU law for platforms to give the tax authorities any relevant data (e.g., the name of the host, the duration of the rental and the details of the property), unless the service providers consent to the transmission of their data. In order to assess the legality of this, a balancing test should take place at the national level, weighing the infringement of data protection vis-à-vis the public interest justification, in this case the fight against tax evasion.[40]

Data exchange between the platform and the tax authorities remains a key challenge in enforcing taxation at the service provider level. Successful examples include Estonia and Finland. In the Estonian example, the Estonian Tax and Customs Board (ETCB) entered into a cooperative agreement with two well-known ride-sharing platforms for information sharing.[41] With individual driver's consent, the platform compiles all relevant data about that driver and sends the file to the ETCB. In an electronic process, the ETCB pre-prepares the individual's income tax returns using all relevant data. The individual, then, is expected to verify the pre-prepared data, amending it, if necessary) and then submit the income tax return.[42]

---

38. For the complete legal framework in administrative cooperation in direct taxation in the EU, see Council Directive 2011/16/EU on administrative cooperation in the field of taxation and repealing Directive 77/799/EEC OJ L 64 (2011); Council Directive 2014/107/EU amending Directive 2011/16/EU as regards mandatory automatic exchange of information in the field of taxation OJ L 359 (2014); Council Directive (EU) 2015/2376 amending Directive 2011/16/EU as regards mandatory automatic exchange of information in the field of taxation OJ L 332 (2015); Council Directive (EU) 2016/881 amending Directive 2011/16/EU as regards mandatory automatic exchange of information in the field of taxation OJ L 146 (2016); Council Directive (EU) 2016/2258 amending Directive 2011/16/EU as regards access to anti-money-laundering information by tax authorities OJ L 342 (2016); Council Directive (EU) 2018/822 amending Directive 2011/16/EU as regards mandatory automatic exchange of information in the field of taxation in relation to reportable cross-border arrangements OJ L 139 (2018).
39. Charter of Fundamental Rights of the European Union OJ C 326/391 (2012); Council Directive 95/46/EC of the European Parliament and of the Council on the protection of individuals with regard to the processing of personal data and on the free movement of such data the Data Protection Directive OJ L 281 (1995) repealed by Regulation (EU) 2016/679 of the European Parliament and of the Council on the protection of natural persons with regard to the processing of personal data and on the free movement of such data OJ L 119 (2016); Directive (EU) 2016/680 of the European Parliament and of the Council of 27 April 2016 on the protection of natural persons with regard to the processing of personal data by competent authorities for the purposes of the prevention, investigation, detection or prosecution of criminal offences or the execution of criminal penalties, and on the free movement of such data, and repealing Council Framework Decision 2008/977/JHA OJ L 119 (2016) which entered into force on 25 May 2018.
40. For more on this topic, *see* Chapter 13, *infra*.
41. 2018 OECD Interim Report, *supra* note 31, at 201.
42. *Ibid.*

In the case of Finland, Finnish tax authorities have focused on sharing economy platforms related to the accommodation industry, P2P lending and crowdfunding activities.[43] They have used website scraping techniques and have relied on international administrative cooperation, including receiving data through spontaneous exchange.[44] However, data obtained in this way is often not complete and faces administrative obstacles.[45]

Outsourcing certain enforcement and collection functions to the platforms, as suggested,[46] appears to work in the aforementioned examples. While platforms are indeed 'best placed to ensure compliance with the rules by their users [and are] ideally positioned to ensure enforcement of service providers' legal obligations since all the information is already centralized on the platform',[47] data exchanges between the platform and the tax authorities are not free of caveats.

First, they are necessarily restricted by nature. They do not even come close to covering a small fraction of the sharing economy activities. Even when they target car sharing platforms, they include only few of the platforms operating in this field, if not just one of them.[48] The second caveat relates to the service provider's consent requirement, which, however, seems to have been overcome in certain cities: whoever does not consent is deleted by the platform. Third, getting data when the platform only has a presence in a third country becomes extremely difficult and relies completely on an EU- or treaty-level framework on the exchange of information. National laws on data exchange, however, cannot be enforced in a third country, and, hence, there may be no requirement in the third country for the platform to collect data. In addition to that, the assessment of the service providers' tax liability cannot take place independently from their overall tax liability (i.e., without taking into account the taxpayer's other income and personal and family situation). Finally, successful data exchange between the platform and the tax authorities presupposes technological advancement and digitalization thereof.

[B] The Service Provider

The particularity of taxation in the sharing economy lies with the taxation of the service provider. As discussed earlier, the problematic tax patterns encountered in the taxation of digital economy platforms are similarly encountered in the taxation of sharing economy platforms. However, tax authorities are confronted, in sharing economy activities, with another, usually taxable, 'layer', made up of the service providers.

43. *Ibid.*
44. *Ibid.*
45. *Ibid.*
46. Pierre Goudin, *The Cost of Non-Europe in the Sharing Economy: Economic, Social and Legal Challenges and Opportunities* 1 (Eur. Parliamentary Res. Serv. 2016).
47. Vara Arribas et al., *Cost of Non-Europe in the Sharing Economy: Legal Aspects* 1, 65 (EIPA 2016).
48. See for instance the often very different models of Uber, BlaBla Cars, Lyft, Ola, GrabTaxi and Hail, all operating in the transportation industry. Similarly, for the accommodation industry if one compares Airbnb, CouchSurfing and Onefinestay he/she will instantly realize the big variations across the platforms.

The main challenge of taxing the service provider lies with the (potential) *invisibility* of his activities. In other words, national tax authorities do not necessarily know whether a person rents out his apartment for some days per year or whether he makes some extra money by driving people to their destination. Consequently, the service provider may escape both VAT and personal (or corporate) income taxation. This is one of the big advantages of the sharing economy's digital platforms and one of the explanations for their increasing popularity on both the service provider side and the consumer side because of the competitive prices such service providers can offer.[49] For the tax authorities to be able to tax such services, and include the money earned in the service provider's income, the service provider must declare the income arising from his sharing economy activity or the platform must provide the tax authorities with the data of the service providers using it.

Before I explore which taxes would or should be triggered in the aforementioned scenario, I believe it is necessary to provide some data on the importance of this invisibility and how it has shaped tax policy and regulation around the world, using the case of Airbnb.

In New York City, for example, the City Council voted in favour of a new law requiring Airbnb and similar home-share companies to share data on their users.[50] The law is expected to enter into force in January 2019, and some believe it will dramatically cut Airbnb's New York City bookings.[51] Some also believe that it will 'give Airbnb-sceptical regulators around the world a straightforward playbook to copy as they seek to limit the company's influence ... "[o]ther cities will now see that data is the key to enforcement".[52] Regulatory moves across the world address from safety to housing inflation prices and competition issues.[53]

Raising revenue from sharing economy activities at the service provider level is also of great importance for the hosting countries, which sharply contrasts with the value of the invisibility of the activities for tax purposes (and the potential for tax evasion that comes with it) by the service providers. In Spain, 2,000 out of the 9,000 apartments offered by Airbnb in Madrid were not registered on the special register providing data to the tax authorities.[54] In Japan, thousands of listings without the requisite licence disappeared from the Airbnb website because of a 2017 Japanese law

49. Vanessa Houlder, *Airbnb's Edge on Room Prices Depends on Tax Advantages*, Financial Times, https://www.ft.com/content/73102c20-c60e-11e6-9043-7e34c07b46ef, reported that: 'When you book an Airbnb room in London, around a third of the $100 saving you make over the price of an average hotel room is due to tax advantages that favour Airbnb's business model.'
50. Title 26 Ch. 21, NYC Admin. Code (2018) (Law No. 2018/146) (N.Y. Council Int. No. 981-A).
51. Olivia Zaleski, *Airbnb's NYC Bookings Could Be Cut in Half by New Rule*, Bloomberg (24 July 2018), https://www.bloomberg.com/news/articles/2018-07-24/airbnb-s-nyc-bookings-could-be-cut-in-half-by-new-rule.
52. *Ibid.* (quoting Scott Shatford, CEO of Air DNA).
53. Such requirements include the holding a special 'hotel-type' licence; registration at a special register; renting out property for a maximum number of days; renting out a particular type of property that meets certain conditions.
54. Esther Sànchez, *Madrid Buildings May Soon Ban Informal Vacation Rentals: New Rules Seek to Address Growing Trend of Short-Term Tourist Accommodation in Downtown Areas* (Sussana Ura trans., El Pais, 28 June 2017), https://elpais.com/elpais/2017/06/28/inenglish/1498643875_155872.html; Zorzet Zolota, Φρένο στην Airbnb σε Ευρώπη και ΗΠΑ (Airbnb breaks in Europe

required Airbnb hosts to register their properties with the government and publicize their licence number by 15 June 2018 in order to remain active on the platform.[55] In Paris, Airbnb had to pay fines for not removing renters who did not have a tax registration number.[56]

[1] Legal Relationship

While some sharing economy platform examples, such as Airbnb, may appear clear-cut with regard to the legal relationship between the service providers and the platform, some others are not as obvious. The problem begins with a lack of a common understanding of the *legal status* of the platforms themselves. The recent *Uber* case before the Court of Justice of the European Union (CJEU) is demonstrative of this disarray.[57] The CJEU found Uber to be a transportation service provider, instead of a digital platform. While that holding may seem, at first sight, irrelevant for tax purposes, it certainly affects taxation by (indirectly) determining the status of Uber drivers, as contractors, service providers, employees or workers and, in turn, deciding their income tax treatment and their VAT liability.

The UK employment tribunal dealt with a similar case about the employment status of Uber drivers.[58] That tribunal was asked whether Uber drivers qualified as self-employed/independent contractors or as employees/workers. In defining whether Uber drivers should be treated as contractors, the tribunal looked into whether income tax and UK national insurance were deducted from their pay. Conversely, to determine their tax liability, the 'tax test' would have had to look at their holiday pay, sick pay and pension rights.[59] The UK employment tribunal concluded that Uber's drivers were to be classed as workers with access to minimum wage, sick pay and paid holidays, although they treat themselves as self-employed for tax purposes.[60] The case highlights the distinction between labour law and tax law in the sharing economy and raises the question of whether there is a need to coordinate these interrelated policy areas.

The 2018 OECD Interim Report identified this distinction as one of the thorniest issues in the sharing economy context.[61] As different states provide for different tax incentives or disincentives, depending on the type of labour contract at issue, sharing

and USA, is this a good translation?, if not, please revise accordingly), Kathimerini (30 July 2018), http://www.kathimerini.gr/977412/article/oikonomia/die8nhs-oikonomia/freno-sthn-airbnb-se-eyrwph-kai-hpa.

55. Monica Rodriguez, *Airbnb Forced to Cancel Thousands of Listings in Japan*, Fortune (8 June 2018), *available at* http://fortune.com/2018/06/08/airbnb-cancels-japan-listings.
56. Aurélie Lebelle, *Locations touristiques: 'La mairie de Paris assigne Airbnb devant le tribunal'*, Le Parisien (11 April 2018), *available at* http://www.leparisien.fr/economie/locations-touristiques-la-mairie-de-paris-assigne-airbnb-devant-le-tribunal-11-04-2018-7659354.php.
57. *Asociación Profesional Elite Taxi*, C-434/15, Judgment, EU:C:2017:981.
58. *Aslam and Farrar and others* v *Uber BV, Uber London Ltd and Uber Britannia Ltd* [2016] I.R.L.R. 4 (ET) (2202550/2015) (hereinafter '*UK Uber Case*'). Note that Uber has launched an appeal against the Tribunal's ruling.
59. Leigh Sayliss, *Be Careful What You Wish for (178)*, 12 Tax'n 12, 13 (2016).
60. *UK Uber Case*, para. 65.
61. 2018 OECD Interim Report, *supra* note 31, at 196.

economy features (and uncertainties) within the tax system could lead to tax revenue losses if there are large shifts in working patterns and taxable status.[62]

[2] VAT

According to the VAT Directive,[63] the definition of a taxable person includes any person or body 'who, independently, carries out in any place any economic activity, whatever the purpose or results'.[64] Hence, employed and other persons bound to an employer by a contract of employment or by any other legal ties creating the relationship of employer and employee as regards working conditions, remuneration and the employer's liability, escape taxability under the VAT Directive.

The test the CJEU usually applies to establish whether a particular activity fulfils Article 4(2) of the VAT Directive examines whether the activity is carried out for the purpose of obtaining income on a continuing basis.[65] This criterion must be assessed on a case-by-case basis 'having regard to all the circumstances of the case, which include, *inter alia*, the nature of the property concerned'.[66]

The term 'economic activity' has been interpreted by the CJEU in very broad terms, considering the activity per se rather than its purpose or results.[67] Along these lines, the CJEU has repeatedly held that:

> [T]he fact that [the] property is suitable only for economic exploitation will normally be sufficient for a finding that its owner is exploiting it for the purposes of economic activities and, consequently, for the purpose of obtaining income on a continuing basis. By contrast, if, by reason of its nature, property is capable of being used for both economic and private purposes, all the circumstances in which it is used will have to be examined in order to determine whether it is *actually being used* for the purpose of obtaining income on a continuing basis (emphasis added).[68]

Consequently, if the property is, due to its nature, clearly used for purposes of obtaining income on a continuing basis, then it (the economic activity) will be subject to VAT. If the use of the property, as matter of fact, is not clear, then a more complex,

62. *Ibid.* at 196.
63. VAT Directive, *supra* note 21.
64. *Ibid.* Art. 9(1). With regard to the second condition (i.e., independent performance), it may be concluded that in cases where the sharing platform can be recognized as an employer of an individual provider (for the latter, the criteria of the existence of a subordination link, the nature of work and the presence of remuneration should be assessed pursuant to the EU law, the individual provider may not be regarded as a taxable person. In such cases, only the sharing platform may be regarded as a taxable person instead – also with regard to underlying supplies of goods and services.
65. *Rēdlihs*, C-263/11, Judgment, EU:C:2012:497, para. 33; *Finanzamt Freistadt Rohrbach Urfahr*, C-219/12, Judgment, EU:C:2013:413, para. 19.
66. *Ibid.*; *Rēdlihs*, C-263/15, para. 29.
67. *Optigen Ltd, Fulcrum Electronics Ltd, Bond House Systems Ltd* v *Comm'n*, Joined Cases C-354/03, C-355/03 and C-484/03, Judgment, EU:C:2006:16, para. 43; *Comm'n* v *Netherlands*, C-235/85, Judgment, EU:C:1987:161, para. 8.
68. *See Enkler*, C-230/94, Judgment, EU:C:1996:352, para. 27; *Rēdlihs*, C-263/15, para. 34; *Finanzamt Freistadt Rohrbach Urfahr*, C-219/12, para. 20.

factual analysis will be necessary to assess whether the activity is carried out for the purpose of obtaining income on a continuing basis.

Several issues arise with respect to whether sharing economy participants are (and should be) subject to VAT. At first sight, the CJEU-made 'continuity' condition seems to be rebuttable: for instance, in the case of Airbnb rentals, if one shows that the purpose of renting out the property for a very short period did not aim at 'obtaining income *on a continuing basis*', then the activity will not be subject to VAT. Hence, in a strictly literal interpretation of the phrase, it remains unclear whether someone who has rented out his apartment every August for the past five years should be assessed. Recent legislation in some countries has reduced, for non-tax-related reasons, the number of days a service provider can provide short-term rentals of his immovable property.[69]

Article 12 of the VAT Directive attempts to ensure that even these service providers can be made subject to VAT: it stipulates that 'Member States *may* regard as a taxable person anyone who carries out, on an *occasional basis*, a transaction relating to the activities referred to in the second subparagraph of Article 9(1)' (emphasis added). While the CJEU has held that the mere exercise of the right of ownership and the management of the private property do not constitute economic activity,[70] it has also ruled that if a party has taken active steps to market property by mobilising resources similar to those deployed by producers, traders, or persons supplying services within the meaning of Article 4(2) of the VAT Directive, such as, in particular, carrying out preparatory work on such land … to make development possible, and deploying proven marketing measures, then such initiatives go beyond mere exercise of the management of the private property.[71] In other words, marketing or advertising the property constitutes, in the CJEU's view, the distinctive element that separates the mere management of private property from its economic exploitation.

This very broad, CJEU understanding has led the Commission to suggest that:

> Given the very wide understanding of the concept of economic activity … it can be therefore concluded that the supplies of goods and services made through sharing-economy platforms, such as driving customers to requested destinations or renting out immovable property *may* qualify as an economic activity in the sense of the VAT Directive *irrespective of whether such supplies are delivered with clear continuity or on a more occasional basis* (emphasis added).[72]

Indeed, under these circumstances and, as the Commission notes, it seems almost impossible for sharing economy service providers to escape the 'taxable person' definition. In the Airbnb and Uber scenarios, therefore, once someone uploads an

69. In Paris, for instance, short-term rentals (Airbnb type) were reduced by law to a maximum of 120 days per year. In Amsterdam owners will be able to rent out their property through Airbnb only for thirty days per year.
70. *Słaby & Others*, Joined Cases C-180/10 & C-181/10, Judgment, EU:C:2011:589, para. 36; *Trgovina Prizma*, C-331/14, Judgment, EU:C:2015:456, para. 23.
71. *Słaby & Others*, Joined Cases C-180/10 & C-181/10, paras 39–41; *Trgovina Prizma*, C-331/14, para. 24.
72. *Question Concerning the Application of EU VAT Provisions: VAT Treatment of Sharing Economy* 6 (Value Added Tax Comm., Eur. Comm'n, Working Paper No. 878, 22 September 2015).

apartment for rent or avails himself of the opportunity, through the Uber platform, to drive someone to that person's destination, he automatically becomes a taxable person for VAT purposes, even if he only does so on an occasional basis.[73]

The second thorny issue attributable to qualifying a services provider using a sharing economy platform as a 'taxable person' is the definition of *income*. The remuneration or 'income' the service providers receive varies widely depending on the platform itself and the provider himself. As the Commission pointed out, such income could range from 'recovering costs (e.g.[,] for the personal use of a good such as in ride-sharing/car sharing) to amounts comparable to business/work activities.'[74] While the Commission suggests that 'tax rules should follow national laws and jurisprudence, which determine from which moment an activity becomes a business activity,'[75] income is not defined in a uniform manner across the Member States. That fact adds to the uncertainty of the definition of what constitutes an economic activity, according to the test the CJEU employs. Accordingly, the same activity may constitute an economic activity for VAT purposes in one Member State and not in another because the remuneration at issue does not qualify as *income*. If one adds to that situation the different thresholds Member States apply by reference to what constitutes a 'professional activity' vis-à-vis an 'occasional' activity of private individuals, the fulfilment of the aforementioned definitions becomes even more segregated.

Another interpretation difficulty across the different Member States relates to the exemption of 'small businesses' (i.e., businesses with low annual turnover) from VAT registration.[76] This special exemption scheme is applied in most EU Member States, but it is not compulsory. Unfortunately, the VAT Directive does not specify whether 'small taxable persons' who participate in the sharing economy (e.g., somebody who occasionally rents out his apartment) can benefit from such exemption schemes. One (administratively burdensome!) option would be to treat them all as 'full-blown taxable persons' based on 'tax points'.[77] The other option would be to extend the special rules for small businesses to the 'small taxpayers' in the context of the sharing economy.[78]

Some Member States set very high thresholds before a person incurs VAT payment obligations. One such example is the UK, where VAT on most Airbnb stays

---

73. The only obvious escape from the application of VAT in such circumstances would be the application of the *de minimis* exemption from VAT reporting. In this vein, some Member States have established minimum annual turnover for VAT imposition (VAT registration threshold). For example, the Belgian Programme Law of 1 July 2016 stipulates that individuals providing sharing economy services do not have to register as VAT payers if its EUR 5,000 threshold is not exceeded.
74. EU Collaborative Economy Agenda, *supra* note 9, at 41.
75. *Ibid.*
76. Articles 284–287, VAT Directive, *supra* note 21. Member States are allowed to exempt small businesses from VAT registration up to a given threshold. Usually the threshold amounts to EUR 5,000.
77. Han Kogels & Markien van Hilten, *Never a Dull Moment*, 28 Int'l VAT Monitor 121, 122–123 (2017). Tax points (or 'time of supply') for a transaction is the date the transaction takes place for VAT purposes. Tax points can be, for instance, the date of invoice or the day the supply took place.
78. Kogels & van Hilten, *supra* note 77, 122.

can be as little as 0.6% because the UK only levies the tax when businesses sell more than GBP 83,000 per year – a threshold reached by very few Airbnb hosts.[79] Some other Member States, such as Greece, grant service providers an exemption from VAT as long as the host does not provide any services similar to the ones offered by hotels, such as regular cleaning and linen changes.[80]

A remedy against potential tax evasion that could arise from the non-payment of VAT by the service providers is the collection of such VAT by the relevant platform (in addition to any other taxes they collect), provided, however, that the hosts have exceeded the threshold for VAT registration. This way, all relevant details that would define the amount to be paid by the taxpayer would already be available to the platform and the risk of tax evasion would be minimized. To date, no measures have been taken in this direction and it is becoming clearer that this legislative gap has spurred a lot of confusion among platform users.[81]

[3] What Kind of Taxes?

The rapid developments in the area of the sharing economy have not been followed at either the national or EU legislative levels. Hence, very few countries have enacted targeted tax legislation with regard to sharing economy activities. Two main challenges can be identified with regard thereto.

First, the many different business models that appear in the sharing economy context make it particularly hard to establish legal relationship patterns. The legal relationship between the platform and the service provider, in turn, determines the relevant taxes to apply. For example, that legal relationship will determine whether the relevant income is taxable as income from employment or income from independent business. The 2018 OECD Interim Report notes that focus should be placed on the contractual relationship between the platform and the service provider as the so-called grey zones that can be found therein could lead to minimization of tax liability and the tax base.[82] However, due to the myriad variations those relationships can take, even if legislation is enacted at the national-level addressing, for instance, the 'employment status' of online transportation service providers, such a law will almost certainly not catch all sharing economy participants in the transportation sector, and will be even less likely to do so in other areas, such as accommodations, where the legal relationship is even more attenuated.

Similar questions apply when trying to define what type of income arises from a particular activity. For instance, in Greece, only recently a new provision was added to the Income Tax Code,[83] providing that income from short-term rentals ('Airbnb-type'

79. Vanessa Houlder, *Airbnb's Edge on Room Prices Depends on Tax Advantages*, Financial Times (2 January 2017), available *at* https://www.ft.com/content/73102c20-c60e-11e6-9043-7e34c07b46ef.
80. Article 111(4) of Law 4446/2016 as amended by Law 4472/2017.
81. For this uncertainty, see indicatively the Airbnb case; *VAT*, Airbnb, *available at* https://community.withairbnb.com/t5/Everything-Else/VAT/td-p/4501.
82. 2018 OECD Interim Report, *supra* note 31, at 196–198.
83. The provision was added in accordance with the Law decree 4472/2017.

rentals) would be considered as income from immovable property and would be subject to the relevant provisions.[84] Similar to Greece's VAT exemption, this systematization only applies as long as the hosts do not provide any other service (with the exception of furnishing bed sheets and towels). If any other service were to be provided, such as breakfast or cleaning, then the income received for the rental of the property would qualify as income from business activities.[85] Car sharing-specific tax rules have not yet been enacted in any Member State. The Commission, in its *EU Collaborative Economy Agenda*, provided for an overview of some Member States' tax initiatives targeted at the sharing economy.[86] Most of these proposed measures concentrate on: providing definitions relating to the sharing economy; raising awareness concerning the tax issues that arise; facilitating the exchange of information; and presenting tax relief measures for participants in the sharing economy.

Finally, different countries may apply different thresholds and tax exemptions with regard to income arising from sharing economy activities. Indeed, introducing thresholds that generally escape taxation may incentivize service providers to report these very small tax-free amounts.[87] It, however, does not solve the problem, as it cannot ensure reporting in case of higher profits.

[4] Enforcement/Collection

At the service provider level, the main challenge is tax compliance and enforcement. Often, the lack of visibility of the activity and the inability to identify potential taxpayers and their taxable income pose obstacles to effective taxation and collection thereof.

The solutions for effectively taxing the sharing economy, in the OECD's view, should focus on improving the effective taxation of activities facilitated by online platforms through improving taxpayer education and facilitating self-reporting.[88] Effective taxation becomes, hence, a matter of collaboration between the platform and the taxpayer. This recommendation has been implemented by some Member States that have attempted to incentivize the service providers to include their income from the sharing economy when completing their tax returns through *simplified procedures* or automated pre-prepared tax declarations available to the service providers directly through the platforms.[89] In France, for example, by law of July 2016, collaborative platforms will have to communicate to each individual providing services in the

84. In this case, taxation is progressive and as follows: for income between EUR 0 and 12,000: 15%, EUR 12,001 and 35,000: 35% and from EUR 35,001 upward: 45%.
85. In this case taxation is progressive and as follows: for income between EUR 0 and 20,000: 22%, EUR 20,001 and 30,000: 29%, EUR 30,001 and 40,000: 37% and from EUR 40,001 upward: 45%.
86. EU Collaborative Economy Agenda, *supra* note 9, at 27 et seq. Table 6.
87. The UK has introduced such thresholds. The 'rent a room scheme', for instance, granted a tax exemption for sharing economy participants earning up to GBP 4,250 in a year for 2016. Similarly, France introduced recently a similar measure applying to specific cases, setting the threshold at EUR 5,000 a year.
88. 2018 OECD Interim Report, *supra* note 31, at 198.
89. It is worth examining this vis-à-vis the reporting obligations in the US: *see* Shu-Yi Oei & Diane M. Ring, *Can Sharing Be Taxed?*, 93 Wash. U. L. Rev. 989, 1032–1037, 1070 (2016):

collaborative economy an annual summary of their tax situation, mentioning how to make their tax declaration and how much they have to declare to the tax authorities.[90]

A commonly used example of a successful strategy for simplifying and streamlining tax collection is Estonia. It has introduced a test service for simplified income declaration for ride-sharing services. Consequently, transactions between the driver and the customer are registered by the collaborative platform, which then only sends the data that is relevant for taxation purposes to the authorities, who will then pre-prepare the taxpayer's tax forms. The main idea is to help taxpayers fulfil their tax obligations effectively and with minimal effort. Estonia now contemplates expanding this scheme to other types of sharing economy businesses.[91]

Mexico is another example of successful cooperation between the tax authorities, the platform and the service providers. By using data recording technologies that drivers of a particular ride-for-hire service are able to use, the platform's own systems file and send invoices to the customers and to the Mexican Tax Administration (Servicio de Administración Tributaria (SAT)), as well as to download them for record-keeping purposes.[92]

[5] Effective Lower Taxation?

The general, current trend that can be identified relates to the *effective* lowering of taxation of the two main sharing economy actors, (1) the platform and (2) the service

> sharing businesses are ... responsible for information reporting with respect to independent contractor income. There are two primary information reporting regimes that are relevant to the sharing economy: (1) Form 1099-MISC information reporting required under I.R.C. § 6041, and (2) Form 1099-K information reporting required under I.R.C. § 6050W ... [A]ll 'third party settlement organizations' making payments to payees in settlement of third party network transactions must report such payments on Form 1099-K if the payments to the participating payee exceed [USD] 20,000 and if there are more than 200 transactions with the participating payee.

The term 'third-party settlement organization' was meant to include services such as PayPal, Amazon and Google Checkout. If the earnings of the service provider fell below said threshold, then the appropriate form to be submitted would be the Form 1099-MISC. With regard to this and the confusion about the reporting numbers in the Form 1099-K, *see also*, Shu-Yi Oei & Diane M. Ring, Tax Issues in the Gig Economy: Implications for Workers, *in* Nestor M. Davidson, Michèle Finck & John J. Infranca, *Cambridge Handbook of the Sharing Economy* (CUP, 2018).

90. EU Collaborative Economy Agenda, *supra* note 9, at 43. The Finance Act of 2016 has introduced a series of obligations to the platforms and the taxpayers in order to ensure their taxation. In specific, the platforms are obliged to send their users' earnings directly to the relevant social security and tax administrations as of 2019. In principle, all online platforms are concerned, regardless of whether they are based in France or abroad. Hence, the tax return filled out by the platform will include information like the total gross income received by the user during the calendar year for its activities on the online platform, and a copy of it will be sent to the users.
91. *Ibid.*
92. 2018 OECD Interim Report, *supra* note 31, at 201. Drivers are obliged to register with the particular recording system of the platform.

provider, enjoy.[93] Some Member States, such as the UK, have already enacted tax relief measures especially for sharing economy actors[94] while others indirectly and effectively allow the non-payment of several taxes.[95]

If one adds to the 'invisibility' of service provider actions, the fact that some Member States are currently allowing companies operating in the sharing economy, such as Uber, to avoid paying social security contributions,[96] or claiming any license fees, it becomes clear that these companies enjoy tax-related and other economic advantages in comparison to other (non-sharing economy participant) companies.[97] In this sense, the sharing economy, even more so than the digital economy, is ring-fenced in a manner beneficial for the digital economy platforms and the service providers.

These economic advantages are likely to trigger State aid rules.[98] By reducing their effective tax burden, either through active tax benefits or through a poor or inexistent collection of taxes, companies like Airbnb and Uber are placed at a competitive advantage vis-à-vis their competitors. Nevertheless, despite hotel owners' and taxi drivers' complaints that they are subject to unfair competition from Airbnb and Uber with regard to taxes and other regulatory loopholes, the applicability of the State aid rules is not entirely clear. As provided in Article 107(1) TFEU, as interpreted by the CJEU, for State aid rules to apply the (tax) measure at issue has to be selective. The selectivity test encompasses the identification of the reference system. In other words, there must be an examination of whether taxis and Uber, or hotels and Airbnb, belong in the same reference framework and can be considered in a comparable situation. If that is found to be the case, then State aid rules may be applicable, provided that all of the other conditions of Article 107(1) are met. To date, there has been no specific test developed by the CJEU to define the reference framework. Instead, the CJEU continues to seek to establish the reference framework on an ad hoc basis.

---

93. If the 2018 EU Proposals on the taxation of the digital economy get adopted then the digital – and by implication also the sharing – economy will be ring-fenced but in a way detrimental to them, as they will, in *some* cases, be subject to a higher tax burden than the traditional economy 'competitors'.
94. For a more detailed discussion of these trends and the references to the relevant documents, see *A European agenda for the collaborative economy*, Commission Staff Working Document accompanying the Commission Communication, SWD(2016) 184, at 27 et seq. Table 6.
95. Vassilis Hatzopoulos & Sofia Roma, *Caring for Sharing? The Collaborative Economy Under EU Law*, 54 Common Mkt. L. Rev. 81, 112 (2017).
96. The question relates, of course, to the definition of these service providers as independent workers or employees.
97. Hatzopoulos & Roma, *supra* note 95, 112–13.
98. State aid is forbidden in the EU. The definition of state aid is provided in Art. 107(1) TFEU and reads as follows:

    > Save as otherwise provided in the Treaties, any aid granted by a Member State or through State resources in any form whatsoever which distorts or threatens to distort competition by favouring certain undertakings or the production of certain goods shall, in so far as it affects trade between Member States, be incompatible with the internal market.

    Exemptions from the general prohibition are set in Art. 107(2) and 107(3) TFEU. In the given context, it is interesting to note that State aid does not include only 'active' State subsidies and capital injections. Rather, they cover tax exemptions, tax allowances, tax deductions, non-collection of taxes and, more generally, any kind of tax alleviation.

This, in conjunction with some inconsistent judgments, leaves far too much room to even attempt to speculate as to whether sharing and non-sharing economy competitors would belong in the same reference framework.

§10.04 THE 2018 EU PROPOSALS

The Commission recently published proposals for two Council Directives on the taxation of the *digital economy*[99] and one (non-binding) Commission Recommendation relating to the corporate taxation of a *significant digital presence* (SDP).[100] These proposals came immediately after the release of the 2018 OECD Interim Report on the tax challenges arising from digitalization.[101] While neither the proposed directives nor the OECD interim report specifically addressed taxation of the *sharing* economy, they are likely to have significant repercussions on it, if adopted, specifically with respect to the taxation of the platforms. The 2018 OECD Interim Report, for example, noted that the focus, with regard to the sharing economy, should be placed on the contractual relationship between the platforms and the service providers, as the grey zones that can be found therein could lead to minimization of both tax liability and the tax base.

The 2018 SDP Directive Proposal is the suggested long-term solution by the Commission. It aims to ensure that profits of the big digital companies are taxed where the company has a so-called significant digital presence, which is equated to a 'virtual permanent establishment'.[102] Its interim solution, the 2018 DST Directive Proposal, introduces a digital services tax (DST) on revenues resulting from the provision of certain digital services. These tax revenues would be collected by the Member State where the users (consumers) are located. The 2018 EU Proposals, thus, concentrate on ensuring that the digital (and, presumably, sharing) economy platforms are taxed sufficiently within the EU (either on their profits or on their revenues), without focusing on the equally problematic taxation of the service provider (i.e., the taxi driver in the Uber case or the host in the Airbnb case), which still remains for the Member States to solve.

The two EU directive proposals also focus on the digital economy, rather than the sharing economy itself, and while – from a contextual interpretation – they appear to apply equally to all digital platforms (including sharing economy platforms) and the

99. The 2018 DST Directive Proposal and the 2018 SDP Directive Proposal, *supra* note 2.
100. European Commission Recommendation of 21 March 2018 relating to the corporate taxation of a significant digital presence, COM(2018) 1650 final.
101. 2018 OECD Interim Report, *supra* note 31.
102. The 2018 SDP Directive Proposal, *supra* note 2, would have found a company to have an SDP in a Member State if one or more of the following conditions applied: (a) the proportion of total revenues obtained in that tax period and resulting from the supply of those digital services to users located in that Member State in that tax period exceeds EUR 7,000,000; (b) the number of users of one or more of those digital services located in that Member State during that tax period exceeds 100,000; or (c) the number of business contracts for the supply of any such digital service that are concluded in that tax period by users located in that Member State exceeds 3,000.

services they provide, a literal interpretation of the definition could provide otherwise.[103] The main problem lay in the proposed definition of digital services and the exclusion, from the scope of the 2018 SDP Directive Proposal, of 'the services listed in Annex III or the sale of goods or other services which is facilitated by using the internet or an electronic network'.[104]

§10.05 CONCLUSION

The inability to tackle, in a coherent and comprehensive manner, the tax challenges that arise from the sharing economy at the national, EU and even supranational level is understandable. Many different parameters must be taken into account, including the role of the platform in the business model, the remuneration received, the non-inclusive definitions in existing EU tax legislation,[105] the legal relationship between the platform and the service provider, and the interdependence of the issues with other areas of law (from labour and contract law to VAT thresholds).

To date, neither the OECD nor the EU seem to have focused on the specific challenges arising from the taxation of the sharing economy. Their proposals, however, both at the EU and OECD levels, addressing the taxation of the digital economy, appear to tackle only the problematic of taxing the *platforms* in the sharing economy context, and not the service providers.

The highly problematic question of taxing the service provider rests mostly, however, with legislative initiatives at Member State level. Some Member States have instituted monitoring systems to ensure compliance while some others rely on the voluntary (or sometimes even, involuntary) cooperation of the platform in exchanging information with the tax authorities in a manner compliant with EU and national data protection frameworks. They also rely on the 'goodwill' of the service provider to pay VAT and to declare his income from his sharing economy activity, and they have successfully used the platforms to educate and facilitate the service providers' compliance, by helping him with his tax returns.

In order to mitigate these uncertainties and conflicts in taxing the sharing economy, the EU should take action in the sharing economy, and the taxation of the service providers *specifically*, not by exhaustively regulating this area – an impossible task in any case – but by adopting comprehensive legislation that would establish general principles that can function as guidelines for all Member States. In this undertaking, it would have to join forces with other areas of law, such as labour law and data protection law.

---

103. The definitions, for instance, on what is included in 'digital services' and what is not in the 2018 SDP Directive Proposal leaves room for debate as to whether the provision of services by the sharing economy platform fall within its definition. In its press release, however, the Commission noted that the proposal would apply to digital platforms in general (including sharing economy platforms).
104. 2018 SDP Directive Proposal, *supra* note 2, Art. 3(5).
105. *See* for instance the definition of the 'taxable person' for VAT purposes, *supra*, §10.03[B][2].

CHAPTER 11

Effective Taxation Versus Effective Data Protection?

Viktoria Wöhrer

§11.01 INTRODUCTION

Due to the digitalization of the economy the question has been raised whether traditional international tax rules are adequately taking into account the characteristics of digitalization. The key features of digitalization, including mobility, reliance on data, network effects, the spread of multi-sided business models, a tendency towards monopoly or oligopoly, and volatility, have created challenges for the application of existing international tax rules.[1] New solutions to ensure fair taxation of the digital economy are proposed both on the level of the Organisation for Economic Co-operation and Development (OECD) and on the level of the European Union (EU).[2] Nevertheless, no consensus has been reached so far as to how to react to those challenges. There are different views among countries on whether and to what extent digitalization should result in changes to the international tax rules.[3]

The digitalization of the economy does however not only pose challenges for the application of substantive tax rules but has also changed and will lead to further changes to the way tax administrations are working and ensuring tax compliance. As

1. OECD, *Tax Challenges Arising from Digitalisation – Interim Report 2018: Inclusive Framework on BEPS* 1, 18 para. 16 (OECD Publishing 2018) (hereinafter '2018 OECD Interim Report').
2. *See* 2018 OECD Interim Report, *supra* note 1, at 165–192 (Ch. 5 & Ch. 6). On 21 March 2018, the European Commission proposed two directives dealing with the taxation of the digital business: (1) Eur. Comm'n, *Proposal for a Council Directive laying down rules relating to the corporate taxation of a significant digital presence* COM(2018) 147 final 2018/0072 (CNS) & (2) Eur. Comm'n, *Proposal for a Council Directive on the Common System of a Digital Services Tax on Revenues Resulting from the Provision of Certain Digital Services*, COM(2018) 148 final 2018/0073 (CNS).
3. *See* 2018 OECD Interim Report, *supra* note 1, para. 512.

the OECD has pointed out in its Interim Report 2018 on the Tax Challenges Arising from Digitalisation, there has been a large increase in the amount of third-party data available to tax authorities in recent years, including 'transaction and income data, behavioural data generated from taxpayers' interactions with the tax administration, operational data on ownership, identity and location, and open source data such as social media and advertising'.[4] Due to technical developments, in particular advances in analytics techniques and lower storage costs, it has become possible to store a huge amount of information and to use this data for better understanding of taxpayer behaviour, to identify the most effective interventions, and to uncover under-reporting, evasion or fraud.[5]

Tax authorities are increasingly gathering and sharing sensitive taxpayer information. This is not limited to a domestic level. The technological developments have facilitated data collection and analysis and have significantly extended the amount of data that is collected for tax purposes both on a domestic and on an international level. Increasing data collection and information exchange between tax administrations of different jurisdictions is one of the means to fight tax avoidance and tax evasion. Thereby, it contributes to a more equal distribution of the burden of tax to different taxpayers as it prevents certain taxpayers from escaping the obligation to pay taxes easily by simply not reporting certain income.[6] However, the recent developments in the area of data collection and exchange of information have been focused on effectiveness and efficiency and increased the scope of reporting obligations of both the concerned taxpayers and third parties. The question of whether there are also risks for taxpayers involved has not been within the focus of attention of the decision makers.[7] In particular, the developments in the area of exchange of information have been criticized for not having sufficiently taken into account the protection of personal tax data.[8] With regard to automatic exchange of financial account information under the OECD Common Reporting Standard (CRS)[9] and under the EU Directive on

4. *Ibid.* para. 489.
5. *Ibid.* para. 489.
6. *See* Sigrid Hemels, *Fairness and Taxation in a Globalized World* 1, 15 s. 6.3, http://ssrn.com/abstract=2570750 (accessed 29 August 2018); Anna-Maria Hambre, *Tax Confidentiality: A Comparative Study and Impact Assessment of Global Interest* 1, 19 (Örebro Univ., Örebro Studies in Law Ser. No. 6, 2015); the effectiveness of measures against tax avoidance and tax evasion has also a constitutional aspect. The German Constitutional Court (Bundesverfassungsgericht) held that an equal distribution of the burden of tax not only has to be provided under the applicable legal framework but must also be the practical consequence. The principle of equal treatment consequently requires that the tax authorities do have possibilities to verify the correctness of the declarations made by the taxpayers where the tax assessment is based on a reporting obligation of the taxpayer. *See* BVerfG (German Constitutional Court), 27.06.1991, 2 BvR 1493/89, BStBl 1, at 654.
7. Pistone has argued that the rights of the taxpayers would be the 'most ignored aspect of global tax law'. *See* Pasquale Pistone, *Exchange of Information and Rubik Agreements: The Perspective of an EU Academic*, 67 Bull. Int'l Tax'n 216, 225 (2013).
8. *See, e.g.*, Marcel Scharper, *Data Protection Rights and Tax Information Exchange in the European Union: An Uneasy Combination*, 23 Maastricht J. Eur. & Comp. L. 514, 530 (2016).
9. OECD, *Standard for Automatic Exchange of Financial Account Information in Tax Matters* (OECD Publishing 2014) (hereinafter 'CRS').

Administrative Cooperation (DAC),[10] in 2016, Philip Baker stated, 'This overriding requirement of compliance with data protection law seems to have been very largely overlooked in constructing the CRS/DAC system' and that it is 'almost inevitable that challenges to the CRS/DAC system will be mounted based upon the failure to protect privacy and data protection rights'.[11] There are concerns that the increasing collection and exchange of large volumes of tax information could eventually have undesired consequences. If more persons have access to tax data, the risk that the information also gets leaked and becomes available to the public or to persons who are not supposed to have access to that data increases. Furthermore, even the use of data for the intended purpose could have a significant negative impact on the situation of the taxpayer when the exchange information is not fully accurate and the taxpayer is not aware of it due to the lack of procedural safeguards.[12]

Therefore, this contribution aims at analysing whether data protection provisions require limits for data processing or storage and/or procedural rights provided to taxpayers. First, an overview of some of the measures that have been adopted in recent years that have led to an increasing data collection and processing will be provided. The most recent development in this area is mandatory automatic exchange of information in the field of taxation in relation to reportable cross-border arrangements.[13] This is followed by an overview of data protection provisions in the EU. The protection of personal data constitutes a fundamental right that is protected *inter alia* by national constitutions, by Article 8 of the Charter of Fundamental Rights of the EU (CFR)[14] and by Article 8 of the European Convention for the Protection of Human Rights and Fundamental Freedoms (ECHR).[15] The General Data Protection Regulation (GDPR)[16] – in force since May 2018 – provides for detailed data protection safeguards and ensures an effective protection of the fundamental right to data protection in the EU. This chapter addresses the questions how data processing for tax purposes has to be designed in order to fulfil the requirements stemming from data protection safeguards and whether procedural rights have to be granted.[17]

---

10. *Council Directive 2011/16/EU on administrative cooperation in the field of taxation and repealing Directive 77/799/EEC*, OJ L 64/1 (2011) as amended by *Council Directive 2014/107/EU amending Directive 2011/16/EU as regards mandatory automatic exchange of information in the field of taxation*, OJ L 359/1 (2014) (hereinafter 'DAC').
11. Philip Baker, *CRS/DAC, FATCA and the GDPR*, 3 Brit. Tax Rev. 249, 252 (2016).
12. *See also* Viktoria Wöhrer, *Data Protection and Taxpayers' Rights: Challenges created by Automatic Exchange of Information*, Ch. 5 (IBFD 2018).
13. Council Directive (EU) 2018/822 of 25 May 2018 amending Directive 2011/16/EU as regards mandatory automatic exchange of information in the field of taxation in relation to reportable cross-border arrangements, OJ L 139/1 (2018) (hereinafter 'DAC 6').
14. EU, *Charter of Fundamental Rights of the European Union*, OJ L 364/1 (2000) (hereinafter 'Charter').
15. Council of Europe, *Convention for the Protection of Human Rights and Fundamental Freedoms* (4 November 1950), Council of Europe Treaty Office ETS No. 005 (ECHR).
16. Council & Eur. Parliament Regulation 2016/679 on the protection of natural persons with regard to the processing of personal data and on the free movement of such data, and repealing Directive 95/46/EC (hereinafter 'General Data Protection Regulation' or 'GDPR') OJ L 119/1 (2016).
17. For a more detailed analysis, *see also* Wöhrer, *supra* note 12.

§11.02 ENSURING EFFECTIVE TAXATION: INCREASING DATA COLLECTION

Increasing data collection is not only happening on a domestic level but is largely driven by international developments. After the Liechtenstein tax affair and the UBS scandal in 2007 and 2008 followed by the financial crisis with the bailouts of financial institutions in 2008, cooperation in tax matters and in particular exchange of information has been highly placed on the political agenda of many jurisdictions. Supported by the OECD and the G20, the Global Forum has been working on enhancing the scope and effectiveness of exchange of tax-related information and put political pressure on those jurisdictions that were more reluctant to implement a broad-scale exchange of information for tax matters.[18] Due to the publication of white, grey, and blacklists in conjunction with the political support of the G20, the countries that initially had reservations regarding the exchange of bank information gave up their resistance and agreed to implement the OECD standard.[19] However, that allowed only the confirmation of a suspicion but not the identification of previously unknown tax evaders.[20]

Therefore, in 2013, the G20 announced automatic exchange of information as the new global standard.[21] In the beginning, the focus was on the exchange of financial information as some jurisdictions previously had insisted on strict banking secrecy. This was however followed by a number of different measures to increase transparency. Triggered by the media reporting about EU State aid cases[22] and the revealing of LuxLeaks,[23]

18. *See, e.g.*, Xavier Oberson, *International Exchange of Information on Tax Matters Towards Global Transparency* 1, 8 et seq. (Edward Elgar Publishing 2015).
19. *See, e.g.*, Daljit Kaur & Rachel Saw, *The EOI Standard – Past, Present and Future*, 16 Asia-Pac. Tax Bull. 14 (2010); Pasquale Pistone, *Exchange of Information and Rubik Agreements: The Perspective of an EU Academic*, 67 Bull. Int'l Tax'n 216, 219 (2013); Pasquale Pistone, *Waiving Bank Secrecy and Exchanging Tax Information in Cross-Border Situations: The Austrian Way to Global Fiscal Transparency, in Financial Crisis and Single Market* 125, 131 (Livia Salvini & Giuseppe Melis eds., Discendo Agitur 2012).
20. *See* Adrian J. Sawyer, *Tax Havens 'Coming in from the Cold': A Sign of Changing Times?* 64 Bull. Int'l Tax'n 554 (2010); Timothy V. Addison, *Shooting Blanks: The War on Tax Havens*, 16 Ind. J. Global Legal Stud. 703, 717 et seq. (2009).
21. *See* G20, *Tax Annex to the Saint Petersburg G20 Leaders' Declaration Saint Petersburg Summit of 5 September 2013*, g20.russia.ru, http://en.g20russia.ru/Annex/20130905/782494374.html (accessed 12 September 2018).
22. *See, e.g.*, Eur. Comm'n, Commission Decision of 21.10.2015 on State Aid SA.38374 (2014/C ex 2014/NN) implemented by the Netherlands to Starbucks, C(2015) 7143 final; Eur. Comm'n, Commission Decision of 21.10.2015 on State Aid SA.38375 (2014/C ex 2014/NN) which Luxembourg granted to Fiat, C(2015) 7152 final; Eur. Comm'n, Commission Decision of 30.8.2016 on State Aid SA.38373 (2014/C) (ex 2014/NN) (ex 2014/CP) implemented by Ireland to Apple, C(2016) 5605 final.
23. For more information, see the International Consortium of Investigative Journalists (ICIJ), *Luxembourg Leaks: Global Companies' Secrets Exposed*, https://www.icij.org/project/luxembourg-leaks (accessed 12 September 2018).

the Panama papers,[24] BahamaLeaks[25] and the Paradise papers,[26] multinationals and high-net-worth individuals are accused of not paying their 'fair share' of taxes and tax activist groups demanded for more transparency in tax matters – not only towards tax administrations but also towards the public.[27]

In the area of exchange of information, the international standard has developed within the last decade from exchange of information on request to automatic exchange of information for more and more types of income. Automatic exchange of financial information has been suggested under the OECD CRS[28] and is currently being implemented on a global basis. Within the EU, automatic exchange of financial account information as it was suggested by the OECD CRS was implemented by an amendment of the DAC (DAC 2).[29] For the look-through approach in respect to passive non-financial entities, the definition for controlling persons relies on the broad beneficial ownership definition stemming from anti-money laundering (AML) legislation. Therefore, the amendment of the DAC of 6 December 2016 requires that tax authorities are granted access to the beneficial ownership register in order to be able to monitor and control whether the financial institutions as tax intermediaries who are required to report tax-relevant information on their account holders are compliant and provide information on accounts of passive entities with controlling persons in another EU Member State (DAC 5).[30] Furthermore, mandatory spontaneous exchange of tax rulings is part of Base Erosion and Profit Shifting (BEPS) Action 5.[31] As a part of the minimum standard, the signatories of the BEPS Action Plan have committed to implement a standardized and regular exchange of information on tax rulings and

24. On 4 April 2016, the International Consortium of Investigative Journalists announced their access to the 'Panama Papers', 11.5 million documents comprising forty years of emails, bank accounts and client records from the Panamanian law firm Mossack Fonseca. More information is available at ICIJ, *The Panama Papers, Exposing the Rogue Offshore Finance Industry*, https://panamapapers.icij.org/ (accessed 12 September 2018).
25. More information is available at ICIJ, *ICIJ Publishes Leaked Bahamas Info to Offshore Database*, icij.org https://www.icij.org/blog/2016/09/icij-publishes-leaked-bahamas-info-offshore-database/ (accessed 12 September 2018).
26. For more information, see ICIJ, *Paradise Papers: Secrets of the Global Elite*, https://www.icij.org/investigations/paradise-papers/#_ga=2.144469813.1664753161.1522330888-1755234133.1519375723 (accessed 12 September 2018).
27. *See, e.g.*, Tax Justice Network, *Tax Us If You Can* (2nd ed., Tax Justice Network 2012), http://www.taxjustice.net/cms/upload/pdf/TUIYC_2012_FINAL.pdf (accessed 12 September 2018); CONCORD, *The Role of the EU in Ensuring Global Tax Justice Spotlight Report 2015 Paper* (Jeffreson, 2015), *available at* http://www.actionaid.org/sites/files/actionaid/concord-pcd-tax-ffd-.pdf (accessed 12 September 2018).
28. OECD, *Standard for Automatic Exchange of Financial Account Information in Tax Matters* (OECD Publishing 2014).
29. Council, *supra* note 10.
30. Council Directive (EU) 2016/2258 amending Directive 2011/16/EU as regards access to anti-money laundering information by tax authorities OJ L 342/1 (2016); *see also* Eur. Comm'n, Communication on further measures to enhance transparency and the fight against tax evasion and avoidance, COM/2016/451 final, 6.
31. OECD, *Countering Harmful Tax Practices More Effectively, Taking into Account Transparency and Substance, Action 5 – 2015 Final Report* (OECD Publishing 2015).

advance pricing arrangements (APAs).[32] On 8 December 2015, an amendment of the DAC was adopted to implement automatic exchange of tax rulings and APAs within the EU (DAC 3).[33] In the area of transfer pricing, the documentation requirements continue to evolve and extend. The EU recommended already in 2006 transfer pricing documentation requirements in its Code of Conduct on Transfer Pricing Documentation for Associated Enterprises in the EU (EU TPD).[34] The two-tier system in the EU TPD consists of a local file and a master file. This concept is also being used in BEPS Action 13 where an extended three-layered transfer pricing documentation, consisting of a master file, a local file and a Country-by-Country Report (CbC report), has been introduced which replaced the existing provisions of Chapter V of the OECD Transfer Pricing Guidelines (OECD Guidelines).[35] The OECD advocates a framework where the tax administrations receive CbC reports under the provisions for automatic exchange of information. Within the EU, automatic exchange of CbC reports was implemented in May 2016 as an amendment of the DAC (DAC 4).[36] Usually only the tax administrations – and not also the public – will have access to CbC reports. Non-profit organizations have however demanded more transparency that would also allow the public to have access to the CbC reports.[37] Increasing obligations to disclose tax-related information to the public such as public CbC reporting have already been implemented by some jurisdictions domestically and are currently also discussed within the EU.[38] Another transparency initiative suggested in the BEPS Action Plan is the adoption of Mandatory Disclosure Rules (MDRs).[39] MDRs would require the taxpayers and/or their tax advisors to disclose certain tax planning schemes to the tax authorities. As this proposal is not part of the minimum standard that all OECD and G20 countries have

---

32. OECD, *OECD Releases Peer Review Documents for Assessment of BEPS minimum standards (Actions 5 and 13)* (1 February 2017) http://www.oecd.org/tax/beps/oecd-releases-peer-review-documents-for-assessment-of-beps-minimum-standards-actions-5-and-13.htm (accessed 12 September 2018).
33. Council Directive 2015/2376 amending Directive 2011/16/EU as regards mandatory automatic exchange of information in the field of taxation OJ L 332/1 (2015).
34. Council Resolution of the representatives of the governments of the Member States, meeting within the Council, of 27 June 2006 on a code of conduct on transfer pricing documentation for associated enterprises in the European Union, 2006/C 176/01 (2006).
35. OECD, *Transfer Pricing Documentation and Country-by-Country Reporting, Action 13 – 2015 Final Report* (OECD Publishing 2015).
36. Council Directive 2016/881 amending Directive 2011/16/EU as regards mandatory automatic exchange of information in the field of taxation OJ L 146/8 (2016).
37. *See, e.g.*, Eurodad, *Exposing the Lost Billions. How Financial Transparency by Multinationals on a Country-by-Country Basis Can Aid Development* (21 November 2011), https://eurodad.org/4720/ (accessed 12 September 2018); Richard Murphy & Tax Justice Network, *Country-by-Country Reporting: Accounting for Globalization Locally*, http://www.taxresearch.org.uk/Documents/CBC2012.pdf (accessed 12 September 2018).
38. Eur. Comm'n, Proposal for a Directive of the European Parliament and of the Council amending Directive 2013/34/EU as regards disclosure of income tax information by certain undertakings and branches, COM/2016/198 final; for an analysis of the constitutionality of public Country-by-Country reporting, see FR Conseil Constitutionnel (French Constitutional Court), *Commentaire des Décisions n° 2016-740 DC et n° 2016-741 DC du 8 décembre 2016* (Conseil Constitutionnel 2016); Viktoria Wöhrer, *Öffentliches Country-by-Country-Reporting verfassungswidrig*, 27 SWI 25 (2017); Viktoria Wöhrer, *Ist öffentliches Country-by-Country-Reporting mit den EU-Grundrechten vereinbar?*, 1 TPI 22 (2017).
39. OECD, *Mandatory Disclosure Rules, Action 12 – 2015 Final Report* (OECD Publishing 2015).

committed to implement but is just a recommendation, it remains to be seen how many jurisdictions will introduce such MDRs. Within the EU, the recommendations in BEPS Action 12 have been implemented within the exchange of information framework (DAC 6).[40] Intermediaries such as tax advisors, accountants and lawyers who design and promote tax planning schemes for their clients will be required to report schemes with a cross-border element which are considered potentially aggressive. There is no definition for 'aggressive tax planning schemes'. Instead, intermediaries are required to report where certain indications - generic or specific hallmarks - are present. Certain hallmarks will only lead to a reporting requirement if the main benefit or one of the main benefits of an arrangement is the obtaining of a tax advantage. Where there is no intermediary (e.g., in-house schemes) or where the intermediary is not obliged to report as it would breach a domestic legal professional privilege, the taxpayer has the obligation to report.

§11.03 TAXPAYERS' RIGHTS IN THE AREA OF EXCHANGE OF INFORMATION

Procedural rights such as the right to inspect files, notification, be heard, object and appeal against exchange of information could prevent situations where the taxpayer is harmed due to a breach of confidentiality or a misuse of the exchanged information.[41] The instruments for exchange of information, however, do not comprehensively provide for procedural rights of the taxpayer but have left this issue to domestic legislation. The focus has been on an efficient and rapid exchange of tax information rather than on the position of the taxpayers whose information is exchanged.[42] The different instruments for exchange of information are not dealing with the relationship to the taxpayer. Whereas the instruments, on the one hand, give countries the right to deny granting the information in some circumstances, this concerns only the horizontal relation between tax authorities of different states. The relation between taxpayers and tax authorities, on the other hand, is almost not regulated at all in the international instruments for exchange of information.[43]

The lack of procedural rights within the exchange of information procedure was confirmed in *Sabou* and in *Berlioz*.[44] The European Court of Justice (ECJ) held that the DAC does not address the procedural rights of the taxpayer and instead leaves it to the

40. Council Directive (EU) 2018/822 of 25 May 2018 amending Directive 2011/16/EU as regards mandatory automatic exchange of information in the field of taxation in relation to reportable cross-border arrangements OJ L 139/1 (2018).
41. *See* Irma Johanna Valderrama, *The Rights of Multinationals in the Global Transparency Framework: McCarthyism?*, 18 Derivatives & Fin. Instruments s. 1 (2016); José Manuel Calderón & Alberto Quintas Seara, *The Taxpayer's Right of Defence in Cross-Border Exchange-of-Information Procedures*, 68 Bull. Int'l Tax'n 498, 505 (2014).
42. *See* Madeleine Simonek, *Taxpayers' Rights in the International Exchange of Information Procedure: Where Is the Right Balance?* 83 Archiv für schweizerisches Abgaberechst 861 (2015).
43. *See, e.g.*, João Félix Nogueira, *Portugal: Right To Be Notified in Requested State, in Tax Treaty Case Law Around the Globe 2014* 355, 356 (Eric C.C.M. Kemmeren et al. eds., Linde 2015).
44. *See Sabou*, C-276/12, Judgment, EU:C:2013:678, para. 36; *Berlioz Investment Fund*, C-682/15, EU:C:2017:373, para. 46.

EU Member States to decide on the appropriate level of procedural safeguards. The DAC only deals with the relationship between the tax authorities and coordinates the exchange of information and does not govern the relationship between tax authorities and taxpayers.[45] In addition, the ECJ held that also the principle of effective judicial protection in Charter Article 47 or the rights of the defence that have been accepted as a general principle of EU law[46] do not impose any obligations on the EU Member States to confer specific rights to the taxpayer during the investigation procedure. The distinction made by the ECJ in *Sabou* between the purely fact-finding investigation stage during which information may be exchanged between different tax authorities and the contentious stage which begins when the taxpayer is sent the proposed adjustment has been criticized both in literature and by the European Court of Human Rights (ECtHR) in the *Othymia* case.[47]

In *Berlioz*, the ECJ also differentiated between data relating to taxpayers who have the possibility to participate in the procedure in the requesting state and taxpayers or third parties who do not have such an opportunity.[48] Whereas the ECJ only implicitly acknowledged that taxpayers should have procedural rights in the requested state if they are not party to a procedure in the requesting state, GA *Wathelet* clearly stated that 'the taxpayer under investigation and the requested third party are not in comparable situations'.[49] If the information to be exchanged relates to a person that is not 'involved in the second stage of the tax control procedure', procedural rights could arguably be required to be granted in the requested state on the basis of Charter Article 47.[50] Furthermore, the ECJ indicates in *Berlioz* that a taxpayer must have a possibility to challenge the legality of an administrative order to provide information where a penalty is imposed for the failure to comply with such an order. When the taxpayer has been ordered to provide information solely because the information was required for replying to a request for information, the taxpayer must be given an opportunity to challenge the validity of it.[51] The ECJ, therefore, has acknowledged in *Berlioz* that the taxpayer has to be provided with procedural rights in the exchange of information procedure under certain circumstances. Nevertheless, in situations when the information to be exchanged is either already available for the tax authority of the requested state or collected from third parties, the DAC and Charter Article 47 do not require that

45. *Sabou*, C-276/12, para. 36; *Berlioz*, C-682/15, para. 46; Simonek, *supra* note 42, at 875; Calderón, *supra* note 41, at 501.
46. The CJEU held in *Sopropé*, C-349/07, Judgment, EU:C:2008:746, para. 36 'Observance of the rights of the defence is a general principle of Community law which applies where the authorities are minded to adopt a measure which will adversely affect an individual' (*see also Sabou*, C-276/12, para. 38).
47. *See Sabou*, C-276/12, para. 40; Philip Baker & Pasquale Pistone, *General Report*, *in* 100B *The Practical Protection of Taxpayers' Fundamental Rights* 21, 27 & 61 (Sdu Uitgevers 2015); *Othymia Investments BV* v *the Netherlands*, no. 75292/10, 16 June 2015, Eur. Ct. H.R. 2015, para. 44.
48. *See Berlioz*, C-682/15, para. 58.
49. *Berlioz*, C-682/15, AG Opinion, EU:C:2017:2, para. 115.
50. *Ibid.* para. 117.
51. *Ibid.* para. 89.

the taxpayer is informed or has any remedies to challenge the exchange of information.[52]

However, even though the DAC is not regulating the relationship between the taxpayer and tax administrations, it accepts indirectly that – due to the data protection requirements – some procedural rights may exist. Article 25(1) DAC explicitly confirms that exchange of information under the DAC is subject to EU data protection guarantees.[53] Article 25 DAC, however, does not merely stress the importance of data protection but also puts an emphasis on the necessity to limit some of the procedural rights in order to ensure the effectiveness of exchange of information.[54] Only in respect to automatic exchange of financial account information, Article 25(3) DAC provides for procedural rights: it requires that financial institutions inform the account holders about data collection and exchange.[55]

§11.04 DATA PROTECTION IN THE EU

The protection of personal data constitutes a fundamental right that is safeguarded by national constitutions, by Article 16 of the Treaty on the Functioning of the European Union (TFEU),[56] by Charter Article 8[57] and by the Council of Europe Convention No. 108.[58] Furthermore, personal data is protected as a part of the right to private life under the Universal Declaration of Human Rights,[59] the ECHR[60] and the International Covenant on Civil and Political Rights.[61] Charter Article 8 states that '[e]veryone has the right to the protection of personal data concerning him or her'. It recognizes the right to the protection of personal data as distinct from the right to respect for private and family life, home and communications which is additionally set out in Charter

52. *See* Viktoria Wöhrer, *Berlioz versus Sabou: Grundrechtsschutz im Amtshilfeverfahren*, 27 SWI 402 (2017).
53. Article 25 of the DAC refers to the Council & Eur. Parliament Directive 95/46/EC on the protection of individuals with regard to the processing of personal data and on the free movement of such data (Data Protection Directive, DPD) OJ L 281/31 (1995). The DPD has been repealed with effect from 25 May 2018. According to Art. 94(2) of the Council & Eur. Parliament Regulation 2016/679 on the protection of natural persons with regard to the processing of personal data and on the free movement of such data, and repealing Directive 95/46/EC (General Data Protection Regulation, GDPR) OJ L 119/1 (2016), this reference to the DPD shall be construed as a reference to the GDPR.
54. *See supra* note 10, para. 27.
55. *See* for further information on the relationship between data protection and exchange of information, e.g., Wöhrer, *supra* note 12, ch. 5, s. 5.6.4 & ch. 7, s. 7.2; Maryte Somare & Viktoria Wöhrer, *Automatic Exchange of Financial Information under the Directive on Administrative Cooperation in the Light of the Global Movement towards Transparency*, 43 Intertax 804, 812 et seq. (2015).
56. Consolidated Version of the Treaty on the Functioning of the European Union 26 October 2012 OJ C 326/47 (hereinafter 'TFEU').
57. Charter, *supra* note 14.
58. Council of Europe, Convention for the Protection of Individuals with regard to Automatic Processing of Personal Data, CETS No. 108, 28 January 1981 (hereinafter 'Personal Data Convention').
59. U.N., Universal Declaration of Human Rights, G. A. Res. 217 A (10 December 1948).
60. *See* ECHR, *supra* note 15.
61. U.N., International Covenant on Civil and Political Rights (16 December 1966).

Article 7.[62] Nevertheless, in case law dealing with data protection, the ECJ often refers to both Charter Articles 7 and 8.[63] At the level of secondary EU law, the GDPR of 2016[64] provides for an effective protection of the fundamental right to data protection in the EU.

Data protection safeguards have to be taken into account in the area of exchange of information. On the one hand, for exchange of information based on the DAC, Article 25(1) DAC explicitly states that exchange of information is subject to data protection provisions. However, even without that explicit statement, the GDPR would be applicable as information exchange in tax matters falls under the scope of the GDPR because it involves the processing of personal data.[65]

§11.05 SCOPE OF EU DATA PROTECTION SAFEGUARDS

Article 2(a) CoE Convention No. 108 states that 'personal data means any information relating to an identified or identifiable individual'. Almost the same definition is laid down in Article 4(1) GDPR where personal data is broadly defined as 'any information relating to an identified or identifiable natural person'. The ECJ has referred to these definitions when dealing with the substantial scope of protection of personal data.[66] This means that not only specific personal information or data related to private and family life is protected by EU data protection legislation. Instead, any information on an individual is covered. Therefore, information that is necessary for calculating taxes, for example data on employment, on income, on assets and on property, clearly constitutes 'personal data' if it concerns individuals.

The ECJ has confirmed in *Satakunnan Markkinapörssi and Satamedia* that a company that is publishing the earned and unearned income and assets of individual taxpayers in a newspaper is processing personal data.[67] Similarly, the transfer of data relating to a taxpayer's declared income from the tax authority to the National Health Insurance Fund as it took place in *Smaranda Bara* is processing of personal data.[68] Furthermore, the ECJ confirmed that also information about bank accounts is personal data.[69]

62. *See Tele2 Sverige*, C-203/15 & C-698/15, Judgment, EU:C:2016:970, para. 129; *Tele2 Sverige*, C-203/15 & C-698/15, AG Opinion, EU:C:2016:572, para. 79; Herke Kranenborg, *Article 8 – Protection of Personal Data, in The EU Charter of Fundamental Rights: A Commentary* 223, 228 (Steve Peers et al. eds., Hart 2014).
63. *See Digital Rights Ireland*, C-293/12 & C-594/12, EU:C:2014:238, para. 29; *Schecke*, C-92/09 & C-93/09, EU:C:2010:662, para. 52; *ASNEF*, C-468/10 & C- 469/10, EU:C:2011:777, paras 40 et seq.
64. Council & Eur. Parliament Regulation 2016/679 on the protection of natural persons with regard to the processing of personal data and on the free movement of such data, and repealing Directive 95/46/EC (General Data Protection Regulation) OJ L 119/1 (2016).
65. For a more detailed analysis, *see* Wöhrer, *supra* note 12, ch. 7 7.2.
66. *See, e.g., Österreichischer Rundfunk & Others*, C-465/00, C-138/01 & C-139/01, Judgment, EU:C:2003:294, para. 64; *Schecke*, C-92/09 & C-93/09, para. 52.
67. *Satakunnan*, C-73/07, Judgment, EU:C:2008:727, para. 35.
68. *Bara*, C-201/14, Judgment, EU:C:2015:638, para. 29.
69. *Coty Germany*, C-580/13, Judgment, EU:C:2015:485, para. 26.

Whereas the question of whether tax data relating to individuals is personal data can be answered in the affirmative, it is not so easy to answer the same question in relation to legal persons. Data protection under the GDPR protects 'fundamental rights and freedoms **of natural persons** and in particular their right to the protection of personal data' (Article 1(2) GDPR). In contrast, the scope of Charter Article 8 is not per se restricted to natural persons. Charter Article 8 states that 'everyone' has the right to the protection of personal data concerning him or her. Nevertheless, the ECJ has clearly stated in *Schecke* and in *WebMindLicenses* that legal persons are protected by Charter Article 8 'only insofar as the official title of the legal person identifies one or more natural persons'.[70] Furthermore, even where legal persons are covered by Charter Article 8, the ECJ held that the data protection standards are not the same as for individuals. Where data of legal persons is at stake, an interference that would already be qualified as not limited to what is necessary and proportional where it relates to data of natural persons could still be justified.[71] In contrast, even though the ECtHR has not explicitly stated whether the right to private life and, in particular, data protection under Article 8 ECHR also covers legal persons, the ECtHR's case law indicates that the ECtHR does not limit the scope of the right to respect for private life in Article 8 ECHR to natural persons.[72]

The GDPR defines the material scope of the respective data protection legislation very broad. Data protection is applicable to the processing of personal data which basically covers everything that can be done with data and covers *inter alia* the 'collection, recording, organization, storage, adaptation or alteration, retrieval, consultation, use, disclosure by transmission, dissemination or otherwise making available, alignment or combination, blocking, erasure or destruction' of personal data (Article 4(2) GDPR). Charter Article 8 and Article 8 ECHR do not define the material scope in such detail. The case law of the ECJ and the ECtHR reveals, however, that the ECJ and the ECtHR have also accepted a broad scope of protection of personal data.[73] Data protection guarantees in the ECHR, the Charter and the GDPR have a very broad material scope and cover almost everything that is done with personal data. Collecting, exchanging, using and storing tax information is processing of personal data and has to be in line with data protection safeguards. Automatic exchange of financial account information, tax rulings and reportable cross-border arrangements increases the amount of personal data collected, exchanged, stored and used by the tax authorities. Where personal data is processed, certain conditions have to be fulfilled for data processing to be legitimate.

70. *Schecke*, C-92/09 & C-93/09, para. 53; *WebMindLicenses*, C-419/14, Judgment, EU:C:2015:832, para. 79.
71. *Schecke*, C-92/09 & C-93/09, para. 87.
72. *See, e.g., Othymia Investments BV* v *the Netherlands*, no. 75292/10, *supra* note 47; *Bernh Larsen Holding AS & Others* v *Norway*, no. 24117/08, 14 March 2013, Eur. Ct. H.R. 2013, para. 98; Wöhrer, *supra* note 12, s. 6.2.3.
73. *See, e.g., Digital Rights Ireland*, C-293/12 & C-594/12, para. 32; CJEU, *Opinion 1/15*, EU:C:2017:592, paras 124 et seq.; *G.S.B.* v *Switzerland*, no. 28601/11 Eur. Ct. H.R. 2015.

§11.06 REQUIREMENTS STEMMING FROM EU DATA PROTECTION

[A] Requirements under Article 8 ECHR

Data processing must be based either on consent or on another legitimate legal basis, and it must be proportional. Article 8 ECHR requires that data processing is in accordance with the law, necessary in a democratic society and pursues one or more of the legitimate aims listed in Article 8(2) ECHR. For justifying exchange of information for tax purposes both the prevention of crime and the economic well-being of a country can be considered as relevant legitimate aims.[74] Both in *Bernh Larsen Holding AS* and in *Othymia Investments BV*, the ECtHR has accepted that the processing of personal data for the purpose of taxation can be justified as being necessary to ensure that taxes are paid which is required to finance public goods for the society.[75] Furthermore, in *X* v *Belgium* the ECtHR has held that legislation requiring the taxpayer to produce a list of his private expenditure has the purpose of collecting the right amount of taxes and to prevent fraud and tax evasion.[76]

The proportionality assessment requires to balance the exercises of the guaranteed right with the necessity of an interference. The ECHR has taken a lot of different factors into account when making its proportionality assessment, *inter alia* the nature of the data,[77] the privacy expectation of the person concerned,[78] the possible control mechanisms given to the person concerned (the right of access to the data),[79] the presence of independent oversight mechanisms[80] and whether security measures have been put in place.[81] Furthermore, the ECtHR considered the cultural and social background in a society[82] and took also the political situation into account: in *F. S.* v *Germany* the 'current trend towards strengthening international cooperation in the administration of justice' was one of the arguments why exchange of information for tax purposes was justified.[83] Similarly, in *UBS* v *France*, the ECtHR considered the 'growing and legitimate concern both in Europe and internationally in relation to financial offences, which constituted socially unacceptable behavior, and the difficulty

74. *See F. S.* v *Germany*, no. 30128/96, 27 November 1996, Eur. Ct. H.R. 1996; Eur. Ct. H.R., 16 June 2015, *Othymia Investments BV* v *the Netherlands*, no. 75292/10, *supra* note 47, para. 41.
75. *Bernh Larsen Holding AS & Others* v *Norway*, no. 24117/08, *supra* note 72, para. 135; *Rousk* v *Sweden*, no. 27183/04, 25 July 2013, Eur. Ct. H.R. 2013, para. 135; *Othymia Investments BV* v *the Netherlands*, no. 75292/10, *supra* note 47, para. 41.
76. *See, e.g., X.* v *Belgium*, no. 9804/82, Commission decision of 7 December 1982, Eur. DR 31, p. 231; Eur. Ct. H.R., 7 December 1982; *R. V.* v *The Netherlands*, no. 12662/87, Eur. Ct. H.R. 1989.
77. *See Z.* v *Finland*, judgment of 25 February 1997, no. 22009/93, Reports 1997-I; *I* v *Finland*, no. 20511/03, 17 July 2008, § 38 Eur. Ct. H.R. 2008.
78. *See Krone Verlag* v *Austria*, no. 34315/96, 26 February 2002, Eur. Ct. H.R. 2002; *Von Hannover* v *Germany*, no. 59320/00, § 69 Eur. Ct. H.R. (2004).
79. *See Leander* v *Sweden*, no. 9248/81 Series A no. 116 (1987); *Gaskin* v *The United Kingdom*, no. 10454/83, § 49 Series A no. 160 (1989).
80. *See Klass* v *Germany*, judgment of 6 September 1978, Series A no. 28 § 50.
81. *See I* v *Finland*, *supra* note 77, para. 40.
82. *See Lundvall* v *Sweden*, no. 10473/83, Commission decision of 11 December 1985, DR 45, p. 121, § 5.
83. *See F. S.* v *Germany*, no. 30128/96 Eur. Ct. H.R. (1996).

of combating such offences'.[84] The fact that not all data collected by public authorities are effectively used cannot lead to the conclusion that data processing is not necessary. In *Michaud*, the ECtHR has explicitly acknowledged that data processing may nevertheless be necessary because it has a deterrent effect.[85]

So far, the ECtHR has not been very strict in assessing the proportionality of processing of personal data in the area of taxation. However, the ECtHR has mostly dealt with exchange of information on request. Therefore, it remains to be seen whether the ECtHR will allow a similarly broad margin when it comes to automatic exchange of information.

[B] Requirements under Charter Article 8 and the GDPR

Charter Article 8(2) stipulates that 'data must be processed fairly for specified purposes and on the basis of the consent of the person concerned or some other legitimate basis laid down by law'. The GDPR provides for more detailed data quality principles. Article 5 GDPR requires that personal data is processed lawfully, fairly and in a transparent manner; collected for specified, explicit and legitimate purposes; adequate, relevant, and not excessive; accurate and kept up-to-date; kept in a form that permits identification of data subjects for no longer than necessary and processed in a manner that ensures appropriate security of the personal data. Where data processing has a legal basis and complies with the data quality principles, it is generally in line with Charter Article 8(2) and the GDPR.

[1] Lawfulness, Fairness and Transparency

The requirement for lawfulness, fairness and transparency indicates that the processing of personal data must have a legitimate basis and that the data subject must be provided with some procedural rights. Article 6 GDPR lists the circumstances under which data processing is allowed and thereby requires a legitimate basis for data processing. Data processing is legitimate if it is based on consent, a contract or a legal obligation. The need for fair and transparent data processing is linked to the rights of the data subject. In order for data processing to be fair, the interests of the data subject have to be taken into account. The rights of the data subject are laid down in Articles 12–22 GDPR.

Article 6(e) GDPR states that data processing is lawful if the processing is necessary for the performance of a task carried out in the public interest or in the exercise of official authority vested in the controller or in a third party to whom the data is disclosed. The ECJ has held that for example the maintenance of the companies'

84. *See UBS* v *France*, no. 29778/15, § 20 Eur. Ct. H.R. (2016).
85. *See Michaud* v *France*, no. 12323/11, § 125 Eur. Ct. H.R. (2012).

register is such a task carried out in the public interest.[86] Tax authorities can rely on Article 6(e) GDPR to collect and process an individual's tax return in order to establish and verify the amount of tax to be paid.[87] Data processing based on Article 6(1)(e) GDPR must however have a legal basis either in EU law or in the domestic law of an EU Member State that meets an objective of public interest and is proportionate to the legitimate aim pursued (Article 6(3) GDPR).[88]

[2] Purpose Limitation

Article 5(1)(b) GDPR requires that personal data is 'collected for specified, explicit and legitimate purposes' and not 'further processed in a manner that is incompatible with those purposes'. The purpose limitation principle requires that there is a legitimate purpose for data processing and that this purpose is specified and documented. The specification of the purpose requires that the purpose is 'sufficiently defined to enable the implementation of any necessary data protection safeguards, and to delimit the scope of the processing operation'.[89] Specifying the purpose for data processing is a precondition for applying other data quality safeguards. Only where the purpose of data processing is clear it is possible to assess whether the data collection is adequate, relevant and limited to what is necessary.

The purpose must be stated explicitly, which requires that it is 'sufficiently unambiguous and clearly expressed'.[90] The principle of purpose limitation should make it predictable for the data subject how data concerning him or her is processed and thereby increases legal certainty.[91] The requirement to explicitly state the purpose of data processing and the data subject's right to information both require that the data subject is fully informed about the fact that processing of personal data takes place and about the purposes for which data is processed. It allows the data subjects to exercise their rights, for example to request a deletion or correction of their data.

As an explicit purpose for data processing is necessary, administrative cooperation among government authorities in different EU Member States must be based on legal rules that clarify what data are to be used, shared and exchanged, for what purposes, who has access to what information, how information technology security is ensured and what additional safeguards are applicable.[92]

---

86. *See Manni*, C-398/15, Judgment, EU:C:2017:197, para. 43.
87. *See* Art. 29 Data Protection Working Party, *Opinion 06/2014 on the Notion of Legitimate Interests of the Data Controller Under Article 7 of Directive 95/46/EC* 1, 21 (Working Paper 844/14/EN WP 217, 2014), *available at* http://ec.europa.eu/justice/article-29/documentation/opinion-recommendation/files/2014/wp217_en.pdf.
88. *See also* Wöhrer, *supra* note 12, ch. 6.3.5.
89. Article 29 Data Protection Working Party, *Opinion 03/2013 on Purpose Limitation* 1, 12 (Working Paper 00569/13/EN WP 203, 2013), *available at* http://ec.europa.eu/justice/article-29/documentation/opinion-recommendation/files/2013/wp203_en.pdf.
90. *Ibid.*
91. *Ibid.* at 4 f.
92. *Ibid.* at 54; *Bonnier Audio & Others*, C-461/10, AG Opinion, EU:C:2011:753, para. 54.

[3] Data Minimization

Article 5(1)(c) GDPR requires that personal data must be 'adequate, relevant and limited to what is necessary in relation to the purposes for which they are processed'. The data minimization principle prohibits the disclosure, making available or use of personal data where it is not strictly necessary for the purposes that the data has been collected for. Personal data should also not be combined with other available data if such a combination is not necessary for the specified purpose.[93] The data minimization principle prohibits the collection or storage of data where it only 'might be useful later'.[94] Instead, it is required to assess the necessity and proportionality of data processing.

In order to assess whether data processing is adequate, relevant and necessary, the ECJ referred to the case law of the ECtHR on the proportionality of data processing.[95] Where a purpose can be reached by processing a smaller amount of information or by a less intrusive way of data processing, the data minimization principle prohibits going beyond the less intrusive data processing operation. In a number of cases the ECJ has held that 'derogations and limitations in relation to the protection of personal data must apply only in so far as is strictly necessary'.[96] In the area of taxation, the ECJ has held in 2017 in the *Peter Puškár* case that where a list of natural persons purporting to act as company directors is created for the purpose of collecting tax and combating tax fraud it is for 'the national court to ascertain ... whether there is no other less restrictive means in order to achieve those objectives'.[97]

However, in a recent tax case the ECJ has applied a rather lenient approach to data protection. In the *Commission* v *Germany* case of February 2018, the ECJ held that the special scheme for travel agents in the value added tax (VAT) Directive[98] does not infringe the fundamental right to data protection.[99] The obligation for travel agents to state their profit margin on the invoice contributes – as part of the harmonization of the VAT regime – to the functioning of the internal market and has the purpose of simplifying VAT rules for travel agents and of providing for a balanced allocation VAT

93. *See* Bart Custers & Helena Uršič, *Big Data and Data Reuse: A Taxonomy of Data Reuse for Balancing Big Data Benefits and Personal Data Protection*, 6 Int'l Data Privacy L. 4, 8 (2016).
94. *See* Art. 29 Data Protection Working Party, *Opinion 8/2014 on the on Recent Developments on the Internet of Things* 1, 16 (Working Paper 14/EN WP 223, 2014), *available at* http://ec.europa.eu/justice/article-29/documentation/opinion-recommendation/files/2014/wp223_en.pdf (accessed 19 October 2018).
95. *Österreichischer Rundfunk & Others*, C-465/00, C-138/01 & C-139/01, Judgment, EU:C:2003:294, para. 88.
96. *Satakunnan*, C-73/07, para. 56; *Schecke*, C-92/09 & C-93/09, para. 77; *IPI*, C-473/12, EU:C:2013:715, para. 39; *Digital Rights Ireland*, C-293/12 & C-594/12, para. 52; *Ryneš*, C-212/13, Judgment, EU:C:2014:2428, para. 28; *Schrems*, C-362/14, Judgment, EU:C:2015:650, para. 92; *Tele2 Sverige*, C-203/15 & C-698/15, para. 96.
97. *Puškár*, C-73/16, Judgment, EU:C:2017:725, para. 113.
98. Council Directive 2006/112/EC on the common system of value added tax OJ L 347/1 (2006), Arts 306–310.
99. *Comm'n* v *Germany*, C-380/16, Judgment, EU:C:2018:76.

revenues between the EU Member States. The ECJ held that this purpose cannot be reached by a less intrusive alternative measure and is therefore justified.[100]

The instruments providing for automatic exchange of information identify the fight against cross-border tax evasion and tax fraud as their purpose. The preamble to the DAC states that automatic exchange of financial account information has the purpose of increasing 'the efficiency and effectiveness of tax collection' as a response to increasing cross-border tax fraud and tax evasion.[101] The objective of combating tax evasion has already been accepted by the CJEU and the ECtHR as a legitimate purpose and as an overriding reason of general interest.[102] Automatic exchange of financial account information has also more generally the purpose of ensuring an effective administration and enforcement of tax laws in cross-border situations. Tax authorities should not only be provided with financial account information that provides tax authorities with indications for non-compliant behaviour. Even though the preamble to the DAC mainly stresses the need to fight tax fraud and tax evasion, also the purpose of 'enabling Member States' tax administrations to correctly and unequivocally identify the taxpayers concerned, to administer and enforce their tax laws in cross-border situations, to assess the likelihood of tax evasion being perpetrated, and to avoid unnecessary further investigations' is mentioned.[103] The CRS explicitly states that exchanged information should be available for 'automatic matching with domestic compliance information and data analysis'.[104] Therefore, automatic exchange of information has also the purpose of verifying whether taxpayers complied with their obligations. Data processing to enable tax administrations to administer and enforce tax laws contributes to the economic well-being of a country and is therefore a legitimate purpose. Automatic exchange of information enables the control of tax returns on a large scale and makes it consequently more efficient to prevent tax avoidance and tax evasion. However, data processing does not only need to follow a legitimate aim but also needs to be necessary and proportional. According to the principle of proportionality, data processing is only in line with the data protection provisions where it is well balanced with the aim pursued by the provision allowing the processing of personal data.

For the question of whether the collection and disclosure of tax information to tax authorities of other states are proportional it is necessary to consider whether it is 'relevant and not excessive in relation to the purposes' of data processing. Assessing the proportionality of a measure is not easy as it requires assessing both the level of intrusiveness of a measure and the importance of the legitimate aim that has been pursued. Both the level of sensitivity of the data as well as the availability of less intrusive alternative measures have to be taken into account.

100. *Ibid.* paras 68 et seq.
101. DAC, *supra* note 10, pmbl, para. 1.
102. *See, e.g.*, *K.S. & M.S.* v *Germany*, no. 33696/11, 6 October 2016, Eur. Ct. H.R. 2016, para. 36; Berlioz, C-682/15, AG Opinion, para. 89.
103. DAC, *supra* note 10, pmbl, para. 10.
104. CRS, *supra* note 9, at 12.

The framework for automatic exchange of financial account information requires the collection and exchange of comprehensive financial account information about all accounts held or controlled by persons which are not (only) resident in the same country as the financial institution where the account is held. There are doubts as to whether the systematic and periodic bulk exchange of taxpayer information is proportional. To some extent, the aspect that a big amount of data is collected from financial institutions for subsequently being transferred to tax administrations of other EU Member States without any indications of non-compliant behaviour can be compared to the data collection under the Data Retention Directive (DRD) which has been declared invalid due to its disproportionality in the *Digital Rights Ireland* case.[105] The DRD laid down a system of generalized and massive collection and retention of traffic and location data covering everyone using electronic communications services without requiring any relation between the data to be stored and a threat to public security.[106] Data collection under the DRD has been declared illegal due to disproportionality.

Under the framework for automatic exchange of financial information, not only information about the account holder and the financial institution where the account is held is exchanged but also comprehensive information on the value of the assets held on the account as well as on the income from savings and investment generated through the account. A less intrusive alternative would be an automatic exchange of information covering just the existence of accounts (identification information). In case a taxpayer did not declare income of a specific account or the tax authorities have reasons to believe that the tax return that has been filed is incorrect, they could in a second step request further information from the financial institutions.

However, the purpose of automatic exchange of information is not limited to combating tax crimes but has more generally the aim to ensure an effective administration and enforcement of tax laws also in cross-border situations. The collection of financial account information from everyone who has an account in one state and is (also) resident in another state is a means to ensure that taxpayers comply with their reporting obligation and does not necessarily go beyond of what is necessary and proportional.[107] A more limited data collection, covering only information on the account holders and on the financial institutions where an account is held, is not as efficient as the collection of the full set of financial account information, including for example account balance, interests and dividends. Even though the financial account information might not allow an effective determination of the tax liability but requires subsequent further investigations, the data supports systematic and efficient risk reviews. Tax authorities could make use of the automatically exchanged financial

105. *See Digital Rights Ireland*, C-293/12 & C-594/12.

106. *Ibid.* para. 58; *Tele2 Sverige*, C-203/15 & C-698/15, para. 105; Ludovica Benedizione & Eleonora Paris, *Preliminary Reference and Dialogue Between Courts As Tools for Reflection on the EU System of Multilevel Protection of Rights: The Case of the Data Retention Directive*, 16 German L.J. 1727, 1762 (2015); Alessandro Spina, *Risk Regulation of Big Data: Has the Time Arrived for a Paradigm Shift in EU Data Protection Law? Case C-293/12 and C-594/12 Digital Rights Ireland and Seitlinger and Others*, 5 Eur. J. Risk Reg. 248, 250 (2014).

107. *See* Tina Ehrke-Rabel, *Geheimhaltungs- und Informationsinteressen beim Automatischen Internationalen Informationsaustausch nach dem GMSG*, 26 SWI 67, 76 (2016).

account information in order to identify taxpayers with indications for non-compliant behaviour. Even where tax authorities are not making use of the automatically exchanged information, it could be considered proportional because automatic exchange of financial account information constitutes an effective deterrent against tax evasion.[108]

[4] Accuracy

Personal data should be accurate and, where necessary, kept up-to-date. Article 5(1)(d) GDPR requires to take every reasonable step to ensure that data are kept accurate and up-to-date, having regard to the purposes for which they were collected or for which they are further processed. Personal data that is inaccurate must be erased or rectified without delay. So far, the ECJ has not interpreted this principle that requires to ensure that personal data is accurate and up-to-date in its case law. Where personal data is inaccurate or incomplete the data subject has the right to obtain the rectification, erasure or blocking of the data.[109]

[5] Storage Limitation

Personal data may not be kept for longer than necessary for the purpose for which the data was processed. Article 5(1)(e) GDPR requires the deletion or anonymization of personal data where it is no longer necessary to fulfil the specified purpose. For the assessment of the necessary and reasonable retention period, the circumstances of the specific case have to be taken into account.[110]

The data retention period is a criterion that has also been taken into account by the ECJ when assessing the proportionality of an interference with the right to private life and the right to the protection of personal data. In *Digital Rights Ireland* the ECJ considered the retention period in the DRD as going beyond of what is strictly necessary because the DRD did not lay down any objective criteria to be followed for the limitation of the retention period and generally fixed the retention period at six to twenty-four months, regardless of the distinction as to the different categories of data dealt with in the DRD.[111]

The DAC has taken data protection concerns into account and requires that the exchanged information is not retained longer than necessary to achieve the purposes of the DAC and in any case in accordance with each data controller's domestic rules on statute of limitations. This provision has the aim to ensure proportionality of data retention. However, due to the lack of clear deadlines this provision does not substantially enhance data protection and it is most certainly not enough to ensure the

108. *See* Wöhrer, *supra* note 12, ch. 7, s. 7.7.2.
109. Article 5.1 c GDPR; Arts 16–18 GDPR.
110. *See* Kranenborg, *supra* note 62, at 248 m.n. 08.106.
111. *See Digital Rights Ireland*, C-293/12 & C-594/12, paras 63 et seq.; Benedizione, *supra* note 106, at 1763.

proportionality of data retention.[112] A data retention period should make a 'distinction between categories of data based on their possible usefulness for the purposes pursued and must use objective criteria for the determination of the length of the retention period'.[113] In order to limit the retention period to the minimum necessary and to comply with the data protection requirements, it is required to clearly identify how the information is to be used and stored. For example, where the financial account information received by other tax authorities can be used for an automatic comparison with income of savings and investment that the taxpayer has declared in his final tax return, the data relating to accounts which do not give any indication of irregularities could be deleted after the first screening.

However, financial information exchanged under the DAC shall not only be used for controlling the correct statement of relevant income in the tax return. Information on the account balances and sale proceeds from financial assets that is exchanged should also help tax authorities to disclose situations where a taxpayer attempted to hide capital that represents income or assets with regard to which tax has been evaded.[114] In order to conduct investigations in that respect it could be useful for tax authorities to have access to data of previous years in order to analyse the development over a longer period. As the DAC does not provide for a clear retention period, the storage period will differ in the different jurisdictions.

In order to ensure compliance with data protection safeguards, all exchange of information instruments should provide for a clear data retention period and explicitly require the deletion of exchanged tax information after this period has expired.[115] For determining the length of the retention period, a distinction as to the purpose of data processing could prove useful. Where tax data is merely used in a general manner for ensuring an effective administration and enforcement of tax laws, a short retention period would be sufficient. In contrast, where tax data is particularly relevant for combating tax evasion, a longer retention period could be justified. In any case, data protection safeguards would be better taken into consideration by defining a clear data retention period or clear criteria for its determination.

112. *See also* Council of Europe Consultative Committee of the Convention for the Protection of Individuals with Regard to Automatic Processing of Personal Data (ETS No. 108), *Opinion on the implications for data protection of mechanisms for automatic inter-state exchanges of data for administrative and tax purposes*, T-PD (2014)05 (Council of Europe 2014); Somare, *supra* note 55, at 812 et seq.; Saturnina Moreno González, *The Automatic Exchange of Tax Information and the Protection of Personal Data in the European Union: Reflections on the Latest Jurisprudential and Normative Advances*, 25 EC Tax Rev. 146, 153 et seq. (2016).

113. EDPS, *Developing a 'Toolkit' for Assessing the Necessity of Measures That Interfere with Fundamental Rights* 18 (16 June 2016), https://edps.europa.eu/sites/edp/files/publication/16-06-16_necessity_paper_for_consultation_en.pdf.

114. *See* DAC, *supra* note 10, pmbl, para. 10.

115. *See* Art. 29 Data Protection Working Party, *Guidelines for Member States on the Criteria to Ensure Compliance with Data Protection Requirements in the Context of the Automatic Exchange of Personal Data for Tax Purposes* 1, 7 (Working Paper 175/16/EN WP 234, 2015), *available at* http://ec.europa.eu/justice/article-29/documentation/opinion-recommendation/files/2015/wp234_en.pdf.

[6] Integrity and Confidentiality

Article 5(1)(f) GDPR requires that personal data must be 'processed in a manner that ensures appropriate security of the personal data'. The data controller is responsible to protect data against unauthorized or unlawful processing and against accidental loss, destruction or damage. Both the controller and the processor are obliged to ensure a level of security appropriate to the risks presented by processing (in Article 32 GDPR). They are required to implement appropriate technical and organizational measures. Furthermore, the GDPR requires the data controller to notify any personal data breach to the supervisory authority within seventy-two hours after having become aware of the personal data breach. In addition, where the personal data breach is likely to result in a high risk to the rights and freedoms of natural persons, the controller must communicate the personal data breach to the data subject without undue delay.

An increasing exchange of large volumes of tax information increases the risk that the information gets leaked and becomes available to the public or to persons who are not supposed to have access to that data. Therefore, it is all the more important that strict security measures are adopted to avoid unauthorized or unlawful processing and accidental loss, destruction or damage of personal tax data. The Article 29 Data Protection Working Party recommends that tax cooperation agreements should explicitly require tax authorities to comply with specific security standards and adopt a *privacy-by-design* approach where data protection requirements are already implemented when the system of data processing is designed as opposed to an *ex post* application of data protection rules. Furthermore, the server hosting the data processing should be within the territory of the EU.[116]

§11.07 PROCEDURAL RIGHTS STEMMING FROM EU DATA PROTECTION

[A] Right to Be Informed about Exchange of Information

The existence and scope of procedural safeguards are important criteria for compliance with data protection safeguards. Nevertheless, many jurisdictions do not provide taxpayers with procedural rights in the process of cross-border exchange of information. Notification procedures to inform taxpayers about exchange of information may delay or prevent exchange of information if the taxpayer takes legal action against the

116. *See* Art. 29 Data Protection Working Party, *Guidelines for Member States on the Criteria to Ensure Compliance with Data Protection Requirements in the Context of the Automatic Exchange of Personal Data for Tax Purposes* 1, 8 (European Union, Working Paper 175/16/EN WP 234, 2015), *available at* http://ec.europa.eu/justice/article-29/documentation/opinion-recommendation/files/2015/wp234_en.pdf; Art. 29 Data Protection Working Party, *Statement of the WP29 on Automatic Inter-state Exchanges of Personal Data for Tax Purposes* 1, 3 (Working Paper 14/EN WP 230, 2015), *available at* http://ec.europa.eu/justice/article-29/documentation/opinion-recommendation/files/2015/wp230_en.pdf.

cross-border cooperation.[117] Furthermore, prior notification may undermine the success of a tax investigation. This is why the Global Forum has criticized countries that generally informed taxpayers about exchange of information.[118] In contrast, data protection legislation may require tax authorities to inform the data subjects prior to providing personal data to other tax authorities in other jurisdictions.

Article 8 ECHR does not explicitly provide data subjects with procedural rights. Whether the data subject has a right to complain against data processing is nevertheless a decisive criterion in the proportionality assessment of the ECtHR.[119] Moreover, the right to the protection of personal data set forth in Charter Article 8 does not explicitly require that the data subject is informed about data processing. Charter Article 8(2) merely stipulates that 'data must be processed fairly'. Article 5(1)(a) GDPR also requires fair data processing. In order for data processing to be fair, the rights of the data subject – laid down in Articles 12–22 GDPR – have to be taken into account. Articles 13 and 14 GDPR provide that the data subject has to be informed about the data processing. The right to be informed about data processing has been interpreted by the ECJ in *Smaranda Bara*.[120] The ECJ held that 'the requirement of fair processing of personal data ... requires a public administrative body to inform the data subjects of the transfer of those data to another public administrative body for the purpose of their processing by the latter in its capacity as recipient of those data'.[121] Because the law regulating the transfer of information in *Smaranda Bara* was not precise enough and did not clearly inform the data subject that information would be provided by the tax authority to the authority responsible for social insurance, the data subject would have had to be informed separately about the data transfer.[122] The right to be informed about data processing is however not absolute. Article 23 GDPR explicitly allows EU Member States to restrict data subject's rights by way of a legislative measure where it is necessary and proportional to safeguard an important economic or financial interest of an EU Member State or of the EU. In particular, rights of a data subject may be restricted where it is necessary for tax purposes.

Where the data subject's right to be informed about data processing – including cross-border exchange of information – shall be restricted, such a restriction has to be

117. *See* Baker, *supra* note 47, at 61.
118. *See, e.g.*, OECD, *Global Forum on Transparency and Exchange of Information for Tax Purposes: Austria 2013, Peer Review Report Phase 2, Implementation of the Standard in Practice* 1, 82 para. 283 (OECD Publishing 2013) (notification was only necessary in case of bank information); OECD, *Global Forum on Transparency and Exchange of Information for Tax Purposes Peer Reviews: Switzerland 2011, Peer Review Report Phase 1, Legal and Regulatory Framework* 1, 10, para. 6 (OECD Publishing 2011); all Peer Review Reports are available on the OECD website: http://www.oecd-ilibrary.org/taxation/global-forum-on-transparency-and-exchange-of-information-for-tax-purposes-peer-reviews_2219469x (accessed 5 September 2018).
119. *See M.N. & Others* v *San Marino*, no. 28005/12, 7 July 2015, Eur. Ct. H.R. 2015; *Brito Ferrinho Bexiga Villa-Nova* v *Portugal*, no. 69436/10, 1 December 2015, Eur. Ct. H.R.; Philip Baker, *Some Recent Decisions of the European Court of Human Rights on Tax Matters (and Related Decisions of the European Court of Justice)*, 56 Eur. Tax'n 342, 349 (2016); Reuven Avi-Yonah & Ginaluca Mazzoni, *Taxation and Human Rights: A Delicate Balance*, Univ. Mich. Public L. Research Paper Series 1, 4 (2016).
120. *See Bara*, C-201/14, paras 38 & 43.
121. *Ibid.* para. 34.
122. *Ibid.* para. 38.

imposed by a legislative measure. It is not sufficient that a domestic law merely requires data processing and does not explicitly address the rights of the data subject.[123] Article 23(2) GDPR explicitly requires that a legislative measure to restrict the data subject's rights – including the right to be informed – 'shall contain specific provisions at least, where relevant, as to: (a) the purposes of the processing or categories of processing; (b) the categories of personal data; (c) the scope of the restrictions introduced; (d) the safeguards to prevent abuse or unlawful access or transfer; (e) the specification of the controller or categories of controllers; (f) the storage periods and the applicable safeguards taking into account the nature, scope and purposes of the processing or categories of processing; (g) the risks to the rights and freedoms of data subjects; and (h) the right of data subjects to be informed about the restriction, unless that may be prejudicial to the purpose of the restriction'.

The instruments for exchange of information do not provide for procedural rights of the taxpayer but have left this issue mainly to domestic legislation. Only the DAC provides that exchange of information is subject to data protection requirements. Nevertheless, Article 25(1) DAC also requires the EU Member States to limit the data protection guarantees. The EU Member States are therefore required not to inform the taxpayers and other persons involved about cross-border exchange of tax information and to explicitly restrict the right to be informed as far as it is necessary to ensure an effective tax enforcement. Deviating from the general obligation to restrict the right to be informed, Article 25(2) DAC requires financial institutions to inform the account holders about the financial account information relating to him/her which is collected and transferred in accordance with the DAC. The account holders will be informed about the relevant data to be transferred and have the possibility to rectify the data before it is provided to the competent authority of the EU Member States where the financial institution is resident and subsequently to the residence state of the account holder. By obliging the financial institutions to inform their clients about the financial data collected and transferred, the protection of the taxpayer's privacy within the EU is enhanced. Whereas the DAC explicitly provides that the account holders have to be informed, similar provisions can be found neither in Foreign Account Tax Compliance Act (FATCA) Model 1 IGAs nor in the OECD CRS. They simply provide for an obligation for the parties to ensure that taxpayer rights are safeguarded without placing any concrete obligation on the countries exchanging the information.

Where the right to be informed is restricted, this restriction must be limited to the extent that is necessary and proportional for tax purposes. Whereas data protection legislation stresses the importance of fairness and transparency of data processing, the data subject does not need to be informed where secret processing of personal data is in the public interest. Consequently, a taxpayer does not have to be informed about exchange of information where secret data processing is necessary to ensure proper tax enforcement.[124]

123. *Ibid.* para. 39; *Puškár*, C-73/16, para. 96.
124. *See* Art. 23 GDPR; Eur. Ct. H.R., 16 June 2015; *Othymia Investments BV* v *the Netherlands*, *supra* note 47, para. 44.

Not explicitly dealing with requirements stemming from data protection, but addressing the proportionality of restricting the right to be informed, *Baker* and *Pistone* argued that not informing the taxpayers at all 'is excessive and disproportionate' because effective exchange of information could also be ensured by other measures.[125] Similarly, *Simonek* argued that a 'denial of any procedural rights to the person concerned in the information-supplying state may seriously affect his legitimate rights and interests' and 'is not necessary in order to guarantee an effective exchange of information process'.[126] Instead of not informing taxpayers at all it is possible to merely provide for exceptions from the notification where it would prejudice the process of investigation. Moreover, in order not to delay the procedure, it is possible to provide for only restricted judicial safeguards with short time limits and limited appeal rights.[127] Taking these considerations into account, where automatic exchange of information takes place without informing the account holders, it could therefore be considered as a disproportionate interference with data protection safeguards.

[B] Right of Access to the Data

Charter Article 8(2) explicitly states that '[e]veryone has the right of access to data which has been collected concerning him or her'. Similarly, Article 15 GDPR provides the data subjects with a right to access personal data. The data subject shall be able to obtain information about the data processing from the controller without constraint at reasonable intervals and without excessive delay or expense. For the area of taxation, this implies that a taxpayer must in general – where the access is not restricted under Article 23 GDPR – be given information on all data on the particular taxpayer stored by the tax administration. Furthermore, the tax administration is supposed to store information on the exchange of tax data with tax authorities of other jurisdictions. The taxpayer is supposed to also have access to information on the disclosure, for example to whom and which tax data has been provided to third parties.[128]

[C] Right to Rectification and Erasure

Charter Article 8(2) explicitly states that '[e]veryone has the right of access to data which has been collected concerning him or her, and the right to have it rectified'. The right to rectification and erasure is also provided for in Articles 16 and 18 GDPR. The data subject has the right to ask for the rectification, erasure or blocking of data where the data processing is not in line with the data protection safeguards. However, a data subject has no right to erasure where data processing is legally required. Consequently, in the area of exchange of information, the taxpayer may only request the deletion of tax data relating to him or her where the collection or storage of that data does not have a legitimate basis or is not in line with the data quality principles.

125. Baker, *supra* note 47, at 63.
126. Simonek, *supra* note 42, at 877.
127. *See* Baker, *supra* note 47, at 63.
128. *See Rijkeboer*, C-553/07, EU:C:2009:293, para. 64.

§11.08 CONCLUSION

Tax authorities are increasingly gathering and sharing taxpayer information in order to better understand taxpayer behaviour, to identify the most effective interventions, and to uncover under-reporting, evasion or fraud. Increasing data collection is not only happening on a domestic level but is largely driven by international developments. Since December 2014, the DAC has already been amended five times in order to increase to scope of automatic exchange of information to also cover financial account information, tax rulings and APAs, CbC reports, and reportable cross-border arrangements.

At the same time, the data protection safeguards in the EU have been strengthened. The GDPR has been adopted to address the technological developments and globalization which allowed easier, less costly, and less visible collection and processing of personal data.[129] In addition, the ECJ has stressed the importance of data protection in some high-profile cases.

The large increase in the amount of third-party data available to tax authorities seems at first sight to be difficult to align with the objectives behind data protection. Whereas data protection legislation puts an emphasis on limiting the amount of data that is processed, the purposes for which the data can be used as well as the time for which the data shall be retained, increasing data collection and automatic exchange of information between different jurisdictions should make it easier for the tax administrations to access taxpayer information.

EU data protection is mainly relevant for natural persons and requires that data collection and processing is proportional – it has to be 'relevant and not excessive in relation to the purposes' of data processing. Assessing the proportionality of a measure requires assessing both the level of intrusiveness of a measure and the importance of the legitimate aim that has been pursued. In the light of the *Digital Rights Ireland* case,[130] doubts have been raised as to whether the systematic and periodic bulk exchange of taxpayer information is proportional. However, so far, both the ECtHR and the ECJ have applied a rather lenient approach when exchange of information or the scope of data collection and data processing for tax purposes was at stake. So far, in tax cases a violation of the right to data protection has been established mainly due to a lack of procedural safeguards.

---

129. *See, e.g.*, EU Comm'n, Communication from the Commission to the European Parliament and the Council: Exchanging and Protecting Personal Data in a Globalised World COM/2017/07 final at 1.
130. *See Digital Rights Ireland*, C-293/12 & C-594/12.

CHAPTER 12

Digitalization and the Future of National Tax Systems: Taxing Robots?

Joachim Englisch[*]

§12.01 INTRODUCTION

It is frequently assumed that already in the next decade, the use of interconnected, adaptive and self-learning machines, devices and programs – 'robots' and robotic process automation with implemented artificial intelligence (AI) – will lead to a dramatic transition of the workforce in almost all sectors of production and services.[1] This will not merely affect blue-collar tasks, where machines have been replacing human workers since the beginning of the industrial revolution, but increasingly also white-collar work, such as office support work or even basic tasks of the liberal professions.[2] While there is a wide range of opinions as to whether this will result in net

* I would like to thank my colleague, Johannes Becker from Münster University, for insightful discussions and the participants of the 2018 conference on 'Tax and the Digital Economy' at Luxembourg University for useful comments.

1. *See, e.g.*, Erik Bryonjolfsson & Andrew McAfee, *The Second Machine Age – Work, Progress, and Prosperity in a Time of Brilliant Technologies* 1, 13 et seq. (W.W. Norton & Company 2014); Richard Dobbs & James Manyika et al., *No Ordinary Disruption: The Four Global Forces Breaking All the Trends* 1, 149 et seq. (Public Affaires 2015).
2. *See* Martin Ford, *The Rise of the Robots Technology and the Threat of Mass Unemployment* 1, 83 et seq. (Basic Books 2015); Ljubica Nedelkoska & Glenda Quintini, *Automation, Skills Use and Training* 1, 51 (OECD Social, Employment and Migration Working Papers, No. 202, 2018), *available at* http://dx.doi.org/10.1787/2e2f4eea-en (accessed 18 February 2019). In general, low-skilled workers are the ones whose jobs are most threatened to become obsolete due to automation across all sectors of the economy; *see* Carl Frey & Michael Osborne, *The Future of Employment: How Susceptible Are Jobs to Computerisation?* 1, 42 (Oxford Univ. Press 2013), https://www.oxfordmartin.ox.ac.uk/downloads/academic/The_Future_of_Employment.pdf (accessed 20 November 2018); Andrew Berg, Edward Buffie & Luis-Felipe Zanna, *Should We Fear the Robot Revolution? (The Correct Answer Is Yes)* 1, 24 (IMF Working Paper No. 18/116, 2018), *available at* https://www.imf.org/en/Publications/WP/Issues/2018/05/21/Should-We-Fear-the

job losses for human employees in the long run, and if so to what extent, or whether the emergence of new job opportunities will eventually compensate for the loss of traditional jobs,[3] there is also broad consensus that the short-term effect of this development will be a disruption of the labour market.[4] In a recent study it has been estimated that in member countries of the Organisation for Economic Co-operation and Development (OECD), 14 % of jobs face a high risk of being fully automated in the 'near future', and another 32 % still face a considerable risk of large-scale automation.[5] From a national government perspective, this could imply a double fiscal challenge: revenues from taxing labour (including social security contributions (SSCs), also referred to as payroll taxes) could shrink while at the same time, the costs for retraining programs, unemployment benefits or public employment initiatives could rise. Moreover, societies could be faced with rising income inequality[6] and high

-Robot-Revolution-The-Correct-Answer-is-Yes-44923 (accessed 18 February 2019); Georg Graetz & Guy Michaels, *Robots at Work: CEP Discussion Paper No 1335* 1, 20 London Sch. Econ. & Pol. Sci. (2018), with further references.

3. For a survey of literature, press statements and the relevant arguments, *see* Camilla Hardy, *Intellectual Property and the End of Work*, Fla. L. Rev. (forthcoming 2019) (manuscript at 7–22) (Technological Un/Employment), *available at* https://ssrn.com/abstract = 3011735 (accessed 18 February 2019). For a particularly dystopian view of the long-term implications for the labour market, *see* Yuval Harari, *21 Lessons for the 21st Century* (Jonathan Cape ed. 2018).
4. *See, e.g.*, Frey & Osborne, *supra* note 2, at 5–13; World Economic Forum, *The Future of Jobs Employment, Skills and Workforce Strategy for the Fourth Industrial Revolution* 1, 10 et seq., *available at* worldeconomicforum.org http://www3.weforum.org/docs/WEF_Future_of_Jobs.pdf (accessed 18 February 2019); Anton Korinek & Joseph Stiglitz, *Artificial Intelligence and Its Implications for Income Distribution and Unemployment* 31 et seq. (National Bureau of Economic Research (NBER), Working Paper No. 24174 1, 2017), *available at* http://www.nber.org/papers/w24174.pdf (accessed 18 February 2019); OECD, *The Next Production Revolution Implications for Governments and Business* 34–35 (OECD Publishing 2017); Len Shackleton, *Robocalypse Now? Why We Shouldn't Panic about Automation, Algorithms and Artificial Intelligence* 1, 24 (IEA Current Controversies 2018). One of the very few dissenting voices is David Autor, *Why Are There Still So Many Jobs? The History and Future of Workplace Automation*, 29 J. Econ. Persps. 1, 3 & 27 (2015).
5. *See* Nedelkoska, *supra* note 2, at 40. An earlier study with a more limited set of OECD member countries found that on average 9 % of jobs are at high risk of becoming fully automated, *see* Melanie Arntz, Terry Gregory & Ulrich Zierahn, *The Risk of Automation for Jobs in OECD Countries: A Comparative Analysis* 1 (OECD Social, Employment and Migration Working Papers No. 189, 2016), *available at* http://www.ifuturo.org/sites/default/files/docs/automation.pdf (accessed 18 February 2019). McKinsey estimates that 14 % of the global workforce is at risk of job losses due to automation by 2030, *see* Adrian Peralta-Alva & Agustin Roitman, *Technology and the Future of Work* 1, 13–14 (IMF Working Paper No. 18/207, 2018), *available at* https://www.imf.org/en/Publications/WP/Issues/2018/09/28/Technology-and-the-Future-of-Work-46203 (accessed 18 February 2019). As a caveat, the extent of exposure to automation varies significantly between different jurisdictions, depending, i.a., on the structure of the national economy, its degree of development, and the degree of collaborative interaction in the organization of work.
6. *See, e.g.*, Mustafa Erdoğdu & Coşkun Karaca, *The Fourth Industrial Revolution and a Possible Robot Tax, in Institutions & Economic Policies: Effects on Social Justice, Employment, Environmental Protection & Growth* 103, 110–111 & 116–117 (Irem Berksoy et al. eds., IJOPEC Publication 2017); Korinek, *supra* note 4, at 23 et seq.; Joao Guerreiro et al., *Should Robots Be Taxed?* 1, 2 (NBER Working Paper No. 23806, 2018), *available at* http://www.nber.org/papers/w23806.pdf (accessed 18 February 2019); Orly Mazur, *Taxing the Robots*, 46 Pepp. L. Rev. 277, 287–290 (2019). *See also* Eur. Parliament Committee on Legal Affairs, Report with recommendations to the Commission on Civil Law Rules on Robotics (2015/2103(INL): Rapporteur Mady Delvaux (27 January 2017) 1, 4 (hereinafter 'Report on Robotics').

'technological'[7] unemployment, creating a potential breeding ground for social unrest and propelling politically extreme parties and movements.

Against this backdrop, the idea of taxing the use of robots that replace human workforce, or even taxing the robots themselves, has emerged, and *Bill Gates'* respective proposal in early 2017 made international headlines.[8] The idea has gained traction in public fora and political initiatives[9] and has also been discussed in several scholarly writings.[10]

This chapter seeks to evaluate the merits of the different proposals in the light of their underlying policy objectives. Reflecting the broad range of tax law principles and socio-economic arguments that have been advanced to justify a tax on robots, the chapter pursues a normative approach that combines a doctrinal analysis of legal systems with elements of economic analysis. Regarding the latter, the neoclassical efficiency paradigm that motivates some of the proposals serves as a starting point, but effective constraints of national lawmaking and international standard setting are also taken into account. A first section of the analysis is devoted to more far-reaching reform proposals that envisage to concede legal personhood to certain robots for tax law purposes. The chapter will set forth why any such move is currently premature but might become a plausible option in the future, especially in the field of indirect taxes. The subsequent section will explore the merits of imposing taxes on the use of robots in the light of different policy objectives. The analysis then concludes with some thoughts on other possible implications of an automation of the workforce.

---

7. *See* John Maynard Keynes, *Economic Possibilities for Our Grandchildren, in Essays in Persuasion* 325 (The Royal Economic Society 1931): 'technological unemployment … means unemployment due to our discovery of means of economising the use of labor outrunning the pace at which we can find new uses for labor.'
8. *See* Kevin J. Delaney, *The Robot That Takes Your Job Should Pay Taxes, Says Bill Gates*, Quartz 17 February 2017), *available at* https://qz.com/911968/bill-gates-the-robot-that-takes-your-job-should-pay-taxes (accessed 18 February 2019).
9. *See, e.g.*, Report on Robotics, *supra* note 6, at 4 & 44 (however, the EP ultimately did not include this recommendation in its resolution, *see* Eur. Parliament, Resolution with recommendations to the Commission on Civil Law Rules on Robotics (2015/2103(INL)) (2017) (hereinafter 'Resolution on Robotics'); UNCTAD, *Robots and Industrialisation in Developing Countries* 1, 3 (UN 2016); UK Parliament, *BEIS Committee Automation Inquiry*, UK Parliament (24 May 2018), *available at* https://www.parliament.uk/business/committees/committees-a-z/commons-select/business-energy-industrial-strategy/news-parliament-2017/automation-future-of-work-inquiry-launch-17-19/ (accessed 18 February 2019). For a recent overview, see Laura Paddison, *If Robots Steal Our Jobs, Maybe We Should Make Them Pay Tax Huffpost*, HuffingtonPost (1 June 2018), *available at* https://www.huffingtonpost.com/entry/robot-tax-bill-gates_us_5b0f030ce4b0be10a4882b63?guccounter=1 (accessed 18 February 2019); Mazur, *supra* note 6, at 296–297.
10. Most notably, Xavier Oberson, *Taxing Robots? From the Emergence of an Electronic Ability to Pay to a Tax on Robots or the Use of Robots*, 9 World Tax J. 247 (2017); Luisa Scarcella & Michaela Lexer, *Challenging Suggested Responses to the Impact of AI on Labor Markets from a Tax Law and Social Security Law Perspective*, WeRobot2017 Conference (2 April 2017), *available at* http://www.lawandai.com/2017/04/02/the-return-of-the-blog/ (accessed 18 February 2019); Ryan Abbott & Bret Bogenschneider, *Should Robots Pay Taxes? Tax Policy in the Age of Automation*, 12 Harv. L. & Pol'y Rev. 145 (2018); *See* Guerreiro, *supra* note 6; *See also* William Meisel, *The Software Society, Cultural and Economical Impact* 1, 220 et seq. (Trafford Publishing 2013); William Weissman, *How Robots Will Kill Tax Administration and the Funding of Social Insurance – Part II*, Employee Benefit Plan Rev. 23, 28 (2014); Uwe Thuemmel, *Optimal Taxation of Robots*, Cesifo Area Conferences (Cesifo 2018).

§12.02 ROBOTS AS TAXABLE PERSONS

In civil law, proposals have been tabled to make physical as well as software-only AI systems subjects of law, e.g., in order to facilitate their autonomous interaction with other entities or for the purposes of civil law liabilities in case of accidents.[11] However, even if a recognition of legal personality was to materialize in some legal systems, this would not necessarily imply that such robots should also be taxable persons. In particular, the theory that taxation (e.g., of corporations) should be regarded as the 'price' to pay for the concession of legal personhood or limited liability has been overcome;[12] neither direct taxation of profits nor the levy of indirect taxes on turnover can be justified by such considerations.[13] Instead, having legal capacity and thus being capable of holding rights and assets as well incurring liabilities would be merely a necessary (pre)condition for the status as taxable person. It would then still have to be decided whether the guiding principles of the respective tax at issue would suggest to grant that status to those robots.

[A] Income Tax

From an income tax perspective, there is currently no compelling argument to make robots themselves taxable persons. Taxes on income are usually conceived as direct taxes with pronounced redistributive objectives, to be borne by the taxpayer herself and to be imposed according to her individual ability to pay.[14] For income tax purposes, financial capacity that might come as a corollary to legal personhood is therefore merely a necessary but not a sufficient justification for taxation. A liability to tax would furthermore imply that the taxable person should normally also bear the tax burden, thereby foregoing personal consumption in lieu of a fair and solidary contribution to the public purse. Admittedly, the incidence of any tax ultimately depends on market conditions.[15] But robots without an autonomously defined personal spending capacity could not even theoretically bear the intended income tax burden; instead, the incidence of the income tax would always fall on someone else (most likely primarily on their owner). Accordingly, as long as robots do not have self-defined personal

11. *See, e.g.*, Report on Robotics, *supra* note 6, at 6–7. For further references, *see* Oberson, *supra* note 10, at 247–248.
12. *See, e.g.*, James Mirrlees et al., *Tax by Design* 1, 408 et seq. (Oxford Univ. Press 2011); Peter Harris, *Corporate Tax Law* 144 et seq. (Cambridge Univ. Press 2013); John Tiley & Glen Loutzenheiser, *Advanced Topics in Revenue Law* 1, 11–12 (Hart Publishing 2013).
13. For a possibly different view, *see* Oberson, *supra* note 10, at 252–253; Xavier Oberson, *Towards Taxation of Robots or Their Use?*, 28 Int'l Tax Rev. 1 (19 February 2018), *available at* http://www.internationaltaxreview.com/Article/3784074/Towards-taxation-of-robots-or-their-use.html?utm_campaign=Email+verification&utm_content=2018-09-07&utm_term=Verification+link&utm_medium=Email+operational&utm_source=Registration+Form&r=verified (accessed 18 February 2019).
14. *See, e.g.*, Lee Burns & Richard Krever, *Individual Income Tax*, *in* 2 *Tax Law Design and Drafting* Ch. 14, 2 & 6 (Victor Thuronyi ed., Int'l Monetary Fund 1998).
15. *See, e.g.*, Joseph Stiglitz, *Economics of the Public Sector* 1, 484 et seq. (W.W. Norton 3d ed. 2000).

needs, making them liable to pay income tax cannot be justified on grounds of the ability to pay principle.[16]

This line of reasoning would also hold if the robot was to be regarded as a labour factor in production that is economically equivalent to a human employee. For the reasons given above, the robot should then nevertheless not be assumed to earn its own wage income and should not be granted taxpayer status for any wage and payroll taxes.[17] The incidence of such taxes on income from employment cannot possibly fall upon the robot, and it should therefore not be considered as ultimate taxpayer required to make a solidary contribution in order to finance public spending. Moreover, as long as robots are not even vested with legal capacity that could make them the bearer of rights in funds and assets, they are not suitable as taxpayers for deemed 'employment' income in the first place.

This problem cannot be overcome by imposing a final withholding tax at source (creating a corresponding obligation for the 'employer' of the robot), either, because the robot would then never actually be held liable itself as a taxpayer. It would be a taxpayer 'in name only'. For reasons of transparency and consistency, any such tax should then better be directly designed as one on the use of robots,[18] discussed below at §12.03.

Finally, some SSCs are expressly designed as a charge that is (at least partially) based on the insurance principle. This is the case, for example, where higher contributions result in higher pensions or higher unemployment benefits, but also in systems where access to public health insurance is limited to certain categories of citizens (typically employees) who 'pay' for this privilege through SSCs. To the extent of that case, the taxation of robots themselves cannot be justified, either, because - and as long as - they are not entitled to similar benefits.[19]

Different from the taxation of bodies corporate and similar legal persons, there is currently also no need to impose a tax on robots as taxable persons in order to ensure timely taxation of the ultimate beneficiaries of the income earned through the use of robots. Since retained earnings of a corporation are not at the disposal of the shareholder until they are distributed, the corporation tax has a compensatory role vis-à-vis the personal income tax and can be understood as a prepayment of the latter upon accrual of the profits.[20] However, under civil law standards as they now stand, any income or profit that is generated by using robots will be directly attributed to the owner or user of this robot. There currently exists no civil law regime such as a 'corporate veil' separating the financial spheres of the robot and its owner or user. The latter have immediate and unlimited access to any funds generated by the activities of the robot. At least at present, the corresponding item of income is therefore realized

16. Likewise, Lexer, *supra* note 10, at 32.
17. For a different opinion, *see* Oberson, *supra* note 10, at 252 et seq.
18. *See also* Tatiana Falcão, *Should My Dishwasher Pay a Robot Tax?*, 90 Tax Notes In'l 1273, 1277 (2018).
19. This is also acknowledged by Lexer, *supra* note 10, at 31.
20. *See, e.g.*, Peter Harris, *Corporate / Shareholder Income Taxation and Allocating Taxing Rights Between Countries* 1, 102 et seq. (IBFD 1996); Stiglitz, *supra* note 15, at 674; Mirrlees, *supra* note 12, at 409 et seq.

directly by the owner or user of the robot. It can therefore be taxed as part of her overall income in conformity with the well-established revenue realization principle. It would create artificial and unnecessary complexities to first tax those profits as income of the robot itself and subsequently at the hands of the owner, implying the need for an imputation system or similar 'owner relief' regime to avoid economic double taxation.

This direct accessibility of the owner to all revenues 'earned' by the robot could furthermore be maintained even if in the future the robot would have civil law personality to some degree, and earnings were to be funnelled, by the customer or client of the robot, to a financial account that is legally held by the robot itself. There would then still be no need to recognize robots as taxable persons on their own in order to ensure a timely taxation of the income generated by them.[21] A different assessment would be warranted only if the accessibility of robot-generated funds by the respective owner or user was to be significantly limited in the future. If restrictions were to be imposed on the withdrawal of profits legally deemed to be earned by the robot itself, and if earnings that are retained at the level of the robot and that its 'beneficial owner' cannot immediately dispose of were to become a common phenomenon, robots would be assimilated to corporations or at least partnerships for the purposes of income and property attribution. In such a scenario it would be consistent to implement a tax regime for robots similar to the one applicable to corporations (or, possibly, partnerships that are treated as fiscally non-transparent) and concede a 'derivative' tax law personality to them. Adequate precautions to avoid economic double taxation would then need to be taken, and they would have to be recognized as 'persons' for tax treaty purposes, too. It is important to point out, though, that robots would then essentially be taxed like corporations, and not like the workers they replace. They would be liable to corporation tax, and not to wage tax and payroll tax/SSCs.

Our conclusion that there is currently no need to designate robots as taxable persons subject to corporation tax (or a functionally equivalent tax) is not called into question by the fact that under the present system of international taxation, corporation tax is levied from legal persons to ensure taxation not only at the right time but also in the right place: Based on internationally accepted allocation rules, the priority to tax corporate profits is by default accorded to the jurisdiction where the profits are sourced or where the corporation is resident, rather than to the jurisdiction(s) where the ultimate shareholder(s) reside.[22] But regarding items of income generated through the use of robots, a similar result could already be achieved by introducing, to the extent necessary, the robot's permanent place of operation as a criterion for taxable nexus (*see also* below at §12.05).

Likewise, there should not normally arise any difficulties in attributing the funds generated by the robot to its 'beneficial owner' even when they would be retained in an account legally held by the robot itself, once more different from the situation of (large

21. For a different view, *see* Lexer, *supra* note 10, at 33–34.
22. *See*, *e.g.*, Mirrlees, *supra* note 12, at 433.

and especially publicly traded) corporations.[23] There are therefore also no administrative difficulties that could lend themselves to the proposition to make robots taxable persons for income tax purposes.

[B] Value Added Tax/Goods and Services Tax

At least regarding some potential applications – e.g., autonomous taxi driving – self-learning robots equipped with advanced AI systems will soon provide goods or services with a considerable degree of autonomy. However, different from what has been suggested in literature,[24] the mere independence or autonomy in rendering a service or supplying goods is not sufficient to qualify an entity as taxable person for the purpose of (European Union (EU)) Value Added Tax (VAT). Considering that VAT is conceived as an indirect tax and that the taxable person is acting as a tax collector for the government,[25] only an entity that also disposes of a certain degree of legal and financial autonomy should be eligible to become a taxable person.

More specifically, only to the extent that (certain) robots were granted legal personality so that they could enter into contractual relationships with customers themselves, and only if the consideration paid for a supply furthermore was to become part of financial funds legally attributed to such robots themselves, it could make sense to consider them taxable persons for VAT purposes. Tax administrations could then easily identify the robots as suppliers of the service or goods and could hold them liable to pay tax, not the least because the ensuing tax claims could then also be enforced by way of seizing funds or assets that are legally attributed to the robot. Such a development could first materialize with Decentralized Autonomous Organizations that are based on blockchain technology, relying on smart contracts[26] and cryptocurrencies. However, it would also have to be ensured that the AI systems of the robots, payment clearance systems and tax compliance procedures are 'smart' enough to facilitate the tax collection.

§12.03 TAXING THE USE OF ROBOTS

[A] As a Fiscal Substitute for Wage and Payroll Taxes

As mentioned above, the idea to tax robots is often advocated in order to provide governments with an adequate fiscal substitute for the decline in wage tax and SSC revenues that is expected in the wake of increasing automation. This rationale for a

23. *See, e.g.*, Harris, *supra* note 12, at 170–171.
24. *See* Oberson, *supra* note 10, at 256.
25. *See, e.g.*, Alan Schenk et al., *Value Added Tax: A Comparative Approach* 1, 20 (Cambridge Univ. Press 2d ed. 2015); Joachim Englisch, *Europäisches Steuerrecht, in Steuerrecht* 889, 896 (§ 17 m.n 12) (Klaus Tipke et al. eds, Ottoschmidt 23d ed. 2018); *see also Balocchi*, C-10/92, Judgment, EU:C.1993:846, para. 25; *Netto Supermarkt*, C-271/06, Judgment, EU:C:2008:105, para. 21.
26. For further details, see Cristopher Clack et al., *Smart Contract Templates: Foundations, Design Landscape and Research Directions* (4 August 2016), *available at* https://arxiv.org/pdf/1608.00771v1.pdf (accessed 18 February 2019).

robot tax implies that the activities of robots should be taxed as would be the case for comparable activities of human workers. It has already been pointed out that this would suggest to tax the use of robots, rather than robots themselves,[27] as long as the latter have no self-defined personal needs.

But the concept of a substitute or proxy tax that is levied on the use of robots and that is to be paid by their owner or user, in a similar fashion as wage and payroll taxes are withheld and remitted by an employer, is subject to considerable concerns, too. First, the fact that a time-honoured source of tax revenue might slowly be drying out does not, in itself, imply that a similar source of revenue has to be found; rather, this should encourage broader discussion on how to realign the tax mix. Second, such substitute levies would be effectively imposed on a measure of expenditure for equivalent human employment that is deemed to have been incurred by the owner or user of the robot, in addition to the regular income or corporation tax on business profits to be paid by the latter. This results in an additional tax burden on income-generating activities that rely on new technologies, imposed (only) on this group of taxpayers. Thus, targeted taxation of certain production processes such as the use of robots would have to be justified from either a tax equity or a tax efficiency perspective.[28] Otherwise, an eventual decline in wage tax revenues and payroll tax revenues should better be compensated by introducing or raising other, more general taxes.

[1] ... Justified as a Tax on Imputed Income?

The imposition of a proxy tax for the wage tax and SSC liabilities that would result from the employment of a human workforce cannot convincingly be justified as taxation of imputed income accruing to the owner or user of the robot.[29] This is obvious if the robot is employed in the course of a business. In such scenarios, robots will contribute to the *actual* profits or income of their owners and users that are already subject to regular income or corporation tax duties. By contrast, robots employed in private households (home appliances with advanced AI systems) admittedly do generate imputed income for their owners and users. However, this imputed income is no different from the imputed income that a human homemaker (housewife or househusband) currently 'earns'. The sound fiscal policy reasons that can be brought forward in defence of not taxing such traditional forms of imputed income also apply to the imputed income generated by the use of robots: It is difficult to evaluate, it is hard to monitor for tax authorities and the tax liability does not necessarily correspond with the capacity of the taxpayer to pay the tax (in cash). In any event, at least in Western societies with high labour costs (and correspondingly, low levels of household

27. Likewise, Oberson, *supra* note 10, at 253.
28. The same concerns apply also if a different tax base such as technology acquisition cost were chosen for the robot use tax, or if the latter were to be designed as a depreciation deduction barrier. Regarding such alternatives, *see* Weissman, *supra* note 10, at 28; Abbott, *supra* note 10, at 168–169; Lexer, *supra* note 10, at 34–35.
29. For a different opinion, *see* Oberson, *supra* note 10, at 254–255; Oberson, *supra* note 13.

employment), the human workforce replaced by household robots will only make up a tiny fraction of the job losses that will result from increasing automation. Therefore, taxing household production of robots only would hardly generate the tax revenue needed to compensate the expected decline in wage tax and SSC revenues.

[2] ... Justified as an Equalization Levy?

Contrary to what has been claimed in literature,[30] taxing the use of robots as if they were human wage earners can also hardly be justified as a measure to restore a level playing field, i.e., on the ground of neutrality of taxation. Admittedly, the tax treatment of the two factors of production – (1) capital and (2) labour – differs, and so does, therefore, also the tax treatment of human workers and robots: Wage payments to human workers are normally subject to wage tax that is withheld at source as a prepayment for their tax on income from employment, and to payroll tax that is withheld to finance social security systems. The use of robots does currently not imply any such withholding tax obligations for their 'employers', nor is the cost of their acquisition and maintenance subject to equivalent levies.

However, wage taxes are designed by law as direct taxes on the income of the employee, withheld at source and reflected in a correspondingly lower net salary. From a legalistic viewpoint, they could therefore be held as to not constitute any cost for the employer at all because they are supposedly borne by the employee. As a consequence, the tax treatment of the human workforce's and of the robot's costs could be regarded as neutral under the current system, apart from eventual cash flow aspects resulting from the usual lack of immediate expensing of acquisition cost for machinery. The same reasoning would then apply at least in part also to payroll taxes in almost all jurisdictions, to the extent that they are legally conceived as employee contributions rather than employer contributions to social security systems.

It is acknowledged here, though, that it is the real economic incidence of wage taxes and payroll taxes, rather than their statutory incidence, that should ultimately matter for the justification of a 'compensatory levy' on the use of robots. But it is hard to build a tax neutrality case for taxing the use of robots even based on an analysis of real economic incidence. First and foremost, tax incidence is hard to measure and depends on a variety of factors, such as short-term versus long-term perspective, relative price elasticities in the relevant labour markets, and the degree and type of regulation of the latter.[31] Empirical studies on the incidence of the wage tax have therefore come to highly divergent conclusions, ranging from zero to 100% effective tax burdens on employees. Notwithstanding the aforementioned qualifications, a recent meta-analysis found that on average, the relevant empirical studies tend to

30. *See* Meisel, *supra* note 10, at 220; Abbott, *supra* note 10, at 163 et seq.
31. *See* CPB et al., *Study on the Effects and Incidence of Labour Taxation* 1, 55 (Eur. Comm'n Tax'n Papers Series, Working Paper N. 56-2015, 2015), *available at* https://ec.europa.eu/taxation_customs/sites/taxation/files/resources/documents/taxation/gen_info/economic_analysis/tax_papers/taxation_paper_56.pdf (accessed 18 February 2019).

suggest that in the long run, workers bear between 65% and 90% of the wage tax in most labour markets.[32]

Thus, even based on real economic incidence, there is no convincing case for imposing similar wage tax and payroll taxes on 'deemed wage income' of robots. While it appears highly likely that in most jurisdictions, at least a significant portion of the wage and payroll taxes is effectively borne by the human workers, such a tax burden cannot possibly be shifted forward to the robot itself.[33] It would therefore fall fully on the user of the robot, reduce her business profits and thus act as a disincentive for investments in modern, automated production processes based on AI. Moreover, it cannot be excluded that the acquisition of robots comes at an implicit tax cost for businesses, similar to the tax cost of the portion of wage taxes and payroll taxes that cannot be shifted onto the human employee. Depending on market conditions, the manufacturers of robots might be able to shift some of their direct tax burdens onto their business customers, as a cost component in the calculation of the price asked for the supply of the robot. Altogether, it is therefore highly speculative and normally not convincing to argue a need for a levy on the use of robots as wage tax and payroll tax equivalent based on considerations of real economic incidence. In any event, a robot tax would have to take into account the differences in tax incidence, and while this might then be a theoretically acceptable approach, it is hardly feasible in practice due to difficulties in measurement.

Another argument in favour of an equalization levy-type tax on the use of robots, put forth by *Abbott/Bogenschneider*, suggests that such a tax is desirable to offset tax advantages that accrue to businesses due to an eventually accelerated depreciation for investments in automated process systems.[34] They argue that when deprecation rates do not reflect the usual economic life of the robot, but instead allow for faster depreciation, taxation favours their use over the employment of human workers. To substantiate this claim, they point out that wage cost can only be deducted as paid, i.e., in accordance with the real 'use' of the worker.

However, this reasoning contradicts textbook economic theory according to which only a comprehensive cash flow taxation is fully neutral with respect to investment projects.[35] Where tax accounting requires asset capitalization and pro rata depreciation, it distorts marginal investment decisions. And if this is foreseen for certain assets only, the tax system furthermore also distorts the choice between alternative investments to the detriment of the assets whose acquisition costs cannot be fully expensed, even if accelerated depreciation is available for them. This is due to the

32. *See* Angel Melguizo et al., *Who Bears Labour Taxes and Social Contributions? A Meta-Analysis Approach*, 4 SERIEs 247, 262 (2013). For a more cautious analysis of existing literature based on a 'narrative' review, *see* CPB et al., *supra* note 31, at 55 et seq. & 95–96.
33. This is apparently not taken into account by Oberson, *supra* note 10, at 255, who argues that the deductibility of the acquisition cost of the robot – or, alternatively, the deductibility of an imputed salary – would neutralize the economic double taxation inherent to taxing its use, similar to the deductibility of real wages in case of workers who are subject to wage and payroll tax.
34. *See* Abbott, *supra* note 10, at 164–166.
35. *See, e.g.*, Michael Devereux, *Issues in the Design of Taxes on Corporate Profit*, 65 Nat'l Tax J. 709, 710 (2012).

fact that the firm incurs an immediate capital outlay cost for the investment of 100% of the acquisition cost of the capital asset, but can subsequently deduct acquisition cost for tax purposes only on a pro rata basis. Hence, alternative investments or factors of production that yield the same revenues but permit full and immediate tax expensing of related payments become relatively more attractive because they improve the cash flow position of the business. It is therefore the immediate expensing of wage costs, rather than accelerated depreciation of acquisition costs for robots, that constitute the more favourable tax treatment. There is thus no need for a corrective tax on robots from this perspective; quite the contrary.

Abbott/Bogenschneider indeed do concede that this would be the textbook scenario, but they argue that in economic reality, 'most large corporations have significant cash accumulations earning a low rate of return'.[36] Under these conditions, the capital outlay cost for the acquisition of the robot is considered insignificant by them. Consequently, accelerated depreciation beyond the actual use of the robot is assumed to yield tax benefits over alternative investments and factors of production, including the wage payments for the 'use' of human workers. However, they provide no empirical evidence for their claim. The author cannot offer any such evidence, either, but anecdotal evidence would suggest that this is not the standard case in Europe and arguably, not even in the United States (US), in particular after the 2018 US tax reform has made tax sheltering of overseas profits obsolete.

[3] Restraints Imposed by International Tax Competition

But even if theoretically, it could be demonstrated that the use of robots should be taxed to avoid privileged treatment vis-à-vis the employment of a human workforce - which I do not find convincing for the reasons stated above - such an 'equalization levy' might not be a feasible option in modern open economies, at least not regarding robots used in industrial production processes.

The downward trend of statutory corporate income tax rates, as well as effective average tax rates, that could be observed in the past two decades in most jurisdictions globally,[37] and in OECD Member States in particular, is a result of persistent and intense international tax competition over business investments and profits.[38] Due to the globalization and digitalization of the economy in general and the establishment of

36. *See* Abbott, *supra* note 10, at 165, fn. 116.
37. Regarding non-OECD Member States, see Ali Abbas et al., *A Partial Race to the Bottom: Corporate Tax Developments in Emerging and Developing Economies* (IMF, Working Paper WP/12/28, 2012), *available at* https://www.imf.org/external/pubs/ft/wp/2012/wp1228.pdf (accessed 18 February 2019).
38. *See, e.g.*, Philipp Genschel & Peter Schwarz, *Tax Competition: A Literature Review*, 9 Socio-Economic Rev. 339 (2011); Markus Leibrecht & Claudia Hochgatterer, *Tax Competition as a Cause of Falling Corporate Income Tax Rates: A Survey of Empirical Literature*, 26 J. Econ. Surv. 616 (2012); Michael Devereux & Simon Loretz, *What Do We Know about Corporate Tax Competition*, 66 Nat'l Tax J. 745 (2013).

the internal market in the EU in particular, discrete investment choices are increasingly influenced by effective (average) tax rates. Additional tax burdens imposed on capital investments result in a reduced capital stock of the respective country, and thus in reduced welfare and growth. By contrast, workers tend to be less mobile than capital investments, and the supply of labour moreover tends to be relatively inelastic.[39] It is therefore possible to impose higher tax burdens upon human workers without substantially reducing the supply of labour. As a consequence, there is an international long-term trend to shift taxes from mobile capital to immobile factors of production.

The use of robots implies a capital investment; hence the logic of international tax competition over business investments applies to robot automation investments, too.[40] Imposing additional tax burdens on the use of robots will likely lead to reduced competitiveness of the respective jurisdiction and make it significantly less attractive as an investment location.[41] It would thus significantly reduce social welfare in that jurisdiction, beyond the effects that a taxation of intermediate inputs in business production has, anyways. Moreover, with investments being (trans-)located elsewhere, jobs that the robot tax seeks to protect might be slashed in that particular jurisdiction, too – or not created in the first place – and instead move elsewhere to the extent that workers are not (yet) replaced by robots. Most countries would not consider such an effect as sound fiscal policy.

The aforementioned problems could only be overcome by a comprehensive international coordination of taxes on the use of robots, at least among industrialized countries,[42] including the BRIC countries Brazil, Russia, India and China and similar emerging economies. Considering the longstanding tradition of international tax competition as well as the current crisis of multilateral institutions built by Western democracies, such a development seems illusory in the foreseeable future. In any event, eventual efforts aimed at forging international tax consensus should better be directed at ensuring comprehensive taxation of company profits and their ultimate beneficiaries (shareholders), rather than singling out a particular – albeit increasingly relevant – factor of production;[43] this will be briefly discussed below at §12.05.

39. *See* Robert McClelland & Shannon Mok, *A Review of Recent Research on Labour Supply Elasticities* (Congressional Budget Office Working Paper Series, Working Paper 2012-12, 2012), *available at* https://digitalcommons.ilr.cornell.edu/cgi/viewcontent.cgi?article=1976&context=key_workplace (accessed 18 February 2019).
40. *See* Thuemmel, *supra* note 10, at 32.
41. *See* Weissman, *supra* note 10, at 28; Josh White, *The Case Against the Robot Tax* (2018) only published online, *available at* http://www.internationaltaxreview.com/Article/3798944/The-case-against-the-robot-tax (accessed 5 March 2019); *see also* Shackleton, *supra* note 4, at 38. For a different opinion, see Dorigo, *Robots and Taxes*, 90 Tax Notes Int'l 1079, 1081 (2018).
42. Likewise, Emanuel Gasteiger & Klaus Prettner, *A Note on Automation, Stagnation, and the Implications of a Robot Tax* 1, 10 (FUB School of Bus. & Econ., Working Paper 2017/17 1, 2017), *available at* https://refubium.fu-berlin.de/bitstream/handle/fub188/22056/discpaper2017_17.pdf?sequence=1 (accessed 18 February 2019); Mazur, *supra* note 6, at 300–301.
43. *See also* Sami Ahmed, *Cryptocurrency & Robots: How to Tax and Pay Tax on Them* 55 (unpublished manuscript 2018) *available at* https://papers.ssrn.com/sol3/papers.cfm?abstract_id=3083658 (accessed 18 February 2019).

[B] As an Optimal Income Redistribution Instrument?

A recent study suggests that as long as routine tasks that are capable of being performed by intelligent robots are not as yet fully automated due to costs of automation, taxing the use of robots could be the best option to reduce income inequality and increase overall welfare in a society where some workers are replaceable 'routine workers' that will suffer from a reduction of their wage income as a consequence of automation, and others are 'non-routine' workers who will conversely benefit.[44]

This finding is based on the assumption that, when faced with such a development, governments will have to pursue a policy of income redistribution from 'non-routine workers' to 'routine workers'. This should however be achieved without creating incentives to reduce the amount of work dedicated to more productive non-routine tasks, as this would result in significant reductions of overall welfare. Due to information asymmetries, governments cannot observe whether a worker has the talents and skills needed to perform non-routine tasks. An attempt to achieve income redistribution by introducing a differentiated set of tax rates on labour income, with lower rates for routine workers than for non-routine workers, might therefore have the unwanted effect of a reduced supply of non-routine work.[45] Therefore, it would appear to be preferable to tackle income inequality at its roots and compress the wage income of the two types of workers by way of imposing a tax on the use of robots, thereby reducing the wage gap.[46] 'Non-routine workers' would then have no reason to prefer 'routine work', and thus incentive compatibility of taxation would be maintained.

The welfare gains expected from the ensuing reduction of income inequality are furthermore considered to outweigh the welfare losses that are associated with the reduced production efficiency due to the taxation of an intermediate good (robots). The authors of this model acknowledge, though, that this assessment changes once automation costs have fallen to an extent that leads to full automation. In such a scenario, all 'routine workers' become unemployed and dependent on government transfers, and 'non-routine workers' would no longer have any reason to mimic the latter.[47]

44. *See* Guerreiro, *supra* note 6. In a similar vein, albeit somewhat more differentiated, *see* Thuemmel, *supra* note 10.
45. *See also* Robert Shiller, *Robotization Without Taxation?* (22 March 2017), *available at* https://www.project-syndicate.org/commentary/temporary-robot-tax-finances-adjustment-by-robert-j--shiller-2017-03?barrier=accessreg (accessed 18 February 2019), who is sceptical about raising progressivity of income taxation on grounds of a lack of political acceptance in the long run. The feasibility of this alternative might indeed depend on public perceptions of such a tax and administrative capacities in the respective jurisdiction.
46. In the authors' model, the wage ratio between both 'routine workers' and 'non-routine workers' is directly affected by the cost of the use of robots (including a tax 'cost') because routine workers compete with the latter, *see* Guerreiro, *supra* note 6, at 5.
47. *See* Guerreiro, *supra* note 6, at 18. An even earlier reduction of the rate of an eventual 'robot tax' towards zero if the objective of the tax is wage compression (as in the model of Guerreiro, *supra* note 6) is proposed by Thuemmel, *supra* note 10, at 19–20.

It is obvious that this economic model is based on some generalizations that do not fully capture the complexities of the actual economic and technological developments. Most importantly, it assumes a clear distinction between routine tasks that can be automated – eventually, fully so – and non-routine tasks that cannot. In reality, this is a continuous process, since almost all business-relevant activities that were traditionally performed by humans will become increasingly automated over time, albeit at a very different pace, and in general with a more immediate impact felt by low-skilled labour. The time at which a 'non-routine' task becomes a 'routine' task prone to automation, and the subsequent transition to a situation where this 'routine' task would become fully automated absent government intervention, depend on sector-specific technological advances that raise the quality and lower the cost of the respective robot alternative to the human labour input. The concepts of 'routine work' and 'full automation' cannot therefore be determined on a generalized basis, but only upon a differentiated analysis of all relevant sectors of the labour market. As a consequence, the introduction and subsequent elimination of a tax on the use of robots in line with the rationale of the above model would require constant monitoring and adaption of the relevant definition of the categories of 'robots' whose use becomes, or ceases to be, liable to taxation. This is little realistic, though, in the lawmaking processes of modern democracies.

Apart from these objections, the welfare losses associated with taxing the use of robots as an intermediate good in the business value chain could be exacerbated by international tax competition, as pointed out above. This has apparently not been accounted for in the model.[48] Finally, its analysis is two dimensional in that it is only concerned with the wage differentiation between different categories of wage earners. Income redistribution might however also be achieved, possibly with less allocative inefficiency, if the (ultimate) owners of capital – and owners of robots in particular – were taxed more heavily to finance social transfers or retraining to the benefit of the 'routine' workers.[49]

[C] As a Pigouvian Tax

The original proposal for a tax on the use of robots made by *Gates* in 2017 envisaged this levy as a corrective tax, or Pigouvian tax, in order to reduce the negative externalities resulting from the rapid employment of intelligent machines that is expected to occur in the course of the next decade.[50] Historical experiences with several industrial revolutions suggest that the human workforce made obsolete in one sector of the economy due to increased automation can be retrained, and can eventually become more productive in another sector of the economy or through acquiring a higher skill level. But apart from the fact that it is unclear whether this optimistic scenario will

48. *See*, however, Thuemmel, *supra* note 10, at 32.
49. *See* now also an interview with *Bill Gates* dating from November 2018, as quoted in https://asia.nikkei.com/Editor-s-Picks/Interview/Robot-taxes-will-help-keep-humans-employed-Bill-Gates-predicts (accessed 18 February 2019).
50. *See* Delaney, *supra* note 8; *see also* Hardy, *supra* note 3, at 50.

materialize also regarding the current digital transformation of the economy, it is generally acknowledged that there are certain constraints to re-training efforts, and that massive lay-offs of human workers in a relatively short transition period can cause significant disruptions in the labour market and in society.[51] Therefore, a tax on the use of robots could be imposed in order to slow down the transformation, and thus buy time for government and the labour market in order to manage transition. Such a tax could then possibly even yield a double dividend, as its revenue could be earmarked for government-financed retraining programs.[52]

It is also worth mentioning that *Abott* and *Bogenschneider* have advanced several alternatives and somewhat more targeted measures with a similar intention.[53] They propose the reduction of depreciation allowances for corporation tax purposes, as well as a partial denial of input VAT deductions for the acquisition of robots, depending on the degree of the firm's automation. They also contemplate an incremental 'automation tax' that would be levied in function of the lay-off of workers due to the automation of the firm.

The design of any such corrective tax would pose a significant challenge for any legislator, though. First, a trade-off needs to be made between the positive social welfare effects – including positive externalities, for example in the field of R&D – that can be attained by using intelligent robots, on the one hand, and the negative effects on the labour market and society as a whole, on the other. To strike a right balance will require close monitoring and empirical evaluation of the effects of the tax and the political willingness to enact subsequent amendments reflecting better insights. Second, a targeted approach will entail significant complexity, especially in defining the scope of the tax, resulting in high administrative and compliance costs.

In any event, a general tax on the use of robots is unlikely to attain the objective of alleviating disruptions in the labour market if it is not coordinated globally.[54] For the reasons already discussed above, uncoordinated unilateral approaches will likely lead to a relocation of automated industry production, rather than slow down the substitution of human workers by robots, and might thus even accelerate the decline of labour demand in the respective national sectors.

This could be different only if the tax on the use of robots was limited to certain sectors of the services industry that are not significantly affected by international tax competition. The tax legislator would then have to focus on non-remote services, especially those rendered to final consumers, that require a local physical presence where the robot is in operation (such as, for example, the transportation and logistics

51. *See supra* note 4.
52. *See* Oberson, *supra* note 13.
53. *See* Abbott, *supra* note 10, at 169 et seq.
54. Likewise, Lawrence Summers, *Picking on Robots Won't Deal With Job Destruction* (5 March 2017), *available at* https://www.washingtonpost.com/opinions/picking-on-robots-wont-deal-with-job-destruction/2017/03/05/32091f08-004b-11e7-8ebe-6e0dbe4f2bca_story.html?utm_term=.8b3e1fb3df5e (accessed 18 February 2019); *see also* a statement made to this effect by *Ansip* in his capacity as European Commissioner for the Digital Single Market and Vice President of the European Commission, as quoted at Techemergence, *Robot Tax – A Summary of Arguments 'For' and 'Against'* (24 October 2017), *available at* https://www.techemergence.com/robot-tax-summary-arguments/ (accessed 18 February 2019).

industry or the restaurant sector). A recent study shows that some, but not all, of the occupations that face a particularly high risk of automation are related to rendering such on-the-spot services.[55] Since final consumers of this kind of services are usually highly immobile regarding the market jurisdiction where they buy the respective services, imposing a tax on the use of 'local' robots would not imply a relocation of the business establishment rendering the service. Instead, it could indeed provide a tax incentive for a relatively higher degree of human input, and thus slow down the replacement of the human workforce.

Such a tax would then also seem to be conceptually superior to a tax on locally registered intellectual property (IP) with labour-displacing potential, as it has recently been proposed in literature.[56] First, it seems little convincing to levy such a tax in proportion to the *profits* made from licencing fees, or from sales generated by exploiting the underlying technology.[57] This would mean that businesses could use their IP without any additional tax cost during loss-making periods, which typically occur when an innovation is first introduced to the market, thus thwarting any corrective effect of the tax. Admittedly, this conceptual deficiency could be remedied by designing the tax as an excise duty instead, to be levied on gross royalties received by the IP holder from the exploitation of the IP in the country of its registration. But even then, additional complexities would arise, such as the need to make arm's-length adjustments in case of group licensing or to base the tax on deemed royalty payments that would be consistent with the arm's-length principle (ALP) in case of an exploitation by the IP-holding firm itself. Meanwhile, the definitional problems of identifying 'labour-displacing' IP to determine the substantive scope of the tax would not be smaller, if not rather more challenging, than in case of a robot tax.[58] Moreover, the tax would only increase the cost for certain forms of innovation that facilitates automation, whose exploitation requires registration, i.e., essentially patented innovation. Software copyrights or unpatented process knowledge, in particular, would not be caught.[59] It has been argued that this should be welcomed as a means to shield smaller innovative businesses from the effects of the tax.[60] But since the IP tax burden would eventually be passed on, to the extent that the market permits, to all businesses using patented innovation, those alleged distributional effects are likely to be weak, if they would materialize at all. Certainly, a business size threshold built into a robot tax could achieve the same objective in a much more targeted manner. Moreover, the reliance on patent registration would make the tax at least partly susceptible to avoidance because companies that constantly re-innovate in short business cycles might then just refrain from patenting and rely on their innovation edge. Finally, an IP tax would not be more

55. *See* Nedelkoska *supra* note 2, at 51: especially for food preparation assistants, cleaners and helpers.
56. Hardy, *supra* note 3, at 50–52.
57. As suggested by Hardy, *supra* note 3, at 50–51.
58. *See also* Summers, *supra* note 54, in the context of the *Gates* proposal on robot taxes.
59. A large portion of business innovations are exploited as non-patented IP, see Annette Alstadsæter et al., *Patent Boxes Design, Patents Location and Local R&D* 1, 24 (Oxford Univ. Centre for Bus. Tax'n Working Paper 57 1, 2015), *available at* https://www.sbs.ox.ac.uk/sites/default/files/Business_Taxation/Docs/Publications/Working_Papers/Series_15/WP1518.pdf.
60. Hardy, *supra* note 3, at 51.

robust against international tax competition than a tax on the use of robots. Within Europe, there is not even the need to register the IP locally if the applicant seeks a European patent. And apart from that, the royalties (or profit-)generating exploitation of IP that determines the tax liability can simply be moved to a jurisdiction without IP tax or only a very low IP tax, unless exploitation is geographically bound to a certain territory.

§12.04 A COMMON CHALLENGE: DEFINING THE SCOPE OF A 'ROBOT TAX'

As has already repeatedly been mentioned, a common problem regarding any kind of taxes imposed on the use of robots, or on robots as taxable persons, is the need for an adequate definition of the concept of 'robot'.[61] This is difficult and regarded by some as an almost insurmountable challenge.[62] For such a definition must reconcile the two potentially conflicting objectives of legal certainty, on the one hand, and flexibility, on the other. It must allow for a clear delimitation of the substantive - or personal - scope of the tax while at the same time it must be future-proof and comprehensive enough to take into account the relevant technological progress. So far, only some broadly worded criteria have been formulated in a civil law or a tax context. For example, the European Parliament has called upon the Commission to propose common Union definitions:

> by taking into consideration the following characteristics of a 'smart robot':
>
> - the capacity to acquire autonomy through sensors and/or by exchanging data with its environment (inter-connectivity) and the analysis of those data;
> - the capacity to learn through experience and interaction;
> - the form of the robot's physical support [and]
> - the capacity to adapt its behaviour and actions to the environment.[63]

In a similar vein, albeit with less emphasis on a physical manifestation of the 'robot', *Oberson* has identified the existence of AI, encompassing sufficient autonomy, and a capacity to learn, progress and to make decisions as key characteristics.[64]

Arguably, the aforementioned definitional elements are sufficiently adaptive to cover a wide range of intelligent machines and, in the case of *Oberson*, also algorithms. However, unless further specified, they would also produce a significant amount of unintended by-catch, and leave many grey areas. Moreover, as *Falcão* has correctly pointed out, a proper definition must take into account the objectives of the robot tax, as well as the socio-economic situation of the jurisdiction that seeks to enact it.[65] For

61. *See, e.g.*, Erdoğdu, *supra* note 6, at 113; White, *supra* note 41; Oberson, *supra* note 13; Falcão, *supra* note 18, at 3.
62. Shackleton, *supra* note 4, at 28.
63. Resolution on Robotics, *supra* note 9, at point 1 & Annex.
64. Oberson, *supra* note 10, at 249-250, with further references to the various standards and definitions analysed by him.
65. Falcão, *supra* note 18, at 5.

example, if designed as a compensatory tax for the reduction in wage and payroll taxes, the physical support element is less relevant – as white-collar work can also be substituted by mere program code, i.e., algorithms – than in the context of a Pigouvian tax that aims to slow down the pace of transition from human labour to machine labour in the field of services that require a local physical presence. And in the case of corrective taxation in general, the degree of autonomy and AI required should be expected to vary according to the stage of technological development that a society finds itself in: While in technologically advanced jurisdictions, there is little risk of human jobs still getting supplanted by low-tech robots – in fact, they already have been – this may well be different in less developed parts of the world.

To enhance legal certainty for taxpayers making use of intelligent robots – or in the more distant future, for the robots themselves – it would seem advisable to establish a system of registration for qualifying robots; taxation should then depend on the entry of the robot in the register. Obviously, this would not eliminate the potential for dispute over the correct assessment of the robot's status, but such a system would avoid surprise assessments during tax audits with significant retrospective effects. It would have to be carefully checked, though, whether one could simply link taxation to the entry of advanced robots into a public register that will eventually be established in the future for regulatory or civil law purposes.[66] It could well be that the objectives of the robot tax differ too markedly from the non-tax objectives underlying the creation of the register.

§12.05 OTHER TAX IMPLICATIONS OF THE INCREASING USE OF INTELLIGENT ROBOTS

The Authorized OECD Approach for the attribution of profits to a permanent establishment (PE) has established the 'significant people functions' performed therein as the key criterion for the determination of an adequate profit share.[67] In a similar vein, the OECD Transfer Pricing Guidelines that are based on the traditional dealing-at-arm's-length standard put increased emphasis on the 'functions performed' by a group member in order to assess, for tax purposes, the transfer prices agreed between associated enterprises.[68] To the extent that such people functions are carried out by intelligent robots in the future, this must be reflected in the respective rules on profit allocation. Beyond that, the physical presence of intelligent robots that form part of the business assets should constitute a taxable nexus for the purposes of international direct taxation, even absent any relevant human workforce. The allocation of assets and risks, and ultimately profits, to such a 'robot PE' should then once more reflect the functions performed by the robot(s).

---

66. Regarding one such proposal, *see* the Annex of the Resolution on Robotics, *supra* note 9.
67. *See* OECD, *2010 Report on the Attribution of Profits to Permanent Establishments*, paras 15 et seq. (OECD Publishing 2010); OECD, *Model Tax Convention on Income and on Capital: Condensed Version 2017* 1, 118 paras 20 et seq. (OECD Publishing 2017).
68. *See* OECD, *Transfer Pricing Guidelines for Multinational Enterprises and Tax Administrations* 1, 265 paras 6.42 et seq. (OECD Publishing 2017).

Mutatis mutandis, the same applies for formulary apportionment of tax revenues, for example among sub-federal states (such as, e.g., the sales tax revenue in the US) or in the context of an eventual future EU common consolidated corporate tax base (CCCTB).[69] The current trend to automation through AI systems should be reflected in the apportionment formula, at least if – and as long as – robots do not merely reshuffle but (temporarily or permanently) replace the human workforce. One option would then be to give more weight to business assets in relation to payroll in the formula, reflecting the shift in value creation factors from personnel to machines. An alternative approach that would neutralize the revenue allocation effects of automation in the formula would be to treat certain robots with advanced AI features no longer as assets but rather count them in the payroll factor with an imputed wage. As a caveat, it should be mentioned that this would create the above-mentioned definitional issues to distinguish between machines that are still counted as assets and advanced AI systems that are considered equivalent to human workers.

Finally, many specific anti-abuse regimes, both in domestic tax legislation and in international tax law, rely on economic substance thresholds in order to establish safe haven rules. In this context, too, the employment of sufficiently intelligent and autonomous robots should be considered equivalent to the presence and performance of human employees entrusted with similar tasks.

§12.06 CONCLUSIONS

The rapid automation in almost all sectors of the economy is widely expected to lead to massive job losses and exacerbate income inequality, at least during a transition period, and possibly even on a permanent basis. It will likely reduce the labour share in national income and increase the capital share. This development could result in a greater political need for income redistribution and in publicly financed re-training programs for workers whose skills have become obsolete in a disrupted labour market. Government furthermore faces the additional challenge that it will be confronted with higher revenue needs in such a scenario while its revenues from wage tax and payroll tax will presumably shrink considerably at least temporarily due to a net loss in jobs that generate such revenues. This will make it necessary for governments to seek alternative revenue sources. Proponents of a tax on robots or on their use argue that such a tax could achieve both fiscal and distributional objectives and could moreover ease the disruption of the labour market through a smoother transition to the new age of robot economies.

However, there is currently no compelling argument to make robots themselves taxable persons, neither for the purposes of income taxation nor for the purposes of indirect taxes on consumption expenditure. In particular, as long as robots do not have self-defined personal needs, making them liable to pay income tax cannot be justified on grounds of ability to pay as the fundamental tax equity principle underlying

69. *See* Commission Proposal for a Council Directive on a Common Consolidated Corporate Tax Base (CCCTB) COM(2016) 685 final 2016/0337 (CNS) (2016).

progressive income taxation. There is currently also no need to impose a tax on robots as a backstop for the personal income taxation of their owners or users so that the robot tax would have a similar function as the corporate income tax. Different from corporate profits, it is still feasible to tax the profits resulting from the use of robots at the hands of the ones employing them, at the right time and the right place. The first tax where robots might eventually attain taxable person status is most likely the VAT/ GST (Goods and Services Tax) (, once (certain) robots are granted legal personality, can enter into contractual relationships with customers themselves and become legal owners of the proceeds from their supply of goods or services. But this is not a current concern.

Realistically, what could already be taxed now is the use of robots. Essentially, four different but interrelated strands of justifications have been brought forward in favour of such a new tax, which could take several different shapes: It has been defended as a tax on deemed income earned by means of the robot, as an equalization levy to restore the level playing field regarding the taxation of robots and of human workers, as an instrument for economically efficient wage compression between winners and losers of automation among the human workforce and as a corrective tax to slow down the disruption of the labour market that is expected as a consequence of rapid automation driven by robotics. However, the first two arguments - aimed at complementary or compensatory taxation of robots - are not convincing because the presumptions that they are based on are either conceptually flawed or they lack credible empirical support. Besides, their proponents tend to underestimate how capital mobility and international tax competition could easily undermine the respective objective of such a tax. The latter objection can also be raised vis-à-vis the conception of the robot tax as a means for wage compression, apart from the complexities that would arise if such a tax were to properly reflect the constantly changing technological progress and its effect on the labour market. Finally, the design as a Pigouvian tax faces similar challenges, except if its scope of application were limited to sectors of the economy that are not, or only to a small degree, exposed to international tax competition.

Altogether, the case for taxing the use of a robot tax is relatively weak. In particular, income redistribution and revenue raising through the taxation of robots should only be considered as a measure of last resort, and in any event a provisional one, if no other alternative is feasible. Any justification would have to outweigh the concern that a tax on robots is liable to result in distortions, complexities and reduced growth,[70] all the more so in a globalized economy with intense international tax competition. In any event, any robot tax legislation would have to deal with the tricky issue of defining its scope of application in a way that is not only fit for (the respective)

70. This applies also to specific excise taxes on goods or services produced by using robots, or elevated VAT rates that would follow the same rationale. Regarding such proposals, *see* White, *supra* note 41. Such taxes could furthermore raise questions regarding their compatibility with WTO non-discrimination standards, when introduced by a jurisdiction with a comparatively low level of automation.

purpose but also ensures both a flexible future-proof coverage and sufficient legal certainty.

Priority should instead be given to intensified efforts to tax the return on capital investments and on profits in general, including an adequate taxation of shareholders. As regards individual income taxation, much progress has already been made in this regard in recent years under the auspices of the OECD, and within the EU in particular, due to revolutionary developments in the field of international exchange of information.[71] Similar progress would now have to be achieved regarding the coordination of national systems of business taxation, especially by limiting the scope for international tax planning and (legal) tax avoidance - the OECD Base Erosion and Profit Shifting (BEPS) project can only be considered a first step in this direction.

71. For a comprehensive discussion, see Xavier Oberson, *International Exchange of Information in Tax Matters* (Edward Elgar 2015).

CHAPTER 13

Big Data in Tax Collection and Enforcement

Tina Ehrke-Rabel[*]

§13.01 INTRODUCTION

In 2014 in all Member States of the G7 Group, namely Canada, France, Germany, Italy, Japan, the United Kingdom (UK) and the United States of America (USA), at least 70% of the gross domestic product depended on intangible goods, rather than on material goods.[1] The first are information related, whereas the latter are the physical output of agricultural or manufacturing processes. The amount is likely to have increased since then. Today's economy is thus very different from the economy at the beginning of the twentieth century and even from that at the end of the twentieth century.

To a large extent this is caused by the development of information and communication technologies (ICTs), or in other terms by digitalization.[2] Today, the most valuable companies worldwide are not companies that produce physical goods but ICT

* The author is grateful for helpful discussions with Prof. Iris Eisenberger, BOKU University of Vienna and Dr Elisabeth Hödl, ubifacts Graz. Moreover, she would like to thank Dr Barbara Gunacker-Slawitsch, Prof. Richard Sturn, Prof. Rainer Niemann, Prof. Alfred Wagenhofer and René Wind (all University of Graz), who by numerous discussions at lunchtime and in workshops have largely inspired the author. She would also like to thank her PhD students Lily Zechner and Stefan Hammerl for their thorough review of the final version and insightful comments. Moreover, she thanks Luisa Scarcella and Lily Zechner for their helpful assistance with formalities.

1. Luciano Floridi, *The 4th Revolution, How The Infosphere Is Reshaping Human Reality* 4 (Oxford Univ. Press 2014).
2. OECD, *Addressing the Tax Challenges of the Digital Economy, Action 1 – 2015 Final Report 1* 11 (OECD Publishing 2015) (hereinafter '2015 OECD Digital Economy Final Report'): The digital economy is increasingly becoming the economy itself.

companies.[3] ICTs are part of everyone's everyday life. Not only people are connected to the Internet but also things (so-called Internet of Things, (IoT)). Via smart devices a swimming pool can inform the pool-keeper of needs for specific maintenance, and via her smartphone the owner of the swimming pool is informed about the solution of the problem. Similarly, a refrigerator can be connected to its owners' favourite grocery provider in order to for example automatically compensate shortcomings of milk and butter to the household. Today's society lives with masses of data being transferred all around. Eventually they get stored, processed and even sold to other economic operators. There are a number of new business models that have emerged around data.

ICT has even reached taxation. Online filing of tax returns and online transmission of tax notifications are common in many States. IoT for tax matters is on the rise: In Slovenia, the cash economy must use certified electronic cash registers that are connected to the tax administration in order to inform it of a transaction in real time.[4] Chile has launched an Electronic Invoicing System that allows taxpayers to issue and receive invoices, which are immediately available to the revenue body of Chile.[5] Tax authorities thus collect masses of data and information on taxpayers.

The current economy is not only different from the one of former times because of ICT, but peoples' awareness of the influence of psychology on humans' behaviour has also changed. Some authors consider today's (developed countries) society 'psychologized'.[6] Psychology and behavioural economics are not only used for treating mental disorders and for marketing, many people have 'coaches' to improve their lives and well-being, politicians use psychological insights to attract voters or to keep their electorate favourable, and behavioural economics challenge and inspire policymakers, lawmakers and even administrations.

Over the past years governments have increasingly coped with ICT and the insights of behavioural economics in order to efficiently enforce laws. Under the term 'new public governance' (among others) behavioural (psychological) insights are used to shape the interaction between the State and the taxpayer in a way that is supposed to increase tax compliance.[7] Moreover, tax authorities have adopted tools of ICTs to improve their management of taxpayer data on the one hand and to support their administrative decisions on the other. Most of the changes on the governance level have taken place either outside statutory law or not fully within statutory law.

Tax authorities have always been dealing with huge amounts of taxpayer data in order to assess the right amount of tax on the right person at the right moment.

3. According to the Forbes ranking Apple, Microsoft, Google, Facebook and Amazon range among the top five brands worldwide (https://www.forbes.com/powerful-brands/list/#tab:rank; (accessed 18 December 2018); *see also* Marc Dugain & Christophe Labbé, *L'Homme Nu, La dictature invisible du numérique* 24 et seq. (Plon 2016).
4. http://www.taxslovenia.com/hogenglish.php (accessed 27 February 2019).
5. For details, see OECD, *Tax Compliance By Design: Achieving Improved SME Tax Compliance By Adopting A System Perspective* 36 et seq. (OECD Publishing 2014).
6. *See, e.g.*, Alexandra Rau, *Psychopolitik* (Campus Verlag 2010); Byung-Chul Han, 5 *Psychopolitik: Neoliberalismus und die neuen Machttechniken* (Samuel Fischer ed., 2014).
7. *See, e.g.*, Eduard Müller, *Good Governance und Steuermoral*, 8 ÖStZ 191, 195 (2011).

Moreover, they have always had to deal with specific personal circumstances at the taxpayers level (e.g., pregnancy, death, insolvency). Data and psychology have never been unknown to tax authorities. But the way tax authorities deal with data and with psychological insights has changed. This change has been deeply impacted by the described determinants of the modern society and nowadays economy.[8] Although statutes have not changed that much, the reality of tax administration has. This contribution argues that the changes can threaten the core values of democracy, which are personal autonomy and the right to privacy, if they do not get legally framed. This contribution seeks to set the ground for such legal framing.

Accordingly, §13.02 summarizes the traditional scheme of tax collection and enforcement and highlights taxpayers' fundamental rights to be preserved. Section §13.03 addresses the subject matter: Big Data Analytics in tax matters. After a definition of Big Data (§13.03[A]), its purpose, use and benefits are highlighted (§13.03[B]). Section §13.03[C] gives an overview of Big Data Analytics use cases in tax matters. Section §13.04 addresses the legal concerns related to the use of Big Data Analytics in tax matters and sets the ground for a proposal of legal actions to be taken (§13.05). It is argued that Big Data Analytics that are not properly framed by law raise legal concerns with regard to the rule of law, the principle of equality, the rights of the defence and privacy rights. A proper framing needs to make a distinction between rule-based and deep-learning algorithms on the one hand and the purposes Big Data Analytics are used for on the other.

This manuscript does not deal with algorithm-based rule-making at legislative level but concentrates on tax collection and enforcement.

In order to assure a common understanding of the terms used we would like to emphasize that data, information and knowledge are not the same. Data are raw piece of information, facts. In contrast to 'information', pure data need to be processed and put into a specific context to be usable for tax purposes.[9] Information is thus to be distinguished from data. 'Information' is data processed in a specific context for a certain purpose.[10] As a consequence, data are generally a reflection of past events, whereas information can supply understanding of patterns and trends across data sources. Intelligence can then add value by providing insight into the future and create knowledge.[11]

8. Maya Bacache, Francis Bloch & Marc Bourreau, *Taxation and the Digital Economy: A Survey of Theoretical Models*, Final Report Study on behalf of France Stratégie, 28 et seq. (France Stratégie 2015).
9. For a definition of pure data, see Luciano Floridi, *Information – A Very Short Introduction* 22 (Oxford Univ. Press 2010).
10. For a general overview, see Jennifer Rowley, *The Wisdom Hierarchy: Representations of the DIKW Hierarchy*, 33 J. Inf. Sci. 163 (2007); Russell Ackoff, *From Data to Wisdom*, 16 J. Appl. Syst. Anal. 3 (1989); Floridi, *supra* note 9, at 20 & 29.
11. European Commission, Directorate General Taxation and Customs Union, Fiscalis Risk Management Platform Group, Compliance Risk Management Guide for Tax Administrations, FPG32/GRP4 (2010) (hereinafter 'Commission Guide for Tax Administrations'), 90.

§13.02 TAX COLLECTION AND ENFORCEMENT

[A] Information Asymmetry and Personal Autonomy

Personal autonomy is the core value of liberal democracies.[12] It underlies the right to free exercise of religion, to free speech, to privacy, to private property, to assembling with others etc.[13] In some constitutions it is explicitly set down,[14] in others not, but it is valid in both types of liberal democracies. Similarly, Article 8 of the European Convention on Human Rights (hereinafter 'ECHR')[15] protects the right to personal development, and the right to establish relationships with other human beings and the outside world.[16] It secures to individuals a sphere within which they can freely pursue the development and fulfilment of their personality.[17] It thus enshrines the right to personal autonomy.[18]

State interference with personal autonomy is only allowed where it is necessary to safeguard the functioning of a democratic society and to prevent others from harm. Taxes are levied from every taxpayer regardless of their readiness to contribute to the public expenditure. Taxation thus interferes with private property, and it restricts personal autonomy.

Taxes that do not attach to simple events, to be seen by everyone externally, are always difficult to collect. It is generally the taxpayer who is in the possession of the information the tax administration needs to collect the right amount of taxes at the right moment. From a game-theoretic perspective, the relationship between the taxpayer

12. *See, e.g.*, Loïc Philip, *Droit Fiscal Constitutionnel: Évolution d'une jurisprudence* 82 (Economica 2014), with further references.
13. The principle underlying the right to respect private and family life is the notion of personal autonomy (*see Pretty* v *the United Kingdom*, no. 2346/02, § 61, Eur.Ct.H.R. 2002-III; *Gillan and Quinton* v *the United Kingdom*, no. 4158/05, § 61, Eur.Ct.H.R. 2010).
14. *See, e.g.*, République Française, Déclaration des Droits de l'Homme et du Citoyen du 1789, Art. 4, légifrance.fr, https://www.legifrance.gouv.fr/Droit-francais/Constitution/Declaration-des-Droits-de-l-Homme-et-du-Citoyen-de-1789 (accessed 18 December 2018) & German Federal Republic, Grundgesetz, Art. 2, bundestag.de, https://www.bundestag.de/grundgesetz.
15. Council of Europe, *European Convention for the Protection of Human Rights and Fundamental Freedoms, as amended by Protocols No. 11 & 14, 4 November 1950*, ETS 5, *available at* https://www.refworld.org/docid/3ae6b3b04.html (accessed 19 December 2018) (hereinafter 'ECHR').
16. *Niemietz* v *Germany*, judgment of 16 Dec. 1992, Series A 251-B no. 13710/88, § 29; *Pretty* v *the United Kingdom*, no. 2346/02, *supra* note 13, at §§ 61, 67; *Oleksandr Volkov* v *Ukraine*, no. 21722/11, §§ 165–167, Eur.Ct.H.R. 2013; *El-Masri* v *the former Yugoslav Republic of Macedonia* [GC], §§ 248–250, Eur.Ct.H.R. 2012.
17. *A.-M.V.* v *Finland*, no. 53251/13, § 76, Eur.Ct.H.R. 2017; *Brüggemann & Scheuten* v *Federal Republic of Germany*, no. 6959/75 ECHR, Commission Decision of July 12, 1977, DR 10, §§ 55, 57; *National Federation of Sportspersons' Associations and Unions (FNASS) & Others* v *France*, nos 48151/11 & 77769/13, § 153, Eur.Ct.H.R. 2018.
18. ECHR, Guide on Article 8 of the European Convention on Human Rights – Right to respect for private and family life, home and correspondence (last update 31 August 2018) 39, 40 (https://www.echr.coe.int/Documents/Guide_Art_8_ENG.pdf) (accessed 18 December 2018) (hereinafter 'ECHR Article 8 Guide').

and the tax administration is reigned by asymmetric and incomplete information.[19] Consequently, information provided by the taxpayers has to be verified. Thus, tax enforcement rules aim at overcoming information asymmetries. The conception of such rules requires to strike the balance between the State's interest in collecting the right amount of taxes on the right person at the right moment and the taxpayer's right to personal autonomy and privacy. The first is for the sake of the collective whereas the latter aims at preserving individuality.

Since the twentieth-century taxation has been relying on an understanding of justice that requires a lot of taxpayer information in order to assess the right amount of taxes at the right moment. In order to comply with the ability to pay principle, income taxation heavily relies on personal circumstances. Other taxes, such as consumption taxes, also include certain specificities, which require specific data of and specific information on specific taxpayers, although they do not bother that much about ability to pay. This need of personal data and information to raise the public revenue must be balanced against the individual right to private autononomy. A very important ingredient of private autonomy is the right to and the guarantee of confidentiality. According to the Austrian Constitutional Court 'freedom as a right of the individual and as a state of being of a society are determined by the quality of relationships of information.'[20] Similarly, to the ECHR broadmindedness and tolerance as hallmarks of a democratic society require - among others - privacy.[21] Consequently, certain information on individuals is traditionally unknown by the State. In this respect the individual remains anonymous towards the State. The State is only granted access to personal data and information insofar it is important to fulfil its legitimate duties.

The concept of personal autonomy underlying modern democracies prevents States from citizens' surveillance and scrutiny, unless overriding reasons in the public interest require the opposite.[22] However, the concepts of privacy differ from State to State. In Switzerland, Belgium, Luxembourg and Austria,[23] for example, bank account

19. *See, e.g.*, Klaus-Dieter Drüen, *Inanspruchnahme Dritter für den Steuervollzug*, 31 DStJG 167, 170 et seq. (2008); Tina Ehrke-Rabel, *Geheimhaltungs- und Informationsinteressen beim automatischen internationalen Informationsaustausch nach dem GMSG*, 2 SWI 67, 68 (2016); Tina Ehrke-Rabel & Barbara Gunacker-Slawitsch, Horizontal Monitoring als Bestandteil des österreichischen Abgabenvollzugs? Österreichische Steuerzeitung 15-16 241, 242 et seq. (2017).
20. VfGH, 27.06.2014, G 47/2012-49; VfGH, 27.06.2014 G 59/2012-38; VfGH, 27.06.2014; VfGH, 27.06.2014 G 62/2012-46; VfGH, 27.06.2014 G 70/2012-40; VfGH, 27.06.2014 G 71/2012-36; 'die Freiheit als Anspruch des Individuums und als Zustand einer Gesellschaft wird bestimmt von der Qualität der Informationsbeziehung'.
21. *Dudgeon* v *the United Kingdom*, judgment of 22 October 1981, Series A no. 45, Application no. 7525/76, §§ 51-53.
22. The fight against terrorism was for example brought forward by States to justify intensive interferences with personal autonomy.
23. More information on the Austrian Bank secrecy in Peter Jabornegg, Rudolf Strausser & Hans Floretta, *Das Bankgeheimnis* (Manz'sche 1998); Katharina Daxkobler & Elisabeth Pamperl, *Das schleichende Ende des Bankgeheimnisses?Aufrechterhaltung im Inland bei gleichzeitiger Durchbrechung im Rahmen des internationalen Auskunftsverkehrs?* 22 SWK 998, 1001 (2014); Friedrich Sommer & Christine Hirsch, *in* 9 *Bankwesengesetz – BWG Kommentar* Markus Dellinger, s. 38 para. 124 (Markus Dellinger ed., LexisNexis 2017); René Laurer, *in* 3 *Bankwesengesetz – BWG Kommentar* s. 38 para. 8 (René Laurer, Rainer Borns, Johann Strobl & Melitta Schütz eds., Manz Grosskommentare 2009); Johannes Ortner, *Das Bankgeheimnis* 63 (Österreichischer Volksbankenverlag 1995); Renate Schaubmair, *Bankgeheimnis, in* 1 *Handbuch zur*

information was protected by privacy rules from State intervention, except in cases of criminal offences. In Sweden, on the contrary, bank account information was never hidden from tax authorities and individual tax liabilities have been publicly accessible for a long time. Moreover, as societies evolve, our experience and expectations of privacy also evolve.[24] The bank secrecy is a good example for this evolution. In States like Austria the very rigid bank secrecy has been given up step by step since 2010. However, in tax matters privacy keeps great importance.

[B] Traditional Tax Collection and Enforcement[25]

In order to minimize interferences with personal autonomy tax collection traditionally resides on information provided by the taxpayer: The taxpayer files a tax return, and after verification the tax administration assesses the tax. In former days it was humans that were supposed to actively intervene for the assessment of every single taxpayer. As taxation has been a mass procedure for a long time it has been assumed for a long time that tax authorities would not be able to thoroughly verify all returns before assessment. Initial assessments were (and still are) thus regularly subject to revision through tax audits.[26] But even with the ex post control through audits full verification of all taxpayers has traditionally not been possible due to limited State resources.[27] The tax administration has thus been granted certain margins of discretion to decide on which cases to audit. Consequently, according to the Organisation for Economic Co-operation and Development (OECD) traditional tax collection schemes can be

Praxis der steuerlichen Betriebsprüfung 258 (Werner Koller, Hannes Schuh & Hubert Woischitzschläger eds., LexisNexis 2010); Cristoph Kerres & Florian Proell, *Aktuelle Entwicklungen zum Bankgeheimnis*, 7 Ecolex 623 (2009).

24. Ann Cavoukian & Jeff Jonas, *Privacy by Design in the Age of Big Data* 1, 7 (https://jeffjonas.typepad.com/Privacy-by-Design-in-the-Era-of-Big-Data.pdf) (accessed 18 December 2018).
25. I am particularly grateful to the input Barbara Gunacker-Slawitsch gave me on this by handing over her draft manuscript on the interplay between the taxpayers' obligation to contribute to tax collection and the tax administrations' duty to inquire and collect the correct taxes ex officio. Without having read her great work I would certainly not have been capable of being that clear and short.
26. François Vaillancourt, Chris Evans & Binh Tran-Nam, *Prefilled Personal Income Tax Returns: A Comparative Analysis of Australia, Belgium, California, Quebec and Spain* (François Vaillancourt ed., Fraser Institute 2011); Barrie Russell, *Revenue Administration: Developing a Taxpayer Compliance Program* 2 (IMF 2010); Jonas Jensen & Florian Wöhlbier, *Improving Tax Governance in EU Member States: Criteria for Successful Policies* 22 et seq. (European Commission Occasional Papers 114, 2012); Commission Guide for Tax Administrations, *supra* note 11, at 42; OECD, *Using Third Party Information Reports to Assist Taxpayers Meet Their Return Filing Obligations – Country Experiences With the Use of Pre-populated Personal Tax Returns* (OECD Publishing 2006); according to the OECD, *Tax Administration 2017: Comparative Information on OECD and Other Advanced and Emerging Economies* 191 (OECD Publishing 2017), most tax administration systems are currently still based on a system requiring the taxpayer to fill his tax return.
27. Tina Ehrke-Rabel, *Third Parties as Supplementaries to Transparency, in Transparency in Taxation* (Funda Basran & Johanna Hey eds., EATLP Congress Papers (forthcoming 2019)); Rafal Lipniewicz, *Tax Administration and Risk Management in the Digital Age,* 6 Info. Systems in Mgmt. 26, 28 (2017).

defined as 'an information rich organisation that derives most of its data from information provided by the taxpayer'.[28]

In order to ease proper tax assessment and to reduce the only reliance on taxpayers' declarations tax systems very often include third parties into the tax collection procedure either by imposing the obligation to withhold certain taxes on behalf of the person liable for the tax or by imposing reporting obligations.[29] Generally, traditional tax collection is reactive, meaning that tax authorities intervene late after the occurrence of the taxable event and mostly only upon declaration of the taxpayer.

With the increased complexity of substantive tax law itself and the shift to a globalized and digitalized (service dominated and increasingly intangible) economy[30] tax collection faces big challenges. Although these challenges are not new, the described developments have made them more evident.

First, tax administrations' investigative and coercive powers are limited to the nation and thus the nations' territory they were invested by.[31] This territorial restriction can be overcome to a certain extent by cross-border cooperation between tax administrations in various forms (exchange of information on request, automatic exchange of information, spontaneous exchange information, right to be present during audits in another State, joint audits).[32] Second – and importantly for this contribution, services

28. OECD, *Technologies for Better Tax Administration A Practical Guide for Revenue Bodies: A Practical Guide for Revenue Bodies* 64 (OECD Publishing 2016).
29. Michael Doran, *Tax Penalties and Tax Compliance*, 46 Harv. J. Legis. 111, 143 (2009); Leandra Lederman, *Statutory Speed Bumps: The Roles Third Parties Play in Tax Compliance*, 60 Stan. L. Rev. 695 (2007); Tina Ehrke-Rabel, *Third Parties as Supplementaries to Transparency, in Transparency in Taxation, supra* note 26; According to Hatfield, 97% of taxpayers is provided to the IRS in routine reports from third parties, Michael Hatfield, *Taxation and Surveillance: An Agenda*, 17 Yale J. L. & Tech. 319, 330 (2015).
30. OECD, *Action 1: Addressing the Challenges of the Digital Economy 2015 Final Report* (OECD Publishing 2015).
31. *See The Case of the S.S. 'Lotus' (France* v *Turkey) (1927)* P.C.I.J Series, A, no. 10 (1927), 18–19; *Corfu Channel Case (Great Britain* v *Albania)*, Judgment, I.C.J Rep. 1949, 35 (25 March); *see also* Michael Hendricks, *nternationale Informationshilfe im Steuerverfahren: Grundlagen, Systematik und Grenzen der informationellen zwischenstaatlichen Rechts- und Amtshilfe* 1, 175–176 (OttoSchmidt 2004); Harald Schaumburg, *Internationales Steuerrecht* para. 22.3 (OttoSchmidt 4th ed. 2017).
32. At International level please consider: Arts 5, 6, 7 of the Convention on Mutual Administrative Assistance in Tax Matters (OECD, *Convention on Mutual Administrative Assistance in Tax Matters* (OECD Publishing 1 June 2011), *available at* https://read.oecd-ilibrary.org/taxation/the-multilateral-convention-on-mutual-administrative-assistance-in-tax-matters_9789264115606-en#page1; at European level please consider Council Directive 2011/16/EU on administrative cooperation in the field of taxation and repealing Directive 77/799/EEC OJ L 64 (2011); Directive 2018/822/EU on mandatory automatic exchange of information in the field of taxation in relation to reportable cross-border arrangements, OJ L 139 (2018); for scholarly literature on this topic please, see among all: CFA Manual on Information Exchange (2006), *available at* http://www.oecd.org/tax/exchange-of-tax-information/cfaapprovesnewmanualoninformationexchange.htm (accessed 19 December 2018); OECD, *Automatic Exchange of Information: What It Is, How It Works, Benefits, What Remains To Be Done* (OECD Publishing 2012); Xavier Oberson, *International Exchange of Information in Tax Matters. Towards Global Transparency* (Edward Elgar 2015); Tonny Schenk-Geers, *International Exchange of Information and the Protection of Taxpayers* (Wolters & Kluwer Law & Business 2009); Nevia Cicin-Sain, Tina Ehrke-Rabel & Joachim Englisch, *Joint Audits – Taxpayer Rights*, 10 World Tax J. (2019).

provided digitally cannot be detected as easily as either the provision of services in the brick-and-mortar economy or the delivery of goods. The more intangible economic operations are, the less detectable they are by externals, the tax administration more precisely. According to the deterrence model, the author believes in, the likelihood of detection and the gravity of sanctions incurred if detected predetermine tax compliance to a large extent.[33] Under-reporting or non-reporting of taxpayers with regard to the intangible economy constitutes thus an increased risk. Third, public resources to efficiently control taxpayers are still or even increasingly limited. A thorough verification of every single taxpayer is thus an illusion. It remains to be seen, whether it will stay an illusion. From a technical perspective, for some taxes and some groups of taxpayers at least, ICT could allow the thorough verification of every single taxpayer. Whether this is compatible with our concept of privacy and personal autonomy will be explored in this contribution.

[C] Change of the Game: New Tools

Governments have soon realized that digital and psychology-based tools used by private businesses would have the potential to improve public administration. Consequently, by transplanting private business concepts to public management tax authorities have refined their 'Tax Compliance Risk Management' tools to increase their effectiveness.[34]

The Fiscalis Risk Management Platform Group at the European Commission describes Compliance Risk Management as 'a systematic process in which a tax administration makes deliberate choices on which treatment instruments could be used to effectively stimulate compliance and prevent non-compliance, based on the knowledge of all taxpayers (behaviour) and related to the available capacity.'[35] For this – the Group emphasizes – the availability of information technology (IT) tools and access to data are of great importance. 'Intensive use of information technology creates opportunities to improve the performance of the Tax Administration. It affects factors such as reliable and updated taxpayer files as well as databases with cross-checking possibilities. *Advanced tools are of no use if access to data is poor. The level of gathering data in digital form is therefore crucial to the administration.*'[36] As a consequence,

33. Michael Allingham & Agnar Sandmo, *Income Tax Evasion: A Theoretical Analysis*, 1 J. Pub. Econ. 323 (1972), modified in Shlomo Yitzhaki, *A Note on Income Tax Evasion: A Theoretical Analysis*, 3 J. Pub. Econ. 201 (1974); Alex Raskolnikov, *Revealing Taxpayer Choice to Target Tax Enforcement*, 109 Columbia L. Rev. 689, 711 (2009); Leandra Lederman, *Reducing Information Gaps to Reduce the Tax Gap: When Is Information Reporting Warranted*?, 78 Fordham L. Rev. (2010).
34. Mark Pijnenburg, Wojtek Kowalczyk & Lisette van der Hel-van Dijk, *A Roadmap for Analytics in Taxpayer Supervision*, 15 Electronic J. e-Gov't 19, 24 (2017).
35. European Commission, TAXUD, Compliance Risk Management Guide for Tax Administrations, Fiscalis Risk Management Platform Group, FPG32/GRP4, February 2010, 5 *available at* https://ec.europa.eu/taxation_customs/sites/taxation/files/resources/documents/common/publications/info_docs/taxation/risk_managt_guide_en.pdf) (accessed on 19 December 2018).
36. European Commission, TAXUD, Compliance Risk Management Guide for Tax Administrations, Fiscalis Risk Management Platform Group, FPG32/GRP4, February 2010, 16 *available at*

electronic filing of tax returns and increased e-government tools have been adopted by many States.

The more data a tax administration has and is able to process the more likely it is to minimize information asymmetries being the core problem of equal and complete tax collection.[37] It is therefore no wonder that the OECD has declared data to play a crucial rule in the transformation of tax administrations.[38] One of the big magic seems to be Big Data. Chapter 2 of the OECD report on Technologies for a Better Tax Administration displays a picture under the heading 'Disruptive Environment Surrounding Revenue Bodies' (Figure 13.1), where Big Data shows up (with different scales) in the third-party data exchange, in the area of software suppliers and developers, in the compliance area and the transactional field.[39]

Figure 13.1 Disruptive Environment Surrounding Revenue Bodies

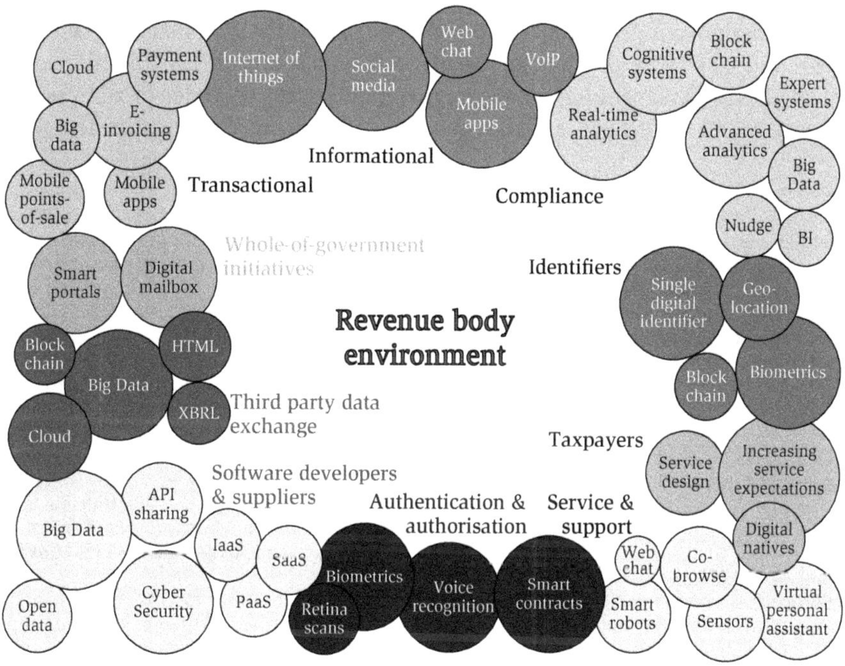

Source: Australian Tax Office (ATO), 2016

https://ec.europa.eu/taxation_customs/sites/taxation/files/resources/documents/common/publications/info_docs/taxation/risk_managt_guide_en.pdf; (accessed on 19 December 2018).

37. Michael Doran, *Tax Penalties and Tax Compliance*, 46 Harv. J. Legis. 111, 143 (2009), even speaks about 'sharp information asymmetry'; Leandra Lederman, *supra* note 32 at 1733; OECD, *The Changing Tax Compliance Environment and the Role of Tax Audit* 39 (OECD Publishing 2017).
38. OECD, *supra* note 36 at 15.
39. OECD, *Technologies for a Better Tax Administration* 24 (OECD Publishing 2016).

Tax administrations all over the world have thus started to adapt their tax collection mechanisms to new technologies. The OECD seems to have largely contributed to this development by issuing studies on the potentials of new technologies for tax administrations and by aggregating experiences from various countries. To mention the most recent reports: Advanced Analytics for Better Tax Administration: Putting Data to Work (2016), Technologies for Better Tax Administration: A Practical Guide for Revenue Bodies (2016), The changing Tax Compliance Environment and the Role of Audit (2017).

In parallel to the increased awareness of the potential of new technologies for tax collection behavioural economics have immersed in tax governance.[40] The old unique command and control approach towards the taxpayer has been considered to be counter-intuitive to tax compliance.[41] In particular, behavioural science has shown that criminal sanctions are not the appropriate response when non-compliance is caused by complex legislation or a lack of knowledge on the part of the taxpayer.[42] Behavioural insights taught that taxpayers react differently on the traditional command and control approach depending on their psychological patterns. Behavioural science suggested to take these psychological patterns into account for tax collection and to segment the taxpayers into different groups of attention[43] in order to address them according to their intrinsic attitude towards paying taxes.[44] This has led to the

40. William Congdon, Jeffrey Kling & Sendhil Mullainathan, *Behavioral Economics and Tax Policy* (NBER Working Paper No. 15328, 2009), *available at* http://www.nber.org/papers/w15328; Benjamini Yael & Maital, Shlomo, *Optimal Tax Evasion Policy: Behavioral Aspects*, *in The Economics of the Shadow Economy* 140–158 (Wulf Gaertner & Alois Wenig eds., Springer 1985); Valerie Braithwaite, *Responsive Regulation and Taxation: Introduction* 29 L. & Pol'y 3–10 (John Wiley and Sons & the University of Denver 2007); Robert Cialdini, *Social Influence: Compliance and Conformity* 55 Annu. Rev. Psychology 591–621 (2004).

41. Sagit Leviner, *An Overview: A New Era of Tax Enforcement – From 'Big Stick' to Responsive Regulation*, 2 Reg. & Governance 360–380 (2008); Kirchler Murphy, *Enforcing Tax Compliance: To Punish or Persuade?*, 38 Econ. Analysis & Pol'y 113–135 (2008); Rachelle Holmes, *Forcing Cooperation: A Strategy for Improving Tax Compliance* 79 Univ. Cin. L. Rev. (2011); a review paper updated to 2001 is provided by Maryann Richardson & Adrian Sawyer, *A Taxonomy of the Tax Compliance Literature: Further Findings, Problems and Prospects* 137–220 (16th Australian Tax Forum 2001); a recent version up to 2012 is by James Alm, *Measuring, Explaining, and Controlling Tax Evasion – Lessons from Theory, Experiments, and Field Studies*, 19 Int'l Tax Pub. Fin. 54–77 (2012).

42. European Commission, TAXUD, Compliance Risk Management Guide for Tax Administrations, Fiscalis Risk Management Platform Group, FPG32/GRP4, February 2010, 5 *available at* https://ec.europa.eu/taxation_customs/sites/taxation/files/resources/documents/common/publications/info_docs/taxation/risk_managt_guide_en.pdf (accessed 19 December 2018).

43. This term is not used by the OECD, but derived from marketing language. Targeted advertising does not do anything different from this kind of taxpayer segmentation. It addresses different kinds of attention to groups of people with different preferences (*see, e.g.*, Yuval Harari, *21 Lessons for the 21st Century* 88 et seq. (Penguin Books 2018)).

44. Michele Bernasconi, Luca Corazzini & Rafaello Seri, *Reference Dependent Preferences, Hedonic Adaptation and Tax Evasion: Does the Tax Burden Matter?*, 40 J. Econ. Psychology 103–118 (2014). Asal Sandro & Mittone Luigi, *Social Esteem Versus Social Stigma: The Role of Anonymity in an Income Reporting Game*, 124 J. Econ. Behavior & Org. 55–66 (2016); Cullis John & Lewis Alan, *Why People Pay Taxes: From a Conventional Economic Model to a Model of Social Convention*, 18 J. Econ. Psychology 305–321 (1997); Cullis John, Jones Philip & Savoia Antonio, *Social Norms and Tax Compliance: Framing the Decision to Pay Tax*, 41 J. Socio-Econ. 159–168 (2012); Sanjit d'Hami & Ali al-Nowaihi, *Why Do People Pay Taxes? Prospect Theory Versus*

development of new ways of interaction with the taxpayer. Besides a more customer-oriented language borrowed from private economy and marketing and certain 'nudges'[45] behavioural economics insights suggested to address taxpayers of the 'high-risk' segment more by a command and control approach and so-called low-risk taxpayers by a softer approach (more 'service-oriented').[46]

Again, the OECD has strongly supported these developments by different studies: 'Forum of Tax Administration, Study into the Role of Tax Intermediaries (2008)', 'Co-operative Compliance: A Framework - from Enhanced Relationship to Co-operative Compliance (2013)'; 'Co-operative Tax Compliance - Building Better Tax Control Frameworks (2016)', 'Engaging with High Net Worth Individuals on Tax Compliance (2009)'; 'Tax Compliance By Design - Achieving Improved SME Tax Compliance by Adopting a System Perspective (2014)'.

Some States have formally adopted cooperative compliance instruments (e.g., Australia, the UK),[47] and others have adopted them partially formally and partially informally (e.g., Austria[48]).

Whatever method chosen, it can be assumed that all States using Big Data Analytics have started actively taking into account the insights from behavioural economics allowing them to change their interaction patterns with the taxpayers.

Regardless of formal or informal implementation the adoption of behavioural insights to tax collection and enforcement would be impossible without the opportunities of data processing.[49] Knowing the psychological pattern of a person requires far more information than the one provided by the taxpayer in his tax returns. Psychological patterns are based on the analysis of taxpayer behaviour, for example how accurate the information he provides by his own motion is, how timely he submits the returns, how timely he pays. Moreover, data collected from other sources (such as the Internet) and cross-checking with the data of other (similar) taxpayers can provide additional insights. Data Analytics and using behavioural insights are thus closely related.[50]

Expected Utility Theory, 64 J. Econ. Behav. & Org. 171–192 (2007); James Andreoni, Brian Erard & Jonathan Feinstein, *Tax Compliance*, 36 J. Econ. Lit. 818–860 (1998).

45. For some examples of nudges, see Tina Ehrke-Rabel & Barbara Gunacker-Slawitsch, *Die Bedeutung von Governance im Steuerrecht*, 1 Austrian L.J. 99 et seq. (2014).
46. For details, see Valerie Braithwaite, *A New Approach to Tax Compliance, in Taxing Democracy* 3 et seq. (Valerie Braithwaite ed., Ashgate 2002); OECD, *Co-operative Compliance: A Framework – From Enhanced Relationship to Co-operative Compliance* 24 et seq. (OECD Publishing 2013); Tina Ehrke-Rabel & Barbara Gunacker-Slawitsch, *Die Bedeutung von Governance im Steuerrecht* 1 Austrian L.J. 99 et seq. (2014).
47. For an overview, see Lisette van der Hel & Marteen Siglé, *Cooperative Compliance: Tax Risk Management and Monitoring*, 44 Intertax 642–650 (2016).
48. On this, see Tina Ehrke-Rabel & Barbara Gunacker-Slawitsch, *Horizontal Monitoring*, 10 Österreichische Steuerzeitung 241 et seq. (2017).
49. In this sense for other fields of law, see Primavera De Filippi, *Gouvernance algorithmique: vie privée et autonomie individuelle à l'ère des Big Data, in Open Data & Big Data* 99, 102 et seq. (Daniele Bourcier & Primavera De Filippi eds., HAL 2016).
50. Tamsin Shaw, *Invisible Manipulators of Your Mind*, The New York Review of Books (20 April 2017), https://www.nybooks.com/articles/2017/04/20/kahneman-tversky-invisible-mind-manipulators/ (accessed 19 December 2018); *see* Pijnenburg, *supra* note 33, at 21.

In summary, the insights of behavioural economics and the developments of ICT have changed the way tax authorities act to collect taxes and to enforce tax law. In this Big Data Analytics plays a crucial role. Accordingly, the OECD defines the benefits of Big Data in the following:

> This ability [to proceed Big Data Analytics], in association with advanced analytics, and new service delivery practices of providing data-driven actionable insight in a visually interactive and rapidly iterative agile manner, is a key benefit associated with Big Data. The ability to analyse data in real-time or near real-time offers revenue bodies the opportunity to change how risks are managed and services are presented to users. Big Data are also providing cost-effective platforms for data management and data governance solutions for varying data volumes.[51]

In another study the OECD acknowledges:

> There is strong evidence that if people believe they are observed or if information is known, then they are more likely to comply. The growing body of behavioural insights and nudge techniques have allowed many tax administrations to influence taxpayers in more targeted ways even in the absence of full data sets.[52]

The opportunity to change how risks are managed and services are delivered indicates a recommendation to use behavioural insights.

To be able to analyse taxpayer data in real time or near real time without imposing additional personal reporting obligations requires either steady surveillance of the taxpayer or the existence of devices at the taxpayers' level which are directly connected to the tax authority, IoT devices. Digital cash registers, electronic invoices and social network analysis show relationships between people, organizations, and other connected entities and thus allows to make tax authorities work more efficiently and effectively.[53]

[D] Legal Constraints of Tax Collection and Enforcement

[1] Rule of Law

As compulsory State intervention into private property, taxation needs to be clearly framed by law. The rule of law is not only relevant for substantive tax laws but also for tax collection and tax enforcement. Although tax authorities must dispose of a certain margin of discretion with regard to whom they audit or verify and how they act in a single case, the fundamentals of tax collection and tax enforcement have to be laid down by law. Moreover, the ECHR and the Charter of Fundamental Rights of the EU (hereinafter the 'Charter')[54] and the European fundamental principles derived from the

---

51. OECD, *Technologies for a Better Tax Administration* 50 (OECD Publishing 2016).
52. OECD, *supra* note 36 at 25.
53. *Ibid.* 75.
54. The Charter of Fundamental Rights of European Union 2000/C 364/01, *available at* http://www.europarl.europa.eu/charter/pdf/text_en.pdf.

Member States' common traditions[55] provide for a set of guarantees to be complied with by tax authorities.[56]

According to the basic rules on tax collection tax administrations have to act ex officio and respect the principle of equality. In order to preserve taxpayers' individual freedom most of the current tax systems require the taxpayers to do the first steps, to proactively disclose their taxable events. Consequently, at the realization of the taxable event, taxpayers are traditionally not being observed by the tax authorities. Traditionally, tax authorities thus only react on the taxpayers' disclosure. This is traditionally the moment when tax authorities start acting ex officio. Except the cases of a hint on fraudulent behaviour tax systems thus strongly rely on the assumption that most of the information provided by taxpayers is accurate. However, in order to assure proper collection and efficient enforcement tax systems traditionally and increasingly rely on trusted third parties, such as banks, employers to either withhold taxes or provide specific information on taxable events of their counterparts. The interplay between taxpayers' and third parties' disclosure and paying obligations on the one hand and tax authorities' control duties allow to preserve privacy as a prerogative of a free society to a large extent.

[2] Right to Respect for Private and Family Life and Correspondence

The information provided by the taxpayer to the tax authorities (by filing a tax return or answering a request of the authority or during an audit) constitute or at least contain personal data. The collection of these data thus interferes with the taxpayers' rights to respect for private and family life, guaranteed by Charter Article 7 and Article 8 of the ECHR, which, to a certain extent, also protects business.[57] As a consequence, mail, telephone and email communications including those made in the context of business dealings are also covered by the notions of 'private life' and 'correspondence' in Article 8(1) ECHR.[58] The same holds true for information from the monitoring of personal internet usage.[59] Interference with the right to correspondence includes all forms of censorship, interception, monitoring and seizure.[60]

55. *For example, Nold* v *Comm'n*, C-4/73, Judgment, EU:C:1974:51; CJEU 21 September 1989, *Hoechst* v *Comm'n*, Joined Cases C-46/87, C-227/88, Judgment, EU:C:1989:337, para. 13.
56. It shall only be noted that the ECHR only applies in the signing States and that the scope of the Charter as well as the general principles of European law derived from the common traditions of the Member States are territorially restricted to the EU, essentially to matters of European Law (such as indirect taxes or cross-border situations of direct taxation). However, most liberal democracies have enshrined similar rights and guarantees into their domestic constitutions.
57. The guarantees are similar at both the Charter and ECHR levels. According to Charter Art. 52(2) Art. 7 is to be given the same meaning and the same scope as Art. 8 of the ECHR) (*see also WebMindLicenses*, C-419/14, Judgment, EU:C:2015:832, para. 70; with reference to *PPU – MCB*, C-400/10, Judgment, EU:C:2010:582, para. 53; *Dereci*, C-256/11, Judgment, EU:C:2011:734, para. 70). Besides, nothing in the Charter is to be interpreted as restricting or adversely affecting the rights recognized by the Convention (Art. 53 Charter).
58. *For example, Kennedy* v *the United Kingdom*, no. 26839/05, § 118, 2010.
59. *Copland* v *the United Kingdom*, no. 62617/00, §§ 43–44, 2007.
60. ECHR Article 8 Guide, *supra* note 17, at 77 (https://www.echr.coe.int/Documents/Guide_Art_8_ENG.pdf).

Any interference with the right to respect private and family life and correspondence is legitimate if it is in accordance with the domestic law[61] and pursues a legitimate aim in the public interest that is necessary in a democratic society. Consequently, relevant and sufficient reasons of justification are required. Furthermore, the measure set on this ground must be proportionate and legitimate to the aim pursued.[62] Finally, any limitation of Article 8 ECHR needs to be accompanied by effective safeguards against abuse by State officials, such as confidentiality rules.[63] Tax collection and tax enforcement have thus to be set down by a domestic law, that is compatible with the rule of law and accessible to the person concerned. Moreover, the requirement of any interference being 'in accordance with the law' demands that the person affected is able to foresee the consequences of the domestic law for him or for her.[64] This includes sufficient foreseeability that individuals are able to act in accordance with the law, as well as a clear demarcation of the scope of discretion of public authorities.[65] As regards the necessity requirement the Court requires the existence of a 'pressing social need' for the interference in question. A restriction on a Convention right cannot be regarded as 'necessary in a democratic society' unless, amongst other things, it is proportionate to the legitimate aim pursued.[66]

The right to respect for private and family life and correspondence is also enshrined in Article 7 ECHR. Accordingly, everyone has the right to respect for his or her private and family life, home and communication. Similarly to Article 8(2) ECHR, Charter Article 52(1) paragraph requires any limitation on the exercise of the rights and freedoms recognized by the Charter to be provided for by law and to respect the essence of those rights and freedoms. Moreover, any limitation is subject to the principle of proportionality. Limitation may thus be made only if they are necessary and genuinely meet the objectives of general interest recognized by the Union or the need to protect the rights and freedoms of others. Since fundamental rights of the Charter which correspond to rights guaranteed by the ECHR, the meaning and scope of those rights shall be the same as those laid down by the Convention. However, the Charter allows European Union (EU) law to provide more extensive protection (Charter Article 52(3)). As far as the right for respect of private and family life and correspondence is concerned for the purpose of this contribution, there does not seem to be any more extensive interpretation at the EU level. We will therefore refrain from covering the related case law of the Court of Justice of the European Union (CJEU).

61. *See Bernh Larsen Holding AS and Others* v *Norway*, no. 24117/08, § 123, 2013; *S. and Marper* v *the United Kingdom* (GC), nos 30562/04 and 30566/04, § 95, Dec. 4 2008; *G.S.B.* v *Switzerland*, Application no. 28601/11, § 68, 2015.
62. *See Bernh Larsen Holding AS and Others* v *Norway*, no. 24117/08, § 158, 2013.
63. *Ibid.*
64. *Rotaru* v *Romania* (GC), no. 28341/95, § 52, 4 May 2000; *Liberty and Others* v *the United Kingdom*, no. 58243/00, § 59, 1 July 2008; *Iordachi and Others* v *Moldova*, no. 25198/02, § 37, 10 February 2009; *Kennedy* v *the United Kingdom*, no. 26839/05, § 151, 18 May 2010.
65. *For example, Shimovolos* v *Russia*, no. 30194/09, § 68, 21 June 2011; *Silver and Others* v *the United Kingdom*, nos 5947/72, 6205/73, 7052/75, 7061/75, 7107/75, 7113/75 and 7136/75, § 87, 25 March 1983.
66. *Dudgeon* v *the United Kingdom*, no. 7525/76, §§ 51–53, 22 October 1981.

[3] Right to Protection of Personal Data

The protection of personal data is of fundamental importance to a person's enjoyment of his or her right to respect for private and family life.[67] Article 8 ECHR provides for the right to a form of informational self-determination.[68]

The storing by a public authority of information relating to an individuals' private life amounts to an interference within the meaning of Article 8, especially where such information concerns a persons' distant past.[69] In determining whether the personal information retained by the authorities involves any of the private-life aspects, due regard must be given to the specific context in which the information at issue has been recorded and retained, the nature of the records, the way in which these records are used and processed and the results that may be obtained.[70] Banking documents undoubtedly amount to personal data concerning an individual, irrespective of whether or not they contain sensitive information.[71] To determine the margin of appreciation of the State, the nature of the information needs to be taken into account.[72] Any interference with the right to protection of personal data must, as any other interference with the right to respect of private and family life, be provided for by law, necessary in a democratic society and proportionate to the legitimate aim pursued. In this context the relevant domestic law must contain sufficient safeguards to prevent abuse. According to the case law of the ECHR the need for such safeguards is all the greater where the protection of personal data undergoes automatic processing, not least when such data are used for police purposes. The domestic law should notably ensure that such data are relevant and are efficiently protected from misuse and abuse.[73]

At the level of the Charter, personal data are specifically protected by Article 8. According to Charter Article 8(2), personal data must be processed fairly for specified purposes and on the basis of the consent of the person concerned or some other legitimate basis laid down by law. Everyone is entitled to access data concerning him that has been collected and has the right to have it rectified. Moreover, the processing of personal data by automated means is regulated by the European General Data Protection Regulation (hereinafter 'GDPR') that has become enforceable on 25 May 2018.[74] According to its Article 1 the collection, processing and storage of personal data by automatic means or their collection with the intention to install files have to be accompanied by the guarantees enshrined in the GDPR.[75]

67. *Satakunnan Markkinapörssi Oy and Satamedia Oy* v Finland (GC), ECHR, no. 931/13, § 133, 27 June 2017.
68. *Ibid. at* § 137.
69. *Rotaru* v *Romania* (GC), *supra* note 62, at §§ 43-44.
70. *S. and Marper* v *the United Kingdom* (GC), *supra* note 59, at § 67.
71. *M.N. and Others* v *San Marino*, no. 28005/12, § 51, 7 July 2015.
72. *G.S.B.* v *Switzerland*, no. 28601/11, § 93, 22 December 2015.
73. *Gardel* v *France*, no. 16428/05, § 62, 17 December 2009.
74. For its territorial, substantive and personal scope, *see supra* Ch. 11.
75. Although the material scope of GDPR (Council Directive 2016/679 of the European Parliament and of the Council of 27 April 2016 on the protection of natural persons with regard to the processing of personal data and on the free movement of such data, and repealing Directive

The GDPR confers specific rights of transparency and communication (Article 12), of information and access to the data (Article 15), of rectification and erasure (Articles 16 et seq.) and the right to object (Article 21) to data subjects. A data subject is anyone whose data are used, proceeded or stored by automatic means. Article 23 GDPR allows Member States to restrict the scope of these rights and obligations for the processing of data by the public body in order to safeguard important objectives of general public interest, such as taxation matters (Article 23(1)(e)). However, such a right to restriction is not unlimited, but subject to certain safeguards (*see* later §13.05[C][3][c]).

Although the GDPR does formally only apply to natural persons, the author will not make a distinction between natural and legal persons. It seems that most of the States implemented the GDPR taxpayers as natural persons and taxpayers as legal persons. Moreover, many States seem to have implemented the GDPR without distinguishing between taxes falling within the scope of European Law and taxes falling outside. The author thus assumes that most Member States of the EU have decided to enlarge the GDPR's scope to these matters. As a consequence of this decision, the GDPR got relevant also for matters outside of the literal scope of the GDPR.[76]

For data used by tax authorities profiling is particularly important. According to Article 4 paragraph 4 GDPR 'profiling' means any form of automated processing of personal data consisting of the use of personal data to evaluate certain personal aspects relating to a natural person, in particular to analyse or predict aspects concerning that natural person's performance at work, economic situation, health, personal preferences, interests, reliability, behaviour, location or movements. Profiling is subject to the GDPR in same way as all other forms of automated data processing and storage.[77] Moreover, there are specific requirements for automated decisions, including profiling in Article 22 GDPR. Tax analytics aim – as we will see – at predicting taxpayer behaviour by processing large amounts of data on the taxpayer. As a result, profiling constitutes one of the main targets of tax analytics (*see* later §13.05[C][3]).

[4] Rights of the Defence

Most importantly for tax collection and enforcement, the rights of the defence have to be respected. The rights of the defence assure that the executive power acts within its legal boundaries and allow the taxpayer to understand why a specific decision is taken and to challenge that decision before court. Accordingly, the rights of the defence contribute to uphold the correct separation of State powers by allowing that the executive be controlled by the judiciary. Decisions by the executive can only be challenged by their addressees if they are provided with information on the driving

95/46/EC OJ L 119 (2016)) (hereinafter 'GDPR') is limited to activities falling within the scope of Union law (Art. 2 para. 2 GDPR) most Member States extended it to any kind of tax matters.

76. *Leur-Bloem*, C-28/95, Judgment, EU:C:1997:369, para. 32.
77. *See* point 72 of the Preliminary Considerations of GDPR.

thoughts leading to a certain decision. As a consequence, the rights of the defence include the right to good administration and the right to a fair judicial review. In the Charter, they are laid down in Articles 41, 47, and 48.[78] The rights to good administration[79] and to a fair judicial hearing include the right to be heard and the right of access to the file.[80] The right to be heard is reigned by the idea that the taxpayer must be able to present his views before the tax authority takes a decision to his detriment. This presupposes informing the taxpayer on the tax administrations' points.[81] Thus, the tax administration must carefully and impartially examine all aspects of the individual case. Before definitely taking a position to the detriment of the taxpayer it needs to give a detailed statement of reasons for its decision,[82] sufficiently specific to allow the taxpayer concerned to understand why his point has been rejected.[83]

The right of access to the file allows the addressee of an administrative decision to know the facts on which the authorities intend(ed) to base their decision.[84] Like most of the fundamental rights relevant in tax matters the right of access to the file can be limited under certain conditions in the public interest laid down by law.[85]

[E] Conclusion

Tax administrations have always been struggling with overcoming information asymmetry. In traditional tax collection schemes the predominant part of information comes from the taxpayer. It is increasingly complemented by information provided by third parties. However, globalization and digitalization have added to the traditional shortcomings of administrative action. Law has partly overcome problems related to the restriction of State actions to their own territory. In tackling the problems of detection related to the intangible economy, law still is in its infancy. Technological development and behavioural insights have created new tools of action or at least allow to use new tools of action. However, they need to be balanced against the core value of personal autonomy, which is reflected by the rule of law, the right to respect for private and family life and communication, and the rights of the defence. New technologies such as Big Data Analytics promise to increase efficiency and effectiveness of tax collection. However, they need to be properly framed in order to avoid undermining democracy.

78. In the European Convention of Human Rights the rights of the defence are enshrined in Art. 6. Contrary to the respective Charter rights they do not apply in tax matters.
79. On this right, see Barbara Gunacker-Slawitsch, *Das Grundrecht auf eine 'gute Verwaltung' im Abgabenverfahren (Teil 1)*, 9 Österreichische Steuerzeitung 256 (2015).
80. In this sense *Ispas*, C-298/16, Judgment, EU:C:2017:843, paras 31 et seq.
81. *See* on this Nevia Cicin-Sain, Tina Ehrke-Rabel & Joachim Englisch, *Joint Audits – Applicable Law and Taxpayer Rights*, 10 World Tax J. (2018).
82. *See Technische Universität München*, C-269/90, EU:C:1991:438, para. 14; *Sopropé*, C-349/07, EU:C:2008:746, para. 50; *Sophie Mukarubega*, C-166/13, EU:C:2014:2336, para. 48.
83. *See Sophie Mukarubega*, C-166/13, para. 48.
84. ECJ, 9 November 2017, Case C-298/16, *Ispas*, EU:C:2017:843, para. 31.
85. *Ibid.*, para. 34, with reference to the Opinion of AG Bobek in the same case, paras 121 and 222.

§13.03 BIG DATA ANALYTICS IN TAX MATTERS

[A] Definition of Big Data

For Big Data there is not one definition, but there are a lot of different definitions.[86] However, Ward and Barker have extrapolated some factors that are enclosed in many definitions. According to them there is the common understanding that Big Data 'is a term describing the storage and analysis of large and or complex data sets using a series of techniques including but not limited to NoSQL, MapReduce and machine learning'.[87] An interagency initiative of the US National Science Foundation (hereinafter 'NSF') and the US National Institute of Health specify that 'The phrase, big data' in this solicitation refers to large, diverse, complex, longitudinal, and/or distributed data sets generated from instruments, sensors, Internet transactions, email, video, click streams, and/or all other digital sources available today and in the future'.[88] Moreover, according to the NSF the phrase 'big data' refers to 'data that challenge existing methods due to size, complexity, or rate of availability.'[89] For the OECD:

> Big Data represents large and complex, often unstructured, datasets that are difficult to work with using conventional tools and techniques. Big Data is not a 'data base'.[90] Big Data is based on data that have been collected from a large variety of sources including the Internet, social media, sensors, text messages, video images and audio files as well as other often unstructured sources.[91]

De Mauro, Greco and Grimaldi propose the following definition: 'Big Data represents the Information assets characterized by such a High Volume, Velocity and Variety to require specific Technology and Analytical Methods for its transformation into value'[92] (so-called 3 V). Mayer-Schönberger and Cukier identify three main characteristics of Big Data: First, the ability to analyse vast amounts of data about a topic rather than be forced to settle for smaller sets. Second, the willingness to embrace data's real-world messiness rather than privilege exactitude. Third, Big Data are characterized by a growing respect for correlations rather than the continuous quest for elusive causality.[93]

86. The lack of a single definition is highlighted by Arthur Cockfield, *Big Data and Tax Haven Secrecy*, 18 Fla. Tax Rev. 483, 497–498 (2016); Floridi, *supra* note 1, at 13.
87. Jonathan Ward & Adam Barker, *Undefined by Data: A Survey of Big Data Definitions*, arxih.org, https://arxiv.org/pdf/1309.5821.pdf (accessed 22 December 2018).
88. National Science Foundation, *Core Techniques and Technologies for Advancing Big Data Science & Engineering (BIGDATA), NSF 12-499 (2012)*, nsf.gov, htpps://www.nsf.gov/pubs/2012/nsf12499/nsf12499.htm (accessed 22 December 2018).
89. National Science Foundation, *Critical Techniques and Technologies for Advancing Big Data Science & Engineering (BIGDATA), NSF 14-543 (2014)*, nsf.gov https://www.nsf.gov/pubs/2014/nsf14543/nsf14543.pdf (accessed 22 December 2018).
90. OECD, *supra* note 50, at 48.
91. *Ibid.*
92. A. De Mauro, M. Greco & M. Grimaldi, *What Is Big Data? A Consensual Definition and a Review of Key Research Topics*, 1644 AIP Conference Proceedings 97 (2015).
93. Viktor Mayer-Schönberger & Kenneth Cukier, *Big Data* 19 (John Murray 2013).

The general definition of Big Data includes data analytics, which means the extensive use of data, statistical and quantitative analysis, explanatory and predictive models and fact-based management to drive decisions and outcome.[94]

[B] Purpose, Use and Benefits of Big Data

[1] Purpose

Big Data may be used to anticipate all sort of things from consumer preferences and customer creditworthiness to fraud detection, health risks[95] and crime prevention.[96,97] In tax matters, advanced analytics (Big Data Analytics) can be used for policy evaluation, for taxpayer service, for debt management, for filing and payment compliance, to predict taxpayers behaviour or the likelihood of additional tax liability following an audit (predictive analytics) or to help the tax administration understand the impact of their actions on taxpayer behaviour (prescriptive analytics).[98] According to the Compliance Risk Management Guide for Tax Administrations by the Fiscalis Risk Management Platform Group at the European Commission the then (in 2010) existing IT-based risk management tools used by tax administrations had predominantly the purpose of prioritizing risks, identifying risky taxpayers, identifying risk in general, creating risk profiles and selecting taxpayers for audit.[99] As a consequence, according to the same guide 'Compliance Risk Management asks for a **pro-active and preventive approach** to enhance the more traditional approach.'[100]

Big Data is thus supposed to allow gathering and proceeding information in a more efficient way than by the intervention of a 'simple' human brain.[101] The purpose of Big Data is prediction in order to allow targeted actions and proactive steps to tackle certain issues.

94. Thomas Davenport & Jeanne Harris, *Competing on Analytics* 7 (Harvard Business School Press 2007).
95. For a comprehensive overview of existing use cases of Big Data, *see, e.g.*, Melanie Swan, *Sensor Mania! The Internet of Things, Wearable Computing, Objective Metrics and the Quantified Self 2.0*, 1 J. Sensor and Actuator Networks 217 et seq. (2012).
96. Cathy O'Neill, *Weapons of Math Destruction: How Big Data Increases Inequality and Threatens Democracy* (Crown 2016); Philippe Vion-Dury, *La nouvelle Servitude Volontaire, Enquête sure le projet politique de la Silicon Valley* 137 et seq. (FYP Editions); *see* Cavoukian, *supra* note 23, at 5.
97. Ian Kerr & Jessica Earle, *Prediction, Preemption, Presumption: How Big Data Threatens Big Picture Privacy*, 66 Stan. L. Rev. Online 65, 66 (2013).
98. The potential of Big Data for the US Internal Revenue Service is described here: Executive Office of the President, *Big Data: Seizing Opportunities, Preserving Values*, obamawhitehouse.archives.gov, https://obamawhitehouse.archives.gov/sites/default/files/docs/big_data_privacy_report_may_1_2014.pdf (accessed 22 December 2018).
99. Commission Guide for Tax Administrations, *supra* note 11, at 92.
100. Commission Guide for Tax Administrations, *supra* note 11, at 10 (emphasis in the original).
101. In this sense, *see* Floridi, *supra* note 1, at 14 et seq.

[2] Use of Big Data

Kerr and Earle have identified three types of predictions in the context of Big Data that can support our legal analysis of Big Data in tax matters.[102] They distinguish consequential predictions, preferential predictions and pre-emptive predictions. *Consequential predictions* attempt to anticipate the likely consequences of a person's action. According to Kerr and Earle the aim of these predictions is to allow individuals to reduce risk by choosing future courses of action that best align with their self-interest, 'forestalling unfavourable outcomes'.[103] Other predictions – most of those used in the private retail sector – can be defined as *preferential predictions*. These are Big Data algorithms that are trying to identify someone's preferences in order to sell goods and services.[104] The last type of predictions Kerr and Earle have identified are *pre-emptive predictions*. They are intentionally used to diminish a person's range of future options.[105] These predictions assess the likely consequences of allowing or disallowing a person to act in a certain way. They are not concerned with an individual's actions but whether an individual or a group of individuals should be allowed to act in a certain way.[106] Kerr and Earle mention no-fly lists as an example.[107]

According to the OECD, Advanced Analytics (Big Data Analytics) can be used for policy evaluation, for taxpayer service (e.g., by mining inbound emails), for debt management and for filing and payment compliance.[108] For its use in tax matters the OECD distinguishes predictive analytics and prescriptive analytics. The former aims to anticipate likely problems – for instance with the accuracy of a tax return or the timeliness of a payment – so that the tax administration can consider which actions should be taken and when (consequential and preferential predictions). It is ultimately about pattern recognition. Prescriptive analytics aims to help the tax administration understand the impact of their actions on taxpayer behaviour, so that they can select the right course of action for any chosen taxpayer or group of taxpayers (pre-emptive predictions). It is thus about casual reasoning.[109] When governments use Big Data they are usually part of their specific risk management systems.[110] It seems thus true that prediction and risk are interrelated concepts.[111]

102. Kerr, *supra* note 95, at 66 et seq.
103. *Ibid.* at 67.
104. *Ibid.*
105. *Ibid.*
106. *Ibid.*
107. *Ibid.* at 67 et seq.
108. OECD, *Advanced Analytics for Better Tax Administration: Putting Data to Work* 17 (OECD Publishing 2016).
109. *Ibid.*
110. For the correlation between risk management and Big Data in tax matters, *see, e.g.*, Commission Guide for Tax Administrations, *supra* note 11, at 91.
111. Kerr, *supra* note 95, at 65–67; with reference to Ulrich Beck, *World Risk Society* 3 (Polity 1999), who defines risk as the modern approach to foresee and control the future consequences of human action.

If Big Data is used for tax risk management, the distinction offered by Kerr and Earle can – with a slight adaption to the particularities of government intervention – be supportive to the legal evaluation of Big Data in tax matters.[112]

[3] Benefits of Big Data

The OECD explains the benefits of Big Data in the following:

> The widespread use of inexpensive connected mobile computing devices has changed the business model from capturing transactions and analysing and inferring behaviour of customers, to measuring it directly. Instead of transaction analytics and data-driven forecasting, the commercial sector has started to use data and real-time access to customers to interact with them and provide individually tailored digital services. This ability, in association with advanced analytics, and new service delivery practices of providing data-driven actionable insight in a visually interactive and rapidly iterative agile manner, is a key benefit associated with Big Data.[113]

It is thus very likely, that Big Data in tax matters proceed cross-checking, mine data beyond those provided by the taxpayer or trusted third persons and generate or evaluate mathematical probabilities. In this respect the OECD mentions (1) analysis across multiple periods, taxpayers and tax domains. This would allow administrations to plan their compliance, control and risk management activities and improve service delivery. Moreover, it mentions (2) gathering customer insight on taxpayers' experience, preferences and behaviour, which would create highly personalized user-centred design approaches; (3) identifying and tracking changes in taxpayer abilities and performance to enable revenue bodies to respond more effectively and in a timelier manner; and (4) using predictive analytics and simulations. Predictive analytics and simulation would allow proactive analysis of taxpayer behaviour and can thus help revenue bodies save time, money and effort during risk profiling.[114] Moreover, Big Data are seen to be able to support whole-of-government outcomes by sharing of insights and information.[115]

[C] Big Data in Tax Matters: Really in Use?

Tax authorities around the world are using Big Data to organize their tax risk management systems.[116] Electronic filing of tax returns eases data processing and has

112. Acts by tax authorities towards the taxpayers are always interventions as they interfere with fundamental rights of the taxpayers such as the right to private property or privacy.
113. OECD, *supra* note 50, at 50.
114. *Ibid.* at 54.
115. OECD, *supra* note 50, at 80. – The whole-of-government approaches the OECD suggests shall not be discussed in this paper (for some idea on the suggestions, see OECD, *Improving Co-operation Between Tax and Anti-Money Laundering Authorities* (OECD Publishing 2015)). However, we would like to emphasize that these suggestions would need a thorough analysis from a fundamental rights and democratic principles perspective. Moreover, such an approach would need to be aligned to the requirements of Art. 13 para. 3 GDPR.
116. On the use of tax analytics by tax administrations, *see* Pijnenburg, *supra* note 33, at 19–32; *see* Lipniewicz, *supra* note 26, at 26–37.

been implemented in many States of the world.[117] Moreover, some States have eased data collection by imposing on taxpayers to use specific electronic devices to comply with their accounting obligations. In Croatia, Slovenia and Austria for example, all sales for cash including credit card payments have to be memorized by using specific fraud-proof electronic cash registers. In Slovenia these electronic cash registers are connected to the Ministry of Finance, which gets the information on memorized sales on a real-time basis.

With regard to the use of Big Data States have different tools in place: The Netherlands have for example prioritized their taxpayers into different 'attention categories' in order to create a basis for effective compliance risk management. The determination of the relevant attention category is fully automated.[118] Furthermore, the Netherlands Tax Administration has been running a web robot, XENON, since 2004. XENON detects unknown taxpayers as well as other probable non-compliant events, such as the unauthorized use of brand names or illegal diversion trade.[119] Another already existing Big Data tool is used in Italy: FALCO serves to detect large taxpayers to be audited. Moreover, the application allows for monitoring their behaviour also using website data.[120] FALCO contains internal and external data, most of the external data come from the Internet.[121] Another application run by the Italian Tax Administration is APPLE (Application to fight against tax evasion), an IT tool which allows to detect non-compliant taxpayers by crossing information on their taxable capacity and data declared in their returns.[122] Ireland runs an application called Risk Evaluation Analysis and Profiling (REAP) that aims at maximizing the value of data held by the Revenue for risk assessment purposes.[123] The Austrian Ministry of Finance runs a 'Predictive Analytics Competence Center' (PACC)[124] that uses Big Data and data mining to improve tax compliance management[125] and to allow more targeted actions by the tax

117. For further details, *see* the country reports in Funda Basran, *supra* note 26 – The OECD has suggested that the broad use of ICT in business transactions could be used for tax purposes: 'It is about capturing business transactions digitally and to co-ordinate this with electronic payments and electronic bookkeeping and further on with electronic reporting and payments to the government' (OECD, *supra* note 5 at 26).
118. For more details, *see* Commission Guide for Tax Administrations, *supra* note 11, at 72.
119. For further details, *see* Commission Guide for Tax Administrations, *supra* note 11, at 67 et seq.
120. Commission Guide for Tax Administrations, *supra* note 11, at 70.
121. *Ibid.*
122. For further details, *see* Commission Guide for Tax Administrations, *supra* note 11, at 65.
123. *Ibid.* at 68.
124. The Austrian Risk Management Unit's major responsibilities are the risk management process, gathering, exchange and analysis of information (including internet monitoring), development of audit and control techniques, case selection and audit plans, international cooperation in the above-mentioned areas (Commission Guide for Tax Administrations, *supra* note 11, at 96).
125. For further details, see Martin Setnicka, *Predictive Analytics in der österreichischen Finanzverwaltung, in INFORMATIK 2016* 629 (Heinrich Mayr & Martin Pinzger eds., Lecture Notes in Informatics (LNI), Gesellschaft für Informatik 2016).

authorities when fighting tax fraud.[126] Further examples of Big Data applications in tax matters can be found in the Compliance-By-Design-Study of the OECD.[127]

§13.04 LEGAL CONCERNS

[A] Introduction

The aforementioned OECD reports contain one common disclaimer: The proposed measures have to fit into the respective legal frameworks, and there might be fundamental rights restrictions to be tackled.[128] However, at least some States that use Big Data Analytics for tax matters do not seem to have fundamentally changed their legal statutes on tax collection and enforcement. Can it be envisaged that the use of Big Data Analytics does not raise new legal concerns, that it fits into the traditional tax collection and enforcement schemes?

In order to answer this question we will first depict the vision the OECD seems to have on the subject matter. Then, two approaches shall be illustrated: According to the first Big Data Analytics do not change anything in the traditional tax collection and enforcement scheme. According to the latter Big Data Analytics is new to a large extent. The latter is the position we take. Based on this position we will elaborate on the legal actions to be taken.

[B] The OECD's Vision of Big Data Benefits in Tax Matters

The OECD envisions that the use of Big Data technologies will allow 'to ingest transactional data and to move taxation to the point of transaction, thus to remove the need for filing of most tax returns'. According to the OECD this is due to the fact that taxes are mostly by-product of business transactions performed by taxpayers. The OECD further states that 'in the future, tax audit may not be seen as a separate process anymore, but may fall into categories such as "monitoring and analysis", "system assessment" and "customer interaction"'.[129]

Furthermore, according to the OECD, Big Data processing technologies allow revenue bodies to examine and review all transactions across the wider economy and industry groups and compare, and not just analyse, risks of selected taxpayers, allowing revenue bodies to 'move from analysing historic transactions to a position

126. Austrian Finance Department, Instrumente zur Betrugsbekämpfung (anti-fraud instruments), bmf.gv.at, https://www.bmf.gv.at/betrugsbekaempfung/instrumente/betrugsbekaempfungs instrumente.html#heading_Predictive_Analytics_Competence_Center__PACC (accessed 23 December 2018).

127. OECD, *Tax Compliance By Design: Achieving Improved Tax Compliance By Adopting A System Perspective* 32–36 et seq. (OECD Publishing 2014).

128. OECD, *Technologies for Better Tax Administration: A Practical Guide for Revenue Bodies* 49 (OECD Publishing 2016).

129. OECD, *supra* note 36 at 24.

where they can review near real-time interactions with taxpayers both on the compliance and service sides of business'.[130]

The use of Big Data for tax purposes is embedded in a more far-reaching vision of the OECD. In its executive summary to the Technology for a Better Tax Administration Report the OECD outlines the following:

> Big Data technology offers revenue bodies the opportunity to extract better business value out of existing data. Investment in new capabilities creates the possibility to develop new and convenient services for taxpayers, along with the ability to create new tools that will help the administration provide proactive services; better manage and address tax risks including tax avoidance, evasion and fraud; and improve other targeted activities including debt collection or making social payments. ... Further, these technologies also offer administrations the opportunity to differentiate services on the inherent risk of a transaction, a taxpayer or an event.[131]

To the OECD, Big Data collected by revenue bodies, when combined with a transparent approach to data, offers tax administrations the opportunity to contribute to improve the lives of citizens and countries' economies.[132]

In a more recent report the OECD gets even more subtle: 'The combination of technological developments and the integration of data into redesigned tax administration systems, including third-party data used by taxpayers in their day-to-day life, have the potential **to make tax administration close to invisible to many taxpayers.**'[133] Furthermore, the OECD speaks of a transition to an organization that sources information from third parties and uses this to determine when and how it interacts with a taxpayer.[134] Moreover, the OECD states: 'Embedding compliance, including upfront verification, in the design of tax administration systems should substantially reduce administrative burdens, freeing up taxpayer and tax administration resource, while improving overall compliance.'[135]

The vision derived from an accumulation of different OECD papers requires – among others – a real-time connection between the taxpayer and the tax authorities, which can be realized either by steady observation of the taxpayer or through IoT devices. Moreover, it requires data cross-checking of multiple taxpayers. If paying taxes shall become close to invisible, more 'convenient', to many taxpayers, someone else than the taxpayer must deal with the tax consequences of a taxpayers' economic activities. According to the OECD this should be – in addition to third parties – the tax

130. OECD, *supra* note 50, at 53 et seq.
131. *Ibid.* at 12.
132. *Ibid.* at 41.
133. OECD, *Tax Administration 2017: Comparative Information on OECD and Other Advanced and Emerging Economies* 190 (OECD Publishing 2017; emphasis added).
134. OECD, Technologies for Better Tax Administration: A Practical Guide for Revenue Bodies 64 (OECD Publishing 2016).
135. OECD, *Tax Administration 2017: Comparative Information on OECD and Other Advanced and Emerging Economies* 190 (OECD Publishing 2017).

administration itself. With IoT devices and data analytics this can become possible in many cases. Administrative burdens can be reduced by 'designing' algorithms that replace direct human intervention. Overall compliance can only be improved if these algorithms get more information than humans (external to the taxable event) and can react timelier than humans. Widespread real-time connection of the taxable event to the tax authority could help achieve this goal.

Traditionally, there have been important legal constraints when including third parties into tax collection. They primarily focussed on the concern of not excessively burdening people with the duties of others and on privacy issues.[136] With the use of secured IoT devices these concerns could be reduced. However, sourcing information either from third parties or in real time through 'monitoring' IoT devices affect taxpayers' control over the data and his sovereignty in deciding on which information to provide or not to provide. This must not lead to a status of surveillance, the point at which the 'freeing of the taxpayer' argument would turn out to be a poisonous gift.

The core question is, whether this concept still strikes the traditional balance between the public (collective) interest in tax collection and the individual interest in preserving personal autonomy. Moreover, it is to be decided whether an invisible but efficient and effective tax administration is desirable in a free society. How should the individual be able to challenge the law or tax administration's behaviour if it is invisible?

With a look to this vision, it seems very unlikely to call the changes brought by Big Data to be nothing new. However, some – including the OECD itself – do.

[C] Position 1: Big Data Analytics Do Not Raise Any Legal Concerns

Despite the concerns raised above, the OECD and some authors argue that Big Data Analytics do not change the traditional way to collect and enforce taxes. Big Data Analytics would thus not raise any legal concerns.

One argument in favour of this position is that tax administrations have always been using statistics for deciding on the cases to audit more closely. Moreover, algorithms are said to be much more precise than human brains. As algorithms are able to process much larger amounts of data than human brains can do in a systematic way, they are said to give much more accurate results than pure human brains. Conversely

136. OECD, *supra* note 36 at 39. In this report, the OECD highlights how obliging third parties to withhold taxes increases their costs on compliance. Withholding represents a way of shifting costs from the tax authorities on third parties without easing detection. This cost shifting can be inappropriate and thus at odds with fundamental constitutional principles. Moreover, in some States there is a variety of constitutional courts case law drawing the line between licit obligation of third parties in governmental duties and illicit one. Taking advantage of a personal relationship of a third party and a taxpayer can constitute – depending on the specific situation – an excessive interference with the right to privacy.

to machines humans can be biased, they can be tired, sick, in a bad mood or have some personal problems with certain groups of taxpayers.

Moreover, algorithms can at least compensate the lack of accurate verification of all taxpayers due to the lack of government resources for staff. They are thought to be cheaper and thus more efficient.[137] Accordingly, the OECD report concludes that in the normal day-to-day work tax administrations are constantly making predictions and coming to conclusions about the likely impact of their activities. Advanced analytics – in the opinion of the OECD – does not aim to achieve anything fundamentally new, but it seeks to carry out these same tasks with more reliance on data and less reliance on human judgment.[138] As tax laws require equal treatment of all taxpayers (under the respect of the ability to pay principle) the use of Big Data Analytics can thus cover more taxpayers more efficiently. Consequently, they contribute to the legal duty of treating all taxpayers equally in a much better way than pure human intervention would. As a result, when humans take decisions without any 'technical' assistance the risk of a suboptimal result would be higher than with Big Data Analytics.[139] Consequently, having machines doing analytics for efficient tax control could be considered to be even more egalitarian than any pure human intervention.

Under these assumptions the legal framework of data and information collection and processing for tax purposes dating from times before Big Data Analytics could be assumed to be sufficient.[140] The use of Big Data Analytics in tax matters would then not raise any legal concerns.

Although some authors[141] and the OECD[142] argue that Big Data Analytics does not achieve anything fundamentally new – at least when it comes to the type of activities carried out by a tax administration,[143] they all identify privacy and ethical issues as concerns. The following section will thus outline potential concerns with the use of Big Data Analytics in tax matters. It will deny the validity of position 1 and set the ground for legal actions to be taken.

---

137. On this arguments in general, see Danielle Keats Citron, *Technological Due Process*, 85 Wash U. L. Rev. 1249, 1252 et seq. (2008).
138. OECD, *Technologies for a Better Tax Administration: A Practical Guide for Revenue Bodies* 86 (OECD Publishing 2016).
139. Michael Lewis, *The Undoing Project* (W.W. Norton & Company 2017); critical Shaw, *supra* note 49.
140. In Austria, e.g., the legal provisions on tax collection and enforcement date from the 1940s and were only very rudimentarily amended, when Big Data Analytics started to be used. The 'old' tools were supposed to be sufficient (*see* presentation slides Madlberger, https://www.oeffentlicherdienst.gv.at/verwaltungsinnovation/innovate2016.html/Streams/Innovatives_Risikomanagement_mit_Predicitve_Analytics.pdf; checked on 26 November 2018).
141. *See* Pijnenburg, *supra* note 33, at 31.
142. OECD, *supra* note 50, at 49:

> While there are obvious ethical and privacy issues that need to be addressed, data integration and analytics are now allowing the more accurate profiling of individuals and companies. It is also opening up new opportunities to create new, customised products or services on a mass basis or at individual customer level.

143. Pijnenburg, *supra* note 33, at 30; OECD, *supra* note 136, at 86.

[D] Position 2: Big Data Analytics Raise Legal Concerns

[1] Concerns Related to the Technical Functioning of Big Data Algorithms

[a] Preliminary Remarks

Big Data algorithms are not superhumans that have just come to earth without emotional and physical biases because they lack a body similar to the human body. Big Data Analytics tools have been created by humans,[144] simple humans with emotional biases and personal values and beliefs like all humans of this world have.

[b] Technical Specificities of Big Data Algorithms

Be it rule-based or deep-learning algorithms, data analytics are always correlation based: Input data get transformed into output data and programmers or the algorithm itself define rules on how this transformation has to be done.[145] Algorithms thus compare new data to existing data in order to identify similar patterns. They are necessarily founded on the past. To a certain extent decisions by humans are also correlation based, when it comes to past experience. Unlike algorithms humans can falsify, verify and connect dots through causality rather than pure correlation.[146] Moreover, humans can invent the future without having to rely on the past.[147]

From a technical perspective rule-based algorithms have the structure of decision trees. Consequently, every decision taken by this type of algorithm is programmed in advance and fully reproducible. Rule-based algorithms can only perform what they were programmed for.[148] With the increased and still increasing amount of data available rule-based algorithms have become more and more complicated and thus increasingly vulnerable to malfunctions.[149]

New methods of programming, such as deep-learning, promise to be more adaptive to increasing complexity of data. The functioning of deep-learning methods is similar to the human brain. Deep-learning methods are based on neural network theory. Neural networks consist of (artificial) neurones that are connected on different layers.[150] These layers constitute multiple levels of representation allowing to transform the representation at one level into a representation at a higher, slightly more

144. As Erik Bryonjolfsson and Andrew McAffee put it, technology is not destiny. It is humans who shape their destiny (Erik Bryonjolfsson & Andrew McAffee, *The Second Machine Age* 257 (W.W. Norton & Company 2016)).
145. *See* Christian Joachim Gruber & Iris Eisenberger, *Wenn Fahrzeuge selbst lernen*, *in Autonomes Fahren und Recht* 54 (Iris Eisenberger et al. eds., Manz Verlag 2017).
146. To put it with Bryonjolfsson, *supra* note 142, at 242: '*Even though algorithms are getting better, they can't do it alone.*'
147. O'Neill, *supra* note 94, at 204.
148. Lawrence Lessig, *Code 2.0,* 62 et seq. (Basic Books 2d rev. ed. 2006).
149. Gruber, *supra* note 143, at 55 et seq.
150. *Ibid.* at 57.

abstract level. This allows the algorithm to learn complex functions.[151] Contrary to rule-based algorithms the different layers of features of deep-learning algorithms are not designed by human programmers, but learned from data using a general-purpose learning procedure.[152]

Deep-learning algorithms need to be trained by interacting with their environment and getting bonuses for welcome behaviour. As a result, contrary to rule-based algorithms, machine learning algorithms are not based on predefined decision trees, but the neural network is created on the basis of the input[153] data. Deep-learning, representation learning to be more precise, allows a machine that has been trained on the basis of a sufficient complex set of data to be fed with raw data and to automatically discover representations needed for detection or classification. Consequently, decisions are developed in a more or less autonomous way. The rules a deep-learning algorithm infers from the patterns it observes through 'training' by exposure to a large quantity of data are not induced by a human programmer.[154] On the contrary, the core value and the core basis for rule-making of deep-learning algorithms are the data. The more accurate the data and the more diligent the training of the algorithm, the less malfunctions are to be expected. Data processed by deep-learning algorithms do in general not allow to single out the individual data at the origin of the outcome of the analysis. Contrarily to rule-based algorithms their 'reasoning' is not fully reproducible.

Deep-learning algorithms can be either supervised or unsupervised learners. Unsupervised learning does not involve a training person nor does it supervise the sourcing of data. Unsupervised deep-learning algorithms do not constitute a legal option for tax authorities. To allow unsupervised deep-learning algorithms to prepare, support or supplant decisions of tax officers would be the same as allowing anyone without any particular education to be a tax officer. We thus only include supervised deep-learning algorithms into our analysis.

Big Data Analytics uses large amounts of data, which are mined at different places. Given its large-scale and totally structured proceeding Big Data Analytics cannot be equalized with the activity of single tax officer, who himself might proceed in a structured way, too, but a single tax officer can neither mine nor scrutinize as many data as an algorithm can. Moreover, the algorithms' results take effect at much larger scale, since an algorithm is able to proceed more data in a structured way than a single tax officer can.

[c] Prediction

Prediction is always an anticipation of a future event, that is not certain to occur. Big Data predictions rely on probability assumptions. Since Big Data base their outcomes

151. For further details, see Yann LeCun, Yoshua Bengio & Geoffrey Hinton, *Deep-learning*, 521 Nature 436 (2015).
152. *Ibid.*
153. Gruber, *supra* note 143, at 60.
154. Joshua Kroll, Joanna Huey & Solon Borocas, *Accountable Algorithms*, 165 U. Penn. L. Rev. 42 (2016) – For examples of how discriminatory effects can be produced through machine learning, *see ibid.* at 43 et seq.

on the analysis of correlations, their evaluations can never provide certainty, but only probability.[155] Whereas this is inherent to future events, it is not necessarily inherent to past events. For the past, there are normally ways to get certainty. In tax matters, however, nowadays at least, the before-described information asymmetry between the taxpayer and the tax administration cannot be totally overcome. In a democratic society that respects individual autonomy and thus privacy including areas of anonymity, certainty will be rarely acquired by tax authorities.

In order to strike the balance between these conflicting interests, collection and enforcement rules normally contain burden of proof provisions and assumption provisions in case proof cannot be provided. As a consequence, tax authorities have been working with probabilities even before digitalization. Prediction has thus always been part of tax authorities' daily work and is not a new phenomenon of ICT.

[d] Opacity

The algorithms' codes are in general not open source. Their functioning, the underlying assumptions and values are hidden to the public. For deep-learning algorithms the disclosure of the code would even not contribute to sufficient transparency because their functioning depends on the patterns the algorithm derives by itself - without a specific code - from the data it observes and the data it has been trained with.

Opacity prevents from understanding the reasoning underlying a certain outcome. From a legal perspective the use of opaque algorithms by tax authorities can be problematic. Opacity of the algorithms' functioning prevents a taxpayer from effectively challenging a decision taken or prepared by that algorithm. This opens doors for misuse, abuse or arbitrariness in taxation.

Transparency - if at all possible[156] - would certainly mitigate these concerns. However, disclosing the core functioning of the algorithm in tax matters would - given that algorithms' outcomes are based on probabilities and that they do not provide for overall monitoring of all taxpayers - incentivize cheating the system. The danger of cheating the system in case of transparent codes does not, however, justify their total opacity. We will come back to this point under §13.05[B][4].

[e] Algorithms Magnify Programmed Biases

Programmers and trainers are humans and are thus susceptible of feeding their own biases into the algorithms' code, if left without legal framing. The programmers' and eventually the trainers' biases become then part of the algorithms core functioning.[157] This can entail discriminatory effects. One might argue that it does not make a difference whether it is the programmer of an algorithm or the somehow biased tax

155. Viktor Mayer-Schönberger & Kenneth Cukier, *Big Data: A Revolution That Will Transform How We Live, Work, and Think* 53 (John Murray 2013), with reference to Nassim Nicholas Taleb, *The Black Swan* (Random House 2007); De Filippi, *supra* note 48, at 115.
156. *See* before §13.04[D][1][b].
157. O'Neill, *supra* note 94; Citron, *supra* note 135, at 1262.

officer preparing and taking a decision. It is true that tax officers are humans like programmers and are thus very likely to be biased, similarly. Besides the fact that programmers are in general not legally trained,[158] the difference between the tax officers' bias and the programmers' or trainers' bias induced to the algorithm lies in the effects biases in algorithms can entail: Algorithms proceed much larger amounts of data and cover taxpayers at high scale in a constantly structured way which is no way comparable to the activity of a biased human. Combined with an opaque code potential biases induced in the algorithms constitute a serious threat to the rule of law, the principle of equality and the rights of the defence.

[2] Input Data-Related Concerns

[a] Origin of the Data

Data used by Big Data algorithms can originate from very different sources. Under the current tax systems, the taxpayer constitutes the most important, in many cases the only source of data and information. Another important source of information and for data are trusted third parties. Tax collection and enforcement systems are having a long statute-based experience of including third parties into tax collection and enforcement. If Big Data algorithms use this data and information, their origin is known by the taxpayer and the respective rules providing this data and information normally contain appropriate safeguards to ensure their accuracy.

But Big Data algorithms source further data and information from either internet monitoring (*see* above the description of the use cases in different European States §13.03[C]) or potentially from interceptions of communication. Both internet monitoring and interceptions of communication raise questions from a fundamental rights perspective. In both cases it has to be asked whether there is an interference with the right to respect for private and family life and communication. In the affirmative, it needs to be seen whether the interference is in accordance with Article 8 paragraph 2 ECHR and Charter Article 52(1).

[b] Accuracy of the Data

Traditional tax collection and enforcement schemes rely on data provided by the taxpayer herself or by trusted third parties. Accuracy of this data from the rights of the defence perspective is therefore likely. If tax authorities happen to use further data they want to base their evaluation or decision on, they have to previously hear the taxpayer. With Big Data Analytics this is hardly possible because the origins of the data or the data themselves are not always clear. The OECD calls this 'accessing and utilising Big Data that they [*the tax authorities*] neither generate nor control'.[159]

158. A fact that could be overcome by accompanying the programmer by a lawyer.
159. OECD, *supra* note 50, at 83.

Another concern that the use of Big Data Analytics in tax matters can raise, if not properly framed, is the 'age' of the data used. The GDPR guarantees the 'right to be forgotten'.[160] This right is not new, with the rise of ICT it just got a new dimension. In general, tax authorities are entitled to store (be it automated or not) personal taxpayer data and information only as long as they might need it for tax collection and enforcement. The time of prescription is generally the moment when taxpayer information must not be kept by the tax authorities anymore. The right to be forgotten is based on modern democracies' fundamental concept of personal autonomy, which encompasses the right to free choice and consequently personal responsibility for any behaviour. Free choice encloses the right to choose being different, acting differently, changing behaviours. People must thus be given the chance to change their behaviour. Prescription rules serve (among others) this purpose. If past behaviour predetermines the way the tax administration interacts with a taxpayer because past behaviour is assumed to predict future behaviour, change is hardly possible. Consequently, the use of past behaviour to predict future behaviour without any time limit affects the right to privacy (Article 8 ECHR and Charter Article 7). This is contrary to the GDPR and more generally attempts the concept of personal autonomy and individual freedom.

[c] Cross-Checking of Data

Furthermore, cross-checking of data, which is regularly done in Big Data Analytics, can raise legal concerns, if not properly framed. An algorithm not correctly coded can lead to treat taxpayers in equal situations unequally. A creative and innovative taxpayer could for example not fall within any of the patterns the algorithm identified and could then be 'scored' as a danger for the public revenue.

[3] Concerns Related to the Psychological Impact of Big Data Algorithms

Another bias to be taken into account when using Big Data Analytics in tax collection and enforcement is the so-called automation bias. If an algorithm displays a certain outcome, people tend to be inhibited to question its accuracy, even if objectively it seems inaccurate. This is called 'automation bias'.[161] The existence of the automation bias should not lead to the conclusion that algorithm-prepared material is less accurate than 'simple' human investigations. By contrast to a decision based on the latter, the bias of machine-based decisions is known: People tend to trust machine-based outcomes more than pure human research and are thus reluctant to verify machine-based outcomes by further (human) investigations.[162] Automation biases may be

160. Article 17 GDPR.
161. Citron, *supra* note 135, at 1271.
162. *Ibid.* at 1271 et seq.

overcome by specific measures, whereas human biases are in general too diverse and multiple-sided to be efficiently tackled. However, the automation bias is to be taken seriously because malfunctions of an algorithm create wrong (maybe illegal) decisions at large scale, whereas human biases occur at smaller scale and not in a comparably structured and generalized way.

[4] Conclusion

Algorithms can source, collect and proceed data in a way that differs from the traditional collection of information and data. As a result, the use of Big Data Analytics by tax authorities entails, without any doubt, a fundamental change in tax collection and enforcement.

If human reasoning and machine reasoning are not identical, legal evaluation needs at first a decision on whether a just legal system really needs human reasoning to enforce laws. Why can human reasoning and intervention not be replaced by algorithms or at least algorithm-driven decisions?

The answer will probably be unequivocal: Whether human reasoning can be replaced by algorithms in legal matters seems to depend on the purpose, the way a machine is being used and its technical functioning.

The purposes of using algorithms in law can be manifold. It can be simple storage of data or information, audit selection, treatment of law addressees in the future and/or collection of the taxes. The interferences with personal autonomy are the more important the more targeted actions are taken because of a certain outcome of Big Data Analytics.[163]

With regard to the way an algorithm can be used, it can be either used as an assistant for a decision by an executive or as replacement. Furthermore, the way data or information are sourced by an algorithm might make a difference from a legal perspective. It makes a difference whether an algorithm proceeds only data it sourced from the taxpayer himself and certain trusted third parties, or whether it sources its data from IoT devices or mines them from untrusted third parties such as the Internet. To comply with the legal prerequisites of a free democratic society, there is need for legal framing of data mining that assures the respect of the rule of law and mitigates discriminatory effects.

Furthermore, due to the differences in the comprehensiveness of their technical functioning, rule-based algorithms and deep-learning algorithms cannot be looked at equally, when their use aims at implementing or enforcing laws.

On the grounds of the identified criteria the use of algorithms by tax authorities needs to be checked against its compatibility with the rule of law, the principle of equality, the right to privacy and the rights of the defence.

163. In this sense more generally De Filippi, *supra* note 48, at 119.

§13.05 LEGAL ACTIONS TO TAKE

[A] Introduction

The main challenge in tackling the legal concerns raised above resides in properly striking the balance between personal autonomy and the public interest in effective taxation. Without personal autonomy and a certain degree of anonymity, the concept of a liberal democracy cannot be effectuated. However, leaving the individual without any legal boundaries in the development of his or her personality would - according to most - lead to anarchy and thus undermine the functioning of a society as a hole. Balancing such competing interests requires a compromise. A free society thus accepts limitations of freedom on the one hand and defaults of effectiveness on the other. The acceptance of defaults is mirrored by the fact that technological feasibility and unquestionable effectiveness are not sufficient to justify any interference with personal autonomy. Where technical feasibility and unquestionable effectiveness would totally destroy personal autonomy without seriously putting society in danger, they are illicit.

[B] Rule of Law, Principle of Equality, Rights of the Defence

[1] Basic Requirements on Big Data Analytics

A core ingredient for functioning democracies is responsibility of the State actors. This entails that the executive, the tax authorities in this context, are bound by definite legal rules set up by parliament and that their behaviour can be controlled by an independent body, that is the judiciary.[164] The addressee of public intervention must be able to understand why certain decisions are taken, he must be able to identify potential breaches of the rule of law or potential discriminations. The same holds true for algorithms that are used by and thus attributable to the State, regardless of whether they serve as supports or supplants of State officers.

If the taxpayer does not know, which assumptions fed the functioning of an algorithm he cannot identify potential breaches of the law or interferences with the fundamental principles of law (such as the principle of equality). Challenging the law is impossible without clear rules and without the legal obligation to disclose the assumptions underlying a decision. The opacity of nowadays' Big Data Analytics systems does not allow for review of the underlying code. If decisions are taken on the basis of these analytics, the opacity destroys one of the core elements of a democratic society, the possibility to debate and to have rules reviewed on their accordance with the rule of law.[165]

The principle of equality prohibits to treat alike situations differently and different situations alike, unless justified by overarching principles in the public interest. Opacity of the code does not contribute to identify potential discriminations.

164. In this sense, *see* Kerr, *supra* note 95, at 70.
165. In this sense, *see* Citron, *supra* note 135, at 1249.

From a rights of the defence perspective, the taxpayer must be heard on the outcomes of Big Data Analytics before a decision based on this outcome is taken. He must be given the opportunity to challenge the presumptions made by the algorithm. When Big Data Analytics are increasingly being used to make decisions about individual people, those people have a right to know on which assumptions these decisions are based.[166]

Regardless of their use, to ensure compliance with the rule of law, the principle of equality and the rights of the defence, algorithms used for tax collection and enforcement have to meet three fundamental requirements: There must be clarity about the origin of the data ([2]), the data must be accurate ([3]) and the outcome of the analytics must be justified, which presupposes either transparency of the code or procedural regularity ([4]). Furthermore, the right to privacy must be respected ([C]).

[2] Origin of the Data

As outlined above (§13.04[D][2][a]) there should be no specific concerns on the use of data and information provided by the taxpayer himself or a trusted third party, if the providing of such data or information is framed by a legal statute. The taxpayer then knows that the tax administration is in possession of this data or this information. Using only taxpayer and trusted third-party data would, however, not be a use case of Big Data Analytics (*see* above §13.03[A]).

When it comes to internet monitoring and interception of communication, privacy concerns must be tackled. Only if this kind of sourcing is in line with the prerogatives of Article 8 of the Human Rights Convention, the basic requirements for licit Big Data Analytics in tax matters are met. The respective prerogatives will be analysed under §13.05[C].

[3] Accuracy of the Data

The OECD recommends to actively engage with providers in order to improve 'the quality and accuracy of information' and envisages that allowing taxpayers to review and provide feedback 'on the accuracy or otherwise of personal information held by the tax administration' would significantly reduce errors and inconsistencies. According to the OECD the interaction with the taxpayer on his data would additionally 'help strengthen the trust relationship between the tax administration and the taxpayer, and reinforce that data accuracy is a joint responsibility'.[167] It remains unclear how the taxpayer shall be held jointly responsible for data mined outside his sphere of influence. Moreover, the ex post checking of the data accuracy by the taxpayer could be difficult if the analytics tool (such as a deep-learning algorithm) has 'mixed' all data up.

---

166. Neil Richards & Jonathan Kings, *Three Paradoxes of Big Data*, 66 Stan. L. Rev. Online 41, 43 (2013).
167. OECD, *supra* note 50, at 83.

Moreover, the OECD stresses that involving the taxpayer in the review and validation of data could be difficult, and therefore 'judgment needs to be exercised in determining which Big Data sources a tax administration would allow its taxpayers to view and validate, but the principle of involving taxpayers in the review and validation of their data appears sound'.[168] From a rights of the defence perspective the OECD's approach to undisclose certain information at the basis of an algorithm-driven outcome raises serious concerns: The right to be heard demands to hear the taxpayer on the facts the tax authorities intend to base their decision on. Data sourced and processed by Big Data Analytics must thus be disclosed to the taxpayer. However, the moment of disclosure could be deferred if there is serious public concern that early disclosure might undermine public intervention. This applies particularly to criminal offences.

There should not be any justification for not disclosing data concerning the taxpayer used by an algorithm. An algorithm that does not allow to identify the data at the origin of a certain outcome must then not be used. Its use would not allow for a justified decision required by the rule of law, the principle of equality and the rights of the defence. Moreover, it would be contrary to the requirements of the GDPR. It must be ensured by law that algorithms that support or constitute the decisions of tax authorities operate with accurate data that can be verified by the taxpayer concerned.[169] This holds fully true for the personal data directly concerning the taxpayer. If certain outcomes of an algorithm result from the cross-checking of the concerned taxpayers' personal data with data of other taxpayers, the right to privacy of these other taxpayers must be respected. This requires to not disclose the single data of these other taxpayers. For this kind of data an aggregated disclosure (which would basically not induce privacy concerns of these other taxpayers) could be sufficient. However, Internet mining by deep-learning algorithms should then – under today's technical standards which do not allow to extract the single data used – not be possible.

The 'age' of the data can be seen as another perspective of data accuracy: If an algorithm uses data that are 'outdated' because a taxpayer has changed his behaviour and then used for the prediction of future behaviour, these data are inaccurate. They cannot reflect the taxpayer's situation anymore. This idea is fully in line with the concept of the GDPR, which enshrines the right to be forgotten in its Article 17. This right calls for a maximum storage time for data, meaning that after a certain time limit, which could be prescription of tax duties, data must not be used for data mining anymore. From the perspective of Big Data Analytics this is of course counter-intuitive because it entails a significant loss of data, and the more data available the more accurate the analysis. However, when personal taxpayer data are concerned, the prohibition to use data of a certain age is the necessary trade-off to properly balance the individual right of privacy and personal autonomy and the public interest in using Big Data to fight tax fraud and to preserve equal taxation among all taxable persons. Similarly, on bulk interceptions of communication the ECHR requires to take reasonable steps to ensure that the authorities proceeding such interceptions have and will maintain the necessary procedures to safeguard the intercepted material, and to ensure

168. *Ibid.*
169. *See* point 71 of the preliminary remarks of GDPR.

that it is disclosed, copied, distributed and retained only to the minimum extent necessary. Moreover, the intercepted material must be destroyed when no longer necessary.[170]

Using standardized ICT, such as specific electronic cash registers, to source tax-relevant information could support data mining and information sourcing in a structured way and on a supervised basis and at the same time avoid problems of accuracy.

However, there is a distinction to be made between the obligation to disclose taxpayer-related data and the obligation to disclose the functioning of the algorithm.

[4] Procedural Regularity

The rule of law, the principle of equality and the rights of the defence require the results of an algorithm to be equally logic and comprehensive. Transparency of the code and of the data feeding the algorithm in the specific case would meet these requirements. Whereas data must be fully disclosed, transparency of the code would, in tax matters, contravene the aim of Big Data Analytics to fight tax fraud.[171] If the code is totally transparent to the taxpayers, taxpayers can adapt their behaviour and cheat the system. Moreover, to understand the functioning of deep-learning algorithms used for Big Data Analytics the pure inspection of the source code would constitute a limited way of predicting its behaviour.[172] As stressed before, deep-learning devices often generate the decisional rule from the data under analysis. Insights in the code would thus not be of great support to transparency of the decisions. Transparency of the code is thus impossible for efficiency and effectiveness reasons on the one hand and on the other not suited to comply with the legal requirements when it comes to deep-learning algorithms.

Are there tools other than transparency of the code to allow compliance with the outlined legal requirements?

According to Kroll et al, computer systems could be designed for what they call procedural regularity.[173] The cited authors describe how lawmakers and policymakers could make algorithms accountable without the evaluator having full access to the algorithm.

For tax purposes procedural regularity would require as a baseline that each taxpayer or other person with tax duties can be sure that the same procedure of information sourcing and processing was applied to him and that the procedure was not designed in a way that disadvantages him specifically. Tax auditing risk assessment should thus not single out individuals either by name or by identifying characteristics.[174] For rule-based algorithms it is argued, that, in order to not create false

170. *Big Brother Watch and Others* v *the United Kingdom*, nos 58170/13, 62322/14 and 24960/15, 13 September 2018, § 367.
171. *See also* Kroll, *supra* note 152, at 23.
172. *Ibid.* at 6.
173. *Ibid.* at 26 et seq.
174. *Ibid.* at 22 ft. 72.

predictions and thus create inequalities that can raise serious legal concerns, feedback loops and regular revision of the codes are necessary.[175] Moreover, to allow proper review it would be necessary to legally set up the obligation for coders of Big Data algorithms to maintain audit trails that record the facts and rules supporting a computer programs' decision.[176]

The design of a computer system is not given.[177] Consequently, algorithms can be subject to legal rules in order to comply with certain fundamental rights and policy prerogatives.[178] As regards rule-based algorithms it would be necessary to assure that the code is programmed in line with the fundamental principles a fair legal system requires. This could be assured if the code itself is programmed by the authorities on their own which entails their own responsibility as representatives of the executive order. Alternatively, the code could be developed under the only supervision of the public authorities. Similar to standard setting for cars and other devices that entail specific dangers for either society or individuals, there should be common, legally founded standards for coding algorithms in use by the public authorities. These standards would need to be accompanied by the mentioned tools to ensure procedural regularity in order to allow control.

As regards deep-learning algorithms the target of legal action cannot be or cannot only be the code. For them it is essential that the training data and consequently the trainers comply with the fundamental principles of law and of tax collection and enforcement, more specifically. If there are clear rules on which data can be used by deep-learning algorithms and if the trainers are State officials or at least people that can be attributed to the State, the risk of feeding illegal beliefs into the systems should be minimized. However, there need to be tools of control. The initial training data can be controlled. The results of the algorithm derived from the analysis of these data can be controlled, either. Competent humans can look at these results and evaluate whether they seem accurate or not. It could be envisaged that the introduction of a deep-learning algorithm in public intervention such as tax collection and enforcement requires a preliminary 'quality check' by either a newly created independent body or a judge. Moreover, it would be necessary to have subsequent checks by an independent body on a regular basis. To supplant human tax officers' decisions with deep-learning algorithms evaluations would thus raise concerns.

[C] Privacy

[1] Preliminary Remarks

When tax authorities proceed Internet monitoring or monitor the information provided by IoT devices (such as electronic cash registers) or even want to intercept taxpayers' communication, they interfere with the right to privacy, thus with Article 8 ECHR.

175. *Ibid.* at 633–704.
176. On the general problem of lacking audit trails, *see* Citron, *supra* note 135, at 1277.
177. *See* Kroll, *supra* note 152, at 27.
178. *See* in this sense Lessig, *supra* note 146, at 78 et seq.

Moreover, the processing and cross-checking of data for the purpose of administrative intervention may constitute profiling under Article 4 Nr. 4 GDPR and may thus be subject to specific safeguards.

[2] Taxpayer Monitoring

[a] Justifying Interferences with the Right to Privacy in General

The use of Big Data Analytics, whatever kind of analytics it is, constitutes an interference with Article 8 ECHR. According to its paragraph 2 such interferences are legitimate, if set up in accordance with the law. 'In accordance with the law' does not only require that the impugned measure should have some basis in the domestic law. It also refers to the quality of this law, demanding that it should be accessible to the person concerned. Moreover, this person must be able to foresee its consequences for him or for her, and the law must be compatible with the rule of law.[179] The ECHR has expressly not distinguished between generalized strategic monitoring and monitoring of individuals when developing the prerequisites for foreseeability.[180]

In the context of measures of surveillance foreseeability does not mean that an individual should be able to foresee when the authorities are likely to intercept his communications so that he can adapt his or her conduct accordingly.[181] The condition of foreseeability does not require States to set out exhaustively by name the specific offences which may give rise to interception, provided that there is sufficient detail about the nature of the offences in question.[182] Furthermore, the ECHR has expressly recognized the need to avoid excessive rigidity in the wording of certain statutes to keep pace with changing circumstances.[183]

[b] Legitimacy of Taxpayer Monitoring

When it comes to Internet monitoring, it could be argued that data visible to anyone on the Internet can be used by tax authorities without the need for any specific legal

179. *For example, Malone* v *the United Kingdom*, no. 8691/79, 2 August 1984, § 67; *Kruslin* v *France*, no. 11801/85; 24 April 1990, § 26; *Kopp* v *Switzerland*, no. 10842/84, 25 March 1998, § 55; *Amann* v *Switzerland* (GC), no. 27798/95, 16 February 2000, § 50; *Association for European Integration and Human Rights and Ekimdzhiev* v *Bulgaria*, no. 62540/00, 28 June 2007, § 71.
180. *Liberty and Others* v *the United Kingdom*, no. 58243/00, 1 July 2008, § 63.
181. *Leander* v *Sweden*, no. 9248/81, 26 March 1987, § 51; *Kennedy* v *the United Kingdom*, no. 26839/05, 18 May 2010, § 152; *Weber and Saravia* v *Germany*, no. 54934/00, 29 June 2006, § 93.
182. *Big Brother Watch and Others* v *the United Kingdom*, nos 58170/13, 62322/14 and 24960/15, 13 September 2018, § 332; *Roman Zakharov* v *Russia* (GC), no. 47143/06, 4 December 2015, §§ 243–244; *Szabó and Vissy* v *Hungary*, no. 37138/14, 12 January 2016, § 64; *Kennedy* v *the United Kingdom*, no. 26839/05, 18 May 2010, § 159.
183. *Szabó and Vissy* v *Hungary*, no. 37138/14, 12 January 2016, § 64; *Kokkinakis* v *Greece*, no. 14307/88, 25 May 1993, § 40; *Big Brother Watch and Others* v *the United Kingdom*, nos 58170/13, 62322/14 and 24960/15, 13 September 2018, § 332.

framing. The ECHR clearly distinguished between watching a persons' activities in public and processing the information or data derived from this activity:

> A person who walks down the street will, inevitably, be visible to any member of the public who is also present. Monitoring by technological means of the same public scene (for example, a security guard viewing through closed-circuit television) is of a similar character. Private-life considerations may arise, however, once any systematic or permanent record comes into existence of such material from the public domain.[184]

For this reason, the European Court of Human Rights (ECtHR) considered files gathered by security services on a particular individual as falling within the scope of Article 8 ECHR, even where the information has not been gathered by any intrusive or covert method.[185] The fact that certain information is already in the public domain does thus not necessarily remove the protection of Article 8.[186] To the contrary, private life considerations arise where there has been a compilation of data on a particular individual, processing or use of personal data or publication of the material concerned in a manner or degree 'beyond that normally foreseeable'.[187] The systematic collection and storing of data by security services on particular individuals constituted an interference with these persons' private lives even if such data were collected in a public place[188] or concerned exclusively a person's professional or public activities.[189]

Tax authorities are not security services and the ECtHR ruled on such actions by security services. However, tax authorities are, like security services, part of the public body and intervene with public power. Security services act on behalf of national security and tax authorities on behalf of a States' proper financing, but both aim at detecting or even preventing the occurrence of situations that undermine a States' core functioning. Both types of investigation aim at discovering individuals that constitute a threat to those two aims. However, there is a gradual difference between tax crimes and crimes targeted by security services. It must be admitted that the target of security services is a threat of potentially greater harm than the target of tax authorities. This is probably also the reason why the EU includes tax crimes into the anti-money laundering directive[190] and the regulation on the protection of the financial interest of the EU only when they are considered to be serious, more precisely if they cause dangers above a certain (high) threshold.[191]

---

184. *P.G. and J.H.* v *the United Kingdom*, no. 44787/98, 25 September 2001, § 57.
185. *Ibid.*
186. *Satakunnan Markkinapörssi Oy and Satamedia Oy* v *Finland* (GC), no. 931/13, 27 June 2017, § 134.
187. *Ibid.* at 136.
188. *Peck* v *the United Kingdom*, no. 44647/98, 25 January 2003, § 59; *P.G. and J.H.* v *the United Kingdom*, no. 44787/98, 25 September, 2001, §§ 57-59.
189. *Amann* v *Switzerland* (GC), no. 27798/95, 16 February 2000, §§ 65-67; *Rotaru* v *Romania* (GC), no. 28341/95, 4 May 2000, §§ 43-44.
190. Article 3 para. 4 point f 4th Anti-Money-Laundering Directive (2015/849/2015, OJ 2015 L141/73.
191. Article 2 para. 2 Directive 2017/1371/EU, 5 July 2017, on the fight against fraud to the Union's interests by criminal law, OJ L 198/29.

As a consequence, restrictions on the secret services' right to interfere with Article 8 ECHR must the more apply to the respective right of tax authorities. If data and information from Internet monitoring feed into a tax Big Data algorithm, the monitoring and the subsequent processing must meet the requirements of Article 8 paragraph 2 ECHR as elaborated by the ECtHR with regard to security services. If tax authorities gain information from 'Internet monitoring', this is not intrusive to the same extent as the interception of communication, but it interferes with privacy because the data sourced by monitoring get stored and processed by the tax authorities. As consequence, the case law of the ECtHR on foreseeability of the interference fully applies.

As a result, Internet monitoring by tax authorities with the aim for data processing to collect and enforce tax law must be based on a clear legal statue that complies with the prerogatives of Article 8 paragraph 2 ECHR.

[c] Secret Surveillance for Tax Purposes?

Interception of communication without any suspicion of tax crimes would be illegitimate (so-called bulk interception[192]). It would resort to a system of secret surveillance, which determines a police State as opposite to a democracy. The ECHR tolerates secret surveillance only insofar as strictly necessary for safeguarding the democratic institutions.[193] Accordingly, it found bulk interception to protect national security not per se illegitimate.[194] With view to the advancements in technology 'which have made it easier for terrorists and criminals to evade detection on the Internet, and the unpredictability of the routes via which electronic communications are transmitted', it considers that the decision to operate bulk interception regimes in order to identify hitherto unknown threats to national security falls within States' margin of appreciation to limit Article 8 ECHR.[195] With regard to the use of modern scientific techniques in the criminal justice system, the Court has found that the protection afforded by Article 8 ECHR would be unacceptably weakened if such techniques were allowed at any cost and without carefully balancing the potential benefits of the extensive use of such techniques against important private-life interests.[196] Such interceptions need to be an instrument of last resort. As long as less intrusive methods attain the same objective, bulk interceptions are disproportionate and thus not allowed under Article 8 ECHR. The OECD's vision depicted above of paying taxes coming close to invisible to the taxpayer can thus not be implemented through steady surveillance of the taxpayer. Such a procedure would undermine democracy and install a police State.

With regard to covert measures of surveillance, the ECtHR has set up the following standards: The law must be sufficiently clear in its terms to give citizens an adequate indication of the conditions and circumstances in which the authorities are

192. Bulk interception is by definition untargeted (*Big Brother Watch and Others* v *the United Kingdom*, *supra* note 168, at § 317).
193. *Szabó and Vissy* v *Hungary*, no. 37138/14, 12 January 2016, §§ 72–73.
194. ECHR, 29 June 2006, *Weber and Saravia* v *Germany*, Application no. 54934/00, § 106.
195. *Big Brother Watch and Others* v *the United Kingdom*, *supra* note 168, at § 314.
196. *S. and Marper* v *the United Kingdom* (GC), nos 30562/04 and 30566/04, § 112.

empowered to resort to this secret and potentially dangerous interference with the right to respect for private life and correspondence.[197] In view of the risk of abuse intrinsic to any system of secret surveillance, such measures must be based on a law that is particularly precise. It is essential to have clear, detailed rules on the subject, especially as the technology available for use is continually becoming more sophisticated.[198] To avoid abuses the ECtHR demands certain minimum standards to be set out in statute law in order to avoid abuses: the nature of the offences which may give rise to an interception order; a definition of the categories of people liable to have their communications monitored; a limit on the duration of such monitoring; the procedure to be followed for examining, using and storing the data obtained; the precautions to be taken when communicating the data to other parties; and the circumstances in which data obtained must be erased or the records destroyed.[199] Furthermore, in the context of measures of secret surveillance by public authorities, because of the lack of public scrutiny and the risk of the misuse of power, the domestic law must provide some protection against arbitrary interference with Article 8 ECHR rights.[200]

Interferences with Article 8 ECHR are only justified if 'necessary in a democratic society' in pursuit of a legitimate aim. According to the ECtHR interception of communications represents one of the gravest intrusions, as it is capable of disclosing more information on a person's conduct, opinions or feelings.[201] Secret surveillance of citizens is thus only tolerated under Article 8 to the extent that they are strictly necessary for safeguarding democratic institutions. There must be adequate and effective guarantees against abuse.[202] Secret surveillance over the mail, post and telecommunications is, according to the ECtHR, under exceptional circumstances necessary in a democratic society in the interests of national security and/or for the prevention of disorder or crime.[203] As soon as notification can be carried out without

197. *Malone* v *the United Kingdom*, no. 8691/79, 2 August 1984, § 67; *Valenzuela Contreras* v *Spain*, no. 58/1997/842/1048, 30 July 1998, § 46; *Khan* v *the United Kingdom*, no. 35394/97, 12 May 2000 § 26.
198. *Kruslin* v *France*, no. 11801/85; 24 April 1990, § 33; *Huvig* v *France*, no. 11105/84, 14 April 1990, § 32; *Amann* v *Switzerland* (GC), no. 27798/95, 16 February 2000, § 56; *Weber and Saravia* v *Germany*, no. 54934/00, 29 Junc 2006, § 93; *Association for European Integration and Human Rights and Ekimdzhiev* v *Bulgaria*, no. 62540/00, 28 June 2007, § 75.
199. *Weber and Saravia* v *Germany*, no. 54934/00, 29 June 2006, § 95; *Association for European Integration and Human Rights and Ekimdzhiev* v *Bulgaria*, no. 62540/00, 28 June 2007, § 76.
200. *Klass and Others* v *Germany*, no. 5029/71, 6 September 1978, §§ 54–56; *Halford* v *the United Kingdom*, no. 20605/92, 25 March 1998, § 49; *Kopp* v *Switzerland*, no. 10842/84, 25 March 1998, § 55; *Weber and Saravia* v *Germany*, no. 54934/00, 29 June 2006, § 94; ECHR, 28 June 2007, *Association for European Integration and Human Rights and Ekimdzhiev* v *Bulgaria*, Application no. 62540/00, § 77.
201. *Uzun* v *Germany*, no. 35623/05, 2 September 2010, § 53; *Big Brother Watch and Others* v *the United Kingdom*, *supra* note 168, at § 350.
202. ECHR, 18 May 2010, *Kennedy* v *the United Kingdom*, Application no. 26839/05, § 153; *Klass and Others* v *Germany*, no. 5029/71, 6 September 1978, §§ 49–50; *Weber and Saravia* v *Germany*, no. 54934/00, 29 June 2006, § 106.
203. ECHR, 12 January 2016, *Szabó and Vissy* v *Hungary*, Application no. 37138/14, § 80; *Klass and Others* v *Germany*, no. 5029/71, 6 September 1978, § 48.

jeopardizing the purpose of the restriction after the termination of the surveillance measure, information should be provided to the persons concerned.[204]

If a tax administration seeks to become – with the words of the OECD – 'close to invisible' to the taxpayers (*see* above §13.04[B]), that tax administration would need to deploy tools of secret surveillance, unless it provides for IoT devices to be kept and used by the taxpayers. Given the massive constraints secret surveillance is subject to for the sake of preserving national security, it cannot be allowed in tax matters, unless the danger tax crimes entail for society is weighed similarly to the danger of terrorism and money laundering. This does not seem to be the case for 'ordinary' tax crimes. Accordingly, the EU Directive EU/2017/1371 on the fight against fraud to the Union's financial interests by means of criminal law,[205] only covers tax offences related to value-added tax (VAT), when (among others), a total damage of at least EUR 10 million is involved.[206]

An algorithm could also search for metadata, such as Internet Protocol (IP) addresses in order to find out more about a specific taxpayer or a specific group of taxpayers. Metadata are not accessible to the public. The question is thus, whether the search for metadata is to be compared with secret surveillance measures. In tax matters the search for such data could for example strongly support tax administrations to find out about the place of supply of a digital service for VAT purposes or the place of participation in remote gaming for the sake of calculating the right amount of gaming taxes. Metadata, as for example IP addresses, facilitate the identification of the author of specific activities. Consequently, they constitute personal data. Their use falls within the scope of Article 8 ECHR and must thus meet the requirements of Article 8 paragraph 2 ECHR.[207] According to the ECtHR the acquisition of related communications data is not necessarily less intrusive than the acquisition of content:

> For example, the content of an electronic communication might be encrypted and, even if it were decrypted, might not reveal anything of note about the sender or the recipient. The related communications data, on the other hand, could reveal the identities and geographic location of the sender and the recipient and the equipment through which the communication was transmitted. In bulk, the degree of intrusion is magnified, since the patterns that will emerge could be capable of painting an intimate picture of a person through the mapping of social networks, location tracking, Internet browsing tracking, mapping of communication patterns, and insight into who a person interacted with.[208]

---

204. *Weber and Saravia* v *Germany*, no. 54934/00, 29 June 2006, § 135; ECHR, 4 December 2015, *Roman Zakharov* v *Russia* (GC), Application no. 47143/06, § 287; ECHR, 12 January 2016, *Szabó and Vissy* v *Hungary*, Application no. 37138/14, § 86.
205. Directive EU/2017/1371 of the European Parliament and of the Council, on the fight against fraud to the Union's financial interests by means of criminal law, 5 July 2017, OJ L 198/29.
206. The reverse perspective could also be taken, see J.E. Stiglitz & Mark Pieth, Overcoming the Shadow Economy, November 2016, Friedrich Ebert Stiftung, International Policy Analysis (https://library,fes.de/pdf-files/iez/12922.pdf; checked on 26 November 2018), who seem to equalize corruption, money laundering and tax evasion.
207. ECHR, 24 April 2018, *Benedik* v *Slovenia*, Application no. 62357/14, §§ 107–108.
208. *Big Brother Watch and Others* v *the United Kingdom*, *supra* note 168, at § 356.

If tax administrations want to collect these metadata, they need clear legal statutes and sound justifications in the overarching public interest. If they collected such data and information without the taxpayer knowing it, it would constitute secret surveillance and thus be subject to the same restrictions as any other measure of secret surveillance.

[d] Conclusion

Internet monitoring with the aim of using the so gained data and information for tax collection and enforcement is not pure watching of a public situation anymore, but a use of private data and information that interferes with Article 8 ECHR. It is thus only legitimate, if set up by a legal statute that meets the requirements of Article 2 paragraph 2 ECHR.

Any measure of Big Data Analytics used by a tax administration to collect and enforce tax law also contributes to detecting tax crimes, but detection of crimes is not the primary of tax authorities, it is control. Moreover, tax crimes, unless they attain a certain level of seriousness, cannot be compared to the crimes that have allowed for interception of communication so far. Secret surveillance measures for tax purposes should thus not be legitimate, unless they aim only at detecting serious crimes comparable to those prosecuted by secret services.

Using IoT devices could approach the goal of increasing effectivity and efficiency in tax collection without installing a system of steady and secret surveillance. If taxpayers get obliged to use specific devices in their day-to-day business, such as electronic cash registers, with a real-time connection to the tax authorities, tax authorities have a means to monitor the taxpayer in a targeted way on a targeted part of his taxable activities. Although this technique interferes with Article 8 ECHR, it could be set up in line with Article 8 paragraph 2 ECHR.

[3] Taxpayer Profiling and GDPR

[a] Big Data Analytics as Taxpayer Profiling

The described Big Data algorithms process personal taxpayer data automatically in order to evaluate certain personal (tax compliance-related) aspects of a person. They are particularly used to analyse or predict aspects concerning a persons' performance at work, or economic situation or reliability. As a consequence, they qualify as 'profiling' under Article 4 paragraph 4 GDPR. In some cases the profiling is followed by automated decisions and have thus to comply with Article 22 GDPR.

[b] Rights and Obligations with Regard to Profiling

The substantive rules of GDPR oblige controllers to provide data subjects with – *inter alia* – information on the existence of automated decision-making, including profiling and meaningful information about the logic involved, as well as the significance and the envisaged consequences of such processing for the data subject (Article 13 paragraph 2 lit. f GDPR). The same is valid in cases where the personal data have not been obtained from the data subject, but from another source (Article 14 paragraph 2 lit. g GDPR). Similarly, the same rights are included in the right of access by the data subject (Article 15 paragraph 1 lit. h GDPR). The right to object is also valid for profiling (Article 21 paragraph 1 GDPR). According to Article 22 GDPR the data subject shall have the right not to be subject to a decision solely based on automated processing, including profiling, which produces legal effects concerning the data subject or similarly affects him or her (Article 22 paragraph 1 GDPR). However, if profiling including automated decisions it is authorized by a law laying down suitable measures to safeguard the data subject's rights and freedoms and legitimate interests (Article 22 paragraph 2 lit. b GDPR), it is not precluded.

The GDPR distinguishes according to the purposes an algorithm is used for. For tax matters it becomes evident that an algorithm supplanting a human decision must be set down by law in order to comply with the GDPR. According to pt. 71 of the preliminary considerations of GDPR a decision in the sense of Article 22 'may include a measure'. Furthermore, according to this same point, automated decisions 'include' profiling. If provided by law, profiling including automated decisions is legitimate, provided it is 'subject to suitable safeguards, which include specific information to the data subject and the right to obtain human intervention, to express his or her point of view, to obtain an explanation of the decision reached after such assessment and to challenge the decision'. Additionally, it requires the controller to use:

> Appropriate mathematical or statistical procedures, implement technical and organisational measures appropriate to ensure, in particular, that factors which result in inaccuracies in personal data are corrected and the risk of errors is minimized, secure personal data in a manner that takes account of the potential risks involved for the interests and rights of the data subject and that prevents, inter alia, discriminatory effects on natural persons.

[c] *Limitations*

However, according to Article 23 GDPR these prerogatives may be restricted by the EU or a Member State, when it is necessary and proportionate in a democratic society to safeguard important objectives of general public interest of the Union or of a Member State, such as taxation matters. Such a restriction must be introduced by legislation, must respect the essence of the fundamental rights and freedoms and must – at least where relevant – contain specific provisions concerning (a) the purposes of the processing or categories of processing; (b) the categories of personal data; (c) the scope of the restrictions introduced; (d) the safeguards to prevent abuse or unlawful access or transfer; (e) the specification of the controller or categories of controller; (f) the storage periods and the applicable safeguards taking into account the nature, scope and purposes of the processing or categories of processing; (g) the risk to the rights and freedoms of data subjects; and (h) the right of data subjects to be informed about the restriction, unless that may be prejudicial to the purpose of the restriction (Article 23 paragraph 2 GDPR). One of the main purposes of the rules on profiling in the GDPR thus aims at preserving the data subjects' right to challenge the processing of her data before courts.

[d] Conclusion

Since Big Data Analytics in tax matters consists in profiling and if the term 'decision' is understood in the broad sense of any measure producing any kind of legal effects, Article 22 GDPR and related provisions of GDPR are highly relevant. Although Article 23 GDPR applies to profiling in tax matters and allows Member States to limit the effects of Article 22 GDPR and the related safeguards, the use of Big Data Analytics needs to be based on **specific** provisions setting down the purposes of the processing. Restrictions to Article 22 and related provisions must be clearly set down by law (Article 23 paragraph 1 GDPR) and fix the purposes of the processing or categories of processing, the categories of personal data used.

Insofar deep-learning algorithms cannot be prevented from sourcing only predetermined categories of data, they cannot be used by the tax authorities without interfering with Article 23 GDPR.

Moreover, such a restriction rule must contain safeguards to prevent abuse or unlawful access or transfer. In most European States tax authorities are bound by a tax secrecy. They are not allowed to disclose taxpayer data to others, unless explicitly permitted by law. These common rules should be adequate safeguards to prevent abuse or unlawful access or transfer if accompanied by appropriate cybersecurity measures.

Restrictions to the GDPR must respect the essence of the fundamental rights and freedoms and must constitute a necessary and proportionate measure in a democratic society. With regard to the use of profiling in tax matters it would certainly not be in line with this essence of the fundamental rights and freedoms to not allow the data subject to express his or her point to contest the decision taken or prepared by the algorithm. This would affect the essence of the fundamental rights. However, it would be legitimate to limit meaningful information about the logic involved. Thorough information about the logic involved would allow taxpayers to cheat the system. Insofar it is necessary to ensure the proper functioning of a system, algorithm-based evaluations must be open to the same margin of discretion as human-based decisions.[209]

The de facto impact of GDPR on using algorithms for tax collection and enforcement depends on and varies according to the purposes algorithms are used for.

209. For more details, see Tina Ehrke-Rabel, *Profiling im Steuervollzug, Finanzrundschau* 45, 52 et seq. (OttoSchmidt 2019).

[D] Conclusion

Accuracy of the data used for tax Big Data Analytics and procedural regularity of the code are the basic requirements for any Big Data Analytics tool in use by tax authorities. They allow to prevent discrimination and ensure the protection of the rights of the defence. Moreover, the privacy concept underlying the GDPR requires clear rules on profiling.

The ECHR and the Charter right to protection of private and family life prohibit any measure of mass surveillance for tax purposes. Such a proceeding would undermine democracy. However, targeted Big Data measures are licit, if the basic requirements that are legality, equality and the protection of the rights of the defence are met. The concrete scope of licit Big Data measures depends on their purpose and use. As a result, it must be asked whether Big Data Analytics can be used for any purpose of tax collection and enforcement.

§13.06 USE AND PURPOSE OF TAX BIG DATA ANALYTICS

[A] Data Storage

According to the OECD Big Data can assist revenue bodies in examining and understanding historical activity and taxpayer behaviour through different tools. One of them is storage of the original, unaltered information.[210] If Big Data in tax matters 'only' aims at assisting the tax authorities in preparing their tasks by compiling taxpayer data without evaluating and comparing them to other taxpayers' data, we admit that the existing traditional rules on tax collection and enforcement of modern democracies are sufficient. This is a case where Big Data is not fundamentally new, but a means of automated storage. This kind of automation would probably not fall within the scope of the common understanding of Big Data, although it is covered by the GDPR.[211] However, this kind of data analytics does not fall within the scope of Article 22 GDPR. The general rules of GDPR have to be respected.

It is neither a specific predictive or reactive tool, but it is an ordinary assistance tool that is not new to tax collection and enforcement. For this kind of data storage existent legal rules should suffice.

[B] Real-Time Monitoring Through IoT

The IoT allows to connect all kind of devices held by a person via the Internet to someone else or to an artificial intelligence that can store and proceed the data obtained by that device in real time. If such a device is connected to an artificial intelligence application run by the State it allows the observation or monitoring of certain aspects

210. The OECD stresses in this context that the greater the volumes of raw data, the wider the possibilities are to process, analyse and assess it.
211. GDPR, Art. 2, para. 1.

of the device holder's behaviour. It could be a device built on a car to allow the geolocalization of the car (and the person in the car), or a cash register allowing to observe the transactions in cash proceeded by a certain taxpayer.

Without any doubt such applications interfere with the individual's private life.[212] However, the ECHR has decided that the surveillance of a person through geolocalization would constitute a less intrusive interference with privacy than the interception of communications.[213]

Using IoT devices could thus support tax authorities in improving tax collection and tax enforcement without turning its activities into activities of mass surveillance that would undermine democracy. Nevertheless, their use would need to be clearly framed by law including the safeguards set up by the ECtHR under Article 8 paragraph 2 ECHR. Moreover, the use of IoT devices would need to be justified by the specific context or a specific activity. Obliging taxpayers to wear a bracelet connected to the tax authorities whenever they exercise their professional activity would not meet these requirements. Awareness must be kept that even the use of IoT devices can lead to a situation of mass surveillance contrary to liberal democracies. To give some insight on the potential risk the use of IoT devices by tax authorities entails:

> Perhaps the most challenging end goal (the 'holy grail' outcome) of IOT tracking is lasting behavior change. One possible progression of the events required for behavior change with IOT is as follows: start tracking, obtain data, look at the data in infographics, determine the meaning, try a behavior change, maintain the behavior change through the three week cliff for new habit instantiation, and ultimately produce long-lasting change.[214]

[C] Audit Selection

The use of Big Data Analytics to select taxpayers for audit aims at identifying cases with a high probability of uncovering tax underpayment. Even without the support of algorithms tax authorities have always had to select taxpayers for audit because restrained resources have never allowed for covering all taxpayers with thorough audits. Besides random-based selection there have always existed certain criteria for selection that for efficiency reasons have also taken into account the probability of detecting underpayments. Without any doubt, the use of an algorithm for this kind of selection increases efficiency and effectivity of government acts and is thus likely to reduce costs.

From a legal perspective this kind of analytics constitute profiling in the sense of Article 4 par. 4 GDPR. Taxpayers get profiled by the algorithm. The decision of the algorithm on the taxpayers to be audited constitutes an automated decision. However, it is not clear whether this is an automated decision in the sense of Article 22 GDPR. In

212. In this sense with regard to geolocalization objects *Ben Faiza* v *France*, no. 31446/12, 8 February 2018, § 53; *Uzun* v *Germany*, no. 35623/05, 2 September 2010, § 52.
213. *Uzun* v *Germany*, no. 35623/05, 2 September 2010, § 66.
214. Melanie Swan, *Sensor Mania! The Internet of Things, Wearable Computing, Objective Metrics and the Quantified Self 2.0*, J. Sensor & Actuator Networks 217, 240 (2012).

general, the decision to audit a taxpayer is not a formal decision a taxpayer can challenge before courts. However, it is a measure with legal consequences for the taxpayer. Initiating an audit or not has concrete legal consequences for the taxpayer. Since a tax audit is a State intervention every taxpayer has to expect at any time and a taxpayer has not the right to reject, it is likely to not fall within the scope of Article 22 GDPR. Consequently, from a data protection perspective the use of such an algorithm is not subject to the additional requirements set up by the GDPR for profiling including automated decision-making. This does, however, not mean that there is no need to inform the taxpayers about the use of such instruments to select audit cases. On the contrary, the overarching principles of GDPR, which are transparency on the use of personal data and fairness (Article 5 GDPR) require the information of the individual concerned about the processing of personal data. The information must allow the person concerned to evaluate the consequences of the effectuated data processing. To invest Big Data algorithms for audit selection without informing the taxpayers of the existence of such tools would thus contravene the prerogatives of GDPR.[215]

In the affirmative it must be enquired if any further legal requirements are to be derived from the rule of law, the principle of equality and the rights of the defence. Big Data Analytics meeting the requirements of the GDPR do also meet the requirements of the rule of law at a very general level.

With regard to discrimination it could be argued that selecting certain taxpayers for audit and not selecting others constitutes a discrimination of alike cases. The cases could be found to be alike because all taxpayers are born equally and because data analytics can never attain certainty and would thus base their selection on statistical probabilities. There is very little to object to this position. However, even in times of pure human intervention, the process of selecting taxpayers for audit was not fundamentally different to an algorithm-based selection (*see* above §13.02[B]). Given the mass effects of taxation and the limited State resources taxpayers have never been controlled equally. This is a shortcoming the system has been accepting for a very long time in order to preserve individual autonomy in a complicated tax system. To use algorithms instead of humans may even make tax enforcement more equal and just than not using them. Provided that the algorithms meet all the requirements depicted under §13.05[B], they can calculate the probabilities relevant for deciding on whom to audit in a much more efficient and further reaching way than humans. To found selection for audits only on the probability to uncover under-reporting at a defined significant level would certainly not be in line with the principle of equality.[216] The algorithm-based selection would thus need to be accompanied by random-based selections of other taxpayers who may never be selected by the algorithm itself.

The rights of the defence would be entirely preserved if the algorithm is set up in line with the requirements of Article 22 GDPR and the related provisions (including the restrictions installed in line with Article 23 GDPR).

215. For more details, see Tina Ehrke-Rabel, Profiling im Steuerrecht, Finanzrundschau 2019 (Otto Schmidt), at 56.

216. For more details, see Barbara Gunacker-Slawitsch, Habilitationsschrift (forthcoming).

The prediction this kind of analytics offers is not a prediction on the taxpayer's future behaviour but on the outcome of an eventual public intervention with regard to a taxpayer's past behaviour. This kind of Big Data Analytics is consequential prediction, but contrarily to Kerr and Earle it does not focus on the analysed subject's future behaviour but on the prediction of another person's intervention with regard to the analysed subject's past behaviour. In summary, from a legal perspective using Big Data for this purpose does not pose any specific concerns.

[D] 'Targeted Advertising' of Taxpayers

[1] By Nudges

If Big Data Analytics is used to find out whether a taxpayer is more sensitive to friendly words than to scary threats and to then address him differently according to his preferences, this kind of prediction focuses on future behaviour of the taxpayer. The instruments then used to react on the outcome of the analysis aim at rendering the taxpayer more compliant. Since the taxpayer remains free to not react on the instruments used, this kind of prediction is preferential: It aims at identifying the taxpayer's preferences in order to sell the 'good' paying taxes.

Soft tools which uphold the taxpayer's free will seem per se not legally problematic.[217] However, this kind of analytics is also based on profiling. The question is whether this profiling includes automated decision-making. It certainly includes a measure in its broadest sense since it is not done without any specific purpose. Can the use of data analytics to influence taxpayer behaviour through different soft tools qualify as a measure with legal or alike consequences? According to Buchner alike consequences are situations where a data subject is impeded on a sustainable basis in her economic or personal development.[218] According to Helfrich it would be a situation where the automated processing and deciding makes the data subject feel non-neglectably monitored and inhibited in his personal development.[219] Soft tools should not prevent rational individuals from taking decisions they do not want to take. Contrary to decisions with binding legal consequences nudging measures as a consequence of profiling should thus not impede the data subject in a comparable way. Consequently, Article 22 GDPR would not apply to this kind of data analytics.

Nevertheless, even for profiling without automated decisions the State as a controller is obliged to provide data subjects with the information cited in Article 14 GDPR. Have to be disclosed, among others, the purposes of the processing for which

---

217. It should be noted, however, that soft tools raise serious legal concerns if designed in a way that qualifies as manipulation. The lines between licit 'nudging' and legally problematic manipulation are blurred (for more details, *see, e.g.*, Gregor Kirchhof, Nudging – zu den rechtlichen Grenzen informalen Verwaltens, Zeitschrift für Rechtspolitik (Verlag Beck) 2015, p. 136 et seq.).

218. Benedikt Buchner, *in Datenschutz-Grundverordnung: Kommentar* Art. 22 recital 26 (Kühling & Buchner eds., Beck 2017).

219. Marcus Helfrich, *in Europäische Datenschutz-Grundverordnung: Handkommentar* Art. 22, recital 51 (Sydow ed., Manz 2018).

the personal data are intended, the categories of the personal data concerned, details on the storage time of the data, etc. Article 23 GDPR allows for restrictions by a legislative measure to safeguard the public interest of effective taxation. This restriction must respect the essence of the fundamental rights and freedoms, must be necessary and proportionate in a democratic society and meet the minimum requirements set up in Article 23 paragraph 2 GDPR.

To disclose to the taxpayer that he gets softly addressed according to his specific profile and to inform him that this addressing is not the same for all taxpayers would in my view not contravene the objective of the data analytics that consists in safeguarding efficient and effective taxation. But to be more precise on the exact outcome and the concrete tools used in the specific case would endanger the effectiveness of the operation. Art. 23 GDPR would allow not to disclose these details. The author of this manuscript believes that it would not allow to entirely neglect the requirements of GDPR and leave the taxpayer ignorant. The essence of a democratic society demands the addressee of government actions to be informed on the existence of such actions (except maybe in cases of fighting serious crimes). Informing the taxpayer on this general level would contribute to drawing the lines between legitimate nudging of the taxpayer for the sake of preserving the public good and illegal manipulation.[220] Deepening these questions would require another contribution and shall be left for further research.[221]

I would like to end this subsection with a quote from Richards and Kings' article *Three Paradoxes of Big Data*:

> The power of big data is thus the power to use information to nudge, to persuade, to influence, and even to restrict our identities. Such influence over our individual and collective identities risks eroding the vigor and the quality of our democracy. If we lack the power to individually say who 'I am', if filters and nudges and personalized recommendations undermine our intellectual choices, we will have become identified but lose our identities as we have defined them in the past.[222]

[2] By Legal Statutes

If Big Data Analytics is further used to segment taxpayers into different groups according to their potential risk of the tax underpayment they are likely to represent in order to then use different tools of control, such as steady monitoring for high-risk taxpayers, regular audits for middle-risk taxpayers and no audit for low-risk taxpayers, this is a case of pre-emptive prediction. This kind of predictions is generated with the aim of allowing or disallowing individuals to behave in a certain way before they set a specific action.[223] At least for the high-risk taxpayers it becomes impossible to cheat the

220. Manipulation is one of the main critiques against nudging.
221. On this issue Gregor Kirchhof, *Nudging – zu den rechtlichen Grenzen informalen Verwaltens*, 48 ZRP 136–137 (2015); Cass Sunstein, *The Ethics of Choice Architecture, in Choice Architecture in Democracies* 21–74 (Alexandra Kemmerer et al. eds., Nomos 2016).
222. Richards, *supra* note 164, at 44.
223. In this sense, *see* Kerr, *supra* note 95, at 68.

system. These taxpayers' future options of under-reporting are largely reduced, whereas the options to cheat increase for low-risk taxpayers. To reduce options of unwanted behaviour allows to approach the social optimum where everyone complies with the laws.

There is certainly not a problem from a rule of law perspective. Focussing the efforts of enforcement on those who are more likely to be non-compliant than on the others increases efficiency and effectiveness as long as the less targeted do not get an incentive to cheat the system at their turn. But this also entails segmentation of taxpayers, who by law are all equal, into different groups according to an algorithmic, data-driven evaluation of their likelihood to be fully compliant.

This can be discriminatory for two reasons: First, the existing concepts of law depart from the assumptions that taxpayers as individuals are all equal. Second, analytics are always based on the analysis of a taxpayer's past behaviour and most likely on her behaviour compared to one of her peers. It could be imagined that an algorithm estimates that taxpayers who do risky sports (which could be found out by internet monitoring) are more likely to take risky positions towards the tax administration and should thus be more under scrutiny than taxpayers who do not seem to take any serious risks in their private lives.

If taxpayers get segmented on the basis of their past behaviour and then get treated differently (in the future) according to the respective segment they were fit in, the segmentation could be incompatible with the taxpayer's real attitude towards paying taxes and would thus be discriminatory. However, segmentation could be justified by the overriding reason in the public interest of securing the State revenue. Like any justified limitations to the principle of equality, this limitation needs to be accompanied by appropriate safeguards to prevent abuse. Such a safeguard could be transparency. However, overall transparency would again undermine the objective of segmentation by allowing or even incentivizing strategic behaviour of the taxpayers. To strike the balance a minimum level of transparency and a robust design of the algorithm – probably by very consciously deciding on the parameters guiding the algorithms' decision-making – are required. Furthermore, this kind of Big Data Analytics use clearly qualifies as profiling including automated decisions with all the requirements of Art. 22 and the related and the legitimate restrictions in line with Art. 23 GDPR, as outlined above under §13.05[C][3].

§13.07 FINAL CONCLUSIONS

Our modern societies are founded on the idea of individuals being free and of the State intervening only where it is necessary for the functioning of our society. This freedom has been acquired in hard struggles, wars, and revolutions. And in this concept of individual freedom society and the State have accepted that people have secrecies that nobody knows, under the assumption of freedom we even accepted that people cheat the laws. As long as information is analogue and local, the laws of the physics create an automatic zone of privacy.[224]

Data analytics allow to combine the huge mass of data on a human being available out there and 'stored'/'held' by different places/institutions in a way a single human being would not be able of. It is evident that anyone has to accept that people watch him when he acts in public. Every trace we leave on the internet is a public footprint. We need to accept that this footprint is being watched.

But there is a difference between watching and processing. At the moment these footprints get combined with each other, combined with other sources of information and feed then into a decision based on evaluations and at the moment this is done permanently, it is not pure observation anymore, it becomes surveillance. Since the State is only allowed to intervene, when provided by law, there need to be clear rules![225] In a digital world, privacy requires explicitly designed institutions, laws and technologies, or norms stating, which information flows are permitted or prevented and which are encouraged or discouraged.[226]

In order to preserve our hardly acquired individual freedoms it is absolutely necessary to be aware of the risks Big Data entail. In order to avoid that Big Data Analytics remain a black box that does not allow a taxpayer to rely on the human rights ensured by conventions and constitutions aiming at avoiding illegal restrictions of personal autonomy, policymakers and lawmakers have to be develop tools that allow making Big Data users – in tax matters governments – more accountable for their actions.[227]

From a legal perspective it thus seems highly problematic that the tax administration is rather opaque with regard to the use of Big Data. Although there is a large margin of discretion of the tax administration with regard to the decision on how to use which instruments of investigation, it needs at first place to be clear and (rule of law) legally founded that data analytics are used for the purpose of tax collection.

224. Bryonjolfsson, *supra* note 142, at 253.
225. On taxpayers' privacy and Big Data, *see* Cockfield, *supra* note 84, at 503–505.
226. Bryonjolfsson, *supra* note 142, at 253.
227. In this sense more generally, *see* Mayer-Schönberger & Cukier, *supra* note 91, at 172; Lawrence Lessig, *Code Version 2.0,* 80 (CreateSpace Independent Publishing 2006).

Index

T

SERIES ON INTERNATIONAL TAXATION

1. Alberto Xavier, *The Taxation of Foreign Investment in Brazil,* 1980 (ISBN 90-200-0582-0).
2. Hugh J. Ault & Albert J. Rädler, *The German Corporation Tax Law with 1980 Amendments,* 1981 (ISBN 90-200-0642-8).
3. Paul R. McDaniel & Hugh J. Ault, *Introduction to United States International Taxation,* 1981 (ISBN 90-6544-004-6).
4. Albert J. Rädler, *German Transfer Pricing/Prix de Transfer en Allemagne,* 1984 (ISBN 90-6544-143-3).
5. Paul R. McDaniel & Stanley S. Surrey, *International Aspects of Tax Expenditures: A Comparative Study,* 1985 (ISBN 90-654-4163-8).
6. Kees van Raad, *Nondiscrimination in International Tax Law,* 1986 (ISBN 90-6544-266-9).
7. Sijbren Cnossen (ed.), *Tax Coordination in the European Community,* 1987 (ISBN 90-6544-272-3).
8. Ben Terra, *Sales Taxation. The Case of Value Added Tax in the European Community,* 1989 (ISBN 90-6544-381-9).
9. Rutsel S.J. Martha, *The Jurisdiction to Tax in International Law: Theory and Practice of Legislative Fiscal Jurisdiction,* 1989 (ISBN 90-654-4416-5).
10. Paul R. McDaniel & Hugh J. Ault, *Introduction to United States International Taxation* (3rd revised edition), 1989 (ISBN 90-6544-423-8).
11. Manuel Pires, *International Juridicial Double Taxation of Income,* 1989 (ISBN 90-6544-426-2).
12. A.H.M. Daniels, *Issues in International Partnership Taxation,* 1991 (ISBN 90-654-4577-3).
13. Arvid A. Skaar, *Permanent Establishment: Erosion of a Tax Treaty Principle,* 1992 (ISBN 90-6544-594-3).
14. Cyrille David & Geerten M.M. Michielse (eds), *Tax Treatment of Financial Instruments,* 1996 (ISBN 90-654-4666-4).
15. Herbert H. Alpert & Kees van Raad (eds), *Essays on International Taxation,* 1993 (ISBN 90-654-4781-4).
16. Wolfgang Gassner, Michael Lang & Eduard Lechner (eds), *Tax Treaties and EC Law,* 1997 (ISBN 90-411-0680-4).
17. Glória Teixeira, *Taxing Corporate Profits in the EU,* 1997 (ISBN 90-411-0703-7).
18. Michael Lang et al. (eds), *Multilateral Tax Treaties,* 1998 (ISBN 90-411-0704-5).
19. Stef van Weeghel, *The Improper Use of Tax Treaties,* 1998 (ISBN 90-411-0737-1).
20. Klaus Vogel (ed.), *Interpretation of Tax Law and Treaties and Transfer Pricing in Japan and Germany,* 1998 (ISBN 90-411-9655-2).
21. Bertil Wiman (ed.), *International Studies in Taxation: Law and Economics; Liber Amicorum Leif Mutén,* 1999 (ISBN 90-411-9692-7).
22. Alfonso J. Martín Jiménez, *Towards Corporate Tax Harmonization in the European Community,* 1999 (ISBN 90-411-9690-0).

23. Ramon J. Jeffery, *The Impact of State Sovereignty on Global Trade and International Taxation*, 1999 (ISBN 90-411-9703-6).
24. A.J. Easson, *Taxation of Foreign Direct Investment*, 1999 (ISBN 90-411-9741-9).
25. Marjaana Helminen, *The Dividend Concept in International Tax Law: Dividend Payments Between Corporate Entities*, 1999 (ISBN 90-411-9765-6).
26. Paul Kirchhof, Moris Lehner, Kees van Raad, Arndt Raupach & Michael-Rodi (eds), *International and Comparative Taxation: Essays in Honour of Klaus Vogel*, 2002 (ISBN 90-411-9841-5).
27. Krister Andersson, Peter Melz & Christer Silfverberg (eds), *Liber Amicorum Sven-Olof Lodin*, 2001 (ISBN 90-411-9850-4).
28. Juan Martín Jovanovich, *Customs Valuation and Transfer Pricing: Is It Possible to Harmonize Customs and Tax Rules?*, Second Edition, 2018 (ISBN 978-90-411-6134-5).
29. Stefano Simontacchi, *Taxation of Capital Gains under the OECD Model Convention: With Special Regard to Immovable Property*, 2007 (ISBN 978-90-411-2549-1).
30. Michael Lang, Josef Schuch, & Claus Staringer (eds), *Tax Treaty Law and EC Law*, 2007 (ISBN 978-90-411-2629-0).
31. Duncan Bentley, *Taxpayers' Rights: Theory Origin and Implementation*, 2007 (ISBN 978-90-411-2650-4).
32. Sergio André Rocha, *Interpretation of Double Taxation Conventions: General Theory and Brazilian Perspective*, 2008 (ISBN 978-90-411-2822-5).
33. Robert F. van Brederode, *Systems of General Sales Taxation: Theory, Policy and Practice*, 2009 (ISBN 978-90-411-2832-4).
34. John G. Head & Richard Krever (eds), *Tax Reform in the 21st Century: A Volume in Memory of Richard Musgrave*, 2009 (ISBN 978-90-411-2829-4).
35. Jens Wittendorff, *Transfer Pricing and the Arm's Length Principle in International Tax Law*, 2010 (ISBN 978-90-411-3270-3).
36. Marjaana Helminen, *The International Tax Law Concept of Dividend*, Second Edition, 2017 (ISBN 978-90-411-8394-1).
37. Robert F. van Brederode (ed.), *Immovable Property under VAT: A Comparative Global Analysis*, 2011 (ISBN 978-90-411-3126-3).
38. Dennis Weber & Stef van Weeghel, *The 2010 OECD Updates: Model Tax Convention & Transfer Pricing Guidelines - A Critical Review*, 2011 (ISBN 978-90-411-3812-5).
39. Yariv Brauner & Martin James McMahon, Jr. (eds), *The Proper Tax Base: Structural Fairness from an International and Comparative Perspective—Essays in Honour of Paul McDaniel*, 2012 (ISBN 978-90-411-3286-4).
40. Robert F. van Brederode (ed.), *Science, Technology and Taxation*, 2012 (ISBN 978-90-411-3125-6).
41. Oskar Henkow, *The VAT/GST Treatment of Public Bodies*, 2013 (ISBN 978-90-411-4663-2).
42. Jean Schaffner, *How Fixed Is a Permanent Establishment?*, 2013 (ISBN 978-90-411-4662-5).

43. Miguel Correia, *Taxation of Corporate Groups*, 2013 (ISBN 978-90-411-4841-4).
44. Veronika Daurer, *Tax Treaties and Developing Countries*, 2014 (ISBN 978-90-411-4982-4).
45. Claire Micheau, *State Aid, Subsidy and Tax Incentives under EU and WTO Law*, 2014 (ISBN 978-90-411-4555-0).
46. Robert F. van Brederode & Richard Krever (eds), *Legal Interpretation of Tax Law*, 2014 (ISBN 978-90-411-4945-9).
47. Radhakishan Rawal, *Taxation of Cross-border Services*, 2014 (ISBN 978-90-411-4947-3).
48. João Dácio Rolim, *Proportionality and Fair Taxation*, 2014 (ISBN 978-90-411-5838-3).
49. Paulo Rosenblatt, *General Anti-avoidance Rules for Major Developing Countries*, 2015 (ISBN 978-90-411-5839-0).
50. Gaspar Lopes Dias V.S., *Tax Arbitrage through Cross-Border Financial Engineering*, 2015 (ISBN 978-90-411-5875-8).
51. Geerten M.M. Michielse & Victor Thuronyi (eds), *Tax Design Issues Worldwide*, 2015 (ISBN 978-90-411-5610-5).
52. Oktavia Weidmann, *Taxation of Derivatives*, 2015 (ISBN 978-90-411-5977-9).
53. Chris Evans, Richard Krever & Peter Mellor (eds), *Tax Simplification*, 2015 (ISBN 978-90-411-5976-2).
54. Reuven Avi-Yonah & Joel Slemrod (eds), *Taxation and Migration*, 2015 (ISBN 978-90-411-6136-9).
55. Alexander Bosman, *Other Income under Tax Treaties: An Analysis of Article 21 of the OECD Model Convention*, 2015 (ISBN 978-90-411-6610-4).
56. John Abrahamson, *International Taxation of Manufacturing and Distribution*, 2016 (ISBN 978-90-411-6664-7).
57. Frederik Boulogne, *Shortcomings in the EU Merger Directive*, 2016 (ISBN 978-90-411-6713-2).
58. Angelika Meindl-Ringler, *Beneficial Ownership in International Tax Law*, 2016 (ISBN 978-90-411-6833-7).
59. Andreas Waltrich, *Cross-Border Taxation of Permanent Establishments: An International Comparison*, 2016 (ISBN 978-90-411-6832-0).
60. Sergio André Rocha & Allison Christians (eds), *Tax Sovereignty in the BEPS Era*, 2017 (ISBN 978-90-411-6707-1).
61. Peter Antony Wilson, *BRICS and International Tax Law*, 2018 (ISBN 978-90-411-9435-0).
62. Louise Otis, Brigitte Alepin & Blanca Moreno-Dodson (eds), *Winning the Tax Wars: Tax Competition and Cooperation*, 2018 (ISBN 978-90-411-9460-2).
63. Marta Castelon, *International Taxation of Income from Services under Double Taxation Conventions: Development, Practice and Policy*, 2018 (ISBN 978-90-411-9594-4).
64. D.M. Broekhuijsen, *A Multilateral Tax Treaty: Designing an Instrument to Modernise International Tax Law*, 2018 (ISBN 978-90-411-9872-3).

65. John Abrahamson, *International Taxation of Energy Production and Distribution*, 2018 (ISBN 978-90-411-9101-4).
66. Leopoldo Parada, *Double Non-taxation and the Use of Hybrid Entities: An Alternative Approach in the New Era of BEPS*, 2018 (ISBN 978-90-411-9991-1).
67. Richard Snoeij, *International Tax Aspects of Sovereign Wealth Investors: A Source State Perspective*, 2018 (ISBN 978-90-411-9431-2).
68. Aleksandra Bal, *Taxation, Virtual Currency and Blockchain*, 2019 (ISBN 978-94-035-0103-1).
69. Werner Haslehner, Georg Kofler, Katerina Pantazatou & Alexander Rust (eds), *Tax and the Digital Economy: Challenges and Proposals for Reform*, 2019 (ISBN 978-94-035-0361-5).

www.ingramcontent.com/pod-product-compliance
Lightning Source LLC
Chambersburg PA
CBHW071238230926
51849CB00001B/148
* 9 7 8 9 4 0 3 5 0 3 6 1 5 *